INTERNATIONAL
RELATIONS
AND
WORLD POLITICS

INTERNATIONAL RELATIONS

AND

WORLD POLITICS

Security, Economy, Identity

Third Edition

Paul R. Viotti
University of Denver

Mark V. Kauppi
Georgetown University

PEARSON

Prentice
Hall

Upper Saddle River, New Jersey 07458

Library of Congress Cataloging-in-Publication Data

Viotti, Paul R.
  International relations and world politics : security, economy, identity / Paul R. Viotti, Mark V.
Kauppi.–3rd ed.
    p. cm.
  Includes bibliographical references.
  ISBN 0-13-184415-6
    1. World politics–1989- 2. International relations. 3. Security, International. 4. International
  trade. 5. Nationalism. I. Kauppi, Mark V. II. Title.

D860.V56 2006
327.101—dc22   2005036329

Editorial Director: Charlyce Jones Owen
Associate Editor: Rob DeGeorge
Editorial Assistant: Jennifer Murphy
Senior Media Editor: Harriet A. Jackson
Marketing Manager: Emily Cleary
Marketing Assistant: Jennifer Lang
Senior Managing Editor: Lisa Iarkowski
Production Liaison: Fran Russello
Manufacturing Buyer: Mary Ann Gloriande
Interior Design: John Ott
Cover Design: Bruce Kenselaar
Cover Illustration/Photo: Getty Images, Inc.
Photo Researcher: Beth Brenzel
Image Permission Coordinator: Joanne Dippel
Composition/Full-Service Project Management: Christine Knapp/Techbooks/GTS,
Los Angeles
Printer/Binder: Von Hoffman Press, Inc.

Pearson Education Ltd.   Pearson Education Australia Pty. Limited
Pearson Education Singapore Pte. Ltd.   Pearson Education North Asia Ltd.
Pearson Education Canada, Ltd.   Pearson Educación de Mexico, S.A. de C.V.
Pearson Education—Japan   Pearson Education Malaysia Pte. Ltd.

10 9 8 7 6 5 4 3 2 1
ISBN 0-13-184415-6

Contents

vi CONTENTS

Chapter 2

PART II

STATE SECURITY AND STATECRAFT

Chapter 3

Chapter 4

Chapter 5   **War, Just Wars, and Armed Intervention   158**

PART III   **INTERNATIONAL SECURITY**

Chapter 6   **International Cooperation and International Security: International Organizations, Alliances, and Coalitions   192**

Chapter 7

Chapter 8

PART V   IDENTITY AND CIVIL SOCIETY

The Preface

We live in an age of globalization made possible by technological advances, particularly in transportation and telecommunications, that bring us not only the benefits but also the downsides of the world's peoples coming closer together. The good news includes:

Increasing production, trade, investment, and other commercial activities with substantial economic growth and improvements in levels of living, health, and nutrition in many parts of the world

Continuing development of the rule of law in a relatively weak but still emerging global civil society

Extensive travel by many, facilitating human contacts, cultural exchanges, transglobal understandings, and appreciation of both similarities and differences among human beings

Proliferation of communications media and access to them that allow for a freer flow of ideas and points of view across national borders

The bad news, on the other hand, is the way in which many previously domestic problems in particular states and societies have now become global concerns:

Ethnic and other intercommunal conflicts frequently spill beyond state borders, often becoming interstate conflicts that threaten international peace and security.

Access in both legal and illegal markets to all kinds of weaponry and telecommunications provides the means by which both states and nonstate actors (to include terrorist groups) now use various forms of violence in conflicts of domestic, regional, and even global scope.

Terror has been used to advance particular causes that once were largely confined within the boundaries of particular states or disputed territories;

organized crime has also outgrown local areas to engage in a very lucrative commerce in illicit drugs, weapons, various forms of human exploitation, and other illegal activities.

Economic growth has not only been uneven in its distribution of gains across the globe with continued poverty, malnutrition, and disease in many Third World countries, but it has also come at a very high price—environmental degradation, resource depletion, labor (to include child) exploitation, and other human rights violations.

This volume takes up these and other weighty issues on our global agenda, examining them in relation to two trends; three broad, organizing themes or concepts; key actors; and three basic images or perspectives that provide structure for the pages that follow:

- Two trends—increasing not only interdependence and interconnectedness of both state and nonstate actors but also crises of authority at state and local levels and in relations among states—that characterize the international relations on world politics in a period marked by increasing globalization
- Key organizing themes or concepts—in particular, security, economy, and identity that structure the three major sections of the book
- Key actors—states, international organizations, and transnational organizations and movements (such as nongovernmental organizations, multinational corporations, and terrorist groups)
- Three basic images or perspectives on world politics—realism, pluralism (or liberalism, as pluralist thinking is frequently called), and global economic structuralism (which includes Marxism, world-systems, and dependency theory) supplemented by references to other theoretical and conceptual understandings mentioned below

Given our goal to provide theoretical and conceptual tools to make some sense out of the often-confusing realm of world politics, we include numerous "applying theory" brief commentaries. We share the view that there is nothing so practical as good theory that helps us make the world around us more intelligible, offering explanatory and predictive handles that contribute to our understanding of how the world works. In this theoretical and conceptual quest, we privilege realism, pluralism or liberalism, and worldwide economic structuralism. Indeed, these images are reflected in the inclusive title of this volume—*International Relations and World Politics*—which encompasses not just title of this volume—*International Relations and World Politics*—which encompasses not just international (or interstate) relations but also a broader view that goes well beyond the state and relations among states to encompass a wide array of nonstate actors interacting transnationally on a greater diversity of issues as well as both Marxist and non-Marxist understandings of global economic structures. At the same time, we also give increasing attention in the "applying theory" commentaries to other theoretical perspectives and approaches—rational choice and various studies using game-theoretic and quantitative methodologies, social constructivism, critical theory, feminism, and postmodern understandings.

Following two introductory chapters in Part I that lay out key concepts and provide a historical backdrop for the study of international relations and world politics, we turn in Part II to the more traditional but still current concerns with security among states and in the regional and global contexts in which they are now immersed—the pursuit of security and other national objectives through diplomacy, the use of force, and other instruments of statecraft that define a state's capabilities. In Part III, we shift to international (both regional and global) security concerns, with chapters on arms control, terrorism, and crime and the role of the United Nations and other international and nongovernmental organizations, alliances, and coalitions. A still-emerging global civil society, the role of international law and global norms, and global political economy are the subject of Part IV, which has chapters on world capitalism, trade, investment, and the environment. Finally, in Part V we take up issues related to human identities—human rights and national and ethnic strife, assessing possible political, economic, and social remedies for managing, if not eliminating, intercommunal conflicts.

In discussing contemporary international relations and world politics, we agree with P. G. Wodehouse's character Bertie Wooster that in telling a tangled story it is fatal to assume the reader knows how matters got to where they are. Hence, compared to many other textbooks, we devote a significant amount of space to the historical development of various international systems and some of the great thinkers associated with world politics. We operate under the assumption that it is difficult to determine what is new about the current world system unless we know what it has in common with the past. We also believe that in order to understand the functioning and future development of the international system, a basic understanding of economics and international political economy is an imperative.

Supplementary Package

Instructor's Manual with Test Item File

In addition to providing test items for creating tests and quizzes, the Instructor's Manual provides, for each chapter, a detailed outline, summary, and learning objectives, and lecture suggestions.

Prentice Hall Test Generator

Suitable for both Windows and Macintosh environments, this commercial-quality, computerized test-management program allows instructors to select items from the test-item file and design their own exams.

Companion Website

www.prenhall.com/viotti

The *Companion Website* provides study modules to help students review their understanding of content through multiple-choice, true-false, and essay questions for each chapter.

OneSearch: Evaluating Online Sources with Research Navigator

This brief guide focuses on developing critical thinking skills necessary to evaluate and use online sources. It also provides an access code and instruction on using **Research Navigator,** a powerful research tool that provides access to exclusive databases of reliable source material.

Research Navigator™

This unique online resource helps your students find the right articles and journals, cite sources, and draft and write effective papers. For more information, contact your local Prentice Hall representative.

Acknowledgments

We are grateful and extend our thanks to the following reviewers for their very helpful comments and advise on how to improve the new edition of our text: Arthur Blaser, Chapman University; Jeanie Bukowski, Bradley University; Thomas P. Dolan, Columbia State University; Gregory Gleason, University of New Mexico; Michael M. Gunter, Jr., Rollins College; Timothy C. Lim, California State University, Los Angeles; James M. Lutz, Indiana University at Fort Wayne; Bob Switky, University of Nebraska at Kearney; and Herbert K. Tillema, University of Missouri.

INTERNATIONAL
RELATIONS
AND
WORLD POLITICS

Chapter 1

"We playwrights, who have to cram a whole human life or an entire historical era in a two-hour play, can scarcely understand this rapidity [of change in Europe] ourselves. And if it gives us trouble, think of the trouble it must give to political scientists who spend their whole life studying the realm of the probable and have less experience with the realm of the improbable than us, the playwrights."

VACLAV HAVEL, FORMER PRESIDENT OF THE CZECH REPUBLIC

"The obscurest epoch is today."

ROBERT LOUIS STEVENSON, AUTHOR OF *TREASURE ISLAND*

Introduction:
Trends, Actors,
Perspectives, and Concepts

O n a sweltering morning in the African country of Chad, the sound of gunfire startles and scatters a herd of goats. Chadian soldiers blast away at a sand hill standing in for Al Qaeda as twenty-three U.S. Marines observe their students in action. "Lookin' good," says Major Paul Baker, the mission commander. Chad, a country ranked 167th out of 177 states on the United Nations Human Development index, has a per capita income of 73 cents a day, yet it is the latest front of the global war on terrorism. Troops in the nearby countries of Niger, Mauritania, and Mali have also received training similar to that of the Chadians. These states are part of a region where much of the land is inhospitable, yet they house terrorists linked to Al Qaeda. The African continent, so often neglected in discussions of international politics, also accounts for 15 percent of U.S. oil, making such countries as Nigeria of strategic importance.

Wang Qishan is a successful businessman in China. Once a sheet-metal worker in a state-owned factory, he exemplifies a new value system that is taking hold and rejects the ideals of the communist state. His first business venture was a four-table restaurant in Shenyang. "It was the early '80s," Wang said. "People looked down on us private guys. They thought we were bandits. While everyone else was going to work without a care, I was out there pushing a tricycle piled high with vegetables, sweating, trying to make a few bucks. It was the worst thing you could be in China at the time. I was outside the system." But Wang continued to work hard, and today he owns a drive-in movie theater and runs a private school; China's state-run television has done a documentary on his business.[1]

Such vignettes illustrate how much has changed over recent years. For the current generation of college students, particularly Americans, the terrorist attacks on New York and Washington, D.C., on September 11, 2001, were a defining moment. International security issues were now domestic security issues. All Americans felt that their world had changed, but in what manner was not particularly clear. Much commentary was devoted to whether the world had entered an "Age of Terrorism" and, if so, what the global political, social, economic, and military implications would be. A little historical perspective, however, is useful.

For an earlier generation, the end of World War II in 1945 was also a defining moment with great global import. Beginning in the late 1940s, the "cold war" label was used to describe crises over the next forty years in such diverse locations as Germany, Cuba, and the Middle East, as well as "hot" wars in Korea and Vietnam. During this period, a series of related concepts developed. Much of the world, for example, was conveniently divided into East versus West or capitalist versus communist. The Soviet Union and the United States had the largest industrial economies and were termed superpowers in that no other states could come close to the magnitude or size of their economic or military—particularly nuclear—capabilities. When the American president met with the leader of the Soviet Union, it was called a summit and was guaranteed worldwide media coverage. The major military alliances were the North Atlantic Treaty Organization (NATO) in the West and the Warsaw Pact in the East.

The world's political, military, ideological, and even economic fault lines were captured by these cold war dualities. Even developing or poverty-stricken countries—despite their diversity—came to identify themselves as the **Third World** in contrast to the **First World** of the capitalist West and the **Second World** of the communist East.

Such concepts allowed observers to orient themselves, make sense of the world around them, and impose a certain degree of order. Without such simplifying road maps, the world appeared unintelligible and chaotic, if not frightening. Despite such fears as a superpower conflict escalating into a nuclear holocaust, political leaders were nevertheless at least able to devise relatively coherent policies and gain support around the world from states and societies sharing either Marxist–Leninist or anticommunist orientations.

The fall of the Berlin Wall in November 1989 symbolically marked the beginning of the end of the Cold War, setting the stage for the reunification of Germany and the collapse of the Soviet empire. When, on December 25, 1991, the communist hammer and sickle flag was lowered for the last time from the Kremlin palace in Moscow, the Cold War was definitely over. There was no formal declaration, no surrender, no peace conference or fireworks. While this was also a defining moment, the subsequent decade seemed to lack definition. It is revealing that the most common description of the 1990s was the "Post–Cold war era." Note that this concept essentially describes the world in terms of what it is not—it is not the Cold War. But then what

---

[1]"US Engages Africa in Terror Fight," *Christian Science Monitor,* September 17, 2004; "Chinese Search for New Values," *Washington Post,* September 26, 1999.

The fall of the Berlin Wall at the end of 1989 has come to represent symbolically the beginning of the end of the Cold War. With the discrediting of communism, democratic and capitalist values spread throughout the former East bloc although the extent to which they took hold varied from country to country. By the mid-1990s, the concept of globalization began to be used more frequently.

was it? The *New York Times* asked its readers to submit suggestions, and the responses ranged from the serious to the whimsical—Millenni-end, the Muddle Ages, the Internetcine Era, the Centrifugal Age, the Citizen's Century, the Transnational Era, and the Age That Even Historians from Harvard Can't Name.[2]

Posing the same question today would probably elicit a similar range of eclectic responses. Uncertainty and uneasiness pervade seasoned observers as well as common citizens when they contemplate the state of the world today. There continues to be a real sense of drift, disorientation, and, in many parts of the world, fear and resentment. We live in an era of increasing globalization of commerce and other forms of human exchange, but people have ambivalent feelings about it. Globalization advocates point to the great gains to human welfare and liberties. Others, however, are quick to point out some of the downsides of globalization: environmental degradation, labor exploitation, rapid spread of viruses and other diseases across national borders, and the globalization of crime and terrorism. On an even broader scale there is perhaps the ultimate question: Is the world becoming characterized more by peace or by war?

The purpose of this textbook is to help the reader gain a better understanding of the shape of the emergent world order. This requires making some basic judgment calls about current and emergent trends, actors, and perspectives. Because it is impossible to discuss every aspect of world politics, we must be selective. The fulfillment of this task depends on the development of a game plan, road map, or conceptual framework that provides guidance concerning what to look at and what to discard. Such a framework also influences how we interpret what it is we have chosen to examine. The game plan we have devised is depicted in Figure 1.1.

---

[2]"No Time Like the Present to Leave Something for Posterity," *New York Times,* April 2, 1995, sec. 4, p. 7. See also "Naming an Era," *Foreign Policy,* No. 119 (Summer 2000): 29–69.

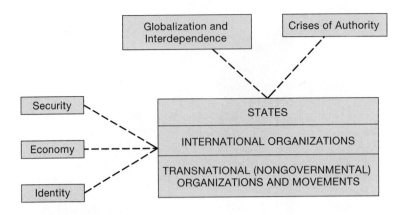

FIGURE 1.1   *Concepts*

Trends

Globalization and Interdependence

The two key trends we wish to emphasize are increasing globalization and interdependence on the one hand and crises of authority on the other. For many social scientists the concept of *globalization* suffers from a myriad of definitions, is fraught with emotional if not ideological connotations, and is so general and all-encompassing that it lacks utility as an analytical concept for the purpose of theory building. From our perspective, while the concept is indeed analytically underdeveloped, it is important as a useful shorthand for a number of interrelated and important developments in world politics. Therefore, in this book *globalization* refers to the process of continual increase in transnational and worldwide economic, social, and cultural interactions that transcend the boundaries of states, aided by advances in technology. Globalization is a process that cannot be ignored, but our definition does not presume it has a specific or uniform impact on any one particular society, group, or class. (See the BOXES on pages 7 and 8.)

A concept that has a well-established academic pedigree is ***interdependence.*** Although one sometimes hears the term used in general terms ("The world is becoming more interdependent"), *interdependence* as a concept in the international relations theory literature is more closely wedded to relations between specified states and their societies, allowing for various attempts to measure degrees of interdependence. *Interdependence,* in its most common usage, refers to a situation in which there is some degree of mutual dependence or reciprocal effects in relations between or among states.[3] Analytically there are different types of interdependence. Interdependence may merely reflect the sensitivity, for example, of one state to actions taken or planned by other states. There is sensitivity in Country *B* to what is going on in or emanating from Country *A.* This could be in the economic (trade), social-cultural (latest trends in pop music), or security (arms deals) realms. For example, for entirely domestic economic reasons, one country may raise its interest rates, leading other countries to follow suit lest capital flows, exchange rates, or import and export prices be affected adversely from

globalization
The continual increase in transnational and worldwide economic, social, and cultural interactions that transcend the boundaries of states, aided by advances in technology.

interdependence
A situation in which actions and events in one state, society, or part of the world affect peoples elsewhere. There is some degree of mutual dependence or reciprocal ties and effects among the parties involved.

---

[3]Joseph Nye, Jr., and Robert O. Keohane, *Power and Interdependence: World Politics in Transition* (Boston: Little, Brown, 1977), 39.

Case & Point

The globalization of sports is perhaps best epitomized by the Tiger Woods phenomenon. Interest and fascination in Woods transcends golf and the United States, and he has joined Michael Jordan as a truly global celebrity. In the case of team sports, Yao Ming from China, who is on the Houston Rockets basketball team, has achieved global recognition in a very short time. In the 2003 NBA season there were sixty-six players from thirty-four countries outside the United States. Twenty-seven of the twenty-nine teams had at least one international player. The 2005 NBA champion San Antonio Spurs were led by Tim Duncan (Virgin Islands), Manu Ginobili (Argentina), and Tony Parker (France). More than 100 non–North Americans played in the National Hockey League by the mid-1990s. Latin Americans—for years key players on many U.S. teams—are even more prevalent in baseball today. A handful of Japanese and Koreans have added luster to the game, including Ichiro Suzuki of the Seattle Mariners, who in his first year in the major leagues (2002) was voted Most Valuable Player and Rookie of the Year. But perhaps the best example of a truly global sport is soccer (known as football to the vast majority of the world). Players such as Pele of Brazil and more recently Zidane of France have achieved international status, aided by the rise of sports networks such as ESPN.

Point: The globalization of sports would not be possible without modern means of communication.

GLOBAL SPORTS

their perspective. One way to understand interdependence, then, is to see countries as sensitive to what other counties do.

Although there are costs associated with sensitivity interdependence, benefits to both parties may outweigh these costs. If, however, a state is vulnerable to the actions of another state, then interdependence is to be avoided, managed, or at least closely monitored. During the Cold War, for example, the United States and the Soviet Union were strategically interdependent in the nuclear realm and, hence, mutually vulnerable. In most cases, the relationship is asymmetric, meaning one party is more affected than the other. As a result, there is always the real possibility and temptation that the dominant state could use the vulnerability of the weaker state to the former's advantage. As we will see in Chapter 2 on international relations in historical perspective, interdependence is not new. Its utility as an analytical concept is equally applicable to attempts to delineate international state systems, empires, or feudal systems.

Another, perhaps less precise, usage of the term *interdependence* does not tie it just to relations among states but rather sees it as related to transactions of all kinds—economic, social, political—conducted across state borders and engaged in by both governmental and nongovernmental actors. Sometimes these transactions lead state and nonstate actors to become increasingly interconnected. Indeed, the policies they pursue are often linked directly or affect each other either positively or negatively—sometimes referred to as positive or negative externalities in what amounts to policy interdependence.

The term *globalization,* then, can be understood as a continuing, multifaceted historical process, while *interdependence*—however defined—is an attribute or characteristic of globalization involving the relations among states and other actors that, at least in principle, is measurable.

Globalization

Globalization is exemplified in the economic realm by the formation and accelerated growth of a global capitalist economy that increasingly disregards state boundaries and makes economic autarky (self-sufficiency) virtually impossible. Multinational corporations (MNCs), for example, are more beholden to stockholders and other interested parties—whatever their nationality—than to any one state. Trade integration—the share of trade volume in gross domestic product—has continued to increase steadily over the past several decades from 30 percent or less to more than 40 or 50 percent. Similarly, global financial linkages continue to grow rapidly. More than a trillion dollars a day enter and leave the world's financial institutions. Furthermore, upward or downward shifts in one stock market continue to have ripple effects with comparable swings in other markets. Perhaps a more easily grasped example comes from the television commercials. Whether cruising in the Mediterranean, exploring a Middle Eastern bazaar, or wandering the back roads of Latin America, one seemingly can always obtain ready cash via an ATM machine or call home on a cell phone.

The communications revolution has been a particularly important cause and consequence of globalization. As noted, it has encouraged the globalization of financial markets, which can be influenced instantly by electronically communicated buy and sell orders. An investor no longer even has to utilize a broker but can engage in financial transactions via the Internet from the comfort of home. Communications networks also allow work to be parceled out anywhere in the world, rendering geographical distances irrelevant. Two professors, for example, can work on an international relations textbook with one living in Washington, D.C., and one in Colorado.

Globalization is also evident in the social realm. Satellites facilitate virtually instantaneous Cable News Network (CNN), British Broadcasting Company (BBC), and other worldwide network coverage of famines, civil wars, and airplane hijackings from heretofore remote spots on the globe, altering our perception of distances. Satellites and cable also bring programs from different countries and cultures into student union buildings and homes around the world, often to the distress of parents and governments worried about "cultural pollution" or the allegedly pernicious effects of foreign values. Global communications webs—exemplified by the Internet—allow people to communicate easily with one another in a manner that few experts fifteen years ago even imagined being possible. For governments there is a difficult trade-off: while such media as the Internet help transmit scientific information essential to economic development, such networks also allow political dissidents to communicate with the outside world or encourage global dissemination of potentially dangerous information, such as how to build powerful explosive devices, including weapons of mass destruction.

Globalization is also evident in the military and security realm. The spread of modern technology has led to the development or acquisition of weapons of mass destruction (nuclear, radiological, chemical, biological) as well as powerful conventional weapons. Nor will such weapons always necessarily be limited to states: terrorist groups or other organizations with a political or religious agenda could conceivably gain access to such weapons or download information on their construction or deployment from the Internet.

authority
A legitimate right to direct or command and to make, decide, and enforce rules. Authority has a moral or legal quality to it, in contrast to brute force, coercion, or "raw" power.

Crises of Authority

Globalization with increasing interdependence among state and nonstate actors is one obvious trend in world politics. But there is another trend that seems at first to be running in the opposite direction—crises of *authority.* Compared to globalization, crises of authority have occurred as long as political units have existed. Where authority exists, individuals and groups follow because they believe that those in authority have the legitimate right to lead. Parents, teachers, religious leaders, and business executives all may be authority figures, but in the realm of world politics the concept is most closely associated with states and their governing officials. Recent crises of authority are exemplified by the late-twentieth-century demise of the former Soviet Union and Yugoslavia as single, multinational states. Ethnic conflicts in many other states threaten to rip them apart. It is manifested around the world, however, in a number of other ways—transnational terrorist groups utilizing indigenous citizens in attempts to destabilize or overthrow regimes in the Islamic world; the power of drug organizations in Colombia, Brazil, Mexico, Nigeria, and elsewhere; the threat to public order in Central America caused by criminal gangs; and the collapse of public order in cities in West Africa that are virtually controlled at night by armed burglars, carjackers, and muggers. Ironically, the erosion of state authority in part is due to the actions of states themselves: Foreign humanitarian intervention in the name of human rights undercuts state authority. Similarly the strengthening of the powers of the European Union (EU) sometimes comes at the expense of its constituent states' ability to make authoritative, unilateral decisions.

The crisis of authority also stems from a cyclical cynicism among citizens about their political leaders and institutions, resulting in the public's withdrawal from politics in some countries, forming counter-regime movements in others. It is also bred from a sense of personal, not national, insecurity arising from government's inability to protect citizens from such events as gas attacks on subways (Tokyo, 1995), bomb attacks against trains (Madrid, 2004 and London, 2005), bloody hostage taking of students and teachers (Chechnya, 2004), truck bombs placed in public areas (multiple examples in recent years), and of course 9/11—terrorists flying airplanes into the World Trade Center towers in New York and the Pentagon in Washington, D.C. Economic insecurity can also be a result due to globalization as jobs are outsourced overseas. For some, the response has been not withdrawal but rather a shift of loyalty from the state or society to some smaller entity, perhaps an ethnic group or geographic locality. Conversely, one may transfer loyalty to an entity, movement, or ideal that transcends the state. Examples include support for world government, transnational religious identification, or a cosmopolitan belief that one is a citizen of the world.

Not everyone loves globalization. Protestors in Seattle, Washington, in November 1999 representing trade unions, environmentalists, and human rights groups hold the World Trade Organization responsible for many of the excesses and failures of global capitalism.

Connections and Cautions

It can be argued that globalization, global interdependence, and crises of authority are themselves interrelated or closely linked. For example, with the growth of the global economy, states increasingly believe they are unable to exert effective influence—let alone control—over their domestic economies. Global competition leads to the collapse of certain industries as cheaper labor is available elsewhere or as companies simply move their production facilities to lower-cost countries. The American steel industry lost much of its market to Japan, which in turn lost much of it to South Korea. White-collar computer jobs in North America are now migrating to India. The resultant anger or discontent of displaced workers is often directed not only at business executives, but also at government leaders, who are judged to have failed to protect domestic jobs from foreign competition. Good examples are the riots and demonstrations that occurred in Seattle, Washington, in November 1999 in protest of the meeting of the World Trade Organization (WTO) and similar subsequent protests at meetings in successive years directed against the WTO as well as against the World Bank and International Monetary Fund (IMF).

CASE & POINT

GLOBAL INTERDE-PENDENCE
A Cautionary Tale

The global financial tremors caused by the downturn of the U.S. stock market in 1987 are often cited as early evidence of increasing global economic interdependence. The integration of world financial markets means that a major downturn in any one market can have a substantial effect on all markets. But is the global role of the American economy and stock market perhaps unique? Consider the case of Asia. Asian markets collapsed in 1997, and many analysts and brokers recommended that investors get out of the stock market at least temporarily until the global impact of Asia's downturn had played itself out. But the American stock market actually proceeded to move to new heights, with the Dow Jones Industrial Average eventually crossing the 10,000 threshold. Similar fears about Russia's economic problems in 1998 also seemed to have little impact on the U.S. stock market.

Point: Global interdependence does not equate to mutual dependence; not all states are equally affected by various crises or trends.

Particularly in Third World countries, such as those in Africa, where the source of foreign income is often limited to a few basic commodities, the power of the global economy can have a devastating effect. If there is a drop in copper, tin, or rubber prices, for example, the resultant unemployment is not cushioned by such state support programs as exist, for instance, in many advanced-industrial, high-income countries. The problem is compounded in those less-developed countries with high birth rates and a limited capacity to absorb young persons into the workforce. Such conditions are ripe for political and social discontent and a loss of governmental authority.

In all nations, there is a real sense that the world is rapidly growing smaller, and we are only now considering what this implies. It must be emphasized, however, that all states do not experience the impact of interdependence equally over the globe. Interdependence is neither a uniform nor a homogeneous condition. There is no doubt that advanced industrial states in Europe, North America, and Japan are much more economically and politically interdependent with one another than they are with the countries of sub-Saharan Africa. Although commercials for computer firms would have us believe that the communications revolution is already well entrenched in Tibetan monasteries and Brazilian rain forests, this is simply not the case. Similarly, the poorer countries and their peoples in the euphemistically termed *developing world* are not equal players in the global economy. In fact, they are dependent on (and sometimes see themselves as exploited by) better-off countries.

The severity of crises of authority also varies. In the United States, a crisis of authority is seen by many to be reflected in low voter turnouts for elections and hence is really a matter of political disillusionment. In other countries, by contrast, crises of authority are much more serious and are reflected in street riots, military coups, insurgencies, and revolutions.

Finally we want to note that the concepts of globalization, interdependence, and crises of authority are not limited in their applicability to the contemporary era. As we will see in the next chapter, interdependence characterizes a number of historical international systems over the past two thousand years, just as crises of authority help to explain the American Revolution in 1776, the French Revolution in 1789, and the Russian Revolution in 1917. What is different today, however, is the extent and depth of interdependence and its global character. Two hundred years ago, letters took weeks if not months to make their way from one end of Europe to another, just as cultural and political influences and trends took time to affect distant societies. The French Revolution, for example, had a profound historical impact, but not immediately on the Asian, African, and Latin American continents. But today the collapse of the nuclear-armed Pakistani government and the accession to power of Islamist extremists would have an immediate and profound ripple effect well beyond the South Asian subcontinent.

> ## GLOBALIZATION
> ### How New?
>
> Globalization or internationalization has been depicted, for much of the past twenty years, as a condition of the present and the future—a phenomenon without a past. For both its admirers and its opponents, it is associated with new and unprecedented technologies: the Internet, international capital markets, supersonic travel, cable news, and just-in-time deliveries across very large distances. But there is indeed a history of globalization. There have been several such periods over the past 250 years: The export and investment booms of the 1860s and the early twentieth century are just two of the more dramatic examples.
>
> **Emma Rothschild,**
> "Globalization and the Return of History," *Foreign Affairs* (Summer 1999): 187–188.

It's Been Said...

Actors

Collective efforts are the primary means by which people achieve security, economic welfare, or a common identity. Individuals certainly make a difference, whether a Mahatma Gandhi in India or a Nelson Mandela in South Africa. But even those illustrious leaders found that a cause must be associated with an organization if the former is to be achieved. Even terrorist leaders, such as Osama bin Laden, who inspire a global following rely on organizations or organizational networks such as Al Qaeda. Indeed, throughout history humanity has recognized that a pooling of resources and energy is generally the most efficient way for individuals or groups to fulfill their wants and needs. In other words, the weak *I* becomes the strong *we*. The expression of this collective effort—whether at the local, tribal, state, or international level—will vary depending on the importance of the issue and the time available for its resolution. In this book we emphasize three basic organizations by which collective efforts have been expressed:

1. States
2. International organizations
3. Transnational nongovernmental organizations

States

As is evident from the table of contents, much of our discussion revolves around **states.** A geographical entity governed by a central authority, the state is traditionally viewed as the most important of the three basic organizations. A state takes the lead in attempting to defend the physical security of the population, ensures the economic welfare of its citizens, provides a focus for loyalty and identity, and claims **sovereignty.** This means its leaders claim to represent and exercise authority over all persons within the state's territory and claim a right to autonomy internationally.

When it comes to world politics, states dominate conventional discourse. Nongovernmental movements such as insurgencies and terrorist groups may attack particular states, but very often their goal is either to take over the reins of power in an existing state or to create a new state. Even if broad-based political-cultural-religious movements transcend state borders, a political-military entity is needed to carry out the agenda. Finally, in those areas of the world burdened by overpopulation, environmental degradation, and mass migration, states are expected to take the lead in developing and implementing policies to deal with these problems.

States, however, can be viewed as obstacles to the achievement of security, economy, and identity when they persecute their own citizens, pursue counterproductive economic policies, and demand complete and undivided loyalty to the point where no dissent is allowed. In addition, in their pursuit of security, states clash with one another, leading to international tension and perhaps war. A key domestic role of states—to adjudicate domestic disagreements—is difficult to perform in the international arena. There is no world government, international courts are weak, and states often resort to the use of force.

International Organizations

States are not the only prism through which to view world politics, particularly in the current era of global interdependence in which it is apparent that no single state can hope to be the sole agent of collective action to solve global problems. **International organizations (IOs)**—also known as intergovernmental organizations (or IGOs)—play a role. IOs can be bilateral (between two states as in the U.S.-Canada North American Aerospace Defense Command), but most are multilateral because three or more states are members. Examples would include organizations with limited membership, such as NATO, the European Union (EU), the Organization of American States (OAS), the Association of Southeast Asian Nations (ASEAN), and the African Union. The best-known universal IO is the United Nations (U.N.). Membership in the U.N. is open to all states. Nongovernmental organizations (NGOs) and even individuals try to influence the United Nations and other international organizations and governments by lobbying or persuading international and national decision makers and their staffs, holding conferences of their own, and publicizing their views in the mass media to include the internet.

There was a dramatic expansion of IOs/IGOs in the twentieth century, ranging from military alliances in the security realm to U.N.-related organizations concerned not just with security, but also with economic and social issues. Organizations such as the Food and Agricultural Organization (FAO), the International Monetary Fund (IMF), the World Health Organization (WHO), the World Bank (known more formally as the IBRD, the International Bank for Reconstruction and Development), and the United Nations International Children's Emergency Fund (UNICEF) barely begin to cover the veritable "alphabet soup" of U.N.-related agencies and other international organizations pursuing specific objectives on the global agenda. The growth in numbers

The United Nations complex in New York City.

and activities of IOs has also been accompanied by a proliferation of NGOs actively pursuing their own objectives or agendas.

While IOs were created by and for states, it is interesting to consider the extent to which they have come to be significant actors in their own right. Do IOs simply reflect states' interests and at best provide a forum for debate? Do they become a source of financial aid or other assistance when economic or other problems arise? Do they offer an international diplomat when states come into conflict with one another? Or have IOs over time come to the point at which they now actually influence states' interests, preferences, and objectives? Whatever influence IOs may have in particular functional areas such as financial loans or mediation efforts, their key role may come to be purveyors of global **norms**—basic values that over time states come to take seriously. For example, while many states around the world continue to violate human rights, over the years norms have evolved that allow outsiders to make this issue a matter of international and foreign policy discussion and even punishment or sanction. Despite vigorous protest from the Chinese government, many states and human rights groups continue to condemn Beijing for its harsh treatment of political dissidents. Another example involved NATO military action against Yugoslavia in 1999, a sovereign state that did not invade another country but whose officials committed or allowed ethnic cleansing and other human rights violations against their own citizens. Such action was a key reason that NATO launched the air war in the former Yugoslavia—a campaign motivated to serve human rights and related humanitarian goals rather than for such traditional purposes as seizing territory or repulsing an invader as bases for using force.

Transnational Nongovernmental Organizations

Finally, as noted earlier, in recent years there has been a veritable explosion in the number of **transnational nongovernmental organizations (NGOs).** As the term suggests, NGOs are composed of private, nonstate international actors that cut across national boundaries. In this regard, we identify four categories of NGOs of interest and importance to us in the study of international relations and world politics. First are private-sector economic organizations. Although some writers reserve the term NGO for nonprofit organizations, we apply it to all nongovernmental organizations, including multinational corporations (MNCs), most of which are private-sector and, thus, nongovernmental organizations. Multinational business corporations are understandably primarily motivated by enhancing the economic well-being of their stock- and other stakeholders, not the economic well-being of any one particular state. Interest in MNCs is not new. Indeed, with the U.S. Central Intelligence Agency (CIA) at the helm, the United Fruit Company played a role in the overthrow of the Arbenz regime in Guatemala in 1954, just as British Petroleum and the CIA were implicated in the overthrow of the Mossadegh government in Iran in 1953. Of particular interest to many observers of world politics, however, is the influence major corporations and banking institutions routinely have on the economies of states, particularly those in the Third World dependent on foreign investment.

Second are NGOs with explicit political, economic, or social agendas, such as Amnesty International, Greenpeace, and religious organizations whose diverse memberships and global perspectives make it difficult to associate them with any one particular state. Transnational NGOs claim to have a broader constituency than MNCs or international banks. In their attempt to help define the international agenda, they often act as pressure groups to influence state behavior or international organizations or, more generally, to increase global awareness of such diverse topics as ozone-layer depletion, deforestation, epidemics, malnutrition and famine, religious persecution, and human rights in general; they advance agendas for dealing with such problems.

While such organizations do attempt to influence world politics by lobbying states and influencing state-sponsored meetings (such as those held during the early to mid-1990s in Rio de Janeiro, Cairo, and Beijing on economic development and environment, population, and the role and rights of women), their influence is actually much more pervasive and their goals much more sweeping. Activists aim at nothing less than shaping public affairs and how people perceive national and global problems. As a result, **global civil society** and the rule of law (domestic and international) associated with this term are increasingly prevalent in discussions of world politics as are efforts to spread democratic forms of governance. Global civil society consists of states as well as individuals and organizations that aggregate individual interests within or outside particular states but operate typically beyond the border of any single state. That is, certain organizations may originate in a particular country, but their global agenda makes them, in effect, stateless. Their memberships also tend to be multinational.

Third are nongovernmental organizations that attempt to avoid overtly political roles. The best examples are humanitarian relief organizations such as Doctors Without Borders. If such an NGO engaged in politics and took sides in civil and international conflicts, it would most likely be denied access to combat zones. This and the previous category are what many people think of when the term NGO is used. In recent years there has been a phenomenal explosion in the number of such NGOs, from approximately 6,000 in 1990 to more than 26,000 a decade later. NGOs have existed for centuries—the British and Foreign Anti-Slavery Society, for example, was around in the early 1800s. But the process of globalization—spurred further by the end of the Cold War and subsequent efforts to spread democratic and market-oriented values and structures, technological change, and economic integration—has also encouraged the growth of NGOs. Globalization has also exacerbated a number of concerns to include the environment, workers' rights, the status of women, health concerns, and human rights in general. When combined, democratization and technological progress have revolutionized the way people can unite across borders through NGOs to present their demands to states and international organizations.

Finally, we also include such nonstate actors as terrorist and criminal organizations and networks. Terrorists often claim to represent a broader constituency, whereas transnational criminal organizations (TCOs) prefer to focus on their narrow economic agendas, becoming involved in politics only when the pursuit of their ill-gotten gains is threatened. In the past, terrorist activity tended to be more localized, often contained by the borders of a particular state. More recent is the globalization of terrorism by such networks as Al Qaeda, whose affiliates are said to operate in more than sixty countries. We include terrorist and criminal organizations as NGOs that challenge the rule of law and, as such, represent the down (or dark) side of the emerging global civil society.

In sum, these three groups of actors—states, international organizations/IGOs, and transnational nongovernmental organizations (NGOs)—can be viewed as means by which people strive to attain their individual and collective goals of security, economic well-being, and identity. As already noted, states are not the only means by which security can be attained. In fact, where authoritarian governments are in power, it may be the state that poses the greatest threat to one's physical security. In such cases, IOs and NGOs might be called upon to help protect human rights, or individuals may turn to organizations or revolutionary movements dedicated to the overthrow of the existing regime.

Similarly, even if one accepts the argument that the state should work to enhance the economic well-being of its citizenry, the globalization of the economy has made this a much more difficult task. Indeed, the governments of some countries lacking financial reserves have turned to such international organizations as the International Monetary Fund for financial relief and in the process have had to swallow the subsequent bitter economic "medicine" imposed by the IMF as a condition for loans: cuts in government spending, increased taxes, higher interest rates, and restrictive fiscal and monetary policies intended to curb inflation, effectively slowing short-term business growth and thus reducing employment opportunities.

Finally, just as states have traditionally been the focal point of citizen identity and loyalty, at least in the Western world, other entities such as the United Nations or the European Union (EU) hold the potential to be foci of loyalty beyond the state. On the other hand, in some parts of the world where state political authority is tenuous, religious or ethnic identification may be a more important bond among people than any sense of loyalty or identification with a particular state.

Individuals

If the focus in this book is on the three broad categories of organizations in world politics, what happens to the average human being? We wish to emphasize that while states, international organizations, and nongovernmental organizations are viewed as the primary actors in world politics, such entities are made up of flesh-and-blood human beings. States do not make the decision to go to war; people in their governments or societies do. States do not decide to engage in genocide or provide famine relief to parts of Africa; people in their governments or societies do. So it is with the people who make up IOs and NGOs.

But the fact of the matter is that while individuals can have a tremendous impact on the short-term course of world events—witness Mikhail Gorbachev, the former president of the former Soviet Union, whose actions contributed to the end of the Cold War—it is extremely difficult to identify such individuals until after their impact has been felt. For example, in 1985 experts initially saw Gorbachev as merely the latest in a long line of Soviet officials or communist party *apparatchiks*. Most people who want to influence world politics must do so in an indirect manner through collective actors such as states, IOs, or NGOs. Gorbachev had at his disposal the communist party and the bureaucratic machinery of the Soviet state. Even Nelson Mandela of South Africa found it useful to be supported by the African National Congress in the presidential election campaign following his release from prison. Former U.S. President Jimmy Carter's leadership on election monitoring, conflict resolution, and other humanitarian causes is facilitated through his NGO, the Carter Center, in association with states and IOs. In short, while individuals can and do act on their own, they usually are more effective when they operate from an organizational base—states and international or nongovernmental organizations.

Conceptual and Theoretical Perspectives

Having provided an overview of basic trends and actors in world politics, we turn to a discussion of perspectives or images of world politics today. In this book, an *image* or *perspective* refers to a set of assumptions about international relations or world politics that influences what types of questions are asked and how one answers them. As such, perspectives help to orient our reading and research by highlighting certain actors or concepts and ignoring others, as well as influencing the interpretation of particular international trends. Images are perhaps best seen as a pair of glasses through which one views the world. The images we are about to discuss are not the only ones that can be used to view the world, but they have many adherents among students of international relations and world politics.

How Realists See the World

realism
An image of international relations that can be traced back two thousand years. Realists tend to hold pessimistic views on the likelihood of the transformation of the current world into a more peaceful one, emphasizing the struggle for power among political units each acting in a rational, unitary manner to advance its interests.

The tradition of political thought known as **realism** has dominated thinking about international politics over the millennia. As the term suggests, writers and political theorists associated with realism claim to view the world as it *is*, not as it *ought* to be. In terms of domestic politics, a primary concern for any ruler is stability. Without some

Practicing World Politics

RESEARCH AND WRITING TOOLS ON THE INTERNET

Using search engines such as www.google.com or www.altavista.com is an excellent way to find sites on international relations and world politics. For library resources, check out the Internet Public Library Reference Center (www.ipl.org). Many classics and other online books and archives can be found on www.google.com or the University of Pennsylvania's site (http://digital.library.upenn.edu/books).

Several sites offer dictionaries and translation services. Be sure to visit www.itools.com. For an online Merriam-Webster dictionary, visit www.m-w.com. Several dictionary entries are compiled on www.onelook.com. For rough translations of English, French, German, Italian, Portuguese, or Spanish text you type in, visit www.babelfish.com or http://babelfish.altavista.digital.com#. To find journal articles visit www.jstor.org.

degree of order or internal stability, it is difficult to pursue other political, economic, or social objectives. Hence the challenge of establishing authority has drawn the attention of many realist writers. In terms of international politics, realists emphasize the struggle for power and influence among states, empires, and principalities. At a minimum, all such political entities seek security. Some, however, may have a more extensive agenda of opportunities to pursue and may even aspire to regional or world conquest.

Realists see a world filled with conflict and struggle—power and balance of power. For them, competition among political units such as states—seen as the key actors—is the hallmark of international politics. While realists may have a personal preference for international peace, harmony, and justice, for them the sad reality is that all too often this is simply not achievable. Their advice for political leaders is that to construct their policies around their hopes rather than the eternal realities of international politics is to risk disaster. More than any other image of world politics, realism most closely approximates the perspective of political leaders down through the ages. For purposes of analysis, realists tend to see the ideal state as a rational, unitary actor facing the outside world. Whatever internal disagreements there may be, ultimately the state, acting in its own interests and using power—its capabilities—to achieve its ends, tends to speak with one voice.

Realists recognize the existence of international and transnational nongovernmental organizations but view IOs as essentially instruments composed of, and directed by, states and NGOs as entities whose influence on world politics is marginal at best. Some realists (particularly those who identify with the English School of thought on international relations and world politics discussed below) argue that we can speak of a **society of states,** meaning that basic rules, norms, and international law define the content and influence the actions of states.

How do realists explain the eternal competition and conflict among states and empires? The answer varies depending on the writer. For some realists, as we shall see, the explanation is to be found in humanity's supposed innate aggressiveness. From this perspective, human beings, by nature, are competitive and selfish. Hence, such characteristics

Journals on International Relations and World Politics

The International Studies Association (ISA) mails its members the *International Studies Quarterly (ISQ)* and the *International Studies Review (ISR)*; the American Political Science Association (APSA) sends its members the *American Political Science Review (APSR), Perspectives on Politics,* and *Political Science Notes (PS).* In both organizations, student members pay substantially reduced annual dues. The *APSR* and *Perspectives* do publish book reviews, but they allocate fewer articles to international relations compared to *ISQ* and *ISR.*

Many journals have Web sites, but primary access is still in journal form. Among the many other journals on international relations and world politics that publish articles with a more theoretical or academic orientation are *World Politics, International Organization, International Security, Millennium, International Affairs, Review of International Studies, Journal of Conflict Resolution, International Studies Review,* and the *American Journal of International Law.* Policy-related journals include *Foreign Affairs* (which also publishes book reviews), *Foreign Policy, World Policy,* and *Orbis.* This is hardly an exhaustive or complete list, but it is a start. Consult your library's complete list of journal subscriptions, and consider subscribing to one or more yourself.

are simply carried over to the international arena. Other realists argue that the idea of innate human aggressiveness is overstated and instead note that certain types of states or societies tend to bring out the worst in people. This, they claim, helps to account for international conflict.

All realists agree, however, that the mere existence of independent states, empires, or principalities—all of which reject the notion of being subject to the authority of any other political unit—creates a dynamic that encourages competition and violence. In other words, international politics is conducted in a condition of international **anarchy**, or, as the seventeenth-century writer Thomas Hobbes also termed it, a world in which there is "no common power." No central, global power exists to enforce peace among the various political units, whether they are city-states, empires, principalities, or modern states. As a result, a political leader's primary concern is to protect the national security of the country. At a minimum this means defending the physical and territorial integrity of the state. We will return to a more extended discussion of the causes of war, but at this point we simply wish to note that for many realists, the competitive and often warlike condition of world politics is essentially the result of some combination of levels of analysis—human nature or the psychology of individuals and dynamics of small groups; the nature of certain types of states or societies; and the structure or distribution of power among states in what some refer to as an international system of states as well as the actions and interactions among units (typically states and alliances) operating within this system. **Structural realists** (sometimes called **neorealists**) such as Kenneth Waltz look to this distribution of power among states or "structure" as affecting the behavior of states within the international system: a **unipolar** structure in which one dominant state has capabilities or power well above all the others tends to make the dominant state (the United States in the present period) more assertive in pursuing its objectives—tending to lead alliances and other coalitions or tending to act unilaterally; a **bipolar** structure as in the cold war of two major or "super" powers—the United States and the Soviet Union—tends over time to make both powers more cautious in pursuing their objectives lest assertive actions lead them into armed conflict with destructive consequences to both; and a **multipolar** structure—the most common form historically—in which calculations among several major powers are enormously complex with coalitions and countercoalitions or alliances "balancing" each other, but sometimes breaking out into armed conflict.

How Pluralists or Liberals See the World

An alternative image of world politics is what we call *pluralism* (some writers refer to this image as *liberalism*—an allusion to classical liberal thought). Indeed, as we use the term, the *pluralist image* is derived from various related strands of political thought that can be traced back to such thinkers as the ancient Greek Stoics, eighteenth- and nineteenth-century liberals, and, more recently, academic writing on interest groups and organizational behavior. As the term suggests, pluralists view world politics in terms of a multiplicity of actors. States are recognized as key actors in world politics, but they are not the only important ones. International organizations such as the United Nations and the European Union (EU) are not simply arenas within which states compete for influence, but often independent actors in their own right that increasingly set the international issue agenda. This trend has accelerated in the more than six decades since the end of World War II. The economic and political clout of cities both within their states and across their borders also makes such urban conglomerates as Los Angeles, New York, and Tokyo significant players. In the Third World, underemployed urban

pluralism
(liberalism) An image of world politics that emphasizes the multiplicity of international actors, challenging the realist preoccupation with the state.

Practicing World Politics

Mass communication print, radio, and television media in the United States provide a wide diversity of sources for current information and analysis on international relations and world politics. Many of these sources also maintain Web sites that post and update content frequently. If you want to read the weekly news magazine with the broadest (and most balanced) coverage of international events, the choice likely would be the *Economist* (www.economist.com). Seeing itself as the newspaper of record, *The New York Times* (www.nytimes.com) prints the full length (or at least excerpts) of speeches and other documents of the day. Adding a Washingtonian perspective is the *Washington Post* (www.washingtonpost.com); for a more right-of-center view, see the *Washington Times* (www.washtimes.com).

In its relatively few pages, the *International Herald Tribune* (www.iht.com) provides a greater breadth of coverage of international events than most domestic papers. Another good alternative is the *Christian Science Monitor* (www.csmonitor.com). Except for its religious page, it is an otherwise secular newspaper. For stories, analysis, and commentary on international economic, commercial, and political matters, see the New York–based *Wall Street Journal* (www.wsj.com) and the London-based *Financial Times* (www.ft.com). Among major newspapers reflecting regional views, see the *Boston Globe* (www.globe.com/globe), the *Chicago Tribune* (www.chicago.tribune.com), the *Denver Post* (www.denverpost.com), the *San Francisco Chronicle* (www.sfgate.com/chronicle), and the *Los Angeles Times* (www.latimes.com). Find the site for your major city or local newspaper listed on its own pages or through a search engine (for example, www.google.com or www.altavista.com).

Television networks covering international events include CNN (www.cnn.com), particularly the international versions available on some cable and satellite systems; such public television programs as *The News Hour* (www.pbs.org); certain programming on C-Span channels (www.c-span.org); the traditional major networks—ABC News (www.abcnews.com), CBS News (www.cbs.com), and NBC News (www.nbc.com); and such specialty networks as MSNBC (www.msnbc.com) and CNBC (www.cnbc.com). For alternative perspectives, see www.democracynow.org, which is a one-hour news program available on the Web site by audio or video streaming, some National Public Radio (NPR) and other radio stations, and satellite television.

Among the major news-related programs on National Public Radio (www.npr.org) are *Morning Edition, Fresh Air,* and *All Things Considered.* ABC (www.abcradio.com) and CBS (www.cbsradio.com) are among the major radio networks with affiliates throughout the country. With origins in the Cold War and reflecting a pro-U.S. perspective to overseas audiences are Radio Free Europe and Radio Liberty (www.rferl.org) as well as Radio America (www.radioamerica.org).

CHECKING OUT SOME WEBSITES ON THE MEDIA

populations suffering in sordid living conditions provide the breeding ground for unrest and demands for political change.

A growing number of pluralists, therefore, debate the privileged position in which realists place the state. Increasing global interdependence associated with the globalization process is an important factor. They note that the emergence of the modern state is, historically speaking, a relatively recent phenomenon, going back to perhaps the fifteenth century. Other forms of political and social relations develop and are carried on across state borders in the form of transnational organizations. Indeed, far from seeing the state as a unitary, rational actor, pluralists see the state as a battleground for conflicting bureaucratic interests, subject to the pressures of both domestic and transnational interest groups.

Some pluralists, embracing classical liberal thought, have seen the state as an anachronism to be supplanted over time by nongovernmental organizations and other institutional forms. By contrast, pluralists of what has been called *neoliberal* persuasion accept the state as an important actor, but by no means the *only* actor. Not only are nonstate actors important, but in some circumstances they may be decisive. To **neoliberal institutionalists,** for example, it is important to take account of organizational or institutional factors that influence the behavior of states as well as international and nongovernmental organizations engaging in the policy milieu.

The term *global civil society* not only refers to growth in the rule of **international law,** but also describes the multitude of institutions, voluntary organizations, and networks ranging from women's groups and human rights organizations to environmental activists and chambers of commerce that have multiplied rapidly since the beginning of the twentieth century. Whereas most originated and confined their interests to the industrial countries of the West, this is no longer the case. Today such organizations are found in developing countries and in the former communist countries of Eastern Europe and Russia. Pluralists note that such organizations are more than special interest groups attempting to influence state policies. These groups play an important role in forming an international consciousness among peoples around the globe on such diverse issues as the environment, human rights, and weapons proliferation. Indeed, it allows one to speak, at least in terms that originated in the Western world, of a growing liberal-capitalist civic identity.

The realist and pluralist views of the possibilities of peaceful international change are also at odds. Realists tend to be pessimists who view international relations as "more of the same old thing"—conflict and competition in a world constantly threatened with instability and threats to peace. Pluralists, however, tend to be much more optimistic, especially in terms of their underlying view of human nature—one that allows for cooperation and accommodation on a person-to-person level, fostering the spread of democratic ideals that over time will tend to have a pacifying effect on peoples and states. According to the eighteenth-century German writer Immanuel Kant in his essay "Perpetual Peace," a world of good, morally responsible states would be less likely to engage in wars. Thus, many pluralists argue that the realist emphasis on international anarchy and the consequent insecurity is excessive; there are to pluralist thinkers no intractable obstacles to international cooperation. Pluralists tend to be optimists who rely on the ability of political leaders and nations to learn from mistakes—the past is not necessarily prologue. State interests can be redefined and new identities—not restricted to loyalty to the state—can be created. Policy makers and others who adopt this more optimistic perspective, seeking to universalize gains through international cooperative and collaborative efforts, are sometimes referred to as **liberal internationalists.**

How Global Economic Structuralists See the World

A third image is ***global economic structuralism.*** Not to be confused with the term *globalization,* discussed above, this image of world politics is also fundamentally different from the realist and pluralist or liberal images. First, those we identify as economic structuralists, both Marxists and non-Marxists, argue that one must comprehend the global context within which states and other entities interact. Understanding the over-all economic or ***class*** structure of the international system means one must examine more than the distribution of power among states (realists) or chart the movements of transnational actors and the internal political processes of states (pluralists or liberals). While important, such actors, processes, and relations are part of a world shaped by global social and economic forces whose impact is not always readily apparent in the day-to-day world of domestic and international political competition. These forces condition and predispose actors (state as well as nonstate) to act in certain ways; they also account for the generation of these actors in the first place. In other words, while realists tend to view state actors and their interests as givens, economic structuralists are interested in explaining how they came into existence in the first place.

By *structure,* Marxists typically mean global class formations as in the *bourgeoisie* or capitalists in various countries that occupy a position of dominance over the "downtrodden"—the worker (proletarian) and peasant classes. Another Marxist (or modified, "neo"-Marxist) understanding sees global capitalist structures of dominance by the **core** of advanced capitalist countries over the **periphery** of capital-poor countries with some countries caught in between—the **semiperiphery.** Both Marxist and non-Marxist economic structuralists also paint a picture of exploitative relations in which the capital-poor countries of the **South** are kept in a position of dependency or bondage by the capital-rich countries of the **North** through various discriminatory practices adverse to these countries caught on the downside of the global economic structure of world capitalism.

So what is the difference between Marxists and non-Marxists on economic structuralism? A short answer is that Marxists tend to focus on class structure; non-Marxists look to other forms of structure. Put another way, Marxists refer readily to the bourgeoisie or capitalist class that establishes a structure of global dominance over the working class or peasantry; non-Marxists generally prefer to describe economic structures of dependency between the capital-rich countries of the North and the capital-poor countries of the South.

Following from the above, economic structuralists argue that it is absolutely necessary to view international relations in historical perspective. Realists and pluralists or liberals would agree. But while realists tend to emphasize the timeless and repetitive nature of world politics dating back to ancient times, economic structuralists tend to use as a benchmark the historical emergence of capitalism. They argue that the emergence of capitalism in sixteenth-century Western Europe was a fundamental breaking point in the structure and dynamics of world politics. Indeed, one could even date the origins of the concept we now call *globalization* to this era. Capitalism continued to spread to the point where we can today speak of a world capitalist system or, as Immanuel Wallerstein would have it, a capitalist world system. Similarly, while pluralists tend to emphasize the growing transnational nature of world politics and foresee the possibility of a fundamental change in the nature of international politics occurring, economic structuralists instead emphasize how the continual, incremental evolution of capitalism goes a long way toward accounting for recent changes in world politics. While individual countries over the years may claim to base their domestic economic systems on something other

economic structuralism
This mode of theorizing tends to focus on relations of dominance in society in the form of economic "structures"—national or global—that purportedly also contribute to explaining the conduct of both state and non-state actors.

than capitalism (such as socialism), economic structuralists argue they nevertheless must operate internationally as part of a global or capitalist world system that conditions and constrains the behavior of all states and societies.

While recognizing the importance of states as actors (as do realists) and nonstate actors such as international organizations, multinational corporations, and banks (as do pluralists), economic structuralists frequently view these entities in light of how they act as mechanisms of domination in a capitalist world order. Specifically, economic structuralists examine how some capitalist states, elites, or transnational classes manage to extract benefits from the global economic structure or the world capitalist system at the expense of others. The exploited occupy the Third World or lesser developed countries (LDCs), which are characterized by large, poverty-stricken sections of their population. Some economic struturalists argue that these countries and populations are kept in a dependent status, not because they have failed to develop capitalist economic systems or because they are poorly integrated into the capitalist world system. In fact, it is quite the opposite: These less developed countries play an important role in the capitalist world system, acting as a source of cheap labor and raw materials. Far from being outside the capitalist world system, they are an integral part of it—their exploitation helping to account for the continual economic dominance of the northern capitalist states in North America, Western Europe, and parts of Asia. LDCs are unable to choose their own path toward economic development, ensnared in the structure of the capitalist world system net and often poorly served by their own elites or **comprador class** (capitalists constituting the local bourgeoisie in an LDC, seen as subordinated to the bourgeoisie in advanced capitalist countries), who derive selfish benefits due to these dependency relations. It is apparent, therefore, that even more so than the realists and pluralists, these structuralists emphasize the critical importance of economic factors in attempting to understand international relations. For economic structuralists, economic considerations in the form of **global structures** of dominance are the key starting point for understanding international relations and the creation and development of the current international system.

How Others See the World—the English School, Social Constructivists, and Feminists

While realism, pluralism or liberalism, and economic structuralism—as we use these terms—are perhaps the three most common perspectives or images of international relations and world politics, they are by no means the only ways to look at the world. Scholars in what is called the **English School**, for example, see the world not as a system of interacting states as structural realists do. Nor do they focus on global class or other economic structures as economic structuralists do. Instead, their image or vision is of a global society composed of both state and nonstate actors. The world is, as the late Martin Wight, Hedley Bull, and other English School scholars of more recent vintage have had it, an anarchical society—one composed of independent sovereign states and other actors but lacking in central authority or global governance. Order in this anarchical society may come from power and the balance of power as one finds in the writings of the Englishman, Thomas Hobbes—the Hobbesian or Hobbist tradition; from the rules or norms accepted by states and other actors as being in their enlightened self-interest, many of which attain the standing of international law as in the writings of the Hollander, Hugo Grotius—the Grotian tradition; or in moral or ethical principles that come to be accepted internationally as in the writings of the East Prussian, Immanuel Kant—the Kantian tradition. Understanding international relations or world politics as

REALISM	PLURALISM	ECONOMIC STRUCTURALISM
VIEW OF INTERNATIONAL SYSTEM		
At best can speak of society of states engaged in struggle for power	Global civil society encompasses or operates parallel to—and influences— the interstate system	System characterized by patterns of economic domination within and among societies
TRENDS		
GLOBALIZATION		
Impact overstated	Impact cannot be overstated; extent historically unprecedented	An ongoing process dating back to at least the 16th century
CRISES OF AUTHORITY		
Pronouncements on death of state premature	States losing authority to IOs, subnational groups, NGOs	Nothing new due to the creative destruction of capitalism
ACTORS		
STATES		
Key actor	Key actor, but nonstate actors also important	States, nonstate actors must be viewed in context of global economic structures
INTERNATIONAL ORGANIZATIONS		
Reflect state interests	Increasingly independent role	Reflect class interests, particularly economic IOs such as IMF and World Bank
TRANSNATIONAL NONGOVERNMENTAL ORGANIZATIONS (NGOs)		
Secondary importance	Increasingly important and growing in number	Corporations reflect class interests
SECURITY		
NATIONAL SECURITY		
Analytic focus: states as unified rational actors; interests a given	Analytic focus: states consist of many actors; security a socially constructed concept	Defined in terms of elite class interests
Security of state and territory key concern	Security of groups and individuals key concern	Security threatened by capitalist or class conflict

(table continues)

TABLE 1.1
Realism, Pluralism, Economic Structuralism

TABLE 1.1
(continued)

REALISM	PLURALISM	ECONOMIC STRUCTURALISM
DIPLOMACY		
Conducted primarily by states, which are also key actors in international organizations and alliances	Conducted by states, IOs, increasingly NGOs in the field	Purpose is to defend capitalist interests
FORCE		
Necessary and seemingly inevitable instrument of state policy	May well be used, but not inevitable instrument of state policy	Historically at the disposal of dominant economic classes
INTERNATIONAL SECURITY		
Balances of power, alliances, collective security provide order	International regimes and other socially constructed institutions and values provide order	Defined in terms of elite interests at expense of lower classes
ECONOMY		
Key source of state power	Key indicator of globalization	Key factor of world politics
IDENTITY		
State, nation-state	State, nation-state, ethnic group; global civil society	Class and economic interests
TRANSFORMATIVE POTENTIAL OF INTERNATIONAL RELATIONS AND WORLD POLITICS		
Pessimistic about transforming IR into a fundamentally better world	Cautiously optimistic about transforming world politics	Logic of capitalist system drives world politics

occurring within global society also puts emphasis on the human dimension rather than on what some see as mechanistic relations among abstract units called states in structural realist or *classes* in economic structuralist formulations. One turns instead to classical realism with its focus on pursuit of interest using state power or capabilities and pluralism with its acknowledgement of roles played by multiple state and nonstate actors. That global society can become a global civil society under the rule of law is also compatible with English School thinking.

In recent years **social constructivism** and **feminism** have provided provocative and intriguing challenges to realist and pluralist conceptions in particular. The starting point for constructivists is the claim that what realists and pluralists take for granted—interests and the identities of actors—are actually malleable. Realists, for example, claim that actors have a more or less fixed nature. States have been and always will be self-interested and security conscious. Whether due to an unbending human nature or the eternal existence of an anarchic international environment, states will continue to compete for power, influence, and prestige. Constructivists, however, argue that actors don't simply react to their environment but dynamically engage it. Just as the environment influences the behavior of the actors, so too do the actors over time change the environment. Through these interactions, individuals construct their knowledge of, and give meaning to, the external world. Indeed, this means that states can redefine their interests.

Several examples may help to clarify this point. We formulate the ideas and construct the norms that define the context within which states and non-state actors operate. Consider how slavery used to be an accepted aspect of the international system from the perspective of the United States and many European countries. Slavery was viewed as an economic imperative as late as the eighteenth and well into the nineteenth centuries and hence critical to the interests of the slave-trading states. Fortunately, this is no longer the case. Sadly, various form of human bondage persist to the present day, but global and national norms make such practices not only morally illegitimate, but also illegal. Or consider that, in the first half of the twentieth century, European states were engaged in two major world wars, supposedly in defense of their respective national interests. But now Europe has created what amounts to a zone of peace, and it is hard nowadays to imagine that for centuries Germany and France had been bitter rivals. How could a realist explain these developments? From a constructivist perspective, actors or "agents" constitute or shape their own social context, and this context in turn shapes the behaviors, interests, and identities we observe.

Concepts such as "interests," "sovereignty," and "anarchy" are exactly that—concepts given meaning by actors, not eternal, unchanging aspects of reality beyond the control of actors. "Sovereignty" is tied to a set of rules telling states how to interact with one another, including the international norm of noninterference in the internal affairs of other states. But these rules mean something only if states (who created them) actually follow them. If multilateralism has become a norm generally accepted by a large number of states as the way international relations are conducted—a construction gradually taking form over the past two centuries—what happens when states, particularly powerful ones, choose to act unilaterally? If states decide that acts of genocide demand international diplomatic or armed intervention in the domestic affairs of states, the rules of sovereignty will weaken. To reiterate, these and other ideas about international relations and world politics do not exist somehow in nature. Instead they are of human origin or, in the language of social constructivists, these concepts are constituted or socially constructed.

Feminism involves using gender as a category of analysis or factor in order to highlight feminine perspectives on social issues and research. Much of contemporary feminism is committed to progressive goals, particularly achieving equality for women through the elimination of discrimination and unequal gender relations.[4] Gender, which embodies relationships of power inequality, is understandably the starting point. Feminists who define **gender** as a set of socially and culturally constructed characteristics share an affinity with the social constructivists. Masculinity is stereotypically associated with power, a rationality often cold to human concerns, self-empowered autonomy, and assumption of leadership in public roles. Conversely, socially constructed feminine characteristics include less assertive or less aggressive behavior, willful dependence on or interdependence in nurturing relationships with others, sensitivity to emotional aspects of issues, and a focus on the private realm.

---

[4]This section draws on the insightful and important article by J. Ann Tickner, "You Just Don't Understand: Troubled Engagements between Feminists and IR Theorists," *International Studies Quarterly,* 41 (1997), 611–632.

The two gender categories are dependent upon one another for their meaning. Indeed, society reinforces the idea that to be a "real man" means not to display "feminine" characteristics. Hence the emphasis on gender is not just about women, but men and masculinity as well. From the feminist perspective, gender is particularly important as a primary way to signify relationships of power, not only in the home, but also in the world of foreign policy and international relations. By privileging masculinity, women can be socially but also legally cast into a subordinate status.

Feminism claims that as gender permeates social life, it has profound and largely unnoticed effects on the actions of states, international organizations, and transnational actors. Feminist scholarship seeks to develop a research agenda and associated concepts to trace and explain these effects. In recent years feminism has cast its net much more widely, examining the interplay of gender with race and class. What connects all three is a concern for the nature of power relationships and points of convergence as well as divergence and connecting them to the study of international relations and world politics.

Since feminism as an approach to international relations first began to appear in the international relations and world politics literature in the 1980s, scholars with a feminist perspective have been critical of "masculinist" approaches to conflict that tend to emphasize coercive diplomacy, unilateralism, and the use of force. From this perspective, conduct in international relations seems similar to school-yard conflicts, particularly among boys in which the strong do what they will and the weak do what they must. By contrast, feminist approaches to conflict would tend to look for common ground—a search for positive gains for all parties. However we react to this mode of thinking, feminist writers have made us more aware of how gender—both feminine and masculine constructions—affect the way we understand international relations and world politics.

International Relations and World Politics: Security, Economy, Identity

We now offer a few comments concerning the title of this book. To be precise, the concept **international relations** should refer to relations among nations—people with a common identity such as the French or Japanese "nation." However, over the years, conventional discourse has come to equate the term *international* with *interstate* relations. When we use the term *international relations*, we are principally referring to relations among states, as we believe it is necessary to emphasize that *states* continue to be the primary actors on the world stage. Furthermore, various types of states historically have dominated international politics. Realists tend to feel most comfortable with this use of the term *international relations*. As we have noted, however, states are not the only important actors. We believe the terms **global** or **world politics**—often used interchangeably by liberals or pluralists and economic structuralists—capture today's reality of a wide range of transnational actors, the phenomena of globalization and interdependence, and vast social and economic inequalities.

One must be wary, however, as to the assumed connotations of global or world politics. Although a case can be made that the trends we discuss in this book are indeed global or at least have global ramifications, not every one we address is equally salient or important to all peoples or regions of the globe. Sweeping generalizations about the condition of the entire world should be viewed with suspicion. Environmental degradation, for example, may be a global concern, but its manifestations are certainly much worse in some areas of the world than in others. The same is true of population and refugee issues. Similarly, economic conditions vary widely across the globe. One could, in fact, simply divide the world into two spheres. In North America, Europe, and Japan, high or increasing standards of living prevail. Much of the rest of the world, home to the mass of humanity, suffers from varying degrees of poverty, low levels of economic development, high rates of population growth, disease, and environmental pollution. Moreover, many of these countries are also plagued by collapsing social and political orders.

A useful metaphor that captures our approach to the study of international relations and world politics is a chessboard. Just as chess consists of different actors—kings, queens, rooks, bishops, pawns—so too does world politics—states, IOs, and NGOs. And just as various chess pieces are more important than others, so too is this the case in global politics. In fact, global politics is a three-level game of chess, with at least three games in progress at once—security, economy, and identity. Within and between each game various levels of interdependencies exist. But to make the game even more of an analytical challenge, the actual size and boundaries of the chessboards are unclear. The constituent elements and complex, multidimensional nature of contemporary global politics are continually evolving. Most observers would agree that the state continues to be the preeminent actor in world politics, but because of globalization and increasing global interdependence and crises of authority, this may or may not be the case at the end of the twenty-first century.

The subtitle of this book reflects three other key concepts that we use to organize much of the material—**security, economy,** and **identity.** Security is often viewed in terms of the basic survival, welfare, and protection of the state existing in an international system characterized by anarchy and self-help. This is a perspective associated with realism. Pluralists or liberals do not deny the anarchic nature of the international

Practicing World Politics

U.S.-based academic organizations one can join include the International Studies Association (ISA) (www.isanet.org) and the American Political Science Association (www.apsanet.org). Membership is also available in APSA's organized sections: International Security and Arms Control, Conflict Processes, Domestic Sources of Foreign Policy, Comparative Politics, Politics and Society in Western Europe, Political Economy, Science, Technology & Environmental Politics, and Ecological and Transformational Politics. ISA also has organized sections.

On international and foreign policy issues, World Affairs Councils in various cities are open to the general public. Study groups on foreign policy decisions—the Great Decisions program of the Foreign Policy Association (www.fpa.org)—are held in some World Affairs Council or other group settings. Groups with membership limited to professionals in a diversity of fields include the Washington-based American Committees on Foreign Relations (www.acfr.org) with grassroots committees in more than thirty U.S. cities; the New York– and Washington-based Council on Foreign Relations (www.cfr.org); the Los Angeles–based Pacific Council on International Policy (www.pacificcouncil.org); and the London-based International Institute for Strategic Studies (www.iiss.org).

CHECKING OUT SOME WEB SITES ON MEMBERSHIP ORGANIZATIONS

Practicing World Politics

USING THE INTERNET TO FIND INTERNATIONAL CAREERS AND JOBS

A number of Web sites contain information about both private-sector (profit and non-profit NGOs) and public-sector (governmental and international organization) jobs and positions. Be sure to check out Web sites of international and nongovernmental organizations, many of which are listed in the Practicing World Politics boxes throughout the chapters of this book. Here are some sites to begin your search; be sure to check their international listings and links to other sites:

www.employmentoffice.net

www.europages.com

www.globalcareers.com

www.idealist.org

www.jobsite.co.uk

www.monster.com

www.nonprofits.org

For academic teaching and research positions, visit the American Political Science Association (www.apsanet.org) and explore the international relations and world politics fields. Visit the Web sites of other professional associations, as well as the *Chronicle of Higher Education* (www.chronicle.com); the latter contains both academic and administrative position listings in colleges and universities.

Job and position information can also be found on search engines such as www.google.com and www.yahoo.com, as well as other general career and job information sites such as www.careermosaic.com and www.careermag.com.

system and the resultant imperative for states to pursue national security. But where they depart from realists is on the means to achieve security. Pluralists recognize the virtues of self-help, but most states are not in position to carry such a financial burden. Pluralists place much greater faith than realists in the role of international organizations, alliances, and international regimes as a means not only to reduce the financial cost of security, but to sustain and expand a sense of international society. Economic structuralists of a Marxist persuasion would disagree with both realists and pluralists, arguing that class interests dictate how security is defined. In effect, security is whatever the elites representing the dominant class say it is.

Constructivists and feminists hold a broader conception of security in terms of (1) what would be defined as security and (2) to whom the term applies. The concept of human security includes nonmilitary threats such as environmental scarcity, overpopulation, diseases, and poverty. Human security tends to focus on individuals and groups as opposed to states. For many unfortunate souls, security is defined as sheer physical survival. In fact, the state may be seen not as the ultimate protector of one's security but rather as the source of the threat.

Discussions of the international economy generally revolve around monetary issues (the relative value of currencies), trade, finance, and aid. For a realist, economic issues are particularly important as they influence a state's overall power. For pluralists and economic structuralists, the international economy is a critical aspect of world politics and raises issues of global disparities and inequalities. Economic matters may be viewed primarily as security concerns such as feeding one's family, which may dominate every waking moment for many people in the world's most impoverished countries. For them, global economic trends, growth rates, balance of payments problems, and exchange rates are irrelevant abstractions. Indeed, achieving minimum economic subsistence is the goal of the vast majority of humanity. Feminists also emphasize world poverty in relation to the subjugation of women, criticizing the failure of mainstream social science to investigate and appreciate the major role women play in the developing world and in the global economy.

Identity involves the answer to the question, "Who am I, and with whom do I identify?" In terms of international relations and world politics, identity is most often associated with the state and nation and the values, culture, and people who fall within that state's borders. For realists, nationalism defined as identity with political ramifications can be a cause of war but also a means to mobilize popular support in defense of the country. Many pluralists see international organizations and transnational movements as purveyors of emergent identities that parallel or transcend those associated with the state. Some people, for example, may identify strongly with an international movement concerned with such goals as protection of the global environment. These people may see themselves more as citizens of the world rather than as citizens of any single country. For others, an identification with a particular religion such as Islam is more important than association with any one state. For many economic structuralists, identity is based on class and, hence, may transcend any state boundary. The concept of identity is particularly important to constructivists and feminists, who both view identity as being somewhat malleable and capable of being changed or redefined over time. Particularly for educated women in the Third World, overcoming traditional, limited roles and establishing an individual identity may well lead them to identify more closely with other such women in other countries than with those in their own state and society.

Security, economy, and identity, therefore, provide the principal themes of the three major parts of this book. In our opinion, the struggle over these three issues and their interrelations—particularly the security dimensions of economy and identity—define much of what is important and interesting today about international relations and world politics. As noted, all three concepts relate not just to the desires of individuals, but also to the collective aspiration of peoples in states and societies throughout the world. A substantial *challenge in world politics is how to satisfy and to attempt to reconcile common aspirations for security, economic welfare, and identity. Accordingly, world politics involves goal-seeking behavior and also the related processes of deciding who gets what, when, and how.*[5]

In sum, these three themes represent three universal concerns. In this book we examine the means by which states, groups, and individuals have attempted to achieve security, economic welfare, and identity—however defined—and the obstacles to this achievement. In a world of scarcity, the means for some to achieve these goals can be an obstacle to their achievement by others. Similarly, while some states at a minimum may seek to be left alone, other states have a more expansive definition of security or the pursuit of other opportunities abroad, the fulfillment of which might come at the expense of their neighbors. One must, therefore, beware of thinking that such common concerns are necessarily a force for universal harmony. In fact, the manner in which

---

[5]Harold D. Lasswell, *Politics: Who Gets What, When, How* (Cleveland, OH: World Publishing Co., 1958).

these concerns for security, economic welfare, and identity are specifically defined and pursued can vary widely. Indeed, they can just as easily divide people as unite them and be a source of domestic, regional, or global conflict.

What Is a Theory, and Why Should We Care?

The word **theory** means different things to different people. In common parlance, for example, something may be true "in theory" but not "in fact." In this rather loose usage, in theory equates to in principle or in the abstract, and hence, theory is viewed by some as irrelevant to the real world.

Another meaning, consistent with usage in this book, views theory as a way of making the world or some part of it more intelligible or better understood. Theories dealing with international relations and world politics aspire to achieve this goal. Making things more intelligible, of course, may amount to nothing more than better or more precise descriptions of the things we observe. For many people, theory requires at a minimum a conceptual framework that allows one to sort out data for purposes of comparison. Although accurate description is essential, theory is something more. Theory makes the world more intelligible by offering causal **explanation** of what we observe or **prediction** of what is likely to happen, given the presence (or absence) of certain factors or conditions.

Theorists try to explain or account for the recurring phenomena we observe. Attempts to explain why wars occur, for example, lead theorists to look for factors or variables that are present (or absent) prior to the outbreak of war. In a now classic explanation offered by Kenneth Waltz in his book *Man, the State and War,* he considers the relative importance of psychological and social-psychological factors involving individuals and groups, societal differences as in whether democracies or dictatorships have a higher propensity to go to war, and the condition of anarchy as well as other factors in the international system causally related to the outbreak of war.

Given these factors, how do we explain the decision for a particular war? Is it a matter simply of rational choice—a conscious calculation to secure national objectives through the use of force? Let's give an example. Ask yourself and attempt to answer the question, "Why did the United States decide to go to war against Iraq in 2003?" Was it rational choice—a calculation of expected costs and benefits related to achieving national (or international) objectives through the use of force? You might recall some of the reasons offered by President Bush's administration: Iraq was said to be a threat to national and international security, as it possessed chemical and biological weapons capabilities and was also understood to be developing nuclear weapons of mass destruction. After all, Iraq was controlled by a dictator with a history in the 1980s of using chemical weapons against Iraqi Kurds (and against Iranians as well in the Iran–Iraq war). Added to this was deep suspicion that Saddam Hussein's regime was somehow tied in with the 9/11 terrorist attacks against the World Trade Center in New York and the Pentagon in Washington, D.C. In short, removing Saddam Hussein from power— changing the political regime in Iraq—would eliminate the threat his regime posed to international peace and stability.

A second take focuses on the individual role and personality of President George W. Bush. Aside from the publicly stated view that Iraq was a threat and sharing the ideological worldview of many of his key advisers, some speculate that the plot instigated by Saddam Hussein to assassinate the president's father on his tour of liberated Kuwait in 1992 may also have been part of the U.S. calculation to go to war in 2003. Even if not decisive, some see it as contributory to accepting and acting on other arguments for going to war. In any event, documentary evidence for this "revenge" hypothesis is slim at best. On the other hand, that the president and his advisors perceived Saddam Hussein as an unsavory, if not diabolical, figure is easier to document. To the extent that perception influenced the way "facts" were interpreted by decision makers and the meanings drawn from what they observed, we see the importance of psychological factors.

A third take emphasizes the decisive role of a relatively small group of policy makers in the White House and U.S. Department of Defense—a decision-making elite—who shared a common ideological world view, sometimes termed *neoconservative,* that underscored the need to be decisive, even preemptive—a willingness to attack first, in the face of threats to national security. Neoconservatives also saw American interests served by spreading democracy to "rogue states" such as Iraq—transforming Iraq into a democratic model for all of the Middle East to emulate. By changing the regime in Iraq, a major threat to Israel would also be removed. What also bound the neoconservatives together was that many had worked together in President George H. W. Bush's administration (1989–1993) and had planned and executed the first U.S.-led war against Iraq in 1991. Removing Saddam was part of their unfinished policy agenda. Though not emphasized in public statements, regime change in Baghdad would also serve U.S. strategic interests by removing control of Iraq's oil fields from Saddam Hussein's hands, assuring continued flow to global markets with revenue directed initially by the United States and, in time, a new regime in Baghdad to finance postwar reconstruction and development of benefit to the Iraqi people. Referring to aims specified in the U.S. National Security Strategy—published in 2002, about a year before the Iraq war—some critics represent all this as part of what they call a "larger imperial design" envisioned by neoconservatives to maintain a position of American power dominance over the coming decades, resorting to preemptive action against challengers whenever necessary to assure this long-term strategic goal.

We can see how difficult it is to explain theoretically why states resort to war in general, much less the outbreak of a particular war. The condition of international anarchy posed no obstacle to going to war in Iraq—what Waltz calls the permissive cause of war. The efficient or direct causes of a particular war are to be found at different **levels of analysis.** At the international system level, there were only a few allies for the venture, but in any event no effective balance of power to block intervention in Iraq by the United States, United Kingdom, and other coalition partners. The three takes offered above ask whether at the individual (or small group) level of analysis the decision to go to war was a rational choice based on the information and understanding of the facts then at hand, whether psychological factors were contributory, and whether the values and group dynamics of a decision-making elite—social-psychological factors—were causally related to the decision made by President Bush and his administration.

Although we will not resolve these questions here, we use this example of the decision to go to war in Iraq to introduce the utility of the concept of levels of analysis— a framework designed to organize systematic thinking about various aspects of world politics. Figure 1.2 illustrates one version.

Note how the levels proceed from the individual to larger and larger aggregations. In our example, the individual level of analysis focuses on the personality of President George W. Bush or perceptions by him and his individual advisors. The group level examines the president in the broader context of his relationships with other key foreign-policy advisers. We might at the domestic or state-and-society level ask if the president's high popularity at the time among most Americans gave him greater freedom of action

levels of analysis
A means to organize systematic thinking about world politics. In examining a phenomenon such as war, for example, one may identify possible causes as characteristics of the international system, states and their societies, groups, or individuals.

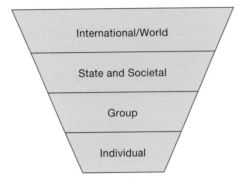

FIGURE 1.2   *Levels of Analysis*

Levels of Analysis: A More Detailed Look

International/World (or Global) Level

Anarchic quality of the international system

Number of major powers or poles

Distribution of power/capabilities among states

Level and diffusion of technology

Patterns of military alliances

Patterns of international trade and finance

International organizations and regimes

Transnational organizations and networks

Global norms and international law

State and Societal (or National) Level

Governmental

Structure and nature of political system
Policymaking process

Societal

Structure of economic system
Public opinion
Nationalism and ethnicity
Political culture
Ideology

Group Level

Government bureaucracies

Interest groups

Other nongovernmental organizations

Individual Level

Human nature and psychology

Leaders and beliefs systems

Personality of leaders

Cognition/perception or misperception

---

politically, enabling him more easily to commit U.S. forces to armed conflict abroad than would have been the case had he not enjoyed such public favor. The international or global level of analysis deals with such factors as the potential threat to the United States and the region posed by Iraq, international norms, balance-of-power considerations, and the role of alliances or coalitions. One can ask in this regard if the preponderance of power enjoyed by the United States (in what many structural realists call a unipolar world characterized by the lack of effective "balancers" or countervailing power) also gave it the greater freedom to take such actions as well as a greater propensity to act unilaterally to achieve national objectives.

One could also ask what, if any, impact or influence domestic or international norms had on the U.S. decision to go to war. Did the fact that the United States proclaimed the importance of establishing democratic regimes in the Middle East and elsewhere have anything to do with the decision to go to war against Iraq? Did the U.S. dependence on foreign oil and a desire to maintain and expand its economic power play a role in the decision? To what extent did the opinions of the United Nations, NATO allies, and Russia affect U.S. decision making? If the answer is, to varying degrees, "all of the above," then the next question is, "What is the relative weight or importance of each factor found at the different levels of analysis?"

The value of considering levels of analysis is the comprehensive framework it provides for classifying factors that account for either a state's foreign policy behavior or international outcomes (such as war among states). As such it helps us along the road to the major goal of theory—explanation. If we have an understanding of what conditions (the presence or absence of certain factors or variables) cause certain phenomena to occur, we may also be in a better position theoretically to predict likely outcomes. Factors at different levels are termed **independent variables,** which may be part of the explanation. What one is trying to explain—a state's foreign policy or international outcomes (war in this case)—is known as the **dependent variable.** The bottom line is that thinking conceptually is important, necessary, and very satisfying when it comes to attempting to understand international relations and world politics. Furthermore, to think conceptually and to use these concepts to think theoretically—seeking explanations or predictions for what we observe in the world around us—can be done by any of us. To think conceptually and theoretically is not something mysterious or impossible to achieve for the uninitiated.

The levels-of-analysis framework is useful as it provides a checklist that allows one to make educated guesses as to what factors might account for the international behavior of any actor. This educated guess is termed a *proposition* or *hypothesis.* According to mainstream science, the task is to engage in **causal** explanation or prediction based on certain prior occurrences, patterns, or conditions. Thus, whenever A is present, then B can be expected to follow. "If A, then B" as **hypothesis** may be subject to **empirical** testing—that is, the rigorous, systematic testing of the hypothesis with evidence or data from the real world. An example of an hypothesis is, "If states engage in arms races, then the likelihood of war increases." Indeed, formal statement and testing of hypotheses through the use of statistical methods are seen by many scholars as central to the theory-building process. Others prefer to rely on nonquantitative case and comparative case studies, historical methods, and reasoned arguments—the so-called traditional methods of theory building. It is the testing of theory with data that gives meaning to the "facts" about the world. It is a fact, for example, that the Soviet empire collapsed in the early 1990s; good theory would help us understand why this occurred—an explanation for what happened.

Whatever differences international-relations scholars might have among themselves, they all agree on one thing—theory is necessary and unavoidable when it comes to explaining and attempting to foresee the future of international relations and world politics. Theory is unavoidable, in that all people approach their subject matter from what has been called variously different prior assumptions, perspectives, or images. An analyst, hence, needs to be theoretically self-conscious, meaning to be aware of the perspective or even bias one might bring to a problem. Theory is also necessary, in that it tells us what to focus on and what to ignore in making sense of the world around us. Without theory we would be overwhelmed and immobilized by an avalanche of mere facts. The sense we make of what we observe is informed by the perspectives, concepts, and theories we hold.

A theory, therefore, is an intellectual construct that helps us explain or predict what we observe—interpreting facts and identifying regularities and recurrences or repetitions of observed phenomena. Fitting pieces into a larger whole makes theory building analogous to puzzle solving. We can certainly think theoretically when it comes to explaining international relations and world politics in general or the foreign policy of a particular state. But international relations theorists tend to be interested in patterns of behavior among various international actors. In identifying patterns, the stage is set for making at least modest predictions about the possible nature and direction of change. To think theoretically, however, is not to engage in point predictions—"A will attack B the first week of the year"—however much we may want the answers to such questions. Predictive theory usually takes the more general form that given certain specified conditions, certain outcomes are likely or can be expected to follow with some degree of probability.

Most of the theoretical work that relies on realist and liberal or pluralist images of international relations and world politics embraces positivism. **Positivism** involves a commitment to a unified view of science, meaning a belief that it is possible to adopt the methodologies of the natural sciences to explain the social world, which includes international relations and world politics. Positivists believe that objective knowledge of the world is possible and, hence, have a faith in and a commitment to the seventeenth- and eighteenth-century Enlightenment's rationalist tradition that underlies science or what some refer to as modernism.

Critical and Postmodern Challenges to Positivist Science

Positivism has been under assault by critical and postmodern theorists for its attempts in international relations and other social sciences to (1) separate facts from values, (2) define and operationalize concepts into precisely and accurately measurable variables, and (3) test truth claims in the form of hypotheses drawn from theories. Whether using quantitative or statistical methods, or such nonquantitative (or qualitative) methods as case and comparative-case studies, those who have tried to be scientific have been criticized for ignoring or taking insufficient account of the personal or human dimension of scholarship. Critical theorists and postmodernists make the assumption that facts, concepts, and theories may not be separated from values, as all three stem from their observation and construction by human agency. To postmodernists, what we see, what we choose to see or measure, and the mechanisms or methods we employ are all of human construction that essentially rely on perception and cognitive processes influenced as well by prior understandings and meanings. Even the language we use constitutes an embedded set of values that are an integral part of any culture. What we observe in either the natural or social sciences is heavily influenced by the interpretive understanding we have of the concepts we employ. The same holds for the causal relations we infer when we specify the relations among variables, theories, hypotheses, and the observed behavior of states and nonstate actors in the political and social milieu in which they are immersed. If the central question of **epistemology** is how we know what we think we know, critical and postmodernist theorists set aside the abstract, universalist, scientific claims of positivists.

Some **critical theorists** argue that beliefs held by theorists necessarily bias their truth claims and may well be part of global ideological schemes to legitimize particular world orders. In supporting an alleged agenda of domination (whether based on class, power, ethnicity, gender, or values), it may be convenient to advance ideologies often masquerading as scientifically based theories. Critical theorists do not reject science or the scientific method as such, but they do subject theoretical and other truth claims to greater scrutiny. One of the tasks of critical theorists is to unmask deceptions, probe for deeper understandings or meanings, and expose the class or other interests these ideologies or alleged theories are designed to serve. Power is a core concept for critical theorists, particularly in relation to those who wield it. Given the focus on human perception and understandings that give diverse meanings to the concepts and theories we formulate and the behavior we observe, it should not be surprising that some authors associated with economic structuralism, constructivism, and feminism are sympathetic to the assumptions of critical theory.

Critical theory may be viewed separately from postmodernism because most critical theorists retain strict methodological criteria to guide their work. Nevertheless, some critical theory does overlap with, or can be understood more broadly as, part of a postmodernist understanding. In this regard, postmodernist **ontology** (or assumptions about being—the way things are—that inform an individual's world view) is prone to find the subtexts and to deconstruct—unpack and take apart—the meanings embedded in what we say or write and even in the ways we act. Human beings are essentially subjective creatures; to postmodernists, claims made to empirically based, objective truth are necessarily hollow. Our understandings and meanings are, after all, humanly constructed. In the extreme, no knowledge or truth is possible apart from the motivations and purposes people put into their construction. From this extreme postmodernist perspective, truth is entirely relative.

Assessing the Challenges to Mainstream Science and Positivism

These are, to say the least, significant challenges to "modernist" science more generally and to international relations theory in particular. It is difficult, however, simply to deny or dismiss scientific methodologies that have produced so much accumulated knowledge in so many diverse fields of human inquiry. Defenders of positivism quite simply see postmodernist thinkers as misrepresenting science; the scientific method is, after all, a skeptical enterprise that subjects all truth claims to both logical and empirical tests.

What critical, postmodernist, and feminist perspectives do contribute to theorizing about international relations and world politics, however, is an ever-increased epistemological sensitivity to, and caution concerning, the fragility of what we think to be true. The values we hold influence the interpretive understanding that leads us to formulate the concepts we adopt. Interpretive understanding thus has its place in international-relations theorizing by aiding in the ongoing search for new syntheses in human understandings of our political world.

Normative Theory

Mainstream social science attempts to explain *what is*. **Normative theory** is driven by a concern for what *ought to be* or should be. Because normative theory deals explicitly with norms and values, it has particular relevance to policy makers who must make the hard choices, particularly those involving moral or ethical questions. Indeed, normative theory strives to provide moral or ethical guidelines not only for policy makers, but also for any individual who is engaged or interested in international relations and world politics. Normative theorists, however, fully realize that choice is constrained by circumstance. Applying normative theory to practice crosses a wide diversity of global issues now confronting humankind. Consider the following questions that normative theory attempts to provide guidance for policy makers:

- Can a war be "just"? And if so, under what conditions?
- When (if ever, some would say) is it legitimate to use force?
- Do the wealthy countries of the world have a responsibility to alleviate poverty in the Third World?
- Despite sovereignty's injunction that states should not interfere in the domestic affairs of other states, under what circumstances should the international community intervene to protect the human rights of people abused by their own governments?

And for individuals:

- Do we owe our primary allegiance to our family, community, ethnic group, state or nation, or to a broader humanity of six billion persons? What obligations and duties do we as individuals have beyond territorial boundaries?
- How should we live in an era of increasing globalization and interdependence?
- Is there a natural limit to politically relevant ethics? Is it possible to balance politics and ethics, or are they inseparable?

Why are such questions important? One reason is that many students of international relations and world politics have felt a growing sense of intellectual inadequacy resulting from the collective failure to foresee the rapid end of the Cold War over a several-year period.[6] If unable to anticipate such a major event (in reality a series of events), how confident can we be that we have an intellectual handle on where the world might be heading in the early twenty-first century as globalization continues apace, the environment deteriorates in many areas of the globe, diseases become more threatening, malnutrition remains prevalent, religious extremism seems on the rise, and the technology of mass destruction appears to be making its way into the hands of groups and individuals? Depending on the issue, normative concerns may well play a role in helping all of us think through the appropriate responses.

---

[6]Ken Booth, Tim Dunne, Michael Cox, "How Might We Live? Global Ethics in a New Century," *Review of International Studies,* 26 (December 2000), 2.

Overview

At this point we provide an overview of the book—a game plan, if you will. In Chapter 2 we begin with an examination of the historical development of international relations and world politics. A key goal is to provide the reader with an appreciation for the continuity as well as the changes in international relations and world politics over the centuries. In order to understand what is unique about the current world, one has to know what it has in common with the past. We also discuss writers who have contributed to contemporary images of international relations and world politics.

Part II focuses on state security and statecraft. As noted earlier, for good or ill, states are still the key actors in world politics. Useful generalizations can be made concerning states' basic interests and objectives, as well as instruments used to achieve them, such as military force and diplomacy. This reliance on an essentially realist view of the world will be critiqued from the perspective of other images.

Part III moves from a discussion of state security to an examination of international security—global dynamics and trends that are of concern to many, perhaps most, peoples. This includes an analysis of the global spread of armaments, international terrorism, and the impact of criminal organizations. Alliances, international law, international regimes, and international organizations—strategies to deal with such common concerns—are also discussed.

Part IV focuses on global civil society and the global economy, both topics informed by liberal or pluralist, economic structuralist, English School, and social constructivist perspectives. A discussion of the historical development of a global civil society is followed by an overview of the attributes and development of the capitalist global economy. Topics include international trade, global finance, the divide between the rich and poor, and development. Challenges posed by resource depletion, population growth, and the environment round out this section. Each topic is a source of current or potential international conflict, and each has led to calls for regional or international responses to the dangers they pose. Hence all of these issues can also be viewed as aspects of international security.

In Part V we examine issues concerning basic human identity in the context of world politics and civil society—religion, nationalism, and regionalism, then humanitarianism as reflected in a concern for refugees, justice, human rights, and the issue of humanitarian intervention, particularly in cases involving national, ethnic or tribal, and other forms of intercommunal strife or civil war. Constructivist and feminist perspectives will be prominent. We conclude by making some observations—pessimistic and optimistic—on the future of world politics and posing a series of questions.

Our increasingly globalized world is in a state of flux, exhibiting a number of disturbing trends. Some of these trends certainly existed during the Cold War, but the forty-five-year-long East-West confrontation between the democratic capitalist and communist world overshadowed them. Observers of international politics through the centuries have made similar observations about their unique and troubling times. In this book, our task as authors is to present an objective and balanced presentation of the key issues of world politics today. Of equal importance is our goal to provide an array of conceptual tools to help the interested student make sense of global politics in the new millennium. Readers should examine critically what we present. After all, for most readers of this volume, it is *your* generation, more than ours, that will have to deal with the problems that face us throughout much of the twenty-first century.

Key Terms

globalization *p. 6*
interdependence *p. 6*
authority *p. 8*

realism *p. 16*
pluralism (liberalism) *p. 18*

economic structuralism *p. 21*
levels of analysis *p. 31*

Other Concepts

Third World *p. 4*
First World *p. 4*
Second World *p. 4*
state *p. 12*
sovereignty *p. 12*
international organizations
  (IOs) *p. 12*
norms *p. 13*
(transnational)
  nongovernmental
  organizations
  (NGOs) *p. 13*
global civil society *p. 14*
society of states *p. 17*
anarchy *p. 18*
structural realists *p. 18*
neorealists *p. 18*
unipolar *p. 18*

bipolar *p. 18*
multipolar *p. 18*
international law *p. 20*
neoliberal
  institutionalists *p. 20*
liberal internationalists *p. 20*
class *p. 21*
core *p. 21*
periphery *p. 21*
semiperiphery *p. 21*
South *p. 21*
North *p. 21*
comprador class *p. 22*
global structures *p. 22*
English School *p. 22*
social constructivism *p. 24*
feminism *p. 24*
gender *p. 25*

international relations *p. 26*
global or world politics *p. 26*
security *p. 27*
economy *p. 27*
identity *p. 27*
theory *p. 30*
explanation *p. 30*
prediction *p. 30*
independent variable *p. 33*
dependent variable *p. 33*
causal *p. 33*
hypothesis *p. 33*
empirical *p. 33*
positivism *p. 34*
epistemology *p. 35*
critical theorists *p. 35*
ontology *p. 35*
normative theory *p. 36*

Additional Readings

For books that examine the impact of globalization using real-world examples, we recommend John Micklethwait and Adrian Woolridge, *A Future Perfect: The Challenge and Promise of Globalization* (New York: Random House, 2003), Joseph Nye, Jr., *The Paradox of American Power* (New York: Oxford University Press, 2002), Nye and John D. Donahue (eds.), *Governance in a Globalizing World* (Washington, D.C.: Brookings Institution Press, 2000), and journalist Thomas L. Friedman's *The World Is Flat: A Brief History of the Twenty-first Century* (New York: Farrar, Straus and Giroux, 2005) and his earlier *The Lexus and the Olive Tree: Understanding Globalization* (New York: Anchor/Random House, 2000). For a unique visual survey of these political, economic, and social trends that is superior to the usual charts and tables, we strongly recommend Dan Smith and Michael Kidron, *The State of the World Atlas,* 6th ed. (London: Penguin Books, 2003). Finally, for academic analyses of significant long-term international trends and transformations that predate the current fascination with globalization trends, see Eugene B. Skolnikoff, *The Elusive Transformation: Science, Technology, and the Evolution of International Politics* (Princeton, NJ: Princeton University Press, 1993) and James N. Rosenau, *Turbulence in World Politics* (Princeton, NJ: Princeton University Press, 1990).

For the reader who wishes to review cold war events prior to the 1990s, we recommend the excellent, brief, and eminently readable overview by William Hyland, *The Cold War: Fifty Years of Conflict* (New York: Random House, 1991). For an American foreign policy perspective, see Stephen Ambrose, *Rise to Globalism* (Penguin Books, multiple editions). For an anthology containing a wide variety of views, see

Michael J. Hogan, ed., *The End of the Cold War: Its Meaning and Implications* (Cambridge: Cambridge University Press, 1992). For a look back as well as forward, we recommend Sean M. Lynn-Jones and Steven E. Miller, eds., *The Cold War and After: Prospects for Peace* (Cambridge, MA: The MIT Press, 1993), which contains articles that first appeared in the journal *International Security*. Also consider two other works: Louis J. Halle, *The Cold War as History* (New York: Harper Collins, 1967 and Perennial, 1991) and John Lewis Gaddis, *The United States and the End of the Cold War* (New York: Oxford University Press, 1992).

From the vast literature on international relations theory:

A. On realism we recommend Jack Donnelly, *Realism and International Relations* (Cambridge: Cambridge University Press, 2000), Robert O. Keohane (ed.), *Neorealism and Its Critics* (New York: Columbia University Press, 1986), Charles W. Kegley, Jr., *Controversies in International Relations Theory: Realism and the Neoliberal Challenge* (New York: Oxford University Press, 1995). On quantitative approaches, see John A. Vasquez and Marie T. Henehan (eds.), *The Scientific Study of Peace and War* (New York: Lexington Books, 1992, 1999).

B. On developments in the English School, consider Adam Watson, *The Evolution of International Society* (London: Routledge, 1992), Edward Keene, *Beyond the Anarchical Society* (Cambridge: Cambridge University Press, 2002), and Barry Buzan, *From International to World Society* (Cambridge: Cambridge University Press, 2004).

C. On constructivism, an important theoretical treatment is Alexander Wendt, *Social Theory of International Politics* (Cambridge: Cambridge University Press, 1999), but for an applied approach, consider Vendulka Kubálková, Nicholas Onuf, and Paul Kowert (eds.), *International Relations in a Constructed World* (London: M.E. Sharpe, 1998) or Ralph Pettman, *Common Sense Constructivism* (London: M.E. Sharpe, 2000). For a volume that relates constructivism to feminism and critical theory, see Karin M. Fierke and Knud Erik Jørgenson (eds.), *Constructing International Relations* (London: M.E. Sharpe, 2001).

D. For postmodernist understandings, see James Der Derian and Michael J. Shapiro (eds.), *International/Intertextual Relations* (London: M.E. Sharpe, 1989) and Francis A. Beer, *Meanings of War and Peace* (College Station, TX: University of Texas Press, 2001). On applications of critical theory, see Frank P. Harvey and Michael Brecher (eds.), *Critical Perspectives in International Studies* (Ann Arbor, MI: University of Michigan Press, 2002) and Ken Booth (ed.), *Critical Security Studies and World Politics* (Boulder: Lynne Rienner, 2005).

E. Among the many anthologies that deal variously with realism, liberalism (and liberal institutionalism) or pluralism, economic structuralism, English School, postmodernism, critical theory, feminism, and social constructivism are Scott Burchill et al., *Theories of International Relations* (New York: Palgrave, 1995, 1996); Colin Elman and Miriam Fendius Elman (eds.), *Progress in International Relations Theory* (Cambridge, MA: MIT Press, 2003); and Walter Carnaes, Thomas Risse, and Beth A. Simmons (eds.), *Handbook of International Relations* (London: SAGE Publications, 2002). We also note the continuing work by Yale H. Ferguson and Richard Mansbach, *The Elusive Quest Continues: Theory and Global Politics* (Upper Saddle River, NJ: Prentice Hall, 2003) and numerous editions of James E. Dougherty and Robert L. Pfaltzgraff, Jr., *Contending Theories of International Relations* (New York: Longman, 1971, 2001). Finally, we note our own efforts in *International Relations Theory* soon to be in its 4th edition with Prentice Hall.

Chapter 2

"One age cannot be completely understood if all the others are not understood. The song of history can only be sung as a whole."

JOSE ORTEGA Y GASSET, PHILOSOPHER AND HISTORIAN

International Relations and World Politics in Historical Perspective

Ferdinand III (1608–1657), Holy Roman Emperor, king of Hungary, and king of Bohemia, had no idea that his actions were partially responsible for the eventual institution of the modern state. Born in Graz, Austria, he was educated by Jesuits and was a noted scholar and musician. But the assassination of the Austrian general Albrecht von Wallenstein led Ferdinand to become the nominal commander of the imperial armies fighting the Thirty Years' War, which involved a long, drawn-out conflict between Catholic and Protestant rulers. Upon his father's death in 1637, Ferdinand became Holy Roman Emperor. In 1640 he refused to accept a proposal that called for a general amnesty for Protestants. In 1648, however, he agreed to the Peace of Westphalia, which decreed that the prevailing religion in each part of the empire was to be determined by the local ruler. By recognizing the independence of individual states, Ferdinand and his fellow rulers of the day departed from the idea of unity within the Holy Roman Empire and set into motion the rise of the modern state.

Imagine that in front of you there is a globe completely devoid of any features except continents, islands, and bodies of water. If you were to depict the major actors of world politics or international relations, what would you sketch in?

The first task for most people would be to add lines showing territorial boundaries among **states.** Indeed, most maps of the world emphasize states, showing the globe as a colorful patchwork quilt of populated territories (recognized by each other as legitimate) over which central governments claim the right to rule, a monopoly on the legitimate use of force, and some degree of influence on the economy and society. You might then add a small star to each state, illustrating the physical location and name of the capital city. Look at the map of the world at the beginning of this book for an example of a map that emphasizes state boundaries.

Political science, economics, history, geography, or international studies majors might feel most comfortable with this depiction, but we are all conditioned to think of international politics as relations among states. You do not have to be a realist to adopt this perspective. Examine any newspaper that covers foreign affairs, and the point is easily illustrated. Invariably the reporter's dateline is from some capital city somewhere in the world, and much

The State

The state as a legal concept includes the following:

- A territory with defined boundaries
- A population (with or without a national or common identity)
- A **government** or administration
- Recognition as a sovereign state by other sovereign states

---

of what is written refers to government activity, whether it is an announcement of war or an announcement of new social programs. States—or at least the people or government officials who claim to act as agents in the name of the state—are usually viewed as the key actors in world politics, if for no other reason than that they control territory and the world's greatest arsenals of weapons. They also have the ability to wreak tremendous havoc and destruction upon their own peoples, neighbors, and the planet as a whole.

How does one think about world politics in a conceptual and historical perspective? The terms *global* or *world* assume, at a minimum, some degree of interdependence among actors. As we have argued in the previous chapter, the contemporary era is the only one that is truly global. Historically, however, most peoples' lives—economic, social, and political—revolved around an isolated village, clan, or tribe. Identity derived from these small communities, not some larger entity. Similarly, the local economy was usually insulated, particularly in subsistence economies, with little trade among villages, clans, or tribes. Hence political and economic—indeed, any—interdependence outside of one's own community was minimal or nonexistent.

The same is true of relations among different civilizations. When the Spanish and Portuguese explorers set forth in the fifteenth and sixteenth centuries, they had little idea what other cultures and civilizations they would encounter. Similarly, it was not until adventurers and traders trekked to China along what came to be known as the Silk Road that economic exchanges occurred between West and East. Therefore it makes little sense to begin speaking of global politics until after the rise of the modern state that encouraged and sponsored the outward expansion of capitalism through both trade and an exploitative **colonialism.** The concepts of global interdependence and **globalization,** however, did not take hold until the worldwide expansion of markets, transportation, and communications, especially during the last half of the twentieth century.

International Systems: Definition and Scope

international system
An aggregation of similar or diverse entities linked by regular interaction that sets them apart from other systems, for example, the interstate or international system of states, or world politics understood as a system composed of both state and nonstate actors.

Given the fact the world has not always been organized the way it is today, it makes more sense to speak historically of *international systems*—systems that were limited in geographic scope and hence cannot accurately be described as global or world systems. The concept of *system* used in this work is defined as an aggregation of diverse entities linked by regular interaction that sets them apart from other systems.[1] The idea of

---

[1] This definition is modified from that provided by Robert A. Mundell and Alexander K. Swoboda, eds., *Monetary Problems of the International Economy* (Chicago: University of Chicago Press, 1969), 343, as cited by Robert Gilpin, *War and Change in World Politics* (Cambridge: Cambridge University Press, 1981), 26. The original definition is, "A system is an aggregation of diverse entities united by regular interaction according to a form of control."

diverse entities is useful in that it allows not only for different types of state actors, such as **city-states, empires,** and modern states, but also international organizations and such nonstate actors as corporations and humanitarian relief organizations. The definition of *regular interaction* varies depending on the nature and intensity of the interactions. For example, the nature of the interaction could be war, with such conflict of greater or lesser intensity. Or the interaction could be trade, ranging from minimal to intense. Finally the nature of the system's units and their relative capabilities or positions in relation to each other give the system *structure* and set the system apart from other systems. This also allows us to speak of a system having boundaries. For example, we can speak of relations in the contemporary European Union (EU) as a political-economic system or view commercial interactions in the North American Free Trade Agreement (NAFTA) among firms and consumers in Canada, Mexico, and the United States as a separate North American economic system.

In this regard it can be said that today a world or global system also exists, as the distinct boundaries between separate international systems of earlier historical periods are lacking. Furthermore the current global system—although dominated by states—is also characterized by extensive economic and technological interdependence and a diverse set of international and transnational actors. From this perspective the EU and NAFTA examples could be termed subsystems of the larger global system.

It should be remembered, of course, that a system is simply an analytic device to allow an observer to deal with an aspect of international relations that is of interest. It is not meant to be a precise description of reality. For example, we could focus on a "Peloponnesian system" limited, for the most part, to interactions of the fifth-century B.C. Greek city-states. This, in effect, was the approach used by the historian Thucydides in his discussion of the ancient conflict between Athens and Sparta. Conversely, we could enlarge the system being analyzed to include the neighboring Persian empire, which played an intermittent but crucial role. Whether to view the Peloponnesian city-states and the Persian empire as separate systems with distinct boundaries or as subsystems within a larger international system is really up to the analyst.

To summarize, while we characterize the world today as a global system, we can also focus on various subsystems. Such subsystems may be geographically oriented—for example, relations among members of the EU, NAFTA, or ASEAN (the Association of Southeast Asian Nations). Or the subsystems may be defined in functional terms—a telecommunications subsystem, a trading subsystem, a transportation subsystem, a financial transaction subsystem. These latter types of subsystems could be depicted visually, with lines crisscrossing the globe, illustrating the density of transactions. Instead of the globe being divided into geographic entities—the image with which we began this chapter—it would look more like a cobweb or latticework. We note that some writers avoid the terms *system* and *subsystem* entirely, preferring instead to see these transactions among diverse actors as part of an increasingly complex and global *society*.

When did the global system come about? It is difficult to determine a precise date, as the globalization process occurred incrementally over many centuries. We would suggest, however, that the globalization of the European state system (i.e., the state as the key political unit) began in earnest in the nineteenth century at the same time that global economic interdependence began to accelerate. It has been only since 1945, or the end of World War II, that the technological and communications revolutions in transportation, communications, information transfer, and other technologies have gathered speed and had a global impact.

Up until the nineteenth century, however, it makes more sense to speak of various regional or international systems, meaning they were not global in scope. In historical

structure (systemic)
In realist usage, structure usually refers to the distribution of power among states. Thus, a world subject to the influence of one great power is unipolar, to two principal powers is bipolar, and to three or more is multipolar.

references we prefer, however, the term *international* to *regional*. In ancient times people had no idea that other civilizations existed in other parts of the world. As far as they knew, they were the world if not the center of the universe. This was as true in Europe as it was in the Americas, Africa, China, or elsewhere in Asia and the Pacific.

In this chapter we examine four different types of international systems, reserving more extensive discussions of the current global system and global civil society for the remainder of the book.[2] There are three purposes in this discussion. First, history contributes to our understanding of international politics. After all, it is difficult to understand what is unique about the current global system unless we know what it has in common with earlier international systems. Second, a discussion of historical international systems allows us to mention some of the political theorists who have influenced contemporary thinking about world politics and influenced the realist and pluralist images. Finally, our discussion will expose the reader to a conceptual and theoretical understanding of international relations and world politics beyond historical facts and figures.

Four Types of International Systems

First an **independent state system** consists of political entities that each claim to be sovereign with the right to make both foreign policy and domestic decisions. No superior power is acknowledged and other states recognize these claims to *sovereignty*. Simply by interacting with other units (the system), some interdependence exists, resulting in a certain degree of constraint on any one state's actions. States are equal in terms of their claims to sovereignty, though they obviously differ in their capabilities and power. An ambitious and rising power may be viewed as a threat to the independence of other states, resulting in the formation of a counterweight or countervailing coalition or alliance. The rising power is constrained by the actions of the others, just as the members of the alliance will witness some degree of limitation on their freedom of maneuver by agreeing to work together to deter or defeat the ambitious state and maintain a *balance of power.*

States also accept other voluntary restraints such as rules of war. Some rules may be promulgated simply to ease the operation of the system, such as diplomatic practices. One historical example of an independent state system is drawn from what we know about the ancient Greek city-state system prior to the fifth-century B.C. wars against Persia. Independent state systems occasionally arose in later historical periods that were relatively free of hegemonic influences.

Second there is a **hegemonic state system.** By *hegemony* we mean one or more states dominate the system, set the "rules of the game," and have some degree of direct influence on the external affairs of member states. Many writers refer in structural terms to what we call hegemony as having three variants:

1. *Unipolarity:* "One pole," or a single dominant state such as the United States at present and in the aftermath of the collapse of the Soviet Union in the early 1990s
2. *Bipolarity* or *dual hegemony:* Two dominant states, such as Athens and Sparta in the second half of the fifth century B.C. or the United States and the Soviet Union during the Cold War

sovereignty
A claim to political authority to make policy or take actions domestically or abroad; based on territory and autonomy, historically associated with the modern state.

balance of power
A key realist concept generally referring to a condition of or tendency toward equilibrium (or "balance") among states.

---

[2]The first three systems we discuss follow the categorization of Adam Watson, *The Evolution of International Society* (London: Routledge, 1992).

Balance of Power

The concept of balance of power is very important to realists, particularly those who emphasize the critical role of the systemic level of analysis to explain patterns of state behavior in the international system. Three questions of considerable debate among scholars are: (1) How is the term defined? (2) Do balances of power automatically occur or are they created by political leaders? (3) Which balance of power—bipolar or multipolar—is more likely to maintain international stability?

Considering the first question, Hans Morgenthau, a realist, admitted to at least four different usages or meanings of the balance of power. These were: (1) a policy aimed at a certain state of affairs; (2) an objective or actual state of affairs; (3) an approximately equal distribution of power among states; (4) any distribution of power among states, including a preponderance of power by one over the others. One critic of realism, Ernst Haas, found eight meanings for the term. Sometimes it is used by leaders and diplomats simply to justify policies. At other times it is used to describe a tendency in international politics toward systemic equilibrium. Balance of power policies have also been criticized for leading to war as opposed to preventing it, serving as a poor guide to political leaders, and functioning as a propaganda tool to justify defense spending and foreign adventures. Given these diverse usages and meanings, we may ask if the balance of power means so many different things, then does it really mean anything? Despite these constant attacks and continual reformulations of the meaning of the term, balance of power remains a central part of the realist vocabulary. This is true not just with academic theorists, but also with policy makers and practitioners.

Former U.S. Secretary of State Henry Kissinger emphasizes a **voluntarist** perspective to the second question, concerning whether balances of power are automatic or created. The balance of power is a foreign policy creation or construction of political leaders; it doesn't just occur automatically. Makers of foreign policy do not act as automatons, prisoners of the balance of power and severely constrained by it. Rather they are its creators and those charged with maintaining it.

In contrast to this voluntarist conception is that of Kenneth Waltz, who sees the balance of power as an attribute of the system of states that will occur whether it is willed or not. Given the realist assumptions that the state is a rational and unitary actor that will use its capabilities to accomplish objectives, states inevitably interact and conflict in the competitive environment of international politics. The outcome of state actions and interactions is a tendency toward equilibrium or balance of power. From this point of view, balance of power is a systemic tendency that occurs whether or not states seek to establish it.

Considering the third question, some authors argue that, in a multipolar system, war is less likely to occur because, as the number of major actors increases, decision makers have to deal with a greater quantity of information and, hence, more uncertainty. They believe that uncertainty breeds caution in the making of policy, and therefore, a multipolar world is more conducive to stability. Other authors, however, believe that greater uncertainty makes it more likely a decision maker will misjudge the intentions and actions of a potential foe. Hence a multipolar system, given its association with higher levels of uncertainty, is less desirable than a bipolar system because uncertainty is at a low level when each state can focus its attention on only one rival.

Question: Is unipolarity more or less stable than the bipolar world of the Cold War era? Will national-ethnic conflicts overshadow ideological clashes? If so, would it make any difference in terms of the amount of conflict if the world were unipolar, bipolar, or multipolar?

3. *Multipolarity* or *collective hegemony:* Three or more states dominate international relations, such as the five great European powers after 1815 (Great Britain, France, Russia, Austria, and Prussia)

In any of these hegemonic systems, the less powerful members may interact with one another, but they take their cues from the hegemonic authorities. They may even derive important benefits such as security by aligning with the more powerful states. The domestic affairs of states, however, are generally left untouched by the hegemonic powers. While political leaders are not installed by the hegemonic powers, they have little room for maneuvering in their state's foreign policy.

The third type of international system is evident in recent centuries as well as in ancient times—**imperial** systems such as those of Assyria, Persia, Macedonia, and Rome. An empire consists of separate societal units associated by regular interaction, but one among them asserts political supremacy and the others formally or tacitly accept this claim.[3] The difference between this and the hegemonic system, however, is that in an empire the dominant state is more likely to manage subject colonies, or territorial units' affairs, appointing local political officials, collecting taxes, drafting recruits into the imperial military, and creating and maintaining a system of roads and other transportation networks to enhance economic, military, and political interdependence.

To summarize to this point, the three systems can be depicted along a continuum as shown here:

Independent	*Hegemonic*	*Imperial*
(no superior power)	(dominance typically by one or more states)	(supremacy of one power, as in an empire)

Historically there has been a tendency for one or more states to attempt to move from an independent system to a hegemonic state system or to an empire, with other states attempting to prevent this from happening or forming empires of their own. Military conquest historically has been the principal means by which empires have been established. But authority crises within a particular political system can make it weak and vulnerable to foreign pressure. Within any particular geographic area, any of these three types of systems can ebb and flow, rise and decline, evolve from one into another and back again.

The Western European medieval era, from roughly the fifth to the fourteenth century, contained our fourth type of international system, the **feudal system,** from about the ninth to the fourteenth centuries. What makes the feudal system so unusual is the diversity of the entities that comprised it and the manner in which the relations among these units were structured. Power was claimed by a diverse group of governmental units, only some of which evolved into modern states. Other actors included trading associations, the great houses of merchant bankers, and local feudal barons.

In the temporal (today we would say secular) realm the Holy Roman Empire, which came to be based in the Germanic area of northern Europe, claimed universal jurisdiction. While the papacy in Rome claimed universal jurisdiction in the spiritual realm, it claimed temporal authority, too, exercising great political power through its international bureaucracy. The Church understood society as Christendom—a single, undivided Christian society emphasizing unity among the disparate political entities of

---

[3]Martin Wight, *Systems of States* (Leicester, UK: Leicester University Press, 1977), 16.

medieval Europe. As pluralists with historical interest point out, the feudal system reminds us that the key actors of international politics have not always been (and in the future may not necessarily be) states. Constructivists would agree, noting that the definition of a political unit owed loyalty can and has changed over the years.[4]

All four categories of international systems—independent, hegemonic, imperial, and feudal—are **ideal** or **pure** types, meaning actual historical examples placed within any single category will not line up exactly but will have their variations. Furthermore, it is possible for such systems to coexist and overlap, as was the case during the period of Spartan–Athenian hegemony and their relations with the Persian empire to the east. Such systems remained important even as the globalization process was beginning to emerge in the eighteenth and nineteenth centuries. Roughly the first half of the twentieth century, for example, most closely resembled collective hegemony (or a multipolar system), but the Cold War had many of the hallmarks of a dual hegemonic (or bipolar) state system because of the dominance of the United States and the Soviet Union.

How do such international systems develop, evolve, and decay over time? Why do such systems come to be viewed as legitimate, meaning their particular distribution of power and authority is accepted (decentralized in an independent state system, centralized in an empire)? To what extent do crises of authority account for their collapse? These questions should be kept in mind as we discuss the emergent global system in subsequent chapters.

We do not wish to leave the impression that the development of world politics followed a predetermined course, with various types of international systems leading inevitably to a world marked by global interdependence. The demise of empires and the rise of the state system did not necessarily have to happen. It is possible, for example, that the Roman empire could have lasted for several more centuries. Similarly, if Charles Martel had not defeated the Arabs at Tours in 733 or if the Turks had successfully breached the walls of Vienna in 1683, it is conceivable that a substantial part of Europe could have come under the sway of a Middle East civilization. More recently, what if Nazi Germany (1933–1945) had succeeded in its imperial ambitions?[5] Conceivably even today's world, marked by global economic interdependence, could give way to regional trading blocs with limited interactions among them.

Just as we must be wary of assuming that the past was somehow predetermined, we must also realize that the future is not inevitably a mere continuation of present trends. It is extremely difficult to judge how various political, economic, social, and technological forces may come together to influence the evolution of the global system. History is full of surprising twists and turns that few could have foreseen: the collapse of the Soviet Union and end of the Cold War are simply the latest examples. This should give pause to anyone who assumes the dominance or hegemony of the United States is now a fixed characteristic of the international system.

A related point we wish to make is that some of the most critical concepts and ideas that have shaped contemporary thinking about the nature of world politics have deep historical roots. As constructivists and pluralists argue, one should not underestimate the power of ideas in influencing the course of history. Human beings do not just passively react to their environment, whether ecological, economic, social, or political;

---

[4]Mark V. Kauppi and Paul R. Viotti, *The Global Philosophers: World Politics in Western Thought* (New York: Lexington Books, 1992), 18.

[5]For a novel that takes this scenario as its starting premise, see Robert Harris, *Fatherland* (New York: HarperCollins, 1993).

they also shape it. For example, political movements designed to redress the grievances of working-**class** people do not spring simply out of economic deprivation; they are also inspired by notions of justice and a sense of what is right or fair that is held by both leaders and their followers.

Ideas about world politics are sometimes used to justify the status quo in any era. But ideas can also help to overturn that status quo by providing inspiration and guidance to those who seek an alternative world future. Consider, for example, how the concept of "democracy" has gripped the imagination of many people all over the world. It has motivated them to take up a struggle against authoritarianism even though in many countries the quest for democracy would appear to be nearly hopeless. Ideas about democracy, political economy, social justice, and other concerns do matter, sometimes succeeding against enormous odds. In this chapter we will refer to writers who have given such questions serious thought, highlighting their contribution to thinking about world politics.

Historical International Systems: An Overview

We now turn to a discussion of historical international systems. Our purpose is to illustrate the diversity of systems, actors, and processes of international relations. We also hope to provide a backdrop or context for the evolving global system of today.

The Persian Empire

Persia is one of the best examples of imperial organization in the ancient world. Centered in present-day Iran, Persia was founded on the ruins of the Assyrian empire (about 1100–600 B.C.), but was much larger, extending from the eastern Mediterranean south to Egypt and all the way to the western borders of India. The Persians were particularly adept at assimilating those local customs that eased the expansion and efficient control of their empire. The Assyrian network of roads, for example, was extended, and Egyptian advances in administration and science were also adopted. In order to communicate more effectively with locals, they used Aramaic as the common language.[6]

The best way to visualize the political aspect of the Persian empire is as a series of concentric circles. The inner core was directly administered, but as one moved farther away from the capital of Persepolis (in present-day Iran), control was more decentralized. In outlying areas the client territorial units were quasi-autonomous. The threat of imperial military forces was always there; garrisons were established at key locations, and local troops were trained and armed. But the Persian overlords preferred to rely on persuasion to maintain control. Indeed, historians note the relative moderation of Persian rule over other peoples. Local governors, termed *satraps,* were either Persians brought in from outside or members of the local royalty. Aided by advisory councils, political rulers had jurisdiction separate from that of the local garrison commander and the representative of the imperial intelligence service. To accommodate regional and cultural differences across the far-flung empire, local administrative customs were generally adopted without substantial change. Administrators below the imperial level ranged from priests and kings to landowning aristocrats or merchant families, depending on the custom of the area.

---

[6]This section relies on insights and is adapted from commentary in Watson, *Evolution of International Society,* 40–46.

Acropolis of Athens: Porch of the Caryatids. The costly Peloponnesian War constrained but did not repress the artistic and intellectual brilliance of ancient Athens.

The Persian rulers were successful in avoiding conflict among the diverse members of their empire. After failing to conquer the Greeks directly, the Persians astutely supplied money and ships to whatever Greek coalition was formed to counter the strongest Greek city-state. During the reigns of Cyrus and Darius, the Persians extended their authority over the Greek and Phoenician cities located along the Mediterranean shore. These trading cities brought the Persians considerable economic benefits, so the Greeks and Phoenicians retained almost complete control over their internal affairs. Special rules also were devised for the government of Egypt, which by some estimates accounted for one-fifth of the population of the Persian empire.

In sum, the Persian approach to empire—providing internal autonomy to constituent territorial units as a means to lower military, administrative, and financial costs—established a practical precedent adopted subsequently by leaders of the Macedonian and Roman empires.

Classical Greece: Independent State and Hegemonic Systems

The Greek world of the sixth to the first century B.C. was composed of a variety of political entities that today we call city-states. Their small populations, limited control of territory beyond city walls, and proximity to each other were similar to the Italian Renaissance city-state system, not to modern states, most of which consist of comparatively large populations and often vast territorial expanses. The political forms of Greek city-states, as discussed by Plato and Aristotle, included monarchies that often degenerated into despotism (both of which involved dominance by a powerful individual) and other forms of rule. These ranged from leadership by enlightened aristocracies to exploitative oligarchies (rule by the few) and in some cases democracy, although participation was limited to those deemed worthy of the title "citizen."[7]

However they were organized, all of the city-states worked assiduously to maintain their independence. Some city-states were naturally more powerful than others, dominating weaker city-states and sometimes extracting tribute in return for military protection. Diplomatic practices were rudimentary, generally consisting of delegations that traveled to other city-states in order to present demands, resolve disputes, or negotiate trade agreements. Aside from its cultural and artistic impact, the classical Greek period also served as a model of interstate relations for European and American diplomats in the eighteenth and nineteenth centuries.

Although all city-states desired to be independent, during the fifth century B.C. the rise of two city-states—Sparta and Athens—turned the Greek independent state system into a dual hegemony. In the middle of the sixth century B.C., the city-state of Sparta was ruled by an aristocracy, considered by them to be an excellent form of government, particularly compared to the many tyrannies and oligarchies that ruled elsewhere. The expansion of Spartan power was confined principally to the Greek peninsula south of Athens known as the Peloponnese, and its purpose was to prevent neighboring states from stirring up trouble among the lower class, known as *helots*. This concern for domestic security limited the extent of Spartan ambitions beyond the Peloponnesian peninsula: The Spartan leadership did not wish to have its military forces distant, in case of a *helot* revolt. City-states allied with Sparta were allowed to conduct their own affairs and were assured Spartan military protection but were pledged to support Sparta in time of need.

The Spartans played a minor role in repelling the Persian invasion of northern Greece in 490 B.C., which ended with the spectacular Greek victory at the battle of Marathon. Ten years later, however, the Spartans reluctantly agreed to accept command of combined Greek forces to repel the second Persian invasion led by King Xerxes in 480 B.C. Spartan forces were unable to hold back the Persians at Thermopylae. The city-state of Athens, known for its navy as well as its democratic form of government, argued for a naval confrontation; and, at the battle of Salamis, the Persian fleet was defeated. The following year the Spartan army routed the Persians at the battle of Plataea, and Xerxes' forces retreated.

With the repulse of the Persians, Sparta returned to its traditional concerns and more limited sphere of influence on the Peloponnese. At this point Athens came to the fore and, hoping to prevent the Persians from launching another invasion of Greece, proposed the creation of the Delian League. This was composed principally of the city-states most vulnerable to Persian pressure, including those along the west coast of Asia Minor (present-day Turkey) and islands in the Aegean. In order to protect these city-states and sweep the Persians out of northern Greece, Athens continued to expand the size of its navy and other military forces. In the process it became a major military power.

After a series of victories against Persian forces, the Delian League of city-states totaled some two hundred members. But, as so often happens in alliances, once the foreign threat had been neutralized, problems among the member city-states soon began to appear. This was in part due to resentment and fear of Athenian domination. These

---

[7]Kauppi and Viotti, *Global Philosophers,* 36.

states, although formally autonomous political units, or *polities*, were forced to pay tribute to Athens, which determined not only their foreign policies, but also important domestic policies.

A deterioration in relations between Athens and Sparta led to the outbreak of war in 457 B.C. The two hegemonic states derived their power from different sources. Athens dominated central Greece and was easily the supreme sea power, whereas Sparta controlled the Peloponnesian peninsula and was the dominant land power. By 454 B.C. direct conflict died down, and a truce finally was achieved in 451 B.C.

Following a peace treaty between the Greeks and Persians in 449 B.C., the Athenians and Spartans eventually negotiated a peace treaty that in effect recognized spheres of influence and a balance of power between the two city-states. The ensuing peace allowed the two hegemonic rivals to consolidate control in their respective spheres. It was at this point, in 435 B.C., that the historian Thucydides took up the story in detail and discussed the specific events that led to the outbreak of the second Peloponnesian War. The Greek international system was essentially an Athenian-Spartan dual hegemony, but other states such as Corcyra, Thebes, Argos, and Corinth also had significant capabilities that distinguished them from the vast majority of city-states.[8] (See the *Afterword* to this chapter for Thucydides on power politics.)

The final defeat of Athens in 404 B.C. at first seemed to usher in a return to the independent state system. But Sparta soon began to assert hegemony over the rest of Greece, interfering in the internal affairs of other city-states and losing the support of its former allies. The Corinthians, who had earlier encouraged the Spartans to lead an antihegemonic alliance against Athens, now joined with Athens, Thebes, and others against Sparta.

The Persian empire, alarmed by Sparta's attempts to extend its rule to city-states in Asia Minor, joined in this new alliance. Unable to control Greece directly, they realized that the next best thing was to support whatever antihegemonic coalition was formed as a way to be sure no single Greek city-state could threaten Persia itself. But their primary concern was stability on the western border of their empire. Hence they pushed for a negotiated peace with Sparta and later a general peace conference among all the belligerents. The resultant settlement has been compared to the Peace of Westphalia of 1648, as both were based on the idea of an international system composed of independent states and a balance of power among them. The difference is that the Persians were financially willing to underwrite the settlement.

The peace, however, was fragile. The Spartans, Athenians, and Thebans maintained their respective hegemonic ambitions. Thebes defeated Sparta in 371 B.C., after which Theban hegemonic ambitions became evident. As a result, the Corinthians resumed their role as creator of an antihegemonic coalition, supporting the defeated Spartans against Thebes. Over time more congresses were held that allowed city-states of any strength to participate. The basic principle of independence was reiterated, although it was recognized that Sparta, Athens, and Thebes were "first among equals." This international system, therefore, can be characterized as one with several states vying for hegemonic control but thwarted in their effort by shifting state coalitions or balances of power. A common Greek identity did not prevent war among them. It is no wonder that later European political leaders found many parallels between their condition and the classical Greek international system.

---

[8]Mark V. Kauppi, "Contemporary International Relations Theory and the Peloponnesian War," in *Hegemonic Rivalry: From Thucydides to the Nuclear Age,* in Richard Ned Lebow and Barry S. Strauss, eds. (Boulder, CO: Westview Press, 1991), 101–124.

Statue of Alexander the Great (356–323 B.C.), king of Macedonia.

With the rise to power of Philip of Macedon to the north and his son Alexander the Great (356–323 B.C.), both the Persian empire and the Greek system ultimately came under Macedonian imperial rule.[9]

India: Independent State and Imperial Systems

Prior to the sixth century B.C., ancient India drew much of its common identity from geographic isolation and the impact of Hinduism. More than a religion, Hindu ideas represent a broad-based set of values that became deeply embedded in Indian culture. As such, Hinduism influenced social and economic life in one of the world's great civilizations. Despite a common civilization, however, the Indian subcontinent was divided into a number of independent political units. Some were more powerful than others, and warfare and expansionism were common. But, aided by Hinduism, there was a degree of common cultural identity and interdependence that encouraged the development of common rules and customs to guide relations among the various states. Although some were ruled by elected leaders and a few were republics, most were governed by kings belonging to the second-highest *kshatriya* caste, who believed their primary role in life was to govern and to fight.[10]

To enhance one's power and glory does not seem to be an unusual objective for kings and warriors. But over time it came to be accepted in India that it was not legitimate to destroy a conquered kingdom's social and economic way of life. Such forbearance was unusual in the ancient world. This is probably due in part to the Hindu tradition that would treat all of nature with great respect, whether vegetation, animals, or humans.

As is so often the case, however, it was Hindu contact with the outside world that led to fundamental changes in the Indian international system of independent states. As the Persian empire expanded eastward, it eventually conquered what is present-day Pakistan. It was at this point that the concept of empire began to circulate among Indian rulers and the educated castes. The Persians showed how a vast territory could be governed from an imperial center and how an extensive road network could facilitate interdependence through commerce and the movement of people. Some two centuries of Persian influence (520–327 B.C.) were followed by the invasion of Alexander's armies. With them they brought new Greek ideas (Alexander, after all, was one of Aristotle's students). This influx of foreign ideas followed hard on the heels of the spread of Buddhism, which also had a major impact on Hindu life.

Out of this intellectual, social, and economic turmoil arose Chandragupta Maurya, who managed to transform an independent state system into an empire. Although it was similar in scope to Persia, day-to-day rule of the Indian empire was heavily infused with indigenous values and customs. This man of action was accompanied in his rise to power by a man of intellect who worked to provide Maurya an extensive treatise on the ways and means of governing. That man was Kautilya.

With the death of Alexander, Chandragupta and Kautilya seized the opportunity to put their plans and ideas into motion and eventually established the Mauryan empire. Although not all of India was brought under Chandragupta's control, most of it was. An attempt to reconquer what had been the Persian part of India was turned back in 305 B.C. Domestic security and the neutralization of foreign threats encouraged the expansion of trade. But, against Kautilya's advice, Chandragupta's rule became heavy

---

[9]Watson, *Evolution of International Society*, 63–68.

[10]This section draws from *ibid.*, 77–84.

Applying Theory

THUCYDIDES' CONTRIBUTION

The Greek historian Thucydides' (c. 460–406 B.C.) untitled history of the Peloponnesian War is an account of the first twenty years of the fifth-century struggle. Filled with tales of heroism and tragedy, it illustrates the nature of war in all of its brutality, intertwining moral issues with political analysis. His is the foremost ancient work on international relations, for Thucydides was interested in examining current events in order to shed light on underlying patterns of politics that transcend any particular age. Indeed, he states at the outset that his work was designed to last forever, and undoubtedly he hoped it would be instructive for political leaders through the ages.

For Thucydides, as for many other observers of international politics known as realists, the underlying cause of the war could be traced to the nature of the Greek international system. He claimed that war was inevitable, given the increase in Athenian military power and the fear this caused in Sparta. His explanation, therefore, focused on the changing distribution of power in the Greek system of city-states and how this shift generated suspicion and distrust among Sparta and its allies.

Thucydides is credited with being the father of what has come to be known as **power transition theory.** Realist adherents to balance of power theories claim that the distribution of power among states is the key to understanding international relations. Power transition theorists would agree, and they see the international system as hierarchically ordered with the most powerful state dominating the rest, which are classified as satisfied or dissatisfied with the ordering of the system. But whereas balance of power theorists argue that the equality of power (balance) leads to peace, power transition theorists claim war is most likely when leading states are relatively equal in power, particularly when the differential growth in two states' economies brings a challenger close to becoming the dominant or hegemonic power. When this transition occurs, war is more likely.

Question: What does the increasing economic and military power of China mean for the stability of the international system in the next few decades?

This focus on the implications of changing balances of power has been generalized to explain the rise and fall of great powers through the centuries. **Long-cycle theory** claims the global system goes through distinct and identifiable cycles or patterns of behavior. According to one proponent of this theory, George Modelski, since A.D. 1500 four states have played dominant or system-leading roles, each one corresponding to a long cycle: Portugal (the sixteenth century), the Netherlands (the seventeenth century), Great Britain (early eighteenth century to the Napoleonic Wars and a second cycle from 1815 to 1945), and the United States (1945 to the present). War tends to mark the end of one cycle and the beginning of another. Modelski notes that, as with long-term business cycles, world order is also subject to decay. The dominant power is inevitably faced with the growth of rival power centers, and attempts to maintain territorial control around the globe prove to be costly. This is what the historian Paul Kennedy refers to as "imperial overstretch," a policy that ultimately drains the vitality and energy of the country. Each cycle, therefore, exhibits a particular ascending then a descending phase. With the end of the Cold War, power transition and long-cycle theories have been of particular interest to many observers of global affairs for obvious reasons.

Question: If one accepts the long-cycle theory, is it therefore likely (or even inevitable) that U.S. global dominance eventually will decay?

World Actors

KAUTILYA

Kautilya was the author of a work entitled the Arthashastra *or* Book of the State. *Rightly compared to Machiavelli, who also wrote a book for a ruler, Kautilya had the advantage of actually having the confidence of a man in power. The* Arthashastra *essentially describes the nature of the Indian independent state system and the relations among the various rulers, then proceeds to provide advice on how to exploit the system in order to create an empire similar to the Persian model.*

Kautilya's work is conceptually and empirically brilliant. He attempted to lay out precise formulas to aid the aspiring conqueror and is also given credit for such pithy bits of advice as "the enemy of my enemy is my friend." In contrast to the ancient Greeks or today's conventional thinking, Kautilya did not believe that an independent state system was necessarily the best. Rather Kautilya believed that benevolent imperial rule was most likely to achieve the ultimate objective of happiness for its subjects.

handed, and not surprisingly he made enemies. He became isolated and withdrawn, surrounding himself with a large personal bodyguard of armed women for protection.

Empire building continued under his son and grandson. The grandson Asoka (272–231 B.C.) initially expanded the empire by brutal methods, but once he became a devout Buddhist, he was known for his concern over the welfare of his subjects. Upon his death, however, the bonds of the empire began to loosen. The desire for independence was reasserted by elements throughout the empire, a crisis of authority ensued, and the empire eventually collapsed. India reverted to a series of independent warring states, the very condition Chandragupta had surmounted more than a hundred years before.

The Roman Empire

At least to those educated in the West, Rome represents the ultimate historical expression of the imperial international system. Rome started out, however, as a city-state, indistinguishable from its neighbors on the Italian peninsula. Over several centuries it gradually expanded its control to all points of the compass: north and west to present-day Germany, Britain, Spain, and France; south to North Africa and Egypt; and east to Iran. The importance of the Roman empire, however, lies not in its size, but in the fact that it came to be viewed as the legitimate authority by the vast majority of its diverse communities. For two centuries, beginning with Augustus (63 B.C.–A.D. 14), the Roman empire provided internal stability, two common languages (Latin and Greek), and a conduit for the dissemination of Greek and Eastern culture that helped to establish the foundations of European civilization. In terms of world politics, Rome shaped current thought and practice about the state, international law, and international society.

In its early years, Rome was ruled by kings, but with the development of aristocratic rule came the rise of the Senate with executive authority residing in two consuls. The lower class, or plebeians, also elected tribunes to keep watch over their interests. Internal strife assuredly occurred, but as Roman rule expanded outward, so did Rome's wealth. Increased wealth combined with able rulers strengthened the power of the Senate.[11]

To conquer territory is a difficult feat, but to retain it is perhaps even harder. The senators were shrewd enough to realize that their long-term interests would suffer if they abused the newly subjected communities. Instead they bestowed upon these populations

---

[11]The rest of this section is based on *ibid.,* 94–106.

the advantages of Roman order and law, co-opting certain individuals via the extension of Roman citizenship. As with such earlier empires as Persia, the degree of direct rule lessened with increased distance from the imperial capital, allowing more distant communities substantial self-rule.

Rome's interest in Sicily brought it into contact with the Phoenician trading city of Carthage, now the capital city of Tunis located on the Mediterranean coast of present-day Tunisia. From approximately 250 to 200 B.C., Rome and Carthage vied for supremacy in the western Mediterranean. With ultimate victory in the Punic wars, Rome absorbed the Carthaginian empire. As this struggle concluded, Rome looked to the east toward Greece and the Macedonian kingdoms. With the Greeks and Macedons unable to form an antihegemonic coalition, Rome soon gained control of the region. At this point the Roman imperial lands were divided into provinces, ruled and taxed by Roman governors. As long as they pledged loyalty, these kingdoms were granted local autonomy, and indigenous customs were generally respected. In fact it was due to Roman occupation that the values and culture of these Eastern civilizations made their way back to Rome.

> *There can surely be nobody so petty or so apathetic in his outlook that he has no desire to discover by what means and under what system of government the Romans succeeded in less than fifty-three years in bringing under their rule almost the whole of the inhabited world, an achievement which is without parallel in human history."*
>
> **Polybius,**
> *The Rise of the Roman Empire,*
> written in the second century B.C.

It's Been Said...

The rapid expansion of the empire, however, made it difficult to control territories effectively, particularly as the central government was constrained by a weak executive authority and a small bureaucracy. Attempts to fill this executive vacuum were made by various military leaders who promised stability but generally brought unrest and near civil war to Rome. The military dictator Sulla returned power to the Senate then retired. But ten years later Pompey, another military hero, came into conflict with the Senate over a number of issues including administrative rules in the provinces and the payment of his war veterans. With the aid of Julius Caesar, Pompey restored civil order to Rome then co-opted the Senate, agreeing to act as its protector. Caesar, however, had his own ambitions and, following his conquest of Gaul (present-day France), defeated Pompey's armies in various campaigns throughout the empire. With victory, Caesar imposed imperial authority and strengthened Rome's administrative power. Following his assassination, civil war wracked the empire, ending when his adopted son Octavian—later known as Augustus—emerged as the ultimate victor.

Ruthless in battle, as a ruler Augustus was a moderate who brilliantly reorganized the empire and provided it with a respite from internal strife. Although he retained ultimate power, Augustus helped to legitimate his authority by allowing for the restoration of the Senate and some of its privileges and responsibilities. His successors helped to consolidate his basic achievement, which was to improve dramatically the governance of the empire. Periods of instability spurred the further growth of a centralized bureaucracy that encouraged the development of Roman law and in turn helped to streamline and rationalize the legal and administrative systems throughout the empire.

As with the case of Persian and Macedonian rulers before them, Roman emperors in the first and second centuries A.D. preferred indirect rule, relying on loyal local rulers to carry out their bidding. Local customs were maintained, and identity was usually derived from one's ethnic group. But aside from Roman law, a web of other interdependencies was created thanks to the standardization of currency, weights, and measures. Commerce throughout the empire thrived as the Roman navy kept Mediterranean pirates in check. The quality of city life—housing, cleanliness, food, and personal security—attained standards that Europe would not see again until the eighteenth

Hannibal's troops are depicted during the Second Punic War, 218–201 B.C., which was one of the titanic struggles in history. The war was marked by Hannibal's invasion of Italy and his initial victory there, but his ultimate failure came at the battle of Zama (202 B.C.) in Africa.

century. Educational opportunities became more widespread, which encouraged at least the educated classes to view themselves as part of a cosmopolitan empire. This was consistent with the Greco-Roman Stoic philosophy that recognized the universality of a common, human identity.

Problems began to arise in the third century, however. Armies of the Persian Sassanid empire invaded Roman territory; when Roman troops in Germany were called back, the northern frontier of the empire became open to attack. Not surprisingly a series of Roman generals came to power, vowing to restore order. Imperial authority became even more concentrated in the hands of the emperor at the expense of the Senate. To those parts of the empire under threat from foreign armies, such a development was welcome. But gradually, following the death of the emperor Constantine in A.D. 337, the western half of the empire began to crumble. The stronger eastern half of the empire, based in Constantinople (present-day Istanbul, Turkey) remained politically, economically, and culturally vibrant for several more centuries. But in the West, the Roman empire came to a formal end in A.D. 476 as Germanic invaders swept south. Although the new rulers adopted many of the Roman administrative forms and functions, communities missed the stability the empire had provided.

The beginning of the Islamic era in the seventh century led to dramatic changes in the East. Muhammad (A.D. 570–632), the founder of Islam, was inspired by Christianity, Judaism, and an abhorrence of the moral decadence of Mecca. Islam offered a comprehensive system of law and precepts for good government that have influenced millions of people around the globe down to this day. While Europe wallowed in backwardness and superstition, Muslim scholarship drew on the philosophical and scientific heritage of Persia, ancient Greece, India, and China, and expressed little interest in the "barbarians" to the north.

Medieval Europe and the Feudal System

The decline and fall of the Roman empire and the resulting decentralization of authority produced a high degree of diversity in Western Europe. The final collapse of Rome in the fifth century A.D. was followed by some thousand years that came to be

Nürnberg was typical of many medieval cities, relying on castle walls for defense and rivers for transportation and economic exchange. Gunpowder and cannons eventually led to the demise of this type of fortification.

known by later scholars as the Middle Ages or the medieval period. Its end point is generally marked by the Renaissance and the Reformation of the fifteenth and sixteenth centuries. This period is of particular interest to students of international relations because it encompasses the period immediately prior to the onset of the current state system. As we will see, the organization of the world into territorially based states was not an inevitable outcome of the Middle Ages; other possibilities existed.[12]

During the Middle Ages the major purveyor of the notion of the unity of humankind was the Christian Church, the teachings of which became the religion of the Roman empire after Constantine's conversion in A.D. 312 or 313. As Rome's empire collapsed, Christian leaders realized that they would need to develop their own sources of worldly power to support their evangelical mission. Thus the Church became an increasingly wealthy and privileged organization with much to lose from invasions and general chaos. Even later, as more and more "barbarians" came under the influence of Christianity, the Church continued in self-defense to strengthen its organization and centralized authority through the papacy. Despite the sometimes corrupt and hypocritical behavior of many members of the Church hierarchy, Christianity was the framework within which medieval life, private as well as public, was conducted.

Although the Church in Western Europe proclaimed the universality of its message in the sacred realm, political power in the secular or temporal realm was greatly fragmented with a wide variety of different types of actors claiming legitimacy. The Holy Roman Empire, founded by Charlemagne in the early ninth century, was centered in Germany and, as the philosopher Voltaire wryly noted, was not very holy, Roman, or much of an empire, compared to that of the Caesars or even that of Byzantium (in present-day Turkey) to the east. Yet Charlemagne's successors provided a limited secular counterweight to the growing power of the Church. Indeed, Christian doctrine initially allowed for two separate but essentially equal papal and imperial powers.

---

[12]This section is drawn from Kauppi and Viotti, *Global Philosophers,* 124–29.

THE STOICS

Applying Theory

Realism emphasizes what separates political entities and people. **Idealism** is another tradition of political thought that emphasizes what unites people. From this perspective, ideas are an important factor that significantly influence how we live our lives, how we relate to others, and the institutions we construct. Idealism has had great influence on contemporary pluralist thinking. Idealism can be traced back to a philosophical school of thought known as Stoicism, which arose around 300 B.C. in Greece. Today the term *stoicism* is generally associated with the idea that one should bravely face life's adversities and persevere despite all odds. But the Stoics also argued that we are all part of a larger community of humankind, regardless of our different political communities and cultures. Stoic ideas were very influential in republican and imperial Rome, and they anticipated the worldviews of the seventeenth-century Dutch legal writer Hugo Grotius and the nineteenth-century German scholar Immanuel Kant.

For the Stoics, the ability to reason is a quality shared by all humans. Reason is a divine spark, a reflection of the God within us. Many followers of Stoicism thought of the divine as the source of the laws of nature. Humanity's universal ability to reason and the universal applicability of these laws of nature led the Stoics to emphasize the equality of people and the factors that unite them as opposed to what divides them, whether those divisions are geographic, cultural, or political.

Roman authors continued to write in the Greek Stoic tradition and attempted to put Stoic ideas into practice. Cicero, Seneca, Marcus Aurelius, and others supported the organizing principle by which Rome managed imperial affairs—a universal image of humanity that transcended the boundaries of a city-state or other small political units. The ideas of natural law (**jus naturale**) as well as laws of nations binding on all peoples everywhere (**jus gentium**) are important Roman contributions to Western political thought that have had profound influence on the succeeding centuries.

The Stoic emphasis on the unity and equality of humankind has obvious political implications: *What does it mean if the world is held together by laws of nature that transcend the laws of any particular king or emperor?* Furthermore, the Stoics raised an issue that is debated to this day: *If everyone is part of humanity, to what extent do we have obligations to humanity as a whole as opposed to the more narrowly defined political community in which we live?* Such a question is of relevance today when satellite communications bring into our homes pictures of victims of starvation and civil war. What are we to do?

Question: What is your response to the Stoic question of the extent of obligations to humanity?

The Holy Roman Empire effectively collapsed, however, because of internal weaknesses and invasions by the Saracens, Magyars, and Norsemen. Constituent kingdoms still existed, but administratively they lacked efficient bureaucracies and permanent military forces. As a result, kings often had little power over local barons. Thus there developed a contradiction between the actual diversity of medieval institutions and the religious and philosophical emphasis on greater unity as provided by emperor or pope.

The power of local barons was reflected in feudalism, the preeminent form of authority that emerged earlier and became prominent by the tenth century. A defining characteristic of feudalism is public authority placed in private hands. As a result of the chaos of late ninth-century Europe—a time in which the stability provided by Roman law and legions was fast fading from memory—public authority came to be treated as the private possession of local lords who controlled territory known as fiefs. The lords held their authority at the expense of kings, who were often distant and weak. For example, courts of justice were viewed as a private possession of individual lords who passed judgment as they saw fit. Similarly a vassal's loyalty and obligation to a lord was of a personal nature; it was not owed to some distant and abstract entity called "the state." In sum, this privatization of public authority in the hands of local nobles was a cause and consequence of the predominance of local government over the claims of kings and the general fragmentation of political authority throughout Europe.

Political authority during feudal times was therefore claimed by a diverse collection of institutions and individuals, including local barons, bishops, kings, and popes. Furthermore, it was also a time in which the middle-class merchants, or **bourgeoisie,** of the towns became a political force, often lending their support to religious or secular leaders in return for charters allowing them to establish free "communes" and, over time, commercial leagues. For students of international politics, it is interesting to note that, depending on their status, any one of these entities could be granted or denied the diplomatic status or right of embassy. This medieval system, which seems in certain respects so alien to the modern mind, has been characterized by historians as "a patchwork of overlapping and incomplete rights of government" that were "inextricably superimposed and tangled" and in which "different juridical instances were geographically interwoven and stratified, and plural allegiances, asymmetrical suzerainties and anomalous enclaves abounded."[13]

Can we speak of this motley collection of polities during the latter half of the Middle Ages as an international system? Definitely so, even though it does not have the elegant simplicity of an international system composed of sovereign states. The present-day distinction between internal and external political realms with rigid territorial demarcations, a centralized bureaucratic structure claiming to exercise public authority, and the claim to a right to act independently in the world would have seemed odd to the medieval mind.[14]

But during the Middle Ages, diplomacy still existed. The papacy and the imperial leadership adopted certain Roman principles and established new ones that have become part of international law: the safe conduct of ambassadors, secrecy in diplomatic negotiations, and condemnation of treaty violations. In terms of secular contributions, personal relationships were a key to diplomacy. Royal marriages were particularly important. Territorial borders were fluid, and relations between kingdoms were a function of dynastic marital connections. One did not speak of the "national interest" but rather the interest of particular rulers or dynasties. The high Middle Ages were a much more cosmopolitan era for the **elites** of the time than anything we have seen since: political courtships and marriages could result in a prince of Hungary becoming heir to the throne in Naples or an English prince legitimately claiming the throne of Castile in present-day Spain. This web of dynastic interdependencies, characterized by royal mobility and a sense of common identity, was paralleled in the rising merchant or bourgeois classes whose interest in commerce also made for a more cosmopolitan view of the world.

---

[13]John Gerard Ruggie, "Continuity and Transformation in the World Polity," in Robert O. Keohane, ed., *Neorealism and Its Critics* (New York: Columbia University Press, 1986), 142, citing, respectively, J. R. Strayer and D. C. Munro, *The Middle Ages*, 4th ed. (New York: Appleton-Century-Crofts, 1959), 115, and Perry Anderson, *Lineages of the Absolutist State* (London: New Left Books, 1974), 37–38.

[14]Ruggie, "Continuity and Transformation," 142–143.

The Rise of the European Independent State System

By the twelfth century, there was some reconcentration of political power in the hands of kings. Invasions around Europe's periphery ceased, allowing kings and nobles to devote more attention and resources to internal affairs and expand the size of their bureaucracies. Peace on the periphery also helped to account for the dramatic increase in the size of the European population. A larger population helped to revive towns, increase the size of the artisan class, and encourage greater trade. With expanded economic activity, taxation reappeared and was levied against churches, towns, and nobles. This required the establishment of a salaried officialdom. Greater royal income encouraged the payment of troops as opposed to relying on the vassalic contract based on mutual obligation. Kings, therefore, began to acquire two of the key elements associated with effective rule—financial resources and coercive power.

The twelfth and thirteenth centuries were also an era in which major strides were made in education. It is impossible to underestimate the importance of the growth of literacy to the rise of the state. As literacy expanded, the idea of written contracts gained currency, and ideals, norms of behavior, and laws could more easily be passed from one generation to another. Aquinas drew inspiration from the ancient Greek writers, universities were established (Paris, Padua, Bologna, Naples, Oxford, Cambridge), Roger Bacon engaged in experimental science, Dante wrote in the language of the common person, and Giotto raised art to a higher level. With the rise of educated bureaucrats, states formed archives that were essential to the continuity of government.[15]

This was also an era, however, in which there were major clashes between the sacred and secular or temporal realms over learning, commerce, and politics. In terms of learning, the clash between scholars with their emphasis on reason and the Church with its claims to authority based on the revealed word of God would continue through the centuries.

In the realm of commerce, the growth of capitalism led to a clash between the Church's emphasis on religious man and the emerging capitalist view of economic man. The medieval Christian attitude toward commerce was that those engaged in business should expect only a fair return for their labor efforts; earning interest on the loan of money (usury) and even making profits on sales were considered sinful. Gradually the feudal notion that the ownership of property was conditional on explicit social obligations was replaced by the modern notion that property is private, to be disposed of as the individual sees fit.

Politically the clash between the sacred and secular realms resulted in a breakdown in the balance of power between the pope and the emperor. This contributed to the breakup of the unity of Christendom, weakened the empire and the papacy, and hence assisted the rise of national states.

The fourteenth century, however, was particularly difficult for several reasons. The Black Death swept through Europe between the years of 1348 and 1352. It was also a time of popular insurrections and the first concrete evidence of the rise of national identity or consciousness. In the following century, Henry V could count on the passionate support of the English in wars against France, just as Joan of Arc appealed to the patriotism of the French. The fifteenth century was also a time of decay in parliamentary institutions. Over time, the power of the monarch and the royal court increased

---

[15]Marc Bloch, *Feudal Society*, v. 2 (Chicago: University of Chicago Press, 1964), 421–422.

World Actors

Niccolò Machiavelli (1469–1527) is considered by many to be the first truly modern political theorist because of his emphasis on "what is" as opposed to "what should be," a hallmark of all realist writers. To Machiavelli—as opposed to many earlier Greek and Roman writers—the purpose of politics is not to make people virtuous, nor is the purpose of the state to pursue some ethical or religious end. Rather politics is the means to pursue and enhance the internal and external security of the state. His concern over state security is understandable: during his lifetime he witnessed domestic turmoil and the devastation of his native Italy by French, Spanish, and northern invasions. His most famous work, The Prince, *was designed to be a handbook for Italian princes who sought to expel foreign invaders and bring unity to a divided Italian peninsula. Hence Machiavelli was the earliest writer to espouse the benefits of achieving national unity.*

Unless security is achieved, Machiavelli claimed, the pursuit of all other goals is pointless. The prince "must not flinch from being blamed for vices that are necessary for safeguarding the state." The two major dangers are internal subversion and external aggression by foreign powers. Domestic turmoil is avoided by having good laws and keeping the people satisfied. As for invasion by foreign powers, "princes should do their utmost to escape being at the mercy of others." The best defense is being well armed and having good allies. Machiavelli agreed with other realists that a permanent or perpetual peace is a dangerous illusion. Any leader who succumbs to such illusions risks losing his country's liberty. Machiavelli did not favor war for war's sake but believed it was justified when the security of the state was at issue.

NICCOLÒ MACHIAVELLI

under the reigns of Louis XI in France, Edward IV and Henry VII in England, Ferdinand in Aragon, Isabella in Castile, and their successors.

During the sixteenth century, there was much conflict and resistance to monarchical state building on the part of ordinary people coerced into surrendering their crops, labor, money, and sometimes land to the emerging states. In England, for example, rebellions were put down in 1497, 1536, 1547, 1549, and 1553. Lesser nobles and other authorities, often members of local assemblies, also resisted this usurpation of their powers. The religious wars in France in the sixteenth century were in part a function of a contest between royal prerogatives and regional liberties. A common thread running through all types of resistance to the emerging state was the issue of taxation. Increased taxes provided monarchs with revenues to support larger armies that in turn were used to defend and expand frontiers and overcome internal resistance to their authority.[16]

Two immensely important developments during the one hundred years commencing with the mid-fifteenth century were the Renaissance and the Reformation. Taken together, they have been viewed by historians as the twin cradles of modernity.[17] The Renaissance, generally associated with western Europe's cultural rebirth, was an ethical and humanistic movement that also elevated the individual and individual accomplishments. The Reformation, closely associated with the German religious leader Martin Luther (1483–1546) and his personal struggle for a right relationship with God, was a religious movement that eventually undercut papal authority and any hope for a unified Christendom. Luther and fellow Protestant John Calvin (1509–1564), a native Frenchman who emigrated to Geneva to escape religious persecution, believed that secular and religious authority should be separate. As the Protestant movement spawned greater religious pluralism, national monarchies grew in strength, and religious differences among the ruling houses exacerbated political problems.

---

[16]Charles Tilly, "Reflections on the History of European State-Making," in Tilly, ed., *The Formation of National States in Western Europe* (Princeton, NJ: Princeton University Press, 1975), 22–23.

[17]Lewis W. Spitz, *The Protestant Reformation, 1517–1559* (New York: Harper and Row Publishers, 1985), 5.

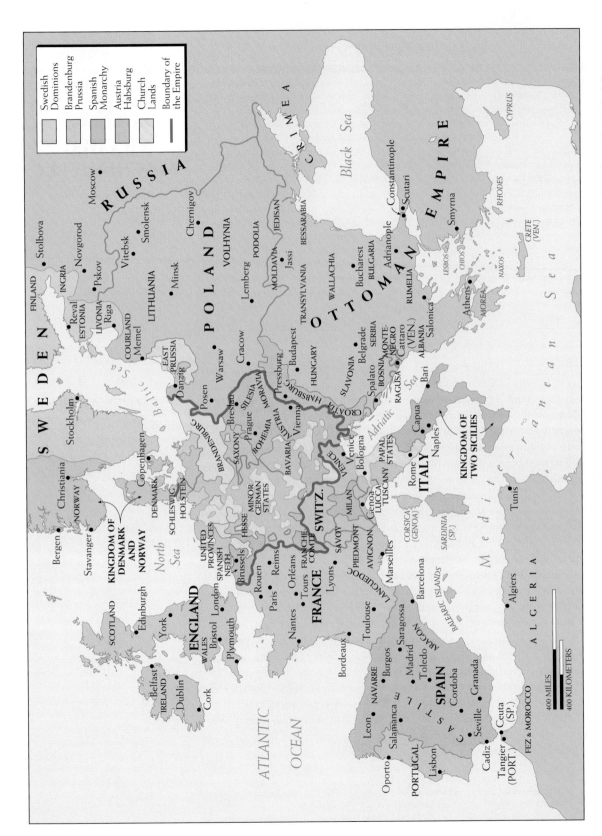

Legend

- Swedish Dominions
- Brandenburg Prussia
- Spanish Monarchy
- Austria Habsburg
- Church Lands
- —— Boundary of the Empire

MAP 2.1   *Europe After the 1648 Peace of Westphalia. Westphalia is viewed as marking the birth of the modern state system and the principle of sovereign territoriality.*

Conflict over religion and the power of the Holy Roman Empire touched off civil war in 1618 in Bohemia (the present-day Czech Republic), eventually expanding throughout Europe into what has come to be known as the Thirty Years' War. Although religion was an important factor, the underlying cause of war was arguably the shifting balance of power among the major states, harkening back to Thucydides' description of the origins of the Peloponnesian War—the rise of Athenian power and the fear this inspired in Sparta.

The Thirty Years' War had a number of important results. First, the Peace of Prague in 1635 addressed the religious problem in the Empire, providing a basis for dealing with the issue in the Peace of Westphalia, which ended the war in 1648. The ruler of a state would determine the religion of the inhabitants of that state. As a result, secular leaders of Catholic countries could ignore the papacy's call for a militant Counter-Reformation policy. Second, a new balance of power emerged that led to the rise of Brandenburg-Prussia, Sweden, and France as the most powerful states in Europe. The chance, therefore, of a secularly or temporally based empire was now as distant as the pope's hope for the unity of Christendom under papal guidance. The writings of the Englishman Thomas Hobbes captured the essence of the new international system of independent states.

By 1660 the territorial state was the primary political unit in Europe, so we can begin to speak of an independent state system. The peace agreement at Westphalia in 1648 helped to solidify the trend of increasing power to the modern state at the expense

World Actors

THOMAS HOBBES

Along with Thucydides and Machiavelli, Thomas Hobbes (1588–1679) is renowned for his contribution to the realist perspective on international relations. Just as Thucydides wrote his masterpiece during the Peloponnesian War and Machiavelli put pen to paper during a time of political upheaval on the Italian peninsula, Hobbes wrote his most famous work, Leviathan (1650), while in exile following the overthrow of King Charles I during the English civil war in the 1640s.

*Hobbes's principal concern was with the establishment of domestic authority, such as determining the relationship between the ruler and the ruled. But his discussion of the **state of nature** has had an important impact on realist thinking about international relations. Although there is some dispute among them, scholars of international relations have come to see his arresting image of the state of nature as analogous to the **anarchy** of the international system—a world without central authority.*

Hobbes did not claim that the state of nature he describes—a time prior to the creation of civil society—actually existed. Rather, Hobbes's state of nature was his attempt to imagine what the world or a particular society would be like without governmental authority or other social structure. His starting point was to describe basic human nature. How one defines this has an obvious impact on the type of government required to ensure a stable political order. If human nature is essentially benign, little coercive power is required. If, however, as Hobbes believed, people are ruled by passions, a strong central authority would be required. If governments did not exist, we would have to create them.

In Hobbes's state of nature, people are roughly equal, as each has the ability to kill another, either by brute strength, cleverness, or in confederacy with others. Out of this basic equality comes the hope of attaining desired ends, but as two people cannot enjoy the same thing equally, conflict results. In one of the most famous passages from Leviathan, Hobbes notes that "during the time men live without a common power to keep them all in awe, they are in that condition which is called war; and such a war, as is of every man, against every man."

Hobbes's description of the state of nature has been viewed as analogous to the international system. Just as in the state of nature in which individuals stand alone, so too in the international system are states driven to maintain their independence. As in the state of nature, the international system is marked by constant tension and the possibility of conflict.

of the other political forms. Not only were rulers put in the position of determining the religion of the inhabitants of their states, but the virtually complete authority of these princes in matters of state was recognized. With the realignment of territorial borders, the notion of the sovereignty of the state also came to the fore. *Sovereignty* involves political authority based on territory and autonomy. Territoriality means that there is a right to exclusive political authority over a defined geographic space—sometimes referred to as the internal dimension of sovereignty. Autonomy means that no external actor—such as another state—enjoys authority within the borders of the state.[18] For example, by agreeing to recognize each ruler as the final and absolute authority within his kingdom, rulers also essentially agreed not to support internal subversion in neighboring states, stir up religious discontent, or otherwise interfere in their domestic affairs.

Notwithstanding claims by princes to a right to be independent or autonomous in their foreign relations—the external dimension of sovereignty—the Peace of Westphalia established a system that did little to curtail the drive for territorial conquests. In fact, the relative military equality of the major states seems to have stimulated war, as many rulers thought they might be able to turn a system of independent states into an imperial system. As a result antihegemonic coalitions arose whenever a would-be emperor such as Louis XIV or Napoleon Bonaparte tried to conquer Europe. The balance of power, in other words, became a key aspect of the European independent state system, a system severely lacking in collective governing principles or conflict resolution norms or procedures.

Another equally important trend occurred along with the rise of the independent state system. Over time, people began to identify with a particular state to the point that in some countries the nation and the state merged into the concept of **nation–state.** Leaders could draw on their public's *nationalism* to gain popular support for national defense and wars fought against foreign enemies. Wars no longer would be fought by mercenaries. Instead citizens provided the troops for imperial conquest or national defense. This trend further restricted movement toward the effective regulation of relations among states. The pursuit of narrow national interests was the order of the day.

The rise of the state and the independent state system was seen not only in the political, diplomatic, and military spheres, but also in the economic realm. Indeed, economic developments were critical in contributing to the ultimate victory of the state system over other contenders. For example, the seventeenth century was the heyday of large trading companies. But while in earlier years these companies were associated with families, now the companies were chartered by monarchs in the name of the state: the East India Company in England (1600), the Dutch East India Company (1602), the Hamburg Company in north Germany (1611). As these state-backed firms increased in power, private city-based firms and trading associations declined. By 1629, for example, only the cities of Lubeck, Hamburg, and Bremen (members of the earlier Baltic commercial association known as the Hanseatic League) maintained their importance. Similarly, leaders of the large territorial states such as England and France worked to free themselves from their dependence on the foreign Florentine and other Italian and German banking houses. In part this was because such family firms were unable to provide the amount of capital monarchs required in order to carry out their wars. Commercial and industrial firms also came to prefer more secure domestic capital sources, leading to the rise of national banks.

nationalism
A mind-set glorifying the national identity, usually to the exclusion of other possible identities, infused with a political content.

---

[18]Stephen D. Krasner, "Compromising Westphalia," *International Security*, v. 20, no. 3 (Winter 1995/96): 115–116.

World Actors

*One of the most important writers on international law was the Dutch legal theorist Hugo Grotius (1583–1645). On the one hand, Grotius is a realist in that he accepted the state as the key political unit and the fact that competition and war are inescapable aspects of world politics. On the other hand, he exhibits aspects of the idealist tradition by claiming there is a basis upon which one can view the state system as a community or **society of states** that is not simply Hobbes's "war of all against all." Hence, he is an important influence on the English School of thought.*

Grotius believed that laws created by human beings and natural laws could contribute to tempering the conflict among states. According to natural law, people in the state of nature are equal and free, with no superior power able to tell them what to do. Following this same logic, states are also equal and free. But just as individuals cannot live in isolation, so too must states associate with their neighbors. This requires creation of laws of nations—international law—based on custom, consent, or contract. Hence, Grotius has no single term for international law, but discusses jus naturale *and* jus gentium—*the laws of nature and laws of nations or people. He therefore differed from writers such as Hobbes in that he believed states are subject to the laws of nations and that the observance of these laws was actually in the self-interest of states.*

*Writing at the time of the devastating Thirty Years' War, Grotius's work gained even greater prominence after the Peace of Westphalia in 1648. As we have noted, the war and its settlement completed the transformation of an international system based on the tenuous unity provided by the papacy and the Holy Roman Empire to a system of sovereign independent states. In order to regulate relations among these newly legitimized entities, a system of law was required. Grotius provided the intellectual foundation for this evolving state system. He also served as an inspiration for later writers such as Emmerich de Vattel (1714–1767), who argued that a recognition of moral obligations among states could coexist with balance of power policies. Taken together, power and international legal **norms** of behavior could aid in the stability and independence of states and thus were in their interests. For that reason, Grotius can be claimed by realists, idealists, and the English School of international relations as one of their own.*

HUGO GROTIUS

The development of state trading companies and banks was part of the dominant economic doctrine of the seventeenth century known as mercantilism. Proponents of **mercantilism** preached that the state should play a major role in the economy, seeking to accumulate domestic capital or treasure by running continual trade surpluses in relation to other states. This was not in pursuit of some lofty moral aim or simply for the benefit of private entrepreneurs; the ultimate objective was to provide resources that could be used for war or conquest. In the name of regulating and protecting commerce, authoritarian state bureaucracies emerged, contrasting dramatically with the primary economic units of the late Middle Ages, the autonomous and self-regulating guilds. These national bureaucracies viewed competition in zero-sum terms: whatever one state gained came at the expense of another.

In retrospect, all of these developments may seem to have led inexorably to the rise of a system of independent, belligerent states. This was certainly the view of such realists as Niccolò Machiavelli and Thomas Hobbes. But there were also developments working to counteract or at least mitigate this trend. They included developments of a transnational character: the impetus to commerce resulting from the discovery of America and new routes to the Indies, a common intellectual background resulting from the flowering of the Renaissance, a sympathy bond between coreligionists in different states that transcended national borders, and a common revulsion toward armed conflicts due to the horrifying cost of earlier religious wars. As one author argues, such "causes co-operated to make it certain that the separate state could never be accepted as the final and perfect form of human association, and that in the modern world as in the medieval world it would be necessary to recognize the existence of a wider unity."[19]

---

[19]J. L. Brierly, *The Law of Nations: An Introduction to the International Law of Peace,* 6th ed. (New York and London: Oxford University Press, 1963), 6–7.

IMMANUEL KANT

World Actors

*Perhaps the most famous work dealing with international cooperation and peace was by the German scholar Immanuel Kant (1724–1804), whose writings have influenced some contemporary pluralists. While influenced by Rousseau, the Stoic roots of Kant's thoughts on world politics are quite clear—as evidenced by his universalism, his concept of world citizenship, and his advocacy of a **federation** among states as a means to peace. Kant's vision is of a diverse world in which human beings can live freely and without war.*

Kant, however, was no head-in-the-clouds idealist, and he realized the transformation of world politics was neither imminent nor easy to achieve. The sovereign state was a reality, and any plan to deal with international anarchy had to take states into account. Even if it were possible to eliminate states and create an empire, this would not solve the problem of war because warring groups could still arise within any such empire.

Kant proposed instead something less than an empire—a league or federation of nations that would leave sovereign states intact. How did Kant reach this conclusion? On the one hand, he agreed that the natural human state might well be war, or at least the continuous threat of war due to the condition of anarchy. On the other hand, Kant disagreed with Hobbes in that he believed that the gradual transformation of human beings and international society was possible. Over time, Kant maintained, discord among human beings will lead them to learn ways to avoid future wars. As reasoning beings concerned with self-preservation and self-improvement, people will learn that states are necessary to secure internal peace. This emphasis on learning is also shared by many present-day pluralists.

The best way to ensure progress toward peace is to encourage the growth of republics (or representative democracies). In a statement echoed by many political leaders to this day, Kant argued that a federation of republics would be inclined toward peace and more likely to take international law seriously than would monarchies or empires. As the number of republics gradually increased, the world would move ever closer toward a "perpetual peace." By transforming the state, the violent manifestations of international anarchy can eventually be overcome.

Such recognition was evident in the development of **international law.** Hugo Grotius and other writers abandoned the medieval ideal of a world-state and accepted the existence of the modern, secular, sovereign state. But they denied the absolute separateness of these states and the extreme version of international anarchy as propounded by Thomas Hobbes. However limited it might be, the idea of community or international society of states could be applied, they argued, to the modern European independent state system. Even the recognition of sovereignty's external aspects—the claimed right of all states to be independent or autonomous in their international relations—expressed a certain degree of community. This is the same perspective—viewing international relations as occurring within a community or society of states—that is core to present-day scholars who identify themselves with what has come to be called the **English School** of thought.

The Emergence of Collective Hegemony

It was in the seventeenth century that we find the beginnings of what could be termed a society of European states. Despite political differences, all of the major European powers from the time of the Peace of Westphalia in 1648 to the start of the twentieth century worked gradually to regulate, delegitimize, and eventually eliminate the practices of such nonstate actors as mercenaries and pirates. If force were to be used, armies organized by states and only states would carry it out.[20]

international law
Laws that transcend borders and apply to states and in some cases individuals and corporations.

---

[20]Janice E. Thomson, *Mercenaries, Pirates, and Sovereigns: State-Building and Extraterritorial Violence in Early Modern Europe* (Princeton, NJ: Princeton University Press, 1994).

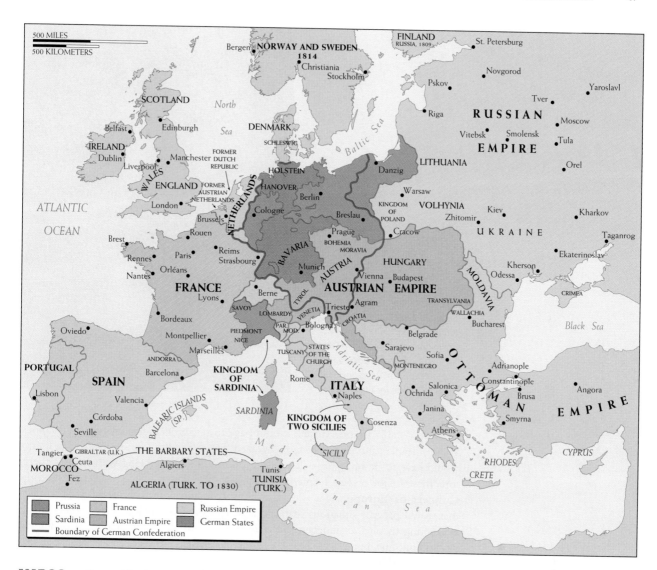

MAP 2.2   *Europe After the Peace Settlement at the Congress of Vienna (1815). Following the Napoleonic wars, diplomats at the Congress of Vienna attempted to rebalance power in Europe by, among other decisions, increasing the territory of Prussia and Austria.*

The rise of Napoleon after the French Revolution that began in 1789 upset the European order as France moved eastward beyond its borders, invading other countries and establishing a French empire. The subsequent defeat of Napoleon was followed by the Congress of Vienna (1814–1815), which created a collective hegemonic (or multipolar) system. Certain rules, values, and expectations developed by the major powers influenced relations not only among these states, but also among the lesser powers as well.

Leaders of the major powers had their various reasons for attempting to institute an international order that promised stability in Europe. Britain, with its global economic and political commitments, hoped to expand its foreign dominance, but to do so required peace in Europe. Russia also desired a quiet Europe so it would be better able to attempt expansion south into the Ottoman empire. Both countries realized that,

Napoleon Bonaparte. Born in Corsica in 1769, he barely qualified as a Frenchman as only the year before Corsica was ceded to France by Italy. A general at age 24, Napoleon controlled or dominated much of Europe for twenty years.

to attain a stable Europe, Austria would have to regain its independence from France. Political leaders also perceptively recognized that to achieve long-term stability, France would have to be brought back into the European system. Along with Prussia, therefore, these major powers formed the core membership of what has been termed the **Concert of Europe.** This was an attempt to devise international rules of conduct that would prevent situations that had arisen in the past, such as Napoleonic France attempting to turn an independent state system into an empire. Conflicts of interest would continue, but it was hoped that disagreements also could be worked out in a pragmatic fashion.[21]

Furthermore, the five major players realized that nationalist and democratic sentiments could conceivably threaten all of them, and in this sense their interests were broadly compatible. Europe, therefore, was viewed as a unique international society—not merely an international system. Such a vision was at odds with Hobbes's view of an anarchic world of states and more in line with that of Grotius.

Pragmatism was evident in European diplomatic practices. Between 1830 and 1884, twenty-five meetings were held among the representatives of the major powers. Though not formally promulgated, the underlying practices and norms that served in practice as the bases for these meetings included the following:

1. The Concert powers have a common responsibility for maintaining the Vienna settlement.
2. No unilateral changes to the settlement are allowed.

---

[21]Watson, *Evolution of International Society*, 238–239.

3. No changes should be made that significantly disadvantage any one power or upset the balance of power in general.

4. Changes are to be made by consent.

5. Consent means consensus, but formal voting does not occur.[22]

Despite revolutionary outbursts in a number of countries in 1848, the Crimean War of 1853–1856, and the Franco-Prussian War of 1870–1871, during the rest of the nineteenth century Europe experienced its longest period of stability since the rise of the modern state system. It is important to note that no single crisis or conflict in this period ever threatened to erupt into a continental war.

The collective hegemony of the great powers was demonstrated in the way they decided the fate of the smaller powers. The Concert sanctioned the independence of Belgium, Romania, Serbia, and Montenegro and prevented war between Luxemburg and Belgium and between Holland and Belgium. Aside from a common interest in European stability, the Concert powers were also able to make the system work because of their generally flexible approach to balance of power politics. Permanent coalitions or alliances did not develop. This situation was also encouraged by the British desire to keep continental Europe divided.[23]

The Globalization of the European System

The European system of independent states did not confine territorial and economic competition to Europe. Over the centuries, the European system spread over the world. Following Europe's stunning realization in 1492 that a much larger world existed than was previously thought, the Spanish and Portuguese agreed to spheres of influence. They treated the Americas as they treated the lands that fell under their dominion in the Iberian peninsula—as integral parts of their kingdoms bound by their laws, administration, and Catholicism. Indigenous civilizations such as the Inca in Peru and the Aztec in Mexico were destroyed as attempts were made to replicate the authority of the kings in Spain and Portugal.[24]

The Dutch, French, and English, however, believed the riches of the Americas and Asia were fair game for all. Few inroads were made initially in the Muslim-dominated areas of the Middle East and North Africa. In fact, the Ottoman empire controlled approximately a quarter of Europe until the end of the seventeenth century. In Asia direct colonial rule was initially not possible as indigenous authorities proved to be formidable representatives of advanced civilizations. The Europeans were allowed to establish trading posts at the behest of local rulers, but in this sense they were no different than Arab and Chinese traders who sailed through the same waters. The Portuguese, for example, established a trading post in China in 1516 and another in Japan in the 1540s. The British and French trading companies concentrated on India; although the initial amount of trade was minimal, the prospect for future gain was great. Such activities marked the beginning of European involvement with the advanced civilizations of Asia as well as the beginning of conflict among European states for commercial advantage in Asia.[25]

---

[22]Kalevi J. Holsti, *Peace and War: Armed Conflicts and International Order, 1648–1989* (Cambridge: Cambridge University Press, 1991), 167.

[23]*Ibid*, 167–168.

[24]Watson, *Evolution of International Society*, 219.

[25]*Ibid.*, 220–224.

Selected Wars and Peace Settlements in Modern European History

As historians and political scientists have observed, peace settlements at the end of wars often go beyond cessation of hostilities to establish major principles or alterations in the structure of power relations:

- The Peace of Westphalia (1648) ended the Thirty Years' War and established more formally the sovereignty or right of princes to exercise authority over the people in territories within their jurisdictions and to be autonomous in the conduct of foreign relations. The prince or sovereign authority could even determine the religion of the inhabitants of a state. This had even broader application to a wide range of other matters subject to state authorities.
- The Peace of Utrecht (1713) provided for an end to the War of the Spanish Succession (1701–1714), curbing French expansionism and Spanish power in Europe and the New World to the advantage of Britain. (Claims to the French crown by Bourbon King Philip V of Spain, grandson of French King Louis XIV, were renounced.)
- The Congress of Vienna (1815) ended the Napoleonic Wars that followed in the aftermath of the French Revolution that began in 1789. These negotiations established a new balance of power and provided for diplomatic arrangements known as the Concert of Europe among Britain, Austria, Prussia, Russia, France, and other European states. Although the Bourbons were restored to the French throne and the territorial boundaries of France were drawn comparable to those that had existed in 1789, French power was again constrained by these formal agreements.
- The Crimean War (1853–1856) and the Treaty of Paris ended a relatively minor armed conflict (although one with substantial casualties), curtailing Russian power in southeastern Europe. The dispute nominally began over contrary Russian and French claims to guardianship of Christian holy places in Palestine. Subsequent movement of Russian forces into Ottoman-Turkish areas of Moldavia and Walachia in present-day Romania were met by the forceful opposition of Britain, France, Sardinia, and the Ottoman Turks. The war was fought primarily to prevent the Russians from establishing military positions in the Crimea on the Black Sea.
- The Franco-Prussian War (1870–1871) once again curbed French power but was followed by a Prussian-led unification of German states into a newly formed German empire, or Reich. The dispute began with protests by France over efforts to assume the Spanish crown by a branch of the ruling Hohenzollern dynasty in Prussia. Although in the popular view the French military under Napoleon III were favored to win, in fact the Prussians prevailed.
- World War I (1914–1918) set a unified German empire allied with the Austro-Hungarian and Turkish empires as "central powers" against British, French, Russian, and by 1917 American allies. The war contributed substantially to undermining the Romanov dynasty in Russia, leading to its overthrow by Bolshevik revolutionaries in 1917. The new regime in Russia under Vladimir Lenin quickly made peace with Germany in the Peace of Brest-Litovsk (1918); however, the western allies continued to fight until they defeated Germany in 1918. The Peace of Versailles (1919) established a League of Nations (and World Court) for a new postwar order but also imposed harsh terms on Germany. Most historians believe these terms contributed to the failure of democracy in Germany and the subsequent rise in the 1930s of nationalist **revanchism** that led to World War II.

- World War II (1939–1945) set a German-Austrian and Italian "Axis," joined later by Japan, against the same World War I Allies—the United Kingdom, France, Russia (which had become the communist Soviet Union), and by 1941 the United States. The defeat of Axis powers by the Allies was followed by three peace conferences in 1945 at Yalta in the Crimea, Potsdam just outside of Berlin, and San Francisco, where the United Nations Charter was signed, laying a basis for a postwar world order.

The pattern of dependent states in the Americas and mutually beneficial commercial operations in Asia continued until the end of the 1700s. Toward the end of the century, Britain lost North American colonies, but European leaders continued to believe that colonies and their commodities were important sources of state power. The eighteenth century, therefore, witnessed an increase in the ultimate expression of economic

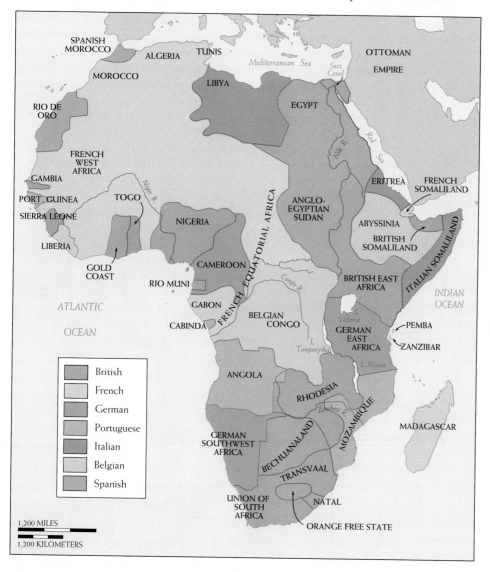

MAP 2.3   *Africa After the 1880–1914 Partition. Almost all of the African continent was divided amongst European powers except for Liberia and Abyssinia.*

exploitation—the capture or purchase of African slaves destined to provide backbreaking labor in the colonies of the Caribbean and North and South America.

European rule continued to be established where indigenous authority was weak or divided. The advance of British rule in India was initially aided by the collapse of the Mogul imperial system into numerous warring states, just as the Dutch managed to spread their influence gradually throughout the East Indies (present-day Indonesia). But in the nineteenth century, Britain worked hard for the independence of Latin American colonies. A primary reason was that, following the Napoleonic war, Great Britain aggressively pursued international trade. By opening up heretofore closed markets, British industry rapidly expanded, leading to dramatic gains in economic growth and wealth that could be translated into state power. The British navy, in conjunction with the Monroe Doctrine of the United States, discouraged the European powers from attempting to reassert control over the newly independent states of Latin America.

European imperial expansion in the nineteenth century, therefore, was directed toward the Middle East, Africa, and Asia. As the Ottoman empire, which included the Balkans and Greece, began to weaken, both Russia and Austria saw an opportunity for imperial expansion. But with both Britain and France concerned about the implications of a slow disintegration of the Ottoman empire, diplomatic compromises kept the Concert powers from military confrontation except during the Crimean War (1853–1856). A similar process of compromise was evident in the Congress of Berlin in 1884, during which the major powers carved up the remaining territory of Africa, the slave trade having long since ended. In Asia, great-power cooperation was also evident during the collapse of the Manchu dynasty in China. With the outbreak in China of

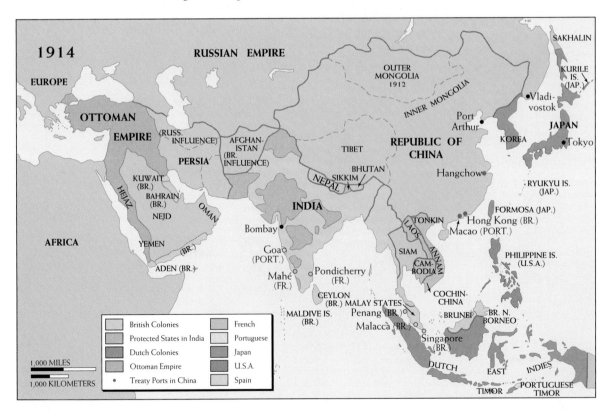

MAP 2.4   *The Spread of Colonialism in Asia*

the Boxer Rebellion in 1900 and the attacks against foreign traders and diplomatic legations, the European powers, along with the United States and Japan, worked together in joint policing and military operations.[26]

By the early part of the twentieth century, the areas of the world outside Europe and North America consisted of a variety of states with differing degrees of political, economic, and cultural dependence. None, however, could avoid the influence of the emerging global capitalist system, and all took on at least some of the formal trappings of the modern state as defined by the European experience. This meant, at a minimum, acceptance of Western economic practices, commercial standards, and international law. Especially in colonial situations, locals who were hired to assist in administrative matters also were influenced by Western values. This was especially true for those few who studied in France and Britain then returned to their native lands.

---

[26]*Ibid.*, 272.

Applying Theory

LIBERALISM VERSUS CLASS STRUGGLE

Kant's belief in the potential for harmony among states and peoples, joined with the faith that unrestricted economic activity would enhance the possibility of international harmony, came together in the works of nineteenth-century classical **liberals** who distrusted the concentration of power in the hands of the state (as opposed to many modern-day social liberals) and argued for the expansion of individual rights and guarantees.

Richard Cobden (1804–1865) was the foremost exponent of this perspective. He made three ambitious claims concerning the impact of free trade on peace. First, he asserted that most wars were fought by states to achieve their mercantilist goals. Free trade would show leaders a much more effective—and peaceful—means to achieve national wealth. Second, even in the case of wars not arising from commercial rivalry, domestic interests that would suffer from the interruption of free trade caused by war would be less inclined to resort to hostilities because of the losses they would suffer. Finally, Cobden argued that with an expansion of free trade, contact and communication among peoples would expand. This in turn would encourage international friendship and understanding. This posited relation between international trade and international peace has been a recurrent proposition, and indeed it is found in some present-day works that claim that interdependence and international trade can have pacifying effects on the behavior of states.

Question: If Cobden is right in his analysis, then shouldn't globalization make for an increasingly peaceful world? Does this appear to be happening?

Very different conclusions were reached by Karl Marx (1818–1883) and his followers. Although hostile to the capitalism of his day, Marx was heavily influenced by certain of Adam Smith's ideas, especially Smith's presentation of history as a series of stages progressing from one form of political economy to another. For Marx the focus of analysis was economic class structure, not the state. He viewed much of history as a tale of increasing human productivity and **class struggle,** with the rich against the poor, the haves against the have-nots.

Marx actually had a grudging admiration for early capitalists because they were critical in sweeping away the feudal order. For him, the world as a whole was divided by materially based class conflict. These horizontal, transnational class divisions cut across state boundaries and were a prime source of conflict, an analysis in contrast to the realist emphasis on conflict arising from interstate competition. Hence, Marx began his famous Communist Manifesto in 1848 with the words "Workers of the world unite! You have nothing to lose but your chains!" Marx predicted that the growth of class consciousness—the realization on the part of workers that their situation was intolerable and that that would lead them to the point at which they would act together—would result in a **proletarian,** or workers', revolution. This would happen first in the most highly developed, industrial countries, as their working classes were largest and had suffered oppression the longest, particularly in the later stages of capitalism beset by declining rates of profits. Over an unspecified period of time, the state—and consequently world politics as we know it—would fade away should a stateless world society be created.

Building on Marx's emphasis on class conflict and applying it to world politics were followers such as Vladimir Ilyich Lenin (1870–1924), the Bolshevik leader of the Russian Revolution of 1917. **Marxist-**

Leninists saw conflict not as the result of anarchy and the **security dilemma,** but rather as the result of capitalist states competing economically against one another. Drawing on the work of non-Marxist English economist John Hobson and German socialist Rosa Luxemburg, Lenin argued that capitalism had reached its highest stage of development—**imperialism.** Because there were no more new areas of the world to exploit—each piece of real estate had been claimed or colonized by a European power—the capitalist states would begin to covet one another's territory, resulting in imperialist wars. The world would be divided and redivided. This struggle among capitalist states would be intensified by the continual yet uneven growth of capitalism that would witness the rise of some states and the relative decline of others.

Question: Can you make the case that Lenin was at least partially correct—that the uneven growth of capitalism is a source of conflict and tension among advanced capitalist states? If so, does this insight also apply to the present period marked by what many describe as increasing globalization?

Twentieth-Century Hegemonic Systems in a Global Context

At the same time European values and economic practices were creating a web of global interdependencies, increasing political separatism was occurring among the major powers in Europe. Perhaps the single most important factor accounting for the collapse of the Concert of Europe was the inability of Europe to adjust to the political, military, and economic rise of Germany (a favorite case study for the application of power transition theory). When World War I finally broke out in August 1914, its viciousness and degree of devastation were shocking. Partly this was due to the Industrial Revolution, which had helped to produce weapons of tremendous destructiveness. The other important factor was inflamed nationalism, which spurred the development of mass armies and a political-ethnic consciousness coterminous with state boundaries. Karl Marx's hope that workers of the industrial world would unite to overthrow existing governments and institute an international system of peaceful socialist states was not to be.

At the end of World War I in 1918, an attempt was made to create an international organization that would prevent the outbreak of future wars. The key legal concept underlying the League of Nations was faith in **collective security,** the idea that if one state behaved aggressively, other states had a legal right to enforce international law against aggression by taking collective action to stop it. In other words, the League of Nations hoped to institutionalize legally the historical phenomenon of antihegemonic coalitions.

The League, however, failed to keep the peace, as evidenced by its inability to halt German, Italian, and Japanese aggression, which resulted in the outbreak of World War II (1939–1945).

A second attempt to institutionalize global collective security was the United Nations, created at the end of World War II. But with rare exceptions—Korea in 1950, Congo in 1960, and peacekeeping missions in places as diverse as the Mediterranean island of Cyprus and the Sinai desert—cold war politics and ideology prevented the United Nations from playing the major collective-security or law-enforcement role originally intended for it in 1945. On the other hand, the U.N. Charter did permit the formation of alliances as states pursued individual and **collective defense.**

While East and West were locked into a conflictual situation of strategic interdependence—particularly because of the development of nuclear weapons capable of devastating much of the globe—economic, ideological, and political independence between

MAP 2.5   *Axis Europe 1941*

the blocs was the norm. Within the blocs, economic, social, and political interdependence dramatically expanded. A political disjuncture, however, was occurring between the so-called First World of the West and the newly emerging states and developing societies of the Third World. The victorious allies had fought Germany, Japan, and Italy in the name of freedom and independence. Now the leaders of the independence movements asked the embarrassing question, "Why did the West not apply the same logic to its colonies?" In some cases, such as the British in India, Palestine, and Yemen, the colonial power grudgingly disengaged. In other cases, particularly the French in Vietnam and Algeria, insurgencies came to power violently and eliminated direct foreign rule. This process continued through the 1970s as the Portuguese disengaged from Angola and Mozambique in Africa and reached its logical conclusion in South Africa in 1990 when the indigenous white elite finally recognized the impossibility of maintaining a monopoly on political power in the face of the political and economic demands of the black majority.

Dual Hegemony During the Cold War: A Closer Look

Given the fact that we continue to sort out the implications of the end of the Cold War on present-day international relations, it is worthwhile to examine this era more closely. When did the Cold War actually begin? It could be argued it began in 1939 when two dictators, Joseph Stalin of the Soviet Union and Adolph Hitler of Germany, agreed to divide Poland. Stalin's broader European goals were consistent with his Kremlin predecessors: dominate the states bordering the Soviet Union and gain control over the Turkish Straits and Baltic region. Beyond that Stalin hoped to influence strongly events in Eastern Europe and Germany.

With the German invasion of the Soviet Union in 1941, the Soviets joined the western alliance in the battle against fascist Germany, Italy, and Japan. Moscow's ultimate goals, however, remained the same. This was apparent at the Yalta Conference (in Soviet Crimea) where Stalin, U.S. President Franklin Roosevelt, and Prime Minister Winston Churchill of the United Kingdom met to discuss the postwar future of Europe. The Soviet Union had suffered more than twenty million dead and vast destruction of property as well. It was not surprising, therefore, that Stalin argued Eastern Europe should fall

Devastation of Cologne, Germany, 1945

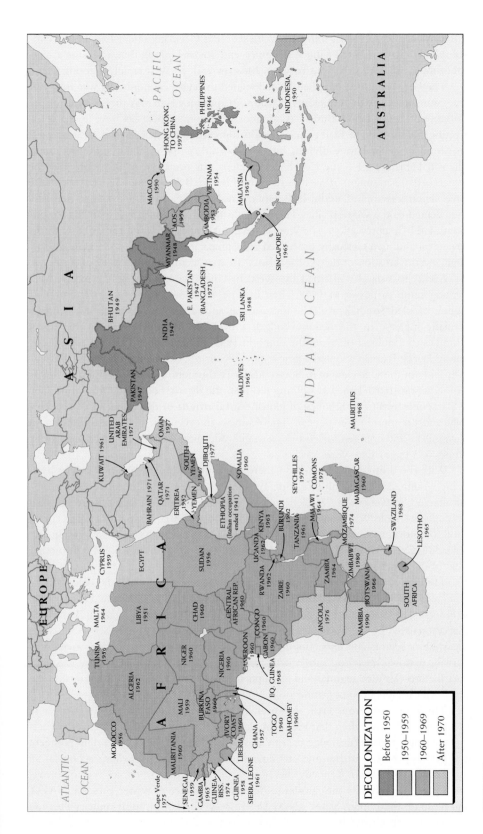

MAP 2.6 Decolonization in Africa and Asia. The collapse of Europe's modern colonial empires began in 1947 on the Indian subcontinent with the creation of the states of Pakistan and India.

within Moscow's sphere of influence. With defeated Germany under four-power control (United States, United Kingdom, France, and Soviet Union), Berlin became a symbol of the Cold War as relations between Moscow and the West rapidly deteriorated.

The U.S.-sponsored Marshall Plan, designed to revive economically war-torn Europe, was viewed with suspicion by Stalin. An ominous sign was the creation of the Communist Information Bureau (Cominform) in September 1947. At its inaugural meeting, a close aide to Stalin announced to the assembled delegates that Europe and the world in general were divided into two hostile camps, capitalist and communist. Then in February 1948 the Czech government was overthrown, and soon after the Soviets began harassment of western trains into Berlin. By mid-June the blockade of the three western sectors of Berlin had begun. Road and rail access across East Germany were denied to the Western allies. The blockade was broken only by a dramatic eleven-month airlift resupply effort. The West, believing it could not work out a deal with the Soviets on a unified Germany, proceeded in its preparations for a West German government and the creation of the North Atlantic Treaty Organization (NATO) in 1949.

Events in Asia also alarmed the West. In China, communist forces led by Mao Zedong came to power in 1948. Then in June 1950 the North Korean communist regime invaded South Korea. The invasion galvanized the United States and led to a dramatic increase in the defense budget, a decision also influenced by the Soviet Union's successful test of an atomic bomb in 1949. In September 1950 the administration of Harry Truman adopted a new national security document, NSC 68, that essentially laid out the U.S. view of its Soviet adversary throughout the Cold War. The Soviet Union, it was stated, aimed at nothing less than the destruction of the free world. The U.S. response was to be a policy of global **containment** of the Soviet Union specifically and communism in general. The Chinese intervention in the Korean War in November 1950 only reinforced this view, and officials in Western capitals discussed the danger of a major East-West war.

With the death of Stalin in 1953, there was cautious hope that a new Soviet leadership would be more accommodating in trying to settle East-West differences. A summit meeting in Geneva in 1955 left political leaders and outsiders with the feeling that although the Cold War would continue in Europe and Asia, it would not turn into a "hot" or shooting war. But even as the summit was taking place, a Soviet ship was unloading Czech weapons in Egypt, marking the expansion of the Cold War into other areas of the Third World.

Throughout the 1950s and 1960s a number of crises occurred: the defeat of the French in Vietnam in 1954, the Taiwan Straits crises of 1955, the Warsaw Pact invasion of Hungary in 1956, and the second Berlin crisis of 1960, during which the Berlin Wall was constructed by the Soviet Union, dividing the occupied city into separate eastern and western sectors and restricting movement of people across the barrier. Soviet support for national liberation movements in the Third World was matched by U.S. support for pro-Western regimes and attempts to overthrow a number of nationalist and pro-Soviet leaders in these countries.

The most dangerous crisis, however, focused on Cuba during thirteen days in October 1962. It was then that President Kennedy learned the Soviets were constructing sites for intermediate-range ballistic missiles in Fidel Castro's Cuba. The president and his key advisors at the time saw Soviet leader Nikita Khrushchev's actions as an intolerable provocation. Kennedy, therefore, in his view had no choice but to compel the Soviets to withdraw the missiles to defend the balance of power, preserve NATO, and illustrate the United States' resolve to Moscow. The key political-military decision was to establish a naval blockade of Cuba as opposed to invasion or air strike on the

Applying Theory

THE COLD WAR

Question: Despite a political and ideological chasm and conflicting interests, why did the Cold War not develop into a hot war? In fact this period has also been characterized as the "long peace." The Cold War witnessed a series of protracted and devastating limited wars fueled by revolutionary, religious, and ethnic competition. But there was no Third World War involving the Soviet Union, the United States, and their respective allies. Explanations for this nonevent include:

- *Nuclear weapons:* Once nuclear weapons were available to both the Soviet Union and the United States, neither side was willing to run the risks required to achieve its objectives by force as major states had routinely done throughout history. The consequences of a nuclear war could easily be imagined by leaders on both sides; hence, these leaders were "self-deterred" from using their nuclear arsenals.
- *Bipolarity:* Some theorists argue that the replacement of a multipolar world with a bipolar structure of power after World War II contributed to international system stability. As noted earlier, the supposed advantage of a bipolar distribution of power over multipolarity is that the responsibility for maintaining the system is concentrated, not dispersed. Calculations between two principal competitors are also simpler than in a multipolar balance when the calculations and interactions of several states are at issue. A superpower can even tolerate an occasional defection from an alliance because the overall distribution of power would not be dramatically affected.
- *Obsolescence of major war:* This view argues that the two previous explanations are essentially irrelevant to explaining the long peace. Recognition of the escalating costs of war for advanced industrial societies is the key, and this was evident to all in World War I. It took the evil genius of Hitler, the bumbling of Mussolini, and a handful of Japanese militarists to start World War II. This war simply confirmed the catastrophic results of war in the industrial age; hence, from this perspective, the long peace after 1945 would have ensued even if nuclear weapons had never existed.

For further discussion and other arguments, see, for example, Sean M. Lynn-Jones and Steven E. Miller, *The Cold War and After: Prospects for Peace* (Cambridge, MA: MIT Press, 1993). The Cold War International History Project (CWIHP) at http://cwihp.si.edu/default.htm disseminates new information and perspectives on the history of the Cold War.

missile batteries. Although the tactic was successful, the president later stated that the probability of a nuclear disaster had been "between one out of three and even." A second major crisis occurred in 1973 during the Arab-Israeli war when Moscow made noises about armed intervention in the conflict. The United States responded by putting its nuclear forces on alert, signaling its resolve to oppose any such action.

After the Cuban missile crisis, the Soviet leadership embarked on a sustained buildup of strategic nuclear weapons that further strained East–West relations. Armed intervention by the United States in Vietnam and support for the South Vietnamese government were also countered by Soviet aid to North Vietnam and its communist (Viet Cong) allies in the South, actions that added to tensions between the superpowers.

Cuban Premier Fidel Castro (left) applauds Soviet Premier Nikita Khrushchev at a Moscow Stadium athletic display in May 1963, less than a year after the dangerous Cuban missile crisis.

Another major development was the Chinese-Soviet split leading to a clash along the Sino-Soviet border in 1969. This opened the way for the United States to play the so-called China card, epitomized by national security advisor Henry Kissinger's secret trip to Beijing in July 1971. President Nixon made a formal visit in February 1972. The Sino-U.S. summit and other factors also persuaded Leonid Brezhnev and the Soviet leadership that a relaxation of tensions (or *détente*) with the West was a viable option and, in any event, better than strategic isolation. Hence, Nixon was invited to Moscow, and the first set of Strategic Arms Limitation Talks (SALT) resulted in arms control agreements signed by Nixon and Brezhnev in May 1972. Further progress in arms control was made by the subsequent U.S. administrations of Gerald Ford and Jimmy Carter and their Soviet counterparts.

Détente suffered a major setback with the Soviet invasion of Afghanistan in late 1979. This event and the inability of the United States to do very much about it aided the election of Ronald Reagan, who continued and expanded substantially the massive U.S. military buildup begun under his predecessor. The imposition of martial law in Poland (December 1981), designed to squash a reformist labor movement (and thought to be due at least in part to Soviet pressure), further soured East-West relations. The Soviet experience in Afghanistan resulted over several years in enormous human and material losses, proving to be a disaster. This was one reason Mikhail Gorbachev (who termed Afghanistan "a bleeding wound") came to power in the Kremlin in March 1985, at a time when it was obvious to all that the Soviet economy was failing. Gorbachev revived the policy of *détente* with the United States and the West with an eye to providing some relief from ruinous spending on the arms race. Under his economic policy of *perestroika* (restructuring), the goal was to introduce limited economic incentives into the socialist economy. Gorbachev neither desired nor expected that his shifts in domestic and foreign policy would set in motion events that ultimately led to the collapse of the Soviet empire and the end of the Cold War.

For those who grew up during the Cold War, concern over a cataclysmic nuclear war between East and West was the dominant international anxiety. Other issues tended to be overshadowed. Given the proliferation of modern weaponry and the persistence of still-unresolved national conflicts, concern over interstate wars remains. But with the obvious exception of the coalition war against Iraq in 1991 and the U.S.-dominated invasion of Iraq in 2003, civil strife and internal (or intrastate) wars have dominated the headlines, in large part due to the national, ethnic, and humanitarian issues at stake. So as the bipolar world faded, scholars attempted to discern the implications of a unipolar system marked by U.S. dominance and also the higher profile of such transnational issues as terrorism, refugees, pollution, and arms proliferation. Within the United States, a vigorous debate continues on the feasibility and burden of attempting to maintain U.S. hegemony. Internationally the power of the United States has in many quarters bred fear and resentment, particularly as the U.S. administration after 9/11 claimed the right to launch preemptive attacks against not only Iraq, but any state or transnational organization deemed to be a possible threat in the years ahead. But in other quarters there is a recognition that if the United States turns isolationist and reduces its role in international affairs, the world could become an even more dangerous place.

Conclusion

As noted, there are three reasons for devoting this chapter to a discussion of historical international systems. First, it is hard to discern what may be unique about the current global system unless we know what it has in common with (or how it differs from) earlier international systems. The history of constant competition and conflict among diverse political entities should make us cautious about expecting global peace and harmony to break out any time soon. War or the threat of war has been constant down through the centuries no matter the time period, the region, the civilization, or the types of political units (city-states, empires, or modern states). On the other hand, we have noted how international systems come and go, and it is shortsighted to assume the planet's future must necessarily replay the past. A look into the past also teaches us that other peoples have experienced dramatic changes in the international systems of their day. They, too, no doubt looked to the future with a mixture of consternation and hope.

Second, our brief overview of writers who have influenced contemporary thinking about world politics through the centuries helps to explain the development of the realist, pluralist or liberal economic structuralist, English School, and other images of international relations and world politics. Such writers as Thucydides, Machiavelli, and Hobbes have been particularly important in terms of realism. As we have noted, for realists *world politics* essentially refers to politics among states, which realists often refer to as interstate or international politics. At times they use the term *international state system,* noting that there is a hierarchy of states due to their disparate economic, technological, and military capabilities. When it comes to power, states are inherently unequal. Similarly, while realists recognize global economic interdependence, they tend to believe that its influence on international relations is overemphasized: More powerful states, at least, can take steps to reduce the influence of outside factors. But no matter the relative power or degree of interdependence, for realists states dominate global politics.

For some scholars of the English School, however, defining global politics as merely a Hobbesian system of competitive states is too restricting and historically misleading. As exemplified by the Concert of Europe, one can also view world politics as a society of states. From this view, states compete for power and influence, but they also have common interests that are reflected in basic rules of behavior and international norms. The world is not always a Hobbesian "war of all against all": Cooperation is evident, particularly in the economic realm for advanced industrial states. States also create international organizations, such as the European Union and United Nations, in order to facilitate limited common objectives, but in so doing they may alter the international environment within which they operate.

Many pluralists or liberals speak of an emerging global civil society. Without some knowledge of the history of thinking about world politics, one would fail to appreciate the contribution of such writers as the Stoics, Immanuel Kant, and the nineteenth-century liberals. From this perspective, the importance of the state is acknowledged, but its primacy is questioned. As noted in Chapter 1, global civil society consists of a series of networks of economic, social, and cultural relations created by individuals and organizations in order to pursue political goals consistent with the rule of law.

Although such organizations as Greenpeace or Amnesty International may attempt to influence the actions and policies of states, they have a broader agenda that includes influencing the perceptions and actions of individuals around the globe. Much of their activity takes place outside the framework of the state system. Furthermore such transnational activity broadens the concept of identity—commitment and loyalty is not exclusively associated with a particular state. In this pluralist view, the terms *global* or *world politics* are much preferred to the realist terminology of interstate or international relations and politics that puts so much emphasis on states as if they were the only actors of consequence.

The economic structuralist image of world politics, however, also draws attention to an unalterable fact—the persistence of extreme global poverty. Karl Marx and his followers have attempted to explain this condition by utilizing class analysis with its emphasis on exploitation of labor. Similarly, Vladimir Lenin stated there was an inherent dynamic built into capitalism that made imperialism an inevitability. Other non-Marxist scholars have developed world-system theories that attempt to explain the logic of the spread of global capitalism and the resultant disparities in income and wealth between the industrialized countries of the West and the millions of persons living in abject conditions in the Third World.

Finally, placing our historical overview in the framework of the rise, fall, and evolution of various types of international systems encourages the reader to think conceptually. In the following chapters, we continue to introduce different concepts associated with globalization, international relations, and world politics. We begin with the realist perspective and its emphasis on the key conceptual building blocks for understanding international relations in this or any age—interests, power, and security.

Afterword

The Peloponnesian War: The Melian Dialogue
Thucydides

(460–401 B.C.E.)

This historical account of raw power politics in the ancient world underscores a classic realist understanding—that in the real world appeals to such ideals as justice and rights to be independent or neutral tend to fail in a world in which the strong (the Athenians) do what they will and the weak (the Melians) do what they must! The Athenians in this conversation have no interest in whether the demands they make on the Melians are just or moral. Other important concepts and notions such as honor, perception, neutrality, interest, alliances, balance of power, capabilities, and the uncertainty of power calculations are all part of this narrative. We have consulted other translations of this ancient Greek text (an excerpt from The Peloponnesian War by Thucydides), starting with the first English translation rendered by Thomas Hobbes. We offer below our own abbreviated, plain-language, present-day English version (adapted from Hobbes).

Athens sent its forces to the island of Melos [in the Aegean Sea]. . . . The Melians, a Spartan colony, unlike other islands, chose not to be a part of the the empire of Athens, preferring instead to be neutral—not taking sides [in the ongoing struggle between Athens and Sparta, the two great Greek city-state imperial powers]. . . . Before engaging in hostilities, the generals . . . sent emissaries to engage in negotiations. . . .

Athenians: We believe in straight talk. . . . It would be good for you . . . to be practical . . . since we both know that in the world in which we live doing what is right or just matters only between those parties who are equal in power. Otherwise, as a matter of fact, *the strong do what they will and the weak do what they must.*

Melians: Since you make us emphasize *interest* or what there is to gain rather than what is *right* or *just*, we think you should not set aside the principle of justice or fairness that actually serves the security interest of everyone. Your own interest certainly would be served by this principle should you ever fall from power and be made to suffer vengeance imposed by others.

Athenians: Even if our empire were to fail, we're not worried about what might happen. We're not so much concerned about being taken over by an imperial power like Sparta (not that we're worried about Sparta) as we are with what would happen to an imperial power attacked and defeated by its own people. On this, be assured we know how to take care of ourselves. We are here for our own good and in the interest of our empire, which it turns out also provides security to your city. We'd like to bring you into our empire peacefully, sparing you and us any difficulties.

Melians: And just why do you think being subordinate to you benefits us and, for that matter, why such an arrangement serves your interest?

Athenians: Because you would be worse off if you resist, thus leading us to conquer you—a contingency we would in our own interest prefer to avoid.

Melians: And we gather you will not accept our choice to be neutral—friendly, not hostile, and not allied with either party [i.e., allied with neither Athens nor Sparta—Eds.]

Athenians: No, we can't accept that because others in our empire will see your neutrality not as friendliness, but rather as hostility to our imperial position—our acceptance indicative of weakness on our part, your dislike of us an indicator of our power over you.

Melians: Do those you speak of consider it fair or just to put us who are independent in the same boat with all the others—your own people as well as the enemies you have defeated?

Athenians: They are ambivalent about which party is in the right, but do accept that independence depends on strength—interpreting passivity by us as signaling fearfulness on our part. Defeating you not only will add you [i.e., Melos] to our empire, but also will enhance its security. Our naval supremacy and your relative weakness as an island compared to others makes it imperative that we not let you get away with defying us—going your own way.

Melians: Can't you see how what we propose serves your security interest? Can we persuade you by explaining how what we think is fair to us also is in your interest? Won't other neutrals feel threatened and thus become your enemies when they see you turning against us? Even though they may not wish to be your adversaries, won't your approach lead them to become so, thus increasing the numbers arrayed against you?

Athenians: As a practical matter, we're not so much concerned with those on the [Greek] mainland who tend not to risk their liberty by acting contrary to us. On the other hand, those most likely to cause us trouble—putting themselves and us in jeopardy—include the islanders outside of our empire like yourselves as well as those under us who object to their subordination.

Melians: Given all the risks you take to keep your empire as well as risks taken by others to break away from it, it would be base and cowardly if we did not do everything possible to avoid coming under your dominance.

Athenians: No, it makes sense for you to submit to the more powerful since it is not an even match—not a fair fight in which the winner is honored and the defeated loses face. It is instead a question of your survival—not foolishly trying to resist us, the stronger party.

Melians: Don't be so sure. The outcome of war is not always certain—not always directly related to the relative strength of the parties. If we give up now, we certainly lose. On the other hand, if we try to resist you, we at least have a chance of success.

Athenians: Hope is a response to danger better pursued by the strong, not you who face ruination. . . .

Melians: Rest assured we know how hard it is for us to oppose your power and position on such unequal terms. . . .

Athenians: . . . Moreover, your reliance on the Spartans for security is ill advised—delusionary. . . .

The Athenians then withdrew. . . . When the Melians refused to submit, hostilities began. . . . The Athenians then proceeded to kill all Melian men of military age, enslaving all women and children. . . .

Key Terms

Other Concepts

Additional Readings

If we were to recommend a single book on historical international systems, it would be Adam Watson, *The Evolution of International Society* (London: Routledge, 1992). Our debt to this superb work is evident throughout this chapter. We would also suggest S. N. Eisenstadt, *Political Systems of Empires* (New York: The Free Press, 1963); Martin Wight, *Systems of States* (Leicester, UK: Leicester University Press, 1977); and Michael W. Doyle, *Empires* (Ithaca, NY: Cornell University Press, 1986). Kenneth Waltz deals with modern state systems (since 1970) in Chapter 8 and considers the concept of international systems more generally throughout his *Theory of International Politics* (Reading, MA: Addison-Wesley Publishing Co., 1979). K. J. Holsti deals with historic and contemporary state systems (including the ancient Chinese Chou dynasty not discussed here) in Part Two of his *International Politics* (Englewood Cliffs, NJ: Prentice-Hall, 1967 and all subsequent editions). For critical perspectives on colonial legacies, see Adam Hochschild, *King Leopold's Ghost* (Boston: Houghton Mifflin, 1998) and David Anderson, *Histories of the Hanged: The Dirty War in Kenya and the End of Empire* (New York: Norton, 2005).

For more ideas about world politics from early theorists and others not mentioned here, see Chris Brown, Terry Nardin and Nicholas Rengger (eds.), *International Relations in Political Thought* (Cambridge: Cambridge University Press, 2002); Ian Clark and Iver B. Neumann (eds.), *Classical Theories of International Relations* (New York: St. Martin's Press, 1996); G.R. Berridge, Maurice Keens-Soper and T. G. Otte, *Diplomatic Theory from Machiavelli to Kissinger* (New York: Palgrave, 2001); and, for that matter, our own earlier effort in this genre—Mark V. Kauppi and Paul R. Viotti, *The Global Philosophers: World Politics in Western Thought* (New York: Lexington Books, 1992).

An elaboration of power transition theory is Robert Gilpin, *War and Change in World Politics* (New York: Cambridge University Press, 1981). On long cycles, see George Modelski, *Exploring Long Cycles* (Boulder, CO: Lynne Rienner, 1987) and Joshua S. Goldstein, *Long Cycles: Prosperity and War in the Modern Age* (New Haven, CT: Yale University Press, 1988). See also Paul Kennedy, *The Rise and Fall of the Great Powers* (New York: Random House, 1987). Finally, we take note of an important book that examines English School, constructivist, economic structural (or "world systems"), and other historically grounded understandings of international or world society in Stephen Hobden and John M. Hobson (eds.), *Historical Sociology of International Relations* (Cambridge: Cambridge University Press, 2002).

Chapter 3

Interests, Objectives, and Power of States

"International politics, like all politics, is a struggle for power. Whatever the ultimate aim of international politics, power is always the immediate aim."

HANS J. MORGENTHAU, REALIST SCHOLAR

I n June 1944 one of the greatest concentrations of conventional military capabilities in the history of the world was ready to be deployed in the invasion of continental Europe by the United States and its allies. Dwight D. Eisenhower was supreme commander of the allies in Europe. Invasion day—or D-Day—was set for June 5. On the 4th, however, a storm swept into the English Channel. In the early morning hours of June 5, Eisenhower met with his officers. The heavy rain and wind were expected to end that afternoon, but the seas would be rough for the flotilla poised to cross the channel and land on the French beaches at Normandy. Eisenhower asked his colleagues and subordinates what they recommended. The army generals wanted to proceed. The air force generals and navy admirals preferred to delay the invasion until the weather improved. Eisenhower paced for a few moments, stopped, and said, "OK, let's go!" Beginning shortly after midnight on June 6, airborne troops began parachuting into the French countryside. At first light, infantry came ashore at Normandy under brutal fire from the Germans dug in along the coast. The greatest invasion in the history of warfare had begun and with it the eventual liberation of Europe.

This chapter discusses the types of resources or capabilities a state—and secondarily nonstate actors—may have in order to serve their interests and achieve their objectives. As we noted in Chapter 1, a wide range of nonstate actors is important—international organizations and transnational actors such as multinational corporations (MNCs) and banks, environmental movements, labor and human rights organizations, and churches. Indeed, some of the larger MNCs and banks have greater financial clout than many states, which have relatively low national incomes. Our emphasis in this chapter, however, is on states, on these matters still the most important global actors or *units of analysis,* with more in-depth discussion of international organizations and transnational actors reserved for later in the book. As a result, much of the discussion in this chapter is influenced by the realist image of international relations.

Framework: Interests, Objectives, Threats, and Opportunities

A basic framework or game plan is useful to provide some degree of order and logic to our discussion.

Elements of the Framework

From the realist perspective, states are actors in global politics with separate **national interests** in a world without a central authority to regulate their activities. In such a world, states are often assumed to be rational or "purposive" actors, pursuing various **objectives** understood to be consistent with their separate interests. Within the global system, *opportunities* present themselves that, if handled properly, can help to achieve specific objectives. Similarly *threats* emanating from the global system have to be dealt with if they interfere with the achievement of basic objectives. But to exploit these opportunities and to handle these threats, states are required to mobilize the various **capabilities** they have at their disposal in order to exert *power* constructively to achieve those objectives and protect those interests. A key responsibility of leaders is to make sure that objectives are in line with available capabilities. A country such as the United States, for example, has many more capabilities than Kenya. Hence, Kenya's ability to exert power on the global stage is severely limited compared to that of the United States, which can seek much more ambitious objectives due to much greater capabilities.

Figure 3.1 depicts this framework. Although the emphasis is on states, it will become apparent that the framework can also be useful in analyzing the behavior of international and transnational organizations and movements. In this chapter we discuss each of the highlighted terms, setting the stage for our discussion in subsequent chapters of two important means states use to achieve their objectives—diplomacy and force.

Interests   A skeptic would claim that the national interest of any state is simply what political leaders say it is—merely a rhetorical device designed to justify the pursuit of a controversial policy. There is certainly an element of truth to this—all leaders claim they act in the selfless pursuit of the national interest whether dictator, democrat, or demagogue. It is fair to say, however, that there are a few basic national interests that transcend any single type of political leader. First, there is no disagreement among policy

unit of analysis
What is being studied; for example, a state or a decision-making unit.

power
The actual or potential influence or coercion a state (or other actor) can assert relative to other states or nonstate actors because of the political, geographic, economic and financial, technological, military, social, cultural, or other capabilities it possesses.

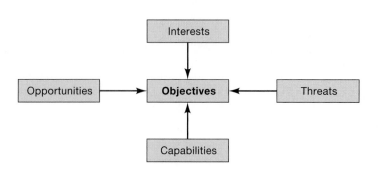

FIGURE 3.1   *Understanding State Behavior*

makers that national survival as a state is the minimum objective—sometimes referred to as a core or vital interest common to all states. Survival as a state implies maintenance of its sovereign status. As noted in the previous chapter, the exercise of sovereignty is a right claimed by a state to exercise complete jurisdiction, power, or authority internally or within its territory and externally to act independently or autonomously in the conduct of its foreign affairs.

A second core interest for states is economic vitality and prosperity. Economic prosperity is not only sought on behalf of citizens of a society, but it can also be an important source of power in international affairs. Granted, there are despots who assiduously work to plunder their own societies and have little concern for their subjects, but such instances are exceptions to the rule. Even those dictators bent on expansionism realize that without the engine of economic growth their dreams of imperial glory are unlikely to be realized.

Finally, the preservation of a society's core values can also be a vital interest. In many Western states, for example, democratic values and democracy are key elements of national identity. They not only are reflected in the structure and functioning of the political system, but also help answer the questions, "Who are we, and what do we stand for?" Similarly, some Islamic states and societies view European and American commercial culture and its emphasis on materialism and overt sexuality as threats to basic religious and moral values.

Objectives   Interests are so general that they are usually an inadequate guide for actual policy making. They do, however, inform more specific goals or objectives. The core interest of survival for a landlocked state, for example, could be more specifically defined as defense against invasion by neighboring states. Similarly, a state with long coastlines that is dependent on foreign trade might see the protection of sea lanes as an important national objective in order to maintain economic prosperity.

The eighteenth-century framers of the U.S. Constitution, for example, were well aware of the security dangers the new country would face. One reason offered by Alexander Hamilton in the *Federalist Papers* in favor of uniting the thirteen states was a belief in greater safety in numbers. Going it alone as thirteen separate states was risky, particularly given the potential for invasion by Britain or Spain.

Achieving the objective of political union, such as the United States, permitted the pooling of defense resources into a single entity while still maintaining state and local defenses. Spanish power waned, but the United States did in fact go to war with Britain in 1812. The United States survived, although the White House was set on fire by British forces bent on settling old scores in the New World. Of course this was only a sideshow in the larger British campaign against Napoleon's extension of French power in Europe, but it was a major assault on American national security, with survival of the still-young country at stake.

Beyond defensive concerns, policy makers may also opt for a broad range of other objectives. Some states may wish to conquer others or take territory by force, as occurred, for example, in both of the twentieth century's world wars, the Korean Conflict in 1950, the Vietnam War in the 1960s and 1970s, and Iraq's invasion of Kuwait in 1990.

As a practical matter, however, most national objectives are usually more modest than conquest or defense against invasion. The scope of these other objectives is really quite broad, covering a wide range of political, social, and economic issues. For example, the United States, Canada, Japan, or some European state may seek to advance human rights, put a cap on the arms race and reduce the likelihood of war, improve the

HANS J. MORGENTHAU AND JOHN H. HERZ: POLITICAL REALISM AND POLITICAL IDEALISM

Applying Theory

John Herz and Hans Morgenthau both left Germany after the Nazis came to power, settling in the United States. Both found themselves in the center of a great realist-idealist academic debate. Morgenthau recognized the importance of values but underscored the centrality of power and interest as the basis for understanding international politics. Calling for a science of international politics that went beyond mere description, Morgenthau posited six principles of political realism: (1) "that politics, like society in general, is governed by objective laws that have their roots in human nature"; (2) that "in international politics" realists emphasize "interest defined in terms of power"; (3) that "interest defined in terms of power is an objective category that is universally valid"—applicable to states throughout the world; (4) that there is "tension between the moral command and the requirements of successful political action," but that as a practical matter "universal moral principles . . . must be filtered through the concrete circumstances of time and place"; (5) that "political realism refuses to identify the moral aspirations of a particular nation [such as the United States] with the moral laws that govern the universe"; and (6) that "interest defined as power" is an understanding that gives international politics a separate standing and thus "emancipates" it from other fields of study.

Herz put greater emphasis on ideas and values along with these power and interest considerations. He provided a synthesis he called "realist liberalism" that understood the importance of power but found a critical place for values and norms as also affecting the choices political actors make: "While Realist Liberalism accepts the inevitability of power and, consequently, of 'power politics' in interrelations of 'powers,' it looks for ways and means of bringing such policies into

a workable system wherein power is applied in the interest of some order, in particular for the balancing of strength and the prevention of hegemony" as in a "collective security system."

In his *Political Realism and Political Idealism* (1951), Herz found fault with extremes in both camps. He saw "political realism" as too narrowly focused on "security and power factors" and on "the struggle for power and power positions" while "political idealism" emphasized "harmonious cooperation," largely ignoring "the problems arising from the security and power dilemma." At the same time, Herz observed how political realists often forget or overlook how "political rationalism or idealism" as a motivator for ideologies underlying political movements (such as "individualism, humanism, liberalism, even anarchism, and beyond these, pacifism and internationalism") has "played a role in influencing the actual course of history and in shaping actual politics." To Herz "ethical considerations intervene" (even universal "values and desirabilities, in principle, for all human beings"), and as a result, we come to see "human relations built, not [so much] on the 'egoistic' instincts and the ensuing 'power policies' of individuals and groups, but on considerations beyond mere self-preservation and self-interest."

Herz made a major conceptual contribution in addressing the **security dilemma** facing states in "anarchic society" within which states interact. This security problem stems from a world in which there is no world government or central authority above sovereign states (much less one with the power or means) to maintain order or assure the prerogatives and territorial integrity of states. In a 1950 article in the journal *World Politics*, Herz wrote that human beings "striving to attain security . . . are driven to acquire more and more power in order to escape the impact of the power of others," but "this, in turn, renders the others more insecure and compels them to" do likewise and "prepare for the worst." As a result, "since none can ever feel secure in such a world of competing units, power competition ensues, and the vicious circle of security and power accumulation is on." Thus in such competitive environments as arms races, increased expenditures on armaments may not enhance but actually undermine security by triggering similar expenditures by adversaries. This problem has become particularly acute in the nuclear age when security failures threaten mass destruction.

Question: Herz suggests that competing views of international relations can be reconciled or synthesized. To what extent could global economic structuralist or feminist images be reconciled with realism?

country's trade and balance-of-payments positions, reduce poverty and increase agricultural and industrial productivity in Third World countries, and slow environmental degradation by putting limits on deforestation and pollution of the oceans and the atmosphere.

Some foreign policy objectives may be more immediate—short term or short range—such as when the United States sought in 1970 (and again in 1973) to achieve a cease-fire between the Egyptians and Israelis, leaving establishment of a more durable peace as a follow-on, longer-term objective to be achieved incrementally over a period of decades. Achieving a lasting peace in the Middle East thus qualifies as a long-range objective with various middle-range objectives defined along the way.

The Camp David Accords in 1978 between Israel and Egypt were an important step toward this end. The way has been slow and progressed in fits and starts. It appeared that partial reconciliation was finally achieved in the 1990s between Israel and the Palestinians, who took back control of some of the territories taken by Israel in 1967. American foreign policy makers have supported a continuing process of negotiations, with the Israelis trading land taken by conquest in return for the apparent security to be drawn from Arab recognition and acceptance of the Israeli state and society. Yet the cycle of violence has continued, with one peace initiative after the other falling by the wayside. Progress in the peace process has occurred at an extremely slow, seemingly glacial pace.

The continuing efforts to establish a political and economic union in Europe are another example of a long-term objective driven by attainment of various short-term and middle-range objectives over several decades. Europeans began modestly in the early 1950s to integrate coal and steel markets, later expanding over the next four decades to a full-blown economic community and common market as successive steps toward economic (and at least some degree of greater political) union.

Of course, short- and middle-range objectives sought by states and international organizations may not always be tied to overarching, long-term goals such as European union or lasting peace in the Middle East. Consider, for example, the following short-term or middle-range objectives:

- Achieving a more competitive position for farmers and agribusiness in grain or corn exports
- Establishing a corner on some part of the global microelectronics market by a country's multinational corporations or other firms

TABLE 3.1
*Categorizing the Foreign Policy
Objectives of States*

EXAMPLES OF ISSUES	OBJECTIVES		
	SHORT-TERM (VARYING IMPORTANCE, OFTEN HIGH URGENCY)	MIDDLE-RANGE (NOT URGENT, BUT OF SOME DEGREE OF IMPORTANCE)	LONG-TERM (NOT URGENT, BUT USUALLY OF GREATER IMPORTANCE)
(A) warfare (security)	Negotiate a cease-fire; separate the warring parties	Maintain effective peacekeeping; manage unresolved conflicts, keeping them from escalating to warfare	Achieve a durable or lasting peace; resolve conflicts and reconcile the parties
(B) commerce (economy)	Persuade the other party to make a trade concession such as lowering a tariff or other trade barrier	Establish a good climate conducive to expanding trade relations	Assure an open trading order will flourish on a global scale
(C) human rights (identity)	Secure the release of particular political prisoners; halt human rights abuse in another country	Establish and foster greater legitimacy for human rights in as many countries as possible	Achieve the societal and political elements essential to durable or lasting democratic regimes in other states

Both may well stand on their own, quite apart from any larger purposes to be served. Table 3.1 provides other examples of objectives in the context of our three themes of security, economy, and identity.

Threats Specific objectives states decide to pursue are not decided upon in a vacuum. Objectives are also influenced by threats emanating from the global system. Up until 1992, for example, Western European states paid relatively less attention to events in Yugoslavia than they would subsequently. With the breakup of the country and eruption of wars among the Croats, Serbs, and Bosnians, a prime European objective became preventing the spread of the conflict beyond the borders of the former Yugoslavia. More generally, states attempt to plan for contingencies that might arise that would require the use of military capabilities in different circumstances.

Opportunities The global system presents states not only with threats to national interests, but also with opportunities that may influence the formulation of foreign policy objectives. The decision by former Soviet leader Mikhail Gorbachev to lift the heavy hand of repression from Eastern European client states in the late 1980s created an opportunity for the Federal Republic of Germany (West Germany) to reunite with the German Democratic Republic (formerly communist East Germany). China's decision to create foreign trade zones in the eastern coastal provinces in the 1980s provided an opportunity for other states to pursue the objective

Applying Theory

REALISM AND THE RATIONALITY ASSUMPTION

If you take a moment to think about it, the discussion of the framework at this point seems almost too neat and straightforward; certainly the calculation of a state's interests and objectives is not so simple. This is a good point at which to elaborate on the important realist theoretical concept of the *unified, rational actor*. From the standpoint of **methodology,** this image is an assumption, not a description of the actual world. Theoretical assumptions should be viewed not in terms of descriptive accuracy, but rather in terms of how fruitful they are in generating insights and hypotheses about international politics. Assumptions, therefore, are neither true nor false; they are more or less useful in helping the theorist derive testable propositions and hypotheses about international relations. As noted earlier, once hypotheses are developed, they are tested with *empirical* evidence. The image of the unified, rational state is, therefore, the starting point for realist analysis, not a concluding statement. Hans J. Morgenthau has explained the utility of the rational, unitary actor assumption:

> We put ourselves in the position of a statesman who must meet a certain problem of foreign policy under certain circumstances, and we ask ourselves what the rational alternatives are from which a statesman may choose . . . and which of these rational alternatives this particular statesman, acting under these circumstances, is likely to choose. It is the testing of this rational hypothesis against the actual facts and their consequences that gives meaning to the facts of international politics and makes a theory of politics possible.*

In other words, even if we were not physically present when a decision was made, the rationality assumption gives us a baseline in attempting to explain what actually happened. Similarly such simplifying assumptions aid the development of hypotheses and theories about the causes of various international phenomena including war, arms races, the formation and maintenance of international organizations, and so on. Many works involving **game theory** and **deterrence,** as we will see in Chapters 4 and 5, use the rational, unitary actor assumption.

Question: When we read about foreign policy or international events in the newspaper, don't we usually apply the rationality assumption in an attempt to make sense of them? For example, in trying to figure out why a foreign leader acted as he or she did, don't we in effect put ourselves in his or her place and ask, "Would I respond in a similar manner in similar circumstances?"

*Hans J. Morgenthau, *Politics among Nations* (New York: Knopf, 1948, 1973), 5.

of expanded trade and economic investment with the world's most populous country.

Policy-Making Conflicts over Interests and Objectives

The previous discussion may leave the impression that the formulation of a state's national security or foreign policy objectives is a straightforward task that can be reduced to a formula:

$$\text{interests} + \text{threats} + \text{opportunities} = \text{objectives}$$

An obvious difficulty, of course, is that even if policy makers can agree on basic interests, they may disagree on what constitutes a threat, an opportunity, or a worthwhile foreign policy objective. For example, in the mid-1980s Western political leaders across the board viewed Gorbachev as simply the latest in a long line of Soviet leaders hostile to the West. Hence, he was viewed as a threat. A few years later, German Chancellor Helmut Kohl and then British Prime Minister Margaret Thatcher came to view Gorbachev as an opportunity to be seized to achieve a dramatic improvement in East-West relations, a position only belatedly accepted by the Reagan administration. Even so, some members of the U.S. government continued to treat Gorbachev as a threat, believing that his reassuring words concerning East-West *rapprochement* and nuclear disarmament were little more than a sophisticated deception campaign.

Even if the leaders of a state come to realize that there is an opportunity that can be seized, there can be disagreement on how best to take advantage of the situation. Consider, for example, the collapse of communism in the former Soviet Union and the end of Soviet rule over Eastern Europe. What was to be the objective of the United States and its then sixteen allies? Extend membership in NATO to some or all of the Eastern European countries? Or merely give them greater assurance of their security by existing NATO members? All of these ideas were suggested and bitterly debated within Western capitals and among NATO allies. Indecisiveness may result from the absence of consensus on foreign policy and national security objectives both within a state and among allies, however, decisions have been made in this case to increase member states to 26, establish a process for further expansion, and form cooperative partnerships with some twenty other countries.

Moreover, these controversies are not always confined to government officials. If we shift the level of analysis to the societal level (especially in analyzing democracies), interest groups and the general public may hold quite different points of view. In 2005, for example, voters in France and the Netherlands rejected the proposed European constitution that had the support of their governments. Notwithstanding these difficulties, governmental authorities often use the national interest to legitimize their more specific foreign policy objectives. Indeed, they customarily speak and act as if they were serving precisely defined state objectives or goals deemed to be in the national interest.

Defining objectives would seem to be easier in dictatorships and other authoritarian regimes than in democracies—not many officials dared to disagree with Adolph Hitler of Nazi Germany (1933–1945) or Joseph Stalin of the Soviet Union (1930–1953) while they were in power. Although democracies are constituted to take popular views or **public opinion** into account, the distinction between democracies and authoritarian regimes in terms of popular influences is often overdrawn. Authoritarian regimes can also be influenced by popular sentiments.

For example, Soviet political leaders came to understand domestic misgivings about the 1979 intervention in Afghanistan, particularly when loss of life and other costs became more widely known to the general public. Of course, popularly supported, authoritarian regimes may derive considerable strength from their mandates in both domestic and foreign policy matters. This was the case in China after Mao's successful revolution in 1949 and in Vietnam under Ho Chi Minh during and after the wars against France (which ended in 1954) and later against the United States and its allies (which ended in 1975). Unpopular authoritarian regimes, by contrast, may face resistance to their domestic and foreign policy objectives. The Shah of Iran, for example, was an important U.S. and Western ally but was overthrown in 1979. Similarly, East

European communist regimes, once they lost the Soviet security guarantee, soon found they could not deal with public demands from the emerging civil societies, and beginning in 1989 they collapsed, one after the other.

Resolving controversies on interests and objectives by governmental decision is common enough in democracies as well, particularly those with a strong cultural tradition in their politics of deference to authorities in such matters of state as foreign policy. By contrast, mandates of this kind are difficult to sustain in the United States without public support, given the strong American political tradition that allows for challenges to all policies, domestic or foreign. Moreover, although the executive branch has the lead in foreign policy matters, **separation of powers** (or **presidential government**) in the United States also gives substantial authority for the formulation of American foreign policy to the legislature, particularly the Senate.

Indeed, the U.S. president and members of the congress are often at loggerheads in determining interests, objectives, and appropriate actions. By contrast, in the more common **parliamentary government,** the head of government is also the leader of the majority party or coalition in the legislature, which somewhat simplifies the consensus-building task. Difficult as it still may be, parliamentary regimes such as those in the United Kingdom, Germany, and Japan need to reach consensus only within the majority party or governing coalition, not across separate, independent branches of government. Still their foreign policies will encounter opposition if there is not sufficient support from or deference by the general public.

Prioritization of Objectives

Let us assume the leaders of a state have agreed on the objectives they wish to pursue. The next problem they face is that the foreign policy objectives of any given state (or international and transnational organization, for that matter) may conflict with each other and, thus, not be entirely compatible. For example, a state's objective of promoting human rights may well conflict with the objective of maintaining good relations or reduced tensions with countries thought to be in violation of human rights. A corporation may want to get early returns on investments in various countries but not be so aggressive or exploitative as to expose itself to foreign complaints that would put its longer-term business position in jeopardy.

Needless to say, such rank ordering is often extremely difficult to accomplish. For example, the Carter administration ranked human rights higher as a foreign policy objective than did the Reagan administration. But both administrations effectively put human rights ahead of some other objectives during the late 1970s and 1980s in a publicly celebrated policy conflict about Soviet emigration restrictions. The U.S. government pressed for liberalizing Moscow's policy to allow those Soviet Jews wanting to emigrate to do so more readily. But U.S.-Soviet relations had deteriorated for other reasons, including U.S. and other Western-bloc disapproval of Soviet intervention in Afghanistan in 1979. Not unexpectedly in this already bad climate of relations, the Soviet Union rejected arguments made by the United States and other countries that the Soviets were guilty of human rights violations by not allowing Jewish citizens to leave the country.

These accusations, which no doubt were intended to embarrass and put pressure on the Soviets, contributed to a further souring of relations between Washington and Moscow with predictably negative impact in a variety of other areas. Beyond scoring propaganda points against the Soviets—an objective in itself—there was considerable debate on how much it actually helped Soviet Jews to emigrate or whether quieter

ALTERNATIVE PERSPECTIVES ON DEFINING INTERESTS AND OBJECTIVES

Applying Theory

In our initial discussion of the development of state interests and objectives, the realist, rational actor was quite in evidence. Other perspectives on international relations would take a different approach, not seeing interests as givens, but something to be explained:

- In the section on policy-making conflicts, the pluralist emphasis on conflicting interest groups, public opinion, and tensions resulting from separation of powers within governments was evident.
- Economic structuralists would look at the role of economic interests in defining a state's interests and objectives.
- Constructivists would emphatically argue that interests, objectives, threats, and opportunities are not givens, but rather malleable and subject to redefinition by actors.

A number of research efforts have drawn on the psychology literature in an attempt to generalize about the circumstances under which certain psychological processes occur. What these pluralist-influenced approaches have in common is an emphasis on how *cognition* and cognitive distortions undermine the realist view of decision making as a rational process engaged in by a unitary actor. Many of these scholars have also studied political science and history in addition to psychology and social psychology.

The work of Robert Jervis, to take one example, focuses on individuals and individual perceptions. Jervis is concerned less with how emotions as such affect foreign policy decision making and more with how cognitive factors and a confusing international environment can result in a poor decision even if the individual is relatively unemotional and as intelligent as he or she can be in evaluating alternatives. Furthermore, Jervis takes into account how the anarchic nature of international politics contributes to this confusing environment by encouraging cognitive processes that make decision making more difficult, and it is not necessarily irrational or a sign of paranoia to be preoccupied with real, potential, or imagined threats.

Jervis devotes a great deal of time, applying psychological concepts to historical events and key diplomatic exchanges. His propositions are generalizations about how decision makers perceive others' behavior, form judgments about their intentions, and hence, define threats to national security. These patterns are explained by the general ways in which people draw inferences from ambiguous evidence and in turn help explain seemingly incomprehensible policies. They show how, why, and when highly intelligent and conscientious political leaders and diplomats misperceive their environments in specified ways and sometimes reach inappropriate decisions.

Jervis is interested in discerning how a decision maker comprehends a complex world filled with uncertainty. Each decision maker has a particular image of the world that has been shaped by his or her interpretations of historical events. Very often these events (such as wars and revolutions) occurred when the individual was young and impressionable. Lessons learned from history, when combined with personal experiences, contribute to the development of particular expectations and beliefs concerning how the world operates that will have a major impact on how policy makers formulate objectives and define threats. Once formed, these images of reality are difficult to change. Cognitive consistency is the norm. Information that conflicts with the decision maker's image tends either to be dismissed, ignored, or interpreted in such a manner as to buttress a particular policy preference or course of action.

Question: Would the cognition literature best reflect pluralist or constructivist images of the world?

diplomacy would have been more effective. What is important here, however, is that policy makers made a clear choice when they decided to make Soviet emigration policy an issue, putting the objective of publicly exposing Soviet human rights violations ahead of other objectives on their agendas. A contemporary example involves China. To what extent should Western states criticize China's human rights abuses, given the objective of wishing to maintain good commercial and other relations with an economic dynamo and growing military power?

Competing Domestic and Foreign Policy Objectives

Now let us assume that policy makers have decided upon basic foreign policy objectives and their priorities. The next problem to consider is the possibility that foreign policy objectives may be consistent with some but conflict with other objectives also sought by policy makers. One set of domestic economic objectives common to most governments is to increase employment (or reduce unemployment) of their country's workers while keeping inflation under control. Thus most countries try to create or maintain existing jobs by promoting exports of the goods and services they produce to other countries. One way for a country to do this is to allow (or even take steps to encourage) the value of its currency to decline relative to other currencies. Why? Because doing so makes the price of Country A's exports to foreigners less expensive and thus, other things being equal, more likely to be purchased by them. More sales mean more jobs for the exporting country.

The importing Country B, however, may object to such a policy, perhaps because a relative decline of Country A's currency not only will allow imports from that country to be more competitive with locally produced goods and services, but also will tend to make Country B's own exports to that country more expensive and thus less competitive. In other words, the employment gains in Country A due to the depreciation of its currency may produce employment losses in other countries. Such policies produce an external, adverse impact on other states—what economists refer to as a negative **externality.** Hence, Country A, although pleased with the policy's economic impact on domestic objectives, might regret the policy's impact in terms of foreign policy objectives, particularly if Country B is an important ally.

A real-world example involves the United States and its important relations with Japan since the end of World War II. By allowing U.S. military bases on its soil, Japan has gained defense support from its ally and facilitated projection of U.S. forces in the region, provided inexpensive imports until the 1960s, and has been welcomed as a member of the club of democratic states. The United States, being a major trading nation itself, also has been a leading proponent of an open international trading system, which has made the reduction of tariffs on imports a key foreign policy objective. Over the years, however, U.S.-Japanese relations have had their ups and downs, principally due to Japan's tremendous economic success. The U.S.-Japanese trade imbalance—heavily favoring Japan—has been a U.S. domestic political issue as presidents, Congress, and the public worry about Japanese imports putting U.S. manufacturers out of business. How do policy makers balance the domestic objective to save American jobs, the commitment to an open international trading system, and the foreign policy objective of maintaining good relations with a valued ally such as Japan? It is not an easy task. Similar concerns are evident in U.S.-China relations.

Even if senior policy makers are able to sort out conflicting foreign and domestic objectives and prioritize them, there is usually considerable disagreement among individuals, interest groups, corporate leaders, and agency officials as to what foreign policy objectives should be, not to mention in what rank order or priority they should be placed. For example, the U.S. Department of Agriculture and privately owned agribusinesses may favor increasing grain exports because increased sales are beneficial to American farmers. The State Department may agree, but for a different reason: they want to maintain or improve relations with countries wanting to import American wheat. For their parts, the Department of Commerce and the Treasury Department may both be inclined to favor such sales because of the favorable impact increased exports will have on the American trade and payments balances.

On the other hand, consumer groups may fear that grain exports will reduce the domestic supplies of wheat, driving up prices of bread and other products made from grain. During the Cold War years, some interest groups and government officials in the United States saw increased agricultural (and technological) exports to the Soviet Union as helping the other side in a global, competitive struggle with significant security implications for the United States. Private interests, members of Congress, and various executive-branch departments and agencies thus weigh in on the different sides of what may have seemed to be a relatively simple issue.

In short, selecting and rank ordering foreign policy objectives is not as easy as it might first seem when domestic goals are taken into account. Determining foreign policy objectives is a rather complex matter when one understands that a country's foreign and domestic objectives often conflict.

In the final analysis, of course, these conflicting interests and competing objectives are usually resolved either through some form of compromise, concession by one or more interested parties, or decision by the president or other authority. In some cases, however, there may be no clear resolution of policy conflicts. When this occurs, separate bureaucratic agencies of government, each purporting to act in the name of the state, may simultaneously carry out conflicting policies designed to achieve their diverse objectives. In such circumstances corporations and other private actors will also be more prone to act independently, perhaps circumventing or trying to go around various government authorities. This last point is worthy of further discussion.

States versus Other Actors

As noted by pluralists and liberals, multinational corporations, banks, interest groups of various kinds, international organizations, and other nonstate actors also pursue interests, objectives, and alternative courses of action that may or may not be consistent with the demands of the states in which they conduct their activities. Consideration of the preferences, not only of other states but also of nonstate actors, is thus included in formulating and implementing a state's foreign policy.

To illustrate such conflicts, we will focus on the relations between one type of transnational actor—the multinational corporation (MNC)—and the state. The primary objective of a multinational corporation is to maximize profits for its stockholders or other stakeholders. To achieve such an objective, the corporation may need to move money into and out of countries with little concern for the effects these financial transactions may have on different countries. Similarly, these MNCs may look for legal ways to maximize profits and avoid or shelter themselves from taxes.

Governments may try as a matter of policy to attract foreign capital investment by keeping taxes on corporate profits low, allowing for earnings to be taken out of the country or **repatriated** with few if any **capital controls** or other obstacles. Other governments may be less permissive on such matters, charging higher taxes, demanding that foreign investments be in the form of joint ventures with the host government or other local nationals, imposing environmental or other conditions under which foreign investments are allowed, and placing formal or informal restraints on capital outflow.

Whether corporations operate in a permissive environment or a more restrictive one, their interests and objectives may be at odds with the host government. When this occurs, the corporation may try to find ways around restrictions. Given the rapid transfer of assets in capital markets that instantaneous global communications have made possible, it has become increasingly difficult in practice for governments to monitor corporate conduct very effectively.

In sum, for a state, international organization, or a transnational actor, deciding upon and implementing a set of objectives is a complex and difficult process. From the perspective of a state, as we have seen, policy makers may disagree among themselves about what are appropriate objectives to pursue and what their relative priority should be. There also may be conflicts between foreign policy and domestic objectives. Finally, states must contend with other international actors who have their own set of objectives that might conflict with those of any particular state. What is most likely to decide the outcome of such a confrontation, however, is the relative power of the actors involved.

Capabilities and Power: Translating Objectives into Realities

Policy makers can talk all they want about the need to formulate and rank order specific foreign policy objectives based upon fundamental national interests and threats and opportunities emanating from the international system. But such an exercise is academic unless a state has the capabilities and power to pursue those objectives. The relation between capabilities and power is difficult to specify because little consensus on the precise meanings of the terms exists in the social sciences, let alone the literature on international relations.

First of all, for some people power is equated with capabilities; the terms are used interchangeably. They see, for example, a country with a large military and great economic wealth and pronounce, "Country X is a great power." But a "large military" and "great economic wealth" mean something only if one asks, "Large or great compared to what?" France has a large military compared to Switzerland but a small one compared to the United States.

Hence, a second view is that the power of a state is evident only when compared to other states and nonstate actors. This concept of power as the relative distribution of capabilities can be viewed from a global perspective. The emphasis is on the importance of the overall distribution of capabilities in the international system—unipolar (one state dominates), bipolar (two states dominate), multipolar (three or more major states dominate). Proponents of this theory believe that simply knowing the distribution of capabilities allows us to predict basic patterns of behavior in the international system. For example, in a bipolar system (as in the Cold War), alliances will coalesce around the two major states; such alliances tend to be stable (or in **equilibrium**) with few defections. Conversely, in a multipolar system, coalitions tend to be much less stable and different combinations of states can ally at different times.

The overall distribution of capabilities will also influence other states that are not major players. Even if a major state is not directly attempting to exert influence on such states, the mere existence of its large, imposing capabilities will influence how states with modest capabilities will act. For example, the Cold War era was a bipolar system— the United States and the Soviet Union were termed the superpowers. Even if less powerful states were ignored by Moscow and Washington, the former did not have the luxury of similar indifference—the political fallout of Soviet-American competition could affect them directly. As an African proverb notes, "When two elephants fight, the grass gets trampled."

Power as a relation can also be looked at from the perspective not of the overall global distribution of capabilities, but rather from that of any two states. States accumulate capabilities that at some point can be brought to bear on other states or actors. Power is a potential means of influence, not an end in itself. Although all actors may not be so motivated, it may be that a state will seek as a national objective to increase its power position relative to other countries or other actors. The typical reason for taking such measures, however, is the knowledge that power is necessary in an anarchic world without central authority if a state is to achieve its ends.

People, however, are puzzled when a state with superior capabilities cannot influence an obviously much weaker state. Even the most powerful states are constrained by limits to what their capabilities can accomplish. Moreover, the power of a state or other actor depends not just on the reality of having certain capabilities, but also on the perception held by other actors of the state's willingness to employ its capabilities for various purposes. Unless a state can make others believe in its willingness to use its capabilities, its actual influence will tend to diminish. In short, **credibility** is an important element in power calculations.

This leads us to the final perspective: power can be viewed as an **effect,** meaning that influence is actually achieved in a particular situation. Consider, for example, two mechanisms through which military capabilities are transformed into effective or actualized military power—victory in war and a change in state behavior due to threats. Victory in war involves taking one's capabilities and actually applying them in a coercive manner, so that a rival is physically defeated or punished to the point at which it surrenders. But an effective threat of force may also be sufficient to change the behavior of another state. In either case power has been achieved over a rival—the net effect is to the advantage of one party over the other.

For our purposes, however, *power* is defined as the *actual or potential **influence** or coercion a state or other actor can assert relative to other states and nonstate actors because of the political, geographic, economic and financial, technological, military, social, cultural, or other capabilities it possesses.* This definition views capabilities as the underpinning of power. Once capabilities are mobilized, their utilization is expressed in the attempt or actual ability to influence (such as by diplomacy) or to coerce (such as by the use of force) the behavior of another state, coalition, alliance, or nonstate actor. We will now discuss key capabilities that a state may wish to create or enhance. The particular mix of capabilities will vary depending on the state.

Political Capabilities

When we discuss political capabilities as a contribution to (or constraint on) national power, our focus is on states and their societies. At least four factors are involved in defining a country's political capabilities: human resources, reputation, technology, and the nature of its political system and political culture. Some or all of these factors can dramatically influence the effectiveness of the application of material capabilities.

The Human Factor   First, human resources are extremely important. Because of their larger population size and higher education levels, some states have great diplomatic and bureaucratic resources that contribute to their political capabilities. Experienced diplomats and other representatives of the state, backed up by competent bureaucratic staffs at home and abroad, certainly enhance the capacity of the state to exercise influence in international affairs.

Applying Theory

ROUSSEAU'S FABLE ABOUT DEER HUNTING AND THE INTERESTS OF STATES: AN APPLICATION OF GAME THEORY

How are states to act in an anarchical, self-help system without any world government or other central authority to provide order? Is it inevitable that they will be self-seeking, attempting to maximize their short-term individual objectives or self-interest? Or is it possible that states can upgrade their common (perhaps enlightened) self-interest over both the short and long term? What is the rational thing to do?

We can find insights in the Geneva-born, eighteenth-century philosopher Jean Jacques Rousseau's allegory or fable about five primitive human beings in a state of nature engaged in a stag hunt. In this presumed or hypothetical state of nature there is no government, no organizations of any kind, no towns or communities, no family unit, no language of communication, nor any form of social structure. In this environment each hunter has to decide (1) whether to collaborate in the hunting of a stag necessary to meet the hunger needs of all five or (2) to defect from the group to capture a hare or rabbit if one appears. To choose the latter course of action would be to serve one's own interest at the expense of the group.

If the individual prefers to serve the common interest (go after the stag), can he or she trust the others to do so? And if the individual cannot trust the others, is it not rational to go for the hare and defect from the group before any of the others do? Or is it possible to develop the basis for collaboration on a continuing basis by all five?

Scholars who deal with *game theory* attempt to answer such questions. Game theory is an approach to determining rational choice or optimum strategy under conditions of uncertainty. As such, game theory has direct relevance to the study of foreign policy choice, serving national interests, and achieving national objectives.

How one understands Rousseau's stag hunt fable has a great deal to do with how one sees states interacting in world politics. Some tend to see the state as serving only narrow self-interest. Pessimists point to the number, duration, and intensity of wars. Those of a more optimistic bent note that in many cases states live in peace and harmony for years, and great potential does exist for collaboration among states.

What is the rational thing for any of these hunters (or states) to do? The answer depends in part on whether they want to serve only narrowly construed individual interests or whether there is enough trust and confidence among the parties to pursue a cooperative or collaborative venture as in collective hunting of a stag. The answer also depends on whether any of the parties wants to think beyond achieving here-and-now, short-term interests, instead focusing on attainment of longer-term interests and objectives. These alternative choices are arrayed in the matrix shown in Figure 3.A. In short, if the hunters (and states) learn to communicate regularly, building trust and confidence among them, it is at least possible to achieve mutually satisfying outcomes. Pluralists tend to be more optimistic than realists about the achievement of such outcomes.

Question: Do you think it is easier for states to cooperate in an era of increasing globalization, undermining the pessimistic realist implications of living in a world characterized by anarchy? If so, why? If not, why not?

	Individual Interests: Pursue the Hare	Group/Collective Interests: Pursue the Stag
Short Run	Serve immediate self-interest	May provide basis for possible future collaboration
Long Run	No apparent basis for collaborative behavior	Serve long-term common interest

FIGURE 3.A   *The Stag Hunt Fable: A Dilemma of Rational Choice*

Some states, by contrast, are unable to find, recruit, train, and assign enough people competent to carry out diplomatic, bureaucratic, and other governmental tasks effectively. Of course this is often the case with lower-income, developing countries where bureaucracies are often bloated and staffed with individuals whose loyalty is to the current ruler. Third World states, therefore, often have to conduct their foreign policies with diminished political capabilities compared to those states and societies having a larger pool of educated individuals and adequate money and institutions to train them.

Technology   Second, one should not ignore technology's contribution to political capabilities, particularly communications technology. Not all states can afford the advantages provided by advanced telecommunications and related technologies that can be used to coordinate and direct the efforts of diplomats and other representatives around the world. These resources also facilitate the communication of a country's point of view and justification for its policies to the public at home and abroad. Most countries have propaganda ministries or information services, but some are more effective than others in targeting and reaching their intended audiences.

Policy makers' access to intelligence also varies considerably. Some states have better technology at their disposal in addition to their human resources. Although all states engage in intelligence collection, only a few have the necessary means to collect and analyze such information adequately on even a regional, much less a global, scale. Even if technologies are available, widespread use of aircraft, ships, electronic ground stations, satellites, and other technical devices is prohibitively expensive for most countries. Diplomats with access to top-notch intelligence that can be disseminated to them rapidly have an obvious advantage when engaging or negotiating with their counterparts.

Reputation   Third, the reputation and prestige of a state should not be underestimated as a capability. If a state, for example, has a reputation of meeting its security commitments in terms of its allies,

> **P**ower is becoming less fungible (that is, less transferable from one issue to another), less coercive, and less tangible. Modern trends and changes in political issues are having significant effects on the nature of power and the resources that produce it. Co-optive behavioral power—getting others to want what you want—and soft power resources—cultural attraction, ideology, and international institutions—are not new. Yet various trends today are making co-optive behavior and soft power resources more important.
>
> **Joseph S. Nye, Jr.**
> *Bound to Lead: The Changing Nature of American Power* (New York: Basic Books, 1990), 188.

It's Been Said...

other states may hesitate to engage in any action that may be viewed as a threat to those allies. Similarly, a state's reputation might convince another state to join with it in an alliance, knowing security guarantees made to it will be met. Conversely a state with a reputation for failing to meet its commitments will find its promises and proposals viewed with skepticism. Particularly in the minds of policy makers, reputation is seen as vital to an effective foreign policy.

Democratic and Authoritarian Regimes The political capabilities of a state are also related to the nature of its political culture, how its political system is structured, and how it functions. The processes of politics—how domestic and foreign policies are made and how well they serve or respond to national interests or objectives—are influenced or constrained by both cultural and structural aspects of a given political system. The ability to reach decisions that can be implemented effectively in a timely fashion thus varies from country to country.

Machiavelli's argument that the power of the state rests in part on popular consent holds as true today as it did in his time. When governing officials or the regime lose *legitimacy*—their "right to rule" in the eyes of the citizenry based on custom or consent—the ability of these policy makers to carry out either domestic or foreign policy is markedly weakened.

In this respect, democracies by their very nature sometimes enjoy greater popular support than authoritarian regimes. Democracies may also be more responsive to public opposition to certain policies, changing course or modifying them consistent with public opinion. This is often frustrating to policy makers and other "experts" who have their own views on what are usually very complex issues, not always well understood by the general public. Nevertheless, treating public opinion as an important consideration, which democracies are more likely to do than authoritarian regimes, may pay off in the longer run. Political capabilities are enhanced when policies, domestic or foreign, enjoy widespread support.

Building a broad consensus through public discussion of issues can be a source of enormous strength in democracies. Speed and relative efficiency of decision making are sacrificed in exchange for policies informed by a greater number of alternative views and accompanied by greater prospects for forging a consensus. Foreign policies are easier to carry out when people support them in the first place. Of course maintaining a public-support base for policies over time is a continuing challenge for political leaders in democracies as it is in authoritarian regimes as well.

Regime Type Democracies such as Japan and most European countries have a parliamentary government in a **unitary state**. Political authority is more concentrated than in the United States, which has separation of powers between legislative and executive branches within a **federal state** (see Tables 3.2 and 3.3). Thus, in the United Kingdom the executives—prime minister, foreign secretary, defense secretary, chancellor of the exchequer (treasury), and other cabinet ministers—are themselves members of parliament. In the United Kingdom and other countries with parliamentary governments, executive and legislative authority is effectively fused instead of being separated into

SOME DOUBTS ABOUT DEMOCRACIES AND EFFECTIVE FOREIGN POLICY

Foreign policy demands scarcely any of those qualities which are peculiar to a democracy; on the contrary it calls for the perfect use of almost all those qualities in which a democracy is deficient. Democracy is favorable to the increase of the internal resources of a state, it diffuses wealth and comfort, fortifies the respect for law in all classes of society, but it can only with great difficulty regulate the details of an important undertaking, persevere in a fixed design, and work out its execution in spite of serious obstacles. It cannot combine its measures with secrecy or await their consequences with patience. These are qualities which are more characteristic of an individual or an aristocracy.

Alexis de Tocqueville
Early nineteenth-century French observer of America; from his *Democracy in America.*

It's Been Said...

legitimacy
In terms of domestic politics, the right to rule or be obeyed based on legal or other authoritative grounds or, more commonly in the eyes of the citizenry, based on custom or consent.

TABLE 3.2

Structural types of States and Democratic Governments

TYPES OF STATES	CHARACTERISTICS	EXAMPLES
unitary states	Those that *concentrate* all political authority or power in one government in its capital city; most states are of this kind.	Japan, the United Kingdom, France, Italy, Argentina
federal states	Those that *divide* all political authority or power between a central government and additional state or provincial governments; although less common than unitary states, many are of this kind.	United States, Canada, Germany, Russia

TYPES OF DEMOCRATIC GOVERNMENTS	CHARACTERISTICS	EXAMPLES
parliamentary governments	Those that *fuse* in particular the executive and legislative functions into a single branch of government; this is the most common form of democratic governance.	Japan, Germany, the United Kingdom, Italy
	The judiciary is usually independent, in some cases with authority to exercise judicial review to assure the constitutionality of governmental acts.	Germany
	In some there is no political authority higher than an act of parliament.	United Kingdom
presidential governments	Those that *separate* the executive, legislative, and judicial function into separate branches of government; the relative strength of branches varies, with the executive clearly stronger in some countries.	France
	In others there may be more of a contest between the legislature and the executive. In some countries authority for judicial review to interpret and assure constitutionality of laws and executive acts is common.	United States

TYPES OF STATES	TYPES OF DEMOCRATIC GOVERNMENTS	
	PARLIAMENTARY	PRESIDENTIAL
unitary	United Kingdom, Italy, Japan (greatest concentration of political authority; most common combination)	France
federal	Germany	United States (greatest fragmentation of political authority; least common combination)

TABLE 3.3
Categorizing States with Democratic Governments: Some Examples

distinct legislative and executive branches, each with its different bases for authority and power, as in the American form of presidential government. Moreover, there is only one government in a unitary state, not the separate state and local governments that may compete with each other and the central government in a federal state such as the United States, Germany, Switzerland, and Canada. In the British case, we note there has been some devolution or transfer of authority to component units, as in establishing Scottish and Welsh legislatures for dealing primarily with issues of local concern; however, authority on foreign policy, national security, and most other issues remains under British parliamentary authority in London.

Considerable debate and compromise still remain both within and outside the majority party or coalition in states with parliamentary governments but not usually to the same degree as in states with presidential governments, in which political power and authority are dispersed or more fragmented. Compromises on foreign policy as in other political matters in parliamentary governments need only be made among legislators within the majority party or coalition of governing parties. Although concurrence by opposition parties can be helpful by providing a broader base of support for a parliamentary government's foreign policy, there is no formal requirement for such a consensus.

Moreover, there is no need to compromise in the consensus-building process across branches of government because the executive is in fact part of the legislature in parliamentary regimes. As a result, states with parliamentary governments tend to be somewhat more decisive and often have more comprehensive and coherent foreign policies than those with presidential governments. When parliamentary governments exist in unitary states—the most common form of democracy—there are even fewer governmental obstacles to overcome once a decision has been made within the central government. No separate state governments are empowered to challenge the decisions of national authorities in a purely unitary state. Of course, efficiency in policy making says nothing about the quality of the actual policy—it could be a failure if not disastrous to the interests of the state.

By contrast, compared to most other countries, there are many more potentially influential voices on foreign policy matters and many more points of access for the exercise of such influence in the United States. Given a federal **division of powers** between central and state and local governments and the aforementioned separation of powers between executive and legislature in all of these governments, there is a fragmentation of authority and a proliferation of points of access for individuals and interest groups. With so many incremental compromises required before decisions are taken, these governments tend to be slower in reaching decisions. When decisions are made, they tend to be step-by-step, incremental choices in which short-term factors often dominate. Although not impossible—given the fragmentation of power and authority under both federalism and separation of powers—it is much more difficult in the United States to develop comprehensive, logically coherent policies that take midrange and long-term considerations seriously into account. Again, however, this does not necessarily mean U.S. policy is less effective in defending its interests and achieving its objectives compared to a parliamentary system.

Political Cultures   Political capabilities are also affected by **political culture**—those norms, values, and orientations of a society's culture that are politically relevant. Many societies have a tradition of deferring, for the most part, to political authorities in such matters of state as foreign policy. In some societies, by contrast, there is a greater tendency for people to become involved. Although government officials in the United States often may have greater latitude in foreign policy matters than on domestic issues, Americans are not prone to defer entirely to political authorities on either domestic or foreign policy and readily let their views be known, whether the issue is U.S. involvement in Bosnia, Kosovo, Haiti, Iraq, or some other country.

In some democracies with consensus-oriented political cultures, such as Japan, Switzerland, or Sweden, there may be a greater tendency to seek a broader basis of support for policies than is constitutionally or legally required. In other democracies, such as the United Kingdom, Germany, or the United States, where conflict-oriented politics prevail as part of their political cultures, a narrow, simple majority of 50 percent plus one vote will do. Wider margins may be desirable but are by no means required in such countries either by law or by expectation within the prevailing political culture.

Social and Cultural Capabilities

The social cohesion of a society has a direct impact on its power position. States suffering from crises of authority and being torn apart by economic, ideological, religious, ethnic, racial, language, or other cultural differences can hardly act effectively in the international arena. The states that comprise the former Yugoslavia illustrate this point. Their bloody civil wars undermined their capabilities. Culturally and socially homogeneous states, by contrast, are usually more effective international actors.

The concept of a **nation-state** refers to the nineteenth- and twentieth-century idea that a common national identity can be achieved among the people living within a given state. In fact, some states, such as Nigeria, Lebanon, Switzerland, the Russian Federation, Belgium, and Canada, can be said to contain two or more nations. Unless such sociocultural diversity can be contained, through toleration and compromise, establishment of linkages that effectively connect different communal groups, or assimilation of diverse elements into one national whole, the power of the state as an international actor can become markedly weakened.

Another important aspect of cultural capabilities is the extent to which countries are able to maintain influence over other countries through common language, religion, ethnic or racial identity, or legal and political tradition. The French and the British, for example, have maintained fairly close ties with the elites of many of their former colonies. In spite of political differences, elites in these former colonies typically speak the language and often adopt many of the ways of the former colonial power. In some instances, these cultural ties have been buttressed or reinforced by continuing military, trade, financial, and other commercial relations. Critics refer to such ties as a manifestation of **neocolonialism**—a new form of long-established patterns of dominance by former colonial powers.

The education levels, distribution of skills, and value systems that characterize different societies often have substantial impact on the roles countries play in world politics. Economic strength, for example, depends directly on such factors. Market-oriented cultures, in which entrepreneurial skills are valued, provide an environment within which individuals and businesses can thrive. A highly skilled and educated population oriented toward productivity makes economic success possible. Societies lacking sufficient numbers of such human resources are hard-pressed to compete successfully in global markets, however committed the country's leadership may be to achieving economic gains and sustaining development.

Geographic, Economic, and Technological Capabilities

Geographic location can affect the capabilities of states. That the United Kingdom and Japan are island states, for example, historically has provided some protection against invasion by continental or other states. Similarly the separation of the United States from Europe enabled the United States early in its history to pursue an isolationist foreign policy, avoiding what George Washington called the "entangling alliances" of European politics. The United States was able, in fact, to delay its entry into both World War I and World War II due to the remoteness of its geographic location from the combat area. Oceans provided valuable insulation from European affairs. Of course this geopolitical advantage has been reduced considerably by technology, in particular the development of intercontinental ballistic missiles (ICBMs) and other weapons systems that have increased the vulnerability of the United States to military attack.

Geography, defined in terms of natural resources, obviously has an important impact on state capabilities. Whatever power the petroleum-producing countries may have stems in large part from the fact that most industrial countries remain so dependent on them for oil and natural gas supplies. Although the United States is somewhat less dependent than Japan and most European countries, more than half of American consumption is from foreign sources. The United States also has vast supplies of lumber, coal, iron, and other raw materials, but the country imports the bulk of its tin, bauxite, chromium, cobalt, manganese, nickel, and zinc. Compared to most countries, however, the United States is still very rich in natural resources. By contrast, Japan is at the other extreme and remains dependent on foreign sources for most of its raw materials. Putting this into perspective, however, the comparative advantage of the resource-rich United States is reduced somewhat by the fact that the country is also the world's largest consumer of natural resources.

The United States also has the world's largest economy as measured, for example, by its **gross national product (GNP).** These are measures of the total dollar value of all goods and services produced in a given year. Economic productivity stems from the efficient use of capital as well as human and natural resources. Second only

---

THE INFLUENCE OF FOREIGN VALUES

*U*ntil 1960, the University College of Fort Hare was the only residential center of higher education for blacks in South Africa. Fort Hare was more than that: it was a beacon for African scholars from all over Southern Central and Eastern Africa. For young black South Africans like myself, it was Oxford and Cambridge, Harvard and Yale, all rolled into one.

Fort Hare was a missionary college. We were exhorted to obey God, respect the political authorities, and be grateful for the educational opportunities afforded us by the church and the government. These schools have often been criticized for being colonialist in attitudes and practice. Yet, even with such attitudes, I believe their benefits outweighed their disadvantages. The missionaries built and ran schools when the government was unwilling or unable to do so. The learning environment of missionary schools, while often morally rigid, was far more open than the racist principles underlying government schools. Fort Hare was both home and incubator of some of the greatest African scholars the continent has ever known.

Nelson Mandela
Long Walk to Freedom
(Boston: Little, Brown, 1994),
37–38.

It's Been Said...

to the United States in national economic output is natural resource–poor Japan, which nevertheless has demonstrated its capability to organize its economy into one of the most productive in the world. Beyond the industriousness of Japan's labor force, considerable capital investment in new and advanced technologies has made possible that phenomenal economic growth over the more than six decades since the end of World War II.

The leading industrial countries with the largest economies in terms of sheer size include the United States, Japan, Germany, France, Italy, the United Kingdom, Russia, and Canada (see Table 3.4). A number of other advanced industrial countries have smaller economies but often higher standards or levels of living than some of the countries with larger economies (see Table 3.5). Switzerland immediately comes to mind. Taiwan,

TABLE 3.4

GNP as Indicator of Relative Capabilities or Power Position: Comparing the Size of Selected Economies[a]

COUNTRY	GROSS NATIONAL PRODUCT (U.S. $ MILLIONS)	COUNTRY	GROSS NATIONAL PRODUCT (U.S. $ MILLIONS)
Group of Seven (World's Major Economies)		Asia and Pacific	
United States	10,948,547	China	1,417,000
Japan	4,300,858	South Korea	605,333
Germany	2,403,160	India	600,637
United Kingdom	1,794,878	Australia	522,378
France	1,757,613	Indonesia	208,312
Italy	1,468,314	Thailand	142,953
Canada	856,523	Philippines	80,754
OTHER EUROPE		**LATIN AMERICA**	
Spain	838,652	Mexico	626,080
Netherlands	511,502	Brazil	492,338
Russian Federation	432,855	Argentina	129,596
Switzerland	320,118	**AFRICA**	
Belgium	301,896	South Africa	159,886
Sweden	301,606	Denmark	211,888
Austria	253,126	Ukraine	49,537
Norway	220,854		
Turkey	240,376		

[a]Aggregate economic production of goods and services can be used as one indicator of overall capabilities or power. What is striking about these numbers is how easily the United States outpaces all other countries. The Russian Federation, the core of the former Soviet Union and chief rival of the United States during the Cold War, is way down the list. Much is justifiably made of the dramatic economic expansion of China in recent years, but it still lags way behind the United States in terms of GNP.

Source: www.worldbank.org

COUNTRY	PER CAPITA INCOME (U.S. $)		
Switzerland	39,880	Iran	2,000
United States	37,610	Guatemala	1,910
Japan	34,510	Colombia	1,810
United Kingdom	28,350	Egypt	1,390
France	24,770	China	1,100
Canada	23,930	Philippines	1,080
Australia	21,650	Indonesia	810
Singapore	21,230	Zimbabwe	735
South Korea	12,020	India	530
Saudi Arabia	8,530	Kenya	390
Mexico	6,230	Uganda	240
Turkey	2,790	Rwanda	220
Russian Federation	2,610		

TABLE 3.5
Level of Living: Per Capita Income of Selected Countries[a]

[a]Take a close look at this per capita income ranking. Note how China and India, which have received a great deal of attention due to their rapidly expanding economies, are still ranked very low in terms of this measure.

Source: www.worldbank.org

Singapore, South Korea, and other **newly industrializing countries (NICs)** have made impressive economic gains in recent decades; these countries have educated and skilled populations with market orientations, but economic capabilities in all of these countries are a function more directly of such factors as labor productivity, the effectiveness of management, the extent and quality of capital investment, the degree of technological innovation, and condition of the **economic infrastructure**—such production-support factors as roads, sea- and airports, public transportation, and telecommunications.

By contrast, agrarian societies with less-developed industrial economies are heavily dependent on agricultural production both for their own domestic consumption and in some cases for export. Because these countries rely more heavily on labor to sustain their economies, they are usually less efficient even in agricultural production than advanced industrial countries such as the United States. Advanced industrial countries that are also endowed with good soil and a favorable climate have made very heavy capital investments in machinery used by the large agribusinesses and smaller, cooperative farm arrangements. Technology-intensive agriculture in the United States, for example, has made it the world's largest exporter of food products.

Vulnerability to price fluctuations in the international market is most severe for those countries that are dependent on export of one or a few crops, minerals, or other raw materials. With the notable exception of the oil-exporting countries, attempts to form producer cartels for other minerals and for agricultural products have not been very successful. In part this is because consumers of these products can more easily substitute other minerals or agricultural products or increase their own domestic production of these products. By contrast, large-scale substitution of other energy sources for oil in the oil-dependent industrial countries is not easily accomplished, at least not in the short run. The economic disparities between the haves and have-nots are evident in Table 3.5.

Military Capabilities

Particularly for many realists, the military is another important capability or component of a state's power. In some countries the military performs a domestic order maintenance function similar to that performed by police forces. Indeed, in some authoritarian regimes the military's primary function is not to protect the country, but to protect the regime from its own citizens. Although the ability to maintain stability or order within the state has an important impact on the state's relative power position, the external capacity of its military forces is perhaps even more important. As we will see in Chapter 5, states use force (or threaten to use it) to secure various objectives, the most important of which is their own defense or survival.

The continued development of nuclear weapons since World War II added a new dimension to military capabilities, but conventional or nonnuclear military forces remain a vital part of the calculus of a state's military capabilities. What size and kinds of force a state can deploy, where, and for how long are variables that have a significant impact on a state's relative power position. The United States is clearly the world's biggest military spender and now has a worldwide military capability greater than that of any other country.

Paradoxically, the rapid advancement of military technology, particularly in nuclear weaponry, has served to constrain those states possessing such capabilities. Indeed, use of such weapons can invite retaliation by one's adversary with unacceptable destructive consequences. Often states not possessing such weapons have been able to assert far more leverage than one would expect, given their apparently inferior military capabilities. As a practical matter, since the end of World War II, the world's nuclear powers have been reluctant to use such weapons to achieve objectives at the expense of nonnuclear states. Nevertheless, states tend to believe that the possession of nuclear weapons enhances the state's international reputation and prestige.

It is easy to overstate the importance of the military component of national power relative to other factors. Certainly prudent decision makers will take seriously any existing or potential military capability that could be threatening in order to assure that they have enough military capability of their own (or in alliances to which they belong) to offset it. On the other hand, military capabilities do depend on the strength of the underlying economy as a source of personnel and for procurement of military equipment and supplies. In this regard, economic capabilities may define the limits of the military capabilities a country may choose to develop.

Measuring Power

Given these diverse capabilities, it is exceedingly difficult to produce a single measure capturing all of these capabilities that would enable the political analyst to rank states in order of their power positions. Most would agree that the United States is currently the world's sole superpower or strongest great power, but who comes next: China? Japan? Germany? France? Great Britain? Russia? Not only is there no agreement on the weighting or relative importance of these capabilities, but it is also next to impossible to quantify such factors as cultural and social capabilities in any meaningful fashion.

USS Louisiana, *a nuclear-powered submarine carrying Trident ballistic missiles with nuclear warheads. Such vessels enhance the global power projection capabilities of the United States.*

Moreover, some realists, as well as scholars working in the pluralist tradition, claim that to talk of power as an integrated concept is not particularly useful. They argue that in different issue areas different capabilities have different degrees of importance. From this point of view, military capabilities have considerable salience in strategic issues but do not have great weight in trade, investment, and other economic issues. How useful, for example, are American military capabilities when it comes to trade disputes with Japan?

On the other hand, most realists argue that one cannot talk of such economic issues as trade and investment relations among the countries belonging to (or associated with) the European Union (EU) strictly in terms of economic capabilities. From this perspective, especially during the Cold War, the European states benefited from the security umbrella provided by the United States. Thus, one can argue that military capabilities are at least as important as economic capabilities in determining the power of states in economic issue areas. Certainly the United States derives some **economic leverage** in its relations with EU members and other European states that have depended to some degree on America's contribution to the NATO alliance and overall European security.

Similarly, realists note that in the 1970s a great deal of attention was given to OPEC, the Organization of Petroleum Exporting Countries. With headquarters in Vienna, this international organization is composed of both Arab and non-Arab oil-exporting countries. While OPEC was a relatively inconsequential organization in the 1960s, its members had considerable success in the 1970s raising the world price of petroleum, thus markedly improving their collective power position. The oil-exporting countries were, in effect, displacing the multinational oil companies from the price-setting role, a task the MNCs had previously performed. OPEC assumed this price-setting function by regulating the supply of oil to world markets. For the first time, these industrially less-developed countries were able to assert very real financial leverage on the industrialized countries. Almost overnight, some observers proclaimed, the OPEC member nations had become major international players.

The price-increase "oil shocks" of the 1970s, however, led industrialized countries to take domestic measures in an attempt to reduce their dependence on oil and natural gas. Beyond conservation measures designed to reduce energy waste, these countries also sought to substitute other energy sources such as coal or nuclear power and have invested in longer-term research and development projects in nuclear, solar, wind, geothermal, and other energy sources.

Divisions within the OPEC cartel and decisions by Saudi Arabia and other major producers to maintain an adequate supply of petroleum to world markets until recently precluded major price increases comparable to those in the 1970s. In particular, the United States took measures designed to assure the security of the principal oil supplier, Saudi Arabia, in exchange for at least a tacit assurance of continuing flow of oil to the global market. The point is that from a realist perspective Saudi Arabia proved to be a one-dimensional power as evidenced by its reliance on the military prowess of the United States and other powers, such as France and the United Kingdom, to deter Iraqi aggression following the 1990 invasion of Kuwait.

In short, little or no consensus exists among analysts as to whether one should treat power as a single, integrated concept or whether one should disaggregate the concept into its separate component capabilities. Contemporary practitioners associated with the realist perspective on international relations seek to enhance the military, economic, and other components of state power. They may do this through domestic or internal measures, such as taking actions designed to strengthen the national economy or to improve the capabilities of the armed forces. External measures designed to increase state power include forming alliances, influencing members of already existing alliances to increase their contributions, and directly arming allies, thus improving their capabilities.

Conclusion

Realists argue that there are a few core or vital interests for all states. Interests in conjunction with threats and opportunities in the global system help to define foreign policy objectives. Realists recognize that such a formula for determining a state's foreign policy objectives is more easily stated than actually achieved. Policy makers may disagree among themselves about what is an opportunity or a threat and about the prioritization of foreign policy objectives once they agree to specific objectives. To complicate matters, foreign policy objectives may conflict with domestic objectives. Furthermore, merely possessing capabilities or power potential does not make a state effective in world politics unless it has the will to use these capabilities in pursuing its objectives. Even so, it may face opposition from both states and nonstate actors with which it may have to contend. A country's sensitivity to public opinion, international legal considerations, domestic politics, perceptions of its resolve, and its reputation and degree of international prestige also may constrain the use of its capabilities.

Given these realities, many pluralists or liberals suggest the explanation of how a state defines its interests is best revealed by looking at cognitive factors of individuals. Many economic structuralists would point to economic class interests as the key determinant of how interests are defined, particularly in an age when access to cheap foreign oil is an imperative for advanced industrial states such as the United States. Finally, constructivists would argue all interests, objectives, threats, and opportunities are socially constructed by policy makers interacting continually with their environment; no single interest is a given.

Beginning in the following chapter, we turn to statecraft—putting power or capabilities to work through diplomacy, the use of force, and other mechanisms available to achieve objectives and serve interests. While the objectives, capabilities, and power of international and transnational organizations remain important, we continue our focus on states in this section of the book.

Afterword

The following excerpts from a government paper (referred to as the "Downing Street Memo") was produced as a backgrounder on July 21, 2002, two days before a British cabinet meeting whose results are summarized in the "Downing Street Minutes". These two previously secret documents were disclosed to the London Times *during the May 2005 British election campaign, apparently by opponents of Prime Minister Blair's government policies on the Iraq war. Of interest to us here, however, is not their controversial quality, but rather their value as an excellent example of how a government (in this case British) engages in planning by weighing carefully its objectives, capabilities, and strategy for mobilizing its capabilities and coordinating actions with its coalition partner, the United States. In bracketed additions to the text, abbreviations or references are defined or clarified. Also annotated here with brackets are the identities or positions of those listed in the address lines of the "Downing Street Minutes", which have been published widely on the Internet. British spellings are left intact as they appeared in the original documents. Italics have been added to emphasize some British understandings of U.S. policy.*

The Downing Street Memo

PERSONAL SECRET UK EYES ONLY IRAQ: CONDITIONS FOR MILITARY ACTION. . . .

Summary

[Cabinet] Ministers are invited to:

(1) Note the latest position on US military planning and timescales for possible action.

(2) Agree that the objective of any military action should be a stable and law-abiding Iraq, within present borders, co-operating with the international community, no longer posing a threat to its neighbours or international security, and abiding by its international obligations on WMD [weapons of mass destruction].

(3) Agree to engage the US on the need to set military plans within a realistic political strategy, which includes identifying the succession to Saddam Hussein and creating the conditions necessary to justify government military action, which might include an ultimatum for the return of U.N. weapons inspectors to Iraq. This should include a call from the Prime Minister to President Bush ahead of the briefing of US military plans to the President on 4 August.

(4) Note the potentially long lead times involved in equipping UK Armed Forces to undertake operations in the Iraqi theatre and agree that the MOD should bring forward proposals for the procurement of Urgent Operational Requirements under cover of the lessons learned from Afghanistan and the outcome of SR2002 [apparently a classified, special British governmental report published in 2002-Ed.].

(5) Agree to the establishment of an ad hoc group of officials under Cabinet Office Chairmanship to consider the development of an information campaign [directed toward the public—Ed.] to be agreed with the US.

Introduction

1. *The US Government's military planning for action against Iraq is proceeding apace. But, as yet, it lacks a political framework. In particular, little thought has been given to creating the political conditions for military action, or the aftermath and how to shape it.*

2. When the Prime Minister discussed Iraq with President Bush at Crawford in April he said that the UK would support military action to bring about regime change, provided that certain conditions were met: efforts had been made to construct a coalition/shape public opinion, the Israel-Palestine Crisis was quiescent, and the options for action to eliminate Iraq's WMD through the U.N. weapons inspectors had been exhausted.

3. *We need now to reinforce this message and to encourage the US Government to place its military planning within a political framework,* partly to forestall the risk that military action is precipitated in an unplanned way by, for example, an incident in the No Fly Zones. This is particularly important for the UK because it is necessary to create the conditions in which we could legally

support military action. Otherwise we face the real danger that the US will commit themselves to a course of action which we would find very difficult to support.

4. In order to fulfill the conditions set out by the Prime Minister for UK support for military action against Iraq, certain preparations need to be made, and other considerations taken into account. This note sets them out in a form which can be adapted for use with the US Government. Depending on US intentions, a decision in principle may be needed soon on whether and in what form the UK takes part in military action.

The Goal

5. Our objective should be a stable and law-abiding Iraq, within present borders, co-operating with the international community, no longer posing a threat to its neighbours or to international security, and abiding by its international obligations on WMD. It seems unlikely that this could be achieved while the current Iraqi regime remains in power. *US military planning unambiguously takes as its objective the removal of Saddam Hussein's regime, followed by elimination of Iraqi WMD. It is however, by no means certain, in the view of UK officials, that one would necessarily follow from the other.* Even if regime change is a necessary condition for controlling Iraqi WMD, it is certainly not a sufficient one.

US Military Planning

6. Although no political decisions have been taken, US military planners have drafted options for the US Government to undertake an invasion of Iraq. . . .

7. US plans assume, as a minimum, the use of British bases in Cyprus and Diego Garcia. This means that legal base issues would arise virtually whatever option Ministers choose with regard to UK participation. . . .

Justification

8. *US views of international law vary from that of the UK and the international community.* Regime change *per se* is not a proper basis for military action under international law. But regime change could result from action that is otherwise lawful. We would regard the use of force against Iraq, or any other state, as lawful if exercised in the right of individual or collective self-defence, if carried out to avert an overwhelming humanitarian catastrophe, or authorised by the U.N. Security Council. . . .

An International Coalition

9. An international coalition is necessary to provide a military platform and desirable for political purposes.

10. US military planning assumes that the US would be allowed to use bases in Kuwait (air and ground forces), Jordan, in the Gulf (air and naval forces) and UK territory (Diego Garcia and our bases in Cyprus). The plans assume that Saudi Arabia would withhold co-operation except granting military over-flights. On the assumption that military action would involve operations in the Kurdish area in the North of Iraq, the use of bases in Turkey would also be necessary.

11. In the absence of U.N. authorisation, there will be problems in securing the support of NATO and EU partners. Australia would be likely to participate on the same basis as the UK. France might be prepared to take part if she saw military action as inevitable. Russia and China, seeking to improve their US relations, might set aside their misgivings if sufficient attention were paid to their legal and economic concerns. Probably the best we could expect from the region would be neutrality. The US is likely to restrain Israel from taking part in military action. In practice, much of the international community would find it difficult to stand in the way of the determined course of the US hegemon. However, the greater the international support, the greater the prospects of success. . . .

Benefits/Risks

12. Even with a legal base and a viable military plan, we would still need to ensure that the benefits of action outweight the risks. . . . *A post-war occupation of Iraq could lead to a protracted and costly nation-building exercise. As already made clear, the US military plans are virtually silent on this point.* Washington could look to us to share a disproportionate share of the burden. Further work is required to define more precisely the means by which the desired endstate would be created, in particular what form of Government might replace Saddam Hussein's regime and the timescale within which it would be possible to identify a successor. We must also consider in greater detail the impact of military action on other UK interests in the region.

Domestic Opinion

13. Time will be required to prepare public opinion in the UK that it is necessary to take military action against Saddam Hussein. . . .

The Downing Street Minutes

SECRET AND STRICTLY PERSONAL - UK EYES ONLY

[To:] DAVID MANNING [British Foreign Policy Advisor]

From: Matthew Rycroft [Staff Aide to Manning]

Date: 23 July 2002

S 195/02 [secret document number 195, the year 2002]

cc: Defence Secretary [Geoff Hoon], Foreign Secretary [Jack Straw], Attorney-General [Lord Goldsmith], Sir Richard Wilson [Cabinet Secretary], John Scarlett [Chair of Joint Intelligence Committee], Francis Richards [Head of GCHQ, the UK's Signals Intelligence agency responsible for communications, electronic and other "signals" intercepts], CDS [Chief of the Defence Staff, Admiral Sir Michael Boyce], C [MI-6 (British Intelligence) Director Richard Dearlove], Jonathan Powell [Chief of Staff], Sally Morgan [Director of Government and Political Relations], Alastair Campbell [Head of Strategy]

IRAQ: PRIME MINISTER'S MEETING, 23 JULY

Copy addressees and you met the Prime Minister [Tony Blair] on 23 July to discuss Iraq. This record is extremely sensitive. No further copies should be made. It should be shown only to those with a genuine need to know its contents.

John Scarlett summarised the intelligence and latest JIC [Joint Intelligence Center] assessment. Saddam's regime was tough and based on extreme fear. The only way to overthrow it was likely to be by massive military action. Saddam was worried and expected an attack, probably by air and land, but he was not convinced that it would be immediate or overwhelming. His regime expected their neighbours to line up with the US. Saddam knew that regular army morale was poor. Real support for Saddam among the public was probably narrowly based.

C reported on his recent talks in Washington. There was a perceptible shift in attitude. Military action was now seen as inevitable. Bush wanted to remove Saddam, through military action, justified by the conjunction of terrorism and WMD [weapons of mass destruction]. *But the intelligence and facts were being fixed around the policy. The NSC* [the U.S. National Security Council] *had no patience with the U.N. route, and no enthusiasm for publishing material on the Iraqi regime's record. There was little discussion in Washington of the aftermath after military action.* . . .

CDS [i.e., Chief of Defense Staff] said that military planners would brief CENTCOM [Central Command, the U.S. military command responsible for the Middle East] on 1–2 August, [U.S. Secretary of Defense] Rumsfeld on 3 August and [President] Bush on 4 August. The two broad US options were:

(a) Generated Start. A slow build-up of 250,000 US troops, a short (72 hour) air campaign, then a move up to Baghdad from the south. Lead time of 90 days (30 days preparation plus 60 days deployment to Kuwait).

(b) Running Start. Use forces already in theatre (3 x 6,000), continuous air campaign, initiated by an Iraqi *casus belli*. Total lead time of 60 days with the air campaign beginning even earlier. A hazardous option.

The US saw the UK (and Kuwait) as essential, with basing in Diego Garcia and Cyprus critical for either option. Turkey and other Gulf states were also important, but less vital. . . .

The Foreign Secretary said he would discuss this with [U.S. Secretary of State] Colin Powell this week. *It seemed clear that Bush had made up his mind to take military action, even if the timing was not yet decided. But the case was thin.* Saddam was not threatening his neighbours, and his WMD capability was less than that of Libya, North Korea or Iran. We should work up a plan for an ultimatum to Saddam to allow back in the U.N. weapons inspectors. This would also help with the legal justification for the use of force.

The Attorney-General said that the desire for regime change was not a legal base for military action. There were three possible legal bases: self-defence, humanitarian intervention, or

UNSC authorisation. The first and second could not be the base in this case. Relying on UNSCR 1205 of three years ago would be difficult. The situation might of course change.

The Prime Minister said that it would make a big difference politically and legally if Saddam refused to allow in the U.N. inspectors. Regime change and WMD were linked in the sense that it was the regime that was producing the WMD. There were different strategies for dealing with Libya and Iran. If the political context were right, people would support regime change. The two key issues were whether the military plan worked and whether we had the political strategy to give the military plan the space to work. . . .

The Foreign Secretary thought the US would not go ahead with a military plan unless convinced that it was a winning strategy. On this, US and UK interest converged. But on the political strategy, there could be US/UK differences. *Despite US resistance, we should explore discreetly the ultimatum.* Saddam would continue to play hard-ball with the U.N. . . .

Key Terms

Other Concepts

Additional Readings

Any student who intends to pursue the study of international relations beyond the introductory level would do well to examine the all-time classic realist textbook by Hans J. Morgenthau, *Politics among Nations* (New York: Knopf), first published in 1948 and reprinted or revised in many subsequent editions. An influential work by two scholars who attempted to draw on the strengths of both realism and pluralism is Robert O. Keohane and Joseph S. Nye's, *Power and Interdependence: World Politics in Transition* (New York: Longman, 1977, 2001). For an excellent discussion of the elements of power from a realist perspective, see Klaus Knorr's, *The Power of Nations: The Political Economy of International Relations* (New York: Basic Books, 1975). Joseph Nye's *Bound to Lead* (New York: Basic Books, 1990) and his more recent *The Paradox of American Power* (New York: Oxford University Press, 2002) underscore the importance of what he calls "soft power." On power and the balance of power, see also Kenneth N. Waltz's, *Theory of International Politics* (Reading, MA: Addison-Wesley, 1979) and his earlier *Man, the State and War* (New York: Columbia University Press, 1954, 1959), especially Chapters VI and VII. John Mearsheimer distinguishes between offensive and defensive realism on the use of power in *The Tragedy of Great Power Politics* (New York: W.W. Norton, 2001, 2003). An excellent anthology on the implications of unipolar (and other) power distributions to G. John Ikenberry, ed., *America Unrivaled: The Future of the Balance of Power* (Ithaca, NY: Cornell University Press, 2002). For a pluralist view of power focusing on cognitive dimensions, see Ernst B. Haas', *When Knowledge Is Power* (Berkeley: University of California Press, 1990). Risa Brooks addresses the relevant questions in this chapter in her "Making Military Might: Why Do States Fail and Succeed? A Review Essay," *International Security* V. 28, No. 2 (Fall 2003): 149–191.

Chapter 4

"A Foreign Secretary is always faced with this cruel dilemma. Nothing he can say can do very much good, and almost anything he may say may do a great deal of harm. Anything he says that is not obvious is dangerous; whatever is not trite is risky. He is forever poised between the cliché and the indiscretion."

HAROLD MACMILLAN, SECRETARY OF STATE FOR FOREIGN AFFAIRS AND LATER PRIME MINISTER OF THE UNITED KINGDOM, 1955

"(A diplomat is) a person who can tell you to go to hell in such a way that you actually look forward to the trip."

CASKIE STINNET

Diplomacy: Managing Relations among States

Napoleon had lost the war, and France had good reason to fear the results of the peace conference held in Vienna beginning in 1814. The French **emissary,** Count Talleyrand, faced a seemingly impossible task—to rescue his country from the vengeance of its wartime adversaries. During Napoleon's wars, French armies had moved deliberately across Europe, forcibly conscripting troops along the way, overthrowing uncooperative princes, and leaving a trail of devastation in their wake. The anger and bitterness they left behind them promised little chance for a charitable outcome now that the tables were turned.

As a bishop of the Catholic Church, Talleyrand had been part of the *ancien régime,* the old order under the Bourbon dynasty that had been overthrown in the revolution that began in 1789. Always a political survivor, Talleyrand was extraordinarily flexible, jettisoning his clerical identity and navigating through the revolutionary turmoil virtually unscathed. He emerged in 1815 as part of a restoration movement designed to reestablish the prerevolutionary order in Europe as a whole and France in particular.

Talleyrand had to face France's now-formidable adversaries without any military or economic leverage to support his negotiating position. The victims of French aggression now had the opportunity to carve up France, dividing it among themselves or at least separating the country into such small pieces that it could no longer be a threat.

The most important delegations at Vienna were those representing the interests of the four great powers that prevailed following the defeat of France. Prince Metternich of Austria was the leading figure, known historically for his intelligence, cleverness, and diplomatic acumen—a man extremely adept at serving Austria's imperial interests. Playing lesser but still very important roles in constructing the settlement at Vienna were Tsar Alexander of Russia, Viscount Castlereagh of Britain, and Prince von Hardenberg of Prussia.

In the final analysis, Talleyrand was able to save France, but not through any charity felt by its erstwhile enemies. Instead France was restored (territorially even slightly larger than it had been in 1789!) only because it was in the interest of all of the great powers to do so. The French Revolution not only had transformed politics in France; it had also threatened the institution of monarchy in continental countries that had never previously experienced such challenges. From this perspective, strengthening European monarchies as legitimate institutions in the post-Napoleonic period meant returning the Bourbons to their "rightful" positions in France as well.

Beyond these considerations, a restored France contributed substantially to maintaining what the British had long favored as a centerpiece of foreign policy—a balance of power on the European continent to keep any one country from becoming too strong. For Austria, a restored France kept growing Prussian power at bay. Finally, the settlement also served Russian interests by maintaining a balance to its west, not just between Prussia and Austria, but also between both of them and France.

For France, it was a badly needed diplomatic triumph. Even though he lacked the military and other tangible resources to strengthen his negotiating position, Talleyrand accomplished his short-term goal. He restored France to legitimate standing in Europe as a great power, much as it had been for centuries preceding the defeat of Napoleon's empire. He was able to accomplish this because, in the course of negotiations, a restored France came to be understood as being in the interest of all of the great powers. More important for Europe as a whole, however, was the lasting influence of the Vienna settlement. It was the basis for a long peace that (with a few interruptions) would last for some ninety-nine years.

❀ ❀ ❀

In the previous chapter we laid out the basic elements of state interests, objectives, and power. You will recall that *power* was defined as the actual or potential influence or coercion a state (or other actor) can assert relative to others and nonstate actors because of the political, geographic, economic and financial, technological, military, social, cultural, or other capabilities it possesses.

In this chapter we examine a primary means by which states attempt to exert influence over other states—***diplomacy.*** Diplomatic activity is one of the most visible aspects of international relations. Almost every day of the week, newspapers and news broadcasts report the work of diplomats. If there is a war to be averted, a crisis to be resolved, or a peace settlement to be negotiated, diplomats are on the scene. Lower-profile activity includes the daily work conducted at embassies and consulates: issuing tourist and immigrant visas, providing citizen services for overseas travelers, encouraging commercial activity among nations, and meeting regularly with host foreign ministry personnel.

Diplomacy among states includes a wide range of both positive and negative approaches—both incentives and disincentives including the use of force (see Table 4.1). In the following chapter, we focus more specifically on the actual use of force in international politics. Diplomacy can be viewed as a basic means by which states attempt to harness their power for the purpose of achieving their objectives and securing their interests.

Generally speaking, in those situations in which states' preferences or interests are close enough to be reconciled and the parties involved desire to achieve a mutually beneficial accommodation, noncoercive diplomacy will play a major role in achieving such an outcome. Examples include the creation of the North Atlantic Treaty Organization (NATO) in 1949, the development of the European Union (EU) over recent decades, and the North American Free Trade Agreement (NAFTA) among the United States, Mexico, and Canada. Although, on a number of indexes, the capabilities will

diplomacy
The management of international relations by communications to include negotiations leading to a bargain or agreement.

ALTERNATIVE	DEGREE OF COERCIVENESS	EXAMPLES
Coercive diplomacy and deterrence	Most coercive; negative approaches and disincentives	Threat or actual use of military force
Economic and other sanctions	Moderately coercive; negative approaches	Threat or actual breaking of diplomatic relations; cutting trade or foreign aid; imposing an embargo
Economic and other positive incentives	Noncoercive; positive approaches and incentives	Promising aid and most-favored-nation trade status; normalizing diplomatic relations; signing cooperative or collaborative agreements; forming alliances
Compromise or finding common ground	Noncoercive; attempt to satisfy separate and common interests of parties	Finding mutual gains as bases for agreements

TABLE 4.1
Diplomacy as a Range of Alternatives

differ among the states involved, all governments believe they have a common interest in seeing an agreement reached.

In those situations in which states' preferences or interests sharply diverge or are viewed as incompatible, policy makers and diplomats may resort to more forceful measures. The active use of physical force is the most basic of means to assert power. This characterized the situation involving the major European states in the late 1930s and Japan and the United States commencing with the attack on Pearl Harbor in December 1941. At the risk of oversimplifying, diplomats are often in the forefront of negotiations to prevent war. If they fail, the military takes over and does what it is trained to do—fight wars. Once force has defeated or demoralized one of the participants, diplomacy plays an important role in any peace negotiations or settlement.

Threatening to use force is a prevalent aspect of diplomacy. Some threats are designed to get another state or states to do what they would not otherwise do—to compel them to take particular actions. This is often referred to as *coercive diplomacy* (or *compellence*) and may include the selective application of actual military force to get a foe to accede to one's wishes. Alternatively threats of force can be an aspect of *deterrence*—a way to persuade states from doing what they intend or might like to do. This demonstrates a more passive use of force.

Not all negative diplomatic approaches use the threat or application of military force. Economic threats or sanctions represent another set of options or disincentives that can be used for the same purposes. For example, U.N. economic sanctions were imposed on Libya in an effort to coerce that country into turning over two Libyan intelligence agents charged with the bombing of Pan Am Flight 103 in December 1988. Two Libyan agents were tried at an international court in the Hague, Netherlands, and one was convicted. International economic sanctions were also imposed for many years against South Africa in an attempt to change its racial **apartheid** policies.

Interstate relations can be played out anywhere along this continuum, moving back and forth depending on the countries involved, the issues in dispute, and the time period. The United States, for example, utilized more positive diplomatic measures in early 1990 to try to persuade Saddam Hussein of Iraq to resolve his grievances with neighboring Kuwait peacefully. Following Iraq's invasion of Kuwait in June 1990, Iraq was threatened not only with economic sanctions, but also with military action unless it withdrew its forces—a prime example of the use of coercive diplomacy. Threat of force was also used to deter Iraq from invading Saudi Arabia. When threats failed to coerce Iraq to withdraw from Kuwait, the United States used skillful diplomacy to organize an international coalition. The combined military force physically destroyed much of the Iraqi military capability, liberating Kuwait and safeguarding Saudi Arabia. Sanctions against Iraq following this 1991 Gulf War were linked to demands for compliance with U.N. Security Council resolutions. Beginning in 2002, the United States once again used coercive diplomacy against Saddam Hussein's Iraq, citing Iraq's supposed possession of weapons of mass destruction and ties to terrorist groups. In this case, the United States also went to war with reluctant U.N. Security Council support, but with far fewer supporters as U.S. diplomats were unable to convince such allies as Germany and France that the threat from Iraq was imminent and, therefore, that a preventive war was justified.

In the next sections, we define and provide a brief overview of what is meant by diplomacy. Second, we discuss the historical development of diplomacy, drawing on examples from the international systems outlined in Chapter 2. Finally, we examine in some detail diplomatic structure and process—the nuts and bolts of how states actually

compellence
Threat or use of force aimed at coercing another actor to change course or take an action it would not otherwise do; often called *coercive diplomacy.*

deterrence
Threat or use of force aimed at persuading another actor not to do what it intends or may like to do; a psychological effect on an opponent.

use diplomacy to further their interests and objectives. We also discuss how in recent years nongovernmental organizations (NGOs) have come to play diplomatic roles.

Definition and Scope

One of the foremost writers and practitioners of diplomacy believed that the most useful definition of the term was to be found in the Oxford English Dictionary: "Diplomacy is the management of international relations by negotiation; the method by which these relations are adjusted and managed by ambassadors and envoys; the business or art of the diplomatist."[1] The emphasis on negotiation is viewed by most people as the essence of diplomacy—negotiating a **treaty,** reaching an **executive agreement,** or bargaining with another state over the terms of a proposed agreement. The emphasis on the state as key diplomatic actor is consistent with a realist perspective on diplomacy.

In ordinary conversation, the words *diplomacy* and *diplomat* usually have a positive connotation. To say someone was "very diplomatic in dealing with the problem" is a compliment that implies that the person is a good communicator—one who possesses understanding, sensitivity, and effective interpersonal skills. Professional diplomats who have developed this ability to communicate effectively often become respected members of their foreign policy establishments. They are able to represent their governments or international organizations quite well even when the messages they convey are not always positive.

As diplomats, they are the advocates of national or international organizational interests and positions on any number of issues. Diplomats may craft a **démarche,** for example, that is, a statement to a foreign government, usually making a formal proposal in the expectation of a formal response. Proposals to foreign governments can be expressed in positive, cooperative language or on other occasions in more forceful language. Even when a country wishes to make an **ultimatum**—"do this or else"—it normally uses language that customarily conforms to diplomatic standards for such communications.

Whether the diplomat personally agrees with or opposes a particular foreign policy position, it is the diplomat's task to represent it as well as he or she can. Lawyers for plaintiff and defense in a civil court case are by necessity in opposition to one another, but each can at the same time respect the competency and honesty of the other. So it is with diplomats, who develop international reputations for the degree of competency or trustworthiness they exhibit in representing their countries or international organizations.

Such work is not restricted to a state's **ambassador** assigned and accredited to a foreign country or an international organization such as the United Nations. Diplomacy may be done by heads of state during a summit meeting, foreign ministers and other government officials, or by a specially designated diplomat as in one who seeks to secure peace between warring parties. Examples of such diplomacy include the following:

- Negotiations between President Nixon and Leonid Brezhnev at U.S.-Soviet summits on arms control and other matters in the early 1970s
- Negotiations hosted by President Carter in the late 1970s between Egyptian President Sadat and Israeli Prime Minister Begin that resulted in the Camp David Peace Accords

treaty
A written agreement or contract between two or more states pledging adherence to any number of commitments.

ambassador
A state's highest-ranking representative assigned to an embassy in a foreign country.

[1]Sir Harold Nicholson, *Diplomacy,* 3d ed. (London: Oxford University Press, 1963), 4–5.

- Meetings on arms control and other subjects by President Reagan and Mikhail Gorbachev at the Reykjavik summit in 1986
- President Bill Clinton's or George W. Bush's efforts to bring Israeli and Palestinian leaders to an agreement over the issues dividing them

Examples of interstate diplomacy below the head-of-government level involved the following:

- Former U.S. Secretary of State Henry Kissinger, who, in the aftermath of the 1973 Arab-Israeli war, engaged in what came to be known as "shuttle diplomacy" between various capitals in the Middle East
- The persistent efforts by Ambassador Dennis Ross in the first Bush and the Clinton administrations to seek a settlement of the Israeli-Palestinian issue
- Ambassador Richard Holbrook of the United States assiduously working throughout 1995 to bring Bosnia's warring parties to the bargaining table then working to keep the Dayton Accord on track and to prevent the Yugoslavian conflict from drawing in neighboring states
- Undersecretary of State Richard Armitage working to defuse a highly dangerous situation involving India and Pakistan in 2001
- Secretary of State Colin Powell and other U.S. diplomats securing a U.N. Security Council resolution in 2002 authorizing the use of force should Iraq fail to declare accurately the status of its inventory on weapons of mass destruction

Diplomacy can involve formal or informal negotiations. These negotiations can be conducted with the full knowledge of the world or in secret. Negotiations can be conducted on a bilateral basis, between two states, or on a multilateral basis, involving three or more states. The secretary general and other diplomats of the United Nations and other international organizations are often in a position to play a constructive role in managing conflicts and assisting parties in the negotiations process.

Diplomacy, Private Citizens, and NGOs

Diplomacy has traditionally been the almost exclusive domain of official representatives of states and international organizations composed of states. Indeed, the term *diplomacy* has traditionally referred to authoritative communications in international relations. Modern diplomacy, by contrast, is often less restrictive, sometimes including private citizens and nongovernmental organizations. Individuals acting in their private capacities have certainly made a difference, particularly when their diplomatic initiatives were sanctioned by a government. During the 1962 Cuban missile crisis, for example, President Kennedy sent former Secretary of State Dean Acheson (then a private citizen) to represent American policy to the president of France, Charles de Gaulle. He was selected in large part because of his positive reputation as a former secretary of state and diplomat. As a result, he was more likely than most others to be able to convey the rationale for American policy to the French, thus securing their support. Similarly, former President Jimmy Carter has been asked as a private citizen to perform diplomatic functions among contending parties in the Middle East, Africa, and Latin America. On some of these occasions he engaged in diplomatic activities as a formal representative of the United States. Subsequently, former Secretary of State James Baker was enlisted by the George W. Bush administration to encourage a number of states to forgive the debt incurred by the Iraqi regime.

At other times, individuals have entered the diplomatic world without invitation. Much to the dismay of state officials, these private actors sometimes have worked at cross-purposes with policies advocated even by their own governments. Sometimes they have performed supportive (though still independent) roles. Although as a practical matter most diplomacy is conducted by government-employed diplomats, the roles that individuals as private citizens play from time to time can be significant.

International conferences addressing economic and social issues are often accompanied by parallel discussions among interested nongovernmental actors who try to influence the process during the months or years of the planning phase and in the international conference itself. Building a consensus for agreements that goes beyond governments is an increasingly important diplomatic function performed by nongovernmental organizations and key individuals. In the 1995 conference held in China on the global state of women, for example, the official delegations were joined by unofficial delegations that came to influence the conference as well as public debate.

This active role for nongovernmental organizations has become commonplace, particularly in association with U.N.-sponsored conferences. Annual and other periodic meetings of specialized agencies such as the World Bank, International Monetary Fund, and the World Trade Organization have also become opportunities for diverse interest groups and advocates of policy change on such issues as economic development, equity for labor, and concern for the environment. This focus on the importance of non-state actors is consistent with a liberal or pluralist perspective on world politics.

The Historical Development of Diplomacy

In a world of increasing complexity, diplomacy in all of its manifestations will continue to play an important role. The formalization of diplomatic practices, however, has taken centuries.[2] From the realist perspective, self-interest will lead political entities to develop mechanisms to deal with rivals or allies. Even before recorded history, warring clans and tribes must have found it useful to negotiate with one another, even if this was simply to recover one's dead after a battle. In the self-interest of all the warring parties, such envoys were undoubtedly granted different treatment than warriors and hence had a special status that allowed them to return unharmed to their own people to convey the demands or requests of the enemy. From the constructivist perspective, the modalities of diplomacy epitomize the process of the purposeful creation of language, norms, and rules of behavior, which in turn become part of the structure of international relations and hence influence future diplomatic interactions.

In ancient Greece, each city chose a herald to communicate with foreigners. Heralds required a good memory and a strong voice so they could accurately repeat the views of their leaders. The heralds were placed under the tutelage of the god Hermes— perhaps an unfortunate choice from the point of view of future diplomats, as Hermes symbolized charm, cunning, and trickery. Beginning in the sixth century B.C., however, the Greek independent state system experienced increased commercial interdependence, and political relations became more complex. As a result, the city-states chose their finest orators to plead their city's case before foreign assemblies.

We see this most clearly in Thucydides' history of the Peloponnesian War. Thucydides attended a number of the political debates he recorded, and the power of the orators is evident to any reader. Prior to the outbreak of the war, for example, the Spartans summoned their allies to a conference to discuss recent events and to decide on a course of action. The case of the Megarians and Corinthians for declaring war on Athens appears quite persuasive until one reads the subsequent Athenian rebuttal. This event also illustrates how far diplomatic practice had been institutionalized at the time of the Spartan-Athenian

---

[2]This section is drawn from *ibid.*, 7–14.

PLURALIST (LIBERAL) AND CONSTRUCTIVIST EXPLANATIONS OF DECISION MAKING

Applying Theory

The official positions taken by diplomats are the result of a state's foreign policy decision-making process. Scholars engaged in studying foreign policy decision-making processes from a pluralist or liberal perspective emphasize that entities known as the "United States" or "Canada" do not make decisions; decisions are made by individuals. Similarly, a particular bureaucratic entity termed the "State Department" or "Foreign Office" is composed of individuals. It is, therefore, not surprising that the study of individuals and small groups has been a primary focus of analysis for a number of scholars.

Scholars focus on how psychological stress arising out of difficult, emotion-laden situations affects rational calculations. One example of this perspective is the work of Irving L. Janis, who has examined the tendency for social pressure to enforce conformity and consensus in cohesive decision-making groups. He calls this tendency *groupthink,* a mode of thinking that people engage in when they are deeply involved in a cohesive in-group, when the members' strivings for unanimity override their motivation to appraise alternative courses of action realistically. Indicators of groupthink include limiting discussions to only a few alternative courses of action, failing to re-examine initial decisions and possible courses of action initially rejected, and making little attempt to seek information from outside experts who may challenge a preferred policy. To make his case for the persuasiveness of concurrence seeking within a group and the resultant impact, Janis examines several foreign policy fiascos, such as the Bay of Pigs invasion in 1961, the military unpreparedness of the United States at Pearl Harbor in 1941, and the American decisions to escalate the Korean and Vietnam Wars. He argues that in each case the pressure to conform to group norms interfered with critical, rational thinking.

A number of international relations scholars have been particularly interested in how psychological processes influence decision making during times of crisis—a situation between peace and war. The tendency for individuals to strive for cognitive consistency and for groups to enforce consensus among their members is particularly evident in crisis situations characterized by high stress, surprise, exhausting around-the-clock work schedules, and complex and ambiguous environments. As a result, there is a general erosion of cognitive capabilities. Tolerance for ambiguity is reduced, policy options are restricted, opposing actors and their motives are stereotyped. Compared to noncrisis situations, decisions are based even more on policy makers' predispositions, expectations, biases, and emotional states. In sum, scholarly work suggests that misperception can play a major role in crisis situations, perhaps contributing to the outbreak of war. Furthermore, it has been argued that not all decision makers operate with the same kind of rationality, making it difficult for leaders to judge what actions may deter an enemy. The cumulative effect of such studies is to undermine the image of decision making as a purely rational process. Nevertheless, scholars persist at the same time in exhorting decision makers "to be more rational." See, for example, Alexander George, "The Operational Code: A Neglected Approach to the Study of Political Leaders and Decision-Making," *International Studies Quarterly,* v. 13, no. 2 (June 1969), 190–220; and Ole Holsti, "The Operational Code Approach to the Study of Political Leaders," *Canadian Journal of Political Science,* v. 3, no. 1 (March 1970), 123–157. Jervis's and Janis's ideas are presented, respectively, in Robert Jervis's *Perception and Misperception in International Politics* (Princeton, NJ: Princeton University Press, 1976) and Irving L. Janis's *Victims of Groupthink* (Boston: Houghton-Mifflin, 1972).

By the mid-1980s there was an evident decline in the amount of literature devoted to the role of cognition in international relations. Indeed, it was seemingly not as fashionable at the time to study the broader role of ideas in international relations.

The late 1980s, however, witnessed a revival of interest in the role and causal importance of ideas, a focus that continued throughout the 1990s and into the present period as constructivist perspectives on international relations became more popular. On the importance of ideas on policy making, Judith Goldstein argues that in order to understand U.S. trade policies over the years, considering only system-level factors or domestic economic interests is insufficient. Rather one must also take into account actors' causal beliefs as to which economic policies can best achieve preferred interests. She and Robert Keohane see worldviews, principled beliefs, and causal understandings as ideas that become embedded in institutions and impact diplomacy and the making of foreign policy by acting as cognitive road maps.

Similarly, Ernst B. Haas underscores the emphasis he places "on the role of ideas in the heads of actors," and John Ruggie notes how some ideas such as "multilateralism" can become institutionalized regionally and globally as the way to conduct diplomatic relations effectively among states and in both international and nongovernmental organizations. To these writers, ideas people carry in their heads are not, as some would contend, merely ideological rationalizations of interests, but play an important role as independent variables constituting interests and influencing diplomacy and foreign policy decisions.

No one would deny that the study of individuals is important if we wish to improve our understanding of international relations. The important question, however, is, "How much emphasis should be placed on the individual level of analysis as opposed to other levels?" We have noted realist Hans Morgenthau's observation that in order to understand how a political leader reached a particular decision, we speculate how we would respond in similar circumstances. In other words, by keeping the decision-making environment constant, we could hypothesize that any rational individual would have acted in the same manner. Despite a diversity of backgrounds or temperaments, the structure of the situation encourages diplomats and decision makers to respond in a similar fashion. On the other hand, what if beliefs and perceptions do make a difference and individuals respond to common stimuli or the environment in divergent ways? If so, the individual as a focus of analysis is obviously more important than Morgenthau and other realists have assumed.

This debate over the relative importance of the individual as opposed to the environment in explaining behavior is common to all the social sciences. If the international system is the key to understanding international relations, then other levels of analysis—individual, organizational, societal, or state—are by definition of less importance. If one accepts a more pluralistic view of international relations, however, then greater consideration and weight are given to the constructivist role of the individual. Individuals matter (as do groups and institutions) simply because their choices significantly affect the functioning of day-to-day decision making and diplomacy in world politics.

Question: Do you think these insights are equally applicable to a wide variety of cultures?

To read more about the role of ideas in policy making, see Judith Goldstein and Robert O. Keohane, eds., *Ideas and Foreign Policy: Beliefs, Institutions, and Political Change* (Ithaca, NY: Cornell University Press, 1993) and Ernst B. Haas, *Nationalism, Liberalism, and Progress, 2 vols.* (Ithaca, NY: Cornell University Press, 1997 and 2000 Cf) *When Knowledge Is Power* (Berkeley: University of California Press, 1990). See also John Gerard Ruggie, *Multilateralism Matters: The Theory and Practice of an Evolutionary Form* (New York: Columbia University Press, 1993) and compare with his *Constructing the World Polity* (London and New York: Routledge, 1998).

hegemony. The Athenians who were allowed to speak were a delegation who happened to be in Sparta on other business. Having heard what their future enemies argued, they presented their rebuttal of the charges that Athens had violated its treaties. They were then allowed to return to Athens to communicate the Spartan assembly's vote for war.

The Romans acquired the Greek diplomatic traditions, but an expanding empire has scant need for negotiating talents when it is crushing all those before it. Roman contributions to international law, however, certainly had diplomatic implications. The Roman emphasis on the fulfillment of contracts, for example, applied to their view of treaties. Their work on **jus gentium** (law applied not just to Romans, but to all peoples whether citizens or foreigners) and **jus naturale** (law whose principles are discovered by reason and, thus, common to all humanity no matter one's race, creed, or color) had foreign policy implications that extended beyond administrative law for an empire; that is, that certain universal principles should govern relations among political units. Finally, the Romans developed trained archivists who became specialists in diplomatic procedures.

During the latter years of the Roman empire, however, a need arose for trained negotiators. The Eastern Byzantine hub of the empire in Constantinople realized force alone could not keep the barbarians at bay. Diplomats, therefore, were critical players in a three-part diplomatic strategy to foster rivalry among the "barbarians," secure the friendship of frontier tribes and peoples by flattery and money, and convert as many of the "heathens" to Christianity as possible. Such a strategy helps to account for Emperor Justinian's ability to extend Byzantine influence as far south as Sudan and keep at arm's length the warrior tribes of the Black Sea and Caucasus. In order to implement the strategy, however, the emperor's diplomats had to be more than heralds or orators; they also needed to be perceptive political observers who could accurately assess the strengths and weaknesses of neighboring despots and warriors. This emphasis on astute observations and sound judgment has become a hallmark of the best professional diplomats down through history.

As we have noted, the collapse of the western half of the Roman empire led in the Middle Ages to an end of the political and administrative rationality imposed by Rome. Political authority was fragmented among a wide variety of local and regional rulers and the Church in Rome, which claimed universal moral authority. As communication and civil authority broke down, commerce suffered, as did contact throughout feudal Europe. Indeed, it was often extremely dangerous to pass from town to town or castle to castle. As a result, no established system of international contacts existed, resulting in little advancement in diplomatic practices and conventions.

Modern diplomacy arose in the thirteenth and fourteenth centuries in Italy. Essentially standing outside the rest of feudal Europe, the Italian city-states resembled the Greek independent state system—common cultural and commercial interests racked by intense political and military competition. It is not surprising that out of this turmoil came such ambassador-scholars as Dante, Petrarch, and Machiavelli.

The first recorded diplomatic mission was established in Genoa in 1455 by the Duke of Milan. Five years later the Duke of Savoy sent a representative to Rome, site of the Holy See (the church). Then in 1496 Venice—a commercial power of the day—appointed two Venetian merchants living in London to represent the republic's interests. Soon after, permanent embassies of the Italian states were established in Paris and London, with other states following suit. It came to be accepted that the ambassador was viewed as the personal representative of his head of state, with the status of the ambassador more a reflection of the power of his ruler and thus his ability to engage in lavish displays of wealth.

The Congress of Vienna (1814–1815), however, is of greatest historical importance. Three reasons stand out. First, as noted in Chapter 2, the era of the Concert of Europe could be characterized as a multipolar (or collective hegemonic) state system.

It is not an exaggeration to observe that ministers, political leaders, and diplomats of the day deserved credit for establishing an international system that successfully mitigated the worst aspects of anarchy among states. Periodic international conferences were held in succeeding decades to make necessary adjustments to the European order—the balance of interests and power supportive of stability that also contributed to the avoidance of general war. Small wars occurred over the next half century, but each was contained, and none posed a substantial challenge to the overall order that had been established. Although the Concert of Europe as a formal diplomatic mechanism fell apart after several decades, the underlying order and expectations established by diplomacy at Vienna in 1815 contributed to preserving Europe from another outbreak of general war until 1914. Indeed, one may speak of a society of states in Europe through much of the nineteenth century.

Second, it was not until the Congress of Vienna that a truly organized system of diplomatic practices and norms emerged. The follow-on Congress of Aix-la-Chapelle, for example, agreed on a hierarchy of diplomatic representation: First were ambassadors, papal legates, and papal nuncios; next were envoys extraordinary and ministers plenipotentiary; then came ministers resident; and finally there were those in the position of *chargé d'affaires.* Furthermore, within each category diplomatic precedence and status were not a function of who represented the most powerful country, but rather who had held the diplomatic post the longest. Also by 1815 diplomatic services came to be viewed as distinct branches of each government. Diplomacy was increasingly professionalized, with common rules, norms, and expectations.

A certain etiquette, for example, is maintained even between enemies preparing for war. After the Japanese bombed Pearl Harbor on December 7, 1941, the United States declared war on Japan, and diplomatic relations were terminated. Consistent with international law, diplomats were quickly given safe passage out of both countries. The rules of diplomatic immunity long established in customary international law were formally codified in the Vienna Conventions on Diplomatic and Consular Relations in the early 1960s.

Finally the Congress of Vienna is worth studying because it is a classic example of successful **multilateral diplomacy**—a number of countries communicating and negotiating, often over the most contentious of issues. Successful multilateral diplomacy depends on accommodating the interests and specific objectives of not only two states (as in **bilateral diplomacy**) but rather a number of participants. International organizations and settlements or agreements that prove to be durable over time derive from a broad consensus and can be modified or adapted as conditions and objectives change. Bureaucratic rigidity or an inability to adapt to changing circumstances will reduce the utility or functionality of international institutions in multilateral diplomacy, leading perhaps to their ultimate collapse.

The Versailles Treaty and other multilateral settlements following World War I pale in comparison to the successes of the Congress of Vienna. The Versailles peace lasted only two decades. World War II repeated the mass destruction of lives and property of World War I but at even higher levels made possible by technological advances in military weaponry. Consistent with the obliteration of urban areas through bombing that had become the norm, dropping atomic bombs on two Japanese cities was the cataclysmic finale of World War II.

Perhaps as a result of learning from earlier experiences, multilateral diplomacy following World War II did prove to be somewhat more successful, although the succeeding half century was also marked by periods of high tension that threatened mass destruction on a truly global scale, thanks to East-West competition during the Cold War. Nevertheless, multilateral diplomacy in international conferences and within international organizations has assumed an increasingly important role in world politics since 1945. More recent examples of multilateral diplomacy dealing with demographic, environmental, economic development, and humanitarian issues are discussed later in the book.

Diplomatic Machinery and Processes

Recognition of States and Governments

A sovereign state comes into existence under international law when a population living in a defined territory that is administered by a government is recognized by other sovereign states. As noted earlier, recognition of a state's sovereignty amounts to an acceptance of its present and future claims to two rights—one internal and the other external. The internal claim is to a right as a sovereign state to exercise complete jurisdiction over its own territory free of interference by other states in its domestic affairs. At the same time, there is an external claim to a right to be independent or autonomous in its foreign affairs, not subordinated to any other state in the conduct of its international relations.

As a practical matter, of course, states do not always respect the sovereign claims of other states. When they choose to interfere in the domestic affairs of another state, the response may well be a diplomatic protest note or public declaration to the same effect. Thus, during the Cold War, the United States privately and on occasion publicly condemned Soviet policies that violated the human rights of its citizens, particularly Jews, who were not permitted to leave the country. The typical Soviet response at the time was to condemn the United States for unlawful interference in its domestic affairs: Soviet emigration policy in Moscow's view was a domestic matter and not the business of the United States. The American position was that the Soviet Union had obligations under international law to respect the human rights of all peoples (including its own citizens) and should not try to exempt itself from international scrutiny just because it was a sovereign state.

More serious, of course, is when a state commits aggression against another state. For example, Germany's invasion of neutral Holland in World War II and neutral Belgium in both world wars clearly violated the sovereignty of these states. They claimed rights to their **neutrality** in foreign policy and to their continued administration of their own countries. As a factual matter, of course, the European states that were successfully invaded ceased exercising their sovereignty over their territories for several years; nevertheless, violation of sovereignty did not extinguish their legal claims to sovereignty. Indeed, invaded states maintained **governments in exile** located in other friendly countries (such as the United Kingdom) that were willing to recognize them as the legitimate governments of their invaded countries then under foreign occupation. These governments in exile maintained their claims to sovereignty throughout the war. Upon liberation of their territories, they were able to reestablish actual control.

Iraq's invasion of Kuwait in 1990 was considered an act of aggression by most outside states, which refused to recognize the legitimacy of Iraqi claims to Kuwaiti territory. The government in Baghdad asserted that Kuwait was not legitimately a state in the first place because it was created as an artifact of British colonialism. Quite apart from the fact that control of Kuwaiti oil fields was also at stake, Iraq maintained that Kuwait was really Iraqi property that it had rightfully retaken by force. Other states rejected Iraq's unilateral efforts to extinguish Kuwait as a sovereign state. They formed a coalition under U.N. auspices to force Iraq to withdraw from Kuwait and restore control to the Kuwaiti government then in exile. When diplomatic efforts failed, military forces of a broad coalition of states drove the Iraqi armed forces out of Kuwait in 1991.

When the invading power establishes a **puppet government,** diplomatic recognition is sometimes withheld. A good example involves the Vichy regime installed in France following the German invasion in 1940. International recognition went to the French government in exile based in London. Even if no government in exile exists, recognition of a regime perceived as illegitimate might still be withheld. This was the case with the former German Democratic Republic (communist East Germany), which was isolated by other states for many years as well as being denied seats in such international organizations as the United Nations and its affiliated agencies.

In some cases decades may pass before diplomatic recognition is granted. The United States and many other states, for example, did not recognize the Soviet annexation in 1940 of the Baltic republics. Estonian, Latvian, and Lithuanian claims to sovereignty were kept alive for half a century through governments in exile that maintained diplomatic ties with foreign governments. At the end of the Cold War, when for political reasons Moscow was willing to relinquish control of the Baltic republics, they reemerged on the world stage as independent and sovereign states.

States continue to be recognized as legitimate entities even when governments change. After the communist takeover in China in 1949, the United States and other like-minded countries chose to deny recognition to the new government in Beijing under Mao Zedong even though, as a factual matter, it had control of all of mainland China. Instead, these countries continued to recognize the nationalist, noncommunist government under Chiang Kai-Shek on the island of Taiwan. Chiang's government maintained that it would one day regain control of all of China.

Neither the Beijing nor the Taiwan governments accepted the two-China solution proposed by some as a settlement to these conflicting claims for legitimacy. Beijing and Taiwan agreed on one thing—that there was just one China, a state that included both Taiwan and the mainland. The dispute was only over which of the two governments had the legitimate claim to political authority. Because they saw it in their interest to do so, the United States and other foreign governments friendly to Taiwan and opposed to communism continued the legal fiction of Taiwanese legitimacy as government of all of China for more than two decades.

In 1971 and 1972 the United States finally reversed its long-standing policy and recognized the Beijing government as the legitimate government of China. Consistent

U.S. President Richard Nixon shakes hands with Chinese Leader Mao Zedong during Nixon's historic visit to China in 1972.

with the new policy, U.S. diplomats were withdrawn from Taiwan, and diplomatic relations were established between Beijing and Washington. Diplomats from Beijing replaced those from Taiwan in the Chinese embassy in Washington. Commercial, cultural, and other nongovernmental ties with Taiwan were maintained as Taiwan remained formally part of the same Chinese state. Government recognition changed, but all the territories recognized as part of China were the same. As a practical matter, the government on Taiwan remained in control there, although without much of the international recognition it had depended on for its legitimacy. For its part, the government in Beijing continues to refer to Taiwan as a "renegade province" but still an integral part of the People's Republic of China.

Recognition is at times a function of how outside powers view a particular conflict—as a war between states or a civil war. Consider the United States and the Vietnam War in the early 1960s. The United States government argued that it was aiding the Republic of Vietnam (South Vietnam) in its defense against aggression from the communist Democratic Republic of Vietnam (North Vietnam). Coming to the aid of a state victimized by aggression (by request of the legitimate government) is allowable under international law, and the United States presented itself merely as helping a victimized state against communist aggression, as it had been asked to do.

Critics of the American policy in Vietnam, however, claimed that there were not two Vietnamese states, one committing aggression against the other. Rather, these critics argued, the Vietnam War was a civil war between contending governments in the same state. If so, then no outside state had a right to intervene militarily or otherwise in what was really a domestic matter within Vietnam.

Because the U.S. government under Presidents Eisenhower, Kennedy, Johnson, Nixon, and Ford recognized the government in Saigon as the legitimate government of a South Vietnamese state under attack by North Vietnam and its Vietcong insurgents, it rejected the notion that the conflict was a civil war. Pressed on the issue, Henry Kissinger (national security advisor and later secretary of state in the Nixon and Ford administrations) admitted that the Vietnam War really had aspects of both a war between states and a civil war; however, the United States used the former understanding to justify its intervention policy.

A similar problem occurred during the American Civil War (1861–1865). British cotton importers and other commercial interests were encouraging London to intervene diplomatically on behalf of the South. They sought recognition for the Confederate States of America as a separate country with the administration under President Jefferson Davis as its legitimate government. Aided by its military victories, however, the United States government under President Abraham Lincoln was successful diplomatically in keeping the British from taking this step.

Had Britain intervened, given its financial and military resources, this would have benefited the South substantially, hurting the North's war effort. As part of its effort to encourage British intervention, the South claimed that the conflict was a war between states and *not* a civil war. To this day historians sympathetic to the South's cause refer to the conflict not as the American Civil War, but rather as the War between the States— that is, the United States and the Confederate States of America.

Gaining acceptance in the international community through recognition of state and government is an important prize to those seeking such status. Recognition of Israel as a new state was granted in 1948 by many countries, including the Soviet Union, but to this day many Middle Eastern states continue to withhold recognition.

Palestinians also seek the same recognition of a territorial state of their own, many having been dispossessed of their homes and property in the newly created Israeli state. Although progress toward a peaceful solution was made in the 1990s, for more than four decades Palestinians have been confronted by Israeli security forces, particularly in territories occupied by Israel since 1967. By contrast, no such progress has been made by the Kurds. In a treaty signed after World War I, Kurdish peoples in the mountainous areas of Turkey, Syria, Iraq, Iran, and the Transcaucasus region of the Soviet Union (now parts of the Russian Federation, Azerbaijan, Georgia, and Armenia) were promised status as a separate Kurdish territorial state, but the great powers making that commitment never delivered.

Aspirations of Palestinians, Kurds, and many other national groups for creation of new nation-states remain unfulfilled. Suppression of these nationalist movements by existing state authorities is common. Kurds have faced continued and forceful opposition, particularly by Turkish and Iraqi governments, over many years. Similarly, in the same region, historical claims to a separate national identity by Chechens has been resisted by Russian authorities. A Chechen secessionist uprising in the Russian Federation has faced confrontation by the military since the mid-1990s, with large numbers of casualties on both sides. Significantly, outside states for the most part accepted Russian claims to sovereignty in the region, effectively treating the Chechen uprising as an internal matter within the Russian Federation.

In the final analysis, recognition of governments and states is a political choice left to other sovereign states and their governments. Some favor a policy that bases recognition of a particular government, for example, on the facts of the case as sole criterion: Does a particular government actually have control over the territory over which it claims jurisdiction? If it does, then it warrants recognition. Another approach is to grant recognition based on a second criterion, which is the perceived desirability of a particular state or government. Thus, the United States denied recognition for the Soviet Union and its government from 1917 until 1934, when diplomatic relations finally were established. As discussed above, recognition of the Chinese government in Beijing was denied from 1949 until the 1970s when normalization of relations began to take place.

Diplomatic Immunities and Protections

While living and doing business in the host country, all diplomats on the diplomatic list are immune from arrest or prosecution by local authorities. Diplomats cannot even be prosecuted for traffic and parking violations, which is very frustrating to national or local governments. Nevertheless **diplomatic immunity** is a reciprocal privilege that extends to all diplomats in all of their activities. Private citizens traveling abroad do not have this privilege of immunity from local laws and law-enforcement measures.

The **reciprocity** that assures the mutual safety of diplomats is absolutely essential if countries are to maintain contact and conduct business with one another. Not only would it be unseemly to arrest the diplomats of other countries, it could lead to reprisals against one's own diplomats. The only legal remedies for the host country for unacceptable conduct on the part of a foreign diplomat are to ignore or overlook such transgressions, to protest these activities to the host government, or to declare the diplomat unwelcome (***persona non grata,*** or PNG for short), forcing his or her removal from the country.

Depending on the circumstances, misconduct can ruin a diplomatic career when it causes one to be declared *persona non grata*. On the other hand, some diplomats may face expulsion for reasons unrelated to their personal behavior. If relations sour between the diplomat's country and the host country, he or she may be subject to recall by his or her own country or alternatively to expulsion through the *persona non grata* declaration. Recalling one's own diplomats or expelling the diplomats of foreign countries is one way of signaling displeasure with the policies of those countries and may have nothing to do with the actual conduct of individual diplomats.

Diplomatic conventions, although legally binding as treaties, do not always assure in practice that diplomats will be treated correctly. In 1979, for example, Iranian revolutionaries held American diplomats as hostages. The revolutionaries' takeover of the American embassy and confiscation of its files also violated the same Vienna diplomatic convention as well as customary international law that protects embassy property even in wartime.

When countries break diplomatic relations, the embassy and its grounds are placed in caretaker status, sometimes under the daily control of a third country mutually acceptable to both disputing countries. This is because of the legal fiction of **extraterritoriality,** which assumes that an embassy and the ground it stands on are part of the sovereign territory and property of the foreign country. Because states are required under international law to respect the sovereignty of other states, embassies and their diplomats are given privileged, protected status.

Even the violation of these rules in Iran did not give the United States or any other country a right to do the same thing to Iranian diplomats or the Iranian embassy and grounds in Washington. The urge to take reprisals in kind is understandable, but any such action was avoided.

Because embassies are viewed as the property of the foreign country and thus not legally subject to host-country intrusion, they provide for their own security. The U.S. Marine Corps has traditionally been assigned the task of guarding American embassies in conjunction with State Department security officers. Host-country police or other security personnel also have the responsibility of protecting embassies by supplementing efforts of the embassy itself.

Embassies sometimes serve as places of **asylum** for host-country citizens or others seeking protection. The political decision to grant asylum is up to embassy officials and usually is limited or reserved as a humanitarian gesture to those whose political or other rights have been (or likely will be) violated. For example, Roman Catholic Cardinal Mindzenty, an opponent of the communist takeover in Hungary after World War II, was one of the more celebrated recipients of American asylum at the U.S. embassy in Budapest. The host country may protest the granting of asylum or even try to prevent individuals from entering embassy grounds; but once asylum has been granted, host-country officials may not legally force entry to the embassy or its grounds to remove those who have found shelter there.

The Organization of Diplomatic Missions

Emissaries of states bear different titles. *Ambassador* is the highest-ranking position in any given **mission.** A *mission* is a term that refers to an **embassy,** including a consular section in the same embassy, **consulates** located elsewhere in a foreign country, a diplomatic mission to an international organization, or a **delegation** to an international conference. In the absence of an ambassador as **chief of mission,** the mission may be left under another person in charge—a *chargé d'affaires* or, more

Case & Point

With the end of the Cold War, the increase in ethnic conflict within states, and the often-resultant humanitarian crises, NGOs and international organizations are playing a new and increasingly important role. Operational NGOs serve in the field, working directly with the recipients of humanitarian aid and economic development projects. Traditionally humanitarian-relief NGOs have worked assiduously to maintain a strict policy of neutrality and leave the diplomacy and conflict-resolution functions to government diplomats. This policy is changing and has caused a great deal of discussion and debate. The following comments from an article by Pamela Aall summarize the findings of a conference sponsored by the U.S. Institute of Peace:

> While NGOs are fast becoming powerful new actors in complex emergencies, managing conflict and taking on certain functions of imperiled governments, several questions arise: Should NGOs be involved in conflict prevention and resolution? If so, how extensive should their involvement be? Effective responses to post–Cold War humanitarian crises often mean that many NGOs must go beyond their traditional mission of providing food, water, and medical assistance, entering the realm of ensuring political stability and fulfilling governmental functions in failed states. Are such expanded roles appropriate for NGOs?

> John Paul Lederbach, director of the International Conciliation Service of the Mennonite Central Committee, argues that NGOs could effectively manage conflict, noting that they bring several special qualities to peace building, especially through their particular insights into different cultures, their relationships with local partners, and their understanding of the links between crisis management and long-term sustainable development.

> In response to the question of roles, there are certain conditions that must be met before NGOs engage in conflict management activities:

> - The NGO knows the country and the regional institutions involved in the conflict resolution effort.
> - The NGO has indigenous partners.
> - The NGO staff has a good knowledge of conflict mediation skills.
> - The NGO's field staff members fully understand the personal risks they are assuming.

> Equally important is the development of further coordination among the different types of operational NGOs and between the NGO community and other actors involved in complex emergency interventions.

> It is more than apparent that NGOs of all varieties are seriously grappling with issues raised by working in situations of conflict. There is widespread recognition that NGOs might unwittingly become a party to conflict in the course of their humanitarian relief work; that their actions could be part of a concerted, coordinated effort involving governments, international and regional organizations, and private groups to avert or resolve conflict; that they have the ability both to provide early warning and to shore up the political will of governments to act; and that they could give guidance to policy makers in their own countries and encourage community building and the development of civil societies in countries decimated by war. In short, the work of NGOs forms an important part of the entire repertoire of intervention strategies for dealing with conflict in the post–Cold War era.

NONGOVERN-MENTAL ORGANIZA-TIONS AND FIELD DIPLOMACY

Point: Whether due to circumstances or design, NGOs are playing increasingly important diplomatic roles.

Source: Pamela Aall, "Nongovernmental Organizations and Peacemaking," in Chester A. Crocker and Fen Osler Hampson, with Pamela Aall, eds., *Managing Global Chaos* (Washington, D.C.: United States Institute of Peace, 1996), 442–443.

simply, a *chargé*. The *chargé* is often the second-ranking person, also known as the **deputy chief of mission** or DCM. Figure 4.1 illustrates the typical organization of a U.S. diplomatic mission.

Consul or **consul general** is usually the title of the official in charge of a consulate in the capital and in one or another of the major cities outside of the host country's capital. These consuls or consuls general work directly for the ambassador, whose residence is in the capital city near or on the embassy grounds. A consulate (or consular section in an embassy) coordinates the issue of passports to its own citizens, issues visas to citizens in the local country, and performs related administrative tasks. Consulates are also a focal point for promoting trade and cultural exchange in areas of the host country outside of the capital city. They report to the embassy or home country directly on political, economic, and other developments they observe.

The level of representation that a state sends to a host country is politically significant. When relations are fully developed or "normal," countries typically are represented at the ambassadorial level. When conflict has resulted in a breach of diplomatic relations between two countries, restoration of these relations is sometimes implemented in a gradual normalization process. The first step in normalizing relations often entails establishing an **interest section** in a mutually friendly country's embassy. Later

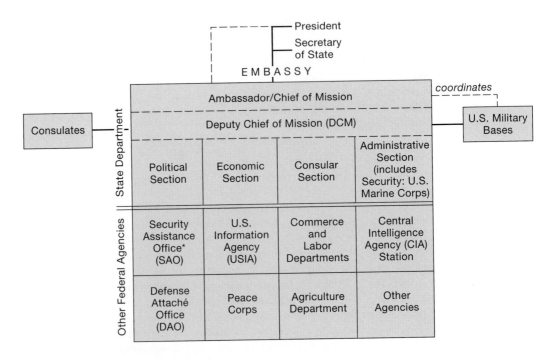

FIGURE 4.1   *Organization of a U.S. Diplomatic Mission*

*Also known as Office of Defense Cooperation (ODC), Office of Military Cooperation (OMC), or Military Assistance and Advisory Group (MAAG).

Practicing World Politics

The U.S. Department of State has a Web site (www.state.gov) that should be of particular interest to students of international relations and world politics. Information is available on summer internships at the main State Department building in Washington, D.C., as well as embassies overseas. Unfortunately, 95 percent of the approximately 800 internships do not offer a salary. If you are interested in working at State as a foreign service officer, information about the written exam, how to order a study guide, an exam bibliography, and suggested courses to take in college to prepare for a foreign service career are provided. Opportunities are available in the U.S. Information Agency, as well as civil service positions in the United States, related agencies, and diplomatic missions abroad. The competition, not surprisingly, is stiff. There are also links to Web sites maintained by U.S. embassies and consulates. So if you are interested in seeing what has been happening in Beijing or Addis Ababa from the point of view of officers serving there, information is only a click away. You can also download literally hundreds of publications from the various bureaus if you are writing a term paper on terrorism, weapons proliferation, refugees, population issues, environmental concerns, human rights, or numerous other topics.

U.S. FOREIGN SERVICE WEB SITE

the embassy may be reopened with a lower-ranking diplomat serving as *chargé d'affaires*. Eventually a full embassy with a serving ambassador is established, perhaps with consulates in other important cities.

A typical embassy, headed by an ambassador as chief-of-mission and a DCM as second in charge, is divided into a number of functional sections. Most countries staff their embassies to perform various political, economic and commercial, consular, administrative, military, and intelligence functions. Missions to international organizations or international negotiations usually have specific tasks to perform and are staffed accordingly. The precise way in which an embassy or other mission is organized varies from country to country and sometimes from place to place depending in part on the functions to be performed. Not surprisingly, embassies and other missions usually mirror the structural and cultural approaches to policy of their home countries.

The United States is no exception. Bureaucratic divisions in Washington are clearly reflected in the typical American embassy or other mission. Serving under the ambassador are the State Department's political, economic, consular, administrative, and embassy security sections, composed primarily of career State Department foreign service officers and staff. These sections maintain constant contact with offices in the State Department as well as those in the local foreign ministry and other local agencies. Embassies are often the link between foreign ministries, heads of government, and other senior officials in different countries.

Not to be outdone, the Department of Defense (DoD) often maintains two important diplomatic offices. The Defense Attaché Office (DAO) is staffed by members of the military and civil service who may be charged with coordinating policy matters with the host-country defense ministry, collecting information on the host country's armed forces (usually an overt, nonclandestine, intelligence-collection function), and performing protocol functions in relation to host-country armed forces. Within the DoD, defense attachés come under the Defense Intelligence Agency and the military departments—army, navy, and air force. Often of even greater importance to the host country, however, is a separate security assistance office administered by DoD and charged with coordinating and overseeing the transfer of armaments and military training to host-country militaries.

Attachés from the Justice, Commerce, Agriculture, Labor, and other departments are also often posted to missions. As carriers of American policy, attachés from these agencies establish ties and channels for influencing businesses, unions, and government agencies in the host country. Export promotion in the industrial, agricultural, and service sectors of the American economy is a central concern, for example, of attachés from these departments. Increased exports, after all, mean more profits for business and farm interests and more jobs for American workers. Their views may clash, however, with State, Defense, or other agencies of the U.S. government. Export of supercomputers and other advanced technologies, for example, may be favored by the Department of Commerce but opposed by the Department of Defense because of their military value.

Finally embassies and other missions also frequently are used for covert **intelligence collection** or **espionage,** defined as clandestine actions sometimes adverse to the host country. The Central Intelligence Agency (CIA) has a station chief who oversees the agency's intelligence program in the host country. This is not unique to the United States. Virtually all countries allocate a portion of the embassy or other mission to intelligence work. This includes human-source intelligence as well as such technical means that enable specialists to intercept signals—communications or other electronic emissions that can be analyzed or evaluated by the appropriate intelligence agencies.

Intelligence officers in an embassy usually enjoy the same diplomatic status and protections of other embassy employees on the host country's diplomatic list. Some intelligence officers in an embassy, usually listed as first or second secretaries or as holding principal offices, are under "deep cover." Others have the same diplomatic titles but have come to be known to the host country as intelligence agents and thus are watched more closely by host-country security services than are other embassy personnel. When intelligence operatives have crossed the line of acceptable behavior or otherwise have been uncovered, the host country may force their expulsion. This can, of course, be followed by retaliation of the same kind directed against the host country's own intelligence agents stationed abroad.

Coordinating the diverse work of an American embassy is no easy task for any chief of mission. The **country team** concept is one approach to integrating these efforts. Members of the country team—usually the chiefs or deputies of the different sections within the embassy—meet as a group at least once a week to review the embassy's collective work. Sometimes, particularly in smaller missions, personalities can be brought together under an effective ambassador or DCM to make a country team that can work together well, ironing out differences as they arise. In many cases, however, disputes go well beyond embassy personalities, reflecting conflicts among agencies in the national government that are not easily resolved.

American embassy officials thus are often as divided among themselves, as are their respective agencies and agency heads in Washington. The reality is that, just as any president of the United States has difficulty controlling government agencies, whether engaged in domestic or foreign policy, an ambassador and the DCM face comparable challenges on a much smaller scale. Countries with a less fragmented political structure and less pluralism in political processes domestically than the United States no doubt have embassies that are far less fragmented and more deferential to the central authority of the ambassador and DCM.

Diplomatic Incentives and Disincentives

Carrots   Whether in bilateral or multilateral settings, diplomats depend on the leverage they can bring to their negotiations and less formal discussions and interactions. Depending on the issue involved, economic or military resources may play an important

Practicing World Politics

Academic institutions and international and nongovernmental organization sites often contain documents, public statements and other useful information on diplomatic activity. The St. Thomas University School of Law has created the Diplomacy Monitor at www.diplomacymonitor.com. In addition to using search engines, links to Web sites for various countries can be found in sites for international organizations of which they are members. For example, the United Nations (www.u.n..org) has links to Web pages and sites of diplomatic missions maintained by member states. One can find similar links on Web sites of such regional organizations as the Organization for Security and Cooperation in Europe (www.osce.org), the European Union (www. europa.eu.int), the North Atlantic Treaty Organization (www.nato.int), the African Union (www.africa-union.org), and the Organization of American States (www.oas.org).

Although in the United States a number of departments and agencies engage in international affairs, it is the Department of State (www.state.gov) that is the senior cabinet office directly tasked with diplomatic representation of the United States. Related agencies of the Department of State is the Agency for International Development (www.usaid.gov).

Other U.S. government executive branch sites at least partly related to international affairs include the Departments of Defense (www.defenselink.mil); Commerce (www.commerce.gov), especially its International Trade Administration (www.ita.doc.gov) and its Bureau of Industry and Security (www.bxa.doc.gov); Agriculture (www.usda.gov), including its Farm and Foreign Agriculture Service pages; Labor (www.dol.gov) and its Bureau of International Labor Affairs pages; and the Treasury (www.treas.gov) and its Customs Service and Comptroller of the Currency pages.

The National Security Council is part of the Executive Office of the President (www. whitehouse.gov/nsc). An independent agency, the Federal Reserve Board (www.federalreserve.gov) also has links to foreign central banks and the Bank for International Settlements (www.bis.org) in Basel, Switzerland. On intelligence, the Central Intelligence Agency (www.cia.gov) has links to some thirteen related intelligence and other agencies that are part of the U.S. intelligence community, including the Defense Intelligence Agency, State Department and military service intelligence offices, the National Security Agency, the National Reconnaissance Office, and the Federal Bureau of Investigation.

U.S. Congressional committees dealing with foreign affairs in the Senate (www.senate.gov) include Foreign Relations, Armed Services, and the Select Committee on Intelligence. For the House of Representatives (www.house.gov), see pages for the Committees on International Relations and Armed Services.

The Washington-based American Committees on Foreign Relations (www.acfr.org), a grassroots nongovernmental organization with committees in more than thirty U.S. cities, provides a list of American links to daily news sources, foreign affairs journals and magazines, think tanks, C-Span programs, Congressional links, columnists, and opinion leaders. The government-funded U.S. Institute of Peace (www.usip.gov) sponsors academic research, as do such nongovernmental organizations as the New York– and Washington-based Council on Foreign Relations (www.cfr.org), which publishes the journal *Foreign Affairs* and various studies. The Chicago Council on Foreign Relations (www.cfr.org) also provides a useful set of links to universities and institutes and international organizations as well as U.S. government and media links. For additional links, see the New York–based Foreign Policy Association (www.fpa.org) and the Institute of International Education (www.iie.org).

THE INTERNET: CHECKING OUT SOME WEB SITES ON DIPLOMACY

role. **Foreign aid** may take the form of grants for social, economic, or military purposes; loans, particularly at concessionary interest rates (reduced below market levels by the donor country as a form of assistance); trade preferences (as in reducing tariffs on imports from a foreign country or guaranteeing purchase at a favorable price of one or another of the exporting country's products); or military assistance (the transfer of weapons free of charge or at reduced prices or the provision of military training). Such incentives may be very helpful, but one should always understand them for what they are—incentives. The firmer foundation on which lasting agreements are based is one in which the mutual interests and objectives of the parties are also accommodated.

An example of the use of diplomatic "carrots" is the 1978 accord reached at Camp David, Maryland, between Egyptian President Anwar Sadat and Israeli Prime Minister Menachem Begin that normalized relations between Israel and Egypt. The Sinai Desert land taken forcibly from Egypt by Israel in 1967 was returned in exchange for recognition by Egypt of Israel's sovereignty or right to exist as a state. In addition to the positive influence he was able to assert because of personal skills and the high stature of his office, President Carter was able to cement the agreement with promises of substantial military and economic aid to both negotiating parties. (The Camp David Accords and the Arab-Israeli peace process are discussed subsequently in greater detail.)

Effective diplomacy is markedly easier to achieve when the parties have an established record of positive accomplishments over decades or longer. Mutual trust is a very important asset in diplomatic exchanges of any kind. Lack of trust, by contrast—perhaps due to a record of broken obligations or other conflicts—poses a significant obstacle or challenge to diplomats. The Camp David Accords proved to be only the first major step in a continuing peace process.

Sticks   Diplomacy, of course, is not simply about such positive inducements as economic and military aid. Diplomacy, as we have noted, can also be coercive—forcing another country to do what it would not otherwise do. In adversarial relations, veiled or explicit threats of economic sanctions or military action can influence or coerce diplomats and policy makers in other states.

One country can punish or exercise economic leverage over another by threatening or actually imposing **economic sanctions.** Actually imposing sanctions amounts to economic warfare. If the punishing state has been giving aid or other assistance, it can be reduced or cut off entirely. A **boycott** against the other country's exports or an **embargo** or prohibition against selling or engaging in other commercial transactions can be imposed. These are legal restrictions preventing the sale or purchase of any goods or services to or from that country. The aim is to get the embargoed state to change its policy or comply with the wishes of the state imposing the embargo.

Economic sanctions are not always very effective in achieving their purposes. When a state's exports are boycotted by one country, it may simply find other markets for its goods. Notwithstanding legal prohibitions, it may also find other states willing to avoid or evade an embargo, which will continue to sell their products to the embargoed state or engage in other commercial activities. A multilateral boycott or embargo imposed by a coalition of states may be more effective by bringing greater collective pressure. Even so, ways are often found to circumvent these restrictions. The multilateral embargo against South Africa, for example, took many years to have noticeable effect. But eventually, in the early 1990s, the *apartheid* policy that had segregated the races was abandoned, and a regime led by Nelson Mandela finally was put into place.

A more serious "stick" is a **blockade,** a more intense form of economic warfare, in which warships or ground forces are used physically to prevent commerce going into or coming out of a country. Imposition of a blockade is an act of war that can escalate into an armed conflict.

Carrots, Sticks, and Crisis   If two states have a perceived conflict of interest and neither backs down, events can produce a **crisis.** In October 1973, for example, President Nixon and Secretary of State Henry Kissinger decided they could not ignore Soviet leader Leonid Brezhnev's threat to intervene militarily in the Arab-Israeli war. The United States placed its strategic forces on alert, resulting in a possibly dangerous confrontation. Once a crisis begins, there is a basic policy dilemma: each side feels it must do whatever is needed to advance or protect its interests but at the same time recognizes that it must avoid taking actions that could escalate the crisis to the point that it gets out of control.[3]

Crisis diplomacy usually entails objectives that are both urgent and extremely important. It requires the greatest care in finding common ground as well as the appropriate combination of carrots and sticks. The Cuban missile crisis of 1962 is one such case. When American intelligence sources discovered in October 1962 that Soviet offensive missiles with nuclear warheads had been deployed to Cuba, American decision makers sought to have the missiles removed while, at the same time, attempting to avoid an escalation of the conflict into a major war. A keen awareness of the importance and urgency of accomplishing both of these short-term objectives clearly influenced deliberations on the various policy options open to the United States.

How the Soviets would respond to U.S. military actions was a matter of grave concern to President Kennedy and his advisors. Although American decision makers did not know it then, Soviet commanders in Cuba already had authority from Moscow to use battlefield nuclear weapons in the event of an American invasion. Had the American response been any more provocative than it was, nuclear war might well have occurred.

Fortunately, President Kennedy and his advisors decided upon a naval blockade of Cuba rather than a ground invasion or air strikes, while continuing to exercise diplomatic and other channels of communication with the Soviets. Trying to soften somewhat the diplomatic impact of the blockade, some officials in the U.S. administration preferred to call it a quarantine of Cuba, which seemed to them a less provocative term. Using the metaphor "quarantine" cast the blockade less as an act of war and more as a temporary measure that would be lifted as soon as "health" was restored. Choosing a less provocative term was a war-avoidance measure, one calculated to allow an adversary to seek a peaceful resolution of the dispute.

Although even this course of action was highly risky, it proved to be successful in getting the Soviets to withdraw the missiles without armed conflict between the two states. But Kennedy wisely provided a carrot to the Soviet Premier Nikita Khrushchev, which was to promise to remove U.S. Jupiter missiles based in Turkey and aimed at the Soviet Union. Significantly, the security interests of both sides were accommodated. Recognition of how close the United States and the Soviet Union had come to the brink of nuclear war led, however, to setting an arms control agenda aimed at reducing tensions and building a foundation for better communications between the two, particularly in times of crisis.

Perceptions concerning the **credibility** of threats matter a great deal. If threats are not credible, a threatened state may choose to ignore them. Alternatively, the other state

[3]Alexander L. George, "A Provisional Theory of Crisis Management," in Alexander L. George, ed., *Avoiding War: Problems of Crisis Management* (Boulder, CO Westview Press, 1991), 22–23.

CRISIS DIPLOMACY AND FOREIGN POLICY DECISIONS

Applying Theory

Graham Allison and his colleagues in the late 1960s engaged in a now-classic study of U.S.-Soviet crisis diplomacy when the two countries came to the brink of nuclear war in 1962 over Soviet missiles secretly deployed in Cuba. Both the unitary and rational assumptions associated with realism are relaxed from the organizational process and bureaucratic politics perspectives adopted by Allison.

The organizational-process model of foreign policy decision making views organizational routines and procedures as determining some and influencing other foreign policy decisions and outcomes. Organizational ethos and world view are also relevant considerations. In an often-cited statement, Allison notes that where a given bureaucratic actor or diplomat stands on a given issue is often determined by where he or she sits; that is, one's view of alternative courses of action is highly colored by the perspective of the organization to which one belongs or role one plays. Perceptions of what is the optimal or best course of action often vary from one bureaucratic actor to another, reflecting organizational biases that raise serious doubts concerning the rationality of the process as a whole. What assurance is there that optimal choices for the state as a whole will be made? Or is optimality, when achieved, purely accidental?

Allison's bureaucratic politics model of foreign policy decision making involves forming coalitions and countercoalitions among diverse bureaucratic actors in a competitive environment. The focus is on specific individuals in positions at the top of organizations and on the pulling and hauling among them. This is in contrast to the more routine, preprogrammed activity of the organizational-process model. Hence, foreign policy decisions at times may be the result of which individual, or which coalition of individuals, can muster the most political power. What may be best for an individual or his or her bureau-

cracy in terms of increased prestige and relative standing within the government may lead to less than the best foreign policy for the state as a whole. Parochial, personal, and bureaucratic interests may reign over any expressed concern for the national interest.

Allison's work does not pose as direct a challenge to the unitary assumption about state behavior as does some of the other literature on decision making (the unitary assumption being that the state, whatever its domestic political differences, comes to speak with one voice in its diplomacy and foreign policy). Although multiple actors influenced by diverse organizational and individual interests compete to influence policy choices, in the final analysis these decisions are still made by certain authoritative individuals. Notwithstanding all the competition and airing of alternative views, the state still ultimately speaks with one voice. At the same time, however, the Allison study did at least raise some questions concerning the unitary character of the state in its implementation of policy. Decisions made were not always carried out as quickly as anticipated or in precisely the way they were intended. After all, policy involves both decisions and actions. Even if the decisions are unitary and the state speaks with one voice (which may not always be the case), if consequent actions are fragmented or otherwise inconsistent, then how unitary is the state after all?

The bottom line is that Allison's organizational process and bureaucratic politics models do challenge the more traditional (and realist) rational model of decision making, raising serious questions concerning the appropriateness of relying on the rational-actor model to explain foreign policy and diplomatic choices. In other studies of crisis diplomacy (the Cuban missile crisis and events leading up to World War I in 1914), Ole

Holsti and his associates also challenge the more simplistic rational-actor model that overlooks cognitive rigidity, time pressures, and stress—factors that can have a decisive (and even devastating) impact if not managed carefully.

Robert Keohane, Joseph Nye, and others have taken the pluralist or liberal image of foreign policy a major step forward, arguing that the state may not be able to confine bureaucratic actors operating in its name. Organizations, whether private or governmental, may transcend the boundaries of states, forming coalitions with their foreign counterparts. Such transnational actors even may be working at cross-purposes with government leaders in their home states who possess the formal authority to make binding decisions. For example, the British Foreign Office may see a given issue similarly to its American State Department counterpart. On the other hand the British Defence Ministry and the U.S. Defense Department may share a common view contrary to that of both diplomatic organizations. Moreover, nongovernmental interest groups in both countries may form coalitions supportive of one or another transgovernmental coalition.

To what extent, then, do coalitions of bureaucratic actors, multinational corporations, and other transnational actors circumvent the authoritative decision makers and diplomats of states through formation of such coalitions? An interesting example of a transgovernmental coalition that had a significant, though unpublicized, impact during the October 1962 Cuban missile crisis involved redeployment of Canadian naval units for an "exercise" in the North Atlantic. This decision effectively relieved the U.S. Navy of at least a part of its patrolling responsibilities there, allowing American ships to be deployed to the Caribbean as part of the naval blockade of Cuba. All of this was apparently established between American and Canadian military officers while the Diefenbaker government in Ottawa was still debating the question of what Canadian policy in the crisis would be! Was this apparent circumvention by the Canadian Navy an exception, or is it commonplace for bureaucratic actors to form coalitions across national borders that in effect make policy? Pluralists would argue that it is more commonplace than most realists would suppose.

If it is typically the way foreign policy is made, then focus by realists on the state as principal actor would seem to be misdirected. From the pluralist or liberal perspective, more attention should be given to the entire range of transnational actors and their interactions. On the other hand, if the example used here is indeed

U.S. President John Kennedy confers with his advisors during the Cuban missile crisis of 1962.

This American U-2 spy plane photo revealed a medium-range ballistic missile launch site at San Cristobal, Cuba. Such intelligence imagery set in motion the events of the Cuban missile crisis.

an exception, then it is an exception that makes the rule. From the realist perspective, the state in most cases retains its prerogatives, precluding circumvention by transnational, bureaucratic actors.

For more details about these two views of foreign policy, see Graham Allison and Philip Zelikow, *Essence of Decision,* 2nd ed. (New York: Longman, 1999); Holsti's article in Paul Gordon Lauren, ed., *Diplomacy: New Approaches in History, Theory and Policy* (New York: 1979); and Robert O. Keohane and Joseph Nye, eds., *Transnational Relations and World Politics* (Cambridge, MA: Harvard University Press, 1972).

may make threats of its own: saber rattling is common enough in diplomacy. States on a collision course may well wind up in armed conflict, particularly in a crisis in which high stakes and time pressure may undercut a reasoned, rational discussion of policy options. Paradoxically, when communications are most necessary, traditional practice is to sever diplomatic relations entirely. As the nineteenth-century Prussian writer Clausewitz observed, war is merely state policy conducted by other means. Inevitably, if cease-fires are to be arranged and peaceful settlements made, diplomacy must play a primary role.

There is also a place for diplomatic communications in wartime, sometimes facilitated by the **good offices** of third parties who assist in getting the parties to communicate and cease hostilities. This is the diplomatic peacemaking role as in the Middle East and elsewhere that aims toward a settlement through direct or indirect negotiations, mediation or arbitration, judicial settlement, or other means. In most cases, the conflicts that led parties to war in the first place are extraordinarily difficult to resolve. Divisions deepen as each party suffers the scourge that is the human cost of war.

Of course, if one side wins or prevails on the battlefield, it may be in a position to dictate the terms of the settlement. The losing party in such circumstances can take some solace in the outcome of the Congress of Vienna. Even without military or economic leverage, a losing party—France—was able to contribute to constructing a settlement that accommodated the diverse and often conflicting interests of the parties. Unfortunately, diplomatic miracles of this sort are usually few and far between, with vindictive and punishing terms for the loser of a war—such as Germany after World War I—a distinct possibility.

The Ways and Means of Diplomatic Communications

Diplomacy as a means of communications between or among governments has many sides. In the extreme, one can play hardball, issuing threats or an ultimatum to one's adversary. Such communications are designed to force an outcome desired by the party sending such provocative messages either in writing or orally—such as when an ambassador representing a foreign country tells a foreign minister or head of government in the host country that unless certain steps are taken, economic or military sanctions of one kind or another will be imposed.

Ultimata of this sort are not the usual, day-to-day stuff of diplomacy. We will discuss three other kinds of diplomatic communications: informational transfers, symbolic messages, and negotiations.

First, some communications are merely informational transfers not designed to produce any particular outcome. Such governmental agencies as departments (or ministries) of foreign affairs, defense, commerce, or their diplomatic representatives in embassies throughout the world let local governments and interested individuals and groups know about newsworthy events or other happenings. For example, the U.S. National Aeronautics and Space Administration (NASA), its Jet Propulsion Laboratory (JPL), or its other centers inform governmental counterparts, scientists, and the general public about shuttle launches into space, photographs of space retrieved from the orbiting Hubble telescope, and missions to Mars or past other planets and moons.

Case & Point

Sometimes the most difficult diplomacy is not between two adversaries, but among allies who disagree on how to approach a common adversary. One example from the mid-1990s is about how NATO member states should deal with Serbia and its then president, Slobodan Milosevic, concerning Serbian actions in Bosnia. The following account comes from the memoir of former U.S. Secretary of State Warren Christopher:

> By the summer of 1995, the crisis in Bosnia had reached its culminating stage. The British and the French, whose troops were the backbone of the United Nations force there, began to signal that they would leave the region by the end of the year. More-over, in response to "pinprick" NATO airstrikes in May 1995, the Bosnian Serb Army had taken some U.N. personnel hostage and chained them to possible air targets. Many of us feared that these acts would be the last straw, and the U.N. would de-cide to withdraw. If this happened, the United States was committed to contributing ground troops to a NATO force that would help ensure a safe withdrawal. I felt that this would be an embarrassing as well as perilous use of American forces, but, on the other hand, failure to keep our commitment would undermine our credibility as the leader of the Alliance.

> As we debated our diplomatic options, the military situation deteriorated. In July, the Bosnian Serb Army overran two U.N. safe areas, Srebrenica and Zepa. The massacre in Srebrenica was devastating, and we realized that something had to be done. The U.N. safe area at Gorazde, the last Muslim enclave in eastern Bosnia, appeared to be the next target.

> To determine the international response to these attacks, Prime Minister John Major of the United Kingdom called an emergency meeting of Allied and other interested Foreign Ministers in London on July 20. I led the U.S. delegation, which included Secretary of Defense William Perry and General John Shalikashvili, Chairman of the Joint Chiefs of Staff. At the meeting we decided that there could be no more half measures; we could not permit the loss of the beleaguered town of Gorazde. NATO had to present the Bosnian Serbs with a clear and unambigu-ous warning to leave Gorazde alone. During a day of tough negotiations in the sweltering heat of London's Lancaster House, and with a major assist from the new British Foreign Secretary, Malcolm Rifkind, we persuaded the Allies to agree that an attack on Gorazde would be met with "substantial and decisive" use of air power. For this reason, the meeting was a vital turning point in our approach to-ward Bosnia: we finally committed to put some real muscle behind our rhetoric.

Point: Before one can bargain with an adversary, tough negotiations among allies are often required.

Warren Christopher, *In the Stream of History* (Stanford, CA: Stanford University Press, 1998), 348.

DIPLOMACY AMONG ALLIES

Other informational communications may have a purpose that goes beyond merely transmitting facts. Government agencies may communicate directly to foreign publics or work through centralized agencies or ministries of information. For example, the State Department wants to convey to foreign publics the rationale for U.S. policies and explain U.S. understanding of and approaches to world events. Most countries have similar information ministries with established press contacts for access to radio, television, and print media. Mailing lists and government sites on the World Wide Web (or Internet) are also used to present a country's point of view—information with a decided purpose. Because such communications are expected by design to be one-sided advocacy of a country's policy positions (not necessarily balanced presentations with all sides of an argument considered), information ministries in democratic countries may well be restricted (as the USIA is) from disseminating their communications to citizens residing within their own countries. Lest they be accused of propagandizing their own citizens, the target audience of information ministries in democratic countries is foreign publics.

Other communications are symbolic, usually designed to reinforce positive aspects of relations between two countries. Thus, French foreign ministry and other government officials attend a Fourth of July celebration hosted by the U.S. embassy in Paris. Naturally U.S. officials reciprocate by attending a similar Bastille Day (July 14) celebration hosted by the French embassy in the Georgetown section of Washington. On such occasions symbolic references are often made to eighteenth-century French help in the American Revolution, the fact that neither country has ever gone to war with the other, and that both countries share long-established commitments to democratic values.

Another example of symbolic communications is to demonstrate respect by presidents and senior government officials or their representatives, ambassadors, and other diplomats attending important state events such as coronation of a monarch, inauguration of a president, royal family or other state weddings or funerals, and other state events. The level of representation at such events is carefully considered, usually to avoid any insult to the host country. Thus, the funerals following the deaths of U.S. President Kennedy in 1963, Egyptian President Sadat in 1981, and Jordanian King Hussein in 1999 brought presidents and prime ministers from all over the world.

Annual events such as Luxembourg's commemoration of U.S. General Patton's role in liberating the country from occupation by Germany during World War II typically draw delegations of American diplomats, generals, and military personnel headed by the U.S. ambassador. Who and what level of position or rank are to be in attendance at such state events are by no means left to chance but are usually carefully coordinated between the two countries beforehand to assure a successful "symbolic" event that contributes to continued good relations between the two countries.

Diplomacy includes not just these and similar kinds of positive exchanges, but (as noted earlier) also has to deal with conflicts in interests and objectives. A third form of diplomatic communications is negotiations; however, one or another of the parties may choose not to negotiate.

Avoiding or Sidestepping Conflicts   Indeed, one approach to a conflict is to sidestep, avoid, or ignore it, not confronting it directly. Sometimes the issues dividing the parties are inconsequential or relatively unimportant and thus not worth any bother, particularly when raising such issues may worsen relations without accomplishing much, if anything. At other times, however, there may be important issues at stake that one or more of the parties may wish to defer to a later time, perhaps realizing that the issues are not likely to be resolved satisfactorily any time soon. This may require some fancy diplomatic footwork, leaving matters rest as they are, unresolved, and without yielding anything in principle to the other side.

A good example during the Cold War was the preference by the United States, Britain, and France not to renegotiate with the Soviet Union the set of rules that had emerged after previous conflicts concerning air and land access to all sectors of Berlin, then still under post–World War II occupation by these four countries. It was feared that any such renegotiation likely would be used by the Soviets to erode access rights claimed by the three Western allies. In 1948, for example, the Soviets had tried to deny air and land access to Berlin across East Germany, but the United States responded by ignoring the Soviet prohibition, airlifting needed supplies to the beleaguered city. In the process, the Western allies established their rights in practice, and eventually the Soviet Union lifted its prohibitions on air and land access. The Soviets still claimed rights to regulate land and air access to the city but chose not to exercise them.

For their part, the Western allies denied that the Soviet Union had any such right to deny them access because wartime agreements had established these rights, which from the Western perspective remained nonnegotiable. This conflict on rights of access thus remained unresolved throughout the Cold War. As a practical matter, however, the Soviets chose not to provoke the Western allies again by forcefully denying them access as they had done in 1948. Importantly, neither side yielded anything in principle on the rights-of-access matter under dispute even as regular flights, railroad trains, cars, and trucks moving across East Germany to and from Berlin were allowed to proceed.

Negotiating without Expectation of Reaching Agreement   Indeed, the real challenges in diplomatic negotiations occur when the parties are deeply in conflict. Sometimes one or both parties do not really want to reach agreement at all but see some value in the negotiating process, at least appearing to negotiate. The objective may be merely to delay taking any action on the conflict at issue. In this mode, one or both sides may set forth a maximum position which neither expects the other side to accept.

For example, in the late 1970s, the United States and its NATO allies responded with a two-track strategy to Soviet deployments in the western Soviet Union of nuclear-armed SS-20 INF ballistic missiles. These intermediate-range nuclear force missiles had a range of 500 to 5,500 kilometers (or 300 to 3,300 miles) aimed at Western Europe. On one track, the United States prepared to deploy the intermediate-range Pershing II ballistic missiles in West Germany as a counter to the SS-20. The United States also prepared to deploy additional cruise (remotely guided, "air-breathing") missiles in West Germany, the United Kingdom, Italy, the Netherlands, and Belgium.

The second (or negotiations) track favored by many of the U.S. allies in NATO was also initiated. The "zero-zero option" negotiating proposal offered by the United States in 1981 was not expected to be accepted by the Soviet Union. A bold stroke by the West (and particularly by the United States), the zero-zero option called for Soviet disarmament of its INF missiles (reducing them to zero) in exchange for NATO commitment not to counter with Pershing II and cruise missiles, leaving both sides with zero INF missiles in their arsenals.

It was a stretch to believe at the time that the Soviet Union would ever dismantle what it had already deployed in exchange merely for a promise by NATO not to match the existing Soviet deployment. Critics of the zero-zero option in NATO countries doubted the sincerity of the U.S.-NATO proposal, seeing it as a ploy merely to appear committed to the diplomatic negotiating track while fully expecting to go forward

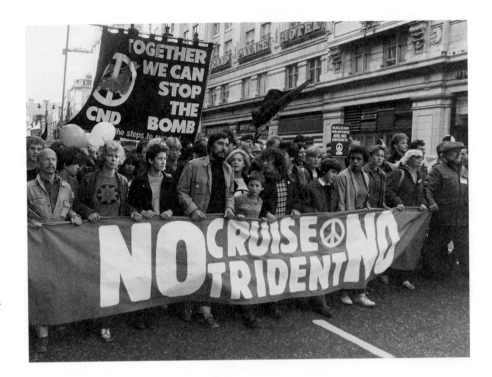

Europeans demonstrating against deployment of missiles to Greenham Common, England, in the early 1980s.

with counterdeployments of Pershing II and cruise missiles. Whatever the truth of this allegation, all Western parties were pleasantly surprised when, counter to their expectations, the new Soviet regime under Gorbachev decided in 1987 to accept the zero-zero option and proposed dismantling all INF missiles. The final outcome, by no means anticipated in 1981, was elimination of an entire category of weaponry: intermediate-range nuclear missiles.

Another example of negotiations not expected to succeed in their apparent purpose is the NATO–Warsaw Pact force reduction talks held in Vienna between 1973 and 1989. The negotiations dragged on throughout the 1970s and 1980s until the end of the Cold War with very little to show for all the time and effort expended. From time to time, each side accused the other of not negotiating in good faith. Some observers joked that the negotiators enjoyed Vienna so much that they did not want to reach an agreement lest they have to leave this beautiful city! These pundits jokingly claimed the way to force agreement was to choose a less desirable city in which to negotiate—an incentive to speeding up the process so the diplomats could go home.

The reality, of course, was that neither side was under any particular time pressure that would force an early conclusion. As recognized leader of the NATO side, the United States entered the negotiations at a time when the Nixon administration wanted to forestall Congressional efforts in the early 1970s to reduce the U.S. troop presence in Europe. The fact was that NATO already had fewer forces deployed in and around Germany in the "central front" between East and West—a numerical disadvantage compared to the Warsaw Pact. Accordingly, neither the Nixon administration nor America's NATO allies really wanted a substantial reduction in American or other NATO forces unless there were also substantial reductions in Warsaw Pact forces. For their part the Soviet Union and its Eastern European Warsaw Pact allies already enjoyed numerical superiority and saw little to gain by reducing their numbers and sacrificing their quantitative advantage over NATO. At the same time, the Warsaw Pact side found value in negotiating, particularly if domestic political pressures forced the United States or other NATO countries to reduce their forces to even lower levels.

Given its numerical superiority, the Warsaw Pact side indicated willingness to reduce forces equally—these were to be mutual force reductions (MFR) talks. The NATO side countered that the reductions needed to be proportional or balanced—mutual and balanced force reductions (MBFR) talks. For example, a 10 percent reduction on both sides would mean a larger number of troops for the Warsaw Pact to reduce because it had more troops in the area. Thus, because the Warsaw Pact had about a million troops and NATO only about 800,000 in central Europe, a balanced or proportional reduction of 10 percent would mean the Warsaw Pact withdrawing 100,000 troops and NATO just 80,000.

Other difficult issues included whether troops in the Soviet Union in striking distance of Western Europe should be counted, particularly since the United States (and Canada) did not want troops counted in their home countries or the other side of the Atlantic. Added to these issues was the so-called "data problem," given differences in composition and size of military units (a division, brigade, or regiment on one side was not the same as a division, brigade, or regiment on the other side, either in terms of numbers of combat or support troops or equipment). Indeed, neither side could agree on how many troops the other actually had under arms in central Europe.

Arguably, both sides could have resolved such matters if they really had wanted to reach agreement on lower force levels. Although frustrating to many arms control advocates, delaying any outcome appeared to be the real objective (or at least the default position of both sides). Viewed in this light, MBFR talks were successful in avoiding any agreement disadvantageous to either side or, in the U.S. case, keeping Congressional pressures from forcing unilateral U.S. force reductions in Europe. Most important, perhaps, the MBFR talks had provided a useful opportunity for two opposing military alliances to be in direct and regular communications for some seventeen years, providing a diplomatic forum for registering complaints, coming to understand (if not accept) opposing sides, and contributing to building relations that would bear fruit in other forums at the end of the Cold War.

Getting-to-Yes Negotiations as Zero- and Positive-Sum Games   The mentality in negotiations is often that what one side gains, the other loses. Game theorists refer to this as **zero-sum**—the pluses one side gains come at the expense of the minuses the other side loses. As discussed earlier, incentives ("carrots") and disincentives or threats ("sticks") may be used by the parties, although such methods are rather blunt instruments. Give and take, pulling and hauling by opposing parties, and formation of coalitions and countercoalitions in multilateral negotiations are tactics often employed to forge compromise agreements when interests and related objectives are in conflict. Sometimes this is the best that can be achieved—a compromise in which typically each side gains something but also gives up something. Each side achieves some points of satisfaction but is also left with some disappointments—points it may have had to give up in order to get some concessions from the other side or perhaps to get any agreement at all.

A potentially far more productive approach to durable agreements is to use negotiations as a means to search for common ground among the parties, forging a positive-sum outcome based on mutual gains. Such agreements may involve some compromises but rest more fundamentally on satisfying the parties' multiple interests—some shared, some not. The Harvard negotiation project has identified several principles or guidelines for "getting to yes"—an essentially positive-sum approach to use when parties are in conflict.[4] The methodology was developed for diverse negotiation settings, but for our purposes it has direct application to diplomatic communications aimed at achieving win-win outcomes.

Although personalities and orientations matter in how negotiators relate to one another, negotiations are about issues, not personalities. In focusing on issues, the parties avoid digging in their heels and taking hard-and-fast positions. Instead they pay attention to the interests of all of the parties in a search for common ground. Interests are of two kinds, those related to the substance of what is being negotiated and those related to preserving and improving relationships in the negotiations among the parties and the countries they represent. There also needs to be room for creative approaches to finding common ground—at times inventing options for mutual gain. Finally, not to be content to rest agreements merely on the will of the parties, objective criteria or standards for measuring what has been agreed, accompanied by fair procedures, are essential to effective implementation of any agreement. In point-by-point summary form, the getting-to-yes method is (1) don't bargain over positions; (2) separate the people from the problem; (3) focus on interests, not positions; (4) invent options for mutual gain; and (5) insist on using objective criteria.[5]

Extended three-way negotiations among Canada, the United States, and Mexico in the late 1980s and early 1990s "got to yes" on establishment of a free trade area judged by negotiators and national leaders at the time to satisfy interests of all three parties. This was by no means an easy task. The United States and Canada, with highly developed advanced industrial (or postindustrial) economies, were both relatively rich in capital but markedly different from each other in aggregate size of their economies. In this regard, Canadians were concerned that more open trade and commercial relations might make them one of the principal objects of U.S. economic dominance. For their part, Mexicans were concerned that their less-developed economy (a per capita income about 10 percent of that in their two northern neighbors) might suffer disadvantage at the hands of both the United States and Canada. Labor unions in the United States objected that jobs in labor-intensive industries would be lost to Mexico, where wages were low. The unions were joined by environmental groups concerned that American corporations would continue moving to Mexico where environmental law and law enforcement was less stringent, allowing them to foul or degrade the environment in ways that would be prohibited in the United States.

The North American Free Trade Agreement (NAFTA) that finally emerged addressed trade product by product in difficult negotiations that also took environmental matters and estimates of jobs to be gained or lost into account. Negotiators searched creatively for options in a positive-sum approach to realizing mutual gains (and minimizing losses), even though these gains (and losses) would be asymmetric—not all evenly shared. Numerous compromises were reached. Difficult issues were sometimes settled by agreeing on scheduled but delayed implementation of some provisions. Objective criteria were specified in the details of a final agreement that numbered more than two thousand pages!

Although one could try to add up all the gains and losses (and both advocates and opponents did just that), in the final analysis NAFTA rested on the view that the overall

---

[4]Roger Fisher and William Ury (with Bruce Patton, ed.), *Getting to Yes: Negotiating Agreement without Giving In* (London and New York: Penguin Books, 1981, 1991).
[5]For details, see *ibid.*, 3–94.

economic interest of each party and North America as a whole would be better served by reducing trade barriers. Whether one agreed with them or not, this was the view held at the time by both U.S. President George H. Bush and his successor President Clinton, as well as by their head-of-government counterparts in Canada and Mexico. As President Clinton put it, one can add up the pluses and minuses if one wants to, but what NAFTA is really about is a big (and important) idea. Liberalizing trade and commerce was a positive-sum vision he, his predecessor, and his counterparts saw as realizing gains, on balance, for all parties.

The decades-long peace process in the Middle East is another example of the getting-to-yes approach at work. Four major Arab-Israeli wars (1948, 1956, 1967, and 1973), repeated terrorist acts, and civil strife have marked the region and divided Arab states from Israel, at times into separate, hostile, seemingly irreconcilable camps. Enormous patience has been required as well as help from third parties (the United States, other countries, and international organizations) to bring the parties together and to facilitate efforts to find common ground satisfactory to their mutual interests.

In the 1970s, for example, both Egypt and Israel had an interest in avoiding the human and material cost of yet another war. Israel's interest in its security and its related desire for diplomatic recognition as a state, coupled with Egypt's interest in regaining and securing territory lost in wars, ultimately led the parties to the 1979 Camp David Accords mentioned in the previous section. Although the agreement contained compromises, its more solid basis was its grounding in mutual interests: Israel gave land back to Egypt in exchange for Egypt's recognition of Israel as a state (the first Arab state to do so), embassies were established in each other's capital, ambassadors were exchanged, and diplomatic relations were normalized. U.S. President Carter was particularly instrumental in bringing Israeli Prime Minister Begin and Egyptian President Sadat together at Camp David, Maryland, using his good offices to keep them engaged in the negotiations process. Creative approaches to finding common ground were employed in the bargaining process. The agreement was also secured with grants of military and economic aid as incentives offered by the United States to both sides. An agreed timetable and procedures for implementing the agreement in accordance with objective criteria were finally reached.

Significantly, the Camp David Accords not only found a substantive common ground based on mutual interest in the peace and security between Egypt and Israel, but the accords also served mutual interest in building and maintaining better relationships at both high-level leadership and midlevel or "working" levels among officials on both sides. These relationships were essential to both reaching and effectively implementing the agreement.

Since then, the peace process has continued in fits and starts as attention turned to Israel's conflicts with other Arab states (security and territory being the same interests typically at issue) and to the interest of Palestinians as a people in eventually securing a state to call their own. Different American presidents, secretaries of state, and other emissaries from the United States, other countries, and international organizations have continued to use their good offices to try to keep the peace process on track in a patient, although frequently frustrating, search for common ground. Apparent progress

> ## BACK-CHANNEL DIPLOMACY
>
> *During my first meeting with President Nixon, I was surprised when he said to me: "Ambassador, I've checked with my predecessor and found out you are a person who never gives leaks to the press or to others. So I believe we could organize a confidential channel. And I have a good man—Mr. Kissinger. He will report directly to me without telling anyone else." Finally [Kissinger] said, "We meet so often—let's have a telephone." So White House communications people put a telephone line in the room next to my office at the embassy. It was a regular phone—it wasn't red—but it had no dial or numbers. When I picked it up, only Henry answered.*
>
> **Former Soviet Ambassador
> Anatoly Dobrynin**
> *quoted in* U.S. News and World Report,
> *November 13, 1995, 70.*

It's Been Said...

has often amounted to small, slow steps, only to be reversed in subsequent weeks and months. Getting to yes has been anything but easy, requiring enormous reserves of patience—a commitment to continuing the process in spite of major differences, assassinations, and terrorist incidents intended by opponents of the peace process to push it off track, disrupting further negotiations if at all possible.

Conclusion

Contemporary diplomatic practices have not escaped the global trends of interdependence and crises of authority. First there has been an erosion of diplomatic norms. Consider, for example, the sanctity of diplomatic missions. Over the years, missions certainly have been attacked by mobs, but the takeover of the American embassy in Tehran in November 1979 by radical students established a dangerous precedent because the revolutionary Islamic regime sanctioned the action. In the 1980 Venice Declaration, the seven participating heads of state from Europe, North America, and Japan noted they were "gravely concerned by recent incidents of terrorism involving the taking of hostages and attacks on diplomatic and consular premises and personnel." They had good reason to be, because by 1980 diplomats had become the major targets for terrorism, accounting for 54 percent of all international terrorist attacks. American diplomats were the favored targets.[6] Furthermore, the Iranian and Libyan regimes used their overseas missions to plan and support terrorist acts on foreign soil. Add to this the rise in crime in urban areas throughout the world, significant health risks, and increasing social anarchy in a number of developing countries, and it is clear that life for diplomats and their families is a long way from the popular image of champagne-and-caviar embassy parties.

Second, the nature of diplomatic communication between governments has evolved. Historically the resident ambassador has been the key communication link with the host government, presenting his state's views and reporting back those of the host government. Now regular summits among leaders, back-channel contacts that skirt the embassy, and direct, secure telephone and electronic lines between political leaders all reduce the relevancy of the ambassador. Even in those situations in which the ambassador has direct access to top host government officials, the result can be to bypass the professional diplomatic circuit.

Third, the end of the Cold War reduced the importance of Western embassies in the former Eastern bloc as sources of information for policy makers. Particularly during the Cold War, Western journalists had little access to Eastern bloc countries, so official political reporting from embassies was critical. As East-West tensions eased, however, journalists were granted entry to previously remote parts of the Soviet Union and Eastern Europe and also found it easier to cultivate their own sources of information in various foreign policy bureaucracies. It is not unusual for policy makers to find important insights in *The New York Times, Washington Post, Le Monde, Times of London, Christian Science Monitor, Wall Street Journal*, or other quality newspapers and magazines.

Fourth, the worldwide communication revolution has also reduced the importance of diplomatic reporting. Thanks to satellites, the first sources of information on breaking events are often television networks, the Internet, and radio reports, with diplomatic and intelligence reporting lagging behind. Indeed, key offices throughout

---

[6]Geoffrey M. Levitt, *Democracies against Terror* (New York: Praeger, 1988), 36–37.

the State Department feature television sets that are tuned to news channels throughout the day. CNN and other networks are also a staple for twenty-four-hour operations centers located in various government agencies that deal with foreign policy and national security issues. Satellite transmissions allow government intelligence analysts as well as regular citizens to watch live news broadcasts from foreign television stations covering local events.

One drawback to relying on live broadcasts is that the information viewers receive does not provide the broader, interpretive context that characterizes diplomatic and intelligence reporting. Furthermore, the live broadcast of events to millions of people may force the pace of events or sensationalize issues, putting pressure on policy makers to make a decision before diplomats can meet to negotiate a mutually acceptable solution.

Fifth, in an increasingly globalized and interdependent world, the diplomatic corps of today and tomorrow have to be more than familiar with complex technological and environmental trends. These are increasingly the subject of international concern—for example, the impact of ozone depletion and the cutting down of the Amazon rain forests, the social and environmental impact of exploding birthrates, the thrust of viral pandemics, or the resolution of disputes between states on conflicting claims to natural resources such as water. It is highly debatable whether the diplomatic corps of most countries are adequately recruiting, training, and retaining persons with expertise in such areas. Yet without such personnel (who must also be skilled in negotiating), it is unlikely that a state will be able to resolve the sorts of challenges and conflicts that are discussed later in this book.

Finally, particularly in the case of humanitarian disasters and civil wars, "field diplomacy" on the part of nongovernmental relief and aid organizations may become increasingly the norm. Often attuned to local politics and knowledge of key players, these nonstate actors may play a key or supporting role in conflict mitigation or even conflict resolution.

Afterword

Toward Containment: George Kennan's Long Telegram

Although present-day technologies allow for encrypted voice communications on a global scale, most diplomatic correspondence between an embassy and its foreign ministry at home is still typically in the form of written messages, classified as secret or top secret and transmitted electronically in encrypted form to be decoded by the recipient—an automated process nowadays. Even though technology now facilitates transmission of massive volumes of data every day between a country's foreign ministry and its worldwide network of embassies, consulates, and other diplomatic missions, older terms such as "telegram" and "cable" still remain part of diplomatic parlance to describe messages sent or received.

Adding italics to emphasize key passages, we include below an excerpt from what we consider an excellent example of diplomatic correspondence—offering the studied views from abroad by an experienced diplomat, a perspective intended to influence the formulation of foreign policy by officials in the national capital. Indeed, on February 22, 1946 George Kennan, a diplomat assigned to the U.S. Embassy in Moscow, replied to an inquiry from the State Department in Washington D.C. in what would become known as the "long telegram"—the foundation for a policy of containing what was understood as a Soviet (historically a Russian) propensity toward expansionism. Kennan tells Washington that the Soviet Union does not tend to "take unnecessary risks" and "is highly sensitive to logic of force," adding that "it can easily withdraw—and usually does—when strong resistance is encountered at any point. Thus, if the adversary has sufficient force and makes clear his readiness to use it, he rarely has to do so. If situations are properly handled there need be no prestige-engaging showdowns." As in most telegrams in those times, Kennan writes in a staccato style, dropping articles to save unnecessary words—an economy no longer required by present-day transmission technologies

. . . In summary, *we have here a political force committed fanatically to the belief that with US there can be no permanent modus vivendi, that it is desirable and necessary that the internal harmony of our society be disrupted, our traditional way of life be destroyed, the international authority of our state be broken, if Soviet power is to be secure.* This political force has complete power of disposition over energies of one of world's greatest peoples and resources of world's richest national territory, and is borne along by deep and powerful currents of Russian nationalism. In addition, *it has an elaborate and far-flung apparatus for exertion of its influence in other countries, an apparatus of amazing flexibility and versatility, managed by people whose experience and skill in underground methods are presumably without parallel in history.* Finally, it is seemingly inaccessible to considerations of reality in its basic reactions. For it, the vast fund of objective fact about human society is not, as with us, the measure against which outlook is constantly being tested and re formed, but a grab bag from which individual items are selected arbitrarily and tendenciously to bolster an outlook already preconceived. This is admittedly not a pleasant picture. Problem of how to cope with this force undoubtedly [is] greatest task our diplomacy has ever faced and probably greatest it will ever have to face. It should be point of departure from which our political general staff work at present juncture should proceed. It should be approached with same thoroughness and care as solution of major strategic problem in war and, if necessary, with no smaller outlay in planning effort. I cannot attempt to suggest all answers here. But I would like to record *my conviction that problem is within our power to solve—and that without recourse to any general military conflict.* And in support of this conviction there are certain observations for a more encouraging nature I should like to make.

(1) *Soviet power,* unlike that of Hitlerite Germany, is neither schematic nor adventuristic. It does not work by fixed plans. It *does not take unnecessary risks.* Impervious to logic of reason, and *it is highly sensitive to logic of force.* For this reason it can easily withdraw—and usually does—when strong resistance is encountered at any point. *Thus, if the adversary has sufficient force and makes clear his readiness to use it, he rarely has to do so.* If situations are properly handled there need be no prestige-engaging showdowns.

(2) Gauged against Western world as a whole, *Soviets are still by far the weaker force.* Thus, their success will really depend on degree of cohesion, firmness and vigor which Western world can muster. And this is factor which it is within our power to influence.

(3) Success of Soviet system, as form of internal power, is not yet finally proven. It has yet to be demonstrated that it can survive supreme test of successive transfer of power from one individual or group to another. Lenin's death was first such transfer, and its effects wracked Soviet state for 15 years. After Stalin's death or retirement will be second. But even this will not be final test. Soviet internal system will now be subjected, by virtue of recent territorial expansions, to series of additional strains which once proved severe tax on Tsardom. We here are convinced that never since termination of civil war have mass of Russian people been emotionally farther removed from doctrines of Communist Party than they are today. *In Russia, party has now become a* great and—for the moment—highly *successful apparatus of dictatorial administration, but it has ceased to be a source of emotional inspiration.* Thus, internal soundness and permanence of movement need not yet be regarded as assured.

(4) All *Soviet propaganda* beyond Soviet security sphere is basically negative and destructive. It *should* therefore *be relatively easy to combat* it by any intelligent and really constructive program.

For these reasons I think we may approach calmly and with good heart problem of how to deal with Russia. As to how this approach should be made, I only wish to advance, by way of conclusion, following comments:

(1) Our first step must be to apprehend, and recognize for what it is, the nature of the movement with which we are dealing. We must study it with same courage, detachment, objectivity, and same determination not to be emotionally provoked or unseated by it, with which doctor studies unruly and unreasonable individual.

(2) *We must see that our public is educated to realities of Russian situation.* I cannot overemphasize importance of this. Press cannot do this alone. It must be done mainly by Government, which is necessarily more experienced and better informed on practical problems involved. In this we need not be deterred by [the negative appearance—Ed.] of picture. I am convinced that there would be far less hysterical anti-Sovietism in our country today if realities of this situation were better understood by our people. There is nothing as dangerous or as terrifying as the unknown. It may also be argued that to reveal more information on our difficulties with Russia would reflect unfavorably on Russian-American relations. I feel that if there is any real risk here involved, it is one which we should have courage to face, and sooner the better. But I cannot see what we would be risking. Our stake in this country, even coming on heels of tremendous demonstrations of our friendship for Russian people, is remarkably small. We have here no investments to guard, no actual trade to lose, virtually no citizens to protect, few cultural contacts to preserve. Our only stake [lies] in what we hope rather than what we have; and *I am convinced we have better chance of* realizing those hopes *if our public is enlightened and if our dealings with Russians are placed entirely on realistic and matter-of-fact basis.*

(3) *Much depends on health and vigor of our own society.* World communism is like malignant parasite which feeds only on diseased tissue. This is point at which domestic and foreign policies meet. *Every courageous and incisive measure to solve internal problems of our own society, to improve self-confidence, discipline, morale and community spirit of our own people, is a diplomatic victory over Moscow worth a thousand diplomatic notes and joint communiqués.* If we cannot abandon fatalism and indifference in face of deficiencies of our own society, Moscow will profit—Moscow cannot help profiting by them in its foreign policies.

(4) *We must formulate and put forward for other nations a much more positive and constructive picture of sort of world we would like to see* than we have put forward in past. It is not enough to urge people to develop political processes similar to our own. Many foreign peoples, in Europe at least, are tired and frightened by experiences of past, and are less interested in abstract freedom than in security. They are seeking guidance rather than responsibilities. We should be better able than Russians to give them this. And, unless we do, Russians certainly will.

(5) Finally *we must have courage and self-confidence to cling to our own methods and conceptions of human society. After all, the greatest danger that can befall us in coping with this problem of Soviet communism is that we shall allow ourselves to become like those with whom we are coping.*

Key Terms

diplomacy   *p. 121*   coercive diplomacy   *p. 122*   treaty   *p. 123*
compellence   *p. 122*   deterrence   *p. 122*   ambassador   *p. 123*

Other Concepts

emissary   *p. 119*   diplomatic immunity   *p. 133*   interest section   *p. 136*
ancien regime   *p. 119*   reciprocity   *p. 133*   intelligence collection   *p. 138*
apartheid   *p. 122*   persona non grata   *p. 133*   espionage   *p. 138*
executive agreement   *p. 123*   extraterritoriality   *p. 134*   country team   *p. 138*
démarche   *p. 123*   asylum   *p. 134*   foreign aid   *p. 140*
ultimatum   *p. 123*   mission   *p. 134*   economic sanctions   *p. 140*
jus gentium   *p. 128*   embassy   *p. 134*   boycott   *p. 140*
jus naturale   *p. 128*   consulate   *p. 134*   embargo   *p. 140*
chargé d'affaires   *p. 129*   delegation   *p. 134*   blockade   *p. 140*
multilateral diplomacy   *p. 129*   chief of mission   *p. 134*   crisis   *p. 141*
bilateral diplomacy   *p. 129*   deputy chief of   crisis diplomacy   *p. 141*
neutrality   *p. 130*   mission   *p. 136*   credibility   *p. 141*
government in exile   *p. 130*   consul   *p. 136*   good offices   *p. 144*
puppet government   *p. 131*   consul general   *p. 136*   zero-sum   *p. 149*

Additional Readings

In the preparation of this chapter, we found to be quite helpful Harold Nicholson's short classic *Diplomacy*, 3d ed. (London: University Press, 1963). To get a feel for diplomacy as actually conducted, many university libraries contain the memoirs of diplomats. The U.S. secretaries of state Dean Acheson, Henry Kissinger, Cyrus Vance, Alexander Haig, George Shultz, James Baker, Warren Christopher, and Madeline Albright have all published lengthy tomes. See also Henry Kissinger's, *Diplomacy* (New York: Simon & Schuster, 1994) and, on the Congress of Vienna, *A World Restored* (New York: Grosset & Dunlap, 1964). For a classic analysis of the diplomacy that set the foundation of the post–World War II era, see Dean Acheson's, *Present at the Creation* (New York: W. W. Norton, 1969). Covering the first half of the twentieth century is George Kennan's *American Diplomacy* (New York: New American Library/Mentor Books, 1951). On the modalities of diplomacy, see Geoffrey R. Berridge, Maurice Keens-Soper, and Thomas G. Otte, eds., *Diplomatic Theory from Machiavelli to Kissinger* (New York: Palgrave, 2001) and Fred C. Iklé, *How Nations Negotiate* (New York: Harper & Row, 1964). Touching on diplomacy over the half millennium since 1500 is Paul Kennedy's *The Rise and Fall of the Great Powers* (New York: Random House, 1987).

On foreign policy decision-making theories and concepts, see Valerie M. Hudson, Derek H. Chollet, and James M. Goldgeier, *Foreign Policy Decision-Making Revisited* (New York: Palgrave, 2002). A theoretically oriented anthology on how smaller states find their way in a world dominated by great powers is Jeanne A. K. Hey, ed., *Small States in World Politics: Explaining Foreign Policy Behavior* (Boulder, CO: Lynne Rienner, 2003). Other recent volumes on diplomatic themes include Amitav Acharya, *Regionalism and Multilateralism: Essays on Cooperative Security in the Asia-Pacific* (London and New York: Eastern Universities Press, 2003) and Scott A Hunt, *On the Future of Peace: On the Front Lines with the World's Great Peacemakers* (San Francisco: Harper Collins, 2004).

Chapter 5

War, Just Wars, and Armed Intervention

"War is a matter of vital importance to the state; the province of life or death; the road to survival or ruin. It is mandatory that it be thoroughly studied."

SUN TZU, *THE ART OF WAR*, C. 500 B.C.

"War is the last of all things to go according to plan."

THUCYDIDES, *THE PELOPONNESIAN WAR*, C. 404 B.C.

"And above all, while defending our own vital interests, nuclear powers must avert those confrontations which bring an adversary to a choice of either a humiliating retreat or a nuclear war. To adopt that kind of course in the nuclear age would be evidence only of the bankruptcy of our policy—or of a collective death-wish for the world."

PRESIDENT JOHN F. KENNEDY, JUNE 1963

At age 30, Mary Louise Roberts enlisted in the U.S. Army following the attack on Pearl Harbor. She was assigned as the operating room supervisor with the Army's 56th Evacuation Unit and went ashore at Casablanca, North Africa. The fighting in North Africa was intense but only a preview of what lay ahead: Anzio, Italy, which marked the beginning of the Allied invasion of Europe in the southern theater. Roberts's medical unit landed five days after the invasion. Situated in the middle of the combat zone with German artillery shells ripping through the operating tent on the Anzio beachhead, she remembers, "At one point our commanding officer got the nurses together and asked whether we wanted to be evacuated. It was pretty bad, but we decided we were going to stay." One male officer was eager to leave, "But he said there was no way he was going to leave until at least one nurse agreed to go—so he stayed, too." One of Roberts's colleagues, June Wandrey, wrote home, "We're working twelve to fifteen hours a day now, never sitting down except to eat. . . . Such young soldiers. They're so patient and never complain. I won't be able to write often and here are the reasons why: Bed 6, penetrating wound of the left flank, penetrating wound face, fractured mandible [jaw], penetrating wound left forearm; Bed 5, amputation right leg, penetrating wound left leg, lacerating wound of chest, lacerating wound right hand."[1]

---

[1]Tom Brokaw, *The Greatest Generation* (New York: Random House, 1998), 174–176.

We begin by posing a simple question: what do you think is the first image that comes to mind for most people when they hear the concepts "world politics" or "international relations"?

A good bet is that war is generally the first thought that comes to mind. All too often **armed conflicts** dominate the newspaper headlines and hence our consciousness when we think of international relations or world politics. This is understandable, because wars are the most destructive of human activities. It has been estimated that 2 million people lost their lives on the battlefields during the Thirty Years' War (1618–1648), 2.5 million during the French Revolution and Napoleonic wars (1792–1815), 7.7 million in World War I (1914–1918), and 13 million in World War II (1939–1945).[2] Such estimates do not even include the death and injury of civilian populations, nor do they adequately reflect the devastation caused by civil wars. Indeed, for countries such as the United States, the great Civil War of 1861–1865 resulted in more American deaths—600,000—than all other wars fought by Americans from 1776 to the present, combined.

It is not surprising, therefore, that over the centuries observers of international relations have been primarily interested in understanding patterns of conflict and cooperation among various types of political units. These units, as we have seen in Chapter 2, have included ancient Greek city-states of the fifth century B.C.; Persian, Roman, and Carthaginian empires; and modern nation-states. The question of "Why do wars occur?" is not all that different from the question of "What factors account for peace?" Indeed, war and peace can be viewed as opposite sides of the same coin.

The Rationalities and Irrationalities of Interstate War

In this chapter we examine the use of *force* in world politics. In the previous chapter, we discussed the threat of force and its limited application for coercive and deterrent purposes as part of a diplomatic arsenal available to policy makers. Force also refers to the use of military capabilities in **interstate wars, civil wars,** or **armed interventions.** Interstate wars are defined as wars by one or more states against another state or states. Civil wars involve fighting among two or more factions within a state. Armed interventions involve the deployment of military personnel to a foreign country in order to tip the balance in a civil war, restore order, maintain peace, or physically coerce a state to change its policies. Whereas the use of military force is the defining characteristic of war, it should be noted that use of propaganda, coercive diplomacy, and economic and other sanctions also usually occur during warfare.

The enormous human costs of war have not prevented countless repetitions of the phenomenon throughout human history in all parts of the world. A propensity to engage in **warfare**—an organized use of force of one group of people against another— is one of the things human beings have in common, however tragic the consequences. Tribes in the rain forests of New Guinea and Amazonia, clans and tribes in Africa and the mountainous or other more remote regions in Eurasia and Latin America, and

force
The use of military capabilities to coerce other states (or actors) against their will.

[2]Jack Levy, "Theories of General War," *World Politics,* v. 37, no. 2 (April 1985): 344.

nations and states throughout the world count war among the experiences they hold in common.

The apparent irrationalities of warfare notwithstanding, the **decision** itself to go to war is often the result, paradoxically, of *rational choice.* Although interstate wars may not occur as frequently today as they have in the past, they have proven difficult to eliminate precisely because rationally motivated decision makers may see war (or other uses of force resulting in war) as serving their national objectives or purposes. The devastation caused by interstate wars and the very real human and economic costs involved may well be viewed as irrational by outside observers, but the decisions to use force or go to war rarely are—at least not in the minds of those who make them. In fact, they are usually made based on maximizing expected gains or minimizing expected losses consistent with the objectives and the interests of the parties making the decision. This perspective on war as rational choice is most closely associated with realists.

A country's desire to defend territory and the people who live on it is to be expected. When a people or their leaders see the use of force as worth the expected costs, we understand them as rational. Certain cultures (or individuals) may range from peaceful, or pacific, to bellicose, or warlike, but we know from experience that decision makers in all societies or cultures are quite capable of choosing force or going to war if the circumstances—threats and opportunities—and interests so warrant.

Sometimes, when faced by the overwhelming force of an aggressor with virtually no chance of success, the rational choice may well be to surrender as opposed to going to war. The Belgians, having been overrun by the Germans in 1914 at the beginning of World War I, understood only too well that they could not stop the German armed forces in 1939 at the outset of World War II. Why would a people rationally choose to endure the very high human costs of war when the situation could only be made worse by doing so? Surrender, while still pursuing resistance by other means, seemed to be the rational choice. Belgium had no good choices; it would lose whether it fought or surrendered, but surrendering minimized these losses.

In practice, rationality is highly subjective. Deciding which objectives (or expected gains) to pursue and which losses (or expected costs) are acceptable may vary depending on who is making the decision. A disinterested observer may estimate costs and benefits but cannot be sure that those actually making the decisions will see them this way. The value or weight they place on various criteria may be influenced by past experiences and highly subjective perspectives or points of view. Moreover, decisions may have to be made without complete information under conditions of uncertainty or under time and other pressures. Misperceptions and miscalculations, coupled with formation of coalitions, countercoalitions, and other political factors further complicate the decision-making process. As a result decisions in practice may be **suboptimal**— less than the best.

The Causes of War

While the decision to go to war may be viewed as rational from a decision maker's perspective, various factors may influence the calculation. In this section we examine some of the most important causes of war, which shape the ultimate decision to resort to the use of force.

rational choice
A choice that requires a rank ordering of preferences or goals, consideration of alternatives to attain one's goals in light of capabilities, and consideration of costs and benefits typically either to minimize the former or maximize the latter.

Legions of books have been written on the causes of war. For our purposes, these causes can be categorized according to our four basic levels of analysis outlined in Chapter 1—the international system, state and society, group, and the individual.

International System Level of Analysis

It has been argued by realists that interstate wars start because there is nothing to stop them.[3] In an anarchic world, there is no world government or central authority, much less one with the necessary power to constrain states or other organized groups from using force or engaging in warfare. In such a world, some states may choose to use force to achieve their objectives. When these actions confront other states, armed conflict may be the result.

Realists note there was no central authority, for example, among city-states in ancient Greece. In these uncertain circumstances, according to the writer Thucydides, it was fear in Sparta about the rising power of Athens that was the underlying cause of the Peloponnesian War. The Spartan's perception of a change in the distribution of power upset existing security calculations, making them more fearful. Sparta took measures to counter Athenian power before it became too strong; these steps contributed to the onset of war. Above all, there was no authority higher than these city-states to intervene, assure both sides of their security, and preclude them from going to war.

For realists, it is this anarchy or absence of any central authority or government in the ancient world (or in the present one, for that matter) that is the underlying or "permissive" cause of war. It is a self-help system in which states seek to attain their objectives or serve their own interests. International relations have a permissive quality, posing no governmental or other authoritative obstacles to countries wishing to use force to achieve their objectives by such means. A number of constructivists have taken issue with this perspective. They argue that while anarchy may exist, the response does not have to be self-help or power politics. The supposed imperative of self-help is not a given or a fact of nature, but rather a human convention. International systems do not have an independent existence, but are what states make of them—they are socially constructed.[4]

The lack of effective governing authorities with power or capability to keep a society together is perhaps most evident in the case of civil wars—armed conflicts within a given state and society. Even when a central government exists, a civil war may break out if the regime lacks legitimacy, which is acceptance by its population as a whole that it has the right to exercise political authority. In any event, the government also lacks the necessary coercive power (military and police capabilities) to maintain domestic law and order.

Competing governments in the same state and society may emerge, perhaps identified with different national, ethnic, or other identities. In such circumstances, outside states may intervene to support one side or another, creating the possibility of a civil war turning into an interstate war. Intervention can take a number of forms: diplomatic action, aid to one or another of the parties, or other forms of interference, including the use of armed force or armed intervention.

Other systemic-level hypotheses or explanations of war involve such phenomena as conflicts between **alliances** or global security competitions that produce arms races.

---

[3]The analysis in this section draws from Kenneth N. Waltz, *Man, the State and War* (New York: Columbia University Press, 1959).

[4]Alexander Wendt, "Anarchy Is What States Make of It: The Social Construction of Power Politics," *International Organization,* 46, 2 (Spring 1992): 391–425.

Alliances and counteralliances were said to have caused World War I. Secret treaties and war clauses committing states to defend one another if injured or attacked resulted in a chain reaction; as one party mobilized for war, others followed suit. The 1914 assassination in Sarajevo of the Austrian Archduke Franz Ferdinand by a Serbian anarchist was merely the spark or catalyst that set into motion a series of actions and reactions among alliance members that resulted in world war.

Many of those who accepted this explanation for World War I argued strenuously for a world in which the use of force for aggressive purposes was outlawed. Rather than the power and balance-of-power politics of alliances, a collective security system of law-abiding states was finally established after the war in the League of Nations. President Woodrow Wilson was a principal advocate of such a league and also argued for a world of open (rather than secret) covenants among states.

If alliances were the cause of World War I, paradoxically it was the absence of alliances, posing no obstacle to a resurgent Germany, that may have contributed to World War II. As a legal system of obligations, collective security within the League of Nations failed to stop aggression or eliminate the use of force by states acting unilaterally.

That arms races contribute to the onset of war is another systemic-level hypothesis. Richardson's equations (see accompanying box) are sometimes used to explain arms race behaviors that can lead to war. Was it the late-nineteenth- and early-twentieth-century naval and ground-force competition between Britain and France against Germany that was one cause of World War I? If so, could the U.S.–Soviet Cold War arms competition have resulted in the same outcome? What kept the peace? Quantitative and other studies have tried to answer such questions, determining how militarized disputes contribute to the occurrence of war.

Individual and Group Levels of Analysis

If anarchy—the absence of effective central authority—is an underlying or permissive cause of all wars, then a particular war may be influenced by perceptions or misperceptions in a leadership group (if not in the society as a whole) of the intentions and capabilities of an adversary. Psychological and social-psychological factors of individuals or small groups may affect such calculations.

In addition to focusing on perception or misperception, explanations at the individual or small-group levels examine individual psychologies and group dynamics. Thus, some argue that human beings are by nature aggressive, or the personality of an individual leader is a critical factor in a country's decision to go to war. For example, would it have made any difference if Al Gore were president rather than George W. Bush when it came to the decision to go to war against Iraq in 2003? Others argue that the frustration of groups or individuals in group settings can lead to aggressive behavior which, in turn, can lead to war. Particularly in cohesive small groups, there is the danger of members reinforcing each other's mutual biases, leading to a phenomenon known as *groupthink.* The result is that information that contradicts the group's devoutly held beliefs and prejudices is ignored. Critics of the U.S. decision to invade Iraq, for example, noted the prevalence of high-level officials who had served together in the earlier Bush administration and also shared neoconservative values in terms of U.S. national security policy.

State and Societal Levels of Analysis

Finally, it has been argued that the nature of a state or society is critical in explaining the outbreak of war and the propensity of a country to use force. President Woodrow

groupthink
A mode of thinking involving a cohesive group in which the members' striving for unanimity overrides their motivation to appraise realistically alternative courses of action.

RICHARDSON'S ARMS-RACE EQUATIONS

Applying Theory

Arms races and militarized disputes between and among states have been the subject of extensive research using mathematics and statistical analysis. One of the earlier practitioners of this approach was Lewis F. Richardson, who developed differential equations to express formally the relations among variables affecting arms races. The propensity of two countries to engage in arms races is interactive, with the action of one country having causal impact on the other. Equilibrium in an arms race is defined as the point of intersection of lines (or curves) for each equation.

Both Country X and Country Y establish a rate (dx/dt and dy/dt, respectively) by which they increase (a positive number) or decrease (a negative number) the military armaments in their inventories. The opponent's strength (x or y) is an important factor, as is one's own strength (x or y), and the overall climate of relations between the countries (q or r)—a measure of hostility or long-standing grievances between the two.

Richardson subtracts the estimate of one's own strength from that of the arms race opponent. If the difference or gap is increasing, a higher propensity to acquire arms to match a rival is understandable. For Country X this is

$$ay - cx$$

and for Country Y it is

$$bx - dy$$

where a and b are proportionality constants representing a positive orientation or readiness to acquire arms and c and d are proportionality constants representing a disinclination to continue acquiring arms due to fatigue or other costs.

Adding the grievance, hostility, or climate-of-relations factor, full equations for both countries are, for Country X,

$$dx/dt = ay - cx + q$$

and, for Country Y,

$$dy/dt = bx - dy + r$$

Given these relations, one is able to draw inferences about the stability of arms races—their tendency to remain in equilibrium or to break out of it—as changes in the force posture of one party affect changes in the force posture of the other.

Note: For Richardson's treatment, see his *Statistics of Deadly Quarrels* (New York: Quadrangle, 1960) and *Arms and Insecurity* (New York: Quadrangle, 1960). For an excellent discussion and critique, see Anatol Rapoport's *The Origins of Violence* (Brunswick, NJ: Transaction Publishers, 1995), 366–377. A highly readable account of Richardson's work and other action-reaction models is Greg Cashman's *What Causes War?* (New York: Lexington Books, 1993), 172–176.

Wilson and others who shared his views argued that dictators and those within their ruling elite are more prone to choose war than those democratically elected to office and held responsible to the people. In his war address to the U.S. Congress on April 3, 1917, Wilson blamed the war on those who "provoked and waged" it "in the interest of dynasties or of little groups of ambitious men."

Wilson saw the 1914–1918 world war as "the war to end all wars," defeating dictatorship in Germany and the other central European powers and making the world "safe for democracy." In short, the Wilsonian hypothesis was that dictatorships (like "the Prussian autocracy" in Germany) produce war, but democracies produce peace.

The Russian revolutionary leader Vladimir Ilyich Lenin, who came to power in 1917, expressed a different view on what type of state or society was more likely to encourage international peace. Socialist states, representing the interests of the working classes traditionally forced to do the fighting and dying in wars, would be inclined to avoid war. In leading the revolution that overthrew the Tsarist regime in Russia, Lenin argued that capitalist states and societies tend to become imperialist as they compete with each other for markets throughout the world. Lenin viewed World War I as a war among imperial powers, and the new socialist workers regime he headed would have no part of it. Peace was made soon after he and the communist party came to power; Russia pulled out of the war.

Or was the economist Joseph Schumpeter right when he argued, contrary to Lenin, that capitalism would be more conducive to peace?[5] Although arms sellers might register some short-term gains, the net effect of war is to destroy capital—the productive capacity of economies. Because it is the capitalists who own this productive capacity, their real interest is in protecting and expanding capital, not destroying it. According to this reasoning, peace is served by the spread of capitalism and commercial values that displace heroism, gallantry, glory, and other obsolete, war-oriented values of an earlier precapitalist or feudal period.

Although Wilson, Lenin, and Schumpeter differ respectively over whether democracy, socialism, or capitalism is more conducive to peace, all of these arguments have one thing in common: it is the nature of state and society or the political and economic regime that is responsible for increasing or decreasing the likelihood of war. We can apply the observations of Wilson, Lenin, or Schumpeter in broader terms than merely describing the relative likelihood of one or another kind of state or society to engage in war. Worldwide democracy (as in a universal concert or partnership of democratic regimes), worldwide socialism, or worldwide capitalism are alternative, international system-level outcomes that, if achieved, might affect the likelihood of war.

A combination of causes at the individual and small group, state and society, and international system levels undoubtedly accounts for the outbreak of any particular war. The difficult challenge is to determine which ones are salient in any given case. Realist observers of world politics and war, however, would claim that it is the underlying anarchy of the system that allows wars to happen regardless of the specific cause or set of causes of a particular war. Other observers agree.

Consistent with this logic, those who want to eliminate war need to change the underlying world order. The most ambitious world federalists, for example, would replace international anarchy with some form of world government. They would vest a central authority with enough power (including armed forces and police units) to keep component states and societies from going to war.

Responding to plans to end war in Europe by constructing a confederation of states, Jean-Jacques Rousseau did not fault the logic of such schemes (eliminating the anarchy of international relations through world governance) so much as their impracticality. World federalists are quick to respond that the very act of defining world government as an impossibility makes it so. It is a self-fulfilling prophecy. We are not likely to achieve (or even try to achieve) what we have defined as an impossibility.

Even if world government were the solution to interstate war, many would find it undesirable. Different peoples in different societies value their independence in a world of sovereign states and prefer to hold on to a national identity. For those with this view, implementing world government as a remedy for war would be worse than continuing to live with armed conflicts and the use of force.

[5]See his *Capitalism, Socialism and Democracy* (New York: Harper and Row, 1942, 1962).

THE DEMOCRATIC PEACE

Applying Theory

As noted in Chapter 2, Immanuel Kant, the eighteenth-century philosopher, argued that the best way to ensure progress toward peace is to encourage the growth of republics whose constitutional arrangements check or balance competing domestic interests. Particularly with the end of the Cold War, scholars have attempted to answer empirically the question, "Are democracies more peaceful in their foreign relations?" This literature, known as the democratic peace, concludes that democracies are quite capable of using force or going to war, perhaps as much as authoritarian regimes. The related question, however, is whether democracies go to war against each other. The answer is that this rarely if ever happens. The virtual absence of war among democracies has led one scholar to conclude that this is "as close as anything we have to an empirical law in international relations."*

The answer to the question of whether democracies are more peaceful in relation to each other is not merely of academic interest; it has potential foreign policy implications. On the one hand, state support of democratic movements around the world can be justified on the grounds of enhancing the prospects of peaceful relations among states. The George W. Bush administration made this argument, claiming a peaceful and democratic Iraq would be a model and thus have a positive ripple effect on authoritarian regimes in the Middle East, transforming them over time into democracies. On the other hand, however, the literature on the democratic peace can be used (or misused) to justify interventions in the domestic affairs of other states or merely as an excuse to dismiss past acts of aggression by democracies.

Question: How would you respond to these two observations?

*Jack Levy, "The Causes of War: A Review of Theories and Evidence," in Philip E. Tetlock et al., eds., *Behavior, Society, and Nuclear War*, vol. 1 (New York: Oxford University Press), 270.

National Strategy and the Use of Force

The Prussian general and writer Carl von Clausewitz (1780–1831) worked for years on a theory of war and the use of force. He had practical experience, serving both Russia and his native Prussia in wars against the French that ended with the defeat of Napoleon in 1815. Clausewitz accepted an important position in 1818 as director of the German War School, which allowed him time to think, research, and write. His incomplete work *On War* was published in 1832, a year after his death.

The book has had an enormous influence on how states use force to achieve their purposes. To Clausewitz, war was merely one means states might employ to achieve objectives set by political authorities. As such, wars (and the armed forces called upon to fight them) were merely means to accomplish objectives, not ends in themselves. War was not glorified as something good in itself. The only legitimate purpose of war, according to Clausewitz, was to serve political objectives; it is diplomacy by other means:

> War is an instrument of policy; it must necessarily bear its character, it must measure with its scale: the conduct of War, in its great features, is therefore policy itself, which takes up the sword in place of the pen, but does not on that account cease to think according to its own laws.[6]

On War presents chapters on the nature and theory of war, **strategy** and plans for fighting a war, and leadership and **tactics** or methods of combat operations.[7] After establishing that war is an instrument of state policy and, as such, the armed forces are sub-ordinated to the political authorities of the state, Clausewitz specifies the way in which any battle or war is won. He elaborates what constitutes **military necessity** in war.

The military aim is always the same—to destroy or substantially weaken an enemy's warfighting or warmaking capability. Clausewitz observes that "if War is an act of violence to compel the enemy to fulfil our will, then in every case all depends on our overthrowing the enemy, that is, disarming him, and on that alone." More to the point he asserts: "The *military power* [of an enemy] must be destroyed, that is, reduced to such a state as not to be able to prosecute the War."[8] Actions taken in war for this purpose, and this purpose alone, constitute military necessity.

In order "to defeat the enemy" it is necessary to direct and "proportion our efforts to his powers of resistance." The commander searches for, finds, and attacks the enemy's *center of gravity* or focal point, which, if successful, disrupts the enemy's forces, facilitating their destruction. Clausewitz identifies a physical factor—military capabilities (C)—and a moral factor—will to use these means (W)—as two critical and related variables responsible for battlefield effectiveness (E). E is expressed as a "product of two factors which cannot be separated, namely, *the sum of available means* [or capabilities] and the *strength of the Will*."[9] Expressed symbolically this is

$$E = C \times W$$

If either factor C or W declines or approaches zero, so does E. One can lose a battle or an entire war if either military capabilities or will to fight decline, particularly if the enemy has kept up its capabilities and will.

Although Clausewitz does not develop or use the concept of **deterrence,** there is a suggestion of it in his observation that if there is a balance or equilibrium in conflict relations between two states, we can expect peace to be maintained for the time being, at least until one side gains an advantage over the other, thus upsetting the balance. Capabilities and will (or strength of motive to fight) are again key variables: "the equation is made up by the product of the motive and the power."[10]

In its modern formulation, which owes much to Clausewitz, deterrence is a psychological concept. One state makes a credible threat to use military capabilities if another state commits aggression or undertakes some other action the deterring state considers undesirable. The deterred state perceives the deterring state's military capabilities and will to use them in armed conflict and is dissuaded from committing aggression or other offense. Expressed symbolically, deterrence (D) is similar in form to battlefield effectiveness (E). It is the product of perceived capabilities (C) and credibility or will (W) to use them:

$$D = C \times W$$

Prussian general Carl von Clausewitz (1780–1831), noted for his book Vom Kriege (On War), *which advocated the total destruction of an enemy's forces as one of the strategic targets of warfare and seeing war as an extension of political policy and not as an end in itself.*

[6]Carl von Clausewitz, *On War*, Book V, Ch. 6 (B). Originally published as *Vom Kriege* (Berlin: Ferdinand Duemmler, 1832). Readily available English editions include one edited by Anatol Rapoport (New York: Penguin Books, 1968) and one edited and translated by Michael Howard and Peter Paret (Princeton, NJ: Princeton University Press, 1976). Citations in this chapter are taken from the Penguin edition.

[7]Clausewitz defines tactics as "the theory of the use of military forces in combat" and strategy as "the theory of the use of combats for the object of the War." He elaborates that "Strategy forms the plan of the War" and "is the employment of the battle to gain the end [or objective] of the War." Strategy has its "moral, physical, mathematical, geographical, and statistical elements." See *Ibid.*, Book I, Ch. 1, and Book III, Chs. 1 and 2.

[8]*Ibid.*, Book I, Ch. 2.

[9]*Ibid.*, Book I, Ch. 1, Section 5.

[10]*Ibid.*, Book I, Ch. 1, Section 13.

It is, as Clausewitz had it, a multiplicative function: the product of power and motive or will, expressed nowadays more commonly as military capabilities times credibility. If either of these two factors weakens, deterrence becomes unstable or tends to break down. In the extreme cases when either capabilities or credibility approaches, zero, deterrence also goes to zero—it fails.

Among the **principles of war** Clausewitz identifies are mass (other things aside, the "superiority of numbers" as when "the greatest possible number of troops" is "brought into action at the decisive point"), **surprise** (achieving military successes through "secrecy and rapidity"), **concentration of forces** (maximizing their collective strength or impact "at the decisive point"), and **economy of force** (a conservative approach that avoids "waste of forces, which is even worse than their employment to no purpose").[11]

Success in war also depends on military leadership with strong mental and organizational capabilities. He calls for officers with strong mental "power of discrimination" and "good judgment."[12] This is particularly important because of the complexities and uncertainties commanders face in war. Things in war often do not go according to even the best-laid plans. Clausewitz refers to this as **friction.**

In physics or mechanics, we calculate on paper or chalkboard the forces we expect will operate on an object in an ideal situation. We try to predict its motion—its velocity or speed and direction—perhaps drawing a diagram specifying the forces with vectors or arrows. As a practical matter, of course, we learn that in the real world the motion of objects is impeded or slowed by friction, which is often difficult to measure in advance. We can get a sense of how much friction is involved through experimental trials, and we may decide to take corrective measures to reduce friction by lubricating the surface or streamlining the object. One may reduce friction, but it cannot be eliminated entirely.

So it is with plans for war drawn up in peacetime or in an office setting. According to Clausewitz, a great gap exists between the "conception" of war and its "execution." As he puts it: "Everything is very simple in War, but the simplest thing is difficult. These difficulties accumulate and produce a friction which no one can imagine exactly who has not seen War." He adds that "incidents take place" in war, change in weather for example, that are virtually "impossible to calculate, their chief origin being chance." At best one can conduct military exercises or experimental trials to try to identify and correct major sources of friction.[13]

Through such measures one may be able to reduce the friction that comes from taking war plans off the shelf and putting them into practice, but one cannot eliminate the effect entirely. Compounding the effects of friction and contributing to it is what Clausewitz called the **fog of war**—the sum of all uncertainties and unpredictable occurrences that can happen so rapidly in war.

Clausewitz understood war as a **zero-sum** phenomenon: One side's gain is the other's loss: "In a battle both sides strive to conquer. . . . The victory of one side destroys that of the other."[14] But Clausewitz was never an advocate of war for war's own sake. Given his own participation in the wars against Napoleon's armies, Clausewitz had observed the awful consequences of armed conflict and worried about "its character" as it "approaches the form of absolute War." More than a century before the nuclear age, Clausewitz expressed his concerns about circumstances when general or total war

---

[11]*Ibid.*, Book III, Chs. 8, 9, 11, and 14.

[12]*Ibid.,* Book I, Ch. 6.

[13]*Ibid.,* Book I, Chs. 6–8.

[14]*Ibid.*, Book I, Ch. 1, Section 15.

Case & Point

THE FUTURE OF WAR: HIGH-TECH OR LOW-TECH?

The Revolution in Military Affairs (RMA) is part of the revolutionary shift from an industrial to an information-based society. The information revolution is a result of advances in computerized information and telecommunications technologies but also innovations in organizational theory. Not surprisingly, the United States has been the leader in developing theoretical and operational concepts related to RMA. The RMA is perhaps best illustrated by the use of high-technology weapons in the 1991 coalition war against Iraq, the 1999 NATO air war against Serbia, and the U.S.–led war against Iraq in 2003. Cockpit video footage of laser-guided smart bombs finding their way uncannily to their targets was a staple of nightly news broadcasts. When the air war against Serbia was over, NATO could claim a victory in which there were no allied casualties. This was certainly an unprecedented event in the history of warfare. When major combat operations in Iraq were over in 2003, the Iraqi army went from the fourth largest in the world to the second largest in Iraq.

Martin van Creveld has argued that a fundamental change in how war is waged is not new. He identifies four eras of military history. In the "Age of Tools" (lasting to about A.D. 1500), most technology was driven by the strength of the muscles of men and animals. Bronze and iron weapons, the stirrup, and wheeled vehicles are examples. The hallmark of the "Age of the Machine" was the organization and institutionalization of a society's natural resources for conducting war utilizing a mass army. Napoleon's army epitomizes the trend of using manpower mass in wars across great distances. The "Age of Systems" involved the integration of technology into complex networks. The culmination was in World War II with the innovative application of mechanization, aviation, and communications technology. The German development and employment of the *blitzkrieg* is one example. Van Creveld terms the period since World War II the "Age of Automation," due to the vast amounts of information needed to wage wars. Information is required to run a military unit on the ground, conduct air campaigns, or wage wars in general. To digest all of this information requires the use of computers. This revolutionary change in the conduct of war, however, requires more than advanced technologies; it also requires complementary organizations that can adapt and change their structure to maximize the value of the technology.*

Advanced industrial states may be investing in the latest high-tech weaponry, but van Creveld and other military historians have noted another trend in terms of the nature of war—the expansion and intensification of low-intensity conflicts. According to Ralph Peters, crises of state authority in countries around the world have opened the floodgates to civil disorder with important implications in terms of wars and warfighting:

> The enemies we are likely to face will not be "soldiers," with the disciplined modernity that term conveys in Euro-America, but "warriors"—erratic primitives of shifting allegiance, habituated to violence, with no stake in civil order. Unlike soldiers, warriors do not obey orders they do not like. Warriors have always been around, but with the rise of the professional soldiers, their importance was eclipsed. Now, thanks to a unique confluence of breaking empire, overcultivated Western consciences, and a worldwide cultural crisis, the warrior is back, as brutal and distinctly better armed.**

Questions: Are countries such as the United States, which devotes billions of dollars to field large armies, air forces, and navies, preparing for the wrong type of war? How useful is technology in fighting low-intensity conflicts?

Point: Throughout history changes in technology have affected how warfare is conducted.

---

*To learn more about the changes in warfare through the centuries, see Martin van Creveld, *Technology and War: From 2000 B.C. to the Present* (New York: Free Press, 1989), Michael Howard, *War in European History* (Oxford: Oxford University Press, 1976), and John Keegan, *A History of Warfare* (New York: Knopf, 1993).

**Ralph Peters, *Fighting for the Future* (Mechanicsburg, PA: Stockpole Books, 1999), 2, 32.

---

is the expected outcome. He counseled how necessary it is "not to take the first step" into such a war "without thinking what may be the last."[15]

Restraining War: Moral and Legal Principles and the Use of Force

Pacifism and Bellicism

Pacifism is a philosophical position that in its purest sense rejects all forms of war and any use of force as legitimate means for attaining objectives, resolving conflicts, or any other purpose. Its opposite—a bellicose orientation or **bellicism**[16]—either sees value in war itself or at least understands war as so essential a part of world politics that it cannot be avoided.[17]

Bellicists tend to discount the human costs of armed conflict, observing that war also produces people willing to make sacrifices, who exhibit courage and outright bravery in the face of danger, industriousness, loyalty, obedience, and other martial values a society may wish to cultivate. Taken to the absurd extreme, war is seen to be a "purifying bath of blood and iron,"[18] presumably a therapeutic effect for society as a whole.

Pacifism or commitment to nonviolence is a perfectly defensible philosophical or moral position. The same cannot be said for bellicism, which sees positive value in violence and the use of force. Just because we live in a world prone to violence does not mean that violence is morally right or good in itself, particularly not in an age when war can lead to mass destruction on an unprecedented scale. The principal challenge to pacifism, of course, is also the question of its practicality in an anarchic world, in which states and even nonstate actors may use force to attain their objectives.

Just-War Theory

normative theory
A value-oriented or philosophical theory that focuses on what ought to be.

Just-war theory (sometimes called just-war doctrine) is an example of *normative theory* that prescribes right conduct—how states and their agents *ought* to act. International law concerning war—the law of armed conflicts—rests on treaty obligations,

---

[15]*Ibid.*, Book V, Ch. 3 (A).

[16]The term is used by James E. Dougherty and Robert L. Pfaltzgraff, Jr., *Contending Theories of International Relations* (New York: Lippincott, 1971), 164.

[17]For example, see Niccolo Machiavelli, *The Prince*, Ch. xiv.

[18]The quote is sometimes attributed to Georg Hegel, although the attribution may be apocryphal.

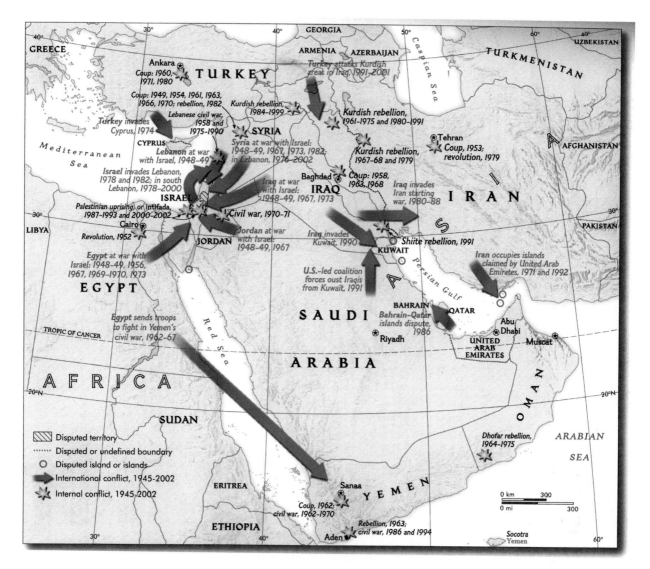

MAP 5.1   *Middle East Regional Conflicts, 1945–2003. The U.S.-led military invasion of Iraq in 2003 and subsequent insurgency are simply the latest in an ongoing series of political and military conflicts in the Middle East.*
Source: Copyright National Geographic Society. Reproduced by permission.

customary practice, the writings of jurists, and general principles closely linked to just-war theory. This theory adopts a position between the pacifist and bellicist positions but is somewhat closer to the pacifist pole because it seeks to avoid war or, failing that, to limit its destructive consequences. Every effort is made to avoid armed conflict in the first place:

Pacifism   Just-War Theory   Bellicism

The War Prayer

by Mark Twain

It was a time of great and exalting excitement. The country was up in arms, the war was on, in every breast burned the holy fire of patriotism; the drums were beating, the bands playing, the toy pistols popping, the bunched firecrackers hissing and spluttering; on every hand and far down the receding and fading spread of roofs and balconies a fluttering wilderness of flags flashed in the sun; daily the young volunteers marched down the wide avenue gay and fine in their new uniforms, the proud fathers and mothers and sisters and sweethearts cheering them with voices choked with happy emotion as they swung by; nightly the packed mass meetings listened, panting, to patriot oratory which stirred the deepest deeps of their hearts and which they interrupted at briefest intervals with cyclones of applause, the tears running down their cheeks the while; in the churches the pastors preached devotion to flag and country and invoked the God of Battles beseeching His aid in our good cause in outpouring of fervid eloquence which moved every listener. It was indeed a glad and gracious time, and the half dozen rash spirits that ventured to disapprove of the war and cast a doubt upon its righteousness straightway got such a stern and angry warning that for their personal safety's sake they quickly shrank out of sight and offended no more in that way.

Sunday morning came—next day the battalions would leave for the front; the church was filled; the volunteers were there, their young faces alight with martial dreams—visions of the stern advance, the gathering momentum, the rushing charge, the flashing sabers, the flight of the foe, the tumult, the enveloping smoke, the fierce pursuit, the surrender!—then home from the war, bronzed heroes, welcomed, adored, submerged in golden seas of glory! With the volunteers sat their dear ones, proud, happy, and envied by the neighbors and friends who had no sons and brothers to send forth to the field of honor, there to win for the flag or, failing, die the noblest of noble deaths. The service proceeded; a war chapter from the Old Testament was read; the first prayer was said; it was followed by an organ burst that shook the building, and with one impulse the house rose, with glowing eyes and beating hearts, and poured out that tremendous invocation—

"God the all-terrible! Thou who ordainest,

Thunder thy clarion and lightning thy sword!"

Then came the "long" prayer. None could remember the like of it for passionate pleading and moving and beautiful language. The burden of its supplication was that an ever-merciful and benignant Father of us all would watch over our noble young soldiers and aid, comfort, and encourage them in their patriotic work; bless them, shield them in the day of battle and the hour of peril, bear them in His mighty hand, make them strong and confident, invincible in the bloody onset; help them to crush the foe, grant to them and to their flag and country imperishable honor and glory—

An aged stranger entered and moved with slow and noiseless step up the main aisle, his eyes fixed upon the minister, his long body clothed in a robe that reached his feet, his head bare, his white hair descending in a frothy cataract to his shoulders, his seamy face unnaturally pale, pale even to ghastliness. With all eyes following him and wondering, he made his silent way; without pausing, he ascended to the preacher's side and stood there, waiting. With shut lids the preacher, unconscious of his presence, continued his moving prayer, and at last finished it with the words, uttered in fervent appeal, "Bless our arms, grant us the victory, O Lord our God, Father and Protector of our land and flag!"

The stranger touched his arm, motioned him to step aside—which the startled minister did—and took his place. During some moments he surveyed the spellbound audience with solemn eyes in which burned an uncanny light; then in a deep voice he said:

"I come from the Throne—bearing a message from Almighty God!" The words smote the house with a shock; if the stranger perceived it he gave no attention. "He has heard the prayer of His servant your shepherd and will grant it if such shall be your desire after I, His messenger, shall have explained to you its import—that is to say, its full import. For it is like unto many of the prayers of men, in that it asks for more than he who utters it is aware of—except he pause and think.

"God's servant and yours has prayed his prayer. Has he paused and taken thought? Is it one prayer? No, it is two—one uttered, the other not. Both have reached the ear of Him Who heareth all supplications, the spoken and the unspoken. Ponder this—keep it in mind. If you would beseech a blessing upon yourself, beware! lest without intent you invoke a curse upon a neighbor at the same time. If you pray for the blessing of rain upon your crop which needs it, by that act you are possibly praying for a curse upon some neighbor's crop which may not need rain and can be injured by it.

"You have heard your servant's prayer—the uttered part of it. I am commissioned of God to put into words the other part of it—that part which the pastor, and also you in your hearts, fervently prayed silently. And ignorantly and unthinkingly? God grant that it was so! You heard these words: 'Grant us the victory, O Lord our God!' That is sufficient. The whole of the uttered prayer is compact into those pregnant words. Elaborations were not necessary. When you have prayed for victory you have prayed for many unmentioned results which follow victory—*must* follow it, cannot help but follow it. Upon the listening spirit of God the Father fell also the unspoken part of the prayer. He commandeth me to put it into words. Listen!

"O Lord our Father, our young patriots, idols of our hearts, go forth to battle—be Thou near them! With them, in spirit, we also go forth from the sweet peace of our beloved firesides to smite the foe. O Lord our God, help us to tear their soldiers to bloody shreds with our shells; help us to cover their smiling fields with the pale forms of their patriot dead; help us to drown the thunder of the guns with the shrieks of their wounded, writhing in pain; help us to lay waste their humble homes with a hurricane of fire; help us to wring the hearts of their unoffending widows with unavailing grief; help us to turn them out roofless with their little children to wander unfriended the wastes of their desolated land in rags and hunger and thirst, sports of the sun flames of summer and the icy winds of winter, broken in spirit, worn with travail, imploring Thee for the refuge of the grave and denied it—for our sakes who adore Thee, Lord, blast their hopes, blight their lives, protract their bitter pilgrimage, make heavy their steps, water their way with their tears, stain the white snow with the blood of their wounded feet! We ask it, in the spirit of love, of Him Who is the Source of Love, and Who is the ever-faithful refuge and friend of all that are sore beset and seek His aid with humble and contrite hearts. Amen.

(After a pause) "Ye have prayed it; if ye still desire it, speak! The messenger of the Most High waits."

It was believed afterward that the man was a lunatic, because there was no sense in what he said.

Source: Mark Twain, *Europe and Elsewhere.* Copyright 1923, 1951 by The Mark Twain Company.

Just-war theory, encompassing both *jus ad bellum* (the right to go to war) and *jus in bello* (right conduct in war), comes from a long tradition in Western thought that can be traced to Plato (427–347 B.C.). The first explicit reference to the just-war concept is from Plato's Roman follower Cicero (106–43 B.C.), who stated that "just wars should be fought justly."[19] The ideas elaborated by Cicero in a non-Judaic, pre-Christian context were developed further by St. Augustine, who presented it as an alternative to pacifism that had been dominant in the early Christian Church. Aquinas (1225–1274), Vitoria (1480–1546), Suarez (1548–1617), Gentili (1552–1608), and other writers contributed further to establishing just-war concepts as a more formal philosophical or moral foundation upon which international law concerning war would come to rest.

Building on the work of Suarez and Gentili, who had dealt with legal aspects of just-war theory, the Dutchman Hugo Grotius (1583–1645) incorporated much of just-war thinking in his writings on international law. His *Law of War and Peace* (first published in Latin in 1625 as *De Bellum ac Pacis*) took just-war theory from its moral or theological base to develop what would become legally binding principles. As with other international law, the **law of war** has been drawn from general principles, customary practice, formal treaties, court cases, and the writings of jurists. The Hague Conventions and Regulations (1899 and 1907) and Geneva Conventions and Protocols (1949 and 1977) represent a formalization or codification of the modern-day law of war.

The *jus ad bellum,* or right to go to war, depends first and foremost upon having a just cause, such as when a country comes under attack by an aggressor state. Second, the decision to go to war cannot be made by anyone; it must be made by the legitimate authority within the state. Determining which is the legitimate authority is not always an easy matter, of course, particularly not in civil wars within a state when each side contends that it is *the* legitimate authority. Third, just-war theory dictates that resort to armed force as an option must first of all be proportionate to the provocation, not a disproportionate response to a relatively minor cause. Fourth, there also must be some chance of success, or resort to war would be a futile enterprise wasting lives and property unnecessarily. Finally, war is the *last* resort. The decision to use armed force should be delayed whenever possible until every reasonable peaceful means for settling the dispute have been exhausted.

Satisfying all of these criteria depends heavily on right intention. If decision makers are not committed to doing the right thing, no set of moral or legal principles can be effective. Clever political leaders and diplomats can always find ways to skirt any set of rules, perhaps even manipulating them in an elaborate rationalization of their conduct. Critics of just-war theory make precisely this point. The historical record suggests to them that more often than not the practitioners of statecraft have manipulated just-war principles to justify some rather unjust causes. Even if this is so, of course, it is more a criticism of the orientation and conduct of many leaders and diplomats than it is an effective assault on the logic of the just-war position. Defenders of just-war theory use this same evidence to underscore the need for greater compliance with a practical mechanism for avoiding war, especially in an age when the mass-destructive consequences of war are so great. Given these criteria, it is worthy of some thought as to whether the decision of the United States to invade Iraq in 2003 met the standards of a just war.

---

[19]See Cicero, *The Republic*, II: xxvii, III: xxiii, xxiv, and xxix, and *The Laws*, II: ix, xiv, and III: iii, xviii.

These conditions for a just war are very demanding. They clearly are skewed in the direction of avoiding war if at all possible. As such they stand much closer to the pacifist than to the bellicist pole. War is not to be sought.

Conduct during War

Just-war theory does not confine itself merely to whether one has a right to use armed force or resort to war in international relations. It goes beyond the *jus ad bellum* to raise questions of right conduct in war once armed conflict breaks out. Another set of principles governs right conduct in war *(jus in bello),* whether or not the decision to go to war was just. Very real limits are set in an effort to limit or confine the death and destruction of warfare to what is militarily necessary thus reducing war's barbarity.

The principle of military necessity can be construed so broadly as to allow almost any conduct in war, if political authorities or military commanders do not approach the use of force with a spirit consistent with the human-cost reduction purpose of just-war theory. It is a narrow construction of military necessity that is prescribed by just-war theory. Consistent with the earlier discussion of Clausewitz's theory of war, armed force is used only to destroy or substantially weaken an enemy's war-making capability.

Destroying an enemy's war-making capability focuses destructive efforts on an adversary's armed forces and *only* those parts of the society's infrastructure that directly contribute to its war-making effort. It is not a call to destroy an entire society, its population, or anything else of material or cultural value. People will still be killed and property destroyed, but probably far less damage will be sustained when the principle of military necessity is narrowly interpreted to limit the destructiveness of war to what is absolutely necessary for military purposes.

Obliteration bombing of cities or other population centers was widely practiced by both sides in World War II. At the time, many defenders of this strategy saw these raids as undermining societal morale in enemy countries, thus weakening an enemy's will to resist. But postwar evaluation of strategic bombing and other uses of air power raised a serious challenge to this rationale. Rage among survivors contributed in many cases to an increased will to resist rather than to submit. If so, then obliteration bombing proved to be counterproductive or dysfunctional, even militarily speaking.

With the benefit of hindsight, obliteration bombing of population centers has been discredited both militarily and morally in the years since World War II. Put another way, there can be no moral justification under just-war doctrine for such mass death and destruction, particularly because these military actions did not serve legitimate military purposes. Just because military purposes are served, of course, is not enough to justify *any* conduct in war. Additional conditions need to be met to satisfy *jus in bello* obligations.

Noncombatants

An effort must be made to spare noncombatants and other defenseless persons. Guilty or not, noncombatants—civilian populations—are not the proper object of warfare. Even captured enemy soldiers are now defenseless persons who may be taken prisoner but may not be executed just because they are prisoners. Prisoners of war (sometimes called PWs or POWs) have rights, and these have been made part of international law. This is why the establishment of the prison at Guantanamo Bay, Cuba, by the United States has been so controversial. The prison was established following the overthrow of the Taliban in Afghanistan in the fall of 2001 to hold suspected terrorists. The U.S. government, relying

The human cost of war: A wounded soldier in World War I (1914-1918). It is estimated there were 7.7 million battlefield deaths in this conflict.

on laws dating back to the Civil War and World War II, declared that these individuals were not prisoners of war, but rather "enemy combatants" held as "detainees." As a result, they could not invoke the international legal rights associated with prisoners of war—a perspective disputed by critics of American prison policies in Cuba and elsewhere.

A distinction is often drawn between **counterforce** and **countervalue** targets. Counterforce targets include military headquarters, troop or tank formations, combat aircraft, ships, maintenance facilities, and other military installations the destruction of which would directly weaken an enemy's war-making capability. Countervalue targets are factories, rail junctions, civilian airports, and power plants in or near cities that contribute to an enemy's war-making capability or overall war effort. Even if people are not the intended victims, the bombing of countervalue targets usually produces more civilian, noncombatant casualties than counterforce targeting.

Moreover the means used to accomplish military purposes need to be proportional to the goal. If a 300-pound bomb can be used to destroy a particular military target, a 10,000-pound ought not to be used, particularly if doing so increases the **collateral destruction** of lives and property. In the same spirit, navy warships may choose to avoid sinking an enemy merchant ship by disabling the propeller, so they can board and search the cargo instead. Just-war theory aims to reduce unnecessary death or other damage.

Some just-war theorists invoke the **dual** or **double-effect principle** in dealing with the moral problem of killing noncombatants and producing collateral damage

Iraqi death list. Friends and family search lists of confirmed dead in 2003. Photo by Fred Abrahams and reproduced by permission of Human Rights Watch.

in warfare. Any action may have two or more effects or consequences. If the intent is to destroy a legitimate target that contributes to an enemy's war-making capability or overall war effort, then every reasonable effort must be made to avoid unnecessary casualties or other destruction. The "good effect" is destroying the legitimate military target. Dropping bombs, sending missiles, landing artillery shells, or firing on such a target may also have unintended human and material consequences—the "bad effect."

Following double-effect logic and assuming proportionality—that the target is worth destroying in light of its military value when weighed against the expected consequences—just-war theorists argue that killing noncombatants or destroying civilian property may be morally justifiable *when both effects occur simultaneously or the good effect precedes the bad*. For example, in targeting an armaments factory at night when most workers were expected to be at home, it is accepted that a few workers may still be killed when the factory is destroyed. Or a bomb may go astray and kill some people in a residential area next to the factory, even though efforts were made to avoid this unfortunate outcome. That is the misfortune of war. Bad things happen in war, which is why just-war theory puts so much emphasis on avoiding war in the first place. Principles by which wars need to be examined in order to be deemed just are outlined in Table 5.1.

If warriors *intend* the bad effect or if it precedes the good, such conduct does not satisfy the principle of double effect and is, therefore, morally wrong. Bombing workers at their homes next to the armaments factory (the bad effect) will likely reduce or eliminate the production capacity of the factory (the good effect, militarily speaking). The problem is that this good effect depends upon achieving the bad effect first. However good one's objectives or purposes may be, just-war theorists argue that good ends cannot justify evil means: *the ends do not justify the means*. It would be wrong to bomb the village. If factory production must be halted, then the factory itself should be targeted, preferably at a time when as many workers as possible can be spared.

TABLE 5.1
Just-War Principles

JUS AD BELLUM	JUS IN BELLO
1. Just cause	1. Military necessity
2. Legitimate authority	2. Spare noncombatants and other defenseless persons
3. Proportionality of war	3. Proportional means
4. Chance of success	4. Means not immoral *per se:* not indiscriminate or causing needless suffering
5. War as last resort; exhaust peaceful means to resolve dispute	

Note: Application of all principles assumes right intention.

Any weapon can be used immorally, but some could not be used morally even if one intended to do so. Immoral weapons are those that are indiscriminate or cause needless suffering. A rifle is not immoral in itself; if used properly it can be used with discrimination, sparing noncombatants. If used improperly to murder noncombatants, for example, it is the action and not the weapon that is immoral.

The same is true for most conventional bombs delivered accurately by airplanes or missiles. They can be used morally or immorally, depending for the most part on the target selected and how it is to be destroyed. The more accurate the better is true from both a military and a moral position. Indeed, destruction of a legitimate military target is more likely, and collateral or unnecessary death and destruction, if not eliminated, can at least be minimized if accurate weapons are employed.

Chemical and Biological Weapons   By contrast wildly inaccurate weapons—including chemical or biological agents as in gas or germ warfare—by their very nature eliminate the distinction between combatant and noncombatant. Such weapons usually are not useful militarily, as winds disperse chemical agents indiscriminately, and diseases can spread to both sides of the battlefield. Such weapons are immoral in themselves and have been declared illegal.

Treaties prohibit use of chemical and biological weapons. The international consensus that led to these chemical and biological conventions rests on this moral argument. Not only are these weapons indiscriminate, they fail another moral test by causing needless suffering. Rifle bullets or other antipersonnel weapons designed to prolong or otherwise increase agony also fail this moral test. Killing in war is supposed to be as humane as possible. Most categories of weapons that are intended to enhance rather than reduce human suffering have also been defined in treaties as illegal.

Nuclear Weapons   Nuclear weapons are a more controversial case. The two atomic bombs that the United States dropped on the Japanese cities of Hiroshima and Nagasaki in 1945 were justified by many on the **utilitarian** grounds that the bombings would shorten the war. Those who made this argument saw the loss of life at Hiroshima and Nagasaki as precluding an even greater loss of life that would have resulted from an Allied invasion of the Japanese home islands. The Japanese had fought tenaciously to defend islands in the Pacific such as Iwo Jima and Guam; it was believed they would fight with even greater determination to defend their homeland. Others questioned the morality of bombing people even for this purpose, suggesting that if the bombs were to be used at all they should have been directed toward strictly military targets, not population centers interspersed with military targets. Decision makers responded that the Japanese leaders could take the blame, as they made the decision to locate military-related plants where they did.

Each of the weapons dropped on Japan was less than 20 kilotons (20,000 tons) in yield. Many nuclear weapons today have a much larger megaton (million tons) yield, with such heat, blast, and radiation effects that they cannot be used with discrimination, so these weapons fail on human-suffering grounds as well. On the other hand, some have argued that lower-yield, tactical nuclear weapons (perhaps as small as one kiloton or less, with reduced-radiation effects) can be used with discrimination and need not cause unnecessary suffering.

Critics are skeptical of this claim. They also counter that using any nuclear weapons at all "opens Pandora's box," legitimating this category of weaponry and increasing the likelihood that even larger nuclear weapons will be employed by one or another of the parties. Indicative of the lack of consensus on these issues, and unlike chemical and biological agents, nuclear weapons have not yet been declared illegal, however ill advised or immoral their use might be.

Law, Armed Intervention, and World Politics

The 1928 Pact of Paris (or Kellogg-Briand Pact) was an unsuccessful attempt to eliminate the use of force in international relations, outlawing "recourse to war for the solution of international controversies." Hope was placed in world peace through law in a system of **collective security** under the League of Nations. As such, collective security is different from **collective defense**—alliances or coalitions that rely ultimately on armed defense or military power rather than law.

The League of Nations tried to substitute law-abiding behavior for individual and collective-defense relations based on power, balance of power, and military might. Law-abiding states under collective-security arrangements enforce international law against law-breaking states. But the League of Nations seemed powerless to counter such aggressive actions as French intervention in Germany and the Italian capture of the Mediterranean island of Corfu (1923), the outbreak of the China-Japan war (1931), the Bolivia–Paraguay Chaco war (1932–1935), Italy's invasion of Ethiopia (1935), Germany's annexation of Austria and part of Czechoslovakia (1938), and finally the outbreak of World War II in 1939.

In an attempt to put the lessons of the interwar period to practical effect, the United Nations Charter (1945) does specify conditions under which force may legally be used:

1. *Unilaterally* in self-defense
2. *Multilaterally* when authorized by the U.N. Security Council "to maintain or restore international peace and security"
3. *Multilaterally* by regional collective defense action[20]

Armed interventions occur frequently enough, sometimes justified by the participants as serving humanitarian purposes or as a measure to maintain or restore international

---

[20]See the U.N. Charter, Articles 39–54 in the Appendix of Chapter 6 of this book.

peace and security—a broad grant of legal authority for U.N.–sponsored actions. In a world of sovereign states, intervention, especially armed intervention, in the domestic affairs of another state is normally prohibited under international law. Article 2 of the U.N. Charter establishes the United Nations "on the principle of sovereign equality of all its Members." Members pledge themselves to "settle their international disputes by peaceful means" and to "refrain in their international relations from the threat or use of force against the territorial integrity or political independence of any state."

States that have suffered violation of their legal rights may choose arbitration, mediation, or a judicial remedy as offered by the International Court of Justice or an appropriate regional or national court. The critical weakness, however, is that these tribunals do not have enforcement powers.

As a practical matter, therefore, force remains very much a part of international relations. In an anarchic world that lacks a central government or other governing authority with the power to enforce international law, sovereign states do not always comply with such legal authorizations and restrictions. States sometimes choose to violate or ignore their obligations under international law. At other times, political leaders and diplomats have proven to be quite capable of interpreting or manipulating legal principles to justify what they already have done or plan to do in any event.

Intervention and Civil Wars

If applying international law is difficult in the case of interstate wars, it is even more complicated when the conflict is internal to a particular state and society—a civil war. Given the crises of authority faced by so many states today, it is not surprising that internal wars, not interstate wars, are the most likely threat to international peace and security. It is often difficult to contain civil wars within the borders of the affected state. Quite apart from outside interference, civil wars can spill beyond their borders and become interstate wars.

Even when motives are legitimate and not contrived, intervention in the domestic affairs of sovereign states conflicts with a long-established principle of international law that prohibits them. Consider the American Civil War (1861–1865) and the debate in Great Britain as to whether or not Britain should support the South. The southern states claimed sovereignty as the Confederate States of America and sought outside assistance in their struggle against the United States of America, from whom they claimed to be separate.

The Lincoln administration in Washington denied the South's claim, arguing that the southern states had no right to secede from the Union in the first place. Thus, to Lincoln it was not a war between sovereign states, but rather a civil war fought between loyal U.S. armed forces and those loyal to the rebellious states. Through careful diplomacy, Washington made its interpretation of events clear to the British, stressing that outside intervention was illegal. Whether they accepted the Lincoln administration's rationale or not, London chose not to intervene either diplomatically or militarily.

Determining the difference between an interstate war and a civil war is often difficult. American armed intervention in Vietnam, for example, was justified by the United States as coming to the defense of South Vietnam (the Republic of Vietnam) against aggression from North Vietnam (the Democratic Republic of Vietnam). If this were factually correct, then going to the aid of a victim of aggression was legitimate under international law. On the other hand, if the situation in Vietnam were understood as a civil war, with a single state torn between two rival governments and an insurgent movement tied to one of the parties, then outside intervention in such an internal matter would not have been legitimate under international law.

The war in Vietnam was fought not only by the regular forces of North and South Vietnam, the United States, the Republic of Korea, and Australia; it also involved **guerrilla warfare,** supported by North Vietnam. This capitalized on North Vietnam's ties with the people in the countryside. By using antigovernment and ideological appeals, knowledge of the terrain, and the protective cover of the jungle canopy, these nonuniformed irregulars (or guerrillas) conducted a very successful campaign against the South Vietnamese government and its allies. This guerrilla warfare included terrorism, ambushes, rocket attacks, and sometimes even firefights with regular forces. These guerrillas were part of an insurgent movement or antigovernment **insurgency** that, coupled with the efforts of North Vietnamese regulars, eventually succeeded in winning the war and wresting control of the South Vietnamese government.

The former Yugoslavia provides another example of the important distinction between *civil* war and *interstate* war. Serbs opposed both the secession of "breakaway republics" and their recognition in the early 1990s by outside states as independent, sovereign states. From the Serbian perspective, the ensuing war among competing parties was really a civil war precluding any legal right to intervention by outside parties. Having been recognized as separate, independent, and sovereign states by U.N. members, however, Croatia, Slovenia, and Bosnia-Herzogovina were seen by other observers as engaging in a war among states against Serbia. As an interstate war, then, outside intervention by the U.N., NATO, or other legitimate authorities acting in compliance with the U.N. Charter was presented as legitimate.

Humanitarian Intervention

In the absence of an invitation from the legitimate government of a state, even **humanitarian intervention**—using force to stop the fighting among competing groups, provide the necessary security to feed starving people, or halting ethnic cleansing—legally violates the principle of nonintervention in the domestic affairs of a state. The U.N. Charter does not give the Security Council authority to use force for humanitarian purposes *per se*. Armed intervention under U.N. auspices in the internal affairs of a state, however justifiable the humanitarian purpose might seem, is legitimate in this strict interpretation only if the problem cannot likely be contained, thus posing a threat to international peace and security.

The case of Kosovo in 1999 illustrates this point. No one denied that Kosovo was a province of Yugoslavia. The Serbs stated that whatever actions they took in the province were, therefore, an internal matter, and outside intervention was a violation of Yugoslavian sovereignty. The Serbian policy of systematic ethnic cleansing, however, led to NATO military action on the grounds of humanitarian intervention and the claim that Serbian actions were a threat to regional peace and security. It is significant that NATO did not ask for the blessing of the United Nations for NATO's air campaign, given opposition within the U.N. Security Council on both political and legal grounds.

Humanitarian motives may genuinely accompany actions taken primarily for national-interest reasons. In other cases, however, humanitarian motives are presented as a pretext used by political leaders and diplomats in an effort to justify armed interventions done exclusively (or almost entirely) for national-interest reasons. Propagandists like to present humanitarian purposes for armed intervention to make the behavior seem less self-serving.

COMPETING CRITERIA FOR DECISIONS ON ARMED INTER- VENTION

Applying Theory

Events in 1989 brought an end to the Cold War but not to armed intervention. Subsequent years have been marked by a continuation of armed intervention by outside states and multilateral coalitions of states as in responses to Iraq's armed intervention and takeover of Kuwait, civil strife in Somalia and Haiti, and genocide in the Balkan states and central Africa. Policy makers face decisions about whether or not to intervene with armed force to respond to aggression, prevent or stop genocide, restore order, or maintain the peace.

Both economic and military capabilities as well as domestic political support (or opposition) typically are part of the decision-making calculus. We can also identify at least five additional and often competing criteria or factors typically weighed by policy makers considering armed intervention. Moreover political support for (or opposition to) armed intervention is often expressed in terms of one or more of these criteria:

SOVEREIGNTY

Under international law, states are normally prohibited from intervention in the domestic affairs of other sovereign states unless requested by the legitimate government of the state subject to such intervention; however, use of force (including armed intervention) is allowed under the U.N. Charter:

- For collective security as when the Security Council authorizes using force in response to a contingency endangering international peace and security (Chapter VII, particularly Article 42)
- For self-defense or collective defense by alliances or coalitions of states as in responding to aggression against a sovereign state (Chapter VII, Article 51)

NATIONAL INTEREST

Armed intervention is an option often weighed against considerations of national interest and related national objectives. Some argue that armed intervention should be pursued only if there is a vital national interest to be served. Even if one considers this criterion to be decisive, as many realists do, there is no escaping the practical difficulty in trying to define precisely what the national interest (much less vital national interest) might be in a particular case. The national interest is subject to multiple interpretations, but even with this ambiguity, it remains part of the decision-making calculus.

HUMAN RIGHTS

A consensus has been forming, mainly in the last half of the twentieth century, that continues to the present and holds that human beings have rights that may supersede those claimed by sovereign states. This human rights consensus rests on increasing understanding and acceptance of respect for life, human dignity, and justice or fairness as universal ethical or moral principles that have global application to individuals, groups, and other categories or classes of human beings. Both unilateral and multilateral, voluntary assistance for relief in natural disasters is one manifestation of these principles in action. The enormous human and material cost suffered by the victims of mass destruction and atrocities throughout the twentieth century resulted in substantial growth in international law (codified by numerous treaties coming into force after World War II) which has come to (1) define certain civil or political, social, and economic rights and (2) prohibit certain acts defined as war crimes, genocide, and other crimes against peace and humanity. When such human rights violations are also understood to endanger international peace and security, there is

EXPECTED NET EFFECT ON THE HUMAN CONDITION

clearer legal ground for humanitarian, armed intervention under U.N. Security Council auspices, following Chapter VII of the U.N. Charter.

Armed intervention has very real costs not just to people and property in states and societies subject to intervention, but also to the armed forces conducting such interventions. The extent of these costs usually cannot be known with certainty, but policy makers nevertheless try to estimate what they are likely to be. It is extraordinarily difficult, if not impossible, to quantify with precision the net effect (benefits minus costs) on the human condition even after an armed intervention has occurred. Deaths and other casualties can be counted and property losses estimated, but some human costs (for example, psychological damage) may not be known for many years, if then. The problem is compounded when one tries to estimate what these costs might be in advance of an armed intervention. Nevertheless, this criterion typically plays on the minds of policy makers who contemplate whether armed intervention will better or worsen the human condition. At the very least, expected net effect on the human condition can play on how an armed intervention is implemented. Using this criterion, policy makers may select options expected to minimize or reduce adverse consequences to both armed forces and the peoples subject to their actions.

DEGREE OF MULTILATERALISM

As unilateral armed intervention, regardless of motivation or justification, has come increasingly into disfavor, policy makers have been more prone to look for multilateral support and cooperation in conducting armed interventions. U.N. Security Council mandates, for example, provide political and legal ground for proceeding. In the absence of such Security Council action, proceeding multilaterally under Article 51 as a collective-defense response is still viewed by most policy makers as politically preferable to unilateral action. This helps explain why the George W. Bush administration, despite a generally dismissive attitude toward the United Nations, sought a U.N. Security Council resolution in the fall of 2002 requiring Iraq to readmit weapons inspectors. This effort included an elaborate oral and visual presentation by Colin Powell, the secretary of state.

These five criteria often compete with each other and choices concerning how much weight to give to one over the other have to be made sooner or later. That said, we are left with an analytical framework that specifies factors that typically are part of decisions to engage in armed intervention.

Because states usually intervene to serve their interests does not mean that they always do so for only self-serving purposes. They may wish to intervene quite genuinely for humanitarian purposes or, consistent with their broad interests, to contribute to restoration of international peace and security. This seems to be the case of NATO intervention in Kosovo. Or they may wish to use military force in efforts against drug smugglers. In such cases states may weigh the costs and benefits of armed intervention or in terms of how well they serve the human condition.

In some cases the use of force for humanitarian purposes may cause even more bloodshed than if no intervention had taken place. In other cases the reverse is true: Armed intervention at relatively low cost may succeed in providing greater security and meeting human needs. The difficulty, of course, is that expected net costs or benefits to human beings are not always easy to estimate accurately.

Law, Force, and National Security

Quite apart from legal considerations, the question of *when* to use force in armed interventions is an important national security matter. Some argue that the sole criterion should be national interest, particularly if a vital interest is at stake. Domestic critics of post-Cold War interventions by the United States in Somalia, Rwanda, and Haiti and the contribution of U.S. troops to the NATO peacekeeping operation in Bosnia and bombing campaigns in Kosovo and elsewhere in Serbia challenged U.S. authorities, questioning whether sufficient U.S. interests were involved to bear the costs or risks involved, however worthy any of these ventures might have seemed to advocates justifying them on purely humanitarian grounds.

Legal restrictions are often overlooked when national interests or objectives are compelling. The French term **raison d'état** (or, in German, **Staatsräson**) refers to the rationale of justifying state policy only by the state's own interests or objectives. In 1914 Germany "justified" its invasion of Belgium on precisely these grounds. Germany had no particular quarrel with Belgium, which claimed a right to be neutral in the dispute between France and Germany. In a rare diplomatic admission in such circumstances, the German chancellor apologized for having to violate Belgian neutrality and thus its sovereignty but claimed that this was necessary in order to protect Germany from an attack by France across Belgium.[21]

The Belgian experience is reminiscent of the plight of the people on the Aegean island of Melos off the Greek coast when confronted by Athens. Melos had claimed a right to be neutral in the Peloponnesian War (431–404 B.C.) between Athens and Sparta. Recounting the events, Thucydides tells us how Athens tried to force Melos to join in an alliance against Sparta and its allies. When the Melians resisted, claiming the right to remain neutral, the Athenians responded that, in the real world, *might makes right*: "The strong do what they will and the weak do what they must."[22] Even though we may dispute the Athenian claim to any right based on its power position, they nevertheless had the capabilities to force the Melians into subjection, which they proceeded to do.

In a more recent example, the leadership in Baghdad sought to justify the 1990 invasion of Kuwait, claiming that the territory of Kuwait really belonged to Iraq. The Iraqi leaders said that British colonialists, acting for their own purposes, had established Kuwait as a British "protectorate" (1897–1961) and had drawn the lines defining a border, thus artificially creating the oil-rich state of Kuwait. Provoked by a dispute over oil rights with Kuwait, Iraq was using its might in an effort to reestablish its "rights," annexing Kuwaiti territory as part of Iraq's historical patrimony or rightful inheritance.

Such an egregious act, however, stimulated an international collective response. Acting under U.N. auspices, an international coalition primarily under U.S. leadership formed to counter Iraq's claims. Iraq was branded an aggressor, and the coalition used force to expel Iraq's occupation forces from Kuwait. Granted, members of the coalition were motivated by their own oil interests in the region and concerned that Saudi Arabia or other Gulf states also might be invaded. But coalition members also denied Iraq's assertion of right through might. The coalition prevailed over Iraq in an armed intervention justified as a defensive measure to reestablish Kuwait and to restore international peace and security in the region. Although the United Nations is not a government with authority or power in itself to enforce the law against aggressors, it

[21]See Michael Walzer, *Just and Unjust Wars* (New York: Basic Books, 1977), 240; cf. Roderick Ogley, ed., *The Theory and Practice of Neutrality in the Twentieth Century* (New York: 1970), 74.
[22]See the Melian dialogue in Thucydides, *History of the Peloponnesian War*, Rex Warner, trans. (Harmondsworth, UK: Penguin Books, 1954), 400–408.

Practicing World Politics

Supported by the Swiss government, the Zurich-based Center for Security Studies and Conflict Research has developed ISN, the International Relations and Security Network (www.isn.ethz.ch), which includes Internet links to a large number of international and nongovernmental organizations. Among these are the London-based IISS, the International Institute for Strategic Studies (www.iiss.org); SIPRI, the Stockholm International Peace Research Institute (www.sipri.org); and the Geneva-based UNIDIR, the United Nations Institute for Disarmament Research (www.unidir.org). The IISS is an "independent centre for research, information and debate on the problems of conflict" that publishes an annual *Military Balance* and *Strategic Survey* as well as *Adelphi Papers* and *Survival,* a journal on international security. SIPRI conducts research on arms transfers, arms production, military expenditure, military technology, chemical and biological weapons, European security, export controls, and other security topics and publishes an annual yearbook, research reports, and fact sheets. For a comprehensive set of Internet links to the U.S. executive branch, Congressional, judicial, think-tank, media, defense industry, embassy, consulate, and international organization sites, visit the Center for Security Policy (www.security-policy.org).

The Washington-based American Committees on Foreign Relations (www.acfr.org), a grassroots organization with committees in more than thirty U.S. cities, provides a list of American links to daily news sources, foreign affairs journals and magazines, think tanks, C-Span programs, Congressional links, columnists, and opinion leaders. The government-funded U.S. Institute of Peace (www.usip.gov) sponsors academic research, as do such nongovernmental organizations as the New York– and Washington-based Council on Foreign Relations (www.cfr.org), which publishes the journal *Foreign Affairs* and various studies. The Chicago Council on Foreign Relations (www.ccfr.org) also provides a useful set of links, as does the New York–based Foreign Policy Association (www.fpa.org) and the Institute of International Education (www.iie.org).

THE INTERNET: CHECKING OUT SOME WEB SITES ON SECURITY AND THE USE OF FORCE

provided a convenient political and legal forum for coalition parties to take collective action on behalf of Kuwaiti rights, Saudi security, and their own interests.

The U.S.-led invasion of Iraq in 2003 proved to be much more controversial and illustrated the invoking of *raison d'etat* to the fullest. A year after the September 11, 2001, terrorist attacks on the United States, the Bush administration issued a national security document stating "as a matter of common sense and self-defense, America will act against emerging threats before they are fully formed."[23] In arguing the need for a preventive war against Saddam Hussein's regime, the Bush administration invoked four main reasons: Saddam's regime was undeterrable, and he would seek any opportunity to kill Americans; he cooperated with terrorist groups such as Al Qaeda, and Iraq had supposedly assisted in the September 11, 2001, attacks; he was close to acquiring nuclear weapons; and he already possessed a vast array of chemical and biological weapons. Through vigorous diplomatic arm twisting, the Bush administration received the requisite votes from the U.N. Security Council to launch a preventive war that Washington apparently would pursue irrespective of the opinion of many members of the United Nations and a number of its NATO allies, including Germany and France. The Al Qaeda connection proved to be fallacious, and nuclear, chemical, and biological weapons were not found.

---

[23]http://www.whitehouse.gov/nsc/print/nssall.html

Conclusion

So many trees have been sacrificed to provide the paper for scholars and political leaders to pontificate on the causes of war and the use of force that many people do believe these are the defining issues in the study of international relations and world politics. Realists, at least, think so. So do peace researchers, many of whom view the world through pluralist or liberal lenses.

If it is any comfort, however, the world today is not the one described by Thucydides in the Melian dialogue. Over the centuries, certain norms, laws, and rules of the game have been devised by clashing kings, prime ministers, chancellors, and presidents to influence, if not govern, their international contests. Using force is often seen by decision makers as a rational instrument of policy or means to attain their national objectives or serve their national interests. Accordingly, political leaders do not bend to the logic and persuasiveness of just-war theory and international norms and law concerning armed intervention purely out of selflessness but rather due to enlightened self-interest. As the Athenians eventually learned to their sorrow, ignoring even the most basic rules of international behavior—those regarding the conduct of war—ensures that one will be treated likewise once the tables are turned. In our world of such increasing dangers as nuclear proliferation and recurrent crises of authority that tempt external armed intervention, we can only hope that most states will see the logic behind the need in collectively abiding by a common set of rules to guide the conduct of their international relations.

Afterword

The Natural Condition of Mankind

Thomas Hobbes

1588-1679

Hobbes focuses on the insecurity that accompanies human relations—his own life torn by uncertainties, particularly during the English civil war in the 1640s when he left England for the relatively greater safety of continental Europe. His concept of human beings in a state of nature is one of war of every person against everyone else. They may not always be engaged in combat, but they live in a world in which one always must be prepared for the fight. The lives of human beings in this anarchy—the absence of a sovereign or governing authority—is "solitary, poor, nasty, brutish and short," a perspective that reflects his rather dim view of human nature. People are hard pressed to survive in this state of war, much less do anything of lasting human value. In domestic society the remedy for this condition is for the people to vest a sovereign, whether a monarch or parliament, with the necessary power to maintain law and order and thus provide security. Put another way, if governments did not exist, we would have to create them. There is, of course, no such social contract among states, which conduct themselves as if they were persons in a state of nature. In Hobbes, realists thus find a theoretical basis for their understandings of the power of states, alliances, and the balance of power that mark the conduct we observe in an anarchic world. States seek to survive in such a world and, succeeding in that, use their power to attain other objectives deemed to be in their national interest.

Nature hath made men so equal in the faculties of body and mind as that, though there be found one man sometimes manifestly stronger in body or of quicker mind than another, yet when all is reckoned together the difference between man and man is not so considerable as that one man can thereupon claim to himself any benefit to which another may not pretend as well as he. For as to the strength of body, the weakest has strength enough to kill the strongest, either by secret machination or by confederacy with others that are in the same danger with himself. . . .

If any two men desire the same thing, which nevertheless they cannot both enjoy, they become enemies; and in the way to their end (which is principally their own conservation . . .) endeavour to destroy or subdue one another. And from hence it comes to pass that where an invader hath no more to fear than another man's single power, if one plant, sow, build, or possess a convenient seat, others may probably be expected to come prepared with forces united to dispossess and deprive him, not only of the fruit of his labour, but also of his life or liberty. And the invader again is in the like danger of another.

And from this diffidence of one another [i.e., non-assertiveness or lacking self-confidence in human relationships—Ed.], there is no way for any man to secure himself so reasonable as anticipation; that is, by force, or wiles, to master the persons of all men he can so long till he see no other power great enough to endanger him: and this is no more than his own conservation requireth, and is generally allowed. Also, because there be some that, taking pleasure in contemplating their own power in the acts of conquest, which they pursue farther than their security requires, if others, that otherwise would be glad to be at ease within modest bounds, should not by invasion increase their power, they would not be able, long time, by standing only on their defence, to subsist. And by consequence, such augmentation of dominion over men being necessary to a man's conservation [i.e., a person's survival—Ed.], it ought to be allowed him.

Again, men have no pleasure (but on the contrary a great deal of grief) in keeping company where there is no power able to overawe them all. . . .

So that in the nature of man, we find three principal causes of quarrel. First, competition; secondly, diffidence; thirdly, glory. The first maketh men invade for gain; the second, for safety; and the third, for reputation. The first use violence, to make themselves masters of other men's persons, wives, children, and cattle; the second, to defend them; the third, for trifles, as a word, a smile, a different opinion, and any other sign of undervalue, either direct in their persons or by reflection in their kindred, their friends, their nation, their profession, or their name.

Hereby it is manifest that *during the time men live without a common power to keep them all in awe, they are in that condition which is called war; and such a war as is of every man against every man. For war consisteth not in battle only, or the act of fighting, but in a tract of time, wherein the will to contend by battle is sufficiently known:* and therefore the notion of time is to be considered in the nature of war, as it is in the nature of weather. For as the nature of foul weather lieth not in a shower or two of rain, but in an inclination thereto of many days together: so *the nature of war consisteth* not in actual fighting, but *in the known disposition thereto* during all the time there is no assurance to the contrary. All other time is peace.

Whatsoever therefore is consequent to a time of war, where every man is enemy to every man, the same consequent to the time wherein men live without other security than what their own strength and their own invention shall furnish them withal. In such condition there is no place for industry, because the fruit thereof is uncertain: and consequently no culture of the earth; no navigation, nor use of the commodities that may be imported by sea; no commodious building; no instruments of moving and removing such things as require much force; no knowledge of the face of the earth; no account of time; no arts; no letters; no society; and which is worst of all, continual fear, and danger of violent death; and the life of man, solitary, poor, nasty, brutish, and short.

It may seem strange to some man that has not well weighed these things that Nature should thus dissociate and render men apt to invade and destroy one another: and he may therefore, not trusting to this inference, made from the passions, desire perhaps to have the same confirmed by experience. Let him therefore consider with himself: when taking a journey, he arms himself and seeks to go well accompanied; when going to sleep, he locks his doors; when even in his house he locks his chests; and this when he knows there be laws and public officers, armed, to revenge all injuries shall be done him; what opinion he has of his fellow subjects, when he rides armed; of his fellow citizens, when he locks his doors; and of his children, and servants, when he locks his chests. Does he not there as much accuse mankind by his actions as I do by my words? But neither of us accuse man's nature in it. The desires, and other passions of man, are in themselves no sin. No more are the actions that proceed from those passions till they know a law that forbids them; which till laws be made they cannot know, nor can any law be made till they have agreed upon the person that shall make it.

It may peradventure be thought there was never such a time nor condition of war as this; and I believe it was never generally so, over all the world: but there are many places where they live so now. . . . It may be perceived what manner of life there would be, *where there were no common power to fear,* by the manner of life which men that have formerly lived under a peaceful government use to degenerate into a civil war.

But though there had never been any time wherein particular men were in a condition of war one against another, yet in all times kings and persons of sovereign authority, because of their independency, are in continual jealousies, and in the state and posture of gladiators, having their weapons pointing, and their eyes fixed on one another; that is, their forts, garrisons, and guns upon the frontiers of their kingdoms, and continual spies upon their neighbours, which is a posture of war. But because they uphold thereby the industry of their subjects, there does not follow from it that misery which accompanies the liberty of particular men.

To this war of every man against every man, this also is consequent; that nothing can be unjust. The notions of right and wrong, justice and injustice, have there no place. Where there is no common power, there is no law; where no law, no injustice. Force and fraud are in war the two cardinal virtues. Justice and injustice are none of the faculties neither of the body nor mind. If they were, they might be in a man that were alone in the world, as well as his senses and passions. They are qualities that relate to men in society, not in solitude. It is consequent also to the same condition that there be no propriety, no dominion, no mine and thine distinct; but only that to be every man's that he can get, and for so long as he can keep it. And thus much for the ill condition which man by mere nature is actually placed in; though with a possibility to come out of it, consisting partly in the passions, partly in his reason.

The passions that incline men to peace are: fear of death; desire of such things as are necessary to commodious living; and a hope by their industry to obtain them. And reason suggesteth convenient articles of peace upon which men may be drawn to agreement. These articles are they which otherwise are called the laws of nature. . . .

Key Terms

force   *p. 160*
rational choice   *p. 161*
groupthink   *p. 163*
normative theory   *p. 170*

Other Concepts

armed conflicts   *p. 160*
interstate war   *p. 160*
civil war   *p. 160*
armed intervention   *p. 160*
warfare   *p. 160*
decision   *p. 161*
suboptimal   *p. 161*
pacificism   *p. 170*
bellicism   *p. 170*
just-war theory   *p. 170*
jus ad bellum   *p. 174*
jus in bello   *p. 174*
law of war   *p. 174*

counterforce   *p. 176*
alliances   *p. 162*
strategy   *p. 166*
tactics   *p. 166*
military necessity   *p. 167*
deterrence   *p. 167*
principles of war   *p. 168*
countervalue   *p. 176*
collateral destruction   *p. 176*
dual or double-effect
  principle   *p. 176*
utilitarian   *p. 178*
collective security   *p. 179*

collective defense   *p. 179*
surprise   *p. 168*
concentration of forces   *p. 168*
economy of force   *p. 168*
friction   *p. 168*
fog of war   *p. 168*
zero-sum   *p. 168*
guerrilla warfare   *p. 181*
insurgency   *p. 181*
humanitarian intervention
  p. 181
raison d'état   *p. 184*
Staaträson   *p. 184*

Additional Readings

Readings on strategy related to the use of force might well begin with Carl von Clausewitz, *On War*, trans. and ed. Michael Howard and Peter Paret (Princeton, NJ: Princeton University Press, 1989). Another volume that combines commentaries on war and strategy by both Clausewitz and the ancient Chinese Sun Tzu is *The Book of War:* Sun Tzu, *The Art of Warfare* and Karl von Clausewitz, *On War* (New York: Random House/Modern Library, 2000). Further readings on strategy can start with the classic B.H. Liddell Hart, *Strategy,* 2nd ed. (New York: Penguin, 1954, 1991). Other volumes on strategy include Peter Paret (ed.), *Makers of Modern Strategy from Machiavelli to the Nuclear Age* (Princeton, NJ: Princeton University Press, 1986); Colin S. Gray, *Modern Strategy* (Oxford, UK: Oxford University Press, 1999); Edward N. Luttwak, *Strategy: The Logic of War and Peace*, rev. ed. (Cambridge, MA: Harvard University/Belknap Press, 2002); and Lawrence J. Korb's analysis of U.S. strategic developments in his *A New National Security Strategy* (New York: Council on Foreign Relations Press, 2003).

On strategy related to nuclear weapons, a classic treatment is Lawrence Freedman, *The Evolution of Nuclear Strategy,* 3rd ed. (New York: Palgrave, 1981, 2003). On nuclear and other weapons of mass destruction, see Kurt M. Campbell, Robert J. Einhorn, and Mitchell B. Reiss, *The Nuclear Tipping Point: Why States Reconsider Their Nuclear Choices* (Washington, D.C.: Brookings Institution, 2004); Peter R. Lavoy, Scott D. Sagan and James J. Wirtz, *Planning the Unthinkable: How New Powers Will Use Nuclear, Biological and Chemical Weapons* (Ithaca, NY: Cornell University Press, 2000); and Joseph Cirincione, Jon Wolfsthal, and Miriam Rajkumar, *Deadly Arsenals: Nuclear, Biological, and Chemical Threats,* 2nd ed. (Washington, D.C.: Carnegie Endowment/Brookings, 2005).

A superb treatment of how intelligence operates as part of national security is Mark M. Lowenthal, *Intelligence: From Secrets to Policy*, 3rd ed. (Washington, D.C.: CQ Press,

2005). See also Robert M. Clark, *Intelligence Analysis: A Target-Centric Approach* (Washington, D.C.: CQ Press, 2004). Space is now considered a place integral to intelligence and national security, although a controversy rages on whether it should be confined to this "militarization" of space—reconnaissance, communications, and other support for military operations on the planet—or whether it should expand to "weaponization," referred to by critics as another form of "star wars." On these debates, see Michael E. O'Hanlon, *Neither Star Wars Nor Sanctuary* (Washington, D.C.: Brookings Institution Press, 2004); Benjamin S. Lambeth, *Mastering the Ultimate High Ground: Next Steps in the Military Use of Space* (Santa Monica, CA: RAND Corporation, 2003); and Dana J. Johnson et al., *Space Weapons, Earth Wars* (Santa Monica, CA: RAND Corporation, 2002).

On why states resort to war, read the classic treatment in Kenneth N. Waltz, *Man, the State and War: A Theoretical Analysis* (New York: Columbia University Press, 1959). This work explicitly identifies different "images" or levels of analysis, the realist understandings of war and the use of force represented in this chapter owing much to Waltz's insights on this question. For another perspective on theories of war using examples of actual conflicts dating back to 1700, consider Geoffrey Blainey's *The Causes of War* (New York: The Free Press, 1973). Another classic study is Quincy Wright's *A Study of War* (Chicago: University of Chicago Press, 1942, 1964).

An example of statistical analysis of causal variables and war is J. David Singer and Melvin Small, *The Wages of War, 1816–1965* (New York: John Wiley, 1972). For later work in this quantitative genre, see John A. Vasquez and Marie T. Henehan (eds.), *The Scientific Study of Peace and War* (New York: Lexington Books, 1992, 1999) and earlier compilations by Manus Midlarsky in his *Handbook of War Studies* (Boston: Unwin Hyman, 1989) and *The Onset of World War* (Boston: Unwin Hyman, 1988). Use of mathematical relations in developing an expected-utility theory is examined in Bruce Bueno de Mesquita, *The War Trap* (New Haven, CT: Yale University Press, 1981). See also John A. Vasquez, *The War Puzzle* (Cambridge, Cambridge University Press, 1993) and his edited anthology, *What Do We Know About War?* (Lanham, MD: Rowman and Littlefield, 2000).

A convenient summary of much of the war-causation literature is Greg Cashman, *What Causes War? An Introduction to Theories of International Conflict* (New York: Lexington Books, 1993). We would also recommend Richard Ned Lebow, *Between Peace and War: The Nature of International Crisis* (Baltimore: Johns Hopkins University Press, 1981); the anthology edited by Robert J. Rotberg and Theodore K. Rabb, *The Origin and Prevention of Major Wars* (Cambridge: Cambridge University Press, 1989); and one edited by Michael E. Brown, Owen R. Coté, and Sean M. Lynne-Jones, *Theories of War and Peace* (Cambridge, MA: MIT Press, 1998).

An excellent overview of war and diplomacy is Gordon A. Craig and Alexander George, *Force and Statecraft* (Oxford, UK: Oxford University Press, 1983) and an interesting case study on the politics of the decision to go to war in Iraq is the account by journalist Bob Woodward, *Plan of Attack* (New York: Simon & Schuster, 2004). Also on the use of force as part of the diplomatic arsenal, see Alexander George, David Hall, and William Simons, *The Limits of Coercive Diplomacy* (Boston: Little, Brown, 1971). For a useful anthology of articles on force in international politics, now in its sixth edition, see Robert J. Art and Kenneth N. Waltz (eds.), *The Use of Force: Military Power and International Politics*, 6th ed. (Lanham, MD: Rowman & Littlefield, 2003).

A volume on the armed forces in post–Cold War society is Charles C. Moskos, John Allen Williams, and David R. Segal (eds.), *The Postmodern Military: Armed Forces After the Cold War* (New York: Oxford University Press, 2000). On military-related technology, economy, and society, consider Ann R. Markusen and Sean S. Costigan, *Arming the Future: A Defense Industry for the 21st Century* (New York: Council on Foreign

Relations Press, 1999); George and Meredith Friedman, *The Future of War: Power, Technology and American World Dominance in the Twenty-First Century* (New York: St. Martin's Griffin, 1996); and Michael Ignatieff, *Virtual War: Kosovo and Beyond* (New York: Henry Holt/Metropolitan Books, 2000).

Finally, on defense and security of the homeland in a world challenged by terrorist activities, see Michael E. O'Hanlon et al., *Protecting the American Homeland: A Preliminary Analysis* (Washington, D.C.: Brookings Institution, 2002) and the revised version a year later in *Protecting the American Homeland: One Year On* (Washington, D.C.: Brookings Institution, 2003). More recently we note the textbook by Mark A. Sauter and James Jay Carafano, *Homeland Security* (New York: McGraw Hill, 2005) and David G. Kamien (ed.), *The McGraw-Hill Homeland Security Handbook* (New York: McGraw Hill, 2006).

Chapter 6

International Cooperation and International Security: International Organizations, Alliances, and Coalitions

Anarchy, Cooperation, Harmony, and Discord

- World Government
- Alliances, Coalitions, and International Organizations
- Collective Security

Peacekeeping: Managing and Controlling Conflicts

Functional Collaboration in Specialized Agencies, Other International Organizations, and Regimes

Conclusion

Appendices: The United Nations Charter, The North Atlantic Treaty, Functional International Organizations

Reacting in part to a territorial dispute over oil rights in Iraq's southern border area, Iraqi President Saddam Hussein surprised the world on August 2, 1990, when his military forces invaded oil-rich Kuwait. Seizing control, Iraq declared that Kuwait was really part of Iraq because British imperialists of an earlier period had created Kuwait artificially from land that was properly part of Iraqi patrimony. From the Kuwaiti perspective (and most outsiders shared their view), the invasion was clearly an act of aggression, violating the sovereignty of a small state. Moreover, the Iraqi move also posed a potential threat to Saudi Arabia and the delicate politics of oil. Policy makers in the United States and elsewhere saw Saudi Arabia as a country possessing the world's largest oil reserves, making it a key player in oil supply and pricing decisions within OPEC, the Organization of Petroleum Exporting Countries. Because viability of the global economy still depends on an adequate supply of oil, the idea that Iraq could gain control of a major source of the world's oil supply sent shivers up and down the spines of many national leaders.

What was to be done? Relying on diplomacy alone was difficult. Nevertheless, both bilateral and multilateral efforts in the United Nations, Baghdad (the Iraqi capital), and elsewhere were made to seek peaceful resolution. Meanwhile, to dissuade or deter further aggression, the United States led an effort under U.N. Security Council auspices to assemble a multinational coalition of military forces in Saudi Arabia and elsewhere in the Gulf region.[1] Since the Gulf is outside of the legally defined North Atlantic area, NATO was not in a position to respond. On the other hand, European members of NATO coordinated their efforts in the Western European Union (WEU), an alliance not constrained geographically

---

[1]The name of the Gulf is itself in dispute between Arab states and Iran, the latter referred to historically as Persia. Not surprisingly, Arab states prefer to use the term Arab Gulf. Non-Arab Iran refers to it as the Persian Gulf, the more commonly used term, due in large part to earlier nineteenth- and twentieth-century British usage when the United Kingdom considered the Gulf area to be in its sphere of influence. To avoid entanglement in this still-divisive issue, in this book we join the more recent convention of referring to this important area simply as "the Gulf."

to Europe. The six-month military buildup in Saudi Arabia and the Gulf area, referred to as Operation Desert Shield, produced a formidable, multilateral array of ground, air, and naval forces.

The failure diplomatically and by show of force to persuade Iraq to withdraw from Kuwait finally led to launching hostilities against Iraqi forces on January 16, 1991. Operation Desert Shield had ended, and Operation Desert Storm began. Sustaining relatively few casualties itself, the coalition imposed a crushing defeat on Iraq, driving its occupation force from Kuwait and threatening Baghdad before hostilities ceased. Ten to twelve thousand Iraqi soldiers were killed in the air campaign and up to 10,000 more in the ground war. Devastation in the countryside was extensive due to aerial bombardment and actions on the ground. Although its human casualty losses were relatively light, the operation cost the coalition more than $100 billion.

As in most wars, human suffering in Iraq fell heavily on civilians, whether they were Arabs, Persians, or Kurds. Kuwait was liberated, the oil fields secured (after wells were set aflame by retreating Iraqi forces), and Saudi Arabia avoided invasion. On the other hand, Saddam Hussein was still in power, and both Kurds in the north and Persians in the south remained in jeopardy at the hands of the Iraqi regime. This situation did not change until the second Gulf War in 2003 when Hussein's regime was overthrown by a much smaller international coalition led by the United States.

international organizations (IOs) Coalitions that have a membership exclusively composed of states, which also leads some people to refer to them as **intergovernmental organizations (IGOs);** by contrast (and as the term implies), *nongovernmental organizations (NGOs)* are composed of private-sector individuals and groups.

The 1991 Gulf War, nevertheless, is an example of international collaboration designed to respond to a change in the *status quo* initiated when Iraq invaded Kuwait. Members of different ***international organizations***—notably the Gulf Cooperation Council, the Western European Union, and Arab League—joined in coalition with still other countries. The coalition was not an established, standing alliance. Nevertheless, it was assembled as a collective security response to what coalition members understood to be both a serious act of aggression against a small state and a threat to the world's oil supplies. Quite apart from the oil issue, small states elsewhere watched with great interest to see if the United States, other great and middle powers, and other small states would join forces to rescue a small state. After completing its tasks, the coalition disbanded.

Anarchy, Cooperation, Harmony, and Discord

As we have noted, realists in particular argue that international anarchy—the absence of central governance or world government in international relations—contributes to a sense of vulnerability on the part of all states and their peoples. One way to address security concerns under anarchy is for a state to rely on itself and increase its economic and military capabilities, as discussed in Chapter 3. At a minimum, the security goal is to deter aggression on the part of another state. This approach, however, assumes that the state has such capabilities at its disposal. An alternative approach is to collaborate with other states and pool resources toward the accomplishment of compatible goals. By such a process, the weak "I"—standing alone—becomes the stronger "we"—pulling together. In this chapter we begin to examine the logic, nature, and limitations of international cooperation. Although we do note the increasing importance of cooperative activities among such transnational, nongovernmental organizations as Amnesty International or Doctors without Borders, the focus here is primarily on cooperation among states and international organizations made up of states. This chapter will focus especially on cooperation in terms of security; international cooperation in economic and social realms, topics of particular interest to pluralists or liberals, will be covered in Part IV.

We begin by clarifying what we mean by international cooperation. It is useful to frame the discussion in terms of harmony and discord, which can be understood as lying on opposite sides of a continuum. If generally harmonious relations exist over time between two or more states, then their policies typically aid the attainment of each other's goals; much bargaining is usually not required. Decisions in these relatively harmonious circumstances are made without negotiating most issues, with the other states sharing these positive relations. Policy is influenced by a mutual understanding of each other's interests as well as points of difference. One example is relations since the nineteenth century between the United States and Canada, which share the longest demilitarized border in the world. Although Canadian and American interest and positions on issues are by no means identical, a shared understanding of both overlapping and divergent perspectives facilitates maintenance of generally positive, cooperative relations.

At the other extreme, if substantial discord exists, then actors' policies hinder the attainment of other actors' goals, and there is no incentive to change behavior. Cooperation, however, occupies a middle ground. It requires that the actions of separate individuals, organizations, or states be brought into conformity through a process of policy coordination that, if pursued successfully, can lead beyond mere coordination to

Organization of Petroleum Exporting Countries (OPEC)

At a conference in Baghdad in 1960, five countries—Iran, Iraq, Kuwait, Saudi Arabia, and Venezuela—formed OPEC. With headquarters since 1965 in Vienna, Austria, OPEC now has eleven oil-producing and -exporting member countries—Algeria, Libya, Nigeria, Indonesia, Iran, Iraq, Kuwait, Qatar, Saudi Arabia, United Arab Emirates, and Venezuela. Previously active OPEC members included Ecuador (1973–1992) and Gabon (1975–1994). Acting as a cartel to serve member interests, OPEC ministers coordinate their oil production policies to help stabilize the oil market, while achieving for its members a satisfactory level of revenue from oil sales as well as an adequate return to those who have invested capital in the industry.

Semiannual ministerial meetings set agreed production targets. The most important OPEC objective thus is "to coordinate and unify petroleum policies among member countries." Rapid and dramatic increases in global oil prices in the 1970s were due to OPEC production decisions. Due in part to member-country needs for continuing revenue from oil sales, OPEC has taken a more moderate course since the 1970s in order to maintain adequate oil supplies to global markets. In practice, oil production limits have been difficult to achieve and have not always been followed by member countries. Moreover new non-OPEC oil suppliers continue to add more oil to the global market. OPEC has been more successful in cooperative activities than sugar, coffee, tin, and other commodity cartels. Cartel agreements are difficult to maintain because the parties are competing with each other for market share in regional and global markets at the same time.

---

extensive collaboration.[2] Such cooperation can itself be understood as a range of activities beyond merely consulting or coordinating at one end of the spectrum to full collaboration on the other end. Similarly discord includes a range of approaches: On the mild end of the spectrum, a party or parties may withdraw when possible from conflict situations or alternatively may decide to work at cross-purposes or even engage in obstructive activities or direct conflict. Along the spectrum between complete harmony and complete discord are seven categories we can identify that describe the degree of positive or negative interactions that characterize relations, whether in international or nongovernmental organization settings within or across state boundaries or among the governments of states themselves:

Complete Harmony	Zone of International Cooperation	Zone of International Conflict	Complete Discord
← Increasingly Positive Activities		Middle Zone	Increasingly Negative Activities →
Extensive collaboration	Working issues jointly Coordinating	Consulting Notifying Separating and withdrawing	Working at cross purposes Obstructing actions Conflict

---

[2]The following discussion draws from Charles A. Kupchan and Clifford A. Kupchan, "Concerts, Collective Security, and the Future of Europe," *International Security*, vol. 16, no. 1 (Summer 1991): 114–125.

International Organizations in North America

In addition to their combined efforts in NATO, Canada and the United States have collaborated militarily since the 1950s in what is now the North American Aerospace Defense Command (NORAD) located in Colorado Springs, Colorado. An array of radars on land, at sea, and in airplanes as well as space-based detection devices provide early warning should bomber or missile attacks be directed against Canada or the United States. Cooperation in commercial matters among Canada, the United States, and Mexico occurs within NAFTA, the North American Free Trade Agreement. Since 1994, NAFTA secretariat sections in Ottawa, Washington, and Mexico City provide the administrative base for the NAFTA Commission and for implementing NAFTA provisions and managing or resolving trade disputes when they occur.

For cooperation to exist, each actor must change behavior contingent on changes in the behavior of others. Cooperation among states, therefore, does not necessarily spring from idealism or some altruistic belief in "the common good." Instead leaders believe that cooperation with other states maximizes benefits. In game-theory terms, this is a positive-sum orientation—one in which all parties stand to gain to one degree or another from cooperative or collaborative actions.

Cooperation or collaboration by states does not always serve benign, positive purposes toward others. Some states may join together in order to conquer other states, just as the Germans and the Soviets did in 1939, when they invaded and divided Poland. Similarly, some states may cooperate in order to exploit weaker states economically, a charge sometimes levied by developing countries against more advanced, industrial states.[3] The point to keep in mind, therefore, is that international cooperation is not necessarily benign, although many times it is. Not surprisingly cooperation among states relies heavily on diplomacy—a topic we explored in Chapter 4.

International cooperation may be a one-shot deal, such as an international relief effort to end a famine or the case of Poland mentioned above. Of interest to us, however, is cooperation that does not have such a short duration. In particular we are interested in international cooperation that has become institutionalized. By this we mean a *pattern of behavior that has become formally or informally organized and reflects certain rules and norms of behavior. Pattern* refers to behavior that occurs not once but repeatedly. *Formally organized* means that the rules and norms of behavior are reflected in the actions of a particular international organization, such as the United Nations or the North Atlantic Treaty Organization (NATO). These are goal-oriented, formal organizations with written charters, hierarchies, budgets, and letterheads. A number of international organizations have been formed to serve common regional interests. Most of these regional international organizations (see accompanying box) have proven to be very durable, adapting to changes in circumstances over time.

Informally organized means that the rules and norms of behavior reflect and influence cooperation among states and transnational actors. It is not as if these rules and norms reside only within the bricks and mortar of formally constituted international organizations. The presence and effect of these values come to be understood and generally accepted by both states and nonstate actors in effect as part of an international

---

[3]*Ibid.*

society—essentially as guidelines for the conduct of international relations. For example, the concept of **multilateralism**—working issues jointly rather than unilaterally by a single state—has become not only the preferred way to cope with most issues on the global agenda, but also the preferred means to construct collaborative mechanisms in international relations for attaining mutual gains. This logic of states cooperating to maximize gains (particularly economic) is a dominant theme in pluralist or liberal writings.

Arrangements based on agreed norms are often grounded further in what are called *international regimes.* Examples include the set of agreed trade and commerce rules in the North American Free Trade Agreement, which progressively liberalize trade among Canada, the United States, and Mexico, opening and expanding trade by removing tariffs and other barriers; there is no single NAFTA headquarters located in one city, although secretariat sections are located in the capital cities of the three member countries. Another example is the agreement among states on generally accepted rules and norms of behavior concerning the treatment of diplomats; there is no International Organization of Diplomats to enforce such rules and norms. Whether formally or informally organized, however, institutions often constrain activity as well as shape expectations. Hence, as new issues arise, the way they are handled is influenced by existing international organizations and associated international regimes. The consequent impact of the development of international norms that in turn constrain the behavior of actors is a dominant theme of **social constructivists.**

international regimes
Sets of rules agreed upon by states to govern their relations or conduct in specified issue areas such as trade and commerce, the exchange of money, environment, health, and so on. These international regimes are often associated with both international and nongovernmental organizations.

Regional International Organizations:
A Sampler

Europe
Of all the world's regions, Europe has the most highly institutionalized set of international (intergovernmental) organizations, often with overlapping purposes and institutional jurisdictions. Most extensive in the scope of its activities is the European Union (EU). After a decision made in 1999, collective defense and other security functions of the Western European Union (WEU) have been absorbed by the EU as it develops its own common foreign and security policy alongside commitments to the North Atlantic Treaty Organization (NATO). Security, trade and commerce, human rights, and preservation of diverse cultures are among the issues that concern the Organization for Security and Cooperation in Europe (OSCE). For its part, the Council of Europe promotes democracy and democratic values.

The Americas
Canada, the United States, and Mexico are members of the North American Free Trade Agreement (NAFTA). The United States has also joined with El Salvador, Nicaragua, Guatemala, Honduras, and Costa Rica to form the Central American Free Trade Agreement (CAFTA), with the Dominican Republic an affiliate. For their part, Latin American states have also pursued economic integration goals among themselves, forming organizations such as the Caribbean Community and Common Market (CARICOM), the Andean Group (a customs union composed of Bolivia, Colombia, Ecuador, Peru, and Venezuela), a Central American Common Market (CACM), and Mercosur in South America's "southern cone," composed of Argentina, Brazil, Paraguay, and Uruguay, with links to Bolivia, Chile, Colombia, Ecuador, Peru, and Venezuela as associate members. Longest standing and most inclusive of regional international organizations in the Americas is the Organization of American States (OAS). Indeed, multilateralism in the western hemisphere began with the Congress of Panama convened by Simón Bolívar in 1826, with

delegates coming from Central and South America. Successor to both the International Union of American Republics (1890) and the Pan American Union (1910), the OAS was established in 1948 with its headquarters in Washington, D.C. Given these historical roots, the OAS qualifies as the oldest regional international organization in the world. Its objectives are to strengthen peace and security in the hemisphere; promote representative democracy; ensure the peaceful settlement of disputes among members; provide for common action in the event of aggression; seek solutions to political, juridical, and economic problems that may arise; curb hemispheric arms trafficking; combat corruption; fight narcotics and money laundering; define fair telecommunications standards; and promote social, cultural, and sustainable economic development. An Inter-American Development Bank was set up in 1959 to provide capital for economic development. Principal OAS organs include a general assembly, meeting of consultation of foreign ministers, permanent council, the Inter-American Council for Integral Development, the Inter-American Juridical Committee, the Inter-American Commission on Human Rights, and a secretariat. Member states are Antigua and Barbuda, Argentina, the Bahamas, Barbados, Belize, Bolivia, Brazil, Canada, Chile, Colombia, Costa Rica, Cuba (excluded from participation since 1962), Dominica, the Dominican Republic, Ecuador, El Salvador, Grenada, Guatemala, Guyana, Haiti, Honduras, Jamaica, Mexico, Nicaragua, Panama, Paraguay, Peru, Saint Lucia, St. Kitts and Nevis, Saint Vincent and the Grenadines, Suriname, Trinidad and Tobago, the United States, Uruguay, and Venezuela. Not surprisingly, given its global and regional position, the United States has long played a major role in OAS deliberations and actions.

Middle East and Africa

Notwithstanding often major differences among its member countries, the Cairo-based Arab League, formed in 1945, continues to promote pan-Arab goals. Members include Algeria, Bahrain, Comoros, Djibouti, Egypt, Iraq, Jordan, Kuwait, Lebanon, Libya, Mauritania, Morocco, Oman, Palestine, Qatar, Saudi Arabia, Somalia, Sudan, Syria, Tunisia, United Arab Emirates, and Yemen.

The best known and most inclusive of regional international organizations in Africa was originally known as the Organization of African Unity (OAU), now called the African Union (AU). The OAU was established in 1963 at Addis Ababa, Ethiopia, its present headquarters and secretariat. Its objectives are to promote the unity and solidarity of African states; defend the sovereignty of member states; eradicate all forms of colonialism; promote international cooperation and human rights; and coordinate and harmonize economic, diplomatic, educational, health, welfare, scientific, and defense policies. The highest policy organ is an annual summit—the Assembly of Heads of State—with provision for extraordinary sessions when the need arises. An AU council of ministers also holds two sessions a year. Given the diversity and often conflicting interests of many of its members, forging cooperation on many issues has been, to say the least, a very difficult and arduous process. AU members are Algeria, Angola, Benin, Botswana, Burkino Faso, Burundi, Cameroon, Cape Verde, Central African Republic, Chad, Cameroon, Congo–Kinshasa, Congo–Brazzaville, Côte d'Ivoire, Djibouti, Egypt, Equatorial Guinea, Eritrea, Ethiopia, Gabon, the Gambia, Ghana, Guinea, Guinea-Bissau, Kenya, Lesotho, Liberia, Libya, Madagascar, Malawi, Mali, Mauritania, Mauritius, Mozambique, Namibia, Niger, Nigeria, Rwanda, Saharawi Arab Democratic Republic, Sao Tome and Principe, Senegal, Seychelles, Sierra Leone, Somalia, South Africa, Sudan, Swaziland, Tanzania, Togo, Tunisia, Uganda, Zambia, and Zimbabwe. Efforts to promote economic integration also have been made since 1975 by the members of the Economic Community of West African States (ECOWAS): Benin, Burkina Faso, Cape Verde, Côte d'Ivoire, Gambia, Ghana, Guinea, Guinea-Bissau, Liberia, Mali, Niger, Senegal, Sierra Leone, and Togo.

East Asia and the Pacific

Regional international organizations are much less common in East Asia, a notable exception being the Association of Southeast Asian Nations (ASEAN), which was formed in 1967 by

Indonesia, Malaysia, the Philippines, Singapore, and Thailand to promote political and economic cooperation and regional stability. Other countries joining ASEAN include Brunei in
1984, Vietnam in 1995, Laos and Myanmar (Burma) in 1997, and Cambodia in 1999. In 1993,
ASEAN members agreed to work to establish a free-trade area, eliminating most tariffs on
manufactured goods. Following its annual ministerial meeting each July, ASEAN also consults
with its ten "dialogue partners": Australia, Canada, China, the European Union, India, Japan,
Republic of Korea, New Zealand, Russia, and the United States. In its early years, ASEAN focused almost exclusively on economic matters and avoided security matters; however, in 1994
ASEAN helped form what is now a twenty-three-member Asian Regional Forum (ARF) that
meets annually at the ministerial level to promote regional stability and peace and to explore
confidence- and security-building measures as well as the modalities of preventive diplomacy
in the region.

The Asia-Pacific Economic Cooperation (APEC) is an association or process established in
1989 that promotes open trade and economic cooperation around the Pacific Rim. Participants in APEC include Australia, Brunei, Canada, Chile, the People's Republic of China (now
including Hong Kong), Indonesia, Japan, Republic of Korea, Malaysia, Mexico, New Zealand,
Papua New Guinea, Peru, the Philippines, Russia, Singapore, Taiwan, Thailand, the United
States, and Vietnam. A multilateral forum in which heads of government and other government ministers meet and interact, APEC addresses economic and related issues of common
concern in a continuing effort to promote economic growth. In addition to supporting national
and international organizations managing financial crises, APEC seeks jointly to develop human capital, foster safe and efficient capital markets, strengthen economic infrastructure, harness future technologies, promote environmentally sustainable growth, and encourage the
growth of small and medium-sized enterprises.

What options beyond unilateral efforts are there for states to help mitigate their
sense of insecurity under conditions of international anarchy? Three broad options are
world government and related world federalist designs, collective defense in alliances or
less formal coalitions, and collective security as in collective enforcement of international law against aggressor states that violate the sovereignty of other states.[4] A fourth
option is to build cooperative multilateral institutions not only for matters of defense
and security, but also to perform necessary functions in both regional and global
contexts. We will discuss each in turn.

World Government

Creating a **world government** involves the centralized management of international
or world politics. In its most complete form, centralized law-making, judicial, and law-
enforcement institutions would be established, and states would agree to relinquish
their control over foreign policy and national security, government finance, and other
important matters to central authorities. Cooperation is institutionalized centrally, although substantial authority still may be exercised by local authorities.

As such, world government has never occurred historically and is considered by
many observers of international relations to be either an idealistic pipe dream or a
recipe for a potentially domineering, authoritarian, global empire. By contrast, advocates see it as a more effective means for managing conflicts regionally and globally,

---

[4]For a classic treatment of world government, balance of power (collective defense), and collective security,
see Inis L. Claude, Jr., *Power and International Relations* (New York: Random House, 1962).

eliminating interstate war, and dealing with an increasingly complex agenda of global issues not easily addressed by the governments of sovereign states.

The idea of a world government to replace the anarchy inherent in international relations among sovereign states is not a new concept. The historical example that comes closest to world government is the Roman Empire, but even that was geographically limited in scope and power. For his part, the philosopher Jean-Jacques Rousseau examined various eighteenth-century proposals for eliminating interstate war by reestablishing centralized government in Europe as had existed in the Roman Empire. He concluded that however desirable such schemes might appear to be, there were just too many obstacles in the way of implementing them, making these ideas, in his view, decidedly impractical and unrealistic.

World federalists pursue a somewhat less ambitious approach to world governance. They look, in the short run at least, to establishing central institutions with practical roles to play. For example, many world federalists advocate vesting an international court or tribunal with the necessary legal authority to hear and make judgments in international criminal cases. Relatively small, incremental steps like this are more practical in their view than larger constitutional schemes that would try to transform global politics overnight. Even if world government were eventually achieved by pursuing such a step-by-step approach, their vision is one in which substantial authority would still be retained by local government units. In world federalism, local government units would coexist alongside centralized global institutions with a federal division of powers or authority between central and state governments composing this world union.

Alliances, Coalitions, and International Organizations

A second option is to create a formal alliance or less formal coalition with like-minded states. **Alliances** are coalitions of states, usually involving formal, long-term commitments; however, not all coalitions are alliances, at least not in the formal usage of the term. Thus, NATO is an alliance that has been around for more than half a century. More than an alliance, NATO is also an international (or intergovernmental) organization with established institutions, bureaucratic processes and routines, and command structures that facilitate the performance of its activities.

Alliances or coalitions can be offensive in character, as in World War II when Germany (then including Austria and other territories in central Europe) allied with Italy and Japan to form the Axis powers. Most alliances now, however, are defensive in orientation, pooling military forces and other resources for **collective defense.** Offensive alliances seek to upset the existing order or balance of power, whereas defensive alliances typically aim to maintain it, usually opting for the *status quo*—keeping things more or less the way they are.

This pooling of resources has the obvious advantage of spreading the burden of the costs of defense. According to realists, if states confront each other with relatively equal military capability, a balance of power exists, and aggression is less likely to occur. A successful example of an alliance is the North Atlantic Treaty Organization (NATO), created in 1949 both to deter Soviet aggression during what had become a "cold" war and to incorporate the new Federal Republic of Germany into a security framework so that past aggressive behavior by Germany in two twentieth-century world wars would not be repeated. (The text of the North Atlantic Treaty is provided as an appendix to this chapter.)

Although allies and friendly states frequently have differences among themselves, the alliances and other coalitions they form do provide arenas or forums for both

MAP 6.1   *Major Cold War European Alliance Systems.   The North Atlantic Treaty Organization, which includes both Canada and the United States, stretches as far east as Turkey. By contrast, the Warsaw Pact nations were the contiguous Communist states of Eastern Europe, with the Soviet Union, of course, as the dominant member.*

cooperative and collaborative activities. Even major disputes between allies, as between Greece and Turkey, both members of NATO, are usually better managed within an alliance framework that allows other alliance members to participate in helping find mutually acceptable approaches to the problems at hand. Cooperation even in assisting allies to manage or settle conflicts, therefore, is to be found primarily within an alliance or other coalition. Allies or coalition partners work together to strengthen their individual and collective positions in competition with other states and opposing alliances or coalitions. In other words, cooperation within an alliance and competition between an alliance or coalition and its adversaries typically characterize these relations.

Less formal coalitions may not have alliance status. The close relations that the United States has maintained with Israel, for example, include a formal agreement to cooperate on security matters that stops short of being a formal alliance. In large part, it is the United States that has avoided formally allying with Israel, in fear that doing so would undercut U.S. ability to work with and influence Arab states. Although strains in U.S.–Israeli relations have shown themselves from time to time, Israeli need for U.S. support and American commitment to the survival of Israel have kept the bilateral coalition intact.

Other coalitions formed to exercise security functions under the U.N. Charter do not qualify as formal alliances. The multinational coalition formed in 1990 and 1991 to liberate Kuwait from occupation by Iraqi forces is an example. Although balance-of-power, collective defense considerations played a central role, the purpose was also to enforce a legal, collective security mandate under U.N. Security Council auspices. Once Kuwait was liberated, the coalition dissolved. The much less robust coalition led by the United States in 2003 to overthrow the Saddam Hussein regime was also blessed by a U.N. Security Council resolution, although there was dispute on the Council on its interpretation.

NATO—The North Atlantic Treaty Organization

NATO now has twenty-six members. Sixteen are from Western Europe and North America: the United States, the Federal Republic of Germany, the United Kingdom, France, Italy, Canada, Belgium, Netherlands, Luxembourg, Denmark, Norway, Iceland, Greece, Turkey, Portugal, and Spain. More recent additions are the Czech Republic, Hungary, Poland, Bulgaria, Estonia, Latvia, Lithuania, Romania, Slovakia, and Slovenia, countries that had been within the Soviet sphere of influence during the Cold War. This geographic expansion eastward by NATO was originally quite controversial to the extent that such extensions might have been seen as threatening by the Russian Federation or other successor republics to the Soviet Union, which broke up at the end of 1991.

As one British diplomat somewhat undiplomatically asserted at the time NATO was formed in 1949, the alliance was established with three purposes in mind: (1) to keep the Americans "in" (i.e., U.S. participation in assuring European security); (2) to keep the Russians "out" (i.e., containing the Soviet Union from further expansion of its sphere of influence into Western Europe), and (3) to keep the Germans "down" (i.e., from rising yet again as a threat to other countries in Europe). Undiplomatic as they sounded, these three phrases did capture three key security concerns among the charter members of NATO.

A regional international organization that performs collective defense functions consistent with Article 51 of the U.N. Charter, NATO's geographic scope was originally limited to the European and North Atlantic area. For its part, the United States in 1949 did not want to be placed in the position of defending against attacks on British, French, Dutch, Portuguese, or Belgian colonies in Asia, Africa, or Latin America. As European empires were dismantled in the 1960s and subsequent decades, the United States tried to get NATO countries to support American efforts in such places as Vietnam or the Gulf; however, European countries (reluctant to engage in conflicts beyond the geographic scope authorized by the North Atlantic Treaty for NATO involvement) chose not to participate, identifying such contingencies as "out of area."

An attack against any NATO member is considered an attack against all. Although the North Atlantic Treaty provides for consultation by the allies if any member is threatened, in the event of such an attack, there is no provision for an automatic use of force. Force may be used, but the alliance is pledged under Article 5 only to take "such action as it deems necessary . . .

to restore and maintain the security of the North Atlantic area." Nevertheless, the NATO alliance proved to be a substantial bulwark for maintaining peace in Europe during and after the Cold War, routinizing collaboration among its members on security matters. Indeed, Article 5 was invoked after the terrorist attack on the United States on September 11, 2001.

As a practical matter, NATO's principal adversary during the Cold War was the Soviet Union and the Soviet-led Warsaw Pact—an alliance formed in 1955 and composed of the Soviet Union, the German Democratic Republic (East Germany), Poland, Czechoslovakia, Hungary, Romania, and Bulgaria. The long cold war struggle over more than four decades was marked by crises and years of high tension interspersed with periods of *détente* or reduced tension. At the end of the Cold War, the Warsaw Pact was dismantled as the Soviet Union itself dissolved into the Russian Federation and other new states formed from its component republics; but NATO survived.

Questions were raised in the 1990s concerning NATO's post–Cold War future, but the alliance proved useful as a means to secure continuing American commitment to European security. In the last half of the decade, NATO's well-developed organizational infrastructure facilitated carrying out military operations in the Balkans, both in Bosnia-Herzegovina and in Kosovo. In the post–9/11 era, NATO established a new precedent in 2003 by taking command of the international peacekeeping force in Afghanistan.

NATO's headquarters is in Brussels, and its military arm is located near Mons in the French-speaking part of Belgium, south of Brussels. The military arm is headed by an American four-star general who holds the title of Supreme Allied Commander Europe (SACEUR) and also is the senior commander of U.S. Forces in Europe. By contrast, the position of Secretary General at NATO headquarters in Brussels is a civilian post held historically by European members of the alliance. In addition to serving as a collective defense alliance, NATO may also be called on under U.N. mandate to perform collective security and other security and peacekeeping tasks.

As noted, the North Atlantic Treaty Organization did not become directly involved in the 1991 Gulf War because its members at the time saw the effort, however important, as falling outside the limits of NATO's geographic area of operations. Efforts by the coalition were supported, however, by another alliance not so geographically constrained, the Western European Union (WEU), which was established in 1948, the year before NATO was formed. The WEU included France, the United Kingdom, Germany, Italy, and other Western European powers, but by a 1999 agreement, its functions have been absorbed by the European Union.

When alliances are successful, security is the **collective good** (or **public good,** as it is sometimes called) they produce. Canada and the United States formed a bilateral alliance in the 1950s known as the North American Air (now Aerospace) Defense Command (NORAD). For its part, the United States maintains important bilateral alliances with a number of countries, including Japan and the Republic of Korea. Both Canada and the United States also belong to NATO, with its twenty-six member states.

A key political question in alliances is who will pay—and how much—for the collective good. Because member countries of alliances differ in capabilities, their contributions cannot be equal. Quite apart from their greater economic capability to pay more, countries such as the United States, which assume leading roles in alliances such as NATO, often pay proportionately more than countries playing less of a leading role.

NATO troops in Afghanistan

Some member countries pay a premium—more than their fair share—while others pay less, a reduced-fare price for the security provided by an alliance or other coalition. Politics within alliances such as NATO and other coalitions have often focused on burden sharing and the **free rider** problem, adjusting the distribution of costs among members in the interest of greater equity.

For some observers, the very success of NATO spells its ultimate doom. The conditions that gave rise to NATO and sustained it for forty cold war years—the Soviet or communist threat—no longer exist. The Soviet Union collapsed in 1991, and its own military alliance involving Eastern European states, the Warsaw Pact, also dissolved. Cold war fears had encouraged cooperation in the West and prompted the European members of NATO to defer to broader U.S. foreign policy objectives. Furthermore, it was under the umbrella of U.S. security guarantees that Western European economic recovery and development occurred. Without the Soviet threat, NATO was in search of a new role. Did NATO need a new threat or new set of risks to provide it a renewed sense of purpose and unity? It was initially thought that "political instability" might be an appropriate rallying cry. But, for some observers, NATO's inability to come to grips initially with the war in the former Yugoslavia was disappointing. Notwithstanding differences among the NATO allies, the organization eventually launched combined operations in the last half of the 1990s, first in Bosnia-Herzegovina then in Kosovo near the Albanian border. Others have been wary about the future of democracy in Russia, believing NATO must continue in effect as an insurance policy against any significant change of regime or orientation in Russia that in the future might pose new threats to other states in Europe and the North Atlantic area.

NATO's importance was apparent after the terrorist attacks on the World Trade Center in New York and the Pentagon outside Washington, D.C., on September 11, 2001. U.S. allies in NATO rallied quickly, invoking Article 5 for the first time in NATO's history and

SECURITY AS A COLLECTIVE GOOD

Applying Theory

The free-rider concept is an idea in public- or collective-goods theory—that "others" who make no payment or contributions themselves to providing the public or collective good are able to benefit from the contributions of one or a few who single-handedly or jointly provide the public good. In the classic case of those who finance or build a lighthouse on a seacoast, the lighthouse provides a benefit to ships or ship companies that have not paid for the light they are using to guide themselves at night. Access to the light from a lighthouse cannot effectively be limited only to those who have paid for it; access is universal to any ship or boat passing by. So it is with providers of security who pay the costs for security that benefits others who pay nothing (free riders) or pay less than they otherwise would have to pay (referred to here as reduced-fare riders) for this public- or collective-goods benefit.

In practical terms, this means that some countries pay far more than others (reduced-fare riders) for the security that an alliance such as NATO provides. Non-members of NATO also benefit from the security it brings to the North Atlantic area, even though they pay nothing for it. Another example is the North American Aerospace Defense (NORAD) alliance between Canada and the United States, which provides early warning of attack on either or both countries. Canada has relatively less financial capability and thus spends far less than the United States does for the security both obtain from NORAD, much less than if Canada tried to provide for this security unilaterally—entirely on its own.

In the first Gulf War, the United States assumed a leadership role in 1991 and assembled a multistate coalition in response to aggression by Iraq against Kuwait. All coalition partners participated in one way or another but to different degrees. Some countries (notably Japan and Germany) did not send combat units but agreed to help finance the effort. Thus the costs of the effort were borne asymmetrically or unevenly, with some making greater contributions than others; some participated less—reduced-fare payers both financially or in terms of troop and other military force contributions. To the extent that nonparticipating states also benefited from the coalition's efforts to provide security in the Gulf region, they qualified as free riders. The amount and kind of contribution any one participant made depended on individual state capabilities, the effectiveness of efforts by the United States and other coalition leaders to solicit these contributions, and the will of participating states to expend available resources for the venture.

Question: What incentives do great powers, such as the United States, need to provide security to other countries in the post–Cold War, twenty-first century?

supporting the U.S. war effort in Afghanistan against terrorist bases and the Taliban regime. Support for the U.S. took various forms, to include Germany's assumption of some U.S. air patrol responsibilities in North Atlantic air space, which then allowed the U.S. Air Force to reallocate these aircraft to the war effort. NATO members have also played an important role in providing peacekeeping forces in Afghanistan. The alliance was hurt, however, when divisions arose over how to deal with Saddam Hussein's Iraq in 2002–2003. The British, Spanish, and Italian governments were among those that supported the U.S. decision to go to war against Iraq, while the French, Germans, and others were adamant in strengthening the U.N. weapons inspection teams.

Collective Security

A third approach involves the notion of **collective security**.[5] The essential idea of collective security is "all against one" as in a common law-enforcement or police action against an aggressor state. In a way, the idea of collective security is like the posse of law-abiding citizens, popularized in the American West, who pooled their talents and other resources under command of state authorities to pursue lawbreakers. Unlike an alliance that is directed against an external threat, collective security is regionally or globally oriented. The purpose is to dissuade any state from breaking international law and committing aggression.

Under collective security arrangements, states retain ultimate control over their foreign policies but are pledged to confront any aggressor not with equal power, but rather with preponderant or overwhelming, collective use of force for international law-enforcement purposes. The threat of using such preponderant force as a means of law enforcement is viewed as a much more effective means to stop aggression and enforce international law than relying on a balance of power among competing states or alliances. Over time, the success of collective security arrangements is in mitigating the rivalry and hostility of an anarchic world composed of sovereign, independent, and often competitive states.

The emphasis in collective security, then, is on international law enforcement against aggressive or other illegal acts committed by states. As such, it is understood as an alternative to alliance-against-alliance or balance-of-power mechanisms. Instead of one power coalition against another, collective security pools the capabilities of "law-abiding" states against aggressors and other international lawbreakers.

The actual scope of collective security cooperation varies along a continuum. At one end are arrangements involving all states and covering all regions of the globe—universal arrangements. Members agree to respond collectively to aggression wherever it occurs. At the other end of the continuum is a concert of the great powers of the day. Their interest in peace may be global in scope or limited to particular regions. Unlike many alliances, there is no binding, ironclad commitment to collective action. Decisions are often made through negotiations and the emergence of a consensus. Although a concert requires that its members share essentially compatible views on the desired nature of the international order, power politics and competition among member states still occur. Such competition, however, falls short of overt hostility. In order to make the distinctions between the universal and concert approaches to collective security clearer, we will discuss several historical examples.

The Concert of Europe   The Concert of Europe, as we noted in earlier chapters, effectively lasted to a greater or lesser degree from the Congress of Vienna (1815), which was convened to put Europe back together after the defeat of Napoleon, until the Crimean War (1854). In 1815, the major players were the remaining great powers of the day: Great Britain, Russia, Austria, and Prussia (with territory in parts of present-day Germany, Poland, and Russia). France was admitted in 1818. In keeping with the Concert approach, minor states were not members of this select circle, and the geographic interest of the members was limited to Europe. Disputes outside Europe stemmed from the often-competing colonial ambitions of the major powers.

The critical, underlying consensus was that all members would abide by the territorial settlement of 1815. The *status quo* was to be changed only by consensus. If

[5]The following discussion draws from Charles A. Kupchan and Clifford A. Kupchan, "Concerts, Collective Security, and the Future of Europe," *International Security,* vol. 16, no. 1 (Summer 1991): 114–125.

Practicing World Politics

REGIONAL INTERNATIONAL ORGANIZATIONS AND ALLIANCES

It is worthwhile in any study of regional international organizations and alliances to check out their Internet sites. Following is an alphabetized list of addresses for a selected (but by no means complete) list of regional international organizations and alliances mentioned in this chapter:

African Union (www.africa-union.org)

Andean Group (www.comunidadandina.org)

Arab League (www.arableagueonline.org)

Asia-Pacific Economic Cooperation (www.apec.org)

Association of Southeast Asian Nations (www.aseansec.org)

Caribbean Community and Common Market (www.caricom.org); Cent. America (www.sieca.org.gt)

Council of Europe (www.coe.int)

Economic Community of West African States (www.ecowas.info)

European Union (europa.eu.int and, in the United States, www.eurunion.org)

Mercosur (Common Market Southern Cone, South America) (www.mercosur.org.uy)

North American Aerospace Defense Command (www.norad.mil)

North American Free Trade Association (www.nafta-sec-alena.org)

North Atlantic Treaty Organization (www.nato.int)

Organization of American States (www.oas.org)

Organization for Cooperation and Security in Europe (www.osce.org)

Organization of Petroleum Exporting Countries (www.opec.org)

Western European Union (www.weu.int)

The U.N. also has regional economic commissions in Africa, Europe, and Latin America that maintain the following Web sites:

Africa (Addis Ababa): (www.uneca.org)

Asia and the Pacific: (www.unescap.org)

Europe (Geneva): (www.unece.org)

Latin America (Santiago): (www.eclac.org)

Western Asia: (www.escwa.org.lb)

collective action were to be taken, it would be done through informal diplomatic negotiations, not by some formal mechanism such as those stipulated by the League of Nations Covenant or U.N. Charter. Some observers believe this informality accounts for the nearly four decades of peace among the major European powers in the first half of the nineteenth century.

Collective management of relations, as under the European Concert system, could be accomplished, some thought, by invoking universally accepted legal principles and norms. As such, Concert diplomacy can be understood as an early expression of collective security. That there are lawbreaking states that commit aggression or otherwise infringe on the sovereign prerogatives of other states was well understood. Law-abiding states, faced by aggression against any one of them, could band together to stop the violation. Any state could find security in the collective assurance that other states would come to its rescue. In sum, the Concert of Europe is an example of an international regime—one with rules of organization and norms of behavior.

U.S. President Woodrow Wilson was a strong proponent of the League of Nations and its collective security mission. The League failed to keep the peace.

The League of Nations   The idea of collective security was a cornerstone of the new League of Nations established in 1920 after World War I (1914–1918). The League was an attempt to institutionalize multilateral efforts toward maintenance of peace and prevention of the awful carnage that had just been experienced. Great hopes were placed in the League. It was meant to include all countries and to resist aggression everywhere; it was meant to be universal in scope. Thirty-two states attended the initial meeting that established the League; by 1938, there were fifty-seven members. All states were represented in the General Assembly, but the League Council was an inner circle consisting of great-power permanent members and several smaller powers that served on a rotating basis.

According to Article 16 of the League Covenant, states that engage in an act of aggression shall "*ipso facto* be deemed to have committed an act of war against all other Members of the League." All states were required to impose collective economic and diplomatic sanctions against the aggressor. The use of military action, however, was to be decided upon by the Council, which would recommend what each member should contribute to the military force. As a practical matter, however, there were technical difficulties in defining aggression with sufficient legal precision or clarity to be a sufficient grounds for collective action in particular cases. Furthermore, all Council recommendations had to be agreed on unanimously, so both temporary as well as permanent members in effect had veto power. States unwilling or unable for one reason or another to take collective action could (and did) hide behind these legal ambiguities. Genuine commitment by League members to collective security fell short. The League's inability to deal with the aggression of the Axis powers (Germany, Italy, and Japan) in the 1930s led ultimately to the demise of the League of Nations and the outbreak of World War II in 1939.

The United States must also share a portion of the blame. The United States did not even join the League and was not a participant in the collective security system. President Woodrow Wilson had asserted extraordinary influence in the post–World War I settlements that led to enshrining collective security within the new League of Nations, but the U.S. Senate failed to ratify the League Covenant. As events would finally demonstrate, the League and its collective security system failed to keep the peace. World war began again in 1939, some twenty years after the first world war had ended.

The United Nations   During World War II, diplomats charged with constructing a postwar international system drew lessons from earlier failures. The term "United Nations" was used by President Franklin D. Roosevelt in 1942 when twenty-six states pledged their governments to continue fighting together against the Axis powers (Germany, Italy, and Japan). The U.N. Charter was drawn up by representatives of fifty countries at the United Nations Conference on International Organizations, which met in San Francisco in 1945. Delegates deliberated on the proposals worked out by representatives of China, the Soviet Union, the United Kingdom, and the United States at Dumbarton Oaks, in Washington, D.C., from August to October in 1944.

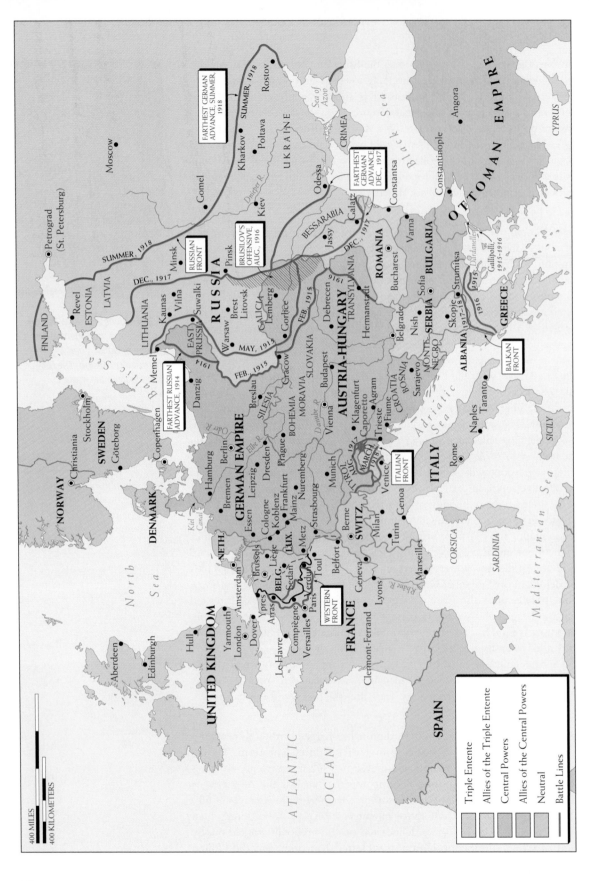

MAP 6.2   *Europe's Alliances and World War I, 1914–1918. Europe moved to a set of antagonist alliances in the first decade of the twentieth century in which Germany and the Austro-Hungarian Empire (known as the Central Powers or the Dual Alliance) were encircled by the Triple Entente (composed of Britain, France, and Russia). The members of the Triple Entente were later joined by Italy, who hoped to expel Austria from its Italian provinces.*

The charter was signed on June 26, 1945. The United Nations officially came into existence on October 24, 1945, when the charter had been ratified by the United States, China, France, the Soviet Union, the United Kingdom, and by a majority of other signatories.

As with the League, U.N. membership was to be universal in scope, all states participating in the General Assembly. Once again, however, the major powers at the time—the United States, the United Kingdom, France, the Soviet Union, and China (the victors in World War II over Germany and Japan)—became permanent members of the Security Council. Article 42 of the U.N. Charter granted the Security Council the power to initiate collective military action. Veto power was also retained by the five permanent members. As a practical matter, then, military force or other sanctions could never be directed under U.N. Security Council auspices against any of these five major powers because any resolution to that effect certainly would be vetoed by the major power affected.

While the United Nations did not abandon collective security as a concept, it was supplemented by both **preventive diplomacy** and collective defense. Preventive diplomacy seeks to prevent fighting from occurring in the first place. Accordingly, the U.N. Security Council was granted legal and political authority to facilitate dialogue and negotiation between disputants.

As a form of international law enforcement, collective security seeks to dissuade states from committing aggression, which may entail taking offensive military operations against the designated aggressor; however, collective defense, supported by a legal framework allowed under Article 51 in the U.N. Charter, rests primarily on power and balance-of-power considerations. Alliances are formed to assure defense through mutual or collective efforts. If collective security and respect for international law fail to prevent aggression, states can still rely on their own power and that of their allies to provide defense. The central point is that the new United Nations retained the League's collective security or collective law-enforcement commitment but did not place exclusive reliance on it for assuring international security. States also would retain their sovereign rights to individual or collective defense in collaboration with other states in alliances or other power-based coalitions.

U.N. supporters contend that this significant modification of the League system has contributed substantially to the absence of world war since 1945. In times of high tension during the Cold War, the Security Council could not reach consensus on many issues. In these circumstances, states could still rely on their respective collective defense alliances.

One major U.N.-sponsored military operation occurred during the Korean War (1950–1953). This came about only because the Soviet delegation walked out of the meeting and was not present to veto a U.S.-sponsored resolution that committed troops to turning back the communist forces that had entered southern Korea in June 1950. Even in the most difficult Cold War times, however, there was at least sufficient consensus in the Security Council to authorize a number of peacekeeping missions to the Middle East, the Mediterranean (Cyprus), Africa, and Asia, where core interests of Security Council members were typically not at stake.

Nothing in the U.N. Charter forbids a state to help itself when Security Council measures fail to have the desired effect. Its inherent right as a sovereign state to defend itself either by its own means or in collaboration with others remains intact.

Multilateral Diplomacy   In a larger sense, multilateral diplomacy in the United Nations as a whole (principal organs, their functional units, and specialized agencies) and in other international organizations has contributed to substantial progress in arms control, trade and commerce, health, human rights, environmental protection, and other

The Objectives and Structure of the United Nations

When states become members of the United Nations, they agree to accept the obligations of the U.N. Charter, an international treaty. According to the Charter, the United Nations has four basic principles: (1) to maintain international peace and security; (2) to develop friendly relations among nations; (3) to cooperate in solving international problems and in promoting human rights; and (4) to be a center for harmonizing the actions of nations. Some critics charge the United Nations has done a poor job in achieving these aims, whereas others charge the United Nations is doing too much and is a threat to the sovereign power of member states.

The United Nations has six main organs. The General Assembly, the Security Council, the Economic and Social Council, the Trusteeship Council, and the Secretariat are based at the U.N. headquarters in New York. The sixth organ, the International Court of Justice, is at The Hague, Netherlands.

The General Assembly consists of all member states. It meets as a deliberative body to consider pressing global problems. Each state has one vote. If the decision involves important matters involving peace and security, admitting new members, the U.N. budget, or the budget for peacekeeping, a two-thirds majority is required. Other issues require a simple majority. The Assembly cannot force any state to take an action, but the United Nations views Assembly recommendations as an indication of world opinion. The Assembly meets from September to December. When it is not meeting, its work is carried out by its six main committees and the U.N. Secretariat.

The Security Council is given the main responsibility for maintaining international peace and security and hence may meet at any time. There are fifteen Council members, with five—China, France, the Russian Federation, the United Kingdom, and the United States—permanent members. The other ten are elected by the General Assembly for two-year terms. In recent years there have been discussions about changing the composition of the Security Council. Decisions of the Council require nine "yes" votes. Each of the five permanent members, however, has veto power. When there is a threat to international peace, the Council generally first explores ways to settle the dispute peacefully, such as undertaking mediation efforts. If fighting has broken out, the Council may try to secure a cease-fire. If a truce or cessation of hostilities occurs, the Council may send in an international peacekeeping force to keep the opposing forces apart. The Council can also take measures to enforce its decisions, such as imposing economic sanctions or ordering an arms embargo.

As its title suggests, the Economic and Social Council coordinates the economic and social work of the United Nations. It is the central forum for discussing international economic and social issues and formulating policy recommendations. The Council receives input from numerous nongovernmental organizations that engage in lobbying and informational efforts. The Council has fifty-four members elected by the General Assembly for three-year terms. It meets one month each year, alternating between sessions in New York and Geneva, Switzerland. The year-round work, therefore, is carried out by subsidiary bodies and working groups. The Commission on Human Rights is one example, and other bodies focus on such issues as social development, the status of women, crime prevention, and environmental protection.

The Trusteeship Council was originally established to provide international supervision of eleven trust territories administered by seven member states. The Council's goal was to help these territories prepare for self-government or independence. By 1994 all of the trust territories had achieved this goal.

The International Court of Justice (also known as the World Court) is the main judicial organ of the United Nations. It consists of fifteen judges elected by the General Assembly and the Security Council. The Court decides disputes among member states, but participation in the proceedings is voluntary. If, however, a state agrees to participate, it is obligated to comply with the Court's decision.

The Secretariat carries out the substantive and administrative work of the United Nations as authorized or directed by the General Assembly, the Security Council, and other organs. The head official is the Secretary General. The U.N. staff totals some 8,700 persons drawn from 160

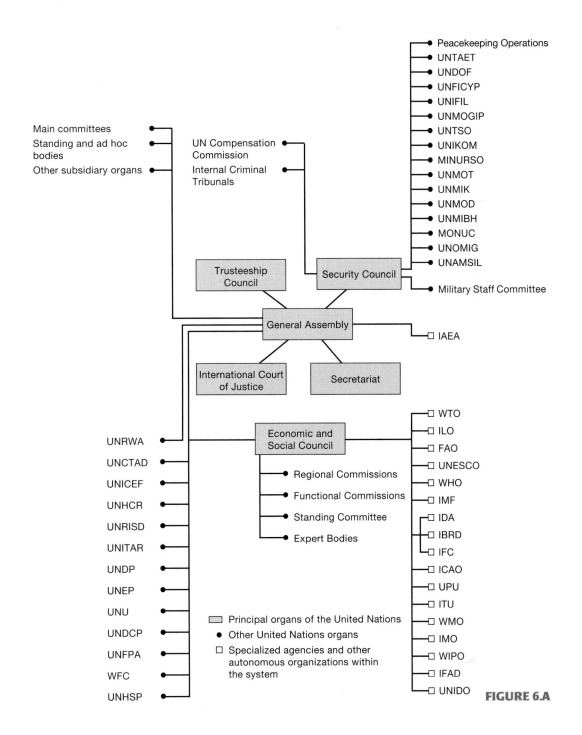

FIGURE 6.A

countries. Aside from the headquarters in New York, personnel are assigned to U.N. offices in Geneva, Vienna, and Nairobi.

It should also be noted that the U.N. systems (see Figure 6.A) include numerous functional units as well as the International Monetary Fund (IMF), the World Bank Group, World Trade Organization (WTO), and twelve other independent organizations known as "specialized agencies" linked to the United Nations through cooperative agreements. These other agencies include the World Health Organization (WHO), the International Civil Aviation Organization (ICAO), and the International Labor Organization (ILO). Capsule summaries of U.N. specialized agencies are provided later in this chapter.

Source: www.u.n..org/aboutun/unchart.

---

socioeconomic issues. It was understood in 1945 that maintaining peace would involve much more than preventive diplomacy, collective security, and collective defense efforts. A lasting peace would have to rest on a much wider foundation of collaborative action, particularly on socioeconomic questions central to economics and identity. It was realized that progress in disarmament and arms control would also be crucial to advancing worldwide security. Much remains to be done as these issues continue to pose great challenges to diplomats.

Multilateral diplomacy also has been institutionalized in such regional organizations as the Association of Southeast Asian Nations (ASEAN) and the Organization of American States (OAS). Particularly noteworthy, however, is the degree of progress that has been achieved since 1945 in Europe—the creation of a Council of Europe to support democracy, a European Union (EU) of states committed to strengthening economic and political ties among its members, and periodic meetings within the Conference on Security and Cooperation in Europe (CSCE), now institutionalized as the Organization for Security and Cooperation in Europe (OSCE).

Since its formal establishment by negotiations culminating in the 1975 Act of Helsinki, the CSCE was understood until the end of the Cold War more as a "process" than as yet another international institution. In the 1990s, however, members of the CSCE added a few institutions in Vienna, Prague, and Warsaw to support its work, renaming itself the Organization for Security and Cooperation in Europe. The core of the OSCE's work, however, remains a general commitment to dealing with security, socioeconomic, cultural, and human rights issues as part of a recurring multilateral agenda.

Multilateral diplomacy as an approach to managing both cooperative and conflictual relations has come a long way from the Concert system of the first half of the nineteenth century. Great experiments have been conducted, lessons have been drawn from these experiences, and modifications have been proposed and implemented. With the end of the Cold War, a number of observers predicted great things for the United Nations in terms of collective security and peacekeeping. The disintegration of Yugoslavia into warring national or ethnic factions, however, exposed weaknesses and problems within both NATO and the United Nations as well as in other international organizations such as the OSCE and European Union. In Yugoslavia and the Balkans, however, it was the greater institutionalization of NATO with its well-established military command-and-control mechanisms as well as capabilities brought by U.S. participation that made NATO, along with the OSCE on civil functions, the alliance and international organizations of choice for these contingencies.

Limitations to Collective Security   Why has more not been accomplished by organizations concerned with collective security? Universal and concert approaches to collective security suffer from at least six problems.[6] First is confusion about what is cause and what is effect in the relation between collective security and peace. Does collective security encourage peace, or does peace have to exist in order for collective security arrangements to be instituted? In other words, both the League of Nations and the United Nations were created after exhausting, devastating wars. These times of postwar positive expectations did not last very long, and the usefulness of such organizations should be judged on how they perform in difficult (not just in good) times. When fascism reared its ugly head in the 1930s in Europe and Asia, the League ultimately failed. When the Cold War began in the late 1940s, many realists subsequently argued that the United Nations had become more of an arena for Soviet-American competition than an ameliorating factor in reducing East-West tensions.

Second is a gap between states' expressed commitments to collective security and their actions. For a number of reasons, states are sometimes reluctant to fulfill their international commitments even when the act of aggression seems blatant. Consider, for example, the international reaction to Iraq's invasion of neighboring Kuwait in 1991. This would seem to have been an easy test for the efficacy of collective security— flagrant aggression by a dictatorial state against a country with significant oil reserves. Yet there was a great deal of hand-wringing in capitals around the world, and it took U.S. leadership and some arm-twisting to put the coalition together.

Third, timing is often a problem. Unlike an alliance, which traditionally has an identified enemy, war plans, and joint training, collective security efforts do not have these established elements. Consider again the first Gulf War against Iraq, which required six months of training and planning before Operation Desert Storm was launched. Even Operation Enduring Freedom, the second war against Iraq, which was launched in 2003, took months of planning and preparation. The point is that putting together a coalition, deciding on who contributes what, and devising a strategy take time, which may lead in some cases to a belated military response.

Fourth, by relying on collective security's multilateralist response, there is always the possibility that the virtues of unilateralism (actions taken by one state) will be overlooked. While a collective security effort offers the greatest amount of pooled or collective power, it does so at the expense of flexibility. Numerous states will doubtless want to influence policy decisions. A unilateral response may provide less power but greater flexibility in terms of planning and implementation. Perhaps the best combination was evident in the 1991 Gulf War, in which an international coalition was formed under the leadership of the United States. The United States put the powerful coalition together but was in the driver's seat in planning the military strategy for the campaign and actual deployment of coalition forces. By 2003, however, U.S. efforts to re-create a large international coalition to overthrow Saddam Hussein were stymied by contending assessments of the degree of threat posed by Iraq, the status of its weapons of mass destruction program, and differing assessments as to the potential for success on the part of U.N. weapons inspectors. Given the tremendous gap in military power between the United States and other countries that widened even further during the 1990s, the United States had, from its point of view, the best of all worlds—supreme military power plus flexibility in terms of planning and implementing the invasion of Iraq. But while the U.S.-led invasion was a military success in terms of overthrowing the Iraqi regime, the alienation of important NATO allies found the United States scrambling for support in postinvasion efforts to stabilize Iraq.

Fifth, as collective-security obligations typically call for some response, it is possible that a minor war could escalate into a major war. For example, a small war between

---

[6]See Mark T. Clark, "The Trouble with Collective Security," *Orbis*, vol. 39, no. 2 (Spring 1995): 241 *et passim*.

two states in Africa might not draw a great deal of international attention. On the other hand, if there were an automatic collective security mechanism in operation that demanded a response to any breach of the peace, the possibility exists that with greater international involvement a small brushfire war might expand or escalate to become a larger regional or even global conflict.

Finally, collective security can imply a commitment to the *status quo*. The Gulf War aside, concern for threats to the peace are paramount. Issues of justice tend to be secondary concerns. When questions of justice are ignored and blame is not assigned, there is a good chance that the collective security mechanism might break down due to disagreements among states on the legitimacy of the cause.

Peacekeeping: Managing and Controlling Conflicts

Peacekeeping can be understood as an extension of collective security thinking to cover conflicts that threaten international peace and security, particularly in the regions where these conflicts are being played out. Resolving conflicts involving states and nongovernmental parties are often decades-long projects at best, particularly when territorial issues are linked to competing national, ethnic, or tribal claims. Sometimes the most that can be achieved is to manage these conflicts—to contain and keep them from becoming violent as constructive steps are taken to address the difficult, divisive issues involved.

Since the end of World War II, even at the height of cold war tensions, important efforts have been undertaken to keep the peace by stationing multinational U.N. forces (so-called Blue Helmets) or other national and multinational contingents on patrol in territorial border areas to provide a buffer or separation between conflicting parties and perform other functions necessary for the security and welfare of populations and the conflicting parties. At various times (and often for extended periods), one could find peacekeepers in such diverse places as the Mediterranean island of Cyprus, the Sinai desert, sub-Saharan Africa, the Balkan area of southeastern Europe, central Asia and Cambodia, or East Timor in Southeast Asia (see box on page 215).

U.N. **peacekeeping** forces have never been intended to fight wars. Accordingly, they have usually been relatively small, lightly armed contingents, capable militarily only of modest defense of their own positions if they come under attack by any party. During the Cold War, peacekeepers were drawn from the national militaries of neutral or nonaligned states, often with equal representation of NATO and Warsaw Pact members as well. Their purpose was to capitalize on the moral authority drawn from their position as peacekeepers accepted in principle by all contending parties. As such, they were not to intervene in these conflicts, much less take sides. They were only to monitor the peace and to provide a necessary presence to dissuade the parties from resorting to force against each other.

Though never without problems, peacekeeping has worked best in these circumstances. A vexing problem, however, is what to do when a government collapses, civil war breaks out, no one is in charge, or widespread famine occurs. In such cases there are no parties to agree to a U.N. presence. This occurred in Somalia in 1993 when the regime collapsed and domestic disorder broke out. An international operation organized by the United States was initially dispatched to ensure the delivery of food supplies. Permission was not requested as Somalia was not a unified state but rather a

Two Irish UNIFIL peacekeepers confer beside a wall with portraits of Islamic leaders in a town in Lebanon. The mission dates back to 1978.

U.N. mission in Bosnia-Hercegovina was turned over to NATO in 1995.

A U.N. force has been deployed in Cyprus since 1964.

collection of warring clans. What is known as mission creep subsequently occurred: The relief effort gave way to an attempt to enforce peace—a substantial expansion of the original humanitarian mission.

Long-term civil unrest in East Timor came to a head in 1999 when residents of this former Portuguese colony taken by Indonesia in 1975 voted to become independent of Indonesia in a referendum watched by U.N. observers. Opposed to the outcome, elements of the Indonesian security forces cracked down on the East Timorese population, murdering residents and committing other human rights violations. With U.N. backing and concurrence of the Indonesian government in Jakarta, a multinational coalition led by Australia ultimately intervened to restore order.

Selected Peacekeeping and Observer Missions

The United Nations and other peacekeeping missions or functional units summarized here and organized by region have detailed missions to perform that are specified typically in U.N. Security Council resolutions and the resolutions of such other international organizations in Europe as NATO and OSCE. The emergence of new contingencies and rapidly changing circumstances have made peacekeeping and observer missions highly fluid, with missions created seemingly overnight in diverse parts of the world—many to be disbanded (or merged with others) as soon as their immediate objectives have been completed. Others are left standing, sometimes for decades, depending on the purposes that remain to be served. For the latest information on peacekeeping and observer missions, check U.N., NATO, and OSCE sources, including their respective Web sites. An excellent summary also can be found in the annual *Military Balance* published by the London-based International Institute for Strategic Studies and available in the reference sections of university and other libraries.

Examples of peacekeeping efforts include missions in almost every part of the world, presented by regions as follows.

Africa
U.N. Mission in the Democratic Republic of the Congo (MONUC)

- Established in December 1999
- Contributes to maintenance of civil order

U.N. Mission for the Referendum in Western Sahara (MINURSO)
- Established in April 1991 and headquartered in Laayoune, Morocco
- Designed to end dispute over future of Western Sahara between Morocco and separatist POLISARIO forces

U.N. Observer Mission in Sierra Leone (UNAMSIL)
- Established in 1999 and headquartered in Freetown, Sierra Leone
- Observes integration of former combatants into society and monitors civil order

U.N. Mission in Liberia (UNMIL)
- Established in 2003 to assist in the implementation of a ceasefire and peace agreement

U.N. Mission in Ethiopia and Eritrea (UNMEE)
- Established in July 2000 to maintain liaison between the two states following cessation of hostilities

Asia

U.N. Military Observer Group in India and Pakistan (UNMOGIP)
- Established in 1949 and headquartered in Rawalpindi, Pakistan, and Sringar, India
- Supervises India-Pakistan border in disputed Jammu-Kashmir area

U.N. Observer Mission in Georgia (UNOMIG)
- Established in 1993 and headquartered in Sukhumi, Georgia
- Monitors cease-fire in disputed Georgia-Abkhazia area

U.N. Mission of Support in East Timor (UNMISET)
- Originally established in 1999 and headquartered in East Timor; in 2002 the name changed to UNMISET when East Timor gained independence
- Promotes peace, stability, and reconciliation and provides civil affairs and electoral units, as well as a civilian police component to recruit and train the East Timorese police force, a military liaison component to undertake the necessary military liaison functions, and a public information component to provide information on progress made

Europe

U.N. Force in Cyprus (UNFICYP)
- Established in 1964 and headquartered in Nicosia, Cyprus
- Separates Greek and Turkish Cypriots and seeks to avoid recurrence of fighting since 1974 cease-fire

NATO Stabilization Force (SFOR II)
- Established by NATO in 1998 to continue work of SFOR I; headquartered in Sarajevo, Bosnia-Herzegovina
- Separates combatant forces, controls air space, assists movement of refugees, and removes mines and other battlefield hazards

U.N. Interim Administration Mission in Kosovo (UNMIK)
- Established in 1999 and headquartered in Kosovo
- Tasks include administration of the province, promoting substantial autonomy and self-government in Kosovo, facilitating a political process to determine Kosovo's future status, supporting the reconstruction of key infrastructure and humanitarian

and disaster relief, maintaining civil law and order, promoting human rights, and assuring the safe and unimpeded return of all refugees and displaced persons to their homes

NATO International Security Force for Kosovo (KFOR)

- Established in 1999 and headquartered in Kosovo
- Provides a secure environment to all ethnic groups, monitors the newly formed Kosovo Protection Corps, supports the U.N. mission in Kosovo (UNMIK) with its civil implementation tasks

NATO Albania Force (AFOR)

- Established in 1999 and headquartered in Plepa, Albania
- Mission to support U.N. High Commissioner for Refugees (UNHCR) and Albanian authorities to assist Kosovo refugees by constructing refugee camps, providing transportation and engineering support to repair transportation infrastructure, and assisting with electronic communications

OSCE Peace Missions

- Missions include Bosnia-Herzegovina, Croatia, Estonia, Georgia, Latvia, Moldova, Macedonia, Tajikistan, and Ukraine, as well as efforts in Chechnya and Nagorno-Karabakh
- OSCE teams act as observers of conflict areas, mediators, and supervisors of elections

Middle East

U.N. Truce Supervision Organization (UNTSO)

- Established in 1948 and headquartered in Jerusalem
- Military observers have patrolled borders in such Arab-Israeli hot spots as Egypt, Syria (Golan Heights), the Lebanon, and Jordanian-Palestinian-Israeli areas

U.N. Disengagement Observer Force (UNDOF)

- Established in 1974 and headquartered in Damascus, Syria
- Supervises cease-fire lines between Israel and Syria since the 1973 war

U.N. Interim Force in Lebanon (UNIFIL)

- Established in 1978 and headquartered in Naqoura, Lebanon
- Separated Israeli and Lebanese forces, overseeing Israeli withdrawal from southern Lebanon in May 2000

The Somalia and East Timor cases typify the sorts of challenges the international community continues to face. Efforts have thus been undertaken to expand beyond the more limited peacekeeping or peace-monitoring roles to include peace enforcement and even peacemaking. These U.N. "Blue Helmets" lacked the military capability to perform these latter tasks, which are less peace-oriented than they sound; they really amount to using force to "make the peace" or enforce it. Pressed by compelling circumstances, performance of these collective security tasks has evolved well beyond both the original, more limited understanding of peacekeeping and the forces detailed for that purpose. Indeed, the great powers in the U.N. security council have been late to respond or reluctant to authorize or provide necessary resources for humanitarian interventions in places as diverse as Rwanda in central Africa and Darfur in the Sudan.

Functional Collaboration in Specialized Agencies, Other International Organizations, and Regimes

We have discussed three approaches to cooperation by which states and other actors have been urged by proponents to build security under conditions of international anarchy—eventually remove anarchy by pursuing world government and related world-federalist designs, organize collective defense in alliances or less formal coalitions, and provide collective security in its various dimensions, including peacekeeping and observer missions.

A fourth approach is to build cooperative multilateral institutions not only for matters of defense and security, but also to perform other important functions in both regional and global contexts. Aside from the U.N. organization with its six principal organs discussed earlier (the General Assembly, Security Council, Economic and Social Council, Trusteeship Council, International Court of Justice, and Secretariat), a large number of specialized agencies perform important tasks in a wide array of socioeconomic, human rights, and other human welfare tasks. Some of these are closely tied to U.N. organs, while others are more loosely affiliated with the United Nations or tied to various regional international organizations.

What political analysts and other observers refer to as **international regimes** have typically grown up alongside these international organizations, providing generally understood or accepted norms or "rules of the road" to guide states, international organizations, and nonstate actors in dealing with even the most technical issues of common concern. The rules or norms that constitute these regimes typically have developed over time by customary practice or in some cases have been specified more formally in multilateral agreements, treaties, or conventions. How these rules or norms have developed and evolved is of particular interest to pluralists or liberals and social constructivists.

Although nongovernmental organizations interact with security-related international organizations, they have proven to be particularly active participants in the human welfare domain of international organizational activity. NGOs influence the agendas of international organizations, many also monitoring closely their performance, holding them accountable for their actions in three principal ways: (1) directly by making their positions known to international organization officials; (2) indirectly influencing them through their links to the national governments of international organization member states; and (3) by publicizing their views via mass communications media—the press, radio, cinema, television, and most recently, the Internet.

Even in the bleakest years of the Cold War, functional collaboration within international organizations persisted, driven by the importance of the tasks on their agendas. Routinization of task performance also removed these issues from the international conflicts that otherwise divided countries and peoples. Cooperation thus survived even in periods of great international discord. Notwithstanding enormous frustrations at the time with conflicts in the Security Council that so constrained the United Nations as an effective multilateral actor in security matters, U.N. advocates at least found some compensation in the continuing work and contributions made by U.N. and other specialized agencies.

Finally we note the U.N. role in holding a number of international conferences designed to build global consensus on important (though often controversial) socioeconomic and human rights issues. The approach is not new. Indeed, such efforts began in the 1960s in an effort to deal with trade and development priorities and cooperative strategies. The 1990s witnessed international conferences, for example, on education,

Applying Theory

FUNCTION-ALISM, NEOFUNC-TIONALISM, AND EPISTEMIC COMMUNITIES

In his 1943 book, *A Working Peace System,* David Mitrany identified certain functions that could not be performed by states single-handedly and thus were the basis for forming international organizations to perform them. The performance of such functions as mail delivery across borders, telecommunications, transportation, exchange of money, international trade and investment, and disease control require greater international institutionalization—the construction of functionally specific international organizations. The oldest of these are the International Telecommunication Union or ITU (as successor to the International Telegraphic Union that originated in 1865) and the Universal Postal Union, or UPU, established in 1874. Technological advances often have created new (or expanded old) functions. For example, the airplane became the basis for a new civil aviation industry requiring transborder and transoceanic coordination among domestic civil aviation authorities and necessitating creation of an International Civil Aviation Organization (ICAO) to ensure security and air safety by both commercial and government passenger and cargo airplanes. Following this technology-driven logic, the ITU's agenda was not to remain static; its charter also grew as telecommunications technologies progressed beyond telephone and telegraph. Indeed, frequency use has become ever more complex as demand for assigned frequencies has increased with the advent of new modes of transmission—radio, television, and now satellites and the Internet. In short, the ITU has had to expand its scope and the tasks it performs in managing the telecommunications function.

Building on Mitrany's **functionalism**—that functions give impetus to establishing the international organizations to perform these functions, pluralists such as Ernst Haas identified politics as the missing variable in Mitrany's formulation. Haas and other **neofunctionalists** following his lead have put particular emphasis on the role played by politically connected, often technically specialized elites as carriers of integration and the construction and expansion of international organizations. In the examples used here, politically connected civil aviation or telecommunications experts are instrumental in the process of constructing, maintaining, and expanding their respective specialized agencies or international organizations—the ICAO and ITU—that regulate or facilitate operations in these sectors. Similarly, economic and financial experts who both influence and respond to political authorities essential to bringing these international organizations online (and maintaining and expanding their tasks) have played central roles in developing such international organizations as the World Bank, International Monetary Fund, and World Trade Organization. For his part, Peter Haas has focused research on the *epistemic communities* formed by specialists who communicate with each other across national borders, building professional relationships and associations in the often technical fields that define their common interests and concerns. Such communities may aid and influence government officials in redefining their interests. This emphasis on learning and redefinition of interests is a hallmark not only of pluralist perspectives on world politics, but of social constructivists and feminists as well.

Question: Pluralists would argue that the increase in global interdependence should facilitate functionalist logic. How would a realist possibly respond?

epistemic communities
Associations, typically across national borders, among knowledgeable persons or experts in particular (often technical) fields; these are networks of personal contacts established and maintained over time in various settings— international meetings and conferences, joint research projects, contacts in international and nongovernmental organizations, and direct communications facilitated now by the Internet.

sustainable economic development in relation to population and the environment, social development, human rights, the advancement of women, youth, human settlements, the world drug problem, natural disaster reduction, fighting landmines, and peaceful uses of outer space. Follow-on conferences on many of these global concerns have continued in the present decade, the agenda also including a focus on the least developed countries, trade and development (a U.N. priority since the 1960s), financing development, indigenous peoples issues, climate change, biological diversity, forests, food, children, aging, crime and justice, illicit trade in small arms and light weapons, nonproliferation of weapons of mass destruction, racism and other forms of intolerance to include "Islamophobia," immune deficiency (HIV/AIDS), Internet governance, and road safety.

Conclusion

In this chapter, we have identified a spectrum between harmony and discord that characterizes the often insecure relations of states in an anarchic world. The emphasis, however, has been on the ways and means by which states cooperate in the regimes and international organizations they have constructed. Alliances and coalitions respectively are formal and less formal types of international organization usually created with security purposes in mind. Other international organizations treat regional or functional issues relating not just to security, but also to socioeconomic, human rights, and other human welfare issues affecting states and their peoples, topics we will address in subsequent chapters. Nongovernmental organizations are playing an increasing role in influencing and monitoring states and international organizations.

Four approaches to building security and cooperation include (1) building authoritative institutions to exercise a greater degree of world governance; (2) cooperating within alliances and coalitions to meet collective defense challenges; (3) participating in multilateral collective security and peacekeeping measures to advance the rule of law and international law enforcement in international relations; and (4) building consensus and expanding multilateral international organizations and regimes to deal functionally with the many diverse issues on the twenty-first-century global agenda.

Key Terms

international organization (IO)   *p. 194*

international regime   *p. 198*

epistemic community   *p. 221*

Other Concepts

intergovernmental organization (IGO)   *p. 194*
multilateralism   *p. 198*
social constructivism   *p. 198*
world government   *p. 200*
world federalist   *p. 201*

alliance   *p. 201*
collective defense   *p. 201*
collective good   *p. 204*
public good   *p. 204*
free rider   *p. 205*
collective security   *p. 207*

preventive diplomacy   *p. 211*
peacekeeping   *p. 216*
functionalism, functionalist   *p. 221*
neofunctionalism, neofunctionalist   *p. 221*

Additional Readings

The literature on international organizations, alliances, coalitions, and regimes is extensive. On integration related to both global and regional international organizations, we have relied heavily on insights drawn from the works of the late Ernst B. Haas such as his now-classic *Beyond the Nation State* (Palo Alto, CA: Stanford University Press, 1964) and his earlier *The Uniting of Europe* (South Bend, IN: Notre Dame University Press, 1958, 2004). We also note the work of the late Werner J. Feld and his colleague Robert S. Jordan, *International Organizations: A Comparative Approach* (Westport, CT: Praeger, 1994), now in its fourth edition, and Robert S. Jordan et al., *International Organizations: A Comparative Approach to the Management of Cooperation* (New York: Praeger, 2001). The classic treatment of international organizations is Inis L. Claude's, *Swords into Plowshares* (New York: McGraw-Hill); a companion to this is Claude's *Power and International Relations* (New York: Random House, 1962), which presents world government, balance of power, and collective security as alternative approaches to order in international relations. On regimes, see Stephen D. Krasner, ed., *International Regimes* (Ithaca, NY: Cornell University Press, 1983); Volker Rittberger, ed., *Regime Theory and International Relations* (Oxford, UK: Clarendon Press, 1993); Andreas Hasenclever, Peter Mayer, and Volker Rittberger, *Theories of International Regimes* (Cambridge: Cambridge University Press, 1997); and Robert Keohane and Elinor Ostrom, *Local Commons and Global Interdependence* (Thousand Oaks, CA: SAGE Publications, 1995). On social constructivism, see John Ruggie's *Constructing the World Polity* (London: Routledge, 1998) and Alexander Wendt's *Social Theory of International Politics* (Cambridge: Cambridge University Press, 1999). An early presentation on epistemic communities is an article by Peter M. Haas, "Do Regimes Matter? Epistemic Communities and Mediterranean Pollution Control," *International Organization*, vol. 43, no. 3 (Summer 1989): 377–403; see also his later *Knowledge, Power and International Policy Coordination* (Columbia: University of South Carolina Press, 1997). On the post–World War II history of U.N. peacekeeping, see William J. Durch, ed., *The Evolution of U.N. Peacekeeping* (New York: St. Martin's Press, 1993) and Scott A. Hunt, *On the Future of Peace: On the Front Lines with the World's Great Peacemakers* (San Francisco: HarperCollins, 2004). On alliances, see Stephen M. Walt, *The Origins of Alliances* (Ithaca, NY: Cornell University Press, 1987), and on cooperative security arrangements see Emanuel Adler, *Security Communities* (Cambridge: Cambridge University Press, 1998).

Appendices: The United Nations Charter and the North Atlantic Treaty

The United Nations was placed in 1945 as the cornerstone of efforts to maintain international peace and security, to improve the social and economic condition of humankind, and to provide a global framework within which still sovereign states would conduct their international relations. We present two documents worth consulting not just because they outline the authorities, roles, and missions of two out of many international organizations of importance in the twenty-first century, but also because they encapsulate key theoretical understandings related to international relations and world politics. Indeed, the ways and means of maintaining international peace and security in these documents go well beyond the mechanisms of collective security and collective defense, providing an institutional framework for a programmatic approach that attempts to integrate the social, economic, and political dimensions of life in a world of diverse states and societies. We see in this an effort, buttressed by both pluralist or liberal internationalist and realist understandings, to provide for the rule of law in a world politics tempered by the realities of power and interest.

We include below the United Nations Charter (1945) and the North Atlantic Treaty that established NATO, the latter an example of an alliance and international organization grounded in authority provided by the U.N. Charter. Note specific references in the North Atlantic Treaty to Article 51 of the Charter, which allows states to provide for their individual and collective self-defense. The North Atlantic Treaty underscores, however, that the U.N. Security Council retains the principal responsibility (and commensurate authority) to maintain international peace and security. As a practical matter, of course, in the absence of the necessary consensus (to include the five permanent members) on the U.N. Security Council, NATO members are free under Article 51 to take appropriate action authorized by the North Atlantic Treaty.

United Nations Charter

(1945)

The U.N. Charter is more than just a legal document defining the roles and authority of principal organs within the United Nations Organization (UNO) in relation to its affiliated agencies within a U.N. "system" of states. Indeed, it is also a multilateral blueprint, grounded in political theory, for the maintenance of international peace and security and for the promotion of fundamental human rights and economic and social advancement. The reading below, starting with the preamble, contains the most important chapters, articles, and sections of the Charter. To facilitate reading, we have also italicized what we consider to be key provisions. The full text can be found readily at www.u.n..org.

The Charter explicitly recognizes the sovereignty of its member states, but also establishes an important exception to the state's sovereign claim by allowing U.N. intervention in matters involving international peace and security (Article 2, Sections 1 and 7 and Chapter VII). The General Assembly (Chapter IV) has broad authority to take up issues of global importance to include international peace and security, which is the primary responsibility of the Security Council (Chapter V). The Secretariat (Chapter XV) supports the work of these two organs as well as the Economic and Social Council (Chapter X), Trusteeship Council (Chapter XIII), and the International Court of Justice (Chapter XIV).

We find here a global plan for dealing with international peace and security (especially in Chapters V–VIII), international economic and social cooperation (Chapters IX and X), and judicial settlement of disputes among states (Chapter XIV). As in the earlier League of Nations that operated in the interwar period between World Wars I and II, responsibility for collective security (i.e., international law enforcement as in collective action against aggression) remained primarily with the Security Council. On the other hand, Article 51 also allows for collective-defense alliances or coalitions. Since the end of the Cold War, there has been greater reliance on collective-security actions under the Security Council, but the veto power held by each of the permanent members (China, France, Russia, the United Kingdom, and the United States) can moderate or block Security Council actions when there is no great-power consensus on what is to be done.

We the peoples of the United Nations determined to save succeeding generations from the scourge of war, which twice in our lifetime has brought untold sorrow to mankind, and to reaffirm faith in fundamental human rights, in the dignity and worth of the human person, in the equal rights of men and women and of nations large and small, and to establish conditions under which justice and respect for the obligations arising from treaties and other sources of international law can be maintained, and to promote social progress and better standards of life in larger freedom, and for these ends to practice tolerance and live together in peace with one another as good neighbours, and to unite our strength to maintain international peace and security, and to ensure, by the acceptance of principles and the institution of methods, that armed force shall not be used, save in the common interest, and to employ international machinery for the promotion of the economic and social advancement of all peoples, have resolved to combine our efforts to accomplish these aims. Accordingly, our respective Governments, through representatives assembled in the city of San Francisco, who have exhibited their full powers found to be in good and due form, have agreed to the present Charter of the United Nations and do hereby establish an international organization to be known as the United Nations.

Chapter I. *Purposes and Principles*

Article 1   The Purposes of the United Nations are: 1. *To maintain international peace and security*, and to that end: to take effective collective measures for the prevention and removal of threats to the peace, and for the suppression of acts of aggression or other breaches of the peace, and to bring about by peaceful means, and in conformity with the principles of justice and international law, adjustment or settlement of international disputes or situations which might lead to a breach of the peace;   2. To develop friendly relations among nations based on *respect for the principle of equal rights and self-determination of peoples*, and to take other appropriate measures to strengthen universal peace;   3. *To achieve international co-operation* in solving international problems of an economic, social, cultural, or humanitarian character, and in promoting and *encouraging respect for human rights and for fundamental freedoms for all without distinction as to race, sex, language, or religion*; and   4. To be a centre for harmonizing the actions of nations in the attainment of these common ends.

Article 2   The Organization and its Members, in pursuit of the Purposes stated in Article 1, shall act in accordance with the following Principles.   1. *The Organization is based on the principle of the sovereign equality of all its Members*.   2. All Members, in order to ensure to all of them the rights and benefits resulting from membership, shall fulfill in good faith the obligations assumed by them in accordance with the present Charter.   3. *All Members shall settle their international disputes by peaceful means* in such a manner that international peace and security, and justice, are not endangered.   4. *All Members shall refrain in their international relations from the threat or use of force against the territorial integrity or political independence of any state*, or in any other manner inconsistent with the Purposes of the United Nations.   5. *All Members shall give the United Nations every assistance in any action it takes in accordance with the present Charter, and shall refrain from giving assistance to any state against which the United Nations is taking preventive or enforcement action*.   6. The Organization shall ensure that states which are not Members of the United Nations act in accordance with these Principles so far as may be necessary for the maintenance of international peace and security.   7. *Nothing contained in the present Charter shall authorize the United Nations to intervene in matters which are essentially within the domestic jurisdiction of any state* or shall require the Members to submit such matters to settlement under the present Charter; *but this principle shall not prejudice the application of enforcement measures under Chapter VII*.

Chapter II. *Membership*

Article 3   The original Members of the United Nations shall be the states which, having participated in the United Nations Conference on International Organization at San Francisco, or having previously signed the Declaration by United Nations of 1 January 1942, sign the present Charter and ratify it. . . .

Article 4   1. *Membership in the United Nations is open to all other peace-loving states which accept the obligations contained in the present Charter* and, in the judgment of the Organization, are able and willing to carry out these obligations.   2. The admission of any such state to membership in the United Nations will be effected by a decision of the General Assembly upon the recommendation of the Security Council. . . .

Article 5   A Member of the United Nations against which preventive or enforcement action has been taken by the Security Council may be suspended from the exercise of the rights and privileges of membership by the General Assembly upon the recommendation of the Security Council. The exercise of these rights and privileges may be restored by the Security Council.

Article 6   A Member of the United Nations which has persistently violated the Principles contained in the present Charter may be expelled from the Organization by the General Assembly upon the recommendation of the Security Council.

Chapter III. *Organs*

Article 7   1. There are established as the *principal organs of the United Nations: a General Assembly, a Security Council, an Economic and Social Council, a Trusteeship Council, an International Court of Justice, and a Secretariat.*   2. Such subsidiary organs as may be found necessary may be established in accordance with the present Charter. . . .

Chapter IV. *The General Assembly*

Composition

Article 9   1. *The General Assembly shall consist of all the Members of the United Nations.*   2. Each Member shall have not more than five representatives in the General Assembly.

Functions and Powers

Article 10   *The General Assembly may discuss any questions or any matters within the scope of the present Charter* or relating to the powers and functions of any organs provided for in the present Charter, and, except as provided in Article 12, *may make recommendations to the Members of the United Nations or to the Security Council or to both on any such questions or matters.*

Article 11   1. The General Assembly may consider the general principles of co-operation in the maintenance of international peace and security, including the principles governing disarmament and the regulation of armaments, and may make recommendations with regard to such principles to the Members or to the Security Council or to both.   2. The General Assembly may discuss any questions relating to the maintenance of international peace and security brought before it by any Member of the United Nations, or by the Security Council, or by a state which is not a Member of the United Nations in accordance with Article 35, paragraph 2, and, except as provided in Article 12, may make recommendations with regard to any such questions to the state or states concerned or to the Security Council or to both. Any such question on which action is necessary shall be referred to the Security Council by the General Assembly either before or after discussion.   3. The General Assembly may call the attention of the Security Council to situations which are likely to endanger international peace and security. . . .

Article 12   1. While the Security Council is exercising in respect of any dispute or situation the functions assigned to it in the present Charter, the General Assembly shall not make any recommendation with regard to that dispute or situation unless the Security Council so requests. 2. The Secretary-General, with the consent of the Security Council, shall notify the General Assembly at each session of any matters relative to the maintenance of international peace and security which are being dealt with by the Security Council and shall similarly notify the General Assembly, or the Members of the United Nations if the General Assembly is not in session, immediately the Security Council ceases to deal with such matters.

Article 13   1. The General Assembly shall initiate studies and make recommendations for the purpose of: a. promoting international co-operation in the political field and encouraging the progressive development of international law and its codification; b. promoting international co-operation in the economic, social, cultural, educational, and health fields, and assisting in the realization of human rights and fundamental freedoms for all without distinction as to race, sex, language, or religion.   2. The further responsibilities, functions and powers of the General Assembly with respect to matters mentioned in paragraph 1 (b) above are set forth in Chapters IX and X.

Article 14   Subject to the provisions of Article 12, the General Assembly may recommend measures for the peaceful adjustment of any situation, regardless of origin, which it deems likely to impair the general welfare or friendly relations among nations, including situations resulting from a violation of the provisions of the present Charter setting forth the Purposes and Principles of the United Nations.

Article 15   1. The General Assembly shall receive and consider annual and special reports from the Security Council; these reports shall include an account of the measures that the Security Council has decided upon or taken to maintain international peace and security.   2. The General Assembly shall receive and consider reports from the other organs of the United Nations. . . .

Article 17   1. The General Assembly shall consider and approve the budget of the Organization.   2. The expenses of the Organization shall be borne by the Members as apportioned by the General Assembly.   3. The General Assembly shall consider and approve any financial and budgetary arrangements with specialized agencies . . . and shall examine the administrative budgets of such specialized agencies with a view to making recommendations to the agencies concerned.

Voting

Article 18   1. Each member of the General Assembly shall have one vote.   2. Decisions of the General Assembly on important questions shall be made by a two-thirds majority of the members present and voting. . . .   3. Decisions on other questions . . . shall be made by a majority of the members present and voting.

Article 19   A Member of the United Nations which is in arrears in the payment of its financial contributions to the Organization shall have no vote in the General Assembly if the amount of its arrears equals or exceeds the amount of the contributions due from it for the preceding two full years. The General Assembly may, nevertheless, permit such a Member to vote if it is satisfied that the failure to pay is due to conditions beyond the control of the Member.

Procedure

Article 20   The General Assembly shall meet in regular annual sessions and in such special sessions as occasion may require. Special sessions shall be convoked by the Secretary-General at the request of the Security Council or of a majority of the Members of the United Nations.

Article 21   The General Assembly shall adopt its own rules of procedure. It shall elect its President for each session.

Article 22   The General Assembly may establish such subsidiary organs as it deems necessary for the performance of its functions.

Chapter V. *The Security Council*

Composition

Article 23   1. *The Security Council shall consist of fifteen Members of the United Nations. The Republic of China, France, the Union of Soviet Socialist Republics, the United Kingdom of Great Britain and Northern Ireland, and the United States of America shall be permanent members of the Security Council. The General Assembly shall elect ten other Members of the United Nations to be non-permanent members* of the Security Council, due regard being specially paid, in the first instance to the contribution of Members of the United Nations to the maintenance of international peace and security and to the other purposes of the Organization, and also to equitable geographical distribution. 2. *The non-permanent members of the Security Council shall be elected for a term of two years.* . . . 3. Each member of the Security Council shall have one representative.

Functions and Powers

Article 24   1. In order to ensure prompt and effective action by the United Nations, its Members confer on *the Security Council primary responsibility for the maintenance of international peace and security,* and agree that in carrying out its duties under this responsibility the Security Council acts on their behalf.   2. In discharging these duties the Security Council shall act in accordance with the Purposes and Principles of the United Nations. The specific powers granted to the Security Council for the discharge of these duties are laid down in Chapters VI, VII, VIII, and XII.

3. The Security Council shall submit annual and, when necessary, special reports to the General Assembly for its consideration.

Article 25   The Members of the United Nations agree to accept and carry out the decisions of the Security Council in accordance with the present Charter.

Article 26   In order to promote the establishment and maintenance of international peace and security with the least diversion for armaments of the world's human and economic resources, the Security Council shall be responsible for formulating, with the assistance of the Military Staff Committee referred to in Article 47, plans to be submitted to the Members of the United Nations for the establishment of a system for the regulation of armaments.

Voting

Article 27   1. Each member of the Security Council shall have one vote.   2. Decisions of the Security Council on procedural matters shall be made by an affirmative vote of nine members. 3. Decisions of the Security Council on all other matters shall be made by an affirmative vote of nine members including the concurring votes of the permanent members [This provision in effect gives each permanent member a veto on all non-procedural questions.—Eds.]; provided that, in decisions under Chapter VI, and under paragraph 3 of Article 52, a party to a dispute shall abstain from voting.

Procedure

Article 28   1. The Security Council shall be so organized as to be able to function continuously. Each member of the Security Council shall for this purpose be represented at all times at the seat of the Organization.   2. The Security Council shall hold periodic meetings at which each of its members may, if it so desires, be represented by a member of the government or by some other specially designated representative.   3. The Security Council may hold meetings at such places other than the seat of the Organization as in its judgment will best facilitate its work.

Article 29   The Security Council may establish such subsidiary organs as it deems necessary for the performance of its functions.

Article 30   The Security Council shall adopt its own rules of procedure, including the method of selecting its President.

Article 31   Any Member of the United Nations which is not a member of the Security Council may participate, without vote, in the discussion of any question brought before the Security Council whenever the latter considers that the interests of that Member are specially affected.

Article 32   Any Member of the United Nations which is not a member of the Security Council or any state which is not a Member of the United Nations, if it is a party to a dispute under consideration by the Security Council, shall be invited to participate, without vote, in the discussion relating to the dispute. The Security Council shall lay down such conditions as it deems just for the participation of a state which is not a Member of the United Nations.

Chapter VI. Pacific Settlement of Disputes

Article 33   1. The parties to any dispute, the continuance of which is likely to endanger the maintenance of international peace and security, shall, first of all, seek a solution by negotiation, enquiry, mediation, conciliation, arbitration, judicial settlement, resort to regional agencies or arrangements, or other peaceful means of their own choice.   2. The Security Council shall, when it deems necessary, call upon the parties to settle their dispute by such means.

Article 34   The Security Council may investigate any dispute, or any situation which might lead to international friction or give rise to a dispute, in order *to determine whether the continuance of the dispute or situation is likely to endanger the maintenance of international peace and security*.

Article 35   1. Any Member of the United Nations may bring any dispute, or any situation of the nature referred to in Article 34, to the attention of the Security Council or of the General Assembly.   2. A state which is not a Member of the United Nations may bring to the attention of the Security Council or of the General Assembly any dispute to which it is a party if it accepts in advance, for the purposes of the dispute, the obligations of pacific settlement provided in the present Charter.   3. The proceedings of the General Assembly in respect of matters brought to its attention under this Article will be subject to the provisions of Articles 11 and 12.

Article 36   1. The Security Council may, at any stage of a dispute of the nature referred to in Article 33 or of a situation of like nature, recommend appropriate procedures or methods of adjustment.   2. The Security Council should take into consideration any procedures for the settlement of the dispute which have already been adopted by the parties.   3. In making recommendations under this Article the Security Council should also take into consideration that legal disputes should as a general rule be referred by the parties to the International Court of Justice in accordance with the provisions of the Statute of the Court.

Article 37   1. Should the parties to a dispute of the nature referred to in Article 33 fail to settle it by the means indicated in that Article, they shall refer it to the Security Council.   2. If the Security Council deems that the continuance of the dispute is in fact likely to endanger the maintenance of international peace and security, it shall decide whether to take action under Article 36 or to recommend such terms of settlement as it may consider appropriate.

Article 38   Without prejudice to the provisions of Articles 33 to 37, the Security Council may, if all the parties to any dispute so request, make recommendations to the parties with a view to a pacific settlement of the dispute.

Chapter VII. Action with Respect to Threats to the Peace, Breaches of the Peace, and Acts of Aggression

Article 39   The Security Council shall determine the existence of any threat to the peace, breach of the peace, or act of aggression and shall make recommendations, or decide what measures shall be taken in accordance with Articles 41 and 42, to maintain or restore international peace and security.

Article 40   In order to prevent an aggravation of the situation, the Security Council may, before making the recommendations or deciding upon the measures provided for in Article 39, call upon the parties concerned to comply with such provisional measures as it deems necessary or desirable. Such provisional measures shall be without prejudice to the rights, claims, or position of the parties concerned. The Security Council shall duly take account of failure to comply with such provisional measures.

Article 41   The Security Council may decide what measures not involving the use of armed force are to be employed to give effect to its decisions, and it may call upon the Members of the United Nations to apply such measures. These may include complete or partial interruption of economic relations and of rail, sea, air, postal, telegraphic, radio, and other means of communication, and the severance of diplomatic relations.

Article 42   Should the Security Council consider that measures provided for in Article 41 would be inadequate or have proved to be inadequate, it may take such action by air, sea, or land forces as may be necessary to maintain or restore international peace and security. Such action may include demonstrations, blockade, and other operations by air, sea, or land forces of Members of the United Nations.

Article 43   1. All Members of the United Nations, in order to contribute to the maintenance of international peace and security, undertake to make available to the Security Council, on its call and in accordance with a special agreement or agreements, armed forces, assistance, and facilities, including rights of passage, necessary for the purpose of maintaining international peace and security.   2. Such agreement or agreements shall govern the numbers and types of forces, their degree of readiness and general location, and the nature of the facilities and assistance to be provided.   3. The agreement or agreements shall be negotiated as soon as possible on the initiative of the Security Council. They shall be concluded between the Security Council and Members or between the Security Council and groups of Members and shall be subject to ratification by the signatory states in accordance with their respective constitutional processes.

Article 44   When the Security Council has decided to use force it shall, before calling upon a Member not represented on it to provide armed forces in fulfillment of the obligations assumed under Article 43, invite that Member, if the Member so desires, to participate in the decisions of the Security Council concerning the employment of contingents of that Member's armed forces.

Article 45   In order to enable the United Nations to take urgent military measures, Members shall hold immediately available national air-force contingents for combined international enforcement action. The strength and degree of readiness of these contingents and plans for their combined action shall be determined within the limits laid down in the special agreement or agreements referred to in Article 43, by the Security Council with the assistance of the Military Staff Committee.

Article 46   Plans for the application of armed force shall be made by the Security Council with the assistance of the Military Staff Committee.

Article 47   1. There shall be established a Military Staff Committee to advise and assist the Security Council on all questions relating to the Security Council's military requirements for the maintenance of international peace and security, the employment and command of forces placed at its disposal, the regulation of armaments, and possible disarmament.   2. The Military Staff Committee shall consist of the Chiefs of Staff of the permanent members of the Security Council or their representatives. Any Member of the United Nations not permanently represented on the Committee shall be invited by the Committee to be associated with it when the efficient discharge of the Committee's responsibilities requires the participation of that Member in its work.   3. The Military Staff Committee shall be responsible under the Security Council for the strategic direction of any armed forces placed at the disposal of the Security Council. Questions relating to the command of such forces shall be worked out subsequently.   4. The Military Staff Committee, with the authorization of the Security Council and after consultation with appropriate regional agencies, may establish regional sub-committees.

Article 48   1. The action required to carry out the decisions of the Security Council for the maintenance of international peace and security shall be taken by all the Members of the United Nations or by some of them, as the Security Council may determine.   2. Such decisions shall be carried out by the Members of the United Nations directly and through their action in the appropriate international agencies of which the are members.

Article 49   The Members of the United Nations shall join in affording mutual assistance in carrying out the measures decided upon by the Security Council.

Article 50   If preventive or enforcement measures against any state are taken by the Security Council, any other state, whether a Member of the United Nations or not, which finds itself confronted with special economic problems arising from the carrying out of those measures shall have the right to consult the Security Council with regard to a solution of those problems.

Article 51   *Nothing in the present Charter shall impair the inherent right of individual or collective self-defence if an armed attack occurs against a Member of the United Nations, until the Security Council has taken measures necessary to maintain international peace and security. Measures taken by Members in the exercise of this right of self-defence shall be immediately reported to the Security Council and shall not in any way affect the authority and responsibility of the Security Council under the present Charter to take at any time such action as it deems necessary in order to maintain or restore international peace and security.*

Chapter VIII. Regional Arrangements

Article 52   *1. Nothing in the present Charter precludes the existence of regional arrangements or agencies for dealing with such matters relating to the maintenance of international peace and security as are appropriate for regional action provided that such arrangements or agencies and their activities are consistent with the Purposes and Principles of the United Nations.   2. The Members of the United Nations entering into such arrangements or constituting such agencies shall make every effort to achieve pacific settlement of local disputes through such regional arrangements* or by such regional agencies before referring them to the Security Council.   3. The Security Council shall encourage the development of pacific settlement of local disputes through such regional arrangements or by such regional agencies either on the initiative of the states concerned or by reference from the Security Council.   4. This Article in no way impairs the application of Articles 34 and 35.

Article 53   The Security Council shall, where appropriate, utilize such regional arrangements or agencies for enforcement action under its authority. But no enforcement action shall be taken under regional arrangements or by regional agencies without the authorization of the Security Council. . . .

Article 54   *The Security Council shall at all times be kept fully informed of activities undertaken or in contemplation under regional arrangements or by regional agencies for the maintenance of international peace and security.*

Chapter IX. *International Economic and Social Co-operation*

Article 55   With a view to the *creation of conditions of stability and well-being* which are necessary for peaceful and friendly relations among nations based on *respect for the principle of equal rights and self-determination of peoples*, the United Nations shall promote: a. *higher standards of living*, full employment, and conditions of economic and social progress and development; b. *solutions of international economic, social, health, and related problems;* and international cultural and educational cooperation; and c. *universal respect for, and observance of, human rights and fundamental freedoms* for all without distinction as to race, sex, language, or religion. . . .

Article 57   1. The various specialized agencies, established by intergovernmental agreement and having wide international responsibilities, as defined in their basic instruments, in economic, social, cultural, educational, health, and related fields, shall be brought into relationship with the United Nations. . . .   2. Such agencies thus brought into relationship with the United Nations are hereinafter referred to as specialized agencies.

Article 58   The Organization shall make recommendations for the co-ordination of the policies and activities of the specialized agencies. . . .

Chapter X. *The Economic and Social Council*

Composition

Article 61   The Economic and Social Council shall consist of fifty-four Members of the United Nations elected by the General Assembly. . . .

Functions and Powers

Article 62   1. The Economic and Social Council may make or initiate studies and reports with respect to international economic, social, cultural, educational, health, and related matters and may make recommendations with respect to any such matters to the General Assembly to the Members of the United Nations, and to the specialized agencies concerned.   2. It may make recommendations for the purpose of promoting respect for, and observance of, human rights and fundamental freedoms for all.   3. It may prepare draft conventions for submission to the General Assembly, with respect to matters falling within its competence.   4. It may call, in accordance with the rules prescribed by the United Nations, international conferences on matters falling within its competence. . . .

Chapter XI. *Declaration Regarding Non-Self-Governing Territories*

Article 73   Members of the United Nations which have or assume responsibilities for the administration of territories whose peoples have not yet attained a full measure of self-government recognize the principle that the interests of the inhabitants of these territories are paramount, and accept as a sacred trust the obligation to promote to the utmost, within the system of international peace and security established by the present Charter, the well-being of the inhabitants of these territories. . . .

Chapter XII. *International Trusteeship System*

Article 75   The United Nations shall establish under its authority an international trusteeship system for the administration and supervision of such territories as may be placed thereunder by subsequent individual agreements. These territories are hereinafter referred to as trust territories. . . .

Chapter XIII. *The Trusteeship Council*

Article 86   The Trusteeship Council shall consist of . . . those Members administering trust territories . . . and . . . as many other Members elected for three-year terms by the General Assembly as may be necessary to ensure that the total number of members of the Trusteeship Council is equally divided between those Members of the United Nations which administer trust territories and those which do not. . . .

Chapter XIV: The International Court of Justice

Article 92   *The International Court of Justice shall be the principal judicial organ of the United Nations. It shall function in accordance with the annexed Statute, which is based upon the Statute of the Permanent Court of International Justice and forms an integral part of the present Charter.*

Article 93   1. All Members of the United Nations are *ipso facto* parties to the Statute of the International Court of Justice.   2. A state which is not a Member of the United Nations may become a party to the Statute of the International Court of Justice on conditions to be determined in each case by the General Assembly upon the recommendation of the Security Council.

Article 94   1. Each Member of the United Nations undertakes to comply with the decision of the International Court of Justice in any case to which it is a party.   2. If any party to a case fails to perform the obligations incumbent upon it under a judgment rendered by the Court, the other party may have recourse to the Security Council, which may, if it deems necessary, make recommendations or decide upon measures to be taken to give effect to the judgment.

Article 95   Nothing in the present Charter shall prevent Members of the United Nations from entrusting the solution of their differences to other tribunals by virtue of agreements already in existence or which may be concluded in the future.

Article 96   1. The General Assembly or the Security Council may request the International Court of Justice to give an advisory opinion on any legal question.   2. Other organs of the United Nations and specialized agencies, which may at any time be so authorized by the General Assembly, may also request advisory opinions of the Court on legal questions arising within the scope of their activities.

Chapter XV. *The Secretariat*

Article 97   *The Secretariat shall comprise a Secretary-General and such staff as the Organization may require. The Secretary-General shall be appointed by the General Assembly upon the recommendation of the Security Council. He shall be the chief administrative officer of the Organization. . . .*

Article 98   The Secretary-General shall act in that capacity in all meetings of the General Assembly, of the Security Council, of the Economic and Social Council, and of the Trusteeship Council, and shall perform such other functions as are entrusted to him by these organs. The Secretary-General shall make an annual report to the General Assembly on the work of the Organization.

Article 99   The Secretary-General may bring to the attention of the Security Council any matter which in his opinion may threaten the maintenance of international peace and security. . . .

Chapter XVIII. *Amendments*

Article 108   Amendments to the present Charter shall come into force for all Members of the United Nations when they have been adopted by a vote of two thirds of the members of the General Assembly and ratified in accordance with their respective constitutional processes by two thirds of the Members of the United Nations, including all the permanent members of the Security Council. . . .

Article 109   1. A General Conference of the Members of the United Nations for the purpose of reviewing the present Charter may be held at a date and place to be fixed by a two-thirds vote of the members of the General Assembly and by a vote of any nine members of the Security Council. Each Member of the United Nations shall have one vote in the conference.   2. Any alteration of the present Charter recommended by a two-thirds vote of the conference shall take effect when ratified in accordance with their respective constitutional processes by two thirds of the Members of the United Nations including all the permanent members of the Security Council. . . .

Chapter XIX. *Ratification and Signature*

IN FAITH WHEREOF the representatives of the Governments of the United Nations have signed the present Charter.

DONE at the city of San Francisco the twenty-sixth day of June, one thousand nine hundred and forty-five.

The North Atlantic Treaty

(1949)

*This treaty provides the authority and bases for action by the North Atlantic Treaty Organization (NATO). Although the U.N. Security Council retains the principal authority and responsibility under the U.N. Charter for **collective security,** NATO assumes an additional regional **collective defense** role, also permitted under Article 51 (see also Article 52) of the U.N. Charter. Collective security and collective defense are related, but have different technical meanings: collective security refers to the same international law-enforcement_authority against law-breaking aggressors as existed under the League of Nations after World War I whereas collective defense is understood as allowing the formation of alliances or coalitions based on countervailing power so long as the parties defer to the prerogatives, when exercised, of the U.N. Security Council.*

The treaty was signed and ratified early in the Cold War with the understanding that the security of NATO countries would be enhanced by U.S. participation as a counter to Soviet power in the East and as an assurance against Germany returning to its aggressive posture in World Wars I and II that had threatened both East and West. The treaty thus focused on security in a European and North Atlantic area identified in Article 6—a geographical scope that also included the United States and Canada. Consistent with U.S. unwillingness to defend the colonial empires of its allies, defining the NATO area this way thus excluded from any NATO security guarantee extensive British, French, Dutch, and Portuguese colonial interests at the time in Asia, Africa, and the western hemisphere.

These empires were subsequently dismantled mainly in the 1960s and 1970s, but the North Atlantic area as geographic restriction still applied, thus rendering engagements elsewhere in the world as "out-of-area" and thus beyond the geographic scope of NATO's authority. More recently, expansion of NATO membership and a broadening interpretation of geographic scope—applying Article 4 to post–Cold War security challenges—have tended to relax this limitation on NATO actions.

Following post–World War I understandings that events in 1914 had triggered automatic alliance responses that were themselves contributory to the outbreak of war, Article 5 does not specify the particular action NATO will take in response to attack on any member; the treaty does not mandate an automatic use of force. Finally, lest one consider NATO only a military alliance, Article 2 makes clear that NATO as international organization has responsibilities and authority in service of democratic principles that also extend to nonmilitary, political, and economic matters.

The Parties to this Treaty reaffirm their faith in the purposes and principles of the Charter of the United Nations and their desire *to live in peace with all peoples and all governments.* They are determined *to safeguard the freedom, common heritage and civilisation of their peoples,* founded on the principles of democracy, individual liberty and the rule of law. They seek *to promote stability and well-being* in the North Atlantic area. They are resolved to unite their efforts for *collective defence* and for the *preservation of peace and security*. They therefore agree to this North Atlantic Treaty:

Article 1   The Parties undertake, as set forth in the Charter of the United Nations, to settle any international dispute in which they may be involved by *peaceful means* in such a manner that *international peace and security and justice* are not endangered, and *to refrain* in their international relations *from the threat or use of force in any manner inconsistent with the purposes of the United Nations.*

Article 2   The Parties will contribute toward the further development of peaceful and friendly international relations by *strengthening their free institutions*, by bringing about a better understanding of the principles upon which these institutions are founded, and by *promoting conditions of stability and well-being*. They will seek to *eliminate conflict in their international economic policies* and will *encourage economic collaboration* between any or all of them.

Article 3   In order more effectively to achieve the objectives of this Treaty, *the Parties*, separately and jointly, by means of continuous and effective self-help and mutual aid, *will maintain and develop their individual and collective capacity to resist armed attack.*

Article 4   *The Parties will consult together whenever*, in the opinion of any of them, the *territorial integrity, political independence or security of any of the Parties is threatened.*

Article 5   *The Parties agree that an armed attack against one or more of them in Europe or North America shall be considered an attack against them all* and consequently they agree that, *if such an armed attack occurs, each of them, in exercise of the right of individual or collective self-defence recognised by Article 51 of the Charter of the United Nations, will assist the Party or Parties so attacked by taking forthwith, individually and in concert with the other Parties, such action as it deems necessary, including the use of armed force, to restore and maintain the security of the North Atlantic area.* Any such armed attack and all measures taken as a result thereof shall immediately be reported to the Security Council. *Such measures shall be terminated when the Security Council has taken the measures necessary to restore and maintain international peace and security.*

Article 6   For the purpose of Article 5, an armed attack on one or more of the Parties is deemed to include an armed attack: *on the territory of any of the Parties in Europe or North America, . . . on the territory of Turkey or on the Islands under the jurisdiction of any of the Parties in the North Atlantic area north of the Tropic of Cancer; on the forces, vessels, or aircraft of any of the Parties, when in or over these territories . . . or the Mediterranean Sea or the North Atlantic area north of the Tropic of Cancer.*

Article 7   *This Treaty does not affect*, and shall not be interpreted as affecting in any way the rights and obligations under the Charter of the Parties which are members of the United Nations, or *the primary responsibility of the Security Council for the maintenance of international peace and security.*

Article 8   Each Party declares that none of the international engagements now in force between it and any other of the Parties or any third State is in conflict with the provisions of this Treaty, and undertakes not to enter into any international engagement in conflict with this Treaty.

Article 9   *The Parties hereby establish a Council*, on which each of them shall be represented, to consider matters concerning the implementation of this Treaty. The Council shall be so organised as to be able to meet promptly at any time. *The Council shall set up such subsidiary bodies as may be necessary; in particular it shall establish immediately a defence committee* which shall recommend measures for the implementation of Articles 3 and 5.

Article 10   *The Parties may, by unanimous agreement, invite any other European State* in a position to further the principles of this Treaty and to contribute to the security of the North Atlantic area *to accede to this Treaty. . . .*

Article 11   This Treaty shall be ratified and its provisions carried out by the Parties in accordance with their respective constitutional processes. . . .

Article 12   After the Treaty has been in force for ten years, or at any time thereafter, the Parties shall, if any of them so requests, consult together for the purpose of reviewing the Treaty. . . .

Article 13   After the Treaty has been in force for twenty years, any Party may cease to be a Party one year after its notice of denunciation has been given. . . .

Article 14   This Treaty, of which the English and French texts are equally authentic, shall be deposited in the archives of the Government of the United States. . . .

Appendix

Functional International Organizations as Specialized Agencies and Other United Nations Organs

We reduce here some of the confusion of the "alphabet soup" of international organizations that function as U.N. specialized agencies and other U.N. organs by presenting their abbreviations and also the full titles that indicate their functional focus. Even though the specialized agencies have independent standing, they are linked to the global purposes of the U.N. Economic and Social Council. In addition to library documents, books, articles, and other sources, their Web sites provide details concerning their missions, purposes, and activities.

Specialized Agencies

FAO: Food and Agricultural Organization of the United Nations (Rome)
Aims to improve agricultural productivity and food security, bettering the living standards of rural populations (www.fao.org)

IAEA: International Atomic Energy Agency (Vienna)
An autonomous intergovernmental organization under the aegis of the United Nations that works for the safe and peaceful uses of atomic energy (www.iaea.org)

ICAO: International Civil Aviation Organization (Montreal, Canada)
Sets international standards necessary for the safety, security, and efficiency of air transport and serves as the coordinator for international cooperation in all areas of civil aviation (www.icao.int)

IFAD: International Fund for Agricultural Development (Rome)
Mobilizes financial resources to raise food production and nutrition levels among the poor in developing countries (www.ifad.org)

ILO: International Labor Organization (Geneva)
Formulates policies and programs to improve working conditions and employment opportunities and sets labor standards used by countries around the world (www.ilo.org)

IMF: International Monetary Fund (Washington, D.C.)
Facilitates international monetary cooperation and financial stability (aims to maintain international liquidity) and provides a permanent forum for consultation, advice, and assistance on financial issues (www.imf.org)

IMO: International Maritime Organization (London)
Works to improve international shipping procedures, raise standards in marine safety, and reduce marine pollution by ships (www.imo.org)

ITU: International Telecommunication Union (Geneva)
Fosters international cooperation to improve telecommunications of all kinds, coordinates usage of radio and TV frequencies, promotes safety measures, and conducts research (www.itu.int)

UNESCO: U.N. Educational, Scientific, and Cultural Organization (Paris)
Promotes education, cultural development, protection of the world's natural and cultural heritage, international cooperation in science, press freedom, and communication (www.unesco.org)

UNIDO: U.N. Industrial Development Organization (Vienna)
Promotes the industrial advancement of developing countries through technical assistance, advisory services, and training (www.unido.org)

UPU: Universal Postal Union (Berne, Switzerland)
Establishes international regulations for postal services, provides technical assistance, and promotes cooperation in postal matters (www.upu.int)

WHO: World Health Organization (Geneva)
Coordinates programs aimed at solving health problems and the attainment by all people of the highest possible level of health, working in areas such as immunization, health education, and the provision of essential drugs (www.who.int)

WIPO: World Intellectual Property Organization (Geneva)
Promotes international protection of intellectual property and fosters cooperation on copyrights, trademarks, industrial designs, and patents (www.wipo.int)

WMO: World Meteorological Organization (Geneva)
Promotes scientific research on Earth's atmosphere and on climate change and facilitates the global exchange of meteorological data (www.wmo.ch)

World Bank Group (Washington, D.C.)
Provides loans and technical assistance to developing countries to reduce poverty and advance sustainable economic growth (www.worldbank.int)
- IBRD: International Bank for Reconstruction and Development
- IDA: International Development Agency
- IFC: International Finance Corporation
- MIGA: Multilateral Investment Guarantee Agency

WTO: World Trade Organization (Geneva)
Administers WTO trade agreements, providing a forum for trade negotiations and handling trade disputes; monitors national trade policies; and offers technical assistance and training for developing countries (www.wto.org)

Other U.N. Organizations

Habitat: U.N. Center for Human Settlements (Nairobi)
Promotes housing for all, improving urban governance, reducing urban poverty, improving the living environment, and managing disaster mitigation and postconflict rehabilitation (www.unhabitat.org)

UNCTAD: U.N. Conference on Trade and Development (Geneva)
Maximizes the trade, investment, and development opportunities of developing countries, helping them face challenges arising from globalization and integrating them into the world economy on an equitable basis (www.unctad.org)

UNODC: U.N. Office on Drugs and Crime (Vienna)
Provides leadership for all U.N. drug-control initiatives; works against illicit drug production, trafficking, and abuse; seeks service as a worldwide center of expertise and information in all fields of drug control; and provides technical assistance to help governments to establish adequate drug-control structures and strategies (www.unodc.org)

UNDP: U.N. Development Program (New York)
Helps countries achieve sustainable human development by assisting them to build their capacity to design and carry out development programs in poverty eradication (the first priority), employment creation with sustainable livelihoods, the empowerment of women, and the protection and regeneration of the environment (www.undp.org)

UNEP: U.N. Environment Program (Nairobi)
Provides leadership and encourages partnerships in caring for the environment by inspiring, informing, and enabling nations and people to improve their quality of life without compromising that of future generations (www.unep.org)

UNFPA: U.N. Population Fund (New York)
Extends assistance to developing countries, countries with economies in transition, and other countries, addressing reproductive health and population issues (www.unfpa.org)

UNHCHR: U.N. High Commissioner for Human Rights (Geneva)
Promotes universal respect for (and observance of) human rights and fundamental freedoms (www.unhchr.ch)

UNHCR: U.N. High Commissioner for Refugees (Geneva)
Strives to safeguard the rights and well-being of refugees; to ensure that everyone can exercise the right to seek asylum and find safe refuge in another state, returning home voluntarily; and to find lasting solutions to the plight of refugees (www.unhcr.ch)

UNICEF: U.N. Children's Fund (New York)
Advocates and works for the protection of children's rights, helping the young meet their basic needs and expanding their opportunities to reach their full potential (www.unicef.org)

UNITAR: U.N. Institute for Training and Research (Geneva)
Enhances U.N. effectiveness through training and research, providing training to assist member states and conducting research on innovative training and capacity-building approaches; forms partnerships within and outside of the U.N. system in order to build on existing networks and expertise (www.unitar.org)

UNRISD: U.N. Research Institute for Social Development (Geneva)
Conducts research into problems and policies of social development and relationships between various types of social and economic development during different phases of economic growth (www.unrisd.org)

UNRWA: U.N. Relief and Works Agency for Palestine Refugees in the Near East (Gaza and Amman)
Directs relief and works programs for Palestine refugees (www.unrwa.org or www.u.n..org/unrwa)

UNU: U.N. University (Tokyo)
Contributes through research and capacity-building to efforts to resolve the pressing global problems that are the concern of the United Nations and its member states (www.unu.edu)

WFP: World Food Program (Rome)
Provides food to sustain victims of artificial and natural disasters, to improve the nutrition and quality of life of the most vulnerable people at critical times in their lives, and to help build assets and promote the self-reliance of poor people and communities (www.wfp.org)

"It is evident that when princes have given more thought to personal luxuries than arms, they have lost their state."

NICCOLO MACHIAVELLI, *THE PRINCE*, CHAPTER XIV

Controlling Global Armaments

Popular songs often reflect both the anxieties and aspirations or wishful thinking of their times. Fears of mass destruction were widespread during periods of high tension throughout more than four decades of the cold war that followed World War II. Focusing on national and ethnic strife, one song observed that "the whole world is festering with unhappy souls" and feared that "someone will set the spark off and we will all be blown away." Anxiety born of global insecurity also produced pockets of guarded optimism, reflected in the wishful thinking of another song:

> Last night I had the strangest dream I never dreamed before;
>
> I dreamed the world had all agreed to put an end to war.
>
> I dreamed I saw a mighty room and the room was filled with men,
>
> And the paper they were signing said they'd never fight again.
>
> The people in the streets below were dancing round and round,
>
> And guns and swords and uniforms were scattered on the ground.

Such sentiments also have ancient religious-cultural roots. In Judeo-Christian scripture, accepted as well by Muslims, is the optimistic expectation stated in songlike verse that nations one day

> . . . shall beat their swords into plowshares,
>
> and their spears into pruning hooks;
>
> nation shall not lift up sword against nation,
>
> neither shall they learn war any more. (Isaiah 2:4)

Unfortunately, much of recorded history is filled with accounts of war and its role in the rise and fall of empires, principalities, and states. As we noted in Chapter 5, there are various complementary and competing explanations for the causes of war. Whichever one we decide is most persuasive, it still seems that such conflict is here to stay. If, however, humanity is unable to eliminate the causes of war, perhaps something can be done to reduce the ability of states to wage war. Two suggested approaches have been disarmament and arms control.

Disarmament and Arms Control

Dealing with weapons in national arsenals is hardly a new problem confronting humanity in the twenty-first century. There have been efforts to promote general and complete *disarmament*—the dismantling and destruction of all forms of military weapons—or all weapons of a particular type (as in the elimination of nuclear, biological, or chemical weapons). How elusive has been the biblical challenge to turn all "swords into plowshares"—instruments of productivity rather than of human destruction! Nevertheless, over the years people have joined together to protest the development and use of all types of weapons. It is assumed that the elimination of major weapons systems would, if not eliminate war, at least reduce its destructive capacity. This view is reflected in such populist movements as the Campaign for Nuclear Disarmament during the Cold War.

Rarely is a state willing to disarm unilaterally (i.e., on its own initiative and being the only state to disarm). Although great schemes have been drawn up for general and complete disarmament, this approach appears to have been too ambitious. As a practical matter, diplomatic attempts to achieve disarmament have succeeded only (and even then not completely) when directed toward particular categories of weaponry such as agreed prohibitions against chemical and biological agents. Another example is the 1987 U.S.-Soviet Intermediate-Range Nuclear Forces (INF) treaty, which removed from Europe and destroyed an entire category of weaponry—all intermediate-range missiles capable of carrying nuclear weapons.

Once the almost exclusive preserve of states and their governments, the elimination of certain categories of weapons has become a central focus of nongovernmental organizations (NGOs) as well. Land mines placed during wars, for example, not only kill and wound soldiers but also maim children and adult noncombatants who happen to stumble on these explosive devices long after wars have ended. Given this continuing danger, a concrete example of global civil society at work involved the more than one thousand local and international NGOs in more than seventy-five countries that joined forces in the 1990s in an international campaign to ban land mines. The rallying cry was not "state security," but rather "human security." British Princess Diana was among the many individual advocates of a treaty banning land mines. After much work by such public-spirited individuals and NGOs, 122 governments signed the Land-Mines

disarmament
Reducing to zero either all weaponry in national arsenals (as in general and complete disarmament) or all weapons of a particular type or kind (as in elimination of biological and chemical weapons).

Treaty in 1997. The treaty went into force in 1999; however, the United States and Russia are among the countries not signing the accord because of their continuing reliance on these weapons. If signed and ratified, the treaty requires signatories to destroy all mines in national arsenals within four years, removing and destroying all of those already in the ground within ten years.

Statecraft based on possessing weaponry and fielding armed forces, however, has been historically the more common norm. Far from viewing weapons as a cause of war, it is argued that they can serve a positive function in terms of not only protecting a state's national security but also maintaining the peace. *Si vis pacem, para bellum* ("if you wish peace, then prepare for war") reflects the realist understanding that peace with neighboring and other states is best assured by a position or posture of military strength. If a state is relatively strong militarily, such strength in principle will deter or dissuade others who might be prone to attack. Hence weapons, it is argued, are actually necessary to maintain peace.

Disarmament advocates are quick to point out, however, that such thinking, coupled with technological advances in weaponry, is in fact responsible for the carnage in two world wars that alone made the twentieth the bloodiest century in human history. Moreover, advances in nuclear, chemical, and biological weaponry also threaten global destruction on a massive scale, particularly if in the hands of transnational terrorist organizations—a key concern on the twenty-first century's global agenda. From this perspective, military strength is hardly a reliable source of security. Arms races in which states compete to achieve security through acquisition of armaments and strengthened armed forces only worsen the global security problem, particularly if such weapons escape their control. That more spending on weapons may actually worsen or undermine security is thus at the core of the security dilemma facing states and international and nongovernmental organizations concerned with such matters.

If complete global disarmament is viewed as an unrealistic goal, if not a fantasy, and the complete elimination of a type of weapon is also exceedingly difficult to achieve, what about a more modest goal of placing restrictions on the number and types of weapons and curtailing their spread? Thus we enter the realm of **arms control,** viewed as a process designed to achieve such modest yet important measures as:

1. Reduce or put quantitative or qualitative limits on numbers, types, and locations of armed forces and their armaments or weaponry.

2. Impose geographic or spatial limits on use or deployment of armed forces and weapons.

3. Specify functional measures that facilitate communications and build confidence and security regionally or globally.

Once instituted, these multilateral agreements constitute **international security regimes.** Somewhat more modest in scope than general and complete disarmament, these measures still offer rules and thus some degree of structure to the development, acquisition, deployment, and use of armaments. Such agreements are typically aimed at one or more of the following:

- Curb arms race competition
- Achieve economic savings from reduced military expenditures
- Lessen the risk of war
- Reduce damage should war occur
- Enhance regional and global security

arms control
A negotiation process aimed at producing agreements on weapons and their use.

international security regimes
Sets of rules, many of which are legally binding, and associated institutions by which states regulate their conduct, such as arms control regimes.

Practicing World Politics

DISARMAMENT AND ARMS CONTROL

Disarmament and arms control have been on the U.N. agenda since its inception. In addition to the U.N. main web page (www.un.org) including references to General Assembly Special Sessions on Disarmament (SSOD), check out the Geneva-based Conference on Disarmament (CD) through the U.N. Office at Geneva (www.unog.ch/disarm/disconf.htm) and the U.N. Institute for Disarmament Research, also located in Geneva (www.unidir.org). Because the United States has been a key player in all but a few arms control efforts, see the U.S. State Department website and click on International Issues, Arms Control, and finally, current treaties and agreements (www.state.gov) for a compilation of treaties and other arms control agreements. See also the U.S. Institute of Peace (www.usip.org) for research and publications on arms control and other security matters.

The International Institute for Strategic Studies, or IISS (www.iiss.org), is a nongovernmental organization located in London and composed of both members of governments and private citizens from around the world. Its annual publications, *Military Balance* and *Strategic Survey* (available for purchase through Oxford University Press or found in reference sections of many libraries for use by scholars, policy practitioners, students, and the general public), are valuable sources for research on arms control, disarmament, national military arsenals, and their uses. Other IISS publications include occasional monographs on particular international security topics known as *Adelphi Papers,* a professional journal containing scholarly articles on security called *Survival,* and single sheets focused on current security topics known as "Strategic Comments." For related information, see also another important nongovernmental organization, the Stockholm International Peace Research Institute (www.sipri.se) for its yearbook and other publications. With locations in Rome, London, Geneva, and at the American Academy of Arts and Sciences in Cambridge, Massachusetts, Pugwash Conferences (www.pugwash.org) bring together for discussions scientists and other "influential scholars and public figures concerned with reducing the danger of armed conflict and seeking cooperative solutions for global problems."

Other journals published by nongovernmental organizations that cover developments in arms control and disarmament include the Arms Control Association's *Arms Control Today* (www.armscontrol.org), the *Bulletin of the Atomic Scientists* (www.bullatomsci.org), and the *Arms Control Reporter,* published by the Institute for Defense and Disarmament Studies (www.idds.org). In addition to any online data provided, these sites also contain details on each organization's publications that can be found in libraries or by purchase or subscription.

Critics note that states and coalitions of states may also see arms control as a way of gaining some strategic advantage over other states by getting them to agree to provisions that disadvantage them in the arms race competition. Be that as it may, arms control regimes can also provide rules states voluntarily agree to follow in their security relations with each other, lending some degree of order and providing greater security to an otherwise anarchical world lacking central authority or governance.

The Nobel Peace Prize

Swedish chemist Alfred Bernhard Nobel (1833–1896) was a disarmament advocate who also invented dynamite, a nitroglycerine-based explosive. Nobel was concerned that explosive technologies usefully applied to building, mining, railroad, and other construction projects might have negative consequences in the development of ever more destructive weapons. The hope was that increasing de-structiveness of weaponry would lead countries to avoid the use of force. Among other awards, his will established a grant "to the person who shall have done the most or the best work for fraternity between the nations, for the abolition or reduction of standing armies and for the holding and promotion of peace congresses." The first of these annual Nobel Peace Prizes was awarded in 1901.

One example of an arms control regime, and a bold effort for its time, was defined in the Naval Limitation Treaty signed in Washington in 1922. This agreement bound the United Kingdom, France, Italy, Japan, and the United States to destroy some warships in their fleets and to accept strict numerical limits on the construction of new ones. Locations of allowable naval bases were specified, thus limiting expansion of overall capabilities to deploy and maintain fleets. In addition to these quantitative restrictions, qualitative limits also were imposed. Guns on smaller warships were limited in caliber to 8 inches, thus restricting their destructive capabilities. Ships were also specified by type and allowable size. Total tonnage of aircraft carriers in any country's fleet was also subject to an overall limitation or cap. The naval-limitation regime established by this treaty failed in practice to prevent a naval arms race in the 1930s, spurred primarily by fascist regimes then in Germany and Japan. The treaty nevertheless stands as an early model of how rules specifying both quantitative and qualitative limits can be incorporated in the construction of security regimes.

Given the large number of arms control agreements reached since the late 1950s, understanding the meaning and significance of what has been accomplished to date can be difficult. One way to cut through this thicket is to use the same three categories mentioned earlier to classify the provisions of arms control treaties and other agreements as those dealing with (1) quantitative and qualitative limitations on armaments and armed forces (Table 7.1). This includes associated weaponry, including research, development, test and evaluation (RDT&E) of improved or new forms of weapons systems as well as other qualitative factors such as readiness, alert levels, or preparedness of military forces for combat; (2) geographic or spatial limitations on deployments or use of armed forces or particular weapons systems (Table 7.2); and (3) functional mechanisms, such as communications and other confidence- and security-building measures (Table 7.3).

The largest number of agreements fall primarily into the first category of quantitative or qualitative restrictions on armed forces and armaments; however, a particular

TABLE 7.1

Controlling Armaments: Major Arms Control Treaties and Agreements

TREATY OR AGREEMENT	PRINCIPAL QUANTITATIVE AND QUALITATIVE RESTRICTIONS, LIMITATIONS, AND OTHER PROVISIONS: NUMBERS, TYPES, LOCATIONS, RESEARCH, DEVELOPMENT, TESTING, AND USE
Biological and Chemical Weaponry	
Chemical and Bacteriological Use (1925)	Prohibits use of asphyxiating, poisonous, or other chemical and bacteriological (biological) weapons
Production and Stockpiling	
Biological Weapons (1972)	Prohibits development, production, stockpiling, otherwise acquiring, or transfering biological weapons; requires destruction of existing stocks
Chemical Weapons (1993)	Prohibits development, production, stockpiling, transfer, acquisition, and use of chemical weapons; requires destruction of existing stocks; permits on-site inspections
Nuclear Weaponry: Testing and Transfer Restraints	
Test Bans	
Limited Test Ban (1963)	Prohibits nuclear weapons tests or other nuclear explosions in the atmosphere, outer space, or underwater (e.g., oceanic)
Threshold Test Ban (1974)	Prohibits underground nuclear weapons tests with yields greater than 150 kilotons; national, technical means of verification expanded by 1990 protocol to require advance notice and allow on-site inspections and measurement for tests greater than 35 kilotons
"Peaceful" Nuclear Explosions (1976)	Reaffirmed 150 kilotons limit on yield for nonweapons or "peaceful" nuclear explosions (PNE)
Comprehensive Test Ban (1996)	Proposes to eliminate all nuclear testing
Nuclear Nonproliferation and Safeguards (1968)	Nuclear weapons states agree not to transfer and nonnuclear weapons states agree not to receive nuclear weapons or weapons-related technologies; all parties agree to work toward nuclear disarmament
Protection of Nuclear Material (1980)	Holds states responsible for secure transit of nuclear materials used for peaceful purposes, providing standards and remedies.
SALT I (U.S.–USSR Strategic Arms Limitation Talks: 1969–1972)	
Defensive Forces	
• Anti-Ballistic Missiles (ABM) 1972 Treaty and 1974 Protocol	When in force, it prohibited deployment by the United States and the Soviet Union (later the Russian Federation) of ABM systems for territorial defense, allowing only

TABLE 7.1
(continued)

TREATY OR AGREEMENT	PRINCIPAL QUANTITATIVE AND QUALITATIVE RESTRICTIONS, LIMITATIONS, AND OTHER PROVISIONS: NUMBERS, TYPES, LOCATIONS, RESEARCH, DEVELOPMENT, TESTING, AND USE
	limited ABM deployments for defense of a state's national capital or one ICBM-launcher complex; development, testing, or deployment of sea-based, air-based, space-based, or mobile land-based ABM systems; transfer of ABM systems or components to other states; provided for national technical means of verification while prohibiting concealment measures
Offensive Forces	
• Offensive Arms Limitations: Interim Agreement (1972)	Prohibits construction of additional fixed, land-based intercontinental ballistic missile (ICBM) and submarine-launched ballistic missile (SLBM) launchers or ballistic missile submarines; conversion of existing ICBM launchers from light to heavy types; provides for national technical means of verification (while prohibiting deliberate concealment measures) and relies on a Standing Consultative Commission to deal with compliance issues
SALT II (U.S.-USSR Strategic Arms Limitation Talks: 1972–1979)	Not ratified as a treaty, but treated as an executive agreement that put quantitative limits on ICBMs and SLBMs, heavy bombers, and air-to-surface and cruise missiles and qualitative restraints on modernization and conversion, testing and deployment of new systems (to include limits on numbers of reentry vehicles on ICBM and SLBM); advance notification of ICBM launches; allowing for national technical means of verification (while prohibiting deliberate concealment measures) and providing for the Standing Consultative Commission
Intermediate-Range Nuclear Forces (INF): U.S.-USSR (1987)	Eliminates all intermediate-range (1,000–5,500 km) and shorter-range (500–1,000 km) ballistic and ground-launched cruise missiles and launchers
Strategic Arms Reduction Talks (START I): U.S.-USSR, 1982–1991	Reduces substantially strategic offensive armaments (ICBM, SLBM, and heavy bombers) to 1,600 each with associated warheads limited to 6,000 each (down from more than 12,000 nuclear warheads in U.S. and Soviet inventories); warhead limits reduced subsequently to some 3,000; in 1992 Belarus, Kazakhstan, and Ukraine joined the Russian Federation and the United States in acceding to the treaty
(START II): U.S.-Russia, 1993 and 1997	Strategic warheads to be reduced to 3,500 or fewer on each side
Moscow Treaty (2002)	By 2012 arsenals to be reduced to 1,700–2,200 warheads each

(table continues)

TABLE 7.1
(continued)

TREATY OR AGREEMENT	PRINCIPAL QUANTITATIVE AND QUALITATIVE RESTRICTIONS, LIMITATIONS, AND OTHER PROVISIONS: NUMBERS, TYPES, LOCATIONS, RESEARCH, DEVELOPMENT, TESTING, AND USE
Missile Technology Control Regime (MTCR) (1987 and 1993)	Establishes common export control policy and list of controlled items with intent to stop spread to other countries of ballistic and cruise missiles and technologies capable of delivering a 500-kilogram nuclear payload (1987) as well as chemical and biological weapons (1993) to a range of 300 kilometers or more (32 state participants)
Nunn–Lugar Cooperative Threat Reduction (1991)	U.S. assistance to Russian Federation in reducing weapons of mass destruction
Conventional Armed Forces in Europe (CFE) (1990)	Limits numbers, types, and locations in Europe of tanks, artillery pieces, armored combat vehicles, combat aircraft, and attack helicopters of all countries
U.N. Registry on Conventional Arms Exports (1991)	Compiles information provided by members on conventional arms transfers (exports and imports)
Wassenaar Arrangement (1996–1997)	Requires arms exporting state participants to exchange information on arms sales and denials, working to minimize adverse impact on international and regional security and stability (33 state participants)
Land Mines (1997–1998)	Requires signatories to destroy all mines in national arsenals within four years, removing and destroying all of those already in the ground within ten years
Strategic Offensive Reductions Treaty (May 2002)	Russia and United States would eventually reduce the number of "operationally deployed" strategic nuclear weapons from about 6,000 in each country to between 1,700 and 2,200.

treaty or agreement may also have provisions that fall into one or both of the other two categories.

Functional approaches to controlling or managing conflicts include establishing **confidence- and security-building measures (CSBMs)** that increase trust and reduce threat perceptions as well as maintaining effective communications even between adversaries in wartime. Multilateral peacekeeping missions under U.N. or other auspices may also contribute functionally as controls on the use of armed forces and armaments in conflict situations.

Communications as an arms control function has been a major focus of arms control efforts, particularly since the 1962 Cuban missile crisis that brought the United States and the Soviet Union to the brink of nuclear war. Clear, direct communications would have been helpful at such a dangerous time. Government leaders in Washington and Moscow had to rely instead on exchanging notes delivered by cable, with many hours lost in the process of transmission and translation. Even at that time, telecommunications technology had more to offer than the systems governments were then using. The "hot line" agreement reached in the following year established a direct

TREATY OR AGREEMENT	GENERAL TERMS
Antarctica (1959)	Allows only peaceful, scientific, or other nonmilitary use of Antarctica; direct inspection by states of all facilities or aerial observation anywhere at any time; provides for open exchange of information from scientific investigation of Antarctica; requires advance notice to other parties of expeditions to and within Antarctica, stations in Antarctica occupied by its nationals, any military personnel or equipment intended to be sent (which are allowed only for scientific research or other peaceful purposes); promotes preservation and conservation of living resources; prohibits new territorial claims, nuclear explosions, or storage of radioactive waste materials
Outer Space (1967)	Prohibits orbiting nuclear or other weapons of mass destruction; military bases or maneuvers on (or national, sovereign appropriation of) celestial bodies; provides for damage claims and recovery of astronauts and objects launched into outer space
Latin America Nuclear Free Zone (1967)	Latin America defined as a nuclear weapons–free zone, prohibiting testing, use, manufacture, production, acquisition, or any other form of possession of nuclear weapons by Latin American states or anyone on their behalf
Seabed Arms Control (1971)	Prohibits nuclear or other weapons of mass destruction in the seabed or ocean floor and subsoil; provides for nondisruptive inspection of suspect facilities
Environmental Modification (1977)	Prohibits military or any other hostile use of environmental modification techniques having widespread, long-lasting, or severe effects as the means of destruction, damage, or injury to any other state
Conference on Security and Cooperation in Europe (1975 Helsinki Final Act); subsequent conference accords in Stockholm (1985) and Vienna (1991)	Specific to the Atlantic-to-Urals European area, conventional arms reductions (Table 7.1) are combined with a regime of confidence- and security-building measures

TABLE 7.2

Controlling Armaments and Conflicts: Locational or Geographic Limitations and Restrictions

communications link between the White House and the Kremlin, a system that would be expanded and modernized over the years as new telecommunications technologies became available.

Approaching arms and conflict control through communications and agreed procedures for managing crises to avoid their escalation to armed conflict have also been the inspiration for a set of nuclear accidents, incidents at sea, and prevention of nuclear war measures adopted in the early 1970s. The United States and the Soviet Union established risk reduction centers in 1987 in each other's capitals, staffed by officials from both countries, and agreed in 1988 on procedures for mutual notification of ballistic missile launches, both of which were efforts to strengthen communications mechanisms between the two principal nuclear powers.

TABLE 7.3

Communications and Confidence- and Security-Building Measures: Functional Approaches to Controlling or Managing Conflict

TREATY OR AGREEMENT	GENERAL DESCRIPTION OF TERMS
U.S.-USSR "Hot Line" Agreement (1963); modernized (1971); expanded (1984)	Established in the wake of the 1962 Cuban missile crisis, the U.S. and USSR established and subsequently maintained and expanded direct communications links between Washington and Moscow
Nuclear Accidents: U.S.-USSR (1971)	Requires organizational and technical arrangements to reduce risk of accidental or unauthorized use of nuclear weapons; advance notice of missile launches extending beyond national territory; communications in the event of accidents
Incidents at Sea: U.S.-USSR (1972)	Provides cautionary measures to avoid collisions or other incidents at sea; prohibits simulated attacks on each other's ships; requires advance notification of actions on the high seas that are dangerous to navigation or to aircraft in flight
Prevention of Nuclear War: U.S.–USSR (1973)	Requires parties to refrain from the threat or use of force against each other or each other's allies that would endanger international peace and security, act to avoid military confrontations and the outbreak of nuclear war, and engage in urgent consultations if relations are in risk of nuclear conflict
Confidence- and Security- Building Measures (CSBMs): Atlantic-to-Urals European Area (1975, 1986, 1991)	Specific to the Atlantic-to-Urals European area, confidence- and security-building measures established in 1975 and 1986 were expanded substantially, requiring notifications of military exercises and allowing for observers; providing for exchange of information to include numbers, types, and locations of armaments, aerial reconnaissance, and announced and unannounced on-site inspections of military installations (measures when combined with limits on armaments [Table 7.1] effectively establish "transparency" or military openness, increased warning time should any party prepare to attack any other, and overall reduction in the risk of war)
Nuclear Risk Reduction Centers: U.S.-USSR (1987)	Establishes Nuclear Risk Reduction Centers in Washington and Moscow with communications links between the two and regular meetings between representatives of the centers at least once a year
Ballistic Missile Launch Notification: U.S.-USSR (1988)	Requires notification through the Nuclear Risk Reduction Centers at least twenty-four hours in advance of the planned date and launch and impact areas of any strategic ballistic missile launch; in the event of launch postponement, notice is good for four days
Open Skies (1992)	Consistent with negotiated annual quotas, NATO and former Warsaw Pact countries agreed that in the European Atlantic-to-Urals area each has the right to conduct and the obligation to receive aerial reconnaissance flights by other parties

Arms Control, Verification, and Compliance

Many arms control treaties and agreements address questions of **verification** and **compliance.** It's one thing to make agreements; it's another to live up to them, as evident by international concern over the North Korean attempts to deceive international inspectors concerning their development of nuclear material in violation of the Non-Proliferation Treaty. Verification of compliance with (or violation of) treaties or agreements is achieved in a number of ways, such as open admission of violations, on-site inspection by other parties, reports by reliable human-intelligence sources, or through **national technical means (NTM) of verification.** These means include advanced technical-intelligence capabilities on ground stations, aircraft, ships, and satellites or other space vehicles.

Alleged violations are presented in diplomatic exchanges in the expectation of bringing violators into compliance. As such, verification (knowing what other countries are actually doing) can be understood as the first phase, to be followed by what amounts to an enforcement phase in which compliance is sought if any of the parties is thought to be in violation of a treaty or agreement. For example, the Standing Consultative Commission (SCC, a U.S.-Soviet bilateral forum located in Geneva) was created in the 1970s by the Strategic Arms Limitations Talks (SALT) to deal with compliance issues. Among the complaints the United States raised at the SCC was one dealing with strategic defenses. For years the United States complained publicly in this forum and elsewhere that a major radar station constructed at Krasnoyarsk in the former Soviet Union violated provisions of the Anti-Ballistic Missile (ABM) Treaty. This issue was not resolved until the end of the Cold War, when the Soviets finally conceded the point and dismantled the radar.

Another example of a dispute raised in the SCC was an exchange of allegations on obstruction of national technical means of verification used by each side to monitor the military activities of the other. By agreement in SALT, neither side was to obstruct these national technical means. The United States complained that the Soviets violated SALT

Radar and other aerospace data are monitored at the U.S.-Canadian North American Aerospace Defense Command (NORAD) in Colorado.

accords by encrypting **telemetry** in missile tests—that is, putting into code the communications or signals sent by these missiles to ground stations monitoring their in-flight trajectories over the Soviet land mass. Although Soviet controllers could decode these signals, the practice obstructed American intelligence efforts to receive and interpret the same information.

For their part, the Soviets countered that the American practice of putting canvas or other protective tents or covers over missile silos violated the same provision. Even if the American claim—that these covers were for protection from rain or snow while performing repair or other maintenance functions—were true, the Soviets complained that covers of any kind or for whatever purpose obstructed their ability to photograph these missile launchers from satellites in space.

Eventually such issues were worked out or, if not resolved to the complete satisfaction of the parties, continued to be addressed. The important point here is that even during the height of the Cold War, adversaries could meet formally to discuss and debate allegations of noncompliance. The SCC was an important mechanism for airing differences, if not always working them out very quickly. As such, the SCC was a means for managing superpower disputes and maintaining the strategic-arms security regime.

Alternative Deterrence Doctrines

Constructing or adhering to arms control regimes can be part of national strategies pursued by states that are designed to serve security and other interests and objectives. As suggested earlier, states may enter arms control negotiations for a number of strategic purposes, including curbing the arms race, achieving savings through trimming unnecessary defense expenditures, reducing the risk of war, reducing damage should war occur, or gaining some other advantage.

Our focus in this section is on nuclear armaments and the relation between arms control and *military (force-employment) doctrines* concerning **deterrence, defense, and warfighting.** Deterrence relations among the great powers that possess nuclear weapons seem relatively less important these days compared to the Cold War. An improved climate of great-power relations and a wide array of strategic arms control achievements in the last half of the twentieth century have contributed substantially to international security and a reduced risk of general war in the twenty-first century.

At the same time, however, great-power strategic nuclear arsenals remain intact, even though in 1992 the United States and the Russian Federation agreed to reduce strategic nuclear warheads by some 75 percent to about 3,000 each (from their Cold War highs of more than 12,000 warheads apiece). Although by 2002 the parties had some 6,000 warheads each, both agreed to continue reductions to some 1,700 to 2,200 warheads each by the year 2012. Arms controllers still have a significant challenge to find ways to reduce nuclear arms below these still high levels without destabilizing deterrence relations and endangering international peace and security.

We think it is useful to include here a review of how deterrence, defense, and warfighting theories or doctrines relate to existing nuclear weapons arsenals as well as the implications these doctrines have for construction, expansion, or maintenance of strategic arms control regimes. The continuing twenty-first-century importance of the topic is not only due to nuclear weapons remaining on the arms-control agendas of the major powers possessing them, but also because India, Pakistan, Israel, North Korea, and other countries

military (force-employment) doctrines
Doctrines that represent what military leaders and theorists understand to be the most effective ways and means of using force, whether to deter adversaries, to defend against them, or to engage them offensively and defensively in other combat operations that are part of warfighting.

have acquired (or may yet acquire) nuclear weapons capabilities, not to mention chemical or biological weapons of mass destruction. Notwithstanding extensive, well intended efforts to avoid further spread of nuclear and other weapons of mass destruction, proliferation of such weapons and weapons-related technologies seems likely to continue.

Military doctrine attempts to answer two key questions: (1) *What* military means shall be employed to protect a country? and (2) *How* shall they be employed? Doctrines concerning deterrence, defense, and warfighting involve either the threat or actual use of force. In deterrence, the effort is merely to dissuade another state, through the threat of force, from doing something it has not yet undertaken; it is not actually required to change a course of action. This also may involve **extended deterrence**—threats designed to protect allies. If deterrence fails, defense involves the use of military force to repel an attack. Warfighting is thus an active use of force for defense or to achieve other political-military goals. (Table 7.4)

The key point in this discussion related to arms control, however, is that the numbers and types of strategic nuclear and other weaponry a country has or may seek to possess is closely tied to the force-employment doctrines it adopts. The military forces (i.e., such **force posture** considerations as numbers, types, and locations of forces) required to deter, defend, or engage in warfighting depend heavily upon force-employment doctrines and related national security strategies. In the absence of change in doctrinal and strategic understandings and commitments, these national requirements effectively define the needs and limits of concessions that can realistically be made by negotiators in arms control talks.

Minimum or Finite Deterrence

The least-demanding alternative in terms of numbers of nuclear forces is *minimum* or *finite deterrence,* which requires only a relatively small number of nuclear weapons that can be used against an adversary. With only a few nuclear weapons (say one or more, but perhaps fewer than 100), a country cannot realistically choose to engage in actual nuclear warfighting against another nuclear power, which would require a much larger arsenal with a full array of nuclear and nonnuclear offensive and defensive capabilities.

Understanding minimum or finite deterrence is particularly relevant in the present period of nuclear proliferation when a larger number of countries may acquire small nuclear arsenals. Because a minimum-deterrence country has only a relatively few nuclear weapons, its nuclear forces can be used effectively only to threaten attack against an adversary, typically against population centers or so-called **countervalue targets.** In a minimum-deterrence situation, there are not enough weapons to direct attacks at a large number of military or **counterforce targets** that would need to be struck if a country were trying to destroy or substantially weaken an enemy's warfighting capability. Hence minimum or finite deterrence can realistically be based only on a threat of punishment primarily to enemy populations should another country undertake aggression or other undesirable action as specified by the deterring state. Even if the genuine purpose is to deter war by such threats, aiming weaponry at population centers raises obvious moral questions.

A moral paradox is thus inherent in the sincere effort of arms control negotiators to reduce nuclear arsenals to minimum levels. A breakdown of deterrence in these circumstances could maximize the human cost of nuclear war. By contrast, larger arsenals do allow for counterforce targeting as a way of reducing unnecessary death and destruction. The irony then is that fewer weapons, as in a minimum-deterrence posture, may be even more problematic morally than larger nuclear arsenals that can be directed

minimum or finite deterrence
A situation in which a country maintains a relatively small number of nuclear or other weapons of mass destruction for use in making deterrence threats.

TABLE 7.4

Implications for Strategic Arms Control Regimes of Alternative Deterrence or Defense Doctrines and Force Postures

STRATEGIC NUCLEAR DOCTRINES			
MINIMUM OR FINITE DETERRENCE	DETERRENCE BY ASSURED (OR MUTUALLY ASSURED) DESTRUCTION (NO REAL WARFIGHTING CAPABILITIES INTENDED; DETERRENCE ONLY THROUGH THREAT OF PUNISHMENT)	DEFENSE BY DAMAGE LIMITATION (SOME WARFIGHTING CAPABILITIES)	DETERRENCE OR DEFENSE BY DENIAL (ROBUST WARFIGHTING CAPABILITIES)
Implications for Force Posture			
Offensive			
(bombers and other aircraft and missiles)	perhaps 100 or fewer nuclear weapons	large numbers of nuclear weapons	very large numbers of nuclear weapons	largest number and diversity of nuclear weapons
Defensive			
A. Active (artillery, fighter-interceptors, surface-to-air and antiballistic missiles, space-based systems, etc.)	none required	none required	some	robust, fully developed
B. Passive (radars, communications, civil defense, etc.)	minimal needs (for early warning)	minimal needs (for early warning)	substantial need (for civil defense and early warning)	robust, fully developed
Implications for Deterrence Stability	potentially unstable	usually considered the most stable	potentially unstable	usually considered the most unstable
Implications for Arms Control	most conducive to arms control limits or restrictions	caps possible on offenses; effort to block development of defenses	somewhat compatible with arms control efforts	least compatible with arms control limits

more effectively against the larger number of military or counterforce targets, thus avoiding population centers whenever possible.

Critics are quick to point out, however, that such distinctions have little if any meaning when weapons of mass destruction are involved—that the distinction between civilian (countervalue) and military (counterforce) targets is difficult, if not impossible, to make when the destructiveness of such weapons can so easily spill over from military targets to adjacent or nearby cities, towns, or other settlements. Beyond direct losses of human life and property, severe damage to the environment, including massive loss of animal and plant life, are additional adverse consequences of using any weapons of mass destruction. The horrendous blast, radiation, and thermal (i.e., heat) effects of nuclear weapons thus blur the distinction between counterforce and countervalue targets. Even if a state focuses on using nuclear weapons only against military or counterforce targets, massive **collateral damage (death and destruction)** to civil populations and property still cannot be avoided.

Minimum Deterrence: India, Pakistan, and Other New Nuclear Weapons States

Compared to the enormous size of U.S. and Soviet nuclear arsenals during the Cold War (and the thousands of strategic nuclear weapons that still remain in U.S. and Russian inventories), those belonging to the United Kingdom, France, and China then and now seem minimal indeed. Strategists have raised serious questions concerning the viability of such small national-deterrent capabilities and the stability of deterrence relations based on them. These problems are compounded for India, Pakistan, North Korea or other countries newly acquiring nuclear weapons and related technologies because of the serious interstate conflicts in which they typically have been involved.

If nuclear weapons continue to proliferate in coming years, the countries acquiring them will likely have only relatively small arsenals to which minimum-deterrence concepts apply. In the experience of the original nuclear powers, minimum-deterrence doctrines establish a force posture with the fewest numbers of offensive forces. Because establishing an effective defense is both extraordinarily difficult and costly, new nuclear weapons states likely will come to rely primarily on the threat of retaliation as the basis of their deterrent, with relatively few if any active defenses (fighter-interceptors, surface-to-air missiles, and antiaircraft artillery to shoot down enemy aircraft carrying these weapons). Nor is an effective antiballistic missile system (much less space-based or other strategic defenses) either attainable or affordable for most, if not all, of these countries in the absence of outside help by the United States or other technologically advanced, major military powers. Some passive defenses may be justified, such as radar (to give early warning of attack) or fallout shelters (to provide

Chakothi bazaar is seen deserted, twenty-eight miles north of Muzaffarabad, capital of Pakistan-held Kashmir, at the border of Pakistan and India. Most of the people left the border town because of shelling across the border.

some civil defense), but the emphasis is on the offensive—maintaining, if possible, a credible retaliatory capability. Minimum deterrence also assumes a viable command-and-control mechanism that can make and implement nuclear weapons decisions in a timely manner.

Because minimum deterrence requires the smallest number of military forces of the several deterrence doctrines discussed in this section, it is the one most conducive to arms-control limitations. If that is its principal advantage from an arms-control perspective, critics of minimum deterrence emphasize that a smaller number of weapons also is more vulnerable to a comprehensive enemy attack aimed at destroying them before they can ever be used to retaliate.

Moreover, decision makers under pressure in a country with just a few nuclear weapons, who believe their country is (or could be) under attack, might launch their few forces even before confirming that the attack were real. Fearing that virtually all of the country's retaliatory forces may be destroyed by an enemy before they can be launched in retaliation may lead a minimum-deterrence country to launch on warning without having (or taking) the time to verify that an attack is actually underway—an extraordinarily dangerous position that can actually produce a war that otherwise would not have occurred! That is why many nuclear strategists consider minimum deterrence and tendencies for countries with these postures to launch on warning to be dangerous, unstable bases for deterrence relations.

To be effective, enough of the deterring country's offensive forces must be able to survive an enemy attack in order to launch a counteroffensive or retaliatory strike—a **second-strike capability.** The stability of deterrence relations is enhanced from this perspective by larger numbers of weapons in addition to other measures that enhance the survivability of nuclear retaliatory forces. When enough retaliatory forces are "survivable," national security decision makers need not act precipitously; they have time to weigh their options. Launch under attack (or even after attack) is possible for countries with survivable, second-strike capabilities.

Beyond numbers, additional measures to increase survivability include hardening (fortifying or shielding warheads or other components and placing missiles in reinforced-concrete underground silos), mobility (placing nuclear weapons on aircraft or in missiles on submarines), dispersion (spreading bomber bases and missile launchers over a wide geographic area), diversification (having a variety of nuclear delivery approaches, including aircraft, land-based missiles, submarine-launched missiles, or "standoff" missiles launched from an airplane or ship to targets perhaps hundreds or more miles away), and strategic defense (deploying antiaircraft and antimissile weapons systems designed to defend a country's retaliatory forces from attack).

These approaches involve technologies and expense well beyond the reach of most would-be nuclear powers in the first decades of the twenty-first century. As a result, critics observe that the proliferation of small nuclear arsenals will result in inherently less stable, minimum-deterrence relations among medium-sized and small powers acquiring such weapons. This is another reason that arms control advocates feel so strongly about maintaining and expanding the nuclear nonproliferation security regime that forbids the transfer or acquisition of nuclear weapons and weapons

North Korea has apparently become the world's ninth nuclear power. In November, 2002 the CIA estimated that Pyongyang has one, perhaps two, nuclear weapons. The North Korean crisis, as it has emerged over the past several months, is an extremely complex affair with implications that could drastically affect Asian security and, by extension, U.S. interests. The confrontation has weakened the Nuclear Non-Proliferation Treaty (NPT) and may send signals to others that obtaining nuclear weapons has geopolitical benefits, especially when facing the United States.

Bulletin of the Atomic Scientists, March/April 2003, Vol. 59, No. 2, pp. 74.

It's Been Said...

technologies to nonnuclear countries, in exchange for a pledge by nuclear powers to work toward reducing their arsenals. Beyond merely nonproliferation policies, active measures taken against nuclear weapons programs are often referred to as **counterproliferation.**

Although no chemical, biological, nuclear, or radiological weapons were subsequently found, military intervention in Iraq by the United States, the United Kingdom, and other countries in 2003 was based on the claim that the Iraqi regime did possess weapons of mass destruction. Use of force in such counterproliferation efforts is a risky venture often accompanied by unintended (and unexpected) adverse consequences, as could well be the case were such counterproliferation measures taken against Iran, North Korea, or other would-be nuclear powers.

Stable deterrence depends on both capability and credibility. It is not enough to have a viable weapons capability as in a second-strike retaliatory, assured-destruction posture; if deterrence is to work, one's adversary must *perceive* a genuine will to use this capability—to retaliate if attacked. Some critics of minimum deterrence argue that smaller numbers not only undermine an adversary's perception that a deterring country could deliver a retaliatory strike but also raise questions as to a minimum-deterrent state's will to resort to nuclear strikes. Whether nuclear weapons have been used by an aggressor or not, why would such a minimum-deterrent state want to introduce them, when doing so would only invite nuclear destruction?

In short, critics worry about the stability of minimum deterrence when both capability and credibility can so easily be drawn into question. Defenders usually acknowledge these problems but argue that the horrendous consequences of using nuclear weapons and the uncertainty of calculations about such matters lead even the smallest nuclear weapons powers to be more cautious than critics contend.

> ## MUTUAL ASSURED DESTRUCTION
>
> It is a clue to the eventual demise of mutual assured destruction (MAD) that the term was coined by a critic who sought to highlight how ludicrous the concept was. In the 1960s, Donald Brennan—an analyst at the conservative Hudson Institute, who was making the case for ballistic missile defense—used the acronym MAD to ridicule the idea that in a nuclear war, or even a large conventional conflict, each side should be prepared to destroy the other's cities and society.
>
> **Robert Jervis**
> "Mutual Assured Destruction," Foreign Policy (November/December 2002): 40.

It's Been Said...

Deterrence through Assured (and Mutually Assured) Destruction and Defensive Efforts to Limit Damage

Assured (and mutually assured) destruction and defensive efforts to limit damage were dominant ways of thinking about deterrence between superpowers in the 1960s and 1970s during the cold war. For reasons presented in the previous section, many critics of minimum deterrence then and now have preferred a larger number of offensive nuclear-deterrence forces. Accompanied by hardening, mobility, dispersion, and diversification of these forces to enhance their survivability, the superpowers established and maintained a capability for second-strike assured destruction. In these circumstances, neither side would be foolish enough to attack first. **Mutually assured destruction (MAD)** exists if both parties in a bilateral deterrence relation have a second-strike, assured-destruction capability against the other. If they do, the threat of punishment or destruction presumably is enough to deter both parties from launching (or even considering) a first strike. Even at reduced levels on the order of 2,000 strategic nuclear weapons in the U.S. and Russian inventories, there will be sufficient numbers to maintain second-strike capabilities for both sides.

Deterrence based strictly on assured destruction (or mutually assured destruction) requires a strong offense accompanied, as in minimum deterrence, by passive defenses for the earliest possible warning of attack and a viable command-and-control system able to make and implement nuclear-employment decisions in a timely fashion. A stable deterrence under these circumstances depends, paradoxically, on maintaining a condition of mutual vulnerability to a first strike, coupled with the assurance that comes from having sufficient survivable second-strike forces. The logic is that neither party would undertake a first strike against the other with the knowledge that doing so would invite unwanted retaliatory destruction.

The SALT accords in the 1970s between the United States and the Soviet Union were based, at least from the American point of view, on deterrence by this threat of mutually assured destruction. Caps were placed on strategic offense, specifying maximum numbers and types of missiles and bombers each side could have. At the same time, severe restrictions were placed on strategic defenses, quantitatively limiting deployment of antiballistic missiles (ABMs) and qualitatively prohibiting space-based testing of strategic-defense components. Limitations on strategic defense were intended not only to curb the arms race but also to maintain the mutual vulnerability central to deterrence by mutually assured destruction.

Termination of the ABM Treaty in 2002, a controversial decision taken by the Bush administration, has cleared away a substantial obstacle to deployment of missile defenses. Arguing that the end of the Cold War and good relations with Russia made the ABM Treaty obsolete, President Bush carried forward the defensive program begun under President Clinton, seeing missile defenses as important lest the United States (or its allies) be attacked by smaller nuclear powers in a period of increased proliferation of nuclear weapons and related technologies.

Defense

The distinction between deterrence and defense became abundantly clear in the 1950s and 1960s. If deterrence broke down, what defenses would a society be able to muster? Hardened blast and fallout shelters could be part of a passive civil-defense plan. Active defenses that could destroy incoming bombers and missiles could be used to reduce or limit damage. Damage limitation could also be achieved by striking enemy missiles

Children huddle below their desks in an American elementary school classroom during a "duck and cover" air raid drill in 1951.

before they were launched (or by developing technologies to destroy them in the middle or terminal phases of their trajectories en route to targets). Of course the discussion of using active defenses or even offensive forces to limit damage made defense sound more and more like nuclear warfighting.

In fact, damage limitation involved acquiring effective area and point defenses offered by antiballistic missile or space-based systems, as well as robust offensive systems with sufficient accuracy to take out enemy air bases and missile sites. There is a danger that one side may think its offensive and defensive "damage limitation" forces are strong enough to make a first strike against the other a feasible option. A credible **first-strike capability** includes not only a capacity to strike first but also an ability to nullify or reduce to "acceptable levels" the ability of an adversary to retaliate in kind.

Even if neither side in fact has such a credible first-strike capability, if either side perceived the other were on the verge of acquiring one, it might lead the disadvantaged party to act preemptively, starting a war before the other side achieved any strategic advantage. In short, pursuing the development of damage-limitation forces is seen by many as potentially destabilizing. Even extensive civil-defense networks honestly designed to protect or defend populations in the event of war can be misinterpreted by an adversary as an indication of secret plans to develop a credible first-strike or warfighting capability. Thus developing or extending even passive defenses can be destabilizing, particularly when they are accompanied by existing active defenses and strong offensive capabilities.

In the SALT negotiations, arms control was used as one means of preventing the development of effective strategic defenses that, beyond their defensive value, also could be seen by an adversary as part of an effective warfighting arsenal. A good offense, after all, depends on having good defenses as well. Arms-control agreements that limited nuclear warfighting capabilities by constraining defenses were understood as contributing to the stability of deterrence relations.

Warfighting

In the late 1970s and 1980s, talk turned more directly to developing nuclear warfighting forces that could win or at least "prevail" if deterrence broke down and nuclear war broke out. Credible nuclear warfighting capabilities were seen by some as another form of deterrence or, more generally, dissuasion. Although punishment would no doubt be involved, the primary focus would instead be on denial. From this perspective no would-be adversary would ever take on a country with nuclear superiority or at least an ability to fight and prevail in nuclear warfighting. Because adversaries would in effect be denied any rational purpose for engaging in nuclear war, they would be dissuaded from undertaking it in the first place. Hence, another paradox of deterrence: the point of talking credibly about fighting and prevailing in a nuclear war is the belief that in so doing, that particular horrible possibility will never come about.

Force posture for effective nuclear warfighting capabilities is the least conducive to constructing arms-control regimes. As in all warfighting, the aim of such a denial doctrine is to destroy or substantially weaken an enemy's war-making capability. Arms-control restraints on numbers, types, and locations, as well as on research, development, test and evaluation (RDT&E) of weapons and weapons systems and other factors are an impediment to developing and deploying large numbers of offensive forces able to penetrate enemy territory and air space (as in employing "stealth" technologies that reduce or disguise the appearance on enemy radars of incoming aircraft and missiles) and destroy even the most hardened targets. This requires high accuracy in delivering bombs to target, using air bursts, ground bursts, and even earth-penetrating warheads, depending on the "hardness" and location of targets to be hit. Strategic offenses must also be accompanied by well developed and extensive active and passive defenses—objectives incompatible with most arms control agendas.

Moreover, research, development, test and evaluation, as well as acquisition of substantial offensive and defensive nuclear warfighting capabilities, were upsetting to the general population, which suffered understandably from Cold War nuclear anxieties, made worse by saber rattling and other strong rhetoric between the United States and Soviet Union. Perhaps even more important were anxieties in the Soviet military high command that the United States was trying to achieve a credible first-strike capability and had the technological superiority to do so.

If this were so, Soviet second-strike forces were now potentially in jeopardy. Soviet command-and-control authorities considered shifting to a posture of launch on warning rather than waiting to confirm an attack until it was too late to retaliate. "Launch on warning" is, as discussed above, a highly unstable readiness posture compared to "launch after attack." The danger of false alarm (due to radar, computer, or other equipment malfunction), other accident, or miscalculation causing war to break out is less when time for command-and-control decisions is increased.

The End of the Cold War and Implications for Arms Control, Deterrence, Defense, and Warfighting Doctrines

The attitudes of Gorbachev and Yeltsin in the late 1980s and 1990s and the willingness of American leaders to trust them signaled a change for the better, making the international climate more conducive to arms-control agreements of all kinds. Such agreements had implications for both defense and warfighting doctrines. Agreement under the Strategic Arms Reduction Talks (START) to reduce strategic nuclear weapons by about 75 percent, as well as dramatically scaling back strategic defense plans, also meant that both sides were, in effect, abandoning notions of deterrence or dissuasion by developing and maintaining robust nuclear warfighting capabilities. New arms-control limitations and a U.S. decision at the time to accept a strict interpretation of the ABM treaty that prohibited space-based testing of strategic defense components effectively put a lid on the nuclear arms race; however, proponents of deploying an effective national missile defense called for renegotiating and amending the ABM treaty or, failing that, even abrogating it. Indeed, the Bush administration consulted with Russia and gave the required six-month notice for treaty termination in 2002.

The move away from planning to fight and prevail in nuclear warfare was a notable shift back to an earlier force posture compatible with mutually assured destruction deterrence doctrine. In a period of lower threat and risk of war, both the Russian Federation and United States agreed to put their strategic nuclear forces on less of a war footing, reducing alert and readiness levels to lower levels. Under heavy diplomatic pressures, the former Soviet republics also agreed to disarm themselves of the nuclear weaponry they inherited after the formal breakup of the Soviet Union in 1992. With a strategic regime of quantitative and qualitative restrictions in place, deterrence relations among the major powers are more stable, the overall climate of post–Cold War international relations is much improved, and the risk of general war among great powers has remained relatively low. The nuclear weapons reduction process continues between the two countries in an effort to eliminate an additional 4,000 weapons on each side between 2002 and 2012.

Deterrence Theory: Some Concerns

Reading military doctrinal statements can be a chilling experience for many people. Often written in a straightforward, technical manner, they are unsettling, particularly when they describe, often in matter-of-fact fashion, a possible nuclear exchange between states. Some feminists characterize all this talk about deterrence by threatening mass destruction as no more than yet another masculinist construction masquerading as if it were a "theory." Other critics of deterrence, defense, and warfighting theories or doctrines make several salient points.

First, what is known as the "usability paradox" lies at the heart of U.S. nuclear weapons policy. Two key objectives of U.S. policy—to deter aggression against the United States and its allies and to prevent accidental war—require that U.S. nuclear forces be usable, but not *too* usable. In other words, for deterrence to work, nuclear forces must be usable enough that an adversary is convinced that a U.S. nuclear response would be forthcoming if the United States or its vital interests were attacked. On the other hand, to prevent an accidental nuclear war, U.S. weapons must not be so usable that they could conceivably be launched by computer error or insane missile silo operators or used in such a way that they provoke a fearful adversary to launch a preemptive attack. It is disturbing to note that a number of studies have suggested that the command-and-control systems of U.S. nuclear forces during the Cold War were not without their problems.

Second, and perhaps even more disturbing, studies of two of the most dangerous crises in the Cold War—Cuba (1962) and the Middle East (1973)—suggest that leaders in both Moscow and Washington misperceived each other's motivations and intentions, making for much more dangerous situations than we had previously realized. Theories of deterrence, it is argued, may give leaders a false confidence that they can carefully calibrate their actions to those of an adversary, thus effectively communicating their intentions.

Finally, there are major areas of concern involving nuclear weapons and the developing world. The key question is the extent to which the logic of deterrence as outlined here, essentially devised by American scholars and political leaders in relation to their Cold War, then-Soviet counterparts, is equally applicable, for example, to Indian–Pakistani relations or to present-day U.S.–Russian relations. There is also concern over China's views on limited deterrence and the fact that Beijing is bent on expanding and modernizing its nuclear arsenal in the years ahead. Without China as a full player, both the nuclear nonproliferation and comprehensive test ban regimes are decidedly of less value. Although the United States continues to endorse obligations under the Nonproliferation Treaty, failure by the U.S. Senate to ratify the Comprehensive Test Ban Treaty and talk in the Departments of Defense and Energy about starting a new round of nuclear weapons tests make it more difficult to keep these (and potentially other) parties in compliance with arms control regimes.

Weapons Proliferation

As suggested in references to India and Pakistan or North Korea and Iran as acquiring or seeking weapons of mass destruction, the one topic that has dominated every international arms control agenda in the post–Cold War era is the issue of *weapons proliferation.*

weapons proliferation
The spread of weapons and weapons systems to countries not previously possessing them (horizontal proliferation) or the accumulation of more and more weapons or weapons systems by particular countries (vertical proliferation).

There are five major areas of concern:

1. Nuclear or radiological weapons
2. Chemical weapons
3. Biological weapons
4. Ballistic missiles
5. Advanced conventional weapons systems

Nuclear weapons and materiel, however, have dominated international debate and discussion.

Nuclear Weapons and Materiel

The Cold War and the bipolar international system it created so completely dominated thinking about military security issues that the startling collapse in 1991 of the Soviet Union with its 33,000 nuclear warheads set governments, think tanks, and academe scrambling. During the Cold War, both superpowers entered into alliances and agreements with a number of states, providing security (as in extended deterrence provided to allies) in exchange for, among other things, the agreement not to pursue an independent nuclear weapons capability. But with the end of the Cold War, such security guarantees no longer seemed so secure as the former superpower rivals reassessed their foreign policies and domestic priorities. In Europe and the developing world, all states previously under the security umbrellas of either the United States or the Soviet Union also began to reassess their positions. All expressed concern over the future of the nuclear arsenals and related technologies possessed by the Russian Federation and former Soviet republics.

Indeed, some 3,000 of these weapons were located in the former Soviet republics of the Ukraine, Kazakstan, and Belarus. Although Ukraine initially demonstrated some reluctance, all three finally did agree to relinquish control over nuclear warheads on their respective territories to Russia. This reluctance was partially due to a desire to extract Western aid concessions but stemmed primarily from Ukraine's concern over Russia's intentions, should Russia's relatively moderate leadership at the time under President Yeltsin be replaced in the future by a regime more threatening to Ukraine.

The physical security of the weapons in Russia and the former republics continues to be a problem, raising the frightening specter of weapons and materiel being stolen and perhaps sold for private gain on the black market to terrorist groups and states such as Iran, which might be seeking to accelerate their own nuclear research and development efforts. There were (and continue to be) concerns about Russian and other nuclear weapons experts in the former Soviet republics who might transfer nuclear know-how to nonnuclear states. Many were left jobless by the demise of the Soviet regime and poor economic conditions in the post-Soviet period, and the fear is that some of these experts might be tempted to sell their expertise to foreign governments or terrorist organizations just to make ends meet, not to mention gaining great profit from such illegal ventures. Beyond legal prohibitions against nuclear technology transfers, finding proper employment and adequate compensation for these experts quickly became not just a Russian but also an international security concern.

The linchpin of the international nonproliferation regime is the 1967 **Nuclear Non-Proliferation Treaty (NPT),** in which the five declared nuclear powers at the time (the United States, the United Kingdom, the Soviet Union, France, and China) pledged not to export to nonnuclear states either nuclear weapons or nuclear weapons components or technologies. Other signatories agreed, as nonnuclear states, not to try to acquire a nuclear weapons capability in exchange for a commitment by the nuclear powers to negotiate in good faith on cessation of the nuclear arms race and the pursuit of nuclear disarmament. All parties that have signed the treaty agreed to safeguards and inspections by the Vienna-based **International Atomic Energy Agency (IAEA)** of nuclear power plants and other nuclear facilities used for peaceful purposes. The purpose of these provisions, of course, is to reassure states that their neighbors are not secretly building nuclear weapons capabilities and thus persuading states to forgo pursuing weapons programs of their own.

Testing of nuclear weapons by India and Pakistan in 1998 added two more members to the nuclear club. It is assumed that Israel also has nuclear weapons capabilities. South Africa developed these capabilities but chose to disarm itself of them after a significant change of regime took place in the 1990s. Likewise, Brazil and Argentina appear to have moved away from developing nuclear weapons capabilities. As mentioned earlier, after the breakup of the Soviet Union in 1992, three of the former Soviet republics (Belarus, Ukraine, and Kazakhstan) relinquished nuclear weapons on their soil to the Russian Federation, weapons that, in turn, were among those subject to destruction under the Russian-American START agreements.

Other states, unable to secure a weapons capability directly, still might be eager to augment their research and development programs with Russian or other foreign expertise. Nor is nuclear materiel secure. A state does not have to steal a weapon or purchase an actual nuclear weapon to become a worry to its neighbors. As noted earlier, arms reduction agreements between the United States and Russia require the dismantling of thousands of existing weapons. The two countries did decide to trim by the year 2012 the pre-1991 U.S.-Soviet strategic nuclear warhead totals by about 75 percent, a figure increased in 2002 to about 85 percent. This nuclear-reduction effort resulted, however, in the creation of a massive nuclear waste–disposal problem. It is estimated that by 2008 the Russians, who lack the processing facilities of the United States, will have had to dispose of some six tons of plutonium and thirty tons of enriched uranium.[1] Given its own interests also at stake, the United States has been willing to assist the Russian Federation in dealing with this issue, but critics charge U.S. efforts are woefully inadequate, given the potential dangers.

Plutonium, an essential part of nuclear weapons, is not found in nature. It is a by-product of the same uranium that is used in a nuclear reactor. Plutonium, even if not weapons grade, could still be made into a low-yield "dirty bomb." Such a device could cause widespread devastation if detonated from the back of a truck. All sorts of such doomsday scenarios come easily to mind, with states as well as terrorist groups involved. But even the possibility of a black market in weapons and weapons-grade material is alarming. Nuclear smuggling of plutonium and other weapons-grade materials can be pursued with relative ease if controls are lax. The criminal motive in such circumstances might be either to realize large financial gains, often linked to government or military officials with access to these resources, or to supply terrorist groups or governments wanting to acquire or manufacture nuclear weapons with weapons-grade materials procured illegally in global black markets.

How should a state respond to a credible terrorist nuclear threat? Refuse to negotiate and hope it is a bluff? Threaten to destroy the targets associated with the group's

---

[1]For ongoing coverage of this issue, go to www.iiss.org.

cause? If one country is unsure about what its neighboring rival has in its military arsenal, would it not have an incentive to acquire a nuclear weapons capability, perhaps in the name of deterrence?

As possession of nuclear weapons spreads, the possibility of inadvertent use increases, because new nuclear states are not likely to have as secure command and control over these weapons as did the major powers during the height of the Cold War. In a crisis, a state may be more likely to launch nuclear weapons against a neighbor, believing it must get in the first strike before its rival. This is known as a preemptive strike. Possible scenarios resulting from instabilities in such regions of the world as the Middle East or South Asia include:

- A regional war between two newly nuclear-armed states
- The rise of a regional nuclear-armed predator leading a major power (or major power–led alliance) to take action to thwart the predator's expansionist ambitions
- The loss of central government control over nuclear forces as a result of the political disintegration of the state, which could lead to a nuclear civil war or to a terrorist organization gaining control of one or more weapons

What can be done about the nuclear proliferation threat? One approach is on the *supply* side—prevention of the further spread of nuclear weapons or nuclear weapons technologies by prohibiting such exports by states already possessing these capabilities. On the demand side, the aim is to improve regional security conditions so that states will be less likely to feel a need to acquire such weapons. Diplomatic efforts to persuade would-be nuclear powers from pursuing the acquisition of nuclear weapons or weapons technologies are demand-side measures. Thus, in arms control usage, the term *supply side* refers to countries already in possession of a particular weapon, weapons system, or related technologies, whereas *demand side* refers to countries wishing to acquire any of these weapons, weapons systems, or technologies.

No doubt signaling their future intentions, India and Pakistan never signed the Nuclear Non-Proliferation Treaty, resulting in unilateral efforts by other states to deny certain technologies to these countries. At most, the treaty, to which neither was a party, merely slowed India's and Pakistan's drive for nuclear weapons capability. Then in 2003 it was revealed that Pakistan's top nuclear scientist had been part of a large-scale operation designed to export nuclear know-how and technology to other states, including Iran and North Korea. It should be noted that the NPT does not prohibit a state from conducting research and development of civilian nuclear-power programs intended for peaceful, electric power–generation purposes, which is what the Iranians claim they are doing. The obvious problem with this, however, is that such a program also can be used not only in developing expertise that can then be applied toward a weapons development program but also in generating plutonium and other products that can be used in constructing nuclear weapons. On the brighter side, in 2003 Libya renounced all efforts to pursue weapons of mass destruction and agreed to allow inspectors into the country. This decision followed the end of U.N. sanctions imposed on Libya for its involvement in international terrorism in the 1980s. Sanctions were dropped by most countries following the Libyan acknowledgment that agents of its government were responsible for the midair bombing of Pan Am flight 103 in 1988. Its decision to allow inspectors into the country was also due to the hope that the United States would lift its unilateral economic sanctions on the beleaguered country.

Efforts by North Korea to develop its own nuclear weapons became apparent when it announced in 1993 its intent to withdraw from the NPT regime in order to avoid an impending IAEA inspection of a suspect site. International pressure and subsequent negotiations kept North Korea formally within the NPT regime for several years. In 2002, however, North Korea announced it was withdrawing from the NPT regime and resuming its nuclear weapons program which resulted in a concerted effort by the United States and other countries to bring North Korea back into the NPT regime.

Despite international efforts against proliferation, a few states have thus made some progress toward acquiring nuclear weapons. Other states may resort to *counterproliferation* policies—taking preemptive actions in attempts to destroy a threatening state's nuclear capabilities. This happened several times with Iraq—the Israeli attack on Iraq's reactor in 1981, the U.S.-led coalition's attack on Iraq's nuclear facilities during the Gulf War in 1991, follow-on U.S. attacks in 1998 meant to ensure that Iraq could not rebuild its program, and finally the March 2003 invasion of Iraq and the fruitless effort to find and destroy nuclear and other weapons of mass destruction, which apparently were not there in the first place.

The *demand* side approach to nonproliferation involves reducing motivations to acquire nuclear weapons. The ideal solution is to eliminate the insecurity and fear among neighboring states. This has been the goal of the United States concerning the Arabs and Israelis. A complementary approach involves security guarantees. The United States, for example, has provided such a guarantee to South Korea as evidenced by the stationing of U.S. troops there. Likewise, Japan has enjoyed a similar security guarantee from the United States as part of its extended deterrence security "umbrella" in east Asia. But that guarantee was made during the Cold War as a measure to contain communism, and it is harder to believe that the United States or any other country would today make an equivalent guarantee to nonnuclear powers not already under the American security umbrella.

Chemical and Biological Weapons

Chemical weapons are much easier to produce than nuclear weapons, and they are found in the arsenals of most states. In January 1993, 130 countries signed the Chemical Weapons Convention (CWC), which revised and expanded the guidelines established by the 1925 Geneva Protocol. The tortuous negotiations began in 1968. Signers of the convention pledge not to develop, produce, acquire, stockpile, or transfer chemical weapons; not to use such weapons; and not to assist or encourage anyone to engage in such prohibited activity. States also pledged to destroy chemical weapons stocks and production facilities. Similar to the previously mentioned role performed by IAEA in the nuclear nonproliferation regime, one task for the Organization for the Prohibition of Chemical Weapons (OPCW) is verification.

Despite the high lethality and effectiveness of biological weapons, they have not been used in modern warfare. As with chemical weapons, an international agreement also exists—the 1973 Biological and Toxin Weapons Convention (BWC), signed in 1973 by some 150 states. The BWC forbids the production of biological warfare agents, but research is allowed for the purpose of producing vaccines and antidotes. Opportunities for cheating are plentiful. With the collapse of the Soviet Union, for example, it became apparent that the Soviets had engaged in a massive program to develop antibiotic-resistant pathogens for use as weapons. The main drawback to the BWC is that it has no effective verification procedure, and hence efforts to control biological weapons lag far behind the international conventions that control nuclear and chemical weapons.

Since the Biological Weapons Convention was drafted in 1969, several things have changed, and not for the good. First, the biotech revolution has made it possible for

Case & Point

BIOLOGICAL WEAPONS

The main international control mechanism for biological weapons is the vital but weak Biological and Toxin Weapons Convention (BWC). The 1925 Geneva Protocol banned the use of "bacteriological methods of warfare," but it was not until 1969 that the United Kingdom offered a draft calling for the actual elimination of biological weapons. The United States supported the idea, and later that year U.S. President Nixon renounced the production and stockpiling of biological weapons. The United States and the Soviet Union agreed on a text banning the production of biological weapons, which was then submitted to the United Nations. In December 1971 the U.N. General Assembly approved a resolution supporting the convention. The key elements are

- No state shall develop, produce, stockpile, or acquire biological agents.
- Each state shall destroy existing stocks.
- No state shall transfer such agents.

The United States signed both the BWC and the Geneva Protocol in 1975. In 2001, however, the United States rejected a protocol designed to strengthen compliance procedures. The U.S. government claimed the protocol gave false assurances that secret bioweapons labs could be detected. The United States also claimed the protocol would endanger the U.S. biodefense program.

Point: The problem is lack of enforcement mechanisms, and it is estimated that ten to twenty-five countries now may possess or be seeking to develop biological weapons.

"designer" bugs to be crafted, raising the specter of a biological agent that could be impossible to combat or even one that could target a particular racial or ethnic group. Second, the worldwide diffusion of technology makes the development of such agents possible for states that are unable to go the nuclear route but still feel vulnerable to attack by others.

Eliminating weapons of mass destruction, particularly chemical and biological weapons, obviously remains a major arms control challenge. Progress has been made on regime construction through treaties and other agreements to outlaw the development, acquisition, and stockpiling of such weaponry. But implementation and enforcement is difficult, given the ease with which even nonspecialists can assemble such weaponry without detection. Governments wanting to produce and stockpile chemical and biological weapons may be identified through intelligence sources. By comparison, however, it is far easier to verify compliance or violations of nuclear nonproliferation regime rules than it is to identify chemical or biological weapons producers and stockpilers.

Ballistic Missiles

The surest and fastest way to deliver such weapons is by **ballistic missiles,** and no similar global effort has been made to control the spread of these. Since their invention in the 1930s, guided ballistic missiles have been used in four wars: The Germans launched over 2,000 V-2 missiles in World War II; Iraq and Iran together launched over 1,000 in their 1980–1988 war; the Kabul government used them against guerrillas during the Afghan civil war; and Iraq launched 80 modified Scud missiles against Israel and Saudi Arabia during the 1991 Gulf War. In all cases only conventional, high-explosive warheads were used, directed mainly against cities.

Case & Point

Passengers on an Israeli airliner anticipated a routine departure from Moi International Airport in Mombasa, Kenya, on November 28, 2002. A loud boom was immediately followed by two white vapor trails on the left side of the aircraft. The Boeing 757 had just missed being shot down by two SA-7 shoulder-launched antiaircraft missiles. Known as Man-Portable Defense Systems (MANPADS), these conventional weapons are meant to knock aircraft out of the sky. The suspected perpetrators were Al Qaeda terrorists. The International Civil Aviation Organization (ICAO) estimates that twenty-seven fixed-wing aircraft were destroyed as of June 2003. This includes the shoot-down of an aircraft carrying the presidents of Rwanda and Burundi in 1994, which helped to spark Rwanda's civil war. Although the exact number of MANPADS is not known, they are found in the armies of NATO, Russia, India, Pakistan, China, and France. The best-known system, the Stinger, was supplied to the Afghan resistance by the United States in the 1980s during the war against the Soviet Union. For many airline companies, the cost of installing electronic countermeasures on all aircraft is prohibitive.

Point: Despite the concern over weapons of mass destruction, conventional weapons such as MANPADS are already a proven deadly threat.

Beyond several hundred miles, however, ballistic missiles are a relatively inefficient means to deliver conventional munitions, hence the emphasis on nuclear warheads by the major nuclear powers during the Cold War. For states without a nuclear capability, chemical weapons are easier to acquire or manufacture and more difficult to detect. While less deadly than nuclear weapons, they can still kill as many people as dozens of conventionally armed missiles. As the range of missiles increases, more and more countries are within an aggressor's target, a fact that feeds perceptions of international insecurity.

One attempt to deal with this development was the establishment in 1987 of the **Missile Technology Control Regime (MTCR).** The original seven members (the United States, Canada, France, Germany, Italy, Japan, and the United Kingdom) agreed to control the transfer of equipment and technology that could aid in the development of nuclear weapons–capable missiles, defined as having payloads of at least 500 kilograms and a traveling distance of at least 300 kilometers. The regime has since expanded to thirty-two members, with Israel, China, and Russia committing themselves informally to follow the provisions without officially joining. Guidelines added in 1993 cover missiles capable of delivering chemical and biological weapons. Enforcement mechanisms, however, are lacking.

Conventional Weapons

The term *conventional weapons* suggests that these are of secondary concern compared to nuclear or radiological, chemical, and biological weapons. In fact, conventional weapons have become ever more lethal, as was evident in the 1991 Gulf War against Iraq, the bombing campaigns in Kosovo in 1999 and Afghanistan in 2001, and the second Gulf War against Iraq in 2003. Computer and guidance system advances have made it more likely that conventional warheads will be delivered with greater accuracy and thus have greater impact than in the past. It does not necessarily take professionally trained military personnel to operate some of these systems. Many surface-to-air missiles, for example, are portable, can be launched by an individual and can bring down an airliner.

THE KALASHNIKOV AGE

Most of the roughly 80 million AK-47s in circulation today are in the wrong hands. According to the United Nations, only 18 million (or about 3 percent) of the 550 million small arms and light weapons in circulation today are used by government, military, or police forces. Illicit trade accounts for almost 20 percent of the total small arms trade and generates more than $1 billion a year. Small arms helped fuel 46 of the 49 largest conflicts in the past decade and in 2001 were estimated to be responsible for 1,000 deaths a day; more than 80 percent of those victims were women and children.

Moises Naim
"The Five Wars of Globalization," Foreign Policy, *January/February 2003, p. 31.*

It's Been Said...

Much of the Cold War was spent dealing with nuclear weapons questions that still remain on the arms control agenda. Conventional or nonnuclear armaments and military forces were also the subject of extensive negotiations during the cold war, particularly in Europe during the period of *détente* in the late 1960s and 1970s. With the end of the cold war, substantial progress has been made in regional security regime construction governing numbers, types, locations, and readiness of military forces in Europe.

Almost twenty years of mutual and balanced force reductions (MBFR) talks in Vienna between NATO and Warsaw Pact members produced very little in the way of results. By contrast, under the auspices of the Conference on Security and Cooperation in Europe (CSCE), the CSCE-wide Conference on Disarmament in Europe (CDE) in Stockholm during the mid-1980s and the Conference on Armed Forces in Europe (CFE) in Vienna during the late 1980s and early 1990s between members of the NATO and Warsaw Pact alliances made major strides in arms control, particularly in relation to conventional forces. The CDE added to confidence- and security-building measures originally established in the 1975 Helsinki Final Act, which were enhanced still further in the early 1990s in CSCE-wide talks, also in Vienna. For its part, members of the two alliances produced a CFE agreement specifying details of military force deployments, setting caps or limits on numbers, types, and locations of armed forces and associated weaponry. As a result of these arms control agreements, European states were provided a militarily transparent or open environment affording increased warning time and thus reducing regional military threats substantially—an enhancement of international security through reducing the overall risk of war. Attention to armaments was coupled with political-military **transparency** involving the open exchange of information, on-site inspections, and other functional approaches to confidence- and security-building.

Although not yet attempted seriously outside of Europe, some arms control advocates see this European approach to regional security regime construction for conventional forces as having potential in such other troubled regions as the Middle East, the Gulf region, and both south and northeast Asia. Even though the conflicts that divide the parties cannot easily be resolved, the security of all can still be enhanced in the short run to the extent that adversary states in these regions can agree on a security regime to govern their military forces. As in Europe, such regimes could address numbers, types, locations, and readiness of forces, perhaps adding security- and confidence-building measures to the mix. Reducing the risk of war through these mechanisms—quite apart from efforts to increase trade and commerce or cultural and other exchanges—would improve the climate of relations, perhaps making conditions eventually more conducive to addressing underlying conflicts among states and societies or other actors or peoples in the region.

Arms transfers are another arms control–agenda item for the post–cold war period. Beyond immediate concerns about proliferation of nuclear weapons are concerns about the vast global armaments market. Both legal and illegal sales of armaments by and to states and nonstate actors continue on a truly massive scale. Critics observe that arms purchases deplete national resources that might otherwise be spent more productively on investment for economic development or other purposes. Moreover, acquiring armaments beyond realistic defense needs fuels arms races that diminish (rather than enhance) the security of states and societies in a region.

EXPECTED GAINS OR OBJECTIVES	STATES AND ALLIANCES		NONSTATE ACTORS		
	SELLERS/ PRODUCERS	BUYERS	CORPORATIONS AND BANKS	RESEARCH GROUPS	TERRORIST REVOLUTIONARY GROUPS
Political					
Enhance security	X*	X			
Challenge governmental authority					X
Economic					
Increase revenue or profit from sales	X		X	X	
Assure return on capital (investments/ loans)	X		X		
Create jobs/reduce unemployment	X		X		
Generate new and spin-off technologies	X		X	X	
Achieve economies of large-scale production (lower unit costs of weaponry)	X	X	X		
Keep assembly lines open and running	X		X		
Secure market share	X		X		
Improve trade balance (export promotion)	X				

TABLE 7.5
The Political Economy of the Global Arms Trade

★ The letter *X* denotes gains from arms trade that serve the interests of diverse actors.

Because the arms trade is a profitable business for many who engage in it, agreeing on rules to limit or constrain it has proven to be extremely difficult. Demand for weaponry continues to be very strong, and there is no shortage of suppliers willing and able to meet it. Moreover, arms-producing corporations and states can realize greater **economies of scale** when they have large export markets, which reduce the per-unit cost to producers of tanks, aircraft, or other expensive military hardware. In short, the interests that favor a continuing and expanding global arms trade have proven far stronger politically than those arms controllers who seek construction of regimes to constrain or reduce the volume of trade and put limits on the kinds of arms that are traded globally and regionally. As indicated in Table 7.5, incentives to

Case & Point

MANAGING THE GLOBAL ARMS TRADE: THE WASSENAAR ARRANGE-MENT

THE PROBLEM

Enormous amounts of money are involved in a global arms trade in which states and their respective corporations participate. The continuing demand for weapons as means to security creates substantial incentive for suppliers to the global arms market. Although export of armaments makes a contribution to defense needs of states not in a position to produce these weapons and weapons systems domestically, the magnitude of such arms transfers may have quite the opposite effect by fueling arms races, creating greater instability, and diverting national resources from investments in development or other positive purposes. We focus in this case only on trade in conventional arms—a term that includes all weapons except nuclear, biological, and chemical (NBC) arms.

THE GLOBAL ARMS MARKET: EXPORTERS AND IMPORTERS

The Supply Side, leading providers

	Export Volume (US$ Billions)	Global Market Share
United States	13.6	47.5%
United Kingdom	4.7	16.3
Russian Federation	3.4	11.8
Ukraine	1.5	5.0
France	1.2	4.2
Germany	1.2	4.2
China (PRC)	0.5	1.7
Israel	0.4	1.2
Italy	0.1	0.3
Belgium	0.1	0.3

The Demand Side, leading recipients

	Import Volume (US$ Billions)
Saudi Arabia	5.8
Egypt	2.1
India	2.0
Israel	1.9
China	1.0
South Korea	0.7
Malaysia	0.6
Taiwan	0.5
Kuwait	0.3
Indonesia	0.3

Source: International Institute for Strategic Studies.

OBSTACLES TO AGREEMENTS ON REGULATING GLOBAL ARMS TRADE

As shown in Table 7.5, buyers and sellers, states and alliances, and nonstate actors all have major stakes in the global arms trade. Their expected gains and related objectives are both political and economic. Incentives to trade in arms far outnumber any disincentives.

Case & Point

TACKLING THE PROBLEM

(continued)

Given global concerns about unregulated trade in arms and dual-use items (goods that have both military and nonmilitary applications), countries engaged in the arms production and export trade conducted negotiations beginning in 1994 in the town of Wassenaar in the Netherlands. Relatively modest in its demands, the outcome of these discussions in late 1995 and early 1996 nevertheless constituted a first step in a process—the so-called Wassenaar Arrangement, pledging thirty-three arms exporting countries to the following actions:

- Establish the Wassenaar Arrangement on Export Controls for Conventional Arms and Dual-Use Goods and Technologies
- Locate the headquarters and secretariat of the Wassenaar Arrangement in Vienna, Austria
- Meet on a regular basis in Vienna, the decisions being made by consensus
- Meet regularly to ensure responsible transfers of conventional arms and dual-use goods and technologies in furtherance of international and regional peace and security
- Promote "transparency" or openness with regular exchange of views and information on arms sales
- Achieve greater responsibility in transfers of conventional arms and dual-use goods and technologies, thus preventing destabilizing accumulations in national arsenals
- Enhance cooperation to prevent the acquisition of armaments and sensitive dual-use items for military end uses if the situation in a region or the behavior of a recipient state is or becomes a cause for serious concern
- Ensure that transfers of arms and dual-use goods and technologies do not contribute to the development or enhancement of military capabilities that undermine international and regional security and stability
- Maintain effective export controls for the items on agreed lists, which are reviewed periodically to take into account both technological developments and experience gained
- Exchange semiannual notifications of arms transfers, covering the same weapons categories used in the U.N. Register of Conventional Arms (battle tanks, armored combat vehicles, large-caliber artillery systems, combat aircraft, attack helicopters, warships, and missiles or missile systems)
- Report arms transfers to other countries or denials of transfers to them of certain controlled dual-use items, preferably within thirty days (but no later than within sixty days) of the date of the denial
- Notify all participants, preferably within thirty days (but no later than within sixty days) of any approval by a participating state of any license to sell arms to a recipient state denied during the previous three years by another participating state

In addition to information exchange and compliance with notification obligations, parties to the Wassenaar Arrangement have been examining increased small arms trade often used in national and ethnic conflicts, illicit arms trafficking, and direct threats to commercial and other aircraft posed by the availability of man-portable air-defense systems (MANPADS), and the need for appropriate measures to prevent such weapons from falling into the wrong hands. For more information, go to www.wassenaar.org.

Point: High stakes in the global arms trade tend to make buyers and sellers reluctant to curb this market to any significant degree.

sell armaments are numerous; buyers are also motivated to import arms to strengthen their security, more cost effectively than if efforts were made to produce these weapons domestically.

The end of the Cold War apparently has not affected the global arms market in conventional weapons. Over the last quarter century, a number of countries such as South Africa and Brazil have entered the global arms market as a way to earn revenue. As international competition has increased, there has been a remarkable globalization of the arms industry on the part of arms manufacturers. In the past, arms industries were firms from different states competing against each other, often backed by their national governments. Firms would develop a complete weapons system and then attempt to sell it on the international market. This is no longer an accurate depiction of the arms market, given a series of transnational developments in recent years. Strategic alliances—loose agreements between firms to explore future collaboration or technology sharing—are one development. A number of major defense companies have taken the next step by establishing transnational joint venture companies in order to develop and build arms. Furthermore, there have been a number of significant mergers and acquisitions in recent years, particularly among prime contractors in aerospace and other defense industries, resulting in greater concentration of capital in ever fewer multinational corporations.

The globalization of arms production has been encouraged by governments. In the aftermath of the Cold War, military budgets shrank in most countries; however, defense spending has increased substantially in the United States, particularly since the terrorist attacks in 2001. Increased competition for sales in arms markets remains strong. Many leaders believed that transnational ties were necessary in defense-related industries to take advantage of technological developments around the world. These would help to maintain a cost-effective yet minimal research and development and production capacity to meet national defense needs. To remain insular and inward looking was to risk falling behind in important areas of research and development, yet another motivation for producing and selling arms.

Conclusion

In this chapter we have examined a large number of disarmament and arms control efforts and agreements achieved during the last half of the twentieth century and continuing into the twenty-first century. The international arms control regimes, established in the enlightened self-interest of states and supported by numerous nongovernmental organizations as well, give us institutions and rules concerning armed forces and armaments (many of which have the binding force of international law). Such international regimes have been a focus of analysis for both pluralist or liberal and realist scholars. Many arms control advocates see the task as having just begun, as they pursue a continuing, incremental effort to beat more swords into plowshares and in the process provide a greater degree of order to an otherwise anarchic world lacking central governance or authority. On the other hand, arms control naysayers, especially in the United States, have put the brakes on some arms control efforts, dampening to some degree the enthusiasm for arms control regime construction and expansion advocated by those who see these measures as central to international security and stability.

Afterword

John Locke on War and Maintaining the Peace

Although John Locke's focus as political theorist is on the social contract that establishes domestic society, it is this coming together by contract or agreement that captures the interest of some present-day international relations theorists, particularly social constructivists. (See, for example, Alexander Wendt's volume on Social Theory, *which identifies a Lockean understanding of international relations comparable to that of Grotius—often referred to as the "father" of international law.) Indeed, Locke does not see the anarchic state of nature— "want of a common judge," government or central authority—as necessarily warlike. In this Locke clearly opposes the view taken earlier by Thomas Hobbes who portrays the state of nature as perpetually in a state of war—either actively engaging in fighting or always on guard, preparing for the fight.*

To Locke, before society is formed one may remain in a state of nature or move from it to a state of war and back again; the two states of being—nature and war—are not one and the same as they are with Hobbes. We find, then, that in applying Locke's insight to international relations we need not see states as necessarily in a state of war with one another. Moreover, states (as if they were persons in a state of nature) may reach agreements with one another to maintain the peace, whether they remain in a state of nature or leave it by forming a community.

Given our focus in this chapter on arms control regimes intended to reduce the likelihood of war or its consequences, we thought it instructive to include this selection of passages from Locke's Second Treatise on Government. *Chapters where these passages can be found are indicated parenthetically by Roman numerals and sections by Arabic numbers. Italics are added here and there to emphasize what we consider key points in Locke's argument.*

To understand political power right, and derive it from its original, *we must consider, what state all men are naturally in, and that is, a state of perfect freedom* to order their actions, and dispose of their possessions and persons, as they think fit, within the bounds of the law of nature, without asking leave, or depending upon the will of any other man. [It is] *a state also of equality*, wherein all the power and jurisdiction is reciprocal, no one having more than another. . . . (II, 4)

It is often asked as a mighty objection, where are, or ever were there any men in such a state of nature? To which it may suffice as an answer at present, that since *all princes and rulers of independent governments all through the world, are in a state of nature,* it is plain the world never was, nor ever will be, without numbers of men in that state. I have named all governors of independent communities, whether they are, or are not, in league with others: for *it is not every compact that puts an end to the state of nature between men, but only this one of agreeing together mutually to enter into one community, and make one body politic; other promises, and compacts, men may make one with another, and yet still be in the state of nature. The promises and bargains for truck, &c. between the two men . . . are binding to them, though they are perfectly in a state of nature, in reference to one another: for truth and keeping of faith belongs to men, as men, and not as members of society.* . . . (II, 14)

And here we have the plain difference between the state of nature and the state of war, which however some men have confounded, are as far distant, as a state of peace, good will, mutual assistance and preservation, and a state of enmity, malice, violence and mutual destruction, are one from another. *Men living together according to reason, without a common superior on earth, with authority to judge between them, is properly the state of nature. But force, or a declared design of force, upon the person of another, where there is no common superior on earth to appeal to for relief, is the state of war: and it is the want of such an appeal gives a man the right of war even against an aggressor, tho' he be in society and a fellow subject. . . . Want of a common judge with authority, puts all men in a state of nature: force without right, upon a man's person, makes a state of war, both where there is, and is not, a common judge. . . .* (III, 19)

To avoid this state of war (wherein there is no appeal but to heaven, and wherein every the least difference is apt to end, where there is no authority to decide between the contenders) is one great reason of men's putting themselves into society, and quitting the state of nature: for where there is an authority, a power on earth, from which relief can be had by appeal, there the continuance of the state of war is excluded, and the controversy is decided by that power. . . . (III, 21)

Whosoever therefore out of a state of nature unite into a community, must be understood to give up all the power, necessary to the ends for which they unite into society, to the majority of the community, unless they expressly agreed in any number greater than the majority. And this is done by barely agreeing to unite into one political society, which is all the compact that is, or needs be, between the individuals, that enter into, or make up a commonwealth. And thus that, which begins and actually constitutes any political society, is nothing but the consent of any number of freemen capable of a majority to unite and incorporate into such a society. And this is that, and that only, which did, or could give beginning to any lawful government in the world. . . . (III, 99)

Thus, though looking back as far as records give us any account of peopling the world, and the history of nations, we commonly find the government to be in one hand; yet it destroys not that which I affirm, *viz.* that the beginning of politic society depends upon the consent of the individuals, to join into, and make one society; who, when they are thus incorporated, might set up what form of government they thought fit. . . . (III, 106)

Key Terms

disarmament *p. 240*	military (force-employment)	weapons proliferation *p. 259*
arms control *p. 241*	doctrines *p. 250*	
international security	minimum or finite	
regimes *p. 241*	deterrence *p. 251*	

Other Concepts

confidence- and security-building measures (CSBMs) *p. 246*	extended deterrence *p. 251*	Nuclear Non-Proliferation Treaty (NPT) *p. 260*
verification *p. 249*	force posture *p. 251*	International Atomic Energy Agency (IAEA) *p. 261*
compliance *p. 249*	countervalue targets *p. 251*	ballistic missiles *p. 264*
national technical means (NTM) of verification *p. 249*	counterforce targets *p. 251*	Missile Technology Control Regime (MTCR) *p. 265*
telemetry *p. 250*	collateral damage (death and destruction) *p. 253*	transparency *p. 266*
deterrence *p. 250*	second-strike capability *p. 254*	arms transfers *p. 266*
defense *p. 250*	counterproliferation *p. 255*	economies of scale *p. 267*
warfighting *p. 250*	mutually assured destruction (MAD) *p. 255*	
	first-strike capability *p. 257*	

Additional Readings

For annotated texts of arms control treaties and agreements, see Paul R. Viotti's *U.S. Foreign Policy and National Security: A Documentary Record* (Upper Saddle River, NJ: Prentice-Hall, 2005), Part Four, chs. 14–16. On other disarmament and arms control matters, see Stockholm International Peace Research Institute, *SIPRI Yearbook: World Armaments and Disarmament* (annual); U.S. Arms Control and Disarmament Agency, *World Military Expenditures and Arms Transfers* (annual); International Institute for Strategic Studies, *Military Balance* (annual); Arms Control Association, *Arms Control Today* (monthly journal); and Institute for Defense and Disarmament Studies, *Arms Control Reporter.* This latter publication continually updates information on arms control negotiations, treaties, and regimes. See also Donald Kerr's *World Directory of Defense and Security* (New York: Stockton Press, 1995); and Nicholas Rengger, ed., *Treaties and Alliances of the World,* latest ed. (UK: Longman Group).

For reviews of arms control issues on the global agenda, see Jeffrey A. Larsen (ed.), *Arms Control: Cooperative Security in a Changing Environment* (Boulder, CO: Lynne Rienner, 2002) and the earlier volume by Larsen and Gregory J. Rattray (eds.), *Arms Control toward the 21st Century* (Boulder, CO: Lynne Rienner Publishers, 1996); Barry Buzan and Eric Herring, *The Arms Dynamic in World Politics* (Boulder, CO.: Lynne Rienner Publishers, 1998); and Andrew J. Pierre, ed., *Cascade of Arms: Managing Conventional Weapons Proliferation* (Washington, DC: Brookings Institution, 1998). For information on small arms trafficking, see Lora Lumpe, ed., *Running Guns: The Global Black Market in Small Arms* (London: Zed Books, 2000). We also recommend the monthly *Bulletin of the Atomic Scientists.*

An informative volume that provides useful historical background of continuing nuclear nonproliferation efforts is Henry D. Sokolski's *The Best of Intentions: America's Campaign Against Strategic Weapons Proliferation* (New York: Praeger, 2001). For a highly readable theoretical debate on nuclear proliferation, see Scott Sagan and Kenneth Waltz, *The Spread of Nuclear Weapons,* 2nd ed. (New York: W.W. Norton, 1995, 2002). On weapons of mass destruction, see Joseph Cirincione *et al., Deadly Arsenals,* Rev. ed. (Washington, D.C.: Carnegie Endowment for International Peace, 2002, 2005); Kurt M. Campbell, Robert J. Einhorn, and Mitchell B. Reiss, *The Nuclear Tipping Point: Why States Reconsider Their Nuclear Choices* (Washington, D.C.: Brookings Institution, 2004); Lawrence Freedman's classic, *The Evolution of Nuclear Strategy,* 3rd ed. (New York: Palgrave, 1981, 2003); and Peter R. Lavoy, Scott D. Sagan and James J. Wirtz, *Planning the Unthinkable: How New Powers Will Use Nuclear, Biological and Chemical Weapons* (Ithaca, NY: Cornell University Press, 2000).

For an interesting analysis of why there are perhaps not more nuclear-capable states, see Thazha Varkey Paul, *Power versus Prudence: Why Nations Forgo Nuclear Weapons* (Montreal: Queen's University Press, 2000). On the relation between technology, national power and the use of force, see George and Meredith Friedman, *The Future of War: Power, Technology and American World Dominance in the Twenty-First Century* (NY: St. Martin's Griffin, 1996) and Ann R. Markusen and Sean S. Costigan, *Arming the Future: A Defense Industry for the 21st Century* (New York: Council on Foreign Relations Press, 1999).

Classics on arms control include Hedley Bull, *The Control of the Arms Race* (New York: Frederick A. Praeger, 1961, 1965); Thomas C. Schelling and Morton H. Halperin, *Strategy and Arms Control* (New York: The Twentieth Century Fund, 1961) as well as Schelling's *The Strategy of Conflict* (New York: Oxford University Press, 1963) and his *Arms and Influence* (New Haven, CT: Yale University Press, 1966); and Anatol Rapoport, *Strategy and Conscience* (New York: Schocken Books, 1964) and his later *The Origins of Violence* (New Brunswick, NJ: Transaction Publishers, 1995).

Chapter 8

International Terrorism and Transnational Crime

*"We have gone around lost for a long time
but it will not be forever. . . .
The rich will come face to face with the poor
and between all the poor
we will bring you to bay
as if you were the thieving fox;
wait, just wait, you who starve my people to death.
I will kill you."* [1]

SONG POPULAR WITH THE REVOLUTIONARY SONS AND
DAUGHTERS OF PEASANTS IN PERU

*"In the post-9/11 world, threats are defined
more by the fault lines within societies than by
the territorial boundaries between them. From
terrorism to global disease or environmental
degradation, the challenges have become
transnational rather than international. That is
the defining quality of world politics in the
twenty-first century."*

9/11 COMMISSION REPORT

Terrorism

- The Causes of Terrorism
- The Extent of Terrorism
- The Changing Nature of Terrorism
- Responses

Transnational Crime and Globalization

- Case Study: The United States, Latin America, and Drugs

Conclusion

Afterword: Bin Laden's 1998 *Fatwah*

At the end of the path I noticed three young men engaged in what appeared to be idle conversation. I thought they were students waiting for the early morning classes to begin, and I greeted them cheerfully. Just as I was passing them, one of them called out my name.

"Mr. Cicippio!"

I turned and they reached out for me. My heart hammering in my throat, I struggled to free myself. Then the butt of a pistol slammed into the back of my head, and the world came crashing in on me.

I slumped forward onto my hands and knees, my vision a blur. I was able to make out my eyeglasses, lying smashed on the pavement and surrounded by drops of blood. When I reached out for them, one of the men kicked them away. A terrorist said, "Don't raise your head or I'll blow it off." They picked me up and carried me, face down, into a university building and out the other side to an adjacent parking lot.

They threw me into the rear of a small foreign automobile. A foot pressed down on my neck, pinning my head to the floor of the car. At that point, the events of my entire life passed before me.

After a while we came to what appeared to be some sort of garage. It was damp and dark and smelled hellishly of car fumes. That place was where I would begin more than five years of cruel confinement, where the tortures of beating and hunger were secondary to those of loneliness, rage and bewilderment. Maddening boredom alternated with stark terror. I would be totally cut off from loved ones, never see the sun or stars, never read a newspaper or receive a letter.[2]

Joseph Cicippio, comptroller of the American University of Beirut,
taken hostage in Beirut, Lebanon, April 12, 1986,
released December 2, 1991

---

[1]Simon Strong, *Shining Path: Terror and Revolution in Peru* (New York: Random House, 1992), p. 50.
[2]Joseph Cicippio and Richard W. Hope, *Chains to Roses* (Waco, TX: WRS Publishing, 1993), pp. 8–9, 10.

Traditional realist security concepts, many of which were introduced in Chapters 3 and 4, tend to revolve around warfighting and diplomacy among states—the international systems level of analysis. Many countries, however, have also long defined their national security in terms of countering terrorism at home as well as abroad. The United States has historically viewed terrorism as something that afflicted other states. There have certainly been exceptions—the Barbary pirates of North Africa seized European and American ships, goods, and hostages in the early nineteenth century, and the Ku Klux Klan terrorized blacks beginning in the post–Civil War era. When the United States was attacked in the twentieth century, however, it was usually abroad against diplomatic, military, or commercial facilities. In the aftermath of 9/11, however, Americans redirected their energies to "homeland security." Not only had foreign threats now reached the shores of the United States, but traditional local policing concerns now took on an international dimension as law enforcement agencies were tasked with finding terrorist "sleeper cells" and rooting out local sympathizers. When it comes to terrorism as well as crime, there is truly a blurring of the international and societal levels of analysis, just as the traditional realist concern for protecting a state's physical security now intersects with the pluralist focus on transnational actors. In an increasingly globalized, interdependent world, states realize that such threats weaken their authority, threaten national security, and also undermine the expansion of a global civil society. Hence such threats are best dealt with on a cooperative, multilateral basis. As we will see, international conventions and organizations also have important roles to play in addressing these international security concerns. We will devote most of this chapter to a discussion of what many now consider the preeminent post–Cold War threat, international terrorism.

Terrorism

Throughout history **terrorism** has been one of the starkest expressions of rejection of authority. Terrorism, as politically motivated violence, aims at achieving a demoralizing effect on publics and governments. The very act of attacking innocents raises the shock value and sends a message that the government is unable to protect its own citizens. The concern is that, over time, terrorism eats away at the social-political fabric of many states, undermines democracy, provides a rationale for a government to delay democratic reforms, and can increase tension among states. The result is often the impression that the world is in a state of chaos, and international order and authority are collapsing. It is understandable why terrorism is considered a major challenge to international security.

Terrorism is usually viewed as a weapon of the weak, so it is associated with such nonstate actors as clandestine terrorist groups and insurgencies. But our definition of terrorism is neutral and can be applied to any number of organizations. Terrorism has been used, for example, by drug traffickers in Colombia against government officials and has also been used by criminal organizations in Italy to intimidate judges. Furthermore, terrorism can be and has been a tool of statecraft. Indeed, down through the centuries, states have certainly terrorized many more people than have terrorist groups or insurgencies. In the 1970s and early 1980s, for example, a number of military regimes in Latin America utilized security forces to kidnap and murder systematically thousands of actual or suspected political dissidents in the name of "national security."

terrorism
Politically motivated violence directed against noncombatants and designed to instill fear in a target audience.

The focus in this chapter, however, is principally on nonstate actors who use violence to achieve political objectives; drug traffickers are discussed later in this chapter and the use of terrorism in the massive abuse of human rights on the part of state agents later in the book. In this chapter we also address state-sponsored terrorism that transcends state borders and is used against innocent foreign—as opposed to domestic—nationals.

Terrorism is certainly not new. In fact it is deeply embedded in history. The Zealots, for example, were a Jewish sect that appeared in A.D. 6 and assassinated local government officials in an attempt to ignite uprisings and drive the Romans out of Palestine. The effort failed, and some 2,000 Zealots were crucified. Later turning to guerrilla warfare, they were finally crushed when their last mountain stronghold, Masada, was surrounded and 960 men, women, and children committed mass suicide. The Middle East spawned the Assassins (A.D. 1090–1275), Muslims who killed the political rivals of the potentate for whom they worked. Christian Europe also had its experience with particular forms of terror in the fifteenth-century Spanish Inquisition that combined the forces of church and state in trials and later in puritanical burnings of witches—a phenomenon that even touched the new world (notably at Salem, Massachusetts, where witches were hanged in the 1690s). Historically, the vast majority of terrorism in traditional societies has been religiously inspired; indeed, terrorists often claimed they were carrying out the will of God. These historical examples are a good reminder that religiously inspired terrorism—a major contemporary concern—is certainly not new.

It was the French Revolution of 1789, however, that popularized the term *terrorism*. During this period, terrorism was associated with the state. As dramatically

Case & Point

RATIONAL TERRORISM?

One way to understand terrorism is to see it as the rational (or purposive) use of the irrational (i.e., the intimidating effects of threats or violence) to advance some objective or set of objectives, typically for political ends. Resorting to terrorism is a way relatively weaker parties (those lacking armies, navies, and air forces to do their bidding) try to level the playing field. As such, terrorism becomes a way to send a message and bring attention to a cause or undermine a regime. The gruesome executions carried out against foreign nationals by Iraqi insurgents, for example, may reflect individual pathologies, but the political purpose of such acts is quite clear.

Terrorism, then, is a form of what the late-nineteenth, early-twentieth century German political sociologist, Max Weber, though not writing about terrorism, referred to as instrumental rationality—a means to some desired end. Leaders like Osama bin Laden are indeed highly rational in their instrumental use of terrorism to advance their agendas. That said, terrorists deeply committed to their cause may be willing to make major sacrifices, even committing suicide, for a cause to which they are deeply committed. This is another kind of rationality—one of complete commitment regardless of costs—that Weber called value rationality. Ironically, it is the instrumentally rational Osama bin Laden as well as other movement leaders in Palestine or elsewhere who are able to mobilize the self-sacrificing value rationality of others to commit suicide or take other high-risk actions to advance a cause.

Point: To dismiss terrorism as something engaged in by crazies misses the point that it can be used to achieve rational, political ends.

depicted in Charles Dickens's *A Tale of Two Cities,* the guillotine was used to behead publicly those who were declared enemies of the state. In later years, even more highly developed forms of state terrorism were practiced in both the Stalinist Soviet Union and Nazi Germany in the 1930s and 1940s. The "knock at the door" by state authorities, use of show trials and executions, and purges of large numbers of people were used by these regimes to instill fear in domestic populations, thus assuring greater compliance with the dictates of the state. Such tactics also found their way into Saddam Hussein's Iraq as well as other states and societies whether on the left or right, secular or religious.

The nineteenth century witnessed the rise of secular (i.e., nonreligious) terrorism on the part of groups that were opposed to particular governments. During the 1800s, both the creative and destructive effects of the scientific and industrial revolutions became obvious in Europe and North America. Great wealth was created but also great poverty. The modern city was born; rural ways of life were changed forever. As humanity grew more confident in its ability to master nature, so too did it gain confidence in its ability to design and create the perfect society. For Karl Marx (1820–1872) and other communists, such faith was evident in their vision of the ultimate victory of the downtrodden classes and the creation of a workers' paradise.

Other leftists, however, were impatient with the slow unfolding of history and wished to hasten the revolutionary process. Collectively known as **anarchists,** they pulled off a number of terrorist spectaculars. In the 1890s alone, victims included the presidents of France and Italy, the kings of Portugal and Italy, the prime minister of Spain, and the empress of Austria. Anarchists also attempted to assassinate the German kaiser and chancellor. What distinguished them from modern-day terrorists, however, is that their victims were almost always government officials, not innocent civilians. The Russian anarchist group known as the People's Will, for example, did not place bombs on railway platforms, kidnap schoolchildren, or shoot people in the knee to cripple them for life.

With the collapse of the major continental monarchies in Russia, Germany, and the Austro-Hungarian empire following World War I (1914–1918), factional, ethnic violence and terrorism came to the fore. Under the banner of national self-determination, terrorist violence was particularly pronounced in Eastern and Central Europe. A somewhat similar process began to unfold in the so-called "developing world" during and especially after World War II. Having fought Nazi Germany, fascist Italy, and Japan in defense of freedom, Western leaders found it difficult to answer nationalist leaders in the colonial world who asked why their countries should not also be free from outside control. European reluctance to end colonial rule led nationalist movements, often with a terrorist wing, to fight British, French, and Portuguese domination. By the 1960s European colonial rule was effectively ended in most areas of the globe.

The Cold War between the United States and the Soviet Union and their respective allies and supporters, however, lent an ideological cast to much of the terrorism from the late 1940s to late 1980s. Despite the fact that Karl Marx himself believed terrorism to be self-defeating, Marxist-Leninist teachings on revolution helped to inspire and justify revolutionary movements throughout the world and justify, to themselves at least, their use of terrorism. These movements included the Red Army Faction in Germany, Red Brigades in Italy, 17 November in Greece, Revolutionary Armed Forces of Colombia, Shining Path of Peru, Japanese Red Army, and New People's Army of the Philippines.

anarchists
Individuals who advocate entirely voluntary human associations or communities, reject authority in general, and may or may not use violence against governments or their officials.

Particularly in Europe, terrorism became the basic strategy of the organization, meaning it was the defining signature of the group. In the Third World, however, terrorism was generally a tactic on the part of an insurgent organization, meaning it was simply one aspect of a larger revolutionary strategy that included paramilitary attacks on government forces, the liberation of territory, and the extensive use of propaganda.

Throughout the Cold War, insurgent organizations often combined Marxism-Leninism with old-fashioned nationalist appeals. Indeed, all successful revolutions, including Lenin's in Russia and Mao's in China, have relied extensively on such appeals. With the end of the Cold War, however, most Russians acknowledged that their Marxist-Leninist vision for society was bankrupt. Furthermore, despite its socialist pronouncements, China experienced an economic boom as the state encouraged the development of a free market. These policies on the part of the two states most closely associated with Marxist-Leninist ideas on international revolution caused a predictable crisis of confidence for revolutionary movements around the world. Some simply condemned Russia and China for backsliding (Shining Path), while others experienced bitter internal divisions that weakened them (New People's Army). Now lacking a transnational ideological justification for their violent campaigns, other groups such as the Kurdistan Workers Party (PKK) shifted their emphasis away from Marxist ideology to more nationalist appeals.

Nationalism has always provided the dynamism of the various original Palestinian organizations associated with the Palestine Liberation Organization (PLO). Despite couching their agenda in Islamic terms, even organizations such as Hezbollah (Party of God) in Lebanon and Hamas in the Palestinian West Bank of the Jordan River and in the Gaza strip are also fueled in part by nationalist sentiment. The expression of this sentiment is evident in their belief that Western values have a corrupting influence on Islamic cultures, requiring an Islamic initiative or even revolution to rectify this situation. Indigenous political leaders in such countries as Egypt, Morocco, and Saudi Arabia are seen as having sold out to the West. Israel, despite its historical association with the region, is viewed as an outpost of Western interests and values. For some observers in the West, the ideological clash of democracy and communism during the Cold War has been replaced by the clash of Eastern and Western civilizations. If not a clash of civilizations, others see conflicts driven by intercommunal and cultural differences that divide peoples in many parts of the world.

Terrorism conducted within a particular state by and against the citizens of the same country can be termed *domestic terrorism.* Of greater interest to us, given our focus on world politics, is **international terrorism.** International terrorism is defined as terrorism involving the citizens or territory of more than one country. An example might help to clarify the difference. If an extremist group consisting of Saudi nationals bombs a Saudi government building in Riyadh, it is an act of domestic terrorism. If, however, the same group attacks the housing compounds of foreigners,

MIKHAIL BAKUNIN

Mikhail Bakunin was a nineteenth-century Russian anarchist. He is credited as the coauthor of the Revolutionary Catechism of 1869. Contemptuous of both Marxists and liberals, he had great revolutionary hopes for members of the criminal groups, which he described in Robin Hoodish terms. For Bakunin a successful revolution required an alliance between the peasants and robbers. In his Principles of Revolution he wrote, "We recognize no other action save destruction, though we admit that the forms in which such action will show itself will be exceedingly varied—poison, the knife, the rope, etc." Bakunin's coauthor of the Revolutionary Catechism was S. J. Nechaev. A former factory worker and student at St. Petersburg University, he wrote in the pamphlet's opening passage:

> The revolutionary is a lone man; he has no interests of his own, no cause of his own, no feelings, no habits, no belonging; he does not even have a name. Everything in him is absorbed by a single, exclusive interest, a single thought, a single passion—the revolution.... We are guided by hatred for all who are not the people.... We have an entirely negative plan, which no one can modify—utter destruction.

It's Been Said...

international terrorism
Terrorist acts of violence that involve the citizens or territory of more than one country.

it is an act of international terrorism. Similarly, if members of this extremist group went to Tunisia and killed a Saudi diplomat, this would also be an act of international terrorism. Airline hijackings such as those on 9/11 are perhaps the exemplar of international terrorism, as the airplane invariably has passengers from a number of countries.

Since the 1960s many European countries have suffered from ongoing terrorist campaigns: Great Britain (the Provisional Irish Republican Army and its splinter groups), France (Direct Action and the Armed Islamic Group), Germany (Red Army Faction), Italy (Red Brigades), Spain (Basque Fatherland), Turkey (leftist and also Kurdish groups), and since the early 1990s Russia (Chechnya). The same is true of Israel, which was first attacked in the 1960s by terrorist organizations affiliated with the Palestine Liberation Organization (PLO). The PLO terrorist campaign included the murder of Israeli athletes at the 1972 Munich Olympics and massacres of civilians at the Rome and Vienna airports in 1985. Following the Israeli invasion of Lebanon in 1982, which was designed to root out Palestinian terrorists, Islamist groups such as Lebanese Hezbollah (backed by Syria and Iran) began in the early 1980s its ultimately successful campaign to drive Israel out of southern Lebanon. Further trouble for the Israelis began in the 1990s in the wake of the first Palestinian uprising or *intifada* in the Israeli-occupied West Bank and Gaza Strip. Out of this chaos came Hamas and the Palestine Islamic Jihad, which have continued to wreak havoc and fear through a seemingly inexhaustible supply of suicide bombing recruits. But aside from actions by the leftist Weather Underground and Puerto Rican nationalists in the 1960s, the United States felt relatively immune from the terrorist threat. This dramatically changed in the 1980s. As one of two superpowers then with a military presence in many countries of the world and economic interests in virtually every country, it is not surprising that the United States has been blamed, rightly or wrongly, for all sorts of problems and has been viewed as an agent of military, economic, and cultural imperialism.

The United States came face to face with international terrorism in the Middle East. With the overthrow of the U.S.–backed Shah of Iran in 1978, a radical Islamic regime came to power not only bent on securing its control over the country, but also desiring to spread its brand of Islamist radicalism to other countries by supporting terrorist organizations. U.S. diplomats were held hostage for over a year in Iran before being released in 1981. Over the course of one year (1983) in Lebanon alone, Lebanese Hezbollah killed 241 U.S. soldiers in a suicide truck bombing of the Marine barracks; the U.S. embassy was destroyed by another suicide truck bomb, costing seventeen lives; and U.S. citizens were repeatedly taken hostage. In 1985 there were several terrorist spectaculars, including the June hijacking of TWA flight 847 by Islamic extremists, which lasted seventeen days; the takeover of the *Achille Lauro* cruise ship by Palestinians in October, which resulted in the murder of a wheelchair-bound American tourist; and the aforementioned December 27 attacks in the Rome and Vienna airports by the Abu Nidal Organization, which left eighteen dead and 114 wounded.

In December 1988 a bomb placed aboard Pan Am Flight 103 exploded over Lockerbie, Scotland, resulting in the death of 259 passengers and members of the crew. Conducted by Libyan intelligence agents, this act of state-sponsored international terrorism, more than any other single terrorist incident, galvanized cooperation among Western governments. The bombing of the World Trade Center in New York City in February 1993, the nerve gas attack on Tokyo's subway in March 1995, the bombings directed against the U.S. embassies in Kenya and Tanzania in August 1998, and the bombing of the *USS Cole* in the port of Aden in October 2000 are all examples of major terrorist incidents predating 9/11. With the exception of the first attack on the World Trade Center in 1993, Americans seemed to be immune from international terrorism on the homefront. The fact of the matter is that as long as terrorists focused their efforts on killing Americans overseas, there was no major public or political groundswell of support for anything like the U.S. response following 9/11. In the remainder of this section we will examine in greater depth the nature and extent of international terrorism and discuss the efforts of the international community to deal with it.

The Causes of Terrorism

A great deal has been written on the causes of terrorism. But, as is often the case with human behavior, no single factor can be identified as the root cause. It is possible, however, to break down the major categories as follows.

Psychological/Social-Psychological Factors Certain analysts—not surprisingly they tend to be trained psychologists or psychiatrists—view some individuals who engage in terrorism as mentally disturbed. While the mental disorder perspective includes explanations rooted in such physiological factors as chemical imbalances in the brain, the main focus of attention is on the early childhood experiences of terrorists. Analysis of European terrorists points to such factors as abusive or unemotional parents, suggesting that at least some terrorists are rebelling, perhaps, against parental authority figures as personified in their minds by the state.

While undoubtedly some terrorists exhibit pathological behavior, to dismiss all terrorists as mentally ill is simply wrong. In fact, one thing most terrorists have in common is their normality. A young person with few life prospects may choose to join a terrorist organization for the expected thrill of life in the underground, or as a way to enhance his or her self-esteem by becoming a "defender of the community," or even simply as a way to earn money. Such prosaic possibilities have little to do with mental illness, and such psychological explanations often have the effect of downplaying terrorism's political component. As one former member of the Provisional Irish Republican Army stated, "The IRA gave these young men a sense of belonging, a status in their community, and a purpose, a cause to believe in and to fight and die for. These were young men without much hope of employment who had seen their communities devastated in sectarian attacks. Now that they were hitting back, their pride and dignity were restored." To the extent that such group dynamics contribute to the self-worth of individual terrorists, strengthening their commitment to a particular cause, we move beyond the psychological or psychoanalytic understanding into the domain of social psychology—the relationships and interactions among individuals in group settings. Hence, there is the case of men from Arab and Islamic countries who travel to the West for schooling or employment and find themselves alienated from their surroundings. Local mosques become a place of comfort and refuge and also an incubator, in some cases, for radical Islamist views. This was the case for Mohammed Atta, head of the 9/11 hijackers, and several of his cohosts. Even more ominous are those cases where young Muslim men who were born and raised in a Western country turn to terrorism. The perpetrators of the July 2005 suicide bombings in London fit this profile.

Ideological Factors Ideological explanations emphasize the power of ideas. Historically Marxism-Leninism has proven to be powerfully attractive to individuals who seek a framework that enables them to understand not only why injustices exist in a society but also how to end them. Terrorists, therefore, are "true believers," possessed by an idea that a better society can be created if only certain obstacles or threats can be eliminated. For Marxist-Leninists, this threat is the upper classes and bourgeoisie; for fascists it is often minority groups or foreign immigrants; for nationalists it is often colonialists; for religious extremists it is not simply foreigners but rather the values they represent that threaten the indigenous culture. For their part, terrorist networks like Al Qaeda and affiliated Islamist groups are reacting not only against American and other Western influences and presence in the Middle East, but also against the forces of globalization that are undermining more traditional, Islamic societies and their ways of life. Indeed, theirs can be characterized essentially as a reactionary (or backward-looking) ideology of the extreme right as opposed to a progressive (or forward-looking) ideology of the extreme or radical left.

Environmental Factors   Environmental explanations that examine where terrorism arises generally fall into one of two related categories: grievances and cultures of violence. Environmental grievances that affect a community can be social, political, or economic in nature. Grievances—real or imagined, just or unjust—are, after all, still grievances that can motivate persons to resort to terrorism against a foreign occupying power or against another community. In this regard, "community" can be broadly defined, referring to either a particular economic class such as exploited peasants or perhaps ethnic groups that have experienced political and economic discrimination over the years.

The Muslims of Lebanon, for example, particularly the Shia, see themselves as having historically suffered from discrimination at the hands of the Christian Lebanese. Not only have the Shia been at the bottom of the economic ladder, but they have also been politically underrepresented in the government and parliament. Such grievances often fester for a long period of time and then erupt in bloody violence, as they did in Lebanon in 1976. In this particular case the Shia were energized by other factors, such as the growing power of the Palestinians, particularly in southern Lebanon. Expelled from Jordan in 1970, many Palestinians fled to Lebanon, where they initially received a warm welcome. But as the Palestinians settled in, many Shia grew resentful when they also suffered from Israeli military reprisals directed against the Palestinians who were using southern Lebanon as a base of operations against Israel.

The second environmental source of terrorism can be termed ***cultures of violence.*** This does not refer to cultures that are somehow innately violent. Rather it refers to societies that have experienced high levels of intercommunal violence over a number of years so that violence, not peace, becomes the norm. For young people growing up in Northern Ireland from the 1970s to the early 1990s, intercommunal warfare and the presence of British troops and security forces on the streets were part of their everyday existence. Violence, not peace, was the *status quo.* Lebanon from the late 1970s through the 1980s represents a similar case. Chechnya and Iraq are current examples. As intercommunal violence continues, people may forget the original reason for conflict, and instead hatred becomes habitual and violence is a function of revenge.

The search for a single factor to explain terrorism is self-defeating. As with all human behavior, multiple factors come into play. To explain why any single individual turned to terrorism, one would have to consider the relative importance of psychological or social-psychological, ideological, and environmental factors. For example, an examination of the lives of the 9/11 hijackers certainly shows a high degree of religious motivation for persons such as Mohamed Atta, leader of the plot. But it is interesting to note that the decision to seek support from Al Qaeda was taken after experiencing

cultures of violence
When violence becomes commonplace, it may acquire an acceptance or even legitimacy in a community.

the alienating environment of living and studying in the West. To assume that all terrorists are ideologically driven zealots is as much an overgeneralization as it is to assume they are all mentally ill.

Furthermore, as time goes by, the continuation of a terrorist campaign may have perhaps as much to do with maintaining the existence of the organization as it has to do with achieving the originally stated political objective. There is no reason to believe that terrorist organizations are any different from any other organization—a primary goal being organizational survival. For some individuals, terrorism undoubtedly becomes a way of life. It is probable that the longer one is with the organization, the more important this factor becomes. Conversely it is likely that the most altruistic and ideologically driven members of the group are the newest recruits.

The Extent of Terrorism

How much international terrorism has actually been conducted in the past quarter century? How many persons have been injured? To what extent should international terrorism be viewed as a threat to national and international security compared to threats posed by diseases such as AIDS? How has terrorism changed over the years? We examine these questions by distinguishing between conventional terrorism and terrorism involving weapons of mass destruction.

Conventional Terrorism   We begin with conventional terrorism for the simple reason that, except for the Aum Shinrikyo sarin gas attack in March 1995, all international terrorism in recent years has been of the conventional sort. What this means simply is that terrorists have essentially restricted their *modus operandi* to bombings, firebombings, arson, armed attacks, kidnappings, and vandalism. In fact, the first three categories account for over 70 percent of all terrorist incidents from 1986 to 2003—bombings of various sorts are the preferred terrorist method of attack. The number of international incidents has fluctuated over time, but within a fairly narrow range (see Figure 8.1). Given the fact that these statistics cover the entire world, most people would probably be surprised at the relatively low number. In fact the number of international incidents in 1998 was the lowest since 1971. Perhaps even more surprising, in 2002 international incidents were even lower than in 1998. So we seem to be faced with a paradox—just as the number of terrorist incidents drops to historical lows, terrorism has become a major international security concern.

Such statistics, however, obscure as much as they reveal, for it is not the number of incidents that matter but rather the casualties they cause and the psychological and policy impact. For example, the bombing of Pan Am Flight 103 in 1988, which killed all on board, counts as a single incident, as does a Molotov cocktail tossed over the wall of the U.S. embassy in Bogota, Colombia, that same year. Similarly, the 247 dead in the Nairobi bombing in August 1998 will statistically be treated the same as one of the periodic bombings of the Cano Limon–Covenas oil pipeline in Colombia in which no one is injured. Or consider the fact

TERRORISM: A FEMINIST PERSPECTIVE

Our brothers who fought in Somalia saw wonders about the weakness, feebleness, and cowardliness of the U.S. soldier.... We believe that we are men, Muslim men who must have the honor of defending Mecca. We do not want American women soldiers defending it.... The rulers in that region have been deprived of their manhood.

Osama bin Laden

I don't want any women to go to my grave ... during my funeral or any occasion thereafter.

Mohamed Atta's last will and testament, found in a suitcase at Logan Airport

Much has been made of many fundamentalist Islamists feeling threatened by the values of the West—a secular society based on individualism, liberalism, human rights, separation of church and state, free markets. It has also been observed by feminist writers and others that many of the all-male madrasses (religious schools) reinforce the belief of the need to subjugate women. Women, it seems, must play an inferior role to men in society, except when it comes time to seek volunteers for suicide missions in Chechnya against the Russians or by Palestinians against Israelis. Professor J. Ann Tickner has also noted that the discussion in the West on how to respond to terrorism also involves highly masculine "macho" language and praise for "the new John Waynes" charged with defending the homeland.

J. Ann Tickner
"Feminist Perspectives on 9/11,"
International Studies Perspectives, 3,
No. 4 (November 2002); 333–350.

It's Been Said...

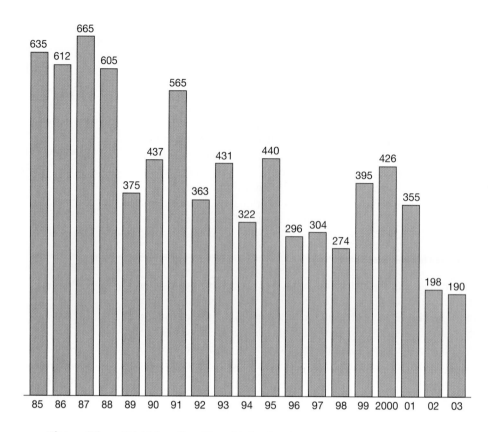

Figure 8.1   *Total International Terrorist Attacks, 1982–2003.*
Source: U.S. Department of State, *Patterns of Global Terrorism 2003,* Washington, D.C., April 2004, p. 176.

that a grisly suicide attack in Israel is statistically treated the same as a pipe bomb. In any given year, therefore, such statistics may underplay or overstate the political significance of a terrorist attack. This is the major reason the U.S. Department of State in 2005 dropped its traditional accounting procedure for tracking terrorist incidents. A new methodology utilizing a broader definition of terrorism reported that in 2004 there were 3,192 terror attacks worldwide with 28,433 persons killed or wounded.

The psychological and policy impact of 9/11 cannot be underestimated in the case of the United States. A new cabinet-level department, the Department of Homeland Security, was created to coordinate the multitude of agencies involved in homeland defense. Budgets went up correspondingly. In Washington it was recognized that "first responders" to a terrorist incident would not be federal or military forces, but rather local fire, police, and emergency medical personnel. Hence, national security planning now involves local and state authorities to a degree never before experienced, a reality recognized in the Pentagon's Domestic Preparedness Program. U.S. counterterrorism policy, therefore, has had to move beyond deterrence, prevention, and punishment to include what is euphemistically termed "consequence management." On the personal level, flying on commercial airliners became an often frustrating and nervous experience due to long lines at airports and memories of the hijackings on 9/11. The Patriot Act was passed leading to what critics claimed was an infringement on civil liberties. Thousands of U.S. military personnel were deployed overseas and placed in harm's way, particularly in Afghanistan and Iraq.

The Twin Towers, World Trade Center, New York, September 11, 2001.

Terrorism with Weapons of Mass Destruction   One reason terrorism is proclaimed a top international security concern is that in recent years it has been coupled with another international security priority—the proliferation of nuclear, biological, chemical, and radiological (or "dirty bomb") weapons of mass destruction (WMD). Newspaper reports and Hollywood movies have highlighted the dangers posed by "nuclear leakage" from the former Soviet Union and fears as to where such material and scientific expertise may end up. It is bad enough if material falls into the hands of renegade states, but worse if terrorists get their hands on it. States have to fear retaliation should they employ such weapons. A small band of terrorists, however, might feel much more confident that they would be difficult to locate.

   Raising the specter of terrorist use of nuclear weapons dates from the 1970s. Looking back, such studies are oddly reassuring. Utilizing the rational actor model associated with realist thinkers, it was assumed by analysts that terrorists recognized that the employment of such weapons was counterproductive in achieving political objectives and gaining public support for one's cause. As noted by Brian Jenkins, "terrorists want a lot of people watching, not a lot of people dead."[3] Such reasoning can be extended to the use of chemical and biological weapons.

---

[3]Brian Jenkins, *The Potential for Nuclear Terrorism* (Santa Monica, CA: RAND, 1977), p. 8.

TERRORISM'S FAILURE

Perhaps the most significant thing that the terrorists of today share with those who practiced warfare against civilians in earlier times is an abiding inability to see that the strategy of terror is a spectacularly failed one. Surprising and difficult as it may be to accept that what we call terrorism is in fact a form of warfare, it may be even more surprising and difficult—particularly given that we are in the midst of a war with terrorists—to understand that it is a form that has never succeeded. It is from this discovery, however, that we must today take both our greatest hope and our sternest warning. Warfare against civilians, whether inspired by hatred, revenge, greed, or political or psychological insecurity, has been one of the most ultimately self-defeating tactics in all of military history—indeed, it would be difficult to think of one more inimical to its various practitioners' causes.

Caleb Carr

The Lessons of Terror *(New York: Random House, 2002), pp. 11–12.*

It's Been Said...

Is this logic still applicable at the beginning of the millennium? Some commentators argue that self-sanctions against the use of weapons of mass destruction may have eroded over the years. It is necessary, however, to distinguish among different types of terrorist groups. With some degree of confidence, we can state it is unlikely such weapons will be utilized if we are talking about secular terrorist organizations with a political agenda that requires public support in order to succeed. Note the three critical adjectives—secular, political, and public. Nationalist-separatist movements, for example, often have political as well as clandestine terrorist wings. The terrorist wing may indeed be more likely to consider using WMD for a number of reasons—violence-prone individuals are by definition drawn to operational cells; if cut off from broader society, internal dynamics tend to move a group toward extreme actions.[4]

The political wings of nationalist-separatist movements, however, also by definition have to take into account a number of factors. First, there is the attitude of the core constituency they claim to represent. As horrible as the effects of bombings may be, crossing the nuclear, chemical, or biological threshold has emotional and psychological effects that go beyond the resultant physical devastation. Death by biological agents is simply viewed differently from death by conventional explosives. Second, political leaders have to take into account the possibility of retribution against their own community. Third, the employment of weapons of mass destruction would undoubtedly forsake any international sympathy and support for one's cause.

The limitations in such lines of argument stem from the fact that the universe of terrorist organizations has been restricted to secular groups with a political agenda requiring public support. What about religious groups? Islamic extremist organizations that engage in suicide bombings come to mind. It is often suggested that religious extremists differ from secular organizations in that the audience they are trying to impress is God, as opposed to a segment of the public. Hence, religious convictions supposedly make it easier to engage in actions causing large numbers of deaths when the act is done in the name of God and supposedly with his blessing.

Such logic is not incorrect but simply incomplete. In fact, religious groups have secular as well as sacred motivations. Hezbollah, for example, is best known for its terrorist operations. Yet it also is represented in the Lebanese parliament and wants to be viewed as a legitimate political player. Such ambitions undoubtedly influence the group's approach to terrorism. Having said this, the one major exception is Al Qaeda and affiliated religious extremist groups. Material found in training camps in Afghanistan make it quite clear that Al Qaeda was actively pursuing the purchase or development of weapons of mass destruction. Furthermore, bin Laden's public statements have explicitly acknowledged this goal. Indeed, bin Laden has called on Islamists

---

[4]See David C. Rapoport, ed., *Inside Terrorist Organizations* (New York: Columbia University Press, 1988); and Walter Reich, ed., *Origins of Terrorism* (New York: Cambridge University Press, 1990).

to build or procure weapons of mass destruction and has claimed it is a duty to use them against the United States and other oppressors of the Muslim peoples. In April 2004, authorities in Jordan disrupted what would have been the largest chemical and terrorist attack ever. The Islamist terrorists had managed to smuggle three cars—packed with explosives, a chemical bomb, and poisonous gas—into the capital city of Amman. It is estimated an incredible eighty thousand people would have been casualties if the bombs had gone off at their intended targets—the Jordanian intelligence headquarters, the U.S. embassy in Amman, and the Jordanian prime minister's office.

The other type of religious organizations likely to use weapons of mass destruction are those that can be characterized as cults. In cults the focus of group loyalty and devotion is not so much to religious precepts as expounded by prophets who have long since departed this earth. Rather, devotion is to a "living god" who issues edicts designed to enforce discipline and complete loyalty among followers. In other words the leader—not the message—is the focus of loyalty. When coupled with physical isolation and a view that outside society is corrupt and sinful, a cult can go one of two ways. Either it can withdraw into itself and avoid contact with the sinful outside world, or it can work to destroy and transform it. It is when a transformative agenda is coupled with the capability to produce weapons of mass destruction that a threat arises.

We may well look back at the period from the 1960s through the 1990s with a certain degree of nostalgia. Groups that engaged in terrorism had stated political objectives that, however much one might disagree with them, were still fathomable. They developed a particular *modus operandi* and generally stayed with it. State sponsors were consistently the same nefarious lot. Analysts were perhaps no better than today in providing warning of impending terrorist acts, but at least there was a certain degree of confidence as to the limits to which groups would go to achieve their stated objectives.

The Changing Nature of Terrorism

Today's terrorism is a multifaceted phenomenon consisting of a diverse array of actors, motivations, and tactics that evolves over time. Such a phenomenon requires equal ingenuity and flexibility on the part of those who study it or—as intelligence analysts, operators, and policy makers—deal directly with it. What is different today has been an evolution in the who, why, and how of terrorism. Each will be briefly discussed in turn.

Who Are Terrorists?   Examine any anthology on terrorism, and you are bound to find discussion centered around the group as the unit of analysis. The subsequent classification scheme is invariably based on the group's essential goals or ideology—Marxist-Leninist, nationalist-separatist, fascist, religious. Typically terrorists utilize such nouns as "army," brigade," or "command" in the name of their organization in order to enhance the legitimacy of their cause by suggesting they view themselves as soldiers. Aside from anarchist organizations whose small numbers preclude a true division of labor, many larger terrorist groups indeed organize themselves along paramilitary lines and hence lend themselves to classic line-and-block organizational diagrams.

In the 1990s, however, a new category of analysis was added. Referred to as *ad hoc* terrorists or "transient groupings," such entities consist of individuals who come

Osama bin Laden

together to plan and carry out a specific operation. The prime example involves Ramzi Yousef, mastermind of the 1993 World Trade Center bombing. Yousef entered the United States with a colleague and established contact with a diverse group of individuals associated with a storefront mosque headed by Sheikh Abdel Rahman in Jersey City, New Jersey. Yousef's uncle, Kahlid Sheikh Muhammed, was an early supporter of Osama bin Laden's nascent Al Qaeda organization. Yousef acted as a catalyst, and followed a similar *modus operandi* in the Philippines in late 1994, recruiting local Islamic extremists for an ambitious plot to bomb a dozen aircraft and assassinate the pope on his visit to Manila. When captured in Islamabad, Pakistan, in 1995 he was planning the same attacks against aircraft. Mohammed Atta and other members of the Hamburg, Germany, cell were not members of Al Qaeda. They traveled to Afghanistan and offered their services to bin Laden.

A related phenomenon concerns what could be termed the *privatization of terrorism*. The exemplar is, of course, Osama bin Laden. Bin Laden, the exiled son of a wealthy Saudi businessman, and his associates not only instigate but also facilitate and inspire terrorist attacks. Perhaps the best way to think of him is as the private sector equivalent of a state sponsor of terrorism. With Al Qaeda's camps destroyed in Afghanistan, Al Qaeda became more decentralized and, in effect, contracted out and inspired terrorist attacks by regional Islamic extremist groups in North Africa, Asia, and Europe.

It is unclear if bin Laden is an anomaly as opposed to an emerging trend. What is apparent, however, is that it is becoming increasingly difficult to determine who is behind many terrorist attacks. If claims of responsibility are made, it is often by a previously unknown group. It is possible that established groups carry out some of these attacks but are fearful of retaliation and hence prefer to remain silent. It is also possible, however, that we will witness more attacks by *ad hoc* groupings that have received encouragement if not financial and logistical support from individuals such as bin Laden or states wishing to plead plausible deniability—not revealing their role in or knowledge of these activities.

Such a phenomenon obviously represents an extremely difficult intelligence target. It is one thing to collect against an established group organization—a group profile can be established, and patterns of behavior or *modus operandi* can be tracked and analyzed. *Ad hoc* groupings lack such signatures. How can a state collect information against a target if it doesn't even know the group exists? By definition, an *ad hoc* grouping does not announce its presence.

Why Terrorism?   As noted, the possible motivations for individuals engaging in terrorism are diverse. They include such possibilities as psychological and social-psychological factors, ideologies, and political, social, and economic grievances. To complicate matters, a single campaign may be composed of various groups who turn to terrorism for their own particular reasons. Insurgents in Iraq who target the United States, coalition partners, and Iraqi government forces include former members of Saddam's Baath party and ex-military officers who wish to return to power, religious extremists who want Islamic rule, foreign fighters who want to hurt the United States, and criminals motivated by money. As has been the case throughout recorded history, the mix and relative weight will vary depending on the individual and the group. Having said that, it appears that revenge was a prominent motivating factor beginning in the 1990s. Whether directed against the U.S. government as a result of events in Waco or carried out by Islamic extremists who resent the pernicious influence of Western values on their societies due to globalization, the potential for high casualties is always there. What is disturbing is that such attacks are not necessarily aimed at achieving a

Applying Theory

NETWAR

When it comes to applying theory to terrorist groups, realists tend to ignore terrorists, and pluralists simply list them as another transnational actor. Insightful conceptual work on terrorist groups has come from national security theorists who see warfare in terms of what is called **netwar.** Netwar refers to "an emerging mode of conflict (and crime) at societal levels, short of traditional military warfare, in which the protagonists use network forms of organization and related doctrines, strategies, and technologies attuned to the information age." The organizational form is not the classic hierarchical structure as reflected in line-and-block organizational charts. Rather, netwar organizational forms may resemble "stars" that have some centralized elements, or "chains" that are linear, or most likely "all-channel" networks in which each principal node communicates and interacts with every other node (see Figure 8.A).

John Arquilla and David Ronfeldt argue that "familiar adversaries who are modifying their structures and strategies to take advantage of networked designs [include] transnational terrorist groups, black-market proliferators of weapons of mass destruction (WMD), drug and other crime syndicates, fundamentalists and ethnonationalist movements, intellectual-property pirates, and immigration and refugee smugglers." Thanks to the worldwide information revolution, members of networks do not necessarily have to meet face to face. From the perspective of terrorists, security is therefore enhanced,

and an organization could conceivably have supporters around the world. These actors generally consist of dispersed groups who agree to communicate and act, perhaps without a central leadership or headquarters. It is suggested that hierarchical organizations such as states might be ill-equipped to deal with such organizational innovations.

Prior to the rise of transnational Islamist extremists, perhaps the best example involved the low-intensity conflict waged by the Zapatistas against the central Mexican government in the Yucatan. Netwar is evident in the decentralized collaboration among diverse Mexican and transnational (mostly U.S. and Canadian) activists who side with the Zapatista National Liberation Army (EZLN). The EZLN aims to affect government policy on human rights and other reform issues and has gained publicity for its goals with the aid of sympathetic nongovernmental activists. As Subcomandante Marcos has stated, the EZLN is not interested in taking over the state. Rather, "It is civil society that must transform Mexico—we are only a small part of that civil society, the armed part." Aided by the Internet, the EZLN and NGO activists have engaged in nonviolent action by utilizing the media to disseminate news, mobilize support, and coordinate actions (www.ezln.org).

Source: John Arquilla and David Ronfeldt, *Networks and Netwars* (Santa Monica, CA: RAND, 2001). See also Ronfeldt, Arquilla, Graham E. Fuller, and Melissa Fuller, *The Zapatista Social Netwar in Mexico* (Santa Monica, CA: RAND, 1998)

Chain
(Smugglers)

Star or Hub
(Drug cartel)

All-Channel
(Peace network)

FIGURE 8.A   *Basic Types and Levels of Networks*

Source: John Arquilla and David Ronfeldt, *The Advent of Netwar,* MR-678-OSD (Santa Monica, CA: RAND, 1996), p. 49.

particular political agenda but rather have the generalized goal of inflicting pain and suffering.

Religious motivation coupled with a desire for revenge is a particularly explosive combination—it makes it easier to justify in one's mind high numbers of casualties, whether they are military or civilian, government employees or tourists. In other words, no one is an innocent, and no moral, ethical, or religious constraints apply. In fact, religion often acts as a justification as opposed to a constraint on terrorist actions. Looking back over the past one hundred years, we have come a long way from nineteenth-century terrorist organizations such as the People's Will that targeted government officials and attempted to avoid killing innocent civilians. For many of today's terrorists, however, the death of innocents not only increases the shock value of the attack—an instrumental goal—but is an end in itself.

How Terrorism Works   A great deal has been written in recent years on the potential terrorist use of weapons of mass destruction. This topic is part of a larger concern over the implications of our increasingly technologically reliant society. The subject can be discussed from the perspective of terrorist use of technology as well as from societies' reliance on it.

CASE & POINT

THE JAPANESE SUBWAY ATTACK

In March 1995, morning commuters on several Tokyo subway lines were exposed to a poison gas attack that killed twelve people and injured hundreds more. The perpetrators were members of a Japanese religious cult, Aum Shinrikyo (Supreme Truth). Its charismatic half-blind leader, Asahara Shokou, had as a youth aspired to be Japan's prime minister, but he failed to gain admittance to Japan's extremely competitive universities. In 1978 he opened a pharmacy and health food store, travelled through India and Nepal, and then returned to Tokyo and founded what became Aum Shinrikyo. By 1994, the cult claimed an estimated 10,000 members in Japan and 100,000 overseas. Its essential message was the corrupt nature of modern society and the need to destroy it.

Although more people were killed by Islamist terrorist bombings in attacks on the Madrid (March 2004) and London (July 2005) subways, the Tokyo subway gas attack was a watershed for several reasons. First, it was the first large-scale terrorist use of chemical weapons against an urban target. As such, it broke an operational and psychological barrier that terrorist groups had never crossed before. The fear has always been that the Aum Shinrikyo attack may eventually encourage other groups to follow suit. Second, Aum Shinrikyo was a religious organization, not a clandestine terrorist group seeking secular political objectives. The problem for governments is that such "millennialist" groups do not present political demands—their actions are carried out to bring about Armageddon, not to wring concessions from a government. Finally, the group was amazingly well financed, had formed a number of front companies, and had built chemical factories employing highly trained scientists.

Point: Concern over terrorist use of weapons of mass destruction skyrocketed after 9/11, but the threshold had already been crossed in 1995.

On the one hand, technology certainly increases terrorist options. The media, for example, have always had a symbiotic relationship with terrorists—the latter provide the drama and the former the dissemination of the dramatic story to its readers and viewers. For some critics, the electronic media in particular are to terrorism what oxygen is to a fire, almost deserving to be viewed as unindicted coconspirators. In recent years, technological developments have provided terrorists with another communications option over which they have more control. The Internet hosts numerous websites for terrorist groups and their political fronts. Such sites are obviously a source of propaganda and a way to solicit financial contributions. They also hold the possibility of serving as a means of recruitment.

On the other hand, the Internet also reflects the vulnerability of our technologically reliant society. In recent years there has been a steady drumbeat of journalistic and government reports analyzing the vulnerabilities of the air traffic and rail control systems, electrical power grids, government computer networks, and financial exchanges and banking records. Rather than having to be physically present at the chosen target, an adept hacker could be located on the other side of the world, using keystrokes to gain access to computer systems. While the alteration or wiping out of financial records may not have the visual impact or resultant fatalities of a car bomb, such computer hacking, dubbed **cyberterrorism**, could obviously cause economic chaos. Hackers with such goals can use the Internet to gain access to military, police, air traffic control, and other networks on which public safety depends.

To date, such scenarios are mostly the province of novels and Hollywood thrillers. Yet such possibilities are being taken seriously by computer security experts and government investigative agencies. The dilemma is that in highlighting technological interdependencies and vulnerabilities, terrorists might be given ideas for new modes of disruption. But to ignore such possibilities reduces the incentives for the private sector and government to take preemptive action to reduce system vulnerabilities.

Practicing World Politics

THE INTERNET: CHECKING OUT SOME WEBSITES ON EXTREMIST GROUPS AND TERRORISM

Sympathizers of terrorist groups and radical organizations (and often the groups themselves) have created websites. The Colombian insurgency ELN, for example, is featured at www.eln-voces.com. As is often the case with the web, sites tend to come and go with great frequency. For overviews of international terrorist groups, see the U.S. Department of State's site at www.state.gov/s/ct. Also check out the website www.terrorism.com, which will hotlink you to other sites. The best site for access to data on terrorism is to be found at www.tkb.com. This site combines information from a number of sources and provides basic tools for the manipulation of the data. See also the Council on Foreign Relations at www.terrorismanswers.com; University of Michigan's Documents Center–America's War against Terrorism at www.lib.umich.edu/govdocs/usterror.html; U.S. Institute of Peace–Terrorism/Counterterrorism web links at www.usip.org/library/topics/terrorism/html.; The Center for Democracy and Technology at www.cdt.org/policy/terrorism; The International Association for Counterterrorism Professionals at www.iacsp.com; and Jane's Terrorism and Insurgency Center at http://jtic.janes.com.

Final Observations   We conclude this discussion of the changing nature of international terrorism with two observations. The first is that one of the difficulties in discussing terrorism and international security is that a single event can immediately and dramatically shift perceptions of the relation between the two. Environmental degradation, progress toward global democratization, and even the spread of nuclear weapons allow one to identify and assess trends with some degree of confidence. In the case of terrorism, however, a devastating act by a single individual or small group can make current analyses irrelevant overnight. Perhaps more so than with any other international security concern, relying on the historical record and simply projecting it into the future is problematic.

Second, terrorist attacks may have an instrumental purpose such as driving the U.S. military out of Iraq, derailing the Israeli-Palestinian peace process, or intimidating a government into releasing jailed comrades. But such terrorist attacks often derive their real power from the psychological effects they produce on the public. While it is highly unlikely that any one individual might be a victim of a terrorist attack, events as far away as Nairobi or as near as London or New York City produce a feeling of vulnerability and uneasiness. Similarly, government policies have the instrumental goal to deter, respond, and punish terrorists. We should not, however, underestimate the power of government policies to create a reassuring psychological effect among the public. National security is not simply an empirical fact, it is also a state of mind. It is therefore understandable why in recent years many governments have made what they view as prudent investments in efforts to respond to the evolving phenomenon of terrorism. Possible responses to international terrorism are worthy of further discussion.

Responses

Innumerable studies, articles, and reports have been produced over the years on the subject of how best to deal with the specter of international terrorism. Both before and after the events of September 11, 2001, terrorism has been on the agenda of international governmental summits and U.N. resolutions, and it is a favorite topic of congressional hearings and presidential, vice-presidential, or other high-level task forces. Some of the most prominent suggestions include the following.

Eliminate the Underlying Causes of Terrorism   This approach assumes that grievances lie at the heart of the problem. In a number of cases, this seems possible. Spain, for example, devolved power to the Basque region, undercutting the appeal of the Basque separatist movement. The peace process in northern Ireland has been one of fits and starts, progress and reversals; however, over the decades there nevertheless has been substantial reduction in the overall volume and intensity of terrorism and other forms of intercommunal violence. Other organizations, however, such as Peru's Sendero Luminoso (Shining Path), would accept nothing less than total political and military victory, leaving little room to negotiate. The sheer amount of poverty and social ills found throughout the world always will provide a fertile ground for political discontent, which may be harnessed to terrorist violence as was at the core of such movements as Sendero Luminoso. Nevertheless progress in accommodating the demands of some groups may reduce the likelihood that they will continue to resort to terrorist actions. In recent years there has also been much discussion in Europe on how to better integrate into society the growing Muslim population.

Counterattack against Terrorism   This approach calls for military attacks on terrorist organizations and states that support them. Such an approach is appealing as it satisfies demands for punishment and justice and assumes the use of military force will remove terrorist bases or serve as a deterrent to further terrorist attacks. Complications with this approach, however, must be taken into account by policy makers. First of all, excellent intelligence is required to locate members of terrorist groups that by definition are clandestine in nature. This is not easy to do. Placing an agent inside a terrorist group is no simple task—terrorists don't openly advertise for new members, and the vetting process is understandably quite rigorous. Satellite imagery might locate possible training sites in the countryside, but it is of limited utility in finding terrorists located in urban environments. Intercepting terrorist communications assumes that one knows where to direct one's electronic gathering capabilities. When governments use technology only to locate and target terrorist groups, there is substantial risk of error with unintended, adverse consequences to nonterrorist groups.

Second, even if a government *can* locate terrorists, a military operation designed to eliminate them faces tactical and political challenges in its actual execution. For example, what if a group of terrorists is training at a site that is also used by the host government's paramilitary forces? Is everyone targeted? If so, what of the political fallout regionally and internationally as photographs of "innocents" are provided to the world media? Would the government that launched the raid be willing to share the intelligence that presumably justifies the action with the public?

Finally, military actions specifically directed against states supporting or engaging in international terrorism can result in retaliation and escalation. Prior to the U.S.-led war against Afghanistan after 9/11, the best example of a military action against a state supporter of terrorism involved the U.S. bombing of Libyan facilities in April 1986. Although this action was designed to punish and deter Colonel Kaddaffi for the Libyan bombing of a West Berlin nightclub frequented by American military personnel, for a time the Libyan government actually increased its support for terrorism; the agents it supported were implicated in the downing of Pan Am Flight 103 in 1988.

Impose the Rule of Law   For many observers, this is the critical pillar of any effective international antiterrorist policy. What is the purpose, they ask, in abandoning democratic principles and legal rights in the name of eliminating terrorism? Is the curbing of civil liberties worth it? History too often shows that in the name of combating terrorism or subversion, temporary states of emergency evolve into dictatorial governments.

Governments can enforce the rule of law in two basic ways: through unilateral domestic efforts and through international cooperative efforts. The United States has used both approaches.

U.S. legislation designed to undercut terrorism also has implications for the U.S. government, U.S. citizens, corporations, and foreign governments and nationals. The Omnibus Diplomatic Security and Anti-Terrorism Act of 1986, for example, strengthens so-called long arm statutes that enable the Federal Bureau of Investigation (FBI) to arrest individuals overseas who are charged with committing a terrorist-related criminal act against U.S. citizens. Of particular importance is Section 6(j) of the Export Administration Act, which allows the secretary of state to place a country on what has come to be known as the Terrorism List. If so designated, a whole host of sanctions are employed—no U.S. foreign assistance to the country, no export of weapons, and a negative U.S. vote that amounts to a veto in international economic institutions such as the World Bank or International Monetary Fund should they contemplate assistance to a country on the Terrorism List. The USA Patriot Act passed in the aftermath of the September 11, 2001, terrorist attacks in New York and Washington has substantially expanded law-enforcement powers of the federal government, which also extends to cooperative measures among federal, state, and local authorities. Not surprisingly, alarms have been sounded by civil liberties groups that the quest for greater security against terrorist attacks has eroded essential liberties that define civil society.

In terms of international legal efforts, states can pursue bilateral or multilateral approaches. An example of a bilateral agreement (between two countries) is the 1985 supplement to the U.S.–United Kingdom extradition treaty, which states that, in certain crimes associated with terrorism (for example, skyjackings or the murder of diplomats), the defendant cannot claim to have been engaged in a political act of conscience and hence not extraditable. For a government to accept this line of argument often led it to invoke the **political exception rule,** which has traditionally been a source of tension among governments. This is in part because of different political agendas and foreign policy priorities but also because a number of European countries did not want to send a suspect to the United States where he or she might face the death penalty. But over the years this has become less of a problem, as the United States is quite willing to let a suspect be tried in a European court in lieu of extradition, and governments are less willing to accept the "political act of conscience" claims of terrorists.

An example of a multilateral or regional agreement is the 1977 European Convention on the Suppression of Terrorism, although it lacks an enforcement mechanism. The best known are listed in the accompanying box. Examples include the Montreal Convention on the Making of Plastic Explosives (1998) and a series of agreements dealing with skyjackings. The problem is that not all states sign such conventions, the most obvious being those that have been accused of supporting or conducting international terrorism, such as Iran and Syria and, in the past, Iraq and Libya. All states, however, can fall back on a particular functional agreement—**Article 51** of the U.N. charter. This article states that "nothing in the present charter shall impair the inherent right of individual or collective self-defense if an armed attack occurs against a Member of the United Nations." Although this provision was originally intended as a legal basis for defense by sovereign states against aggression by other states, it can broadly be applied to defense against terrorist activity, whether or not it is state sponsored. All sovereign states thus reserve the right to engage in unilateral (or collective) military action against such threats.

Encourage International Cooperation   Perhaps even more important than formal legal agreements, however, are various efforts among states to improve international cooperation in the struggle against terrorism. Diplomatic progress, often painstaking and requiring enormous patience and persistence, can reduce the resorting to terrorism by some groups. This has occurred as an outcome of continuing negotiations concerning Northern Ireland. An unintended, positive consequence of deliberations that resulted in the unification of Germany at the end of the Cold War was the effective denial of sanctuary used by a number of terrorist groups operating from East Germany (the former German Democratic Republic).

Cooperation can take any number of forms—diplomatic support for another state's counterterrorist efforts, combined military operations, intelligence sharing, law enforcement cooperation, or security assistance and training. Such cooperation, however, is not always easily achieved. A concern for international terrorism may be a common concern for most states, but its relative priority among foreign policy issues is not always the same. For example, it was easy for Washington to call for stronger economic sanctions against Libya, as the United States has few citizens living in that country and does not import Libyan oil. For the French and the Italians, however, this was not the case. Similarly, prior to 9/11, Europeans often noted that their geographical proximity to the Middle East meant they are more likely than the United States to be

International Agreements Addressing Terrorism

In addition to bilateral treaties and a number of United Nations Security Council and General Assembly resolutions, there are eleven major multilateral conventions related to states' responsibilities for combating terrorism. All require the prosecution or extradition of offenders.

Tokyo Convention (1963): Authorizes pilot to take measures if he or she believes a passenger is about to commit or has committed an action that threatens the security of the aircraft

Hague Convention (1970): Makes it an offense to threaten or seize an aircraft; requires states to punish perpetrators of hijackings

Montreal Convention (1971): Makes it an offense to perform an act of violence against a person or to place an explosive device on the aircraft

Convention of Crimes against Internationally Protected Persons (1973): Defines such persons as diplomats, head of state, minister of foreign affairs, representative of an international organization

Convention on Physical Protection of Nuclear Material (1979): Criminalizes the possession, use, transfer, theft, or threatened use of nuclear material

Convention against the Taking of Hostages (1979): Applies to cases in which hostages are used in an attempt to compel a state or international organization to take a particular act in order for the hostages to be released

Protocol for the Suppression of Unlawful Acts at Airports (1988): Extends provision of the Montreal Convention to airports

Protocol for the Suppression of Acts of Violence against the Safety of Marine Ships (1988): Applies to terrorist activities on ships

Protocol for the Suppression of Unlawful Acts against the Safety of Fixed Platforms Located on the Continental Shelf (1988): Established a legal regime applicable to fixed platforms (such as oil-drilling platforms) that is similar to aviation regimes

Convention on the Marking of Plastic Explosives (1991): Provides for chemical marking to facilitate the detection of plastic explosives in order to combat aircraft sabotage

Convention on the Suppression of Terrorist Bombings (1997): Expands the legal framework for international cooperation in the investigation, prosecution, and extradition of persons who engage in terrorist bombings

Source: www.state.gov.

the venue for terrorist actions on the part of Islamic extremists. Italy, Germany, France, and the United Kingdom also play host to a large number of foreign nationals from this region. After 9/11, however, there is no doubt that many of the successes against terrorist groups and their plans came about as the result of observant law enforcement officials around the world. While the second war against Iraq in 2003 may have caused diplomatic problems between the United States and several of its European friends and allies, at the working level, cooperation continued among law enforcement and intelligence officials on both sides of the Atlantic.

In sum, terrorism is a phenomenon that is here to stay—as history shows, terrorism doesn't end; rather it evolves. Often the instrument of groups or movements that perceive few, if any, other alternatives to serve their causes, terrorism for them becomes the purposeful or rational use of the irrational—bringing attention to their objectives through the intimidation and fear that terrorism evokes in target officials, populations, or institutions. A government simply cannot ignore terrorism even if it might wish to do so. With the advent of mass media and instantaneous communications—the so-called CNN effect—terrorist incidents in even remote parts of the globe are brought into our living rooms. It is inevitable that governments will have to address the clamor of questions raised by a press corps avidly covering all aspects of a newsworthy international terrorist incident.

To believe terrorism's underlying causes can be cured or its manifestations stamped out by military force is naive. If successful, addressing grievances and related causes may reduce the propensity of groups to resort to terrorism; however, defensive measures are still necessary. Indeed, combating international terrorism requires patience and the execution of a strategy combining a number of elements. Prevention through good intelligence and effective law-enforcement measures is best, but also planning for the worst—mitigating damage and managing consequences by employing well-trained and equipped police, firefighters, medical personnel, and other first responders—is essential. In addition, a successful strategy also requires diplomatic and conflict-resolution approaches that, if successful, reduce substantially the propensity of affected groups to resort to further terrorist activity. In an era of global interdependence, when no state can be sure it will not fall victim to terrorist attacks, international cooperation is particularly important.

Transnational Crime and Globalization

Terrorism may currently be the number-one transnational threat to states, but it is not the only one. Although terrorist violence is a type of criminal activity, as it violates laws, it is useful to distinguish here between terrorism with a political motivation and other forms of organized crime that usually are motivated by economic purposes—making illicit gains. Of course, some terrorist groups also engage in criminal activity to support their movements financially, but most organized criminal groups merely seek illicit gains not as a means to serve political purposes, but rather as an end in itself. What interests us here is that organized crime, which traditionally has been viewed as a domestic problem for a few states, has become an increasing global concern. Compared to terrorism, it may be under the radar of most persons, but the threat is evident in a number of developments in the 1990s that have persisted into the new millennium:

- The Colombian drug cartels' assassination and bombing campaign designed to change their government's extradition policy. (**Extradition** involves a government sending one of its citizens to another country for criminal prosecution.)
- Trafficking in human beings for sexual exploitation and forced labor
- Sicilian Mafia attacks on the Italian state and the murder of judges investigating organized crime
- The rise of criminal organizations in Russia and other areas of the former Soviet Union and Eastern Europe
- Extension beyond Japan (Yakuza) and China (Triads) of long-established criminal networks
- The dramatic expansion of international money laundering
- Reports of trafficking in nuclear materials in Europe
- The sale of pirated and counterfeit products; copyright, trademark, and patent infringement; and other forms of intellectual property violations

Applying Theory

**TRANS-
NATIONAL
ORGANIZED
CRIME**

As with the case of terrorism, mainstream international relations literature has not dealt much with transnational organized crime. Hence, little theory has actually been applied to the phenomenon. Realists have maintained their focus on states and have not had much to say about transnational organizations in general and criminals groups in particular. As the realist conception of security emphasizes external military threats, when a border is breached the focus is understandably on a military invasion. Pluralists and liberals are conceptually not much better. Despite an acknowledgment of the importance of transnational actors, they are most concerned with private sector economic actors, nongovernmental organizations, and international organizations as facilitators of collaboration among states. Some pluralists who would also consider themselves globalists go so far as to argue that borders are becoming increasingly irrelevant due to the internationalization of production, trade liberalization, the mobility of finance, and revolutions in communications. But particularly in the case of North America and Europe, borders are becoming increasingly important in the post–September 11 era. Given concern over immigration as well as the entry of terrorists and criminal organizations expanding their reach, countries are investing vast sums of money and resources in attempting to regain control over their borders. In the case of the European Union, policing has involved the pooling of sovereignty and a move toward more restrictive border policies. This is exemplified by the Schengen agreement of 1996. While eliminating internal border inspections, external border checks have been harmonized and strengthened.

Transnational criminal organizations (TCOs) in Russia and Latin America, for example, that operate across state borders are both a cause and a consequence of the development of the global market for illicit drugs, but other aspects of globalization have facilitated their spread:

- The end of the Cold War broke down political and economic barriers between the East and West at the same time that attempts were being made to reform the criminal justice system throughout the former Soviet empire. Organized crime in Russia and each of the former satellites began to look beyond their respective borders for new markets and targets of opportunity.

- The development of free trade areas in North America and Western Europe (and movements to do so elsewhere in Latin America and Asia) occurred in tandem with the expansion of trade and transportation.

- The continual expansion of international telecommunications now allows for the easy electronic transfer of money.

Underlying these trends is an insatiable demand for drugs. Estimates of the value of all global retail sales of illicit drugs is over $320 billion, making the drug trade one of the biggest commercial activities in the world. In sum, one downside of the growth of globalization is the facilitation of the expansion of transnational crime in general and the drug trade in particular.

As noted, terrorist groups and criminal organizations differ in one basic aspect: Terrorists tend to be more motivated by political objectives than criminals who pursue essentially economic goals. Terrorists very often wish to undermine a state, whereas

Case & Point

PIRACY

Transnational crime at sea is anything but new. Rome, for example, sent ships to stop the piracy that had long plagued Mediterranean commerce since the first century B.C. Responding to growth in the volume and importance of trade in modern times, national navies were mobilized to protect international commerce. Portrayed as a threat to humankind, piracy was seen under customary international law as a crime against all nations, a capital offense, enforceable by any of them. In a quest against pirates, governments sent out their newly formed deep-water navies, capable of combat operations on the high seas far away from national shore lines.

The record of international law enforcement, however, was mixed. Sometimes states encouraged attacks on commercial ships of their enemies—an action referred to technically as **privateering** rather than piracy, but potentially just as devastating to international commerce. Pirates of the Caribbean such as Jean Laffite and Blackbeard were joined by prominent sixteenth-century English buccaneers such as Sir Francis Drake (c. 1540–1596) and Sir John Hawkins (1532–1595). They directed much of their energies toward disrupting Spanish commerce but also participated in the terrible slave trade then rampant.

After the Anglo-American War of 1812 and the subsequent defeat in Europe of Napoleon's armies, the U.S., British, and Dutch navies and later the French fleet coalesced to fight and win the war against piracy in the Mediterranean waged from North African locations. Two other major concentrations of pirates in the nineteenth century were the Persian (or Arab) Gulf, where pirates had found refuge in settlements referred to collectively as the Pirate Coast, and the strategic Straits of Malacca through which most European shipping passed to and from the Far East. In the 1820s London dispatched the Royal Navy to the Gulf to stop pirates from preying on British and other shipping en route to (or coming from) India, China, and elsewhere in Asia and the Pacific.

Point: Transnational crime is not a new phenomenon.

U.S. Army Chinook helicopter engaged in a counterdrug mission in Central America.

criminals usually want to be left alone to pursue their criminal activities. Far from wanting to overthrow the capitalist system—the professed goal of many terrorists over the years—criminals embrace the market system and exploit it to their advantage. Instead of attacking governments and law enforcement agencies, they would prefer to corrupt and intimidate them.

There is reason to believe, however, that the traditional distinction between terrorists and criminals is eroding. Criminals at times resort to political violence to intimidate government officials, as seen in the assassination campaigns of the Medellin cartel in Colombia and the Sicilian Mafia against judges in Italy. Conversely, the Revolutionary Armed Forces of Colombia (FARC) has protected coca growers and shippers from government forces, receiving protection money from traffickers. Perhaps a better example is the Shan Army of Burma, which over the years evolved from a revolutionary organization to little more than a cabal of drug traffickers.

This development is not unexpected. With the end of the Cold War, Marxism-Leninism was discredited, and many revolutionary organizations underwent an identity crisis, losing their *raison d'être*. On a more practical level, some terrorist organizations have lost state support and need to find an alternative source of income. It is not surprising that terrorist organizations operating in such countries as Colombia, Peru, and Lebanon, which are the source of much of the world's illicit drugs, would become involved in the drug trade. On the other hand, as governments gear up to deal with the expanding transnational crime problem, it can be expected that criminals will resort more frequently to antigovernment violence as a means to intimidate and coerce policy changes.

If criminals essentially see their operations as businesses, it is not surprising that they at times create strategic alliances that work to their mutual benefit. As with legitimate businesses, the point is to reduce risk and improve profits. One example involves the relationship between the Colombian drug cartels and Mexican drug-trafficking families. Mexican criminal organizations have developed over the years an excellent smuggling infrastructure for transporting goods and people across the border into the United States. For the Colombians, employing the Mexican smuggling networks to get their cocaine into the United States lowers the risk of running afoul of U.S. drug interdiction efforts. For the Mexicans involved, the alliance allows them to share some of the profits of the cocaine industry, which has much higher profit margins than marijuana and other smuggled commodities.

A similar alliance has been developed between Mexican smugglers and Chinese criminal organizations that transport illegal immigrants seeking to enter the United States. The Colombians have also worked with Nigerian drug-trafficking organizations, with the latter providing heroin to the Colombians in exchange for cocaine, which the Nigerians sell in Europe. Similarly, the Sicilian Mafia and the Colombians worked out an alliance in the late 1980s designed to aid Colombian entry into the European cocaine market. The Sicilians had a well established distribution system in Europe and knowledge of regional law enforcement capabilities; they were also making efforts to recapture a portion of the U.S. heroin market they had progressively lost to Asian suppliers. Map 8.1 shows cocaine trafficking flows used by transnational criminal organizations.

TRAFFICKING IN HUMAN BEINGS

From Himalayan villages to Eastern European cities, people–especially women and girls–are attracted by the prospect of a well-paid job as a domestic servant, waitress or factory worker. Traffickers recruit victims through fake advertisements, mail-order bride catalogues and casual acquaintances. Upon arrival at their destination, victims are placed in conditions controlled by traffickers while they are exploited to earn illicit revenues. Many are physically confined, their travel or identity documents are taken away and they or their families are threatened if they do not cooperate. Women and girls forced to work as prostitutes are blackmailed by the threat that traffickers will tell their families. It is estimated that one million women and children are seduced into leaving their homelands each year.

Source: United Nations Office on Drugs and Crime (www.unodc.org/unodc/trafficking_human_beings.html).

It's Been Said...

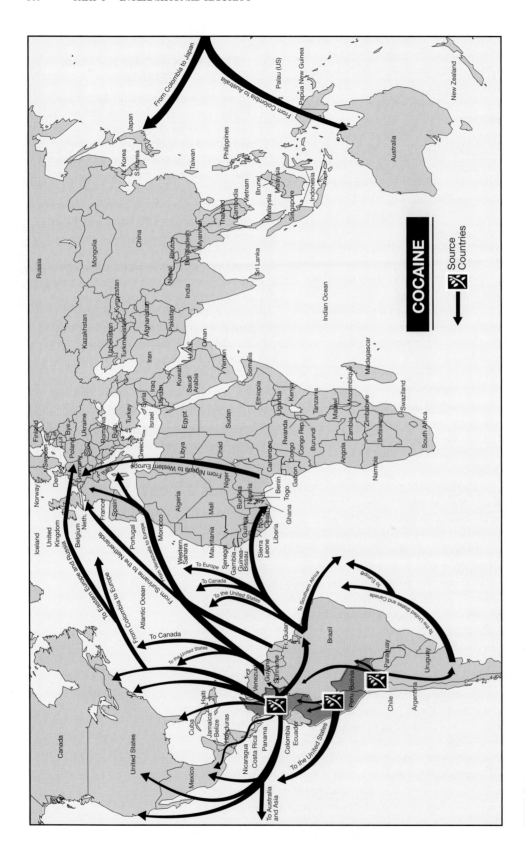

MAP 8.1   *International Cocaine Trafficking Flows*

Source: Office of National Drug Control Policy, *National Drug Control Strategy 1999* (Washington, D.C., 1999), p. 74.

Case & Point

South Africa is committed to fighting domestic and international trafficking in illicit narcotic drugs, but reliable evidence suggests that the country continues to be an important transit area for cocaine (from South America) and heroin (from the Far East), primarily destined for Southern African and European markets. South Africa has for some time been the origin, the transit point, or the terminus of many major smuggling routes; this was particularly so during the *apartheid* period. Trends and practices begun in the sanctions-busting *apartheid* period continue into the current era; rather than embargoed items, drugs and other illicit items now are smuggled into and out of South Africa. Additionally, South Africa has the most developed transportation, communications, and banking infrastructure in sub-Saharan Africa. The country's modern international telecommunications systems (particularly wireless telephones), its direct air links with South America, Asia, and Europe; and its permeable land borders provide opportunities for regional and international trafficking in all forms of contraband, including narcotics. Narcotics trafficking is very profitable for organized crime syndicates, and they have become heavily involved in stealing vehicles and trading them across South Africa's land borders for narcotics.

Point: Globalization has allowed criminal organizations to take advantage of South African commercial and communication links with the rest of the world.

Source: U.S. Department of State, *International Narcotics Control Strategy Report.*

A DOWN-SIDE OF GLOBAL-IZATION

A comparative study reveals many interesting similarities among several criminal groups such as the Italian Mafia, Japanese Yakuza, Russian Mafia, and Chinese Triads. Very much a part of their national and local cultures, they were at their origins fraternities also known for good or service-oriented works that built their legitimacy in the communities in which they operated. Indeed, the term *Triad* refers philosophically to an essential three-way linkage among the spiritual ("heaven"), the material ("earth"), and human beings. Moreover, the *omerta* or code of silence among members is by no means unique to the Mafia, a commitment to secrecy also being an integral part of Russian Mafia, Yakuza, Triads, and other criminal groups. Hierarchical structures of social organization based on personal, reciprocal loyalties and protection of other family members are also characteristics in common albeit with cultural variations. Viewing the criminal organization as a form of extended family with expectations of loyalty thereto is to be found in Mafia and Triad groups; however, reflecting its origins in feudal Japan, the Yakuza put greater emphasis on the personal, mutual loyalties between the *oyabun* (senior) and his followers.

How big a threat are such TCOs to national and international security? There is always the danger of threat inflation. Law enforcement and intelligence organizations, seeking to justify their mission and budget with the demise of the communist threat, may overstate the problem. To date it is apparent that such criminal alliances are alliances of convenience, with each organization asking, "What's in it for us?" Such organizations are highly protective of their independence and markets, so there is no movement to create some sort of global criminal organization with central direction and enforcement mechanisms. In fact, transnational criminal alliances have their strains and can fall apart, just as legitimate international businesses have their disagreements.

But large-scale, organized criminal activity, though it is not designed to bring down a state and create a new political order, can have the pernicious and deadly effect of undermining the social fabric of a society and contributing to a host of financial and social ills and political crises of authority. This is particularly the case with narcotics trafficking and the attendant consequences of widespread drug abuse and the financial corruption of governments. Such dangers are particularly pronounced in countries struggling to escape from their authoritarian past but saddled with weak legal, financial, and democratic institutions.

How have governments responded? The nature of the response varies because different countries are faced with different degrees and types of threat. The following case study illustrates the problems of international cooperation in the attempt to deal with transnational criminal behavior.

Case Study: The United States, Latin America, and Drugs

In the 1980s the U.S. government professed to follow a two-part strategy in its war on drugs, attacking the twin issues of supply and demand. The demand side dealt with such concerns as drug education, counseling, and rehabilitation. The supply side, on which we will focus, emphasized destroying crops at the source in Latin America, weaning peasants away from drug-related crops, and interdicting drugs before they could enter the United States. But the U.S. "drug war" ran afoul of competing national interests and faced a whole host of seemingly intractable problems.

The United States relies on the Peruvian, Bolivian, and Colombian militaries to carry out the fight against the drug traffickers, yet these militaries have at times committed human rights abuses. These same three countries suffer from dreadful economic problems, and, as a result, significant portions of the populations rely on the drug trade for their livelihood. Bolivia's cultivation of coca is about half of what it was at its peak in 1995. Any gains in the government of Bolivia's successful reduction of domestic coca and cocaine production, however, have been partially offset by Bolivia's growing importance as a transit country for Peruvian cocaine destined mainly for Brazil. Bolivia's borders run through the most remote and least controlled territories of its five neighboring countries, presenting multiple natural routes for smuggling. Simply put, the U.S. war on drugs is also a war against a major segment of these Latin American economies. The top priority for Latin American political leaders is, understandably, economic and political stability, not what they see as the U.S. drug problem.

The situation is somewhat different in Colombia, where the Medellin cartel declared a "total war" on the state in 1989. The Colombian government draws a distinction between narcoterrorism and narcotics trafficking; they are certainly committed to reducing drug-related violence and responded vigorously in the 1990s to the attacks of the Medellin cartel. Colombia continues to be the world's leading producer and distributor of cocaine and a significant supplier of heroin to the United States. In addition to supporting independent drug traffickers and cartels, the drug trade serves as a major source of funding for the leftist Revolutionary Armed Forces of Colombia (FARC), the hemisphere's largest and oldest terrorist group, and the United Self Defense Forces of Colombia (AUC), a paramilitary organization. The AUC and the FARC each control areas within Colombia that have the greatest coca and poppy cultivation. Their involvement in the drug trade fuels continued violence as each group vies to gain or retain profitable territory. Colombian governments continue to struggle to make good on their promise to crack down on extralegal armed groups and the illegal drug trade that funds them.

Case & Point

EUROPEAN AND INTER- NATIONAL ANTICRIME COOPERA- TION

In May 2004, ten new member states joined the European Union, bringing the total population of the EU to 450 million people. For law enforcement personnel, their job simply became harder. There are two prime examples of the institutionalization of anti-crime cooperation. The first is the International Criminal Police Organization (ICPO or, more commonly, INTERPOL), the name adopted in 1956 for a law-enforcement information-exchange network originally established in 1923. From its secretariat in Lyon, France, INTERPOL now connects more than 180 countries that may share information and coordinate law-enforcement efforts against criminal activities of all kinds in an increasingly globalized world. Singled out for particular emphasis these days are terrorism and other forms of violent crime, criminal organizations, narcotics production and trade, human trafficking, financial and high-technology crimes, and alien and fugitive investigation support to national authorities. Keep track of INTERPOL activities at www.interpol.int.

The second institutional development is EUROPOL (European Police Office). EUROPOL'S challenging mandate is to improve the effectiveness and cooperation of member states in preventing and combating terrorism, unlawful drug trafficking, and other serious forms of international organized crime to include trafficking in human beings, counterfeiting of money, and money laundering. Authorized by the Maastricht Treaty on European Union (February 1992), limited cooperation began in January 1994 with the establishment of the EUROPOL Drug Unit. The mandate of EUROPOL was expanded later to its current mission of dealing with all serious forms of international crime. EUROPOL principally supports member states by facilitating the exchange of information and threat assessments through EUROPOL liaison officers designated in member countries. To learn more, visit the Europol website at www.europol/eu/int.

The United States and 123 other countries signed the U.N. Convention against Transnational Organized Crime during a high-level signing conference, December 12–15, 2000, in Palermo, Italy. The impetus for the United Nations to begin negotiations on this first multilateral treaty to fight organized crime was the post–Cold War realization that many forms of transnational organized crime pose a serious threat to democracy. This is particularly true in the developing world and in countries with fragile economies in transition. The convention will enable governments to prevent and combat transnational organized crime more effectively through a common tool kit of criminal law techniques and through international cooperation. It requires member states to outlaw some of the most prevalent types of offenses committed by organized crime groups: obstruction of justice, money laundering, corruption of public officials, and conspiracy. The convention has three protocols: to combat trafficking in persons, smuggling of migrants, and illicit manufacturing of and trafficking in firearms.

Point: The end of the Cold War has facilitated the rise of organized crime in Europe and elsewhere around the world, but there is also an increase in international law enforcement cooperation.

Not only do states face competing national interests, but within such countries as Peru (the second largest cocaine producer in the world and a major exporter of high purity cocaine and cocaine base to markets in South America, Mexico, the United States, and Europe) there have been competing bureaucratic interests between the military and the police. In Peru, for example, bureaucratic competition has been

TRANSNATIONAL CRIME

Transnational crime will be a defining issue of the 21st century for policymakers—as defining as the Cold War was for the 20th century and colonialism was for the 19th. Terrorists and transnational crime groups will proliferate because these crime groups are major beneficiaries of globalization. They take advantage of increased travel, trade, rapid money movements, telecommunications and computer links, and are well positioned for growth.

Louise I. Shelley

Director of the Transnational Crime and Corruption Center, American University, Washington, D.C.

It's Been Said...

exacerbated by contradictory missions. The police, on the one hand, take the lead in counternarcotics efforts. Hence they seek to disrupt the cultivation and trafficking activities in the Upper Huallaga Valley in conjunction with the U.S. Drug Enforcement Administration. The military, however, was in the 1990s principally concerned with the Shining Path insurgency. As a result, they hesitated to alienate peasant growers and so, at times, the military has thwarted counter-drug operations. A Peruvian general who was the former regional commander remarked, "There are 150,000 peasant coca-growers in the zone. Each one is a potential subversive. Eradicate his field and the next day he'll be one. . . . Most of my troops come from this area. In effect, the police were wiping out the livelihood of their families, while I was asking them to fight Shining Path, which was sworn to protect the growers. Shining Path looked like heroes."[5] Indeed, remnants of Sendero Luminoso (SL) were providing security for a fee to traffickers transporting drugs out of the Apurimac/Ene Valleys and the Upper Huallaga Valley.

Even where U.S. in-country enforcement efforts have been somewhat successful, as in Peru and Bolivia, the result has been simply to spread coca production into other countries, such as Colombia, Brazil, Ecuador, Venezuela, and Argentina. And as U.S. interdiction efforts improved in the Caribbean and southern Florida, drug traffickers simply found alternative routes, such as coming through Mexico. Furthermore, by the late 1990s, a new generation of drug traffickers in Colombia became adept at using the Internet and other modern technology such as encryption, reversing the gains of earlier years that had crippled the older cartels. They also maintain a much lower profile, mix illicit and licit businesses, avoid engaging in terrorist attacks against the government, and operate in small autonomous cells. Rather than being hierarchically organized and integrated, Colombian traffickers contract out most of their jobs to specialists. It is estimated that there are now several hundred small cartels.[6]

Crop substitution has been proposed as a way to wean peasants away from coca growing, but the problem here is simply economics—coca often brings ten times the price of other crops. Coca is a hardy crop; one bush produces leaves four to six times a year for fifteen years. It is easy to harvest and process into paste, and drug traffickers make marketing easy for peasants by flying into remote airstrips and paying up front with U.S. dollars.

How can governments combat transnational criminal organizations? As with all problems of world politics, there are no easy answers. One approach is to improve intelligence collection and analytical efforts, aiming at better understanding of TCOs, their networks, and means of doing business. This "mapping of the terrain" requires the sharing of information and intelligence among interested states. EUROPOL, a clearing house for police information based in Europe, is one example of such an enterprise. Another step is to develop joint programs and operations among those states that have the interest, will, and capability to make inroads in the power of TCOs.

---

[5]Kenneth E. Sharpe, "The Military, the Drug War and Democracy in Latin America: What Would Clausewitz Tell Us?" *Small Wars and Insurgencies,* vol. 4, no. 3 (Winter 1993): 72. See also Mark S. Steinitz, "The Terrorism and Drug Connection in Latin America's Andean Region," *CSIS Policy Papers on the Americas,* July 2002.

[6]Douglas Farah, "Drug Cartels Hold Tech Advantage," *Washington Post,* November 15, 1999, pp. 1, 18.

Developing any strategy or policy requires taking into account the possible unexpected consequences of a particular line of attack to minimize the sorts of outcomes evident in counterdrug efforts in Latin America. One can also be critical of such rhetoric as the "war on drugs" or the "war on crime." Such military phrases imply that such problems can be solved once and for all—a naive hope—rather than reduced, a more reasonable goal. Finally, and perhaps most importantly, more progress can be made in curbing the demand for illicit drugs—the market that gives incentives to criminal activity in the first place. It is not enough to wage war on the "supply side" without attending to the difficult social and other factors that lead people to buy and use drugs in the first place.

Conclusion

Terrorism and crime are where realist concern with national security threats to states intersects with the pluralist and liberal interest in nonstate actors. International terrorism has understandably received more headlines and news coverage than has transnational organized crime. A major terrorist incident, after all, is very dramatic. On the other hand, few of us or anyone we know will ever fall victim to a terrorist attack. The impact of global crime, however, is much more pervasive. It is evident in the drug problems in our schools and society in general. Criminal activity has major financial consequences and, like terrorism, can threaten democratic institutions. This is particularly a concern in emerging democratic states.

Although one can debate the extent to which international terrorism and transnational organized crime are threats to international security, there is little doubt as to the key to a successful response. Unilateral actions by governments are the usual starting point. But multilateral and international efforts are indispensable in an age of increasing globalization and interdependence.

Afterword

Osama bin Laden's Fatwah against Americans (1998)

Below are harsh words in a fatwah (or edict) issued in 1998 by Osama bin Laden, a Saudi militant whose Al Qaeda organization would be responsible for a number of terrorist attacks against American targets around the world, most notably the September 11, 2001 destruction of the World Trade Center in New York and the attack on the Pentagon in Washington, D.C. Some have challenged Osama's authority to issue a fatwah, given that such edicts are customarily reserved to religious authorities. Be that as it may, the name of God ("Allah" in Arabic) is invoked as being on the side of Muslims and against the Americans and other infidels. This extraordinary claim reminds us of the quip often attributed to Abraham Lincoln in a very different context—that instead of questioning whether God is on one side or another, it might be better to ask whether one is on "God's side." The passage is obviously bereft of any such humility.

Praise be to God, who revealed the Book, controls the clouds, defeats factionalism, and says in His Book; "But, when the forbidden months are past, then fight and slay the pagans wherever ye find them, seize them, beleaguer them, and lie in wait for them in every stratagem (of war)"; and peace be upon our Prophet, Muhammad . . . who said, "I have been sent with the sword between my hands to ensure that no one but God is worshipped, God who put my livelihood under the shadow of my spear and who inflicts humiliation and scorn on those who disobey my orders." The Arabian Peninsula has never—since God made it flat, created its desert, and encircled it with seas—been stormed by any forces like the crusader armies now spreading in it like locusts, consuming its riches and destroying its plantations. All this is happening at a time when nations are attacking Muslims like people fighting over a plate of food. In the light of the grave situation and the lack of support, we and you are obliged to discuss current events, and we should all agree on how to settle the matter.

No one argues today about three facts that are known to everyone; we will list them, in order to remind everyone:

First, for over seven years the United States has been occupying the lands of Islam in the holiest of places, the Arabian Peninsula, plundering its riches, dictating to its rulers, humiliating its people, terrorizing its neighbors, and turning its bases in the Peninsula into a spearhead through which to fight the neighboring Muslim peoples.

If some people have formerly debated the fact of the occupation, all the people of the Peninsula have now acknowledged it. The best proof of this is the Americans' continuing aggression against the Iraqi people using the Peninsula as a staging post, even though all its rulers are against their territories being used to that end, still they are helpless.

Second, despite the great devastation inflicted on the Iraqi people by the crusader-Zionist alliance, and despite the huge number of those killed, in excess of one million. . . . Despite all this, the Americans are once again trying to repeat the horrific massacres, as though they are not content with the protracted blockade imposed after the ferocious war or the fragmentation and devastation. So now they come to annihilate what is left of this people and to humiliate their Muslim neighbors.

Third, if the Americans' aims behind these wars are religious and economic, the aim is also to serve the Jews' petty state and divert attention from its occupation of Jerusalem and murder of Muslims there. The best proof of this is their eagerness to destroy Iraq, the strongest neighboring Arab state, and their endeavor to fragment all the states of the region such as Iraq, Saudi Arabia, Egypt, and Sudan into paper statelets and through their disunion and weakness to guarantee Israel's survival and the continuation of the brutal crusade occupation of the Peninsula.

All these crimes and sins committed by the Americans are a clear declaration of war on God, his messenger, and Muslims. And ulema [religious authorities] have throughout Islamic history unanimously agreed that the jihad is an individual duty if the enemy destroys the Muslim countries. . . .

On that basis, and in compliance with God's order, we issue the following fatwah, to all Muslims:

The ruling to kill the Americans and their allies—civilians and military—is an individual duty for every Muslim who can do it in any country in which it is possible to do it, in order to liberate the al-Aqsa Mosque and the holy mosque from their grip, and in order for their armies to move out of all the lands of Islam, defeated and unable to threaten any Muslim. This is in accordance with the words of Almighty God: "and fight the pagans all together as they fight you all together," and "fight them until there is no more tumult or oppression, and there prevail justice and faith in God."

This is in addition to the words of Almighty God: "And why should ye not fight in the cause of God and of those who, being weak, are ill-treated and oppressed—women and children, whose cry is 'Our Lord, rescue us from this town, whose people are oppressed, and raise for us from Thee one who will help!'"

We—with God's help—call on every Muslim who believes in God and wishes to be rewarded to comply with God's order to kill the Americans and plunder their money wherever and whenever it is found. We also call on Muslim ulema, leaders, youths, and soldiers to launch the raid on Satan's U.S. troops and the devil's supporters allying with them, and to displace those who are behind them so that they may learn a lesson.

Almighty God said: "O ye who believe, give your response to God and His Apostle, when He calleth you to that which will give you life. And know that God cometh between a man and his heart, and that it is He to whom ye shall all be gathered."

Almighty God also says: "O ye who believe, what is the matter with you that when ye are asked to go forth in the cause of God, ye cling so heavily to the earth! Do ye prefer the life of this world to the hereafter? But little is the comfort of this life, as compared with the hereafter. Unless ye go forth, He will punish you with a grievous penalty, and put others in your place; but Him ye would not harm in the least for God hath power over all things."

Almighty God also says: "So lose no heart, nor fall into despair. For ye must gain mastery if ye are true in faith."

Key Terms

terrorism   *p. 276*   international terrorism   *p. 279*
anarchists   *p. 278*   cultures of violence   *p. 282*

Other Concepts

netwar   *p. 289*   extradition   *p. 296*   privateering   *p. 298*
cyberterrorism   *p. 291*   transnational criminal
political exception rule   organizations (TCOs)
   p. 294   *p. 297*
Article 51   *p. 294*

Additional Readings

For a now-classic historical and conceptual overview of terrorism, see Walter Laqueur's *The Age of Terrorism* (Boston: Little, Brown, 1987). See also his more recent *The New Terrorism: Fanaticism and the Arms of Mass Destruction* (New York: Oxford University Press, 1999). We also recommend Bruce Hoffman's, *Inside Terrorism*, 2nd ed. (New York: Columbia University Press, 2005); Walter Reich, ed., *Origins of Terrorism: Psychologies, Ideologies, Theologies, States of Mind* (Cambridge, England: Cambridge University Press, 1990), and Daniel Benjamin and Steven Simon, *The Age of Sacred Terror* (New York: Random House, 2002). For more on Islam, diversity in Islam, and terrorism, see Bernard Lewis, *The Crisis of Islam* (New York: Random House, 2003, 2004); Sohail H. Hashmi, *Islamic Political Ethics: Civil Society, Pluralism, and Conflict* (Princeton, NJ: Princeton University Press, 2002); and Vartan Gregorian, *Islam: A Mosaic, Not a Monolith* (Washington, D.C.: Brookings Institution, 2003).

On counterterrorism and homeland security, see Michael E. O'Hanlon *et al.*, *Protecting the American Homeland: A Preliminary Analysis* (Washington, D.C.: Brookings Institution, 2002) and the revised version a year later in *Protecting the American Homeland: One Year On* (Washington, DC: Brookings Institution, 2003). More recently we note the textbook by Mark A. Sauter and James Jay Carafano, *Homeland Security* (New York: McGraw Hill, 2005).

The most thorough account of the 9/11 plot is *The 9/11 Commission Report* (Washington, DC: U.S. Government Printing Office, 2004). This extraordinary document reads almost like a novel. You might also wish to take a look at the journals *Terrorism and Political Violence* and *Conflict and Terrorism*. Finally, for academic articles on crime, see the journal *Transnational Organized Crime;* Richard Friman and Peter Andreas, eds., *The Illicit Global Economy and State Power* (Lanham, MD: Rowman and Littlefield, 1999); Tom J. Farer (ed.), *Transnational Crime in the Americas* (London: Routledge, 1999); Jeffrey Robinson, *The Merger: The Conglomeration of International Organized Crime* (New York: Overlook Press, 2000); David E. Kaplan and Alec Dubro, *Yakuza: Japan's Criminal Underworld* (Berkeley: University of California Press, 2003).

Chapter 9

An Emerging Global Civil Society: International Law, International Organization, and Globalization

I n the summer of 1999, the Chinese government banned a vast, silent movement known as Falun Gong. Falun Gong is not a political organization designed to undercut governmental authority but rather an organization that synthesizes Buddhist, Taoist, and folk beliefs and whose distinguishing activity is collective deep-breathing exercises. Its tens of millions of followers include lower- and middle-class people plus Communist Party members who hope to achieve a healthier and happier life. The Chinese government was unable to arrest the leader of Falun Gong for a simple reason—he lives in New York City. But with the Internet's e-mail capability, this geographic separation from his followers did not pose a significant obstacle to communication.

Similarly, various nongovernmental organizations have used the Internet to coordinate strategy and organize protests against the World Trade Organization (WTO) in Seattle, Washington, in November 1999, the World Bank and International Monetary Fund in Washington, D.C., in April 2000, the WTO ministerial meeting in Cancun, Mexico, in September 2003, and in subsequent meetings of these organizations. No matter the culture or nationality, persons with a common interest, faith, or agenda are able to share ideas and concerns without ever having to meet face to face. A sense of community, therefore, does not necessarily have to arise from the close proximity of individual members— virtual communities can arise from online connections.

One does not have to be a realist to recognize ours is a complex, multicultural world divided into separate states. Societies in some states have distinct cultures and national identities, reinforcing a populace's identification with a particular state. Other societies are decidedly multicultural, sometimes with multiethnic or multinational identities. Moreover, cultures and identities are not always confined by state boundaries but frequently overlap, as pluralists or liberals often argue. Even these state boundaries, as constructivists would claim, can be viewed as artificial or "socially constructed" and hence permeable and subject to change. For the English school, the web of state interactions and the development of international norms allow one to speak of a society of states and non-state actors as well.

In Chapter 2 we emphasized the historical development of international relations and world politics. The system perspective we used emphasized international relations—a focus on empires and states. This gave the discussion a distinct realist cast. In this chapter, however, we focus on world politics and the emergence in the last 500 years of developments that not only contributed to the rise of states but also have provided early glimpses into the development of a still-emerging global civil society—often a pluralist and English school concern. Themes will be introduced that we discuss at greater length in subsequent chapters. An emerging global civil society, for example, has been both a cause and a consequence of the formulation of international law to guide, direct, or govern the behavior of states, international and nongovernmental organizations, and other actors.

Global society becomes a truly civil society to the extent that values or norms gain legitimacy and become widely accepted, some even acquiring the force of law. Use of the term *civil society* in "domestic" societies within states implies that behavior of people within these societies is subject to the rule of law. So it is with a still-emergent global civil society.

The Globalization of International Relations and World Politics

Globalization refers to enormously increased transnational and worldwide interactions in virtually every human pursuit. This globalization owes much to great advances in technology or know-how, especially in transportation, communications, and related technologies. Widespread application of these technologies has already transformed the ways in which we do business and interact with each other. In trade we now engage in global marketing, sales, and delivery of goods and services; in finance we transfer large amounts of money instantaneously across the globe. In science we use computers (and supercomputers) in analysis of data and exchange information globally through the Internet and other media. Findings are disseminated in such diverse fields of inquiry as astrophysics and the exploration of space, quantum mechanics and the behavior of subatomic particles, and chemistry, biology, and medicine.

Indeed, advances in technology, particularly during the last 500 years, have shrunk the globe dramatically and are likely to continue to do so throughout the twenty-first century. Let's take a quick look back and see from where we've come. Larger sailing ships and improved celestial navigation in the late fifteenth century facilitated global transportation for exploration, trade, and commerce (and warfare). The invention of the sextant in 1731 made it possible to locate geographical position by measuring the degrees of elevation of the sun or stars above the horizon, further expanding exploration, trade, and cultural exchange.

globalization
The continual increase in transnational and worldwide economic, social, and cultural interactions aided by advances in technology.

Study in contrast: An athletic official in traditional dress using a cell phone in Ulan Bator, Mongolia.

Technologies further enhancing this mobility were products of the nineteenth-century industrial revolution that brought the wood- and coal-fueled steam engine for use in steel-clad ships engaged in global seaborne transit, augmented by railroads that quickly came to link and crisscross continental land areas. The late nineteenth and early twentieth centuries witnessed the harnessing of electricity and the development of the internal combustion engine, which substantially replaced horses, horse-drawn wagons and carriages, and bicycles with automobiles, trucks, and buses as the principal means of overland road and highway transportation.

Coal was augmented by the development of petroleum-based gasoline or diesel fuels that then became the principal energy sources not only for the road and highway transportation mode but also for railroads, ships at sea, and aviation. After World War II, nuclear energy found limited use in submarines and some surface warships, extending significantly their operational range. Development of the jet engine in the 1940s replaced most propeller-driven engines in both military and civil aviation.

Electricity also brought the development of lightbulbs and the vacuum tube and the ability to send electronic signals, innovations that matched advances in transportation. The gradual development of new communications technologies began in the mid-nineteenth and early twentieth centuries with the development of the telegraph and then the telephone (carried by above- and below-surface wires and even undersea cables linking continents); radio and radar; and, by the late 1930s and 1940s, the development and marketing of black-and-white television. Color television and vacuum-tube, mainframe computers emerged in the 1950s and 1960s, enhanced by the development in the 1960s and 1970s of transistors and solid-state technologies that largely replaced reliance on vacuum tubes in computer and most communications applications. Use of Earth satellites developed since the late 1950s for military and commercial purposes was enhanced by new semiconductor, microchip, and related microelectronic technologies in

THE INTERNET

Will the Internet enhance cross-cultural understanding and empathy? "Not necessarily. If we were to use the Net to open ourselves up to new social and cultural experiences, we could do wonders for cooperation and mutual understanding at the local, national, and international levels. But the ability the Net gives us to endlessly filter and personalize information means that, more than ever before, we can also build virtual gated communities where we never have to interact with people who are different from ourselves. . . . If this happens, communal conversations could be cut up into an endless number of isolated exchanges. Local activists would have difficulty competing with virtual communities for the attention of their neighbors. Even as the global nature of the Net promises to let us shrink the world, compromise between different nations and peoples may be more difficult if we replace fading national borders with new ones based on prejudice and self-indulgent preference."

Andrew L. Shapiro
*"The Internet," Foreign Policy
(Summer 1999): 14–27.*

It's Been Said...

the 1980s and 1990s, pushing computers and telecommunications to ever-higher levels.

Advances in wireless technology went well beyond earlier walkie-talkies and limited-range field telephones to mass marketing in the 1990s of portable, handheld cellular telephones for routine domestic and limited transnational use—satellites even allowing global communications for those able to afford this extended, worldwide coverage. These new technologies, of course, have also found their way into vehicles of every sort as well as the navigation and communications machinery of transportation systems on land, at sea, and in the air. A far cry from using sextants and other mechanical means, radio, radar, or electronic-based devices for measuring location of a ship or airplane, Earth satellites can now be used with extraordinary accuracy in determining precise geographic position at any point in time.

Transmission via satellite of telephone, radio, television, and other electronic signals has literally made routine a diverse variety of worldwide links of human beings that outside of science fiction were inconceivable to most people just two or three decades ago. Sometimes portrayed as an "information superhighway," the Internet or World Wide Web that emerged for widespread use in the 1980s and 1990s is really still in its infancy. We can expect that most of the limitations of bandwidth, speed, and other technicalities will be overcome in the next five to ten years, substantially enhancing information transit in all modes including television but also facilitating widespread use globally of these new applied technologies.

Already the impact of transportation and telecommunications advances on movement of peoples, the flows of their economic resources, and transmission of their ideas has been enormous. The outlines of a more cosmopolitan worldview are apparent to many observers (a number of whom would characterize themselves as pluralists or liberals) who see the world as having been fundamentally changed, not just in the last 500 years but especially in the last half century. States are still around and remain important, if not always the most important, actors. We see states interacting in interdependent, often interconnected relations with each other and with an increasing number of international and nongovernmental organizations (including multinational corporations and financial institutions). All of these rely on global transportation and telecommunications networks to do their work and now have greatly expanded capabilities to facilitate their diverse efforts. Even individuals and small groups can use these technologies to expand their impact.

The Emergence of a State-Centric Global Society

Taking the longer view, advances in transportation, communications, and other technologies over the last 500 years also witnessed the rise of states as the major actors in international relations. Certainly these technologies, coupled with similar developments in armaments of all kinds (including increasing mobility of armed forces on land or at sea), put governments in a better position to expand their effective authority within the territorial boundaries of their respective societies, also expanding their links and interactions with other states and societies in both peacetime and warfare. The emergence of nationalism in eighteenth- and nineteenth-century Europe and in the Western

Case & Point

Many see the terrorist attacks on the World Trade Center and Pentagon on September 11, 2001, at least in part a violent reaction against what some view as the ultimate purveyor of globalization—the United States. Indeed, to some "globalization" is just another word for Americanization—an effort by Washington to impose not only its will but also its values on other parts of the world. Such critics are prone to view the United States, the lone superpower (or hyperpower) as imperial, establishing what they call a "global empire." Defenders contest this claim, noting that the United States does not seek to hold territory as had been the case in the nineteenth- and twentieth-century British, French, Belgian, Dutch, German, Spanish, and Portuguese empires. Resenting the use of words like *imperial* or *empire* to describe present-day American foreign policy, defenders observe that when the United States does intervene abroad, it does not seek to stay for long, occupying foreign territory only as long as it takes to accomplish humanitarian, security, or other purposes. Moreover, the democratic or liberal values being advanced globally are not uniquely American but rather are the outcome of the seventeenth- and eighteenth-century Enlightenment period in European history and thus are shared by many countries. Economic structuralist critics quickly respond that the new imperialism in this more advanced stage of capitalism is not so much about land as it is about maintaining a dominant position in the global economy, particularly capital and energy markets. This is true, say the critics, whether the United States is acting unilaterally or multilaterally under U.N. auspices. Liberal values from this point of view not only pose no obstacles but also facilitate exercise of extraordinary influence or leverage by the United States and other countries sharing its interests or vision of world politics.

Point: The term *globalization* is a classic example of what is termed in the social sciences a "contested concept."

Hemisphere contributed to greater differentiation among societies with diverse cultures and identities as increased movement and communications of peoples and their governments occurred within the territorial borders of states. Extension of this mobility beyond the borders of states also called for some agreement on rules to govern commercial activity and matters relating to war and peace.

A cosmopolitan view of society was certainly present in Europe during the Middle Ages even though, as a practical matter, most people spent their lives in the local areas related to their position in feudal society. Nevertheless, travel by lords and knights was not uncommon (some even engaged in the Crusades against Muslims occupying much of the Holy Land in what we now call the Middle East). The idea of a Christendom as an all-encompassing European society was common to the medieval mind-set, even as daily life often witnessed strife among different feudal communities.

Although difficult given the technologies of the day, travel was not restricted to the upper stratum. Even peasants were known to travel in large numbers, if only once in a lifetime, on pilgrimages to holy sites. Of course soldiers and sailors also crossed the English Channel for campaigns in England or France or descended from northern Europe in forays to the south. Indeed, Scandinavian Norsemen or Vikings made their presence felt in Britain and Ireland as well as on the European continent, particularly in coastal areas as far away as Sicily.

Increased commerce associated with advancing transportation technologies at sea raised questions concerning rights of navigation through the coastal waters of different states as well as the modalities by which goods would be bought and sold—imported

ASSESSING THE ROLES OF STATES AND NONSTATE ACTORS

Applying Theory

Theorists, liberal or pluralist as well as realist, cannot ignore states and their interactions even as we expand our focus to include nonstate actors with channels of interaction that both crisscross and surround international or, more precisely, interstate relations. Our vision of the world need not be either-or. States (and interstate relations) coexist and interact with other units in diverse and complex patterns of interactions. To say the least, states have not yet withered away, however desirable they may or may not be. Most observers thus concede that states remain central players along with international and nongovernmental organizations in the world politics of global society, whatever may be true at present or in the future concerning any transformative role played by nonstate actors.

Important early work in the 1970s making the case for taking nonstate actors seriously was by Robert O. Keohane and Joseph S. Nye, Jr. Both authors have continued over the years to investigate the complexity of world politics, recognizing the centrality of the state yet sensitive to the impact of transnational interdependence and nonstate actors on world politics. About 5,000 international NGOs lobby states and international organizations, some to promote international cooperation, others to keep states from interfering with the activities of private citizens. There are also some 7,000 multinational corporations (MNCs) with subsidiaries that have gross sales larger than the gross domestic product (GDP) of even some major countries. Finally, loosely organized transnational alliances involving dissident movements played important roles in toppling communist regimes in Eastern Europe in 1989.

The biggest problem with most works on transnational actors is that they tend to be highly descriptive but with low theoretical content. The key question to ask about transnational actors is, "How and when can transnational actors change policy?" A number of scholars in recent years have attempted to answer this question. A major focus of theoretical and empirical work is on how domestic structures—the political institutions of the state, societal structures, and policy networks that link the two—affect the policy impact of transnational actors. The basic argument is that under similar international conditions, differences in domestic structures determine the variation in the policy impact of transnational actors. The extent to which transnational actors gain access to political systems seems to be primarily a function of the state structure. The hypothesis is that the more centralized the state structure, the less access points transnational actors have to penetrate and influence the institutions of the state. Conversely, states with "weak" political institutions should be easier to influence. Hence, we would expect human rights organizations to have the most difficulty in establishing contact with dissident movements in countries with authoritarian systems, such as Eastern Europe while under communist rule from the late 1940s to 1990. The more fragmented the state structure, the less a state is able to resist or control the influence of foreign transnational organizations. This is the case with many Third World countries.

Question: Given the federal structure of the United States and its separation of powers, do you think the United States qualifies as a "weak" state? If so, according to the domestic structure theory, transnational actors should have an impact on policy.

These points are raised and more fully discussed in Thomas Risse-Kappen, ed., *Bringing Transnational Relations Back In: Non-State Actors, Domestic Structures and International Institutions* (Cambridge: Cambridge University Press, 1995). See also the seminal work by Robert O. Keohane and Joseph S. Nye, Jr., eds., *Transnational Relations and World Politics* (Cambridge, MA: Harvard University Press, 1971) and their subsequent *Power and Interdependence*, 3rd ed. (New York: Longman, 1977, 2000).

and exported across territorial boundaries. Although territorially a rather small state, Holland had already emerged as a major sea-based commercial center by the sixteenth and seventeenth centuries. With its "head" turned toward the sea and its "back" toward the rest of Europe, it is not surprising that the idea of **international law** or law among nations would gain prominence in Holland.

Hugo Grotius (1583–1645), both a scholar and very practical man living in the Dutch commercial town of Delft, turned his attention to these concerns of governments, trading companies, and businesses of newly formed states in his day—commercial issues and matters of war and peace. Writing in the wake of the horrors of the Thirty Years' War, Grotius offered formulations of law drawn from several sources. One can see the influence on Grotius of the philosophical and historical legacy of a Roman imperial *jus gentium* (a law to govern relations among diverse peoples in the ancient Roman empire) as well as **natural law** thinking. Natural law is a philosophical view that claims there are laws inherent in nature that transcend any laws made by mere mortals. Such thinking is closely tied to the writings of Augustine, Aquinas, and other Christian writers of the late Roman Empire and Middle Ages. Grotius also knew how to make general principles and customary practice central to his constructions of legal rules of the road for states in a newly emerging, state-based European society. Thanks to the colonial and imperial extension of European states in the eighteenth, nineteenth, and twentieth centuries, this would eventually move closer toward a global society of peoples within states.

Aided by new transportation and communications technologies, territorial states became the principal actors in this new international societal order. Following Grotius and other writers, international law developed rapidly in two principal areas—economic (mainly trade and commerce) and security matters of war and peace (including diplomacy). For example, following Grotius, the territorial sea came to be defined by a three-mile limit extending from the shoreline of the coastal state. The reason three miles was chosen was that artillery technology of the time limited the range of a cannonball to about three miles, the practical distance then that any country could expect to defend from the shore without actually going to sea. Principles of just war (limits on conduct of and in warfare developed by Cicero, Augustine, Aquinas, Gentili, Suarez, and other philosophers over more than 1,500 years of Western civilization) now became matters of international law, not just moral preachings. Ideas concerning mutual respect for the welfare of foreign diplomats and their embassies and consulates now became legal obligations based on the customary practice of states.

International Law and Multilateral Institutions

As certain values and norms have gained legitimacy and acceptance on a global scale, many of these have also acquired legal status. For example, understanding, acceptance, and growing commitment since World War II to such ethical principles as respect for life, human dignity, and justice or fairness as global norms have motivated efforts to construct and expand international law on human rights.

Treaties or conventions are the most concrete forms of international law. Governments, as agents of the sovereign states they represent, contract when they sign and ratify treaties or international conventions to be bound by mutual agreement to the terms of these documents. The ancient idea from Roman times that treaties are binding (in Latin, *pacta sunt servanda*) finds practical application in global civil society in the construction of international law on human rights, defining civil and criminal jurisdictions of legal accountability, managing the global environment, and reducing environmental degradation.

HUMAN SECURITY

The first comprehensive statement on human security appeared in 1994 in the annual U.N. Human Development Report. It noted, "The concept of security has for too long been interpreted narrowly: as security of territory from external aggression, or as protection of national interests in foreign policy or as global security from the threat of nuclear holocaust. . . . Forgotten were the legitimate concerns of ordinary people who sought security in their daily lives."

It's Been Said...

multilateralism
An institutional form that coordinates relations among three or more states (and other actors involved in the process) on the basis of generalized principles of conduct. Example: In trade, the most-favored nation (MFN) principle forbids discrimination among countries producing the same product for export.

As a result, security has come to be viewed by a number of scholars and international activists not only in terms of national security and the use of force, but also human security (see the accompanying box). At the same time, the more traditional domains of international law on matters of security in war and peace as well as commerce are expanding in an increasingly global economy.

Another important source of international law is customary practice over time (such customary international law often becoming codified later in treaties or conventions). General principles inform our understandings of international law, particularly for those who turn to a natural law tradition that sees universal principles of law as discoverable by applying human reason. Finally we rely on the writings of jurists—justices and judges—whose legal opinions in cases before international as well as domestic courts bring all of these sources into sharper focus. Legal precedents are important in establishing wider legitimacy and acceptance of the rule of law on an ever-increasing number and diversity of issues in international relations and world politics.

Some ideas or norms in global civil society over time may become institutionalized as the legitimate and accepted ways and means of conduct in international relations and world politics. For example, John Ruggie has observed how **multilateralism** has become the preferred way of dealing with issues on the global agenda. Rather than resorting to unilateral actions by individual states, these issues are thought to be addressed more properly (and functionally more effectively) in the international organizations to which states belong and in other multilateral settings. These settings are increasingly open not only to states but also to nongovernmental organizations, groups, and even individuals. The idea of global civil society is thus an ever-more cosmopolitan or liberal-pluralist vision of the ways and means of conducting international relations and world politics.

Not only do ideas become institutionalized—accepted as the appropriate or legitimate ways in which states and nonstate actors expect (or are expected to) behave, but these ideas often become embedded in (meaning an integral part of) both international and nongovernmental organizations in which states or their citizens participate and interact with one another. For example, the U.N. organization or any of its specialized agencies provide a multilateral forum, procedures, and processes for dealing with the wide range of issues in which states and nonstate actors engage.

SHUNEH, JORDAN: A World Bank representative speaks with the Iraqi Planning Minister during the opening of a two-day international organization meeting.

Applying Theory

INSTITUTION-ALIZED IDEAS AND THE SOCIAL CONSTRUCTION OF GLOBAL CIVIL SOCIETY

Norms that become established in the form of either tacitly accepted understandings or explicitly agreed upon rules (some of which have the binding quality of international law) lie at the foundation of **international regimes** (voluntarily agreed sets of principles, norms, rules, and procedures concerning diverse issues—human rights, war and peace, commercial transactions, and the like) and their servicing institutions. These regimes and institutions are the outcome of human design efforts intended to provide an authoritative basis for regulating or at least influencing the behavior of both state and nonstate actors. So understood, the development of global society is a **constructivist** enterprise.

As briefly noted in Chapter 1, Alexander Wendt and other social constructivists portray self-help, power politics, and similar concepts as having been socially constructed under the anarchy of international relations and world politics and, as such, not necessary or essential attributes of international politics. For example, the realist view that states are on their own as sovereign entities relying on "self-help" to achieve their objectives is an institutionalized idea—one of various structures of identity and interest that may exist under anarchy. Indeed, Wendt sees such collective meanings (or institutionalized ideas) as constituting the structures that organize our actions. The key point is that systems do not have an independent existence;

they are what people make (or have made) of them.

To John Ruggie, another social constructivist, multilateralism is another example of an institutional form and, as such, a social construction often embedded in international organizations constituted around this value. To the extent that multilateralism becomes an established way of conducting international affairs, this institutional form effectively influences or channels the course of subsequent actions taken by states. Ideas matter, and thus constructivists see the building blocks of the international reality we construct as not just a function of bricks and mortar, financial, and other tangible or material considerations, but they are also (and perhaps more importantly) a function of ideational factors. Such ideational factors include culture, norms, and ideas as well as the reflective acts of social creation that we put in more concrete form in the global institutions we construct.

Question: How do you think realists would respond to this perspective?

For extensive presentations of their social-constructive perspectives, see Alexander Wendt, *Social Theory of International Politics* (Cambridge: Cambridge University Press, 1999) and John Gerard Ruggie, *Constructing the World Polity: Essays on International Institutionalization* (London: Routledge, 1998).

Constructing Global Civil Society: A Multicentury Project

The two oldest fields in the construction of the rule of law in global civil society are security or war and peace issues and economic or commercial matters. The newest (and much less developed) fields are human rights, the environment, and holding individuals accountable and offering them standing in both civil and criminal cases before global and regional courts. As regional and global cultures emerge that specify values and realize consensus on such matters, this consensus provides a more solid ground or foundation for formulating international law.

Diplomacy and Security: Matters of War and Peace

The emergence of sovereign states in fifteenth-, sixteenth- and seventeenth-century Europe focused attention on the ways and means of diplomacy or communications among states, their security concerns, and the conduct of relations among them in both war and peace. Consistent with the writings of Jean Bodin (1530–1596), Hugo Grotius (1583–1645), and other legal scholars, international law came to define the **sovereignty** of a state as conveying a right to exercise complete jurisdiction on its own territory as well as a right to be independent or autonomous in conducting foreign policy or international relations. Although they are unequal in power and position in international relations, sovereign states enjoy legal equality as members of the United Nations and other international organizations. Indeed, Article 2, Section 1 of the U.N. Charter states clearly and unequivocally that the "Organization is based on the principle of the sovereign equality of all its Members." As we already discussed in Chapter 4, routines and procedures for diplomatic representation became established practice over time and thus served as a customary basis for international law. States came to accept as a matter of international law the immunity from arrest or prosecution of foreign diplomats and the extraterritorial idea or legal fiction that the small parcel of land on which an embassy, consulate, or other diplomatic mission was located was to be secured and respected as subject to the sovereign prerogatives of the foreign country as if it were its own territory. Although long established as customary international law, these and other rules governing diplomacy finally were specified formally as treaty obligations in the Vienna Conventions on Diplomatic and Consular Relations in 1961 and 1963, respectively.

Nongovernmental organizations, other groups, and individuals in their private capacities can influence decision making and implementation of foreign and national security policies, but diplomacy and war and peace matters are primarily the domain of states and international organizations made up of states. Grotius wrote about war and peace, drawing from the moral tradition in Western thought we have already discussed in Chapter 5. That use of force in war must be justified *(jus ad bellum),* and that states engaged in warfare are obligated to observe limits and practice right conduct *(jus in bello)* thus acquired legal (in addition to moral) standing through the work of Grotius and other writers.

Efforts began in the late nineteenth century to codify and expand upon these principles, which resulted initially in the Hague Conventions of 1899 and 1907 that specified certain legal obligations as well as illegal conduct in warfare. Reacting to the enormous carnage of World War I that had devastated Europe between 1914 and 1918, signatories of the Covenant of the League of Nations tried to find in the concept of collective security an alternative to war and the use of force in international relations. As already discussed in earlier chapters, collective security was understood as amounting to collective law enforcement. Because aggression against a sovereign state was illegal, law-abiding states would come together, pooling their resources to take appropriate action against any lawbreaking aggressor state. The Pact of Paris or General Treaty for the Renunciation of War (more commonly referred to as the Kellogg-Briand Pact) took matters a substantial step further in 1928 by declaring resort to war as an illegal activity.

However well intended, this legal approach to security and matters of war and peace failed to prevent acts of aggression in the 1920s and 1930s, as well as the onset of a second world war in 1939. After World War II, the U.N. Charter retained collective security as collective law enforcement but supplemented it by recognizing the inherent right of sovereign states to use force to provide for their individual or (joining with other states in alliances or coalitions) their collective self-defense. On the conduct of warfare itself, the tradition of the Hague Conventions was revived in the formulation

Practicing World Politics

Formed more than half a century ago, the World Federalist Association or WFA (www.wfa.org) is a nongovernmental organization in the United States that seeks to abolish war, preserve a sustainable global environment, and provide a just world community through the development of enforceable world law. Its agenda also includes working toward an effective democratically elected federal system of global governance and moving to a system of world law that applies to individuals as well as nation-states. The WFA works with counterpart organizations in other countries that are part of the World Federalist Movement. Links to such national sites in Canada, Sweden, Japan, Germany, and the Netherlands, as well as to Young European Federalists and other NGOs, can be found on the WFA site.

THE INTERNET: CHECKING OUT SOME WEBSITES ON WORLD FEDERALISM

by treaty of obligations and limits in the Geneva Conventions on the Laws of War (1949). These laws of war were formulated with interstate wars in mind but fell short in addressing civil wars and other armed conflicts that may occur within or across boundaries of states. Accordingly, two protocols to these conventions signed in 1977 extended coverage of laws of warfare to cases of "armed conflict not of an international [i.e., interstate] character."

Security issues have also been a major growth area in global civil society since World War II, as indicated by the extraordinary proliferation of arms control agreements and treaties emerging from exhaustive diplomatic efforts over the last half of the twentieth century and continuing to the present day. These have already been treated at length in Chapter 7, detailing rules that can be categorized as (1) qualitative and quantitative restraints or armaments; (2) geographic (or spatial) limitations on deployment and use of weaponry; and (3) such functional approaches as maintaining reliable telecommunications links and adopting such confidence- and security-building measures (CSBMs) as the direct exchange of military information, conduct of aerial reconnaissance and on-site inspections, notification of military exercises with foreign observers at these maneuvers, and staffing of conflict prevention centers intended to reduce the likelihood of misperceptions and miscalculations that could lead to war.

Economic and Commercial Matters

A culture in global society dealing with economic or commercial matters also has deep roots. Certainly Grotius and other contributors made commerce a core focus in developing rules to govern trade. Early rules that acquired legal standing under international law were that ships carrying cargoes were free to transit the high seas without interference. Moreover, piracy threatening international commerce was understood as a crime against the law of nations, punishable by any state. Rules that emerged in customary practice governing the responsibilities of exporters to deliver and importers to pay for the goods they buy reduced to a routine how commercial traders conduct their business. Also contributing to the expansion of trade was developing most-favored nation (MFN) status as a diplomatic measure, granting other countries (and their firms) a right to sell their products at the same low level of tariff or tax as was imposed on imports from their "most-favored" trading partners.

Practicing World Politics

THE INTERNET: CHECKING OUT SOME WEB-SITES ON ECONOMICALLY ORIENTED INTERNATIONAL ORGANIZA-TIONS

Such international organizations as those referred to in the text perform substantial economic or commercial roles in global civil society. Most of these and other specialized U.N. agencies can be found on the World Wide Web by their abbreviated organizational names followed by .org or in some cases .int (www.icao.org, www.imo.org, www.itu.int, www.wto.org, www.imf.org, and www.worldbank.org—the last of these the more commonly used nickname substituted for its more formal designation as the International Bank for Reconstruction and Development).

Similarly, international law came to require nondiscriminatory treatment of foreign investments. Such properties may be expropriated or taken by a host country's government only for some legitimate public purpose (such as putting in a highway across privately owned properties). Let's say, for example, that as part of its economic development plan the Ecuadoran government has decided to put in a new highway directly across Guayaquil, one of the country's coastal cities. This will require the government to nationalize or take for public use all private properties in the path of the proposed highway, giving the owners monetary compensation for their losses, typically the market values of properties seized. It is not enough just to compensate domestic property owners: International law also requires the government to give fair or just compensation to foreign property owners as well.

Since the end of World War II, international law on economic and commercial issues has continued to grow. States belonging to the General Agreement on Tariffs and Trade (GATT)—now the World Trade Organization (WTO)—located in Geneva have reduced taxes and quotas or limitations on imports as well as other barriers to trade in treaties or other agreements that effectively have the force of international law. Other international organizations and U.N. specialized agencies like the World Bank and International Monetary Fund, both located in Washington, D.C., follow legal procedures and processes in lending capital respectively for economic development or for maintenance of international **liquidity**—cash needed from time to time by national treasuries and their central banks to settle financial obligations owed to the central banks or national treasuries of other countries. This procedure maintains the viability and facilitates the exchange of national currencies used in international commerce.

International transportation is subject to rules with the effect of law made by member states and staffs in U.N. specialized agencies—the International Civil Aviation Organization (ICAO) in Montreal and the International Maritime Organization (IMO) in London. Similarly, another U.N. specialized agency, the International Telecommunication Union (ITU) in Geneva, has regulatory authority on international use of telecommunications frequencies. A more recent example of continued growth in international law concerning economic or commercial matters is the Anti-Bribery

Treaty negotiated within the Organization for Economic Cooperation and Development (OECD)—an international organization composed of First World, "rich," advanced industrial countries. The treaty obligates its signatories to pass laws prohibiting corporations seeking contracts from paying bribes to government officials.

Intellectual property law—legal obligations to respect copyrights and patents across national borders—is yet another expanding area of international law in the economic and commercial sector, particularly given the development of ever-new technologies needing such protection.

"Growth Areas" in International Law: Human Rights and the Environment

Prior to World War II, international law dealt primarily with security, diplomatic, and economic or commercial matters. As indicated in the previous two sections, these domains have continued to expand substantially since 1945. Human rights and the environment, however, are the new "growth" areas for extending international law within global civil society. These topics will be discussed in greater detail in Chapters 13 and 15, but some basic background is appropriate at this point.

Human Rights   The Holocaust in Germany and other areas in Europe under the National Socialist (Nazi) regime's influence or control in the 1930s and 1940s cost some six million Jews their lives and forced millions more to flee their homes, leave their property behind, suffer extreme trauma, and sustain enormous psychological damage. Additional millions of Slavs, Gypsies, homosexuals, regime opponents, and others deemed undesirable by the regime were also sent to labor or concentration camps. Also stirring the human conscience were reports of atrocities in Asia and the Pacific, particularly those conducted by the Japanese military against Chinese and other Asian peoples. Moreover, all of these losses were in addition to the tens of millions killed in the war itself. Reflection on these horrific human losses led to calls for action to preclude any such occurrence from ever happening again.

One immediate response was to hold perpetrators accountable in the Nuremberg and Tokyo war crimes trials held in 1945 and 1946. In addition to crimes against the laws of war, two other categories were delineated in 1945 by the United States, the United Kingdom, France, and the Soviet Union: crimes against the peace (as in planning and waging a war of aggression) and crimes against humanity (such inhumane acts against civilian populations as murder, extermination, enslavement, and deportation). Though criticized by some as merely a case of the victorious holding the vanquished accountable, the trials did set an important precedent by holding individuals internationally accountable for criminal acts.

The trials were followed in 1948 by two important agreements: (1) a U.N. Genocide Convention that defined this crime against the law of nations as being one committed "with intent to destroy in whole or in part, a national, ethnic, racial or religious group, as such" and (2) a U.N. General Assembly Universal Declaration of Human Rights, discussed in greater detail in Chapter 15. These initiatives in effect set a human rights train in motion leading over several decades to international agreement in the U.N. General Assembly on a number of important treaties: an International Convention on the Elimination of All Forms of Racial Discrimination (1965); a Covenant on Civil and Political Rights (1966); a Covenant on Economic, Social, and Cultural Rights (1966); an International Convention on the Suppression and the

HUMANE GOVERNANCE AND THE WORLD ORDER MODELS PROJECT (WOMP)

Applying Theory

Princeton Professor Richard Falk and Saul Mendlovitz have codirected the World Order Models Project (WOMP), which seeks a world characterized by "humane governance." Quite apart from whether or not the twenty-first century witnesses establishment of world government or other forms of international organization, the multinational participants in WOMP identify ten tasks that define its humane governance vision: (1) "taming" war as a first step, (2) eventually abolishing war, (3) making individuals in authority accountable internationally for war and human rights violations, (4) constructing an effective collective security system, (5) establishing globally the rule of law, (6) effecting revolutionary or other social change through nonviolence, (7) protecting human rights, (8) managing the global environment, (9) promoting a fully participative "positive citizenship" concept that combines global identity and commitment to both nonviolence and human rights, and (10) realizing in practice cosmopolitan democracy as the essential basis of global civil society. For further information, see www.princeton.edu, go to the Center for International and Regional Studies, and seek references to World Order Studies Program.

Punishment of the Crime of Apartheid (1973); a Convention on the Elimination of All Forms of Discrimination against Women (1979); a Convention against Torture and Other Cruel, Inhuman, or Degrading Treatment (1984); and a Convention on the Rights of the Child (1989). Regional human rights efforts were also central in the Act of Helsinki (1975) within what is now the Organization for Security and Cooperation in Europe.

Universal acceptance of these sweeping provisions as international law, of course, is a decades-long process requiring both signature and ratification of these treaties. What they do represent, however, is a growing consensus in global civil society on the universal norms that should guide human conduct and protect human rights no matter where one resides or travels.

The Environment   A growth area in the construction of international law for global civil society is the physical environment within which human beings, plants, and animals live. Pollution and other forms of environmental degradation as well as depletion of nonrenewable resources are global concerns on a planet of more than six billion people, many of whom suffer from poverty, malnutrition, and little or no access to adequate health care. At the same time, populations continue to grow, and demands for better levels of living continue to rise. Pressures on the environment are enormous as we try to sustain the economic development that is so necessary for improving the welfare of human beings and other forms of life on Earth.

Notwithstanding the high aspirations of environmental advocates, efforts to construct international law on such matters have been extremely difficult. For one thing, asymmetric or uneven development and distribution of wealth and income around the world create diverse interests and purposes. Poorer countries understandably want to be able to pursue their economic development plans with as few environmental obstacles as possible. For their part, richer countries already consume a disproportionate share of resources, the high levels of production they sustain contributing substantially to resource depletion and environmental degradation.

Not only are interests divergent, but scientific efforts to find remedies or viable approaches to reducing environmental degradation have been clouded by uncertainties as to both cause and effect. Nevertheless, relatively modest agreements have been reached on such matters as ozone-layer depletion and global warming or climate change. For example, understanding that such chlorofluorocarbon (CFC) uses as freon in refrigerators and aerosol propellants in spray cans are causes of ozone-layer depletion, negotiators finally reached an initial agreement in 1987 in the Montreal Protocol to put limits on (in an effort to phase out) CFC emissions. The parties have continued to address the matter, amending the protocol in 1990, 1992, 1995, and 1997.

A growing scientific consensus also holds that a principal cause of global warming is continued emissions of carbon dioxide and other greenhouse gases produced in particular by industrial and other burning of fossil fuels (coal, petroleum products, and natural gas). These greenhouse gases work in effect as an atmospheric blanket that retains heat from the sun's rays. Signatories of the Kyoto Protocol (1997) pledged to reduce their production of such gases by the year 2012 by 5.2 percent compared to 1990 emissions levels. The Kyoto Protocol is the product of a continuing process of negotiations within the U.N. Framework Convention on Climate Change (1992). To date, the United States is among the few countries that have chosen not to be bound by these restrictions on the use of fossil fuels.

Conclusion

In this chapter, we have taken a broad view over more than half a millennium at the emergence and development of global civil society. Our conceptual lens has been from the liberal or pluralist and constructivist perspectives as opposed to the realist view. Similarly, many in the English School address the emergence and development of a global civil *society*. Indeed, technological advances have facilitated bringing diverse peoples around the globe into ever-greater and more frequent contact in economic or commercial, cultural, and social matters. As these peoples increasingly interact with each other on diverse issues, we can identify the gradual development over time of some common norms or understandings. Notwithstanding diverse cultural understandings and views as we compare and contrast different societies and identities within and across state boundaries throughout the world, consensus on at least some common values or preferences has emerged over time. This constitutes a culture within a global civil society that serves as a basis for constructing and maintaining international law and international organizations. The rule of law in a global civil society focuses not just on the more traditional, state-centric sectors—security, diplomacy, war and peace, and economic or commercial matters—but also on newer "growth areas" such as human rights, the environment, and individual standing and accountability before such bodies as the International Criminal Court (ICC). Globalization also has its downside: the globalization of terrorism and crime, environmental degradation, labor exploitation, and the like. The idea of global civil society has a long way to go before matching what has been achieved within the domestic civil societies of most states, but it is worth taking stock nevertheless of what has been done since World War II as work on this project continues well into the twenty-first century.

Afterword

Freedom of the Seas
Hugo Grotius

In this brief passage from his book The Law of War and Peace *(1608), Grotius (often referred to as the "father" of international law) observes how the growth of trade and other forms of commerce—a very early phase of what we now call globalization. Because Grotius sees trade and commerce as essential to life, he argues that the law must allow such activities not only within a particular country, but also beyond its borders. International trade should be free of restraints much as it also is supposed to be within a state and its society. Importantly, we see a glimmer in Grotius of what present-day members of the English School characterize as the "society" one finds beyond the boundary of a state: "If it be thought that the small society which we call a state cannot exist without the application of these principles (and certainly it cannot), why will not those same principles be necessary to uphold the social structure of the whole human race and to maintain the harmony thereof?" He mentions in a quote from the Roman poet Virgil "common water" and "common air"—what some present-day writers refer to as the international or global "commons." This passage from Grotius is taken from a 1916 translation by Ralph Van Deman Magoffin from the original Latin (New York: Oxford University Press, 1916). Italics have been added to the text for emphasis.*

To the Rulers and to the Free and Independent Nations of Christendom

Now, as there are some things which every man enjoys in common with all other men, and as there are other things which are distinctly his and belong to no one else, just so has nature willed that some of the things which she has created for the use of mankind remain common to all, and that others through the industry and labor of each man become his own. Laws moreover were given to cover both cases so that all men might use common property without prejudice to any one else, and in respect to other things so that each man being content with what he himself owns might refrain from laying his hands on the property of others. . . .

There is not one of you who does not openly proclaim that every man is entitled to manage and dispose of his own property; there is not one of you who does not insist that all citizens have equal and indiscriminate right to use rivers and public places; *not one of you who does not defend with all his might the freedom of travel and of trade.*

If it be thought that the small society which we call a state cannot exist without the application of these principles (and certainly it cannot), why will not those same principles be necessary to uphold the social structure of the whole human race and to maintain the harmony thereof? If any one rebels against these principles of law and order you are justly indignant, and you even decree punishments in proportion to the magnitude of the offense, for no other reason than that a government cannot be tranquil where trespasses of that sort are allowed. If king act unjustly and violently against king, and nation against nation, such action involves a disturbance of the peace of that universal state, and constitutes a trespass against the supreme Ruler, does it not? . . .

The law by which our case must be decided is not difficult to find, seeing that it *is the same among all nations;* and it is easy to understand, seeing that it is innate in every individual and implanted in his mind. Moreover the law to which we appeal is one such as no king ought to deny to his subjects, and one no Christian ought to refuse to a non-Christian. For *it is a law derived from nature,* the common mother of us all, whose bounty falls on all, and whose sway extends over those who rule nations, and which is held most sacred by those who are most scrupulously just. . . .

My intention is to demonstrate briefly and clearly that the Dutch—that is to say, the subjects of the United Netherlands—*have the right to sail* to the East Indies, as they are now doing, *and to engage in trade* with the people there. I shall base my argument on *the following most specific and unimpeachable axiom of the Law of Nations,* called a primary rule or first principle, the spirit of which is self-evident and immutable, to wit: *Every nation is free to travel to every other nation, and to trade with it.*

God Himself says this speaking through the voice of nature; and inasmuch as it is not His will to have Nature supply every place with all the necessaries of life, He ordains that some nations excel in one art and others in another. Why is this His will, except it be that He wished human friendships to be engendered by mutual needs and resources, lest individuals deeming themselves entirely sufficient unto themselves should for that very reason be rendered unsociable? . . .

Do not the ocean, navigable in every direction with which God has encompassed all the earth, and the regular and the occasional winds which blow now from one quarter and now from another, offer sufficient proof *that Nature has given to all peoples a right of access to all other peoples?* Seneca thinks this is *Nature's* greatest service, that by the wind she united the widely scattered peoples, and yet *did so distribute all her products over the earth that commercial intercourse was a necessity to mankind. Therefore this right belongs equally to all nations.* Indeed the most famous jurists extend its application so far as to deny that any state or any ruler can debar foreigners from having access to their subjects and trading with them. Hence is derived that law of hospitality which is of the highest sanctity; hence the complaint of the poet Virgil:

> *"What men, what monsters, what inhuman race,*
> *What laws, what barbarous customs of the place,*
> *Shut up a desert shore to drowning men,*
> *And drive us to the cruel seas again."*

And:

> *"To beg what you without your want may spare—*
> *The common water, and the common air."*

We know that certain wars have arisen over this very matter. . . . Victoria holds that the Spaniards could have shown just reasons for making war upon the Aztecs and the Indians in America, more plausible reasons certainly than were alleged, if they really were prevented from traveling or sojourning among those peoples, and were denied the right to share in those things which by the Law of Nations or by Custom are common to all, and finally if they were debarred from trade.

We read of a similar case in the history of Moses, which we find mentioned also in the writings of Augustine, where the Israelites justly smote with the edge of the sword the Amorites because they had denied the Israelites an innocent passage through their territory, a right which according to the Law of Human Society ought in all justice to have been allowed. . . . Again, as we read in Tacitus, the Germans accused the Romans of 'preventing all intercourse between them and of closing up to them the rivers and roads, and almost the very air of heaven'. When in days gone by the Christians made crusades against the Saracens, no other pretext was so welcome or so plausible as that they were denied by the infidels free access to the Holy Land. It follows therefore that the Portuguese, even if they had been sovereigns in those parts to which the Dutch make voyages, would nevertheless be doing them an injury if they should forbid them access to those places and from trading there.

Is it not then an incalculably greater injury for nations which desire reciprocal commercial relations to be debarred therefrom by the acts of those who are sovereigns neither of the nations interested, nor of the element over which their connecting high road runs? . . .

Key Terms

globalization   *p. 310*   multilateralism   *p. 316*

Other Concepts

international law   *p. 315*   international regime   *p. 317*   liquidity   *p. 320*
jus gentium   *p. 315*   constructivist   *p. 317*
natural law   *p. 315*   sovereignty   *p. 318*

Additional Readings

Thomas L. Friedman portrays globalization as "the integration of capital, technology, and information across national borders in a way that is creating a single global market and, to some degree, a global village." Central to his thesis is the dynamic "tension between the globalization system"—represented metaphorically by the Lexus (high-technology, capital-intensive manufacture of quality automobiles)—and "ancient forces of culture, geography, tradition, and community" symbolized by his reference to the olive tree. See Friedman's *The Lexus and the Olive Tree* (New York: Farrar, Strauss, and Giroux, 1999) and, more recently, his *The World Is Flat: A Brief History of the Twenty-First Century* (New York: Farrar, Straus and Giroux, 2005). Also supporting globalization is Jagdish Bhagwati, *In Defense of Globalization* (New York: Oxford University Press, 2004).

For a nuanced examination of globalization that cautions against simplistic generalizations, see Jan Aart Scholte's, *Globalization: A Critical Introduction* (New York: St. Martin's Press, 2000). An entertaining and enlightening read is John Micklethwait and Adrian Wooldridge's *A Future Perfect: The Challenge and Promise of Globalization* (New York: Random House, 2003). See also Douglass C. North, *Institutions, Institutional Change and Economic Performance* (Cambridge: Cambridge University Press, 1994) and his earlier works *The Rise of the Western World Performance* (Cambridge: Cambridge University Press, 1973) and *Structure and Change in Economic History* (New York: W.W. Norton, 1981).

Political-economic dimensions of globalization can be found in Barry Eichengreen's *Globalizing Capital* (Princeton, NJ: Princeton University Press, 1996); Mark R. Brawley, *Turning Points: Shaping the Evolution of the International Political Economy* (Ontario, Canada: Broadview Press,1998); Eric Helleiner, *States and the Reemergence of Global Finance* (Ithaca, NY: Cornell University Press, 1994); and Larry Diamond and Marc F. Plattner (eds.), *Capitalism, Socialism, and Democracy Revisited* (Baltimore: Johns Hopkins University Press,1993).

On development in an emergent global civil society of global norms, rules, and international law that it is hoped will constitute humane governance, see Richard Falk's *On Humane Governance: Toward a New Global Politics* (University Park: University of Pennsylvania Press, 1995). On rules that constitute regimes in global civil society, see Robert J. Beck, Anthony Clark Arend, and Robert D. Vanderlugt (eds.), *International Rules: Approaches from International Law and International Relations* (New York: Oxford University Press, 1996). On developments in international law covering war and peace, the global economy, human rights, the environment, and individual criminal or civil accountability before international tribunals, see the latest edition of D. J. Harris's *Cases and Materials on International Law* (London: Sweet and Maxwell, 1973, 1991).

On the downsides of globalization, see Donatella Della Porta and Sidney Tarrow's *Transnational Protest and Global Activism* (Lanham, MD: Rowman and Littlefield, 1995); Maude Barlow and Tony Clarke, *Global Showdown* (Toronto, Canada: Stoddart, 2001); Michael E. Brown *et al.* (eds.), *New Global Dangers: Changing Dimensions of International Security* (Cambridge, MA: MIT Press, 2004); Mark Rupert, *Ideologies of Globalization* (London, Routledge, 2000); and Michael Mandelbaum's *The Ideas that Conquered the World* (Cambridge, MA: Perseus, 2002). On the thesis that globalization amounts effectively to "Americanization"—an American worldwide empire, see Chalmers Johnson's *Blowback: The Costs and Consequences of American Empire,* 2nd ed. (New York: Henry Holt Metropolitan Owl Book, 2000, 2004) and his *The Sorrows of Empire: Militarism, Secrecy, and the End of the Republic* (New York: Metropolitan Books, 2004); Andrew J. Bacevich, *American Empire* (Cambridge, MA: Harvard University Press, 2002); Michael Hardt and Antonio Negri, *Empire* (Cambridge, MA: Harvard University Press, 2000); and D. Clayton Brown's *Globalization and America Since 1945* (Wilmington, DE: Scholarly Resources Books, 2003).

Chapter 10

> "A world-economy, capitalist in form, has been in existence in at least part of the globe since the sixteenth century. Today, the entire globe is operating within the framework of this singular social division of labor we are calling the capitalist world-economy."
>
> PROFESSOR IMMANUEL WALLERSTEIN

Global Economy: Politics and Capitalism

Good evening, ladies and gentlemen. Welcome to "Capital Recap"—your weekend business program on global commerce. Here's the latest from Wall Street and other capital markets. . . .

After an eighteen-month decline, the bears are in retreat as the bulls are finally taking center stage. Both the Dow and NASDAQ are up about 15 percent over the past two weeks, 10 percent this past week alone! The Fed's decision last week to cut interest rates by another quarter of a point, coupled with this week's news of increased earnings last quarter in blue-chip and technology stocks, boosted the rally already under way.

Even small-capitalization stocks are up, seen by many as good buys, given their reports of increased sales figures but still low price-earning ratios. Bonds are steady as mutual funds and other large institutional buyers so far have held them while moving their large cash reserves into equities.

It may still be too early to tell, but White House officials are saying the recession is over!

In any event, the dollar is up against the Euro, yen, and other major currencies on news that although the American economy is rebounding, the U.S. trade deficit has narrowed—exports gaining slightly with imports so far remaining down.

Checking with overseas capital markets, Hong Kong's Hang-Seng and, not to be outdone, both the German Dax and English FTSE indexes are also up, responding to strong macroeconomic indicators in East Asia and Europe and following the trend being set on Wall Street.

Now let's turn to our guests for their comments on these late-breaking developments. . . .

Once the domain of a few experts, the workings of the global, capitalist economy are now of interest to many who tune in to television and radio reports, read the financial press, and consult the Internet. We have witnessed in recent years an enormous expansion in the number and diversity of stakeholders in capital markets who consult brokers or engage in online trading of stocks and bonds, channel resources into mutual funds, and trade on commodity and currency markets as well. Not restricted to domestic firms, the capital they control travels the globe at lightning speed as they seek investment opportunities or recoil when they think their capital is in jeopardy.

There is no doubt that for most academics, pundits, and analysts of international relations and world politics, it is the expansion of the capitalist world economy that is the critical dynamic of the process known as globalization. Realists, pluralists or liberals, economic structuralists, social constructivists, and feminists may disagree as to the extent, pace of expansion, or even existence of a global civil society, but all agree on the historical importance and spread of global capitalism, which has done much to blur the distinction between international and domestic contexts. Profound disagreement exists, however, over the implications of the economic component of globalization and particularly who benefits or is hurt by it. In this and the subsequent two chapters we take a detailed look at the global political economy, which involves the production, distribution, and exchange of wealth. Not unlike politics, economics also involves answering the contentious questions, "Who gets what, when, how, and why?"

Global Political Economy

If war is too important to be left to the generals—as government leaders, diplomats, and many political scientists have believed—then economics may be too important to be left only to businesspersons or economists. Economic questions tend to become politicized rather quickly because the stakes are high, some questions seem to require some authoritative or governmental response, and competing parties do not see these issues the same way.

In a deeper sense, the economy cannot really be separated from politics. Even the *laissez-faire* (or *laisser faire,* in French meaning "to leave alone") stance, believing that governments should not intervene in the marketplace, leaving such affairs to private interests, is a political decision. The degree to which a more intrusive role for government is allowed or preferred—buying and selling in currency and other markets to affect exchange and interest rates or other prices, letting contracts to private-sector suppliers of goods and services, regulating commercial transactions, or in the extreme, actually directing output levels or production quotas and prices—is also subject to authoritative or political choice.

Many of those who have favored economic *laissez-faire* policies have presented economics as if it were entirely separate from politics. Although we place high value on economic theories that have contributed to explaining and predicting how markets, national economies, and global commerce function, we think a more accurate and comprehensive understanding is served by incorporating political variables into these presentations. We prefer the term ***political economy,*** which captures the very essence of what is at stake either domestically or globally—the intersection of politics (or authoritative choice) with economics, which is concerned with seemingly unlimited wants in a world marked by a relative scarcity of resources.

political economy
The intersection of politics (or authoritative choice) with economics, which is concerned with seemingly unlimited wants in a world of relative scarcity of resources.

Are Internationalization and Globalization the Same Thing?

The term **internationalization** refers to increasing trade, commerce, investment, and other interactions that occur primarily between or among states and their societies. When we use *internationalization*, we still tend to think in terms of national identities. We even identify corporations with operations in two or more countries as having a home base or headquarters in a particular country with ownership and managerial control typically held by nationals of that country. Thus, we usually refer to General Motors as an American multinational corporation (MNC) and Renault as a French MNC. Because their operations are by no means confined to their home territories, we see the growth of their multinational operations as evidence of increased internationalization.

By contrast, **globalization** transcends or goes beyond states and their respective corporations, taking a broad or global view of such matters. As firms begin to lose exclusive national identity, they perform as actors on a world or global stage. Indicative of increasing globalization are mergers of MNCs in one country with MNCs in another country as well as increasing diversity in ownership with shares of stock in a particular country owned by nationals from different countries. Aided by advances in telecommunications and transportation technologies, exchange and transfer of information anywhere in the world are instantaneous, and human beings are able to close geographic gaps that historically have divided and kept them apart. For example, as globalization increases, measurements of economic or commercial activities purely on a state-by-state basis begin to lose their significance as we come to think in world (or at least regional) terms. Thus we become more interested in trade and other forms of commerce within and between North America, the European Economic Area, or East Asia and the Pacific than we do about purely national economic data. Of course, as discussed in Chapter 9, globalization is not just a matter of economics but also deals with international security, human rights, the environment, and many other pressing topics on the global agenda.

Political economists, then, begin either as *economists,* who understand the political nature and implications of economic issues for politics, or as *political scientists,* who understand the importance of economics in political questions and reject the notion that economic issues are in any way unimportant or inconsequential and thus "low" politics. Because of their salience, pluralists or liberals and or economic structuralists in particular believe economic issues can occupy extremely high places in national and global international political agendas. As global economic interdependence grows and globalization trends persist, this will continue to be the case.

The Emergence and Development of Capitalism as a Worldwide Form of Political Economy

As noted in Chapter 2, *capitalism* as a **mode of production** or form of political economy gradually emerged in Europe during the late Middle Ages into the Renaissance, eventually displacing **feudalism.** Feudal political economy concentrated agricultural and other production in small communities, carried out by peasants under the protection of lords or aristocratic landholders on whose estates they worked. These communities were largely self-sufficient economically. Some provided the protection of castle

capitalism
An economic system, form of political economy, or mode of production that emphasizes money, market-oriented trade, capital investment for further production, and a set of values or culture legitimating investment and market-oriented behaviors.

walls against marauding bands or other intruders. Relatively little need for trade existed in a feudal society, other than for a few spices, silks, or other commodities not produced locally. Feudal markets for exchange of goods and services therefore were marginal or relatively unimportant compared to those that arose under capitalism.

The focus of daily life under feudalism was on the local community as headed by local barons, dukes, and kings. Standing as exceptions to this inward focus were once-in-a-lifetime pilgrimages to holy shrines or intermittent participation in the Crusades. The Crusades to the Middle East during the late Middle Ages were Christian Europe's quest to wrest control of the Holy Land from Islam. No doubt these experiences fostered some continuing interest in commerce with the outside world, but even more significant was the change in social structure and economic activity marked by the emergence of towns.

Markets emerged as these towns sprang up near the castles or estates that had been the centers of feudal life. Townsmen (or *burghers*, as they were called in the German-speaking states) traded the goods and services that they and others produced. They would become the core of a new middle class between the land-owning aristocracy and the peasantry or farm people tied to landed estates in the countryside. This new middle class of townsmen or burghers was labeled in French the *bourgeoisie* or more commonly in English the "capitalist class."

Trade among towns and cities increased substantially as markets became more important throughout Europe. Examples of early urban centers of market activity, including banking, are such fourteenth- and fifteenth-century trading cities as Venice and Bruges, in modern-day Italy and Belgium respectively. Printing presses and other tools and hand-operated machines were the new technologies that contributed to production in towns and urban settings, even as agricultural production remained centered in the great landed estates of the passing feudal era. We can see evidence of these feudal and early capitalist political economies in the castles and usually well-preserved or restored old centers of late medieval and Renaissance towns and cities throughout modern-day Europe.

Identifying the Attributes of Capitalist Political Economy

Attributes of emerging capitalism included **markets** and **money,** but these were not new. Although less important in feudalism, markets and money were the bedrock of ancient forms of political economy to be found, for example, among Phoenicians, Egyptians, Greeks, Persians, and Romans. Money provided a standard of value for buying and selling in markets and a store of value that could be held until needed for spending at a later time. These functions were essential to commerce in ancient market economies that relied so heavily for production on human (including slave) labor. Even the technologies for harnessing animal labor, especially for agricultural production, were late in coming and would not be fully developed until the feudal period of the Middle Ages.

Investment as an Attribute of Capitalism   What distinguishes capitalism from feudal and ancient political economies is its greater need for **investment.** Advancing technologies that produced the machinery and tools of early preindustrial capitalism would be followed by a late eighteenth- and nineteenth-century industrial revolution that began in the United Kingdom. This soon spread to France, the German states, and elsewhere on the European continent and the Americas, particularly the United States. The tools and hand-operated machines of early capitalism, the heavy machinery of industrial capitalism, and the high-technology machinery and computers or artificial intelligence of advanced or postindustrial capitalism all require that substantial amounts of savings be put aside for investment in these tools and machinery that are essential to production.

If we consumed all that we were capable of producing, there would be nothing left for investment or for the purchase of new plants and machinery. An airline that as a service industry provides transportation of passengers or cargo needs to invest in new airplanes and airport facilities, not only to expand its present business but also to maintain and eventually replace aging equipment or facilities. An industry producing goods (for example, automobiles, personal computers, and other manufactured and agricultural products) faces the same need to invest in new factories or plants and machinery. So it was in preindustrial capitalism, when some time, effort, and resources or savings had to be put into crafting, purchasing, and maintaining the tools and hand-operated machines used in the production of goods and services.

The plants, tools, and machinery that are essential to the production of other goods and services are referred to by economists as **capital goods.** Capital goods have no value to us in themselves other than their contribution to the production of other goods or services we do value or want to produce for consumption. A lathe used in cutting or shaping metal or wood in manufacturing, an airplane used to carry passengers or move cargo, a printing press used by a publisher of books or newspapers, and a computer and software used by a writer for word processing are examples of capital goods. We do not consume everything we produce but put our profits from sales, salary, or other income from earlier production into new investments in capital goods for further or future production.

Two important components of **gross national product (GNP)**—a measure of the aggregate size of a national economy—are annual consumption and investment. Measured in dollars or other currency, how much has been spent on goods and services and how much has been saved or set aside for capital investment—the purchase or acquisition of capital goods for future production? Capitalist economies that do not invest sufficiently tend to decline or experience a drop in production, consumption, and standard or level of living. To maintain or expand present levels of production, consumption, and living standards, capitalist economies require sufficient **capital formation**—new and continuing investment in capital goods for production and consumption. The box on page 334 examines gross national product (GNP) and **gross domestic product (GDP)** in greater detail.

A Commercial Culture as Attribute of Capitalism   The late nineteenth- and early twentieth-century German political sociologist Max Weber observed how the emergence of capitalism was also accompanied by a new set of social values supportive not only of market-oriented trade and monetary activities but also of the savings and investment function so essential to capitalism. Given this emphasis on the development of new values and the power of ideas, constructivists can lay claim to Weber as an intellectual precursor. Church teachings in the Middle Ages had held that the righteous did not commit the sin of usury, which was defined as earning interest from loans or by making profit on sales.

Religion is so deeply embedded in a society's culture or set of values that it is often difficult to distinguish between values that have a religious grounding and those that do not. The antimarket religious orientation of Church authorities was perfectly consistent with the feudal political economy, which did not rely heavily on markets anyway. Weber observed how the rise of capitalism was encouraged by a revolution in religious thought on economic matters. This was a product of the Reformation that he referred to as a "Protestant ethic" or "spirit of capitalism."[1]

---

[1]For a readily available edition in English, see Max Weber, *The Protestant Ethic and the Spirit of Capitalism* (New York: Charles Scribner's Sons, 1958, 1976).

Max Weber.

The Wealth of a Nation and Its Productive Capacity: Gross National Product and Gross Domestic Product

Adam Smith observed that the wealth of a nation was not to be found in its stock of gold and other treasure; it was to be found instead in the productive capacity of its economy—that is, the total of goods and services that could be produced. Gross national product (GNP) is now a commonly used annual measure that captures the essence of Smith's idea.

GNP is the total or aggregate of goods and services produced in a state in a given year. We can compute it by summing the dollar amounts of the following:

1. Domestic consumption of goods and services *(C)*
2. Investment *(I)* of surplus or savings—additions to the capital stock used for future production
3. Government spending to purchase goods and services *(G)*
4. Exports of domestic production *(X)* minus imports of foreign production *(M)*—a subtraction that also takes account of the contribution of foreign-produced goods and services to domestic production and consumption levels:

Demonstrated national productive capacity		Consumption		Investment		Government Spending		Trade Balance
GNP	=	C	+	I	+	G	+	$(X-M)$

Gross domestic product (GDP) is a more refined measure that subtracts national earnings from foreign investments in other countries. After all, domestically owned capital invested abroad contributes to foreign, not domestic production. GNP counts returns from such investments; GDP does not:

$$GDP = GNP - \text{returns on foreign investments}$$

In addition to statistical problems in counting accurately the sum of commercial transactions, neither GNP nor GDP accurately captures production of goods and services not traded in the marketplace. Because goods and services produced and consumed in a household cannot be measured directly, GNP and GDP are criticized for understating aggregate or total domestic production. This is particularly acute in Third World economies that typically have a higher proportion of household production and consumption.

Consistent with Smith's focus on the wealth of nations, GNP and GDP are aggregate measures at the state and society level. In an interdependent and interconnected global economy, some critics claim that measures of demonstrated productive capacity at regional, global, or other levels of aggregation may well be more appropriate, particularly since globalization trends that accelerated in the twentieth century have continued into the twenty-first century.

The importance of the individual in Lutheran thought, for example, was a liberal idea consistent with the new capitalist political economy that would come to rely so heavily on individual initiative in the marketplace. Calvinist or puritanical ideas held that hard work was good and that one ought to lead a productive but prudent life. Further, it was held that one ought not to consume all that one produced but should invest the savings of money originally earned from hard work (thus putting one's money to work as well). Earning a fair profit or a fair return on loans and investments was now legitimate in the new religious teachings.

Weber observed that eventually the religious underpinnings of these new market-oriented values in an emerging capitalist culture would be forgotten. The important point for us, however, is to recognize that as a form of political economy, capitalism has its own "culture" or set of supporting values, just as European feudalism had. Capitalism legitimizes profit-making enterprises and allows for interest on loans and returns on investment that are essential to its functioning. Indeed, worldly success was believed by some Protestant sects to be a mark of one's membership in the "elect," who were predestined to enjoy eternity in heaven. Poverty was not seen as a sign of God's favor.

Setting religious underpinnings aside, the new commercial ethic oriented members of society in a deeper sense to produce above consumption needs and to accumulate savings, thus increasing wealth available for investment. In the secular European and American commercial cultures, the religious sources of these ideas may have been forgotten, but the ideas spawned by these religious understandings decidedly were not lost. Indeed, these ideas related to work, savings, and investment were retained in a commercial culture accepted by people of diverse religious identity as well as by those claiming no religious preference.

After all, investment is the "fuel" that drives the capitalist "engine." If capitalist economies are to be maintained and grow, there is a continuing and seemingly never-ending need for more investment in capital goods. Indeed, one of Weber's principal insights was to identify capitalism's dependency on a commercial culture that treats market-oriented activities as legitimate, encourages hard work, and promotes a propensity to save and invest. This was as true in preindustrial capitalism as it is in the more advanced forms of industrial and postindustrial capitalism that continue to require enormous amounts of investment in capital goods.

The Passing of Feudalism and the New Politics of Capitalism, Mercantilism, and Liberalism

As capitalism gradually displaced feudalism, states were also emerging as a new political unit. Notwithstanding divisions leading to an eleventh-century schism between the Christian Church in the West at Rome and the Orthodox Christian Church in the East at Constantinople (Istanbul in present-day Turkey), the Western European feudal idea of unity in Christendom survived throughout the Middle Ages. The fifteenth- and sixteenth-century Protestant Reformation, however, split Christendom in Western Europe along the new state lines as warring princes chose either Protestant or Catholic professions of faith.

Notions of feudal unity in Christendom gave way eventually to a more fragmented order of sovereign states that declared themselves independent of any claims to superiority by either religious or temporal authorities, pope or emperor. The old idea that emperor and pope stood at the top of an earthly hierarchy composed of many small feudal communities, dukedoms, kingdoms, and other principalities no longer conformed to the new reality. The 1648 Peace of Westphalia that ended the Thirty Years' War concluded that the religion of the inhabitants would be determined by the prince or temporal authority in any given realm—in Latin, *cujus regio ejus religio* (the religion of the inhabitants of the realm as being determined by the ruler) captured this new idea. The authority of princes in these new political units called states was indeed supreme if even religious matters could be determined by them.

States thus displaced the landed estate or feudal community in the new European political and economic order that emerged. The monarchs in these new states gradually accumulated more and more central authority within their realms. As a matter of state policy, kings and queens favored international trade that enriched them and their governments. If one visits the churches and other well-preserved buildings in Toledo, the imperial capital of Spain, one can see in the altars and other artworks vast amounts of gold, precious gems, and other treasure acquired primarily by sixteenth-, seventeenth-, and eighteenth-century Spanish monarchs as they pursued the mercantile policies of early capitalism.

In addition to acquiring new gold from mines in New World colonies, mercantilists acquired gold from running a favorable balance of trade and stored it in national treasuries. Hoards of gold, silver, and other precious metals accrued in national treasuries from the profits or royalties from commercial transactions conducted by state-chartered corporations and other traders. Sometimes such treasures were retained by these national firms as a store of value to finance future purchases required in their business ventures. The ideal in **mercantilism** was for traders to sell more than they bought, requiring others to pay for their purchases with gold or silver, which then could be added to the national treasure.

The Scottish political economist Adam Smith took issue with the mercantilist view in *The Wealth of Nations,* which he published in 1776. Smith argued that national wealth in capitalism was not to be found in the treasure that accrued in treasury vaults; rather, wealth was to be found in the productive capacity of economies, which was increasingly to be found in their capital stock along with labor and other resources that are the **factors of production.** His was a **liberal** view of capitalist political economy, emphasizing **free markets** in which governments took a hands-off or *laissez-faire* approach, allowing nongovernmental, private firms and individuals to buy and sell in the marketplace without interference by state authorities.

After all, state authority or government in European feudalism had been in the hands of land-owning aristocrats. In many instances, state authority had been used against the bourgeois or commercial interests of the new middle class. Consistent with the political liberalism of John Locke and other writers discussed in Chapter 15 on human rights, Smith's economic liberalism supported the interests of the new middle class by holding that free-market enterprises were far more likely to increase national wealth.

In serving their own interests, capitalists would have to compete with other self-oriented buyers and sellers in the marketplace. Competition among free traders would force firms and individuals wanting to stay in business to be more efficient without government interference, thus supplying the market with quality goods and services at lower, more competitive prices. Instead of government direction, an invisible hand of market competition would force these efficiencies, resulting in greater productivity and thus wealth for the nation as a whole than could be acquired under mercantilism.

Following Smith's lead as a classical political economist in the economic liberal tradition, the early nineteenth-century English writer David Ricardo even more explicitly favored the new commercial middle-class or bourgeois interests against those of the aristocracy. He complained that land-owning aristocrats contributed virtually nothing to capitalist production in exchange for the rents they collected as mere owners of land used by others for productive enterprise. As such, aristocrats were a drag on capitalist economies.

Moreover, **protectionism** (typically in the form of tariffs or taxes on imports) favored these agricultural interests and denied firms and individuals the freedom to buy and sell at market prices without restriction across national frontiers. Tariffs and other barriers to **free trade** both protected and encouraged inefficient producers. Pushing Adam Smith's economic liberalism beyond the borders of the state, Ricardo argued that international trade free of such government interference would have the same positive effect on productivity as free trade in domestic political economies.

World Actors

Adam Smith.

Of the classical economists, two of the best known are Adam Smith (1723–1790) and David Ricardo (1772–1823). In his monumental work An Inquiry into the Nature and Causes of the Wealth of Nations (1776), Smith rejected mercantilism in favor of productive capacity as the proper measure of a nation's wealth. Smith understood the importance of producing tools, machinery, or other capital goods but still relied on a labor theory of value—that is, the value of what is produced is the result of labor put into the production process. Indeed, Smith argued that efficiency can be enhanced significantly with specialization and a **division of labor.**

Ricardo extended Smith's analysis, criticizing aristocratic or other landholding interests for putting an unwarranted cost on production and for restraining international trade through tariffs and other protectionist measures that favored their agricultural interests. Arguing that free trade allowed for national specialization in accordance with **comparative advantage,** Ricardo saw that great gains in overall or aggregate production would come from allowing international markets to operate without government interference favoring particular class interests. Of course, Ricardo's free-trade prescription favored the newly emergent capital-owning class, which put its capital to work in manufacturing and would benefit from free markets in which to sell its products. Ricardo's major work was Principles of Political Economy and Taxation (1817). A free-trade advocate, Ricardo also advanced his cause as a member of the British parliament.

Consistent with both Smith's and Ricardo's analyses, Karl Marx (1818–1883) accepted the same labor theory of value but focused on what he understood to be the exploitative character of class relations. Smith had referred to classes as various "orders" in society, understanding as did Marx later that classes had played a historic role in the political economy. Marx expanded Ricardo's criticisms of the aristocracy to include capitalist and other classes that have been dominant over the course of human history. Marx also understood capitalism as a worldwide form of economy with commercial implications on a global scale.

CLASSICAL POLITICAL ECONOMY

David Ricardo.

Karl Marx.

What Is Capital and How Is It Formed?

The term *capital* refers to one of three factors of production, the other two being labor and land (or natural resources). Production of any good or service involves combining various amounts of these three factors. Some products are referred to, for example, as labor-intensive or capital-intensive, depending on the relative proportion of labor or capital used in production of a particular good or service. Thus making handwoven carpets from yarns (from the "land" as in wool, cotton, or other resources drawn in turn from agricultural production) is highly labor-intensive, using relatively little capital. By contrast, because manufacturing carpets in factories requires purchasing and putting specialized machinery to work using the same yarns, we say it is far more capital-intensive than making handwoven carpets.

Capital is often in the form of equipment or capital goods essential to the production of other goods and services. We also refer to *finance capital* that can be used for investments in factories, machinery and other production equipment, computers, research and development of products, and delivery systems—roads and trucks, railroads and trains, airports and airplanes, seaports and ships, all of which require large capital expenditures. Industrial and advanced-technology economies that depend on so much machinery and other production equipment and delivery systems require vast amounts of capital to sustain production and foster economic growth.

If we spend or consume everything (or even more than) we produce, there will be nothing left over for capital investment. Savings are generated when we consume less than we produce. For example, if you earn a wage or receive profits from a business and spend it all not just on the essentials (food, clothing, and shelter) but also on luxury or nonessential goods and services, then nothing will be left for savings and investment. If you don't spend everything you earn and set aside some of these earnings for savings, then these savings are available as finance capital for investment in capital goods necessary for future production.

Similarly we save (set aside for future use) some machines or equipment used as capital goods, which normally serve no other purpose or practical value than to produce other goods or services. A lathe is an example of a capital good; it is a machine used in manufacturing other products—cutting or shaping materials such as wood, metal, or plastic by holding and turning or rotating them against a cutting tool. In addition to shaping, lathes can be used to make threads, drill holes, and grind or polish materials.

On the other hand, other types of equipment or machinery may have purposes other than just contributing to further production of goods or services. An automobile used for pleasure, for example, is not a capital good, as pleasure driving is a consumption, not an investment activity. Miles driven for sightseeing depreciate the car's value through use (it wears out over time) without any contribution to producing other goods or services; however, the same car put to use for production of services—let's say by converting it into a revenue-earning taxi for transporting passengers—is now a capital good because its use is no longer for pleasure or consumption; it is now an essential part of a business that provides taxi services. The taxi used to transport passengers will need capital expenditures for maintenance and repair, but a portion of the revenues its use brings in can be allocated to pay these costs as well as fund purchase of a replacement taxi when it wears out or no longer can be of service for business use.

In short, both capital goods and finance capital are necessary not only for manufacturing various products but also for providing services as in taxi, car-rental, airline, banking, telecommunications, or other service industries. Capital is "formed" typically from business or private earnings set aside as savings. Capital formation becomes a problem when national savings rates are too low (typically when consumption is very high). In such circumstances, attracting the savings of people and firms in other countries in the form of investment or loans may be necessary if current production levels are to be sustained, not to mention fostering economic growth in production capacity.

Direct investment occurs when, for example, capital is used to purchase or pay for factories, equipment, or other capital goods essential for production. *Portfolio investment* happens when capital takes the form of investment in such securities as stocks, bonds, or bank assets, which can then be used by corporations to fund their capital expenditures in existing or new plant and machinery. Governments, of course, also raise capital by taxing earnings or sales or borrowing (as in getting loans from banks or issuing bonds in capital markets). This capital may be subsequently allocated for investment expenditures on such projects as research and development of new production-related technologies in manufacturing, agriculture, health care, or other sectors, and on construction of roads and bridges, schools, hospitals, and the like.

Case & Point

Whether a withering critic or a strident supporter of capitalism, everyone can agree on its historical impact as a mode of production on societies—it has proven to be an incredibly destructive and at the same time creative process. The eighteenth-century enclosure movements in England, for example, witnessed the concentration of land in fewer and fewer hands as peasant tenant farmers were driven off in order for the lords of the manor to use the land in more profitable pursuits. The result was the destruction of English peasant society as embodied in the traditional village. Nineteenth-century industrialization brought the unemployed and dispossessed to the cities, where working conditions generated the image of Satanic mills spewing forth flames. For those too poor or ill to work, poorhouses offered small comfort. Perhaps the best description of the impact of industrialization and the resultant impact on the English countryside and cityscape has come from the novels of Charles Dickens. But as noted by the Marxist scholar E. J. Hobsbawn in his *The Age of Revolution, 1789–1848*, the French Revolution and the Industrial Revolution ushered in the modern age. Much was destroyed, but there were also advances in science, philosophy, religion, and art. Similarly, Karl Polanyi captures the impact of political, economic, and social change in the nineteenth century by the very title of his magisterial work, *The Great Transformation*.

Point: To assess the impact of capitalism on a society or the world in general requires a balanced assessment that avoids simplistic generalizations.

CAPITALISM'S IMPACT

Nineteenth-century mill town in Lancashire, England.

Aggregate productivity would increase, Ricardo maintained, as more efficient producers specialized in producing those goods and services in which they had a comparative advantage. Ricardian theory held that free trade would favor the most efficient producers, regardless of their country of origin, who in competitive markets were in a position to offer the lowest prices for any given good or service. The resulting specialization by this market-driven efficiency criterion would amount to an international division of labor in the overall production of goods and services for the market.

In a classic example used by Ricardo, producers in England enjoyed a comparative advantage (or were more efficient) in cloth production and thus should specialize in it. Producers in Portugal, however, retained a comparative advantage in the production of wine and thus should specialize in that. More cloth and wine could be produced through such specialization and labor than if both were produced in each country.

Comparative advantage was an idea that also served the interests of the commercial middle class in the United Kingdom which, as the first country to undergo an industrial revolution, had already acquired a comparative advantage in textiles and other manufactures. Free-trade theory also undermined the interests of British aristocrats who, with the repeal of the Corn Laws in 1846, no longer could rely on the protection of their less-efficient agricultural sector. Over time, peasants left the countryside for urban employment in factories owned by the new capitalists.

The Progressive Globalization of Capitalism

The seventeenth and eighteenth centuries marked the first wave of imperial expansion from Europe, focusing on acquiring colonies in the New World of the Americas. The British, French, Dutch, Spanish, and Portuguese were the key players. Mercantilist policies dominated in this early stage of capitalism as colonial powers sought trade and commercial advantages over each other.

In the process of acquiring and maintaining these colonies, settlers and successive generations brought with them European political and economic ideas that took root in the new world. As colonies gained their independence in the late eighteenth and early nineteenth centuries, new states formed with claims to sovereignty following the European or "Westphalia" model. Along with the state, the elements of market capitalism were also transferred. The political economy of states and societies in the Western Hemisphere resembled those of the European countries that had organized and cultivated them.

The second wave of nineteenth- and twentieth-century **imperialism** effectively spread capitalist political economy throughout the globe to distant parts of Africa, Asia, and the Pacific. The same European powers, along with Germany, Belgium, and the United States, were the players in the second wave of imperial expansion that established new colonies or other territorial holdings. Corporations and banks from imperial countries were transnational actors, which operated globally just as state-chartered firms had done in the first wave of imperial expansion.

One does not have to be an economic structuralist to recognize the fact that motivated primarily by mercantilist policies, colonial empires were constructed to serve the commercial advantage of the colonial power. At the same time, European and American administrations and firms transferred their ideas about capitalist political economy throughout the world. As colonies in Africa, Asia, and the Pacific became independent, particularly in the first quarter-century after World War II, their capitalist political economies were often linked by **neocolonial** ties with the former colonial power.

Nevertheless, the effect of the second wave of imperialism and the decolonization that followed was to complete the globalization of capitalism and capitalist political economy. **Multinational corporations,** or **MNCs** (firms that own and manage economic units in two or more countries), and multinational banks headquartered in the world's largest economies operated alongside firms in the markets of these new states.

Even communist or socialist states in Central and Eastern Europe, China, Cuba, and elsewhere that experienced revolutions led by those seeking to overthrow capitalism were forced to adopt what some political economists refer to as a particular (sometimes brutal) form of state capitalism.[2] Instead of privately owned capital being at the core of the domestic political economies of these countries, capital was expropriated in the name of the "people" from private owners. It was concentrated in the hands of state authorities in centrally planned or controlled economies following a Leninist political design of "democratic centralism" within a ruling-party apparatus.

Most people accepted the claims by these regimes that they had rejected capitalism. Socialist regimes established in these countries led to their categorization as a Second World apart from advanced capitalist, industrial, and postindustrial political economies in the First World and those of less-developed, predominantly capitalist countries in the Third World. The separate categorization of Marxist-Leninist or socialist regimes as noncapitalist or anticapitalist, authoritarian or command economies is still the consensus view.

By contrast, political economists we have termed economic structuralists have disagreed, noting that in fact these Leninist regimes had succeeded only in overthrowing free-market capitalism in which capital was privately owned, the most common form of capitalism. Economic structuralists who adopt this view note that the centrally planned and directed political economies of these Leninist regimes still remained part of a worldwide capitalist political economy and retained in their domestic political economies a capitalist reliance on markets, money, and investment subject to state direction or control with a supporting commercial culture expressed in a Marxist-Leninist, materialist ideology.

After the Bolshevik Revolution in Russia in 1917 and throughout the Cold War, political regimes in these countries claimed to have established socialism and to be on the way toward achieving the goals of communism—production from each member of society according to his or her ability and distribution to each according to need. As a practical matter, however, these Leninist political economies still depended on markets, money, and capital investment—all of which were tightly controlled by regime authorities who set production goals and prices. State capitalism is not free-market capitalism, but it bears the marks of capitalism all the same.

As with free-market capitalism, investment in capital goods is also a central function in state-capitalist economies. Unlike free-market political economies, however, state-capitalist economies reserve to central authorities key decisions on investment (as on most other matters of importance). For example, collectivization of agriculture in the Soviet Union in the 1930s during the Stalinist period—expropriating land and putting peasants on collective farms—was the model followed in Eastern Europe, China, and Cuba. Some political economists see this agricultural collectivization not just as a means of enhancing agricultural productivity but also as a way for state authorities to extract or collect the "surplus value" or profit produced by these peasants, reallocating much of it to investment in heavy industry, the military, or other economic sectors favored by regime authorities.

The end of the Cold War resulted in the abandonment of Leninist and state-capitalist forms of political economy by most of these states and societies. The logic of

---

[2]For an early representation of this idea, written in a different context or time frame of the 1930s and early 1940s, see Frederick Pollock, "State Capitalism: Its Possibilities and Limitations" in Stephen Eric Bronner and Douglas MacKay Kellner, eds., *Critical Theory and Society* (New York: Routledge, 1989), pp. 7–8 and 95–118. In state capitalism, Pollock sees the essential elements of capitalist investment and production in place even as state or party authorities constituting a new class of central planners take over capital investment, pricing, and distribution functions previously left to markets in what he calls private capitalism. Pollock does not claim credit for the idea but does provide a useful synthesis or model in which he specifies, following Max Weber, the ideal typical attributes of state capitalism.

Case & Point

GLOBALI-ZATION AND U.S. HIGH-TECH JOBS

- More than half of all Fortune 500 companies say they're outsourcing software development or expanding their own development centers outside the United States.
- Of more than 100 information technology (IT) executives who responded to a survey, 68 percent say their offshore contracts will increase.
- 10 percent of all information-technology jobs in American IT companies are moving offshore.
- By 2015 an estimated 3.3 million more American white-collar jobs will shift to low-income countries, mostly India.

Point: Despite a major focus on globalization's impact on the Third World, it also has a substantial impact on job prospects and the livelihood of many Americans workers.

Source: The Washington Post.

the world–capitalist system seems to be playing out. Experiments, some not always very successful, were undertaken with different forms of free-market capitalism. Some of these included a strong social-democratic component with some state ownership of industries, utilities, or other means of production. Others have had little or no government ownership and a much less generous provision for the kind of social security taken for granted in the more advanced Western welfare states. The underlying cultures in these different societies are decisive in determining the degree to which regimes in these states will privatize their economies and the emphasis they will place on achieving social-democratic or welfare-state goals.

The globalization of capitalism in the present-day world is one in which money, markets, and investment are central attributes. As Weber understood, an orientation to work, productivity, and a propensity to save and invest remain key cultural values essential to the effective functioning of capitalist political economies anywhere. At the same time, beneath the surface of global capitalism is a world of great diversity. Capitalist political economies do differ substantially from country to country. There are differences in commercial and political values that affect the way business is conducted and the political, social, and economic choices that are made.

For example, the United States probably has (by choice) the least-generous and Switzerland and Sweden, also by choice, have among the most-generous welfare states of any of the advanced capitalist political economies. On the issue of privatization versus socialization (or public ownership of the means of production), Switzerland is much closer to the United States, with most production capital in private hands. Sweden has widespread private ownership of both small and well-known, large firms such as Saab and Volvo, the latter now internationalized given its passenger-car merger with Ford. On the other hand, state subsidies of private industries and outright public ownership of other firms has been more prevalent in Sweden, as it is in other northern European countries with strong social-democratic expectations.

To illustrate how commercial culture and the structure of government-private sector relations can vary, we can compare the United States with Japan. As in the United

Pedestrians stroll in front of a large Wal-Mart store in Shenzhen, China.

States, most of the Japanese economy is in private hands, but the relation between Japanese firms and their government is close-knit, with direct coordination and state subsidies widely accepted as perfectly legitimate within the Japanese commercial culture. The Ministry of International Trade and Industry (MITI) has been widely studied for the role it has played in advancing the global competitiveness of Japanese industry.

Although there are U.S. government subsidies and government-industry partnerships for research and development as well as other contracts with private-sector firms, the underlying American commercial culture generally views government intervention in the market with skepticism. As a result, no U.S. equivalent institution to MITI for coordinating government-industry relations exists. Suggestions in the 1980s that the United States emulate or copy the Japanese (or, for that matter, French) government-industry, joint-planning approach to market competitiveness were strongly resisted by many in the United States. The economic distress of the Japanese economy in the 1990s only reinforced this view. Nevertheless, by contrast, almost all other advanced industrial countries have ministries or agencies concerned with advancing the global competitiveness of their national industries. Quite apart from balance-of-payments considerations, government involvement in these countries typically tries to optimize employment of the national labor force as well as assure sufficient returns to domestic owners of capital invested in these enterprises.

Although there are similarities, the ways in which multinational corporations and banks operate and interact on a global basis also reflect the diversity of the underlying commercial cultures they represent. Some will be more likely to form alliances or even **cartels** with other firms, much as they are accustomed to doing in their domestic markets. Other firms, reflecting fiercely competitive and free-market-oriented values in their domestic commercial cultures, are likely to act in the same way abroad.

On the other hand, there can also be convergence of multinational corporate orientations across cultures on such issues over time. Globalization has also meant an increasing concentration of capital as competition for market share has driven some firms to seek strategic alliances or mergers and acquisitions. For example, in reaching out to global markets, American multinationals like United Airlines have organized strategic alliances with other non–U.S. airlines—Air Canada, Air New Zealand, All Nippon Airways, Ansett Australia, Lufthansa, SAS, Thai International, and Varig, as well as regional alliances with still other carriers. Other major carriers have done much the same thing. In the automotive industry, U.S. multinational Chrysler has merged with German Daimler-Benz to form DaimlerChrysler, and U.S. multinational automaker Ford has acquired Swedish Volvo cars. Although adaptation can be difficult, these alliances and mergers have forced often very diverse corporate cultures to grapple with the challenges of building fully collaborative alliances and organizations compatible with their diversity in national and corporate perspectives.

The Twentieth-Century Debate on Global Commerce

A knowledge of historical background of the emergence and globalization of capitalism is essential to understanding twentieth-century arguments among economic liberals, mercantilists, post–World War II neomercantilists, and world-system theorists (the latter we categorize as part of the structuralist perspective on world politics). After the heyday of economic liberalism in the late nineteenth and early twentieth centuries, the period between the two world wars was marked by a revival of mercantilist ideas. Countries erected high tariffs and other barriers to trade to protect domestic industries and agricultural sectors from foreign competition. They also **devalued** their currencies in an effort to secure a price advantage for domestic industries, making exports cheaper to foreign buyers while making imports more expensive to domestic buyers. It was a game all countries could play, and most did as they engaged in successive rounds of competitive devaluations.

The aim was to run a favorable balance of trade—exporting or selling more than was imported or bought from abroad, regardless of the effects of such policies on foreign producers. As in the mercantilist period, relatively more successful players could be identified by the amount of gold or other monetary assets they accrued from positive trade balances. Referred to by economic liberals as "beggar-thy-neighbor" policies, protectionism and competitive-devaluation policies resulted in an enormous reduction in the volume of trade during the 1930s as each country strove to avoid purchasing other countries' exports. No country really won in this game; all experienced economic depression and the loss of productivity. Indeed, as Adam Smith had observed a century and a half before, the wealth of nations was not to be found in their gold stocks.

Any trade that did go on tended to occur in mutually exclusive trade blocks—for example, Germany at the core of Central European trade, Britain within its empire and commonwealth, the United States in North America and the Caribbean, and Japan in its East Asian "coprosperity" sphere. Many historians have identified the breakdown of economic liberalism and the

THE INFORMATION REVOLUTION

The Information Revolution is now at the point which the Industrial Revolution was in the early 1820s, about forty years after James Watt's improved steam engine (first installed in 1776) was first applied, in 1785, to an industrial operation–the spinning of cotton. And the steam engine was to the first Industrial Revolution what the computer has been to the Information Revolution–its trigger, but above all its symbol. Almost everybody today believes that nothing in economic history has ever moved as fast, or had a greater impact than, the Information Revolution. But the Industrial Revolution moved at least as fast in the same time span and had probably an equal impact if not a greater one.

Peter Drucker, "Beyond the Information Revolution"

It's Been Said...

formation of political-economic blocks in the 1930s as contributory causes of World War II. In any case this was widely believed, particularly among British and American policy makers who were charged with constructing a postwar global economy based on liberal principles.

Their objective was to establish an open trading and commercial environment on a global basis, rather than to repeat the experience of the interwar period. International economic regimes or sets of rules governing commerce were established, as were international organizations charged with implementing the three-part grand design, which included free or open trade, monetary means for maintaining the currency exchange essential to commerce, and capital investment for economic development.

By any standard, the five decades following World War II were a remarkable period for economic growth. For the first half of that period, the economies of the advanced industrial states grew nearly twice as fast as in any comparable period before or since. In the following twenty-five years, a number of newly industrializing countries also made remarkable economic gains. But these same years also witnessed periods of inflation, high unemployment, and productivity slowdowns in the industrialized countries. For the Western Europeans, the end of the cold war began a debate over the desirability, nature, and pace of integration of the former East bloc into the West. The key question is whether the post–World War II period was an exceptional half century of economic growth and whether that period has drawn to a close.[3] We will briefly provide an overview of key developments in post–World War II trade, monetary, and investment issues and provide more detail in subsequent chapters.

Trade Regime

Attempts to establish an International Trade Organization (ITO) as a key institution for a free- or open-trade regime failed when opposition at the time, particularly in the United States, described such a plan as "too socialistic." There was the possibility that an ITO would become too strong and intervene against corporate or national interests. Although the ITO idea failed, a General Agreement on Tariffs and Trade (GATT) was established in 1947.

In succeeding decades, GATT negotiation rounds worked painstakingly to reduce tariffs and other barriers to trade. In turn, the GATT has been succeeded in 1995 by the World Trade Organization (WTO), an institution given the task of continuing the work of reducing barriers to trade and fostering as open a trading environment on a global basis as possible. It is an incredibly important task, as for more than half a century the multilateral trading system has underpinned global prosperity. Further liberalization will not be easy as evidenced by the collapse of trade talks in Cancun, Mexico, in September 2003 and subsequent setbacks. Dating back to November 2001, the latest round of trade talks was aimed at lowering trade barriers where freer trade would help poor countries the most, particularly in agriculture. With 148 members, the WTO is the only trade forum where all countries—no matter how poor—have veto power. In no other world forum do poor countries have such influence. Some political economists see the failure of Cancun as reinforcing growing tendencies to form competing European, American, and Japan–East Asian trade areas. Trade areas are not inherently bad for simple geographic reasons; internal trade within North America, within Europe, and within Asia usually tends

---

[3]Barry Eichengreen and Peter B. Kenen, "Managing the World Economy under the Bretton Woods System: An Overview," in Peter B. Kenen, ed., *Managing the World Economy: Fifty Years after Bretton Woods* (Washington, D.C.: Institute for International Economics, 1994), 3.

to be greater than their external trade with other areas. Enhancing such trade within regional areas can be beneficial, but free-trade advocates worry lest these trade areas become mutually exclusive trade blocks, as they were in the 1930s. The challenge for the WTO and other organizations will be to maintain global trade across regions on as open a basis as possible, even as efforts are made at the same time to enhance intraregional trade. At the same time (and responding to public pressures), the WTO and other international organizations concerned with global commerce will be called on to accommodate, to a greater degree than in the past, demands from both labor and environmental interests (often supported by nongovernmental organizations) adversely affected by the increasing globalization of capital and commercial transactions.

Monetary Regime

Creating an international monetary regime and an International Monetary Fund (IMF) was much easier than constructing a trade regime. Competitive devaluations, such as those that had occurred during the interwar period, were forbidden, and exchange rates of one currency for another were to be stable. This was set forth by the Bretton Woods regime, named for the New Hampshire location where the international agreement was reached in 1944. The IMF was to maintain international **liquidity,** helping states with insufficient foreign cash reserves by making short-term loans, enabling them to balance their books in the event of a shortfall in foreign currency reserves or other monetary assets. For example, if a country had a negative trade balance and insufficient funds to cover the cost of imports in excess of export earnings, it could borrow from the IMF. In the absence of IMF lending, that country might have been forced to put up trade barriers against further imports, thus cutting off trade, to the disadvantage of other countries.

The international monetary regime changed in the 1970s from relatively fixed exchange rates under Bretton Woods to a regime of "managed flexibility," or floating exchange rates subject to currency-market interventions by central banks. The IMF, however, remained in place as a monetary lending agency with purpose and capacity to maintain international liquidity. In a regime in which exchange rates are set in currency markets, central banks and national treasuries may choose to intervene in these markets unilaterally or, more likely, in concerted, multilateral actions. They intervene in order to buy and sell national currencies so as to affect their price or exchange rate, in turn affecting prices of goods and services. To do so effectively may require borrowing foreign currencies from other countries or from the IMF. For example, Mexican efforts in the 1990s to defend the peso's value required borrowing dollars or other **hard currencies** from the IMF, the United States, or other countries.

Investment Regime

Finally, a multilateral capital-investment regime was established after World War II with the World Bank as its principal agency. The formal and original title of the World Bank—International Bank for Reconstruction and Development (IBRD)—reflects its original purpose, which was to rebuild war-torn economies in Europe and Asia. Its task in more recent decades, however, has been to lend capital for development purposes to capital-poor, Third World countries with an eye to integrating them more effectively in an open and global political economy. Efforts by the World Bank are supplemented by regional development lending banks, such as the Inter-American Development Bank (IADB) and Asian Development bank (ADB), as well as bilateral loans from capital-rich to capital-poor countries.

The OEEC Becomes the OECD

The Organization for European Economic Cooperation (OEEC) was formed in 1948 in Paris in the aftermath of World War II to facilitate capital-investment flows (U.S. assistance under the Marshall Plan as well as Canadian aid) to rebuild European economies. Aims at the time were to promote trade and monetary cooperation among member countries, fostering production and the economic reconstruction of Europe, promoting trade by reducing tariffs and other barriers, considering formation of a customs union or free-trade area, and exploring arrangements for regional monetary payments on a multilateral basis.

Immediate postwar economic reconstruction in Europe largely completed, an expansion of scope took place in 1961 with the formation of the Organization for Economic Cooperation and Development (OECD) to replace the OEEC, but still with Paris-based headquarters. Along with OEEC members, the United States and Canada became members in their own right. Admissions are no longer confined to Europe, and there are now twenty-nine member states from around the world committed to market economy, pluralist democracy, and respect for human rights. The original or charter OECD members from 1961 are Austria, Belgium, Canada, Denmark, France, Germany, Greece, Iceland, Ireland, Italy, Luxembourg, the Netherlands, Norway, Portugal, Spain, Sweden, Switzerland, Turkey, the United Kingdom, and the United States. Of this group, only Austria, Canada, and the United States were not members of the earlier OEEC. Members joining the OECD later are Japan (1964), Finland (1969), Australia (1971), New Zealand (1973), Mexico (1994), the Czech Republic (1995), Poland (1996), Hungary (1996), the Republic of Korea (1996), and the Slovak Republic (2000).

Often referred to now as the rich countries' club, the OECD fosters strong economies in its member countries and works to expand free or open trade and contribute to economic development not only in advanced-industrial and postindustrial countries but also in developing countries. With a truly global view, the OECD now focuses its efforts on the increasingly global economy. For further and up-to-date information, check out the OECD's official website (www.OECD.org).

The best way for capital-poor countries to borrow for investment purposes is at concessionary rates of interest, that is, below market rates from long-term lenders such as the World Bank, other international lending institutions, or foreign governments. Loans at concessionary rates for development purposes are really a form of grant or foreign aid. If they are prudent, borrowing countries will set aside a portion of the concessionary loan, investing it at higher market rates and allowing compound interest over time to produce the funds needed to pay off the loan when due.

Unfortunately, heavy borrowing in the 1970s and 1980s by Third World countries—often at market interest rates from privately owned multinational banks and foreign governments—left many Third World countries deeply in debt. The heavy interest payments were burdens on their domestic political economies. Moreover, much of the money borrowed was not spent for development or, when it was, was not always allocated to sound projects. As a result, many of the expected economic gains for which the loans were originally requested were not realized either. Although many lenders offered refinancing and debt relief to borrowers so they could avoid default, the burden was reduced and crisis avoided primarily by the gradual reduction in global interest rates in the 1980s and 1990s.

Practicing World Politics

INTERNATIONAL ORGANIZATIONS AND THE GLOBAL ECONOMY

For a preview of international institutions covered in greater detail in Chapters 11 and 12, check out websites for the World Bank group in Washington, D.C. (www.worldbank.org); the International Monetary Fund, also in Washington (www.imf.org); and the World Trade Organization in Geneva (www.wto.org)—all specialized agencies in the U.N. system. The principal U.N. organ responsible for global economic matters is the U.N. Economic and Social Council (www.un.org). Other U.N. organs and specialized agencies dealing with economic or commercial matters on a global basis include those specializing on the following:

- *Different aspects of economic and commercial development and production, energy, copyrights, and patents*—U.N. Development Program in New York (www.undp.org); U.N. Environment Program in Nairobi (www.unep.org); the Food and Agricultural Organization of the United Nations in Rome (www.fao.org); the International Fund for Agricultural Development, also in Rome (www.ifad.org); the U.N. Industrial Development Organization in Vienna (www.unido.org); the U.N. Conference on Trade and Development in Geneva (www.unctad.org); the International Atomic Energy Agency in Vienna (www.iaea.org); and the World Intellectual Property Organization in Geneva (www.wipo.int)

- *Labor and related human issues*—the International Labor Organization in Geneva (www.ilo.org); the U.N. Institute for Training and Research (www.unitar.org) and the U.N. Research Institute for Social Development (www.unrisd.org), both in Geneva; the World Health Organization, also in Geneva (www.who.int); Habitat, the U.N. Center for Human Settlements in Nairobi (www.unchs.org); World Food Program in Rome (www.wfp.org); the U.N. Population Fund in New York (www.UNFPA.org); the U.N. Drug Control Program in Vienna (www.undcp.org); and the U.N. Children's Fund in New York (www.unicef.org)

- *Transportation*—the International Maritime Organization in London (www.imo.org) and the International Civil Aviation Organization in Montreal (www.icao.int)

- *Communications*—the Universal Postal Union in Berne (www.upu.int) and the International Telecommunication Union in Geneva (www.itu.int)

Details on U.N. organ and specialized agency roles and missions found at these websites are also summarized in Chapter 6. The United Nations also has regional economic commissions in Africa (Addis Ababa) (www.uneca.org), Europe (Geneva) (www.unece.org), Latin America (Santiago) (www.eclac.org), and Asia and the Pacific (Bangkok) (www.unescap.org).

Regional international organizations dealing primarily with economic or commercial matters include in the Americas, the Andean Group (www.comunidadandina.org), Caribbean Community and Common Market (www.caricom.org), Mercosur (Common Market Southern Cone, South America) (www.mercosur.org.uy), and the North American Free Trade Association (www.nafta-sec-alena.org); in Asia and the Pacific, the Asia-Pacific Economic Cooperation (www.apec.org) and the Association of Southeast Asian Nations (www.aseansec.org); in Africa, the Economic Community of West African States (www.ecowas.int); and in Europe, the European Union (europa.eu.int; the U.S. web address is www.eurunion.org). Other international regional organizations for which

Practicing World Politics

economics is one among a wide range of agenda items include the African Union (www.africa-union.org), the Organization of American States (www.oas.org), and the Organization for Security and Cooperation in Europe (www.osce.org). Regional lending institutions include the Asian Development Bank (www.adb.org), African Development Bank (www.afdb.org), Inter-American Development bank (www.IADB.org), and the North American Development Bank (www.nadb.org).

(Continued)

The North-South Divide

The extraordinarily large gap in technology, capital, and levels of living between advanced industrial and postindustrial countries of the North and those in the South (where most people live) is a striking characteristic of the present-day global political economy. French socialists first started using the expression "Third World" in the 1960s to denote the most populous category of the world's peoples, in much the same way as the term *third estate* in French history and culture refers to the masses of people who at the time of the French Revolution in 1789 were decidedly less well off than those in the upper classes. This original usage of *Third World* thus had a positive connotation because it carried the implication that improvement in life conditions for the world's masses was still possible, whether by revolution or other means. In more recent years, however, the term has fallen into disfavor among those who feel the term devalues or puts lower-income countries in a third-rate position.

In any event, in this chapter and throughout this volume we use these terms descriptively without any intended connotation. *First World* and *North* are used interchangeably to refer to high-income countries that with a few exceptions lie in the Northern Hemisphere. *Third World* or *South* are also interchangeable terms that reflect that most middle- and low-income countries are in the Southern Hemisphere. As a practical matter, the term *Second World,* which during the Cold War referred to the Soviet Union and other centrally planned, Marxist-Leninist political economies, has much less usage today.

A world profile using U.N. and World Bank data (see Table 10.1) divides countries by level of economic development into high-, middle-, and low-income categories. Take a close look at this table. As is immediately apparent, the disparities are enormous, which shows dramatically how human conditions vary. Adjusted for inflation and to reflect purchasing power parity, real per capita income in high-development, high-income countries, for example, is still *thirteen times* the average in middle-income countries, and more than *sixty times* the average in low-income countries (most of which are in Africa). Other indicators of level of living show literacy at close to 100 percent in high-income countries but only two-thirds that in low-income countries, the middle-income countries splitting the difference. Food calories in the poorest countries are two-thirds of those supplied to the richest countries, grams of protein only about half. Diseases such as tuberculosis are still major afflictions in poor countries, and the supply of medical providers—physicians and nurses—is a fraction of those available in high-income countries. Given these conditions as well as high infant mortality, it is hardly surprising that life expectancy declines from 78 years in

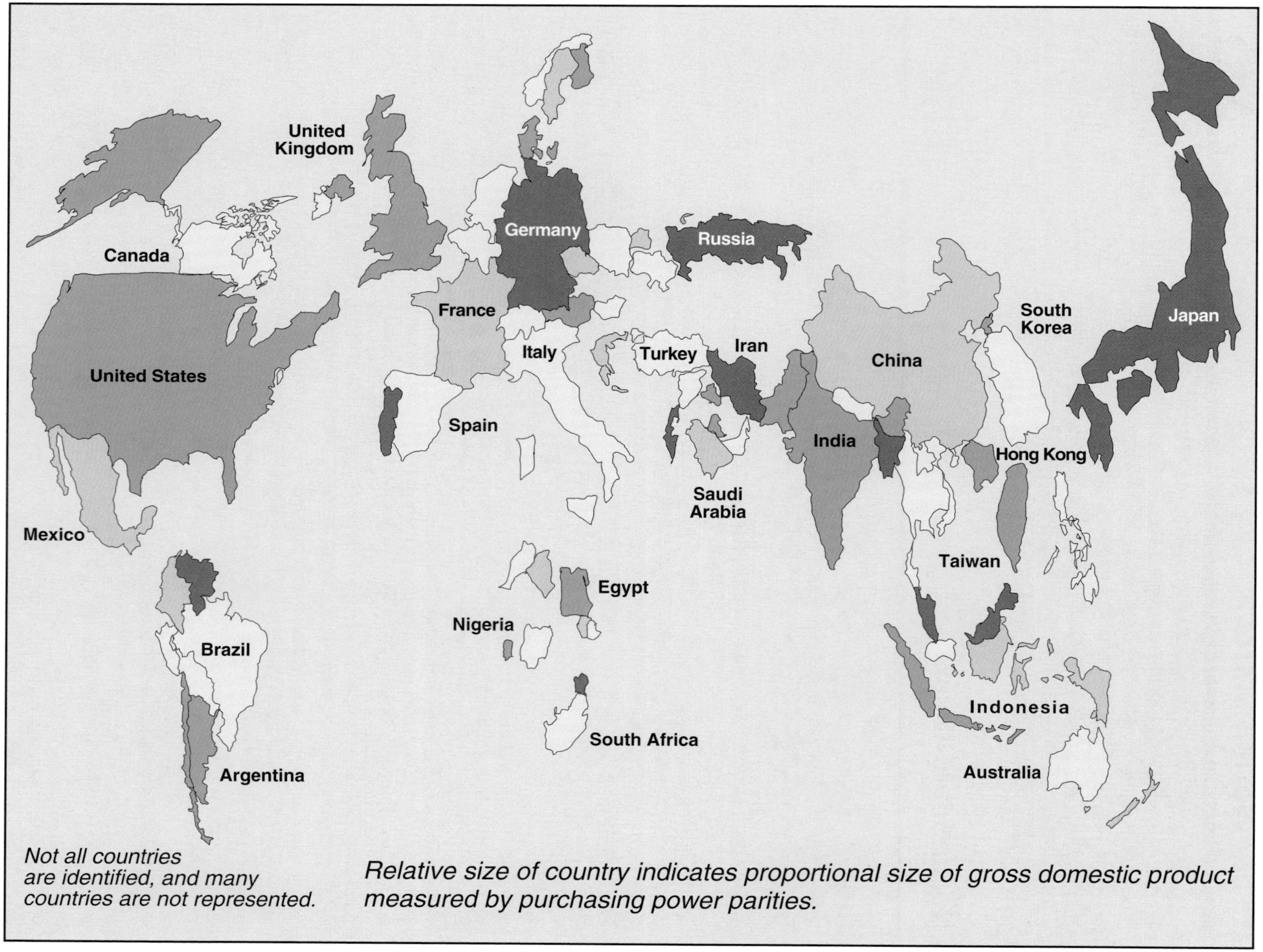

United Kingdom
Canada
United States
Mexico
Brazil
Argentina
Germany
France
Italy
Spain
Russia
Turkey
Iran
Saudi Arabia
Egypt
Nigeria
South Africa
India
China
South Korea
Japan
Hong Kong
Taiwan
Indonesia
Australia
Not all countries are identified, and many countries are not represented.
Relative size of country indicates proportional size of gross domestic product measured by purchasing power parities.

MAP 10.1
Market Size by Gross Domestic Product

	LEVEL OF DEVELOPMENT			TABLE 10.1
	LOW INCOME	MIDDLE INCOME	HIGH INCOME	
Number of Countries in Category	36	86	55	
Gross National Product (GNP in billions of US$)	$1,123.9	$5,138.5	$25,767.9	
Annual Real Economic Growth Average Annual percent increase in real GNP since 1990	2.3%	2.0%	1.7%	
Net Official Development Assistance Received (ODA as percent of GNP)	2.5%	0.3%	<0.1%	
Population (millions)	2,561	2,721	941	
Real GDP per Capita: Annual Income per Person in US$	451	1,877	27,312	
Life Expectancy: Age in Years	59.1	70.0	78.3	
Literacy	63.6%	89.7%	>99%	
Population Growth Rate (Annual Average Since 1990)	2.0%	1.1%	0.7%	
Per Capita Annual Energy Consumption kilowatt hours per person	400	1,541	10,030	
Pollution (carbon dioxide emissions) metric tons per person / share of world total	0.9 / 8.5%	3.4 / 37.6%	12.4 / 47.8%	
Output by Economic Sector (percent of GDP) Agriculture / Industry / Services	25% / 25% / 50%	11% / 38% / 51%	2% / 27% / 71%	

Global Political-Economic and Social Indicators: A World Profile

Source: World Bank, *World Development Report, 2005* (New York: Oxford University Press, 2005) and U.N. Development Programme, *Human Development Report, 2004* (New York: Oxford University Press, 2004).

high-income countries to 70 and just under sixty years respectively in middle- and low- income countries.

That the few consume the most is apparent when we examine per capita energy-consumption levels. Industries, other businesses, and individuals in the less-populated North consume more than six times as much energy (measured in kilowatt hours) per person as those in middle-income countries and more than twenty-five times as much as those in low-income countries in the South. The same disparities in consumption between North and South apply for other nonrenewable resources. Measured per capita, the North is also the heaviest-polluting group. The higher levels of living enjoyed by people in the North come at a very high price indeed.

High-income countries have remained highly urbanized even as high-technology, capital-intensive, information-based services have displaced many labor-intensive industries. Low- and middle-income countries have also experienced a substantial shift in recent decades from agriculture to urban-centered industry and services. In pursuit of a better life and responding to the labor demands of new industries, people in low- and middle-income countries have become more urbanized, many leaving the countryside and their rural way of life behind. But many (if not most) have not found a better life in the cities as the rapid urban in-migration has overloaded the capacity of many governments to provide even such essential services as clean water and sanitation.

A Look Ahead

A few further comments are in order concerning the future of international cooperation in the economic realm. Historically, when we think of international cooperation, we think of cooperation among states: Consider the post–World War II creation of the IMF, the World Bank, and the construction of international regimes. The dominant paradigm or image among political leaders traditionally has been one of national economies facing the outside world, paralleling the realist perspective of states as the key unit of international relations.

It can be argued, however, that this distinction between national and international economies is outdated. As noted here and in Chapters 1 and 9, a remarkable globalization of financial markets has occurred, eroding the ability of states to control their "national economies." Similarly, in terms of production, it becomes difficult to determine exactly what is an "American" product. For example in the 1990s, an American consumer paying $20,000 for a Pontiac Le Mans would have seen $6,000 of that sum going to South Korea for parts and operations, $3,500 to Japan, $1,500 to Germany, and an additional $1,400 to other suppliers of products and services in these countries. Less than $8,000 went to pay for goods and services in the United States.[4]

It is possible that we may soon witness further political fallout from the increase in global economic interdependence. First, now that economic barriers among the advanced capitalist states have been reduced significantly, differences in domestic economic structures—government policies and patterns of private sector industrial organization—may become more important. The best example involves U.S. criticism of Japan's domestic economic structure and policies, which aggressively push Japanese exports and make it difficult to import foreign goods and services. A key aspect of support for the postwar international economic order has been a domestic social compact between state and society in many countries in which support for an open-international market is balanced by domestic programs designed to support workers with unemployment compensation, retraining, and other benefits as part of a social "safety net." High and increasing costs have made it increasingly difficult for governments to live up to their end of the domestic bargain. As a result, political criticism of free trade has increased.

Second, even if unilateral protectionism does not come about, regional trade and other economic arrangements run the risk of becoming mutually exclusive camps if members turn inward and away from interdependent relations within broader global markets. Such blocks could evolve in North America, Europe, and the Far East.

---

[4]Robert Reich, *The Work of Nations* (New York: Knopf, 1991), 133–44.

Applying Theory

Economic growth in early twenty-first century economies is profoundly influenced by innovations and upward shifts in technology. A number of economists have been reexamining conventional (or neoclassical) thinking that focuses primarily on investment capital and labor inputs to production processes, giving relatively more attention to technology or knowledge-based inputs.

The conventional view that at a certain point each new input of capital or labor results in successively smaller gains in production—so-called diminishing results—is challenged by economists who see investment in technology or knowledge capital as actually producing "increasing returns." The new thinking extends views developed in the 1930s and 1940s by economist Joseph Schumpeter, a contemporary of John Maynard Keynes, who addressed the impact of technological innovation on business cycles.

Investments in technology are very costly; however, they are seen as crucial determinants of economic growth and future competitiveness in the global economy. Governments have been active players along with business enterprises in pursuing technological development, particularly high technologies with application in such knowledge-intensive industries as electronics, computers, and telecommunications.

Know-how in advanced materials, superconductors, semiconductors, lasers, and computers and computer software has very real market applicability. Payoffs in these sectors are potentially not only greater but also increasing compared with similar investments in machines for lower-technology manufacturing enterprises. The implication is that countries and firms able to work in this high-technology sector will reap the greater rewards of knowledge-intensive production.

Question: Doesn't this trend mean the development gap between the First and Third Worlds will simply increase?

TECHNOLOGY, COMPETITIVE-NESS, AND GLOBAL POLITICAL ECONOMY

Third, the growing North–South economic divide is not only a challenge to a truly global economy but also a threat to an emerging global civil society. Economic and social inequality continues to be an important feature of world politics. If populations continue to grow so rapidly, capitalist political economy will be put to the test as resource and environmental constraints make sustainable development extraordinarily difficult in many areas of the Third World. The domestic, regional, and international political repercussions could be significant.

In sum, maintaining an open global financial and trading environment consistent with liberal or openness principles is a substantial challenge in coming decades in a world that could just as easily move in the opposite direction.

Conclusion

In this chapter, we have examined some of the key concepts and issues associated with the global political economy. As we noted in Chapter 1, when people speak of the expansion of global interdependence, very often they are referring to economic interdependence. Particularly since the end of World War II, the world has been increasingly caught up in a web of economic relations, the extent and density of which were heretofore unknown.

Furthermore, economic interdependence has progressively worked under increasing globalization to undermine the claims of governments that they have the ability to protect national economies from the effects of the larger, global political economy. The lines between global and state economies are becoming blurry as international economic issues become domestic political issues and vice versa. Globalization is having an enormous impact.

As we have noted, however, the benefits of global economic interdependence and interconnectedness are uneven, a point made for years by economic structuralists as well as pluralists or liberals interested in international economic cooperation. Some states prosper more than others. As in earlier years, the Third World or the South continues to be trapped in poverty. Already beset by problems of political legitimacy, many such regimes see their authority further eroded by an unforgiving global economy that rewards those with highly trained and adaptable work forces with access to the most modern technology. For every Singapore or Malaysia, there are five Sierra Leones or Sudans. So, despite growing global economic interdependence, this does not mean a global economic leveling is occurring. The gap between North and South continues to widen, and there remains the danger of mutually exclusive, regional economic trading blocks forming in the more advanced areas of the world that compete with one another.

Afterword

The Wealth of Nations
Adam Smith
(1723–1790)

In this classic work, Smith sees the aim of political economy as enrichment of "both the people and the sovereign." He identifies the wealth of a nation in its productive capacity (the ability of its economy to produce goods and services), thus rejecting the mercantilist idea that a country's wealth was to be found in the amount of money (typically gold or silver) a country could acquire. In all this the market is paramount. As individuals pursue their own interests, producing and selling goods and services in pursuit of personal gain, they are unwittingly also working to benefit consumers and thus society as a whole. It is, as Smith puts it in a classic passage, as if there were an "invisible hand" guiding individual producers in the market: "By pursuing his own interest he frequently promotes that of the society." Smith's obvious laissez-faire preference is to minimize government interference or regulation of the market since such interventions tend to divert resources from where they otherwise more productively may have gone, thus not enhancing production, but likely retarding it. As with other "classical" economists, Adam Smith subscribes to a labor theory of value—that the value of the goods and services we produce depends prominently upon the resources we use and labor we expend to make this happen; however, an economy's overall productive capacity also is a function of its capital stock. As Smith notes: "No regulation of commerce can increase the quantity of industry in any society beyond what its capital can maintain." We include here excerpts from Book IV (Chapters 1, 2, 4, and 8) of Smith's The Wealth of Nations *(first published in England in 1776). Italics are added for emphasis.*

Political economy, considered as a branch of the science of a statesman or legislator, proposes two distinct objects: first, to provide a plentiful revenue or subsistence for the people, or more properly to enable them to provide such a revenue or subsistence for themselves; and secondly, to supply the state or commonwealth with a revenue sufficient for the public services. *It proposes to enrich both the people and the sovereign. . . .*

Of the Principle of the Commercial or Mercantile System

That wealth consists in money, or [i.e., gold ore—Ed.] and silver, is a popular notion which naturally arises from *the double function of money, as the instrument of commerce and as the measure of value.* In consequence of its being the instrument of commerce, when we have money we can more readily obtain whatever else we have occasion for than by means of any other commodity. The great affair, we always find, is to get money. When that is obtained, there is no difficulty in making any subsequent purchase. In consequence of its being the measure of value, we estimate that of all other commodities by the quantity of money which they will exchange for. We say of a rich man that he is worth a great deal, and of a poor man that he is worth very little money. A frugal man, or a man eager to be rich, is said to love money; and a careless, a generous, or a profuse man, is said to be indifferent about it. To grow rich is to get money; and wealth and money, in short, are, in common language, considered as in every respect synonymous. A rich country, in the same manner as a rich man, is supposed to be a country abounding in money; and to heap up gold and silver in any country is supposed to be the readiest way to enrich it. . . .

If a nation could be separated from all the world, it would be of no consequence how much, or how little money circulated in it. The consumable goods which were circulated by means of this money would only be exchanged for a greater or a smaller number of pieces; but the real wealth or poverty of the country, they allow, would depend altogether upon the abundance or scarcity of those consumable goods. But it is otherwise, they think, with countries which have connections with foreign nations, and which are obliged to carry on foreign wars, and to maintain fleets and armies in distant countries. This, they say, cannot be done but by sending abroad money to pay them with; and a nation cannot send much money abroad unless it has a good deal at home. . . .

In consequence of these popular notions, *all the different nations of Europe have studied, though to little purpose, every possible means of accumulating gold and silver in their respective countries.* Spain and Portugal, the proprietors of the principal mines which supply Europe with those metals, have either prohibited their exportation under the severest penalties, or subjected it to a considerable duty. The like prohibition seems anciently to have made a part of the policy of most other European nations. . . .

The quantity of every commodity which human industry can either purchase or produce naturally regulates itself in every country according to the effectual demand, or according to the demand of those who are willing to pay the whole rent, labour, and profits which must be paid in order to prepare and bring it to market. . . .

It would be too ridiculous to go about seriously to prove that *wealth does not consist in money, or in gold and silver; but in what money purchases, and is valuable only for purchasing.* Money, no doubt, makes always a part of the national capital; but. . . . it generally makes but a small part, and always the most unprofitable part of it. . . .

It is not for its own sake that men desire money, but for the sake of what they can purchase with it. . . . The importation of gold and silver is not the principal, much less the sole benefit which a nation derives from its foreign trade. . . . *By opening a more extensive market for whatever part of the produce of their labour may exceed the home consumption, it encourages them to improve its productive powers, and to augment its annual produce to the utmost, and thereby to increase the real revenue and wealth of the society.* These great and important services foreign trade is continually occupied in performing to all the different countries between which it is carried on. . . . To import the gold and silver which may be wanted into the countries which have no mines is, no doubt, a part of the business of foreign commerce. It is, however, a most insignificant part of it. A country which carried on foreign trade merely upon this account could scarce have occasion to freight a ship in a century. . . . Some of the best English writers upon commerce set out with observing that *the wealth of a country consists, not in its gold and silver only, but in its lands, houses, and consumable goods of all different kinds.* . . .

Of Restraints upon the Importation from Foreign Countries of Such Goods as Can Be Produced at Home

By restraining, either by high duties or by absolute prohibitions, the importation of such goods from foreign countries as can be produced at home, the monopoly of the home market is more or less secured to the domestic industry employed in producing them. . . . That this monopoly of the home-market frequently gives great encouragement to that particular species of industry which enjoys it, and frequently turns towards that employment a greater share of both the labour and stock [i.e., capital—Ed.] of the society than would otherwise have gone to it, cannot be doubted. But whether it tends either to increase the general industry of the society, or to give it the most advantageous direction, is not, perhaps, altogether so evident. . . .

No regulation of commerce can increase the quantity of industry in any society beyond what its capital can maintain. It can only divert a part of it into a direction into which it might not otherwise have gone; and it is by no means certain that this artificial direction is likely to be more advantageous to the society than that into which it would have gone of its own accord. . . . The produce of industry is what it adds to the subject or materials upon which it is employed. In proportion as the value of this produce is great or small, so will likewise be the profits of the employer. But it is only for the sake of profit that any man employs a capital in the support of industry; and he will always, therefore, endeavour to employ it in the support of that industry of which the produce is likely to be of the greatest value, or to exchange for the greatest quantity either of money or of other goods. . . .

As every individual. . . . endeavours as much as he can both to employ his capital in the support of domestic industry, and so to direct that industry that its produce may be of the greatest value; every individual necessarily labours to render the annual revenue of the society as great as he can. He generally, indeed, neither intends to promote the public interest, nor knows how much he is promoting it. By preferring the support of domestic to that of foreign industry, he intends only his own security; and by directing that industry in such a manner as its produce may be of the greatest value, *he intends only his own gain, and he is in this, as in many other cases, led by an invisible hand to promote an end which was no part of his intention. Nor is it always the worse for the society that it was no part of it. By pursuing his own interest he frequently promotes that of the society more effectually than when he really intends to promote it. I have never known much good done by those who affected to trade for the public good. It is an affectation, indeed, not very common among merchants, and very few words need be employed in dissuading them from it. . . .*

Nations have been taught that their interest consisted in beggaring all their neighbors. Each nation has been made to look with an invidious eye upon the prosperity of all the nations with which it trades, and to consider their gain as its own loss. . . . *The wealth of a neighbouring nation, however, though dangerous in war and politics, is certainly advantageous in trade.* In a state of hostility it may enable our enemies to maintain fleets and armies superior to our own; but in a state of peace and commerce it must likewise enable them to exchange with us to a greater value, and to afford a better market, either for the immediate produce of our own industry, or for whatever is purchased with that produce. *As a rich man is likely to be a better customer to the industrious people in his neighbourhood than a poor, so is likewise a rich nation.* . . . A nation that would enrich itself by foreign trade is certainly most likely to do so when its neighbors are all rich, industrious, and commercial nations. . . .

If the exchangeable value of the annual produce . . . exceeds that of the annual consumption, the capital of the society must annually increase in proportion to this excess. The society in this case lives within its revenue, and *what is annually saved* out of its revenue *is naturally added to its capital, and employed so as to increase still further the annual produce.* If the exchangeable value of the annual produce, on the contrary, fall short of the annual consumption, the capital of the society must annually decay in proportion to this deficiency. The expence of the society in this case exceeds its revenue, and necessarily encroaches upon its capital. Its capital, therefore, must necessarily decay, and together with it the exchangeable value of the annual produce of its industry. . . .

The balance of produce and consumption may be constantly in favour of a nation, though what is called the balance of trade be generally against it. A nation may import to a greater value than it exports for half a century, perhaps, together; the gold and silver which comes into it during all this time may be all immediately sent out of it; its circulating coin may gradually decay, different sorts of paper money being substituted in its place, and even the debts, too, which it contracts in the principal nations with whom it deals, may be gradually increasing; and yet its real wealth, the exchangeable value of the annual produce of its lands and labour, may, during the same period, have been increasing in a much greater proportion. . . .

Conclusion of the Mercantile System

Though *the encouragement of exportation and the discouragement of importation are the two great engines by which the mercantile system proposes to enrich every country*, yet with regard to some particular commodities [e.g., gold or silver—Ed.] it seems to follow an opposite plan: to discourage exportation and to encourage importation. *Its ultimate object*, however, it pretends, *is always the same, to enrich the country by an advantageous balance of trade.* . . .

Consumption is the sole end and purpose of all production; and *the interest of the producer ought to be attended to only so far as it may be necessary for promoting that of the consumer.* The maxim is so perfectly self-evident that it would be absurd to attempt to prove it. But in the mercantile system the interest of the consumer is almost constantly sacrificed to that of the producer; and it seems to consider production, and not consumption, as the ultimate end and object of all industry and commerce.

In the restraints upon the importation of all foreign commodities which can come into competition with those of our own growth or manufacture, the interest of the home-consumer is evidently sacrificed to that of the producer. It is altogether for the benefit of the latter that the former is obliged to pay that enhancement of price which this monopoly almost always occasions. . . .

Key Terms

political economy   *p. 330*   capitalism   *p. 331*

Other Concepts

internationalization   *p. 331*
globalization   *p. 331*
mode of production   *p. 331*
feudalism   *p. 331*
markets   *p. 332*
money   *p. 332*
investment   *p. 332*
capital goods   *p. 333*
gross national product
 (GNP)   *p. 333*
capital formation   *p. 333*

gross domestic product
 (GDP)   *p. 333*
mercantilism   *p. 336*
factors of production   *p. 336*
liberal   *p. 336*
free market   *p. 336*
division of labor   *p. 337*
comparative advantage
 p. 337
protectionism   *p. 336*
free trade   *p. 336*

imperialism   *p. 340*
neocolonial   *p. 340*
multinational corporation
 (MNC)   *p. 340*
cartel   *p. 343*
devalue   *p. 344*
liquidity   *p. 346*
hard currency   *p. 346*
uneven development   *p. 00*
world-system theory   *p. 00*

Additional Readings

A foundational reading in classical economics worth pursuing in serious study is Adam Smith, *The Wealth of Nations* (1776). Among the available editions are those from Oxford University Press and University of Chicago Press, both 1976. It is also available on line, easily found through a Google search. Many cite Smith, but few have actually read him and understand the context and meaning of this work. The first three of the five "books" or parts are the most important; however, his classic reference to the invisible hand is to be found in the fourth book from which the *Afterword* in this chapter is drawn. Smith's earlier (1759 and 1761) *Theory of Moral Sentiments* (Indianapolis, IN: Oxford University Press, 1976) presents his understandings about how moral values relate to political economy in society. Smith's works have also been reprinted by Liberty Fund, Inc. (Indianapolis, IN).

Max Weber's *Protestant Ethic and the Spirit of Capitalism* (New York: Charles Scribner's Sons, 1958, 1976), written as a challenge to Marx's more material explanation for the emergence of capitalism, formulates the hypothesis that religious ideas that eventually became secularized in modern commercial culture were at least as important as material factors, if not more so. See also Weber's classic *Economy and Society* (Berkeley: University of California Press, 1968, 1978). Two books on the development of different forms of capitalist political economy including ideas and practical realities in relation to public versus private ownership of the means of production are Karl Polanyi's *The Great Transformation* (Boston: Beacon Press, 1944, 1957) and Joseph A. Schumpeter's *Capitalism, Socialism, and Democracy* (New York: Harper and Row, 1942, 1976). Cf. Larry Diamond and Marc F. Plattner (eds.), *Capitalism, Socialism, and Democracy Revisited* (Baltimore: Johns Hopkins University Press, 1993). For more in this genre on ideas in relation to material aspects of globalization and international political economy, see Albert O. Hirschman's *The Passions and the Interests: Political Arguments for Capitalism Before Its Triumph* (Princeton, NJ: Princeton University Press, 1977, 1997); Michael Mandelbaum, *The Ideas that Conquered the World* (Cambridge, MA: Perseus, 2002); and Mark Rupert, *Ideologies of Globalization* (London: Routledge, 2000).

Widely read overviews of international political economy include Robert Gilpin's *The Political Economy of International Relations* (Princeton, NJ: Princeton University Press, 1987) and his two more recent volumes—*Global Political Economy: Understanding the International Economic Order* (Princeton, NJ: Princeton University Press, 2001) and *The Challenge of Global Capitalism: The World Economy in the 21st Century* (Princeton, NJ: Princeton University Press, 2002); Robert O. Keohane and Joseph Nye, *Power and Interdependence* (Boston: Little Brown, 1977, 2001); and, more recently, Keohane's *Power and Governance in a Partially Globalized World* (London: Routledge, 2002). See also James A. Caporaso and David P. Levine, *Theories of Political Economy* (New York: Cambridge University Press, 1992). Among his many valuable works, but particularly relevant to the historical twentieth-century discussion in this chapter, is Charles Kindleberger's *The World in Depression, 1929–1939* (Berkeley: University of California Press, 1973, 1986).

A comprehensive treatment of international political economy focusing on concepts and theories, global trade and monetary systems, multinational corporations and North-South relations, technology and domestic sources of national economic behavior, and business cycles and globalization is Robert A. Isaak, *Managing World Economic Change: International Political Economy*, 3rd ed. (Upper Saddle River, NJ: Prentice Hall, 1991, 2000). Other textbooks in various editions are Susan Strange, *States and Markets* (London: Pinter, 1994) and Joan Spero, *The Politics of International Economic Relations* (New York: Wadsworth, 2002); and Barry Hughes, *Continuity and Change in World Politics*, 4th ed. (Upper Saddle River, NJ: Prentice-Hall, 1999).

On the United States. and globalization, see D. Clayton Brown, *Globalization and America Since 1945* (Wilmington, DE: Scholarly Resources Books, 2003). On equity and social justice in global political economy, see George Demartino, *Global Economy, Global Justice: Theoretical and Policy Alternatives to Neoliberalism* (London: Routledge, 2000). Cf. David P. Levine, *Wealth and Freedom: An Introduction to Political Economy* (N.Y.: Cambridge University Press, 1995). Other critiques or defenses of globalization include discussions in Donatella Della Porta and Sidney Tarrow, *Transnational Protest and Global Activism* (Lanham, MD: Rowman & Littlefield, 2005); Maude Barlow and Tony Clarke, *Global Showdown* (Toronto: Stoddart, 2001); and Jagdish Bhagwati, *In Defense of Globalization* (New York: Oxford University Press, 2004).

Chapter 11

"Economic interdependence among nations places a premium on frameworks and institutions. I am sure we would all prefer the rule of law over the law of the jungle. We need rules of the road and norms to guide relations between individuals and communities. This is as true of the global village as it is of the village each of us may have come from."

KOFI ANNAN, SECRETARY-GENERAL OF THE UNITED NATIONS

The Political Economy of International Trade, Money, and Regional Integration

The following report appeared in the "Weekly Piracy Report" of the ICC Commercial Crime Services (www.iccwbo.org):

- 24.12.2003 at 0357 LT at 3.5 miles south of fairway buoy, Cotonou anchorage, Benin. Five pirates armed with guns and knives boarded a bulk carrier and took watchman as hostage. They raided master's cabin and stole ship's cash, master's cash and personal belongings and two passports. When crew mustered pirates fired warning shots and escaped in a waiting boat. Second officer and bosun [SLC] sustained gun injuries in their legs and they were sent to hospital. Master reported that almost every day pirates attempted to board.

  Somalian Waters - Eastern and Northeastern coasts are high-risk areas for hijackings. Ships not making scheduled calls to ports in these areas should keep at least 75 miles and if possible 100 miles from the coast. Use of radio communications including VHF in these waters should be kept to a minimum.

- 25.11.2003, the tug profit no. 8 departed Jambi, Indonesia with barge Sumber Jaya 8 bound for Singapore. About 15 armed pirates hijacked the tug and barge about 15 nm off Muara Sabak. All 14 crew were ordered to jump overboard. They managed to swim safely to Tg. Jabung. The barge was located on 26.11.2003. The tug is still missing.

- All vessels are advised to maintain antipiracy watches and report all suspicious movements of craft. Piratical attacks should be immediately reported to the Piracy Reporting Centre, Kuala Lumpur, Malaysia.

  Imagine! One of the oldest of crimes on the thigh seas is still with us. Ever increasing commerce under globalization provides new opportunities not just for traders but also for pirates.

In this chapter we examine in some detail three topics involving the global political economy: trade, finance, and regional integration. At least since the beginning of capitalism, observers, analysts, and academics have pondered and debated such critical questions as "How can trade, finance, and regional integration improve a society's standard of living?" and "What specific policies will increase a nation's wealth and pull people out of poverty?" The emphasis in this chapter will be on the more developed regions of the world. Furthermore, we will introduce you to classical and neoclassical economic thinking that has profoundly influenced how economists and political leaders have approached these three issues in crafting domestic and international policy regimes and responses. In Chapter 12 we will revisit the trade and finance issues as they relate to the developing world and also address other concerns, such as demographics, the environment, and health, that have proven to be further burdens and barriers to the economic advancement of the poorest people who comprise the majority of the world.

Classical Trade Theory and Comparative Advantage

The reason we give so much attention in this chapter to understanding the economics of **trade** is that it, quite simply, has a dramatic impact on the economic well-being of countries worldwide. The importance of trade in national economies is apparent in Table 11.1, which depicts **exports** and **imports** as a percentage of total domestic economic production as measured by GDP. As noted in Chapter 10, it should not surprise us that anything as important as economics is also highly political. Politics is core to economics as peoples and their governments (and the international and nongovernmental organizations they form) inevitably become involved to a greater or lesser degree in the decisions they make about budgets, money, trade, investment, and other commercial matters. Particularly for states, as we noted in Chapter 3, economic capabilities are one indicator of overall state power and hence of interest to realists and pluralists or liberals alike.

A Rolls Royce dealership in Moscow.

Exports and imports are an important part of national economies, although some countries are relatively more dependent on their trade sectors than others. As discussed in Chapter 10, a positive (or favorable) trade balance–when exports are greater than imports, the dollar difference adds to GNP. Conversely, a negative (unfavorable) trade balance–when imports are greater than exports, the dollar difference is subtracted from GNP. The following data depict the relative importance of trade among different categories of states. As shown, developing countries have increased their reliance on trade as a percentage of GDP in the years since 1990 while, given their lower level of economic development, lagging far behind the capital-rich, high-income countries in terms of high-technology exports.

TABLE 11.1

International Trade and Economic Production

	IMPORTS AS % OF GDP		EXPORTS AS % OF GDP		HIGH-TECH EXPORTS AS % OF MANUFACTURED EXPORTS	
	1990	LATEST	1990	LATEST	1990	LATEST
Developing Countries	23	30	24	33	8	20
Least Developed	23	34	14	23	n.d.	n.d.
Arab States	38	30	38	36	1	2
East Asia/Pacific	33	45	34	49	14	28
Latin America	12	19	14	21	7	16
Sub-Saharan Africa	26	35	27	34	n.d.	4
Central/East Europe & CIS	25	40	25	42	n.d.	11
OECD High Income	18	21	18	21	18	23

Source: U.N. Development Programme, *Human Development Report, 2004* (New York: Oxford University Press, 2004); some data on manufactured exports for 1990 taken from earlier editions.

Some people think governments have a constructive role to play in managing their economies and working with other governments to manage regional and global commerce. Others prefer a *laissez-faire* approach, minimizing government participation or interference in the marketplace, whether domestically or globally. Having said that, most *laissez-faire* advocates concede that government treasuries and their central banks wind up playing an instrumental role in global commerce by managing the national supply of money and assuming obligations to make payments to other countries that come from international trade, investment, and other commercial or financial transactions. These transactions are summarized in the box on page 365. Governments, their courts, and their law-enforcement authorities also play a pivotal role in defining, enforcing, and adjudicating disputes concerning property rights. However we look at it, it is difficult to talk about trade and commerce without talking about politics and the roles played by governments and international organizations.

Why do countries trade with one another? How does trade translate into a higher standard of living? Why are some countries winners and others losers? Why can't countries do just as well by simply going it alone economically? We examine two approaches to these questions with a long and respected tradition: classical and neoclassical economic theory. Classical trade theory is exemplified in the writings of David Ricardo (1772–1823) and others. For countries or their business firms to engage in international trade requires some reason or rationale for doing so. Classical trade theory predicts that countries (their corporations and their other firms) will tend *ceteris paribus* (i.e., other things being "equal" or held constant[1]) to produce and export those products in which they have a **comparative advantage.** Productive capacities and the demand for these products in domestic and external (regional and global) markets will determine the amount produced and the degree of economic return. Thus trade depends upon differences, not sameness in relative efficiency and capacity of production among two or more countries and their businesses in the products they trade regionally or globally. If there were no differences in efficiency of production and domestic production capacity were sufficient to meet demand, in theory there would be no trade at all. States could, indeed, go it alone. (For a more detailed look at the specifics of classical trade theory, see pages 367–370.)

What factors account for comparative advantage? Why don't all countries produce electronics or agricultural products for export? Consistent with Ricardian thinking, the **Heckscher-Ohlin theorem** developed early in the twentieth century makes the obvious point that because different countries have diverse factor endowments—different amounts and quality of land, labor, and capital—they are likely to export those goods or services in which their combination of these production factors gives them a comparative advantage. For example, producers in some countries, having sufficient labor and a favorable climate, might specialize in agricultural production, whereas producers in other countries with larger capital endowments might specialize in manufactured goods and services such as banking.

This may all sound well and good in theory, but there are at least two major criticisms of classical trade theory that should be mentioned. First, it is one thing to state that countries should produce that which is favored by their factor endowments, but that still does not guarantee a significant role or comparative advantage for many Third World countries. You would think, for example, that developed countries should emphasize high-tech production and less-developed countries agricultural exports. We still often think of agriculture—raising animals and the growing and harvesting of plants for food and other purposes—as a labor-intensive enterprise favoring countries with good soil, favorable growing climate, and abundant populations willing to work the land. Historically, this has been the case. Even today, the composition (proportion of GDP) of many Third World economies remains 30 percent or more agricultural compared to advanced-industrial or postindustrial First World economies that are perhaps just 1 to 3 percent agricultural.

Capital-rich countries, however, may find their capital still gives them decided advantages over other countries that are rich in natural resources. The United States and other First World economies tend to be relatively more efficient in agricultural production because capital has been effectively substituted for higher-cost labor in these countries. Indeed, the mechanization of agriculture, coupled with agricultural research and development of growing-and-producing technologies, requires vast amounts of capital, which the First World has in relatively more abundant supply than Third World countries do. Such technologies include using chemicals as fertilizer and for insect or pest control, developing plant hybrids with greater or more diverse crop yields, and the more controversial area of genetically engineering new plant and animal forms by altering DNA or cell content.

Thus capital-intensive agriculture becomes a comparative cost advantage for many capital-rich countries. Moreover, governments in these countries, enjoying ample access

comparative advantage
In classic trade theory, the concept that countries will produce and export to other countries those products that they can produce relatively more efficiently than can their trading partners.

[1] Economists often use the term "other things being equal," or in Latin *ceteris paribus,* as a caveat or warning that the model they are describing or the argument they are making contains simplifying assumptions—for example, that factors held as constants in a model or argument are variables in the real world that could otherwise affect the predicted outcome.

Trade and Payments Balances: An Overview of International Commercial Accounting

The balance of trade or current account (b) refers to exports (X) minus imports (M) of goods (merchandise trade) and services across national borders during a specified period of time (typically a month, quarter [three months], or year). Thus, if Japan has exported more than it has imported in a given year, it is said to have run a **surplus** or positive balance of trade. By contrast, if the United States imports more than it exports over the same period of time, it is said to have a **deficit** or negative trade balance:

Balance of Trade		Exports		Imports
b	$=$	X	$-$	M

The trade balance or current account is only one of several accounts in a country's overall **balance of payments.** Net investment, the capital account, is another. This is the difference between capital investment by domestic investors in foreign countries and capital investment by foreign investors in the country's domestic economy.

Unilateral transfers is a third account. This refers to grants or other transfers received by a country's government (e.g., foreign aid) or residents (e.g., social security or other pensions received) from foreign governments minus grants or other transfers sent by the country's government to other governments or to residents living in other countries.

Finally there is the official reserves account (referred to historically as the gold account) composed of assets used to balance payments with other countries; these are generally gold, foreign currencies, and special drawing rights (SDRs) from the International Monetary Fund (IMF) that can be counted as official reserves. If, after adding up the balances in the other accounts there is a net deficit, the balance can be made up by sending official reserves to other countries. On the other hand, if the sum of a country's other accounts shows a surplus, other countries may be called upon to transfer a portion of their reserves to add to the official reserves of the surplus country:

Balance			I		II		III		IV		
of	(B)	$=$	Current	$+$	Capital	$+$	Unilateral	$+$	Official	$=$	0*
Payments			Account		Account		Transfers		Reserves		

Balance of Payments in Outline Form

I. Current Account (Goods and Services)

   A. Examples of Credits/Positive Entries (+):

      1. Merchandise exports (goods)
      2. Transportation abroad provided by domestic carriers (airplanes, ships, and the like) and paid for by foreigners
      3. Expenditures by tourists from foreign countries
      4. Financial services and insurance provided by domestic banks and other firms to (and paid for by) foreigners
      5. Interest, dividends, and other financial payments received by domestic residents from abroad

*Balance of payments equals zero with overall surpluses or deficits in the first three accounts compensated by transfers (gains or losses) of official reserves in the fourth account.

6. Spending by foreign governments (e.g., the costs of running their embassies and other missions, making official visits, stationing troops if any, and various other activities)

B. Examples of Debits/Negative Entries (−):

1. Merchandise imports (goods)
2. Transportation abroad provided by foreign carriers and paid for by residents
3. Expenditures by residents as tourists in other countries
4. Financial services and insurance provided by foreign banks and other firms to (and paid for by) domestic residents
5. Interest, dividends, and other financial payments made to foreigners
6. Spending by the government in foreign countries (e.g., the costs of running their embassies and other missions, making official visits, stationing troops if any, and various other activities)

II. Capital Account

A. Examples of Credits/Positive Entries (+):

1. Increase in foreign-owned deposits or accounts in domestic banks, brokerage firms, or other financial institutions
2. Decrease in domestically owned deposits or accounts in foreign banks, brokerage firms, or other financial institutions
3. Purchase of domestic stocks, bonds, or other securities by foreigners

B. Examples of Debits/Negative Entries (−):

1. Decrease in foreign-owned deposits or accounts in domestic banks, brokerage firms, or other financial institutions
2. Increase in domestically owned deposits or accounts in foreign banks, brokerage firms or other financial institutions
3. Purchase of foreign stocks, bonds, or other securities by domestic residents

III. Unilateral Transfers (Gifts or Grants)

A. Examples of Credits/Positive Entries (+):

1. Grants, contributions, or pensions received from nongovernmental foreign sources
2. Grants or other payments (including pensions) received from foreign governments

B. Examples of Debits/Negative Entries (−):

1. Grants or contributions made to foreigners or residents in foreign countries (e.g., pensions)
2. Grants or other payments made to foreign governments

IV. Official Reserves (gold, foreign currencies, SDRs)

A. Credits/Positive Entries (+)

1. Export of reserves, thus reducing payment amounts due to foreign countries as a result of net deficits in the other three accounts (current account, capital account, and unilateral transfers)

B. Debits/Negative Entries (−):

1. Import of reserves, thus reducing payment amounts due by foreign countries as a result of net deficits in the other three accounts

Applying Theory

CLASSICAL RICARDIAN THINKING ON PRODUCTION, COMPARATIVE ADVANTAGE, AND TRADE

To understand classical trade theory and the concept of comparative advantage, it helps to simplify things a bit. So let's pretend there are only two countries in the world (Insula and Terra), each capable of producing the same two products. Many texts illustrate the concept of comparative advantage as affecting the trade of cloth versus wheat or wine versus textiles, but we will modernize the example by referring to the trade of semiconductors versus lumber. (Semiconductors used in computers and other high-technology applications conduct electricity better than insulators, but not as well as good conductors do.)

Insula is an island country with small, well-tended forests and other natural resources. Terra, a continental country, also has natural resources and vast forest lands. Let's assume each country uses the factors of production (land, labor, and capital) it has to produce just two products—semiconductors and lumber. It takes land (or natural resources) to produce them: Silicon or other crystalline substances are used to manufacture semiconductors (used in computers and other advanced technologies). Forests with trees of one kind or another are necessary to produce lumber (used in construction, manufacture of paper, and for many other applications).

In the real world, of course, even the smallest national economies produce more than just two products, and many national economies are able to produce and compete in the sale in regional and global markets of a large number of products. They use money to buy and sell, import and export. To keep things simple, however, let's assume that these countries **barter,** or exchange one product for another without using money. We omit in this discussion the effects of such variables as different levels of domestic demand, different size economies and scales of production, changes in exchange rate that affect prices (a topic discussed later in this

chapter), and government intervention (as in subsidizing production or imposing tariffs or quotas to protect and encourage domestic production of a particular product). Rather, in order to understand classical free-trade theory and its predictions, it is helpful to reduce the trade puzzle to its basic essentials—production trade-offs of just two products produced and traded between just two countries *ceteris paribus* (i.e., holding all other factors constant or "equal").

PRODUCTION POSSIBILITIES

In addition to land and other natural resources, both semiconductor and lumber production rely heavily on labor (or human resources, especially skilled labor) and capital in the forms of machinery, work space, and finance for these enterprises. Take a look at the graphic presentation of production possibilities for the two countries in Figure 11.A. The diagonal lines on both graphs represent the maximum possible combinations of semiconductors and lumber that can be produced separately by Insula and Terra.

If Insula produces only semiconductors (putting all of its available land, labor, and capital to that purpose), the most it can produce is 100,000 units, but no lumber at all is produced at that level of semiconductor production. If Insula wants to produce at least some lumber, it will have to reduce semiconductor production a bit to free up some land, labor, and capital, reallocating these to lumber production. On the other hand, if Insula forgoes semiconductor production entirely and produces only lumber, the most lumber it can produce is 50,000 units.

As a practical matter, however, firms in Insula actually produce both lumber and semiconductors, as depicted on the graph by point I: 25,000 units of lumber and 50,000 semiconductors. A similar analysis for Terra reveals a maximum production possibility of either 100,000

Applying Theory

(continued)

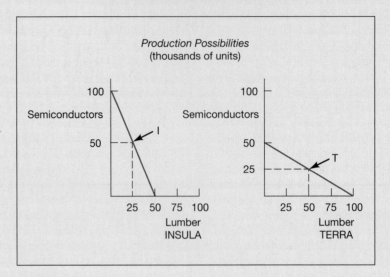

Production Possibilities
(thousands of units)

FIGURE 11.A

units of lumber or 50,000 semiconductors with actual production, point T, being a combination of 50,000 units of lumber and 25,000 semiconductors.

The marginal tradeoff between producing semiconductors and lumber for Insula is 2:1—for every two units of reduced semiconductor production, Insula can free up enough land, labor, and capital to produce one more unit of lumber instead. The reverse is also true: For every unit of reduced lumber production, Insula can allocate enough land, labor, and capital to produce two more semiconductors instead. (We can also see this by looking at the downward or negative slope of the diagonal line, which is 2.0.)

By contrast, Terra's marginal trade-off between producing semiconductors and lumber is 1:2—for every unit of reduced semiconductor production, Terra can free up enough land, labor, and capital to produce two more units of lumber instead. Alternatively, if Terra forgoes two units of lumber production, it will have enough land, labor, and capital to produce one more semiconductor instead. (Again, we

can also see this by looking at the downward or negative slope of the diagonal line, which is 1/2 or 0.5.)

COMPARATIVE ADVANTAGE AND SPECIALIZATION

These trade-offs show us how Insula, compared to Terra, is relatively more efficient in producing semiconductors than lumber (it can produce two more semiconductors for every unit of lumber production it forgoes), and Terra is relatively more efficient in producing lumber than semiconductors (for every unit of semiconductor production it forgoes, it can produce two more units of lumber). Put another way, efficiency in producing semiconductors allows Insula to produce them less expensively than Terra can. Terra's comparative advantage in lumber allows it to produce lumber less expensively than Insula can.

The idea of trade-offs is captured by the term **opportunity costs.** If a country (or more specifically, its corporations or other firms) chooses to invest its capital and allocate labor and other resources to production of some quantity of

Applying Theory

(continued)

semiconductors, the same capital and labor will not be available for production of some quantity of lumber (or other products). If Insula allocates all of its production to semiconductors, it will not have any labor or capital left to cut trees, process them, and deliver lumber to market. Inability to produce any lumber because production factors have been allocated to producing only semiconductors is referred to as an opportunity cost. As a practical matter, of course, production decisions in the real world are usually not all-or-nothing decisions. Instead, a country may allocate its capital, labor, and natural resources to production of different amounts of semiconductors, lumber, or other products. Still, as the model depicts, Insula's decision this year to produce 50,000 semiconductors and 25,000 units of lumber (point I) also means it is forgoing (as "opportunity costs") the production of up to an additional 50,000 semiconductors or up to an additional 25,000 units of lumber it could produce if a decision were made respectively to produce either more semiconductors

(and less lumber) or more lumber (and fewer semiconductors).

In any event, if both countries choose not to trade with each other and sustain their current production levels of both products (points I and T respectively), their total production will be 75,000 semiconductors (50,000 for Insula and 25,000 for Terra) and 75,000 units of lumber (25,000 for Insula and 50,000 for Terra). On the other hand, if each specializes according to comparative advantage, total production of semiconductors and lumber can be increased from 75,000 to 100,000 units of each product—the maximum production possibility (see Figure 11.B).

Because of this difference in efficiency in the use of the three factors of production and consequent cost of production, there is an opportunity for trade. If the two countries do specialize in producing those products in which they enjoy a comparative advantage—those in which they are relatively more efficient as producers—aggregate or total production of both

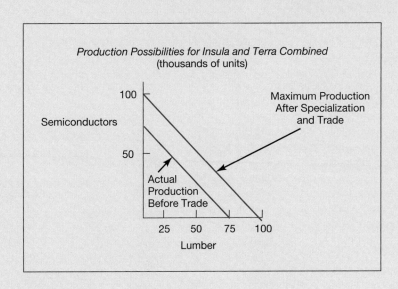

FIGURE 11.B

Applying Theory

(continued)

products can expand substantially. Assuming Insula needs the 50,000 semiconductors it now produces for domestic use, if production of semiconductors is increased to 100,000 (its maximum production possibility), it can increase its consumption or use of semiconductors somewhat but still have enough left over for export to Terra. Similarly, by specializing in lumber production, Terra can also increase its consumption of lumber somewhat but still have enough left over for export to Insula.

Based on prespecialization production levels, Insula can expect an export market or demand in Terra for at least 25,000 semiconductors, and Terra can expect an export market or demand in Insula for at least 25,000 units of lumber. In fact, Terra may wish to import more than 25,000 semiconductors, and Insula may wish to import more than 25,000 units of lumber. Insula and Terra are able to exchange (or barter) these two products at a "price" or trade ratio advantageous to the parties. Again, both countries can consume more domestically and still have enough left over for export to the other. Because more is produced less expensively through specialization, both countries engaging in trade can benefit mutually from this increase in production—an ability to consume more of both products than was possible before specialization of production. In this example, the welfare of both countries is better off after specializing in production and export of semiconductors and lumber than it was before they did so. The bottom line: classical trade theory tells us *ceteris paribus* that countries tend to produce for export those products they produce most efficiently—those in which they enjoy a comparative advantage.

In principle, in a free-trade environment, both countries allow buying and selling and importing and exporting to proceed without any politically imposed restrictions or other obstacles—no tariffs, quotas, government subsidies to domestic producers, or any other barriers to trade. Whether applied on a regional or global basis, the claim of classical trade theory is that if we allow free, unencumbered trade, countries will tend to specialize in production of those products (goods and services) in which they have a comparative advantage. A world in which the most efficient producers of particular products tend to specialize in their production results in maximizing or optimizing aggregate, worldwide production, thus enhancing global welfare. As critics are quick to point out, however, enhancing aggregate production through specialization and free trade does not mean an equal or even equitable distribution of these gains. Some countries and their businesses clearly benefit more than others.

Work by Eli Heckscher in 1919 and Bertil Ohlin in 1933 noted that trade occurs due to different concentrations or intensities of factors of production among countries—so-called factor endowments. A given country tends to export those products that are "intensive" in the factor it has in relative abundance compared to other countries. Thus the Heckscher-Ohlin theorem predicts that capital-rich countries tend to export such capital-intensive products as manufactured goods, whereas land or natural resource–rich countries tend to export commodities—minerals or agricultural products. The abundance of oil in Saudi Arabia and other oil-rich countries, for example, accounts for them being the world's largest oil exporters.

A challenge to the Heckscher-Ohlin theorem was raised in 1953 by Wassily Leontief in an empirical or factual study of trading relations, suggesting that other variables not accounted by Heckscher and Ohlin also affect trading outcomes. Subsequent studies lead many to conclude that the Heckscher-Ohlin theorem seems to capture an important part of the explanation of why and what states trade, but only a part. Other factors also need to be taken into account.

to capital through taxation or borrowing, have also subsidized the politically influential agricultural sectors in their countries. Not surprisingly, in the absence of tariffs, quotas, or other barriers, these capital-rich countries are prone to export agricultural produce to each other and even to Third World countries! Indeed, it was this very point—the demand of a number of Third World leaders that the developed world restrict its agricultural exports to developing countries—that led to the collapse of the World Trade Organization (WTO) talks in Cancun, Mexico, in September 2003. In a capitalist world economy, we should not be surprised that decisive advantages even in agriculture often go to capital-rich countries.

A second and related objection to classical trade theory is that it ignores unequal *terms of trade.* Beginning in the 1960s, Latin American and other economists charged that Third World, less-developed countries of the South were in a decidedly disadvantageous position compared to more advanced, industrial countries of the North. Economists like Argentine Raúl Prebisch observed that countries in the South export raw materials and agricultural *commodities* that tend not to increase (or even tend to decline) in price, whereas countries in the North gain an advantage from production and export of manufactured goods that tend to increase in price.

To address this and other trade problems, Third World countries have sought trade preferences from rich countries. Trade preferences can take the form of assurances by First World countries that they or their businesses will buy at least a certain minimum quantity of Third World products. Alternatively, they may agree to give trade preferences—not to impose tariffs, quotas, or other barriers against Third World exports even as these countries retain such barriers against imports from the First World.

For their part, the European Union (EU) countries have developed by political agreement the most extensive set of trade preferences in Africa, the Caribbean, and the Pacific (the so-called "ACP" countries), many of which were former colonies of EU members. In addition to benefits derived by Third World countries from these measures, trade preferences and cooperative monetary measures also tie them economically to the countries granting these favors. Critics thus see extensive trade preferences as actually a means of maintaining neocolonial, political-economic relations that also convey substantial advantages to First World countries. Defenders see little or nothing wrong with trade preferences or arrangements that benefit both sides, however unequally.

Neoclassical and Subsequent Economic Thought on How the Global Political Economy Works

It is not only critics from the Third World who have taken issue with classical economic theory as advanced by Adam Smith, David Ricardo, and other classical economists. As far back as the late nineteenth and early twentieth centuries, there were developments in economic thought that departed from the labor theory of value. What we now call **neoclassical economic theory** refers to approaches advanced by English economist Alfred Marshall (1842–1924) and French economist Leon Walras (1834–1910).

Instead of seeing the value of a good or service as determined primarily by the human labor put into its production, neoclassical economists see value in a market context—price as the outcome of **demand** for and **supply** of particular products. As such, value is to be found in relative abundance or scarcity and in the utility buyers and sellers

terms of trade
Ratio of export prices of one country to those of another, which tells us in effect the amount of revenue from a country's export sales to the other that can be used to pay for imports from the other.

commodity
Broadly, any article that is bought or sold; agricultural products, metals, and other minerals are often referred to as commodities and are traded in bulk on commodities exchanges.

place on the goods or services they seek (demand) or provide (supply) to markets. Utility and marginal utility (the value to be found in each additional unit of a good or service) thus became key concepts in market analysis. The equilibrium price is dependent on the intersection of demand and supply curves representing quantities sought or provided at alternative prices in different types of markets (e.g., models of "perfect" or "pure" competition among many sellers, oligopoly among a few sellers, and monopoly dominated by one seller).

Bringing the ideas of earlier economists together, Marshall and Walras dealt with different aspects of market equilibrium as a conceptual device for understanding market forces. Although Smith, Ricardo, and other classical writers certainly dealt with individuals and firms as units in the marketplace, they also placed relatively more emphasis in their work on understanding the functioning of the economy as a whole (the subject of *macroeconomics*), whereas neoclassical economists focus relatively more on how purchasers (consumers or buyers) and suppliers (firms or sellers) interact in the marketplace (the subject of *microeconomics*).

Neoclassical economic theorists have developed and explored the applicability of such microeconomic concepts as elasticity of demand and supply—the expected response to changes in price (or income) with respect to quantities of a product buyers want to purchase or suppliers want to sell; externalities—the positive or negative impacts (benefits or costs) of market behaviors on others; efficiency and optimization of utility, production, allocation of resources, and performance of other market activities; and rational expectation, public choice, and collective goods theories that provide a basis for explaining or predicting market behaviors. (For more detail, see the boxes on elasticity and externalities.) Other important analytical concepts introduced by neoclassical economists to provide understanding of market processes include marginal cost (the cost of producing and supplying an additional unit), marginal revenue (the amount earned from sale of an additional unit), and diminishing marginal returns, or more simply, diminishing returns (that each additional unit of land, labor, or capital put into production—holding all other factors constant—will produce proportionately somewhat less of a product than the previous unit of land, labor, or capital). In all of this work, most neoclassical theorists have made heavy use of both mathematics (stating economic ideas symbolically in algebraic equations) and statistics, in what is usually referred to as econometrics.

At the same time, other economists have also made substantial contributions to macroeconomic theory. Directly influenced by Marshall's earlier work, John Maynard Keynes (1883–1946) and his followers have taken a macroeconomic view, dealing with aggregate demand and supply for an entire economy taken as a whole. They have explored, for example, how demand is stimulated or dampened when government spends and taxes (**fiscal policy**) and influences the money supply and interest rates (**monetary policy**). Keynes also participated in laying political plans in 1944 for global actions through an International Monetary Fund (IMF) to assure international monetary flows and facilitate currency exchange so essential to international commerce (discussed more completely later in this chapter). Often at odds with Keynesian economists, the work of Milton Friedman and other **monetarists** has focused on how the supply and velocity or flow of money in an entire economy affect production and supply as well as demand. For his part, Joseph Schumpeter (1883–1950), a contemporary of Keynes, also took a macroeconomic perspective, particularly in his exploration of how changes in technology, innovation, and other factors influence business cycles. He also investigated how capitalism and socialism relate to democracy and democratic ideas.

These and other economists have made very important contributions to macroeconomic theories and concepts; but, in our view, they have had an even greater impact on

macroeconomics
The branch of economic theory that deals with attempting to understand and explain the functioning of the economy as a whole, typically involving such aggregates as money supply and GNP or GDP.

microeconomics
The branch of economic theory that deals with how purchasers and suppliers interact in the marketplace, which is sometimes referred to simply as price theory.

microeconomic theorizing. Originally formulated more with local or domestic markets in mind, microeconomic theories and concepts developed by neoclassical economists have increasing applicability to the global political economy. Markets for many goods and services now have truly worldwide scope. Microeconomic theory offers explanation of the exchange value (or price) of currencies in relation to each other as well as an account of the expected effects of governmental subsidies, regional integration, tariffs, quotas, or other barriers to trade. All of these issues have enormous political importance, given the high economic stakes states, firms, consuming publics, and others have in such matters. In short, neoclassical and other theorists have continued to expand our understanding of the global political economy beyond the foundational insights offered by classical writers.

The Impact of Technological Innovation on Free-Trade Theory

To summarize the discussion to date: classical Ricardian free-trade theory (amplified by the Heckscher–Ohlin theorem concerning relative factor endowments) focuses primarily on cost differences among producers. If a country is relatively more cost-efficient at producing a particular good or service, it will supposedly tend to specialize in producing and exporting what is not consumed or used domestically. It is the differences among countries that explain trade. In the absence of government intervention to place tariffs, quotas, or any other obstacles in the way of trade, countries will tend to specialize in producing those products in which they enjoy a comparative cost advantage relative to other producers. The result, then, of relegating production to the most efficient producers is, in principle, to maximize total productive capacity or aggregate output of goods and services, enhancing global welfare, however uneven the distribution of these gains from specialization and trade may be. Or so says classical theory.

Not so fast, say some economists. Ricardian theory goes part way but does not really provide a complete answer to why countries trade. Instead of focusing just on differences in production cost efficiencies, we also need to understand how **economies of scale** deriving from technological innovation influence marketing and production for export trade. That the average cost per unit of producing a million semiconductors typically is less than when a production line is set up to produce only a thousand is an example of an economy or unit-cost reduction based on large-scale production. Existing producers, large or small, of particular goods and services thus may look globally to expand their markets and enjoy increasing gains from export trade, dramatically increasing sales by finding many more customers that can be served efficiently by increasing substantially the overall level or scale of domestic production.

In the 1930s and 1940s economist Joseph Schumpeter, a contemporary of John Maynard Keynes, addressed the impact of technological innovation on business cycles. Clusters of new technologies displace older technologies in a process of "creative destruction." Economic growth, particularly in early twenty-first-century advanced-industrial and postindustrial, information- or knowledge-based economies, is profoundly influenced by such innovations and upward shifts in technology. Investments in technology usually are very costly; however, they are seen as crucial determinants of economic growth and future competitiveness in the global economy. Governments have been active players along with business enterprises in pursuing technological development, particularly "high technologies" with application in such knowledge-intensive industries as electronics, computers, and telecommunications. Know-how in advanced materials, superconductors, semiconductors, computers, and lasers has very real market applicability. Payoffs in these sectors are potentially not only greater but also increasing compared with similar investments in machines for

Muslim women at a fast-food restaurant in Kota Bharu, Malaysia.

lower-technology manufacturing enterprises. The implication is that countries and firms able to work in this high-technology sector will reap the greater rewards of knowledge-intensive production. Once again, this tends to leave Third World countries in the dust.

MIT economist Paul Krugman is prominent among those who have raised theoretical challenges to classical Ricardian trade theory. Krugman is careful to note, however, that focusing on increasing gains aided by technological innovation as motivation for export trade is a supplement to (not a replacement for) comparative-cost considerations as to why trade occurs.[2] Engaging in trade for increasing gains is not a new idea; but, as Krugman suggests, we may not have given it sufficient consideration.

The increasing-gains argument, however, may actually matter more than merely enjoying a comparative-cost advantage, particularly for high-technology products in some markets in which certain firms have already well established themselves. It is difficult, although not impossible of course, to start up a new firm and achieve a strong market position when one or a few large firms with ready access to capital already dominate a particular market. It is even harder to compete when new, fast-changing high technologies are difficult to acquire and develop into marketable products that can be produced at sufficient scale to be cost (and price) competitive.

By contrast, because of their ready access to capital, large, established firms in industries with increasing returns to scale are usually quite able not only to beat start-up

---

[2]For example, see Paul R. Krugman, *Rethinking International Trade* (Cambridge, MA: MIT Press, 1990, 1994).

competition but also to grow even larger and realize ever-increasing gains from expanding their export-market positions. Aviation is a good example of a market in which only a few firms dominate globally. In fact, mergers and acquisitions of existing firms have continued to reduce the numbers of these large firms to just a few. Capital for production of aircraft and related high-technology products is thus increasingly concentrated in fewer corporations. Thousands of smaller firms offering specialized products are therefore increasingly dependent for contracts on a declining number of major producers. In order to compete on a scale with such U.S. giants as, for example, Lockheed Martin and Boeing/McDonnell Douglas, European producers have pooled their efforts in joint development and production agreements for both civil and military aircraft, thus effectively reducing even further the total number of competitors in global markets.

The automobile market is another example. Transnational mergers between Chrysler (a U.S.-based **multinational corporation**) and Daimler-Benz (the German automobile producer) along with a similar agreement between Ford (another U.S.-based multinational) and Volvo (a Swedish firm) underscore market incentives to remain competitive and realize increasing gains by pooling technologies and other forms of capital.

What about the success of start-up high-tech companies? Isn't the world market still open to technological innovations advanced by individual entrepreneurs? Indeed, some start-up firms with high-technology applications have been successful challengers to established, large-scale firms. But even these new players have had to secure substantial access to capital to finance and expand their efforts by selling stocks and issuing bonds in financial markets. Furthermore, market forces have ruthlessly eliminated many of these firms.

In sum, existing large-scale producers motivated by the prospects of increasing gains have a decided trade advantage, quite apart from any comparative-cost considerations suggested by classical theory. Following the same logic, of course, even smaller firms marketing specialized products seek to increase both their domestic- and export-market shares to achieve increasing gains. Although not yet fully developed, new thinking on trade and other aspects of the global economy thus challenges old theoretical assumptions and predictions, provides new explanations, and aims to expand our understanding of how international and global trade actually work.

Trade and Finance

Classical free-trade theory also assumes the neutrality of money, which hardly seems to be the case in the real world. By "neutralizing" money, in classical trade theory the exchange of goods and services is influenced only by production cost and related considerations, not fluctuations in the value or exchange rates of currencies. In the earlier example in which the fictional countries Insula and Terra bartered semiconductors and lumber (see box on pages 367–370), no consideration was given to the value of currencies. Again, following classical theory, it is comparative production costs, not changes in the value of money, that are supposed to drive consequent changes in the direction, volume, and types of products traded.

But in the real world, the value of money *does* fluctuate with consequent effects on prices. One country's currency may be worth more in relation to another country's currency today than it was yesterday, but it may be worth less tomorrow. Unfortunately, the prices at which goods and services are traded also change when *exchange rates* between currencies also change. Let's look at an example. If one U.S. dollar could

exchange rate
The price of one currency in terms of another; for example, it may take $1.60 (U.S.) to purchase a British pound, or put another way one U.S. dollar at this exchange rate will buy 0.625 of a pound.

purchase 120 Japanese yen last week but today can only purchase 110 yen, we say the dollar has **depreciated** in relation to the yen. Put another way, the yen has **appreciated** in relation to the dollar over the same period. A week ago, 120 yen could buy one U.S. dollar, but now the same 120 yen can buy about $1.09.

Let's see how a change in exchange rates affects prices. A Japanese importer wanting to buy a Ford automobile costing $25,000 last week at an exchange rate of 120 yen to the dollar had to come up with 3 million yen. This week the same $25,000 Ford can be bought at 110 yen to the dollar for 2,750,000 yen—a saving to the Japanese importer of 250,000 yen (about $2272.72 at this week's exchange rate). Savings on the car are to the benefit of the Japanese importer; however, the American exporter is paid the same amount ($25,000) this week as last week. The real gain to the American exporter, of course, is the degree to which Japanese importers are willing to buy more Fords at 2,750,000 yen than they would at 3 million yen. Other things equal, more sales at the same dollar price mean more revenue and profits to Ford and Ford retailers.

Economists describe the impact on markets (and export-import positions) of exchange-rate changes by referring, as in the Ford case discussed earlier, to the **price elasticity of demand** in the Japanese market for Fords. For example, if demand for Fords increases substantially with a small decline in yen price, and as a result many more are purchased, elasticity is said to be high. The American exporter realizes great gains from increased sales due to a reduced price in yen to Japanese. The American exporter's gain is not caused by increased efficiencies or reduced production costs on the American side. The gain in sales is purely due to a change (a decline) in the dollar-yen exchange rate. This effect is less if Japanese demand for Fords is not very elastic in relation to price or, worse from the American perspective, is perfectly inelastic—demand stays the same (does not change at all in relation to price).

Now let's turn the tables and look at the position of a Japanese exporter (and its U.S. retailer or dealer) of Honda automobiles. At 120 yen to the dollar, a Honda with a 3 million yen retail price that arrived by ship in Los Angeles last week can be sold for $25,000, competing directly with a $25,000 Ford. On the other hand, at an exchange rate of just 110 yen to the dollar, if the export manufacturer of the same type Honda arriving in Los Angeles today is to receive the same profit margin in yen, it will have to raise the retail price in the U.S. market by more than $2,200. The Honda will be less competitive in this circumstance, not due to any change in quality or cost of production but solely because a change in exchange rate has had an adverse impact on its price. In an elastic market in which U.S. consumers are willing to substitute Fords for Hondas, a price rise can adversely affect Honda's market position, undercutting its sales and revenues.

Given the dollar's decline in value (it now buys only 110 yen compared to 120 yen last week), if the Japanese exporter and its U.S.-based retail dealer judge the American market to be inelastic, the price increase due to the exchange-rate change can be passed directly onto the consumers. On the other hand, if the U.S. market for Hondas is elastic, the exporter and retailer may choose for the time being to hold the American price at $25,000 and absorb more than $2,200 in lost revenue between them on the sale of each vehicle. (Of course, how the loss is distributed is subject to contract or negotiation between the export manufacturer and the importing dealer. Thus Honda can reduce the price in yen the dealer is charged or the dealer will have to reduce its dollar profit margin on each Honda it sells.)

To sum up, *exchange rates are important to know about precisely because changes in them directly affect prices and thus the revenues earned from international trade.* Political decisions or actions taken by governments and their central banks either unilaterally or coordinated

Applying Theory

EXCHANGE RATES

An exchange rate is merely the price a currency can be bought at (or sold for) using another currency. Although exchange-rate arithmetic may seem confusing at first, it's really not so difficult to figure out if we treat a currency just like any product traded in markets and we take a few moments to sort out how it is priced. Tourists are forced to do this when they travel abroad.

If the British pound (often referred to in currency markets simply as sterling and represented by the symbol £) can be traded for $1.60, we refer to this as the sterling–dollar exchange rate (£ 1.0 = US$1.60). Put the other way, one U.S. dollar can buy 0.625 of a pound–an exchange rate of US$1.00 = £ 0.625. This is how to switch from one exchange rate to the reverse:

$$£ 1.00 = US\$1.60$$

thus, reversing what is on either side of the = sign

$$US\$1.60 = £ 1.0$$

and

$$US\$1.00 = £ 0.625$$

In the example used in the text, the dollar–yen exchange rates are US$1.00 = 120 yen (for last week) and US$1.00 = 110 yen (today)–a depreciation in the value of the dollar in that the same dollar buys fewer yen today than it could a week ago. Put the other way, last week's yen-dollar exchange rate can be expressed as 100 yen equaling about $0.83 last week but increasing to about $0.91 today–an appreciation in the value of the yen.

The exchange rate of a currency (its price in relation to other currencies) fluctuates in financial markets in response to shifts in demand for (and supply of) them in much the same way as commodities do. Currencies in demand *ceteris paribus* tend to rise in price; a drop in demand means its exchange rate in relation to other currencies falls. When governments or their central banks make the authoritative or political choice to increase or decrease the supply of their currencies by selling or buying them in open-market operations, they also can impact exchange rates for these currencies. These effects are summarized in Figure 11.C.

The intersection of the demand and supply curves is the equilibrium exchange rate in a particular financial market. The dashed lines represent alternative demand and supply curves. Look at what happens to exchange rates when the levels of demand and supply go up (increase) or go down (decrease).

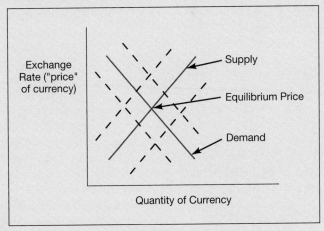

FIGURE 11.C   *Effects of Supply and Demand on Currency Exchange Rate*

multilaterally with their counterparts in other countries thus can affect exchange rates, export–import prices, and the terms of trade:

- If a country's currency depreciates, or falls, in relation to other world currencies, the prices of the products its firms export become cheaper (and thus more competitive) in foreign markets. At the same time, foreign goods its firms and individuals import become more expensive in domestic markets.

- On the other hand, if a country's currency appreciates (or becomes more valuable in relation to other currencies), its firms and people may buy and import more from abroad at lesser prices, but the prices of its exports rise and thus become less competitive in foreign markets.

Because government and central bank actions can have such effects on the livelihoods or welfare of exporters, importers, and those who produce or own the goods and services traded, changes in prices or currency values are not just economic but also highly political decisions.

Indeed, all of this becomes very political when governments (or their central banks) choose to intervene in global currency markets to maintain, increase, or decrease a currency's exchange value. For example, in the mid-1980s U.S. monetary authorities (in the U.S. Treasury and Federal Reserve Board, the central banking authority that oversees the U.S. banking system) perceived that, just as in the 1960s and early 1970s, the dollar had become too overvalued in relation to other major currencies. Put simply, an overvalued dollar meant that U.S. firms and individuals could import foreign products too cheaply while U.S. exports were too "pricey" or expensive to foreigners. The decision to depreciate and thus reduce the foreign buying power of the dollar (making foreign goods pricier to Americans) also made U.S. products cheaper to foreigners. This sounds at first like a charitable gesture or good deal to foreigners by U.S. monetary authorities. On closer examination, however, it was a case of "charity begins at home."

Jobs were at stake. An overvalued dollar meant U.S. consumers would tend to pass up buying U.S.-made products in favor of foreign-made goods of comparable quality but priced at a discount only because of an overvaluation in dollar–foreign currency exchange rates. As a result, overall U.S. purchases from other countries were far greater than American sales abroad—a national trade imbalance deeply in red ink. Even more important from a domestic political perspective, however, imports of foreign products stimulate production (and employment) in other countries but tend to dampen or reduce domestic production with consequent losses of jobs. Labor unions argued that jobs were being lost to producers in other countries. Some put it this way: overvaluation of the dollar tends to shift production to other countries with job creation abroad to replace jobs cut at home, in effect exporting jobs.

U.S. monetary authorities might have tried to depreciate the dollar unilaterally— by themselves—but instead worked the issue multilaterally, negotiating with their treasury and central bank monetary-authority counterparts in other countries to collaborate in depreciating the dollar. This meant refusing to defend the existing exchange rates between the dollar and other countries, instead letting the dollar slide or helping it down the depreciation road to a new, lower level at which valuation or purchasing power of the dollar and other countries would at least be closer or somewhat more comparable. The bottom line: consistent with classical trade theory, the effort to adjust exchange rates in this way is designed to achieve greater purchasing-power parity (see box on p. 379) between the dollar and other currencies because this shifts competition from artificial, exchange-rate considerations to such factors as efficiency, cost of production, and quality.

Purchasing-Power Parity and Pricing Hamburgers, Fries, and Cola

Classical trade theory assumes the neutrality of money. As demonstrated in the text, however, exchange rates can get out of whack and adversely affect trade that otherwise would be based on comparative advantage with lower-cost, more efficient producers specializing in production of certain products. In the real world, some currencies are **overvalued** (overpriced in terms of their exchange rates with other currencies), and others are **undervalued** (underpriced in terms of their exchange rates with other currencies).

To be neutral, money should be in parity or roughly the same in purchasing power to buy goods and services in one country as in another. A practical but amusing way to measure purchasing-power parity is to compare how much it costs to buy the same hamburger, fries, and cola in one country as in another. If money is really neutral and production and marketing costs are roughly the same, the hamburger, fries, and cola should cost or be priced about the same regardless of which currency one uses. This is what is meant by purchasing-power parity—the equivalent values of all currencies should in principle buy about the same number or amount of the same goods or services.

In 1983 the *Economist,* a weekly news magazine, developed its "Big Mac" index—a play on one of the McDonald's hamburger offerings—as an indicator of what exchange rates should be (and might well become). The index is calculated and published in the magazine from time to time. In principle, the price of the Big Mac *ceteris paribus* should cost about the same everywhere, but that is usually not the case. In some countries it is decidedly higher or lower than others. If the local currency is overvalued in relation to the dollar, the Big Mac tends to be cheaper (i.e., an overvalued currency goes further; it can purchase a Big Mac less expensively) than in another country with an undervalued currency (more of which is needed to purchase the same Big Mac).

For example, one publication of the index suggested that many European currencies, in particular the euro, were overvalued in relation to the dollar—that Big Macs were much cheaper in these countries than in the United States. Subsequently the exchange value of the European currencies dropped, bringing them much closer to purchasing-power parity with the dollar. "See, we told you so," said writers for the *Economist.* Critics have advocated that the *Economist* move away from its Big Mac index to a more diverse, market-basket calculation using a number of products.

An International Monetary Regime for Financing International Commerce

In day-to-day international commerce, government agencies, business firms, other groups, and individuals use domestic currency to buy foreign currencies to finance the purchase of goods and services imported from abroad, to loan or invest money in foreign countries, or to have money to spend there. Similarly, foreign government agencies, foreign business firms, other groups, and individuals living abroad use their currencies to buy currencies in other countries needed to conduct the same kinds of transactions. Currencies, usually in the form of deposits in banks and other financial institutions, thus readily move back and forth across national boundaries.

Rules governing the exchange of currencies and conditions for loans have evolved over time, as have the international organizations tasked by member countries with implementing or enforcing them. The sets of rules and institutions associated with them constitute what we can refer to as an ***international monetary regime,*** which has as its purpose providing financial arrangements so essential to maintaining and expanding trade and other forms of international commerce.

In earlier centuries, currencies were often defined as being equivalent in value to a fixed weight of some precious metal like silver or gold. In the late nineteenth and early twentieth centuries, for example, a U.S. dollar could be exchanged for 1/20th of an ounce of gold. Put another way, it took $20 to buy an ounce of gold from the U.S. Treasury. Stated formally, the dollar's gold parity (a technical term) was $20 an ounce. At the same time the value of the British currency (the pound sterling) was also defined as a fixed weight of gold. Countries willing to exchange their currencies for gold on demand were said to be on a gold standard.

In fact, relatively little gold was actually exchanged because countries found it more convenient instead to exchange each other's currencies as needed to finance trade and other forms of international commerce. The exchange rate between the U.S. dollar and British pound was easy to calculate because both were defined in terms of specified weights of gold. Thus, at the time, it took about $4.87 (more precisely $4.867) to buy one British pound note. At the core of the international monetary regime at the time was what amounted to a gold-exchange standard.

In the late 1800s and early 1900s the United Kingdom enjoyed financial prominence in Europe and throughout the world. Given its standing and its access to capital throughout the world, the Bank of England as a central bank managed not only the British currency—the pound sterling, which was readily convertible into a fixed quantity of gold—but also effectively the worldwide international monetary regime. Other countries often held deposits of the pound sterling as **reserves,** which could be used to finance their trade and other purchases abroad. Holding sterling deposits as reserves was actually preferable to holding gold because these sterling deposits could even earn interest. Because of its pivotal role in the international monetary regime of the time, sterling came to be regarded in effect as a key currency.

This is how the Bank of England managed the international monetary regime at the time. Because foreigners understood and respected the financial soundness of the Bank of England and the economy it represented, whenever the Bank of England wanted to attract foreign currencies to enhance its own reserves in order to make payments to other countries, it could do so simply by raising its interest rate—referred to technically as its discount rate.

As a central bank, changes in the rate it charged to other British banks would have an impact on their own interest rates as well. By raising its discount rate, the Bank of England in effect encouraged the sale of sterling to holders of foreign currencies seeking greater earnings due to higher interest rates to be found in British financial markets. Put another way, holders of foreign currencies would readily use these holdings to buy sterling for deposit in British banks, thus taking advantage of higher British interest rates. In turn, many of these foreign currencies would wind up in the Bank of England's reserves as British banks exchanged them there for sterling.

During World War I (1914–1918), budgetary requirements to finance the war effort forced Britain (and other countries) to abandon the gold-exchangeability of their currencies. Wartime controls on currency expenditures were eventually removed when the war ended as the United Kingdom tried to reassume its prewar role as manager of a restored international monetary regime. Although the United Kingdom still retained its worldwide empire, Britain's capital base had been significantly eroded by heavy borrowing necessitated by massive wartime expenditures. The United States, although it possessed the capital base to assume the international-monetary management role, was

international monetary regime
Financial rules, regulations, and institutions agreed on by states to facilitate international trade and commerce.

unwilling to do so. Given its financially weakened position, Britain had great difficulty performing the monetary-management role in the 1920s and finally was forced to abandon the effort in 1931 with the onset of a worldwide economic depression.[3]

During the 1930s, countries often resorted to currency **exchange controls** to limit the amount of money spent abroad, thus avoiding payment obligations. At the same time, imports were restrained by high tariffs, quotas, and other barriers to trade. It was a period described as "beggar thy neighbor" as countries turned inward to protect themselves no matter what the expense might be to other countries. Countries also devalued their currencies in an effort to make imports more expensive to firms and individuals at home while at the same time promoting their exports by making them cheaper to foreigners.

The United States did this by raising the price of gold from $20 to $35 an ounce. Raising the official price of gold amounted to a devaluation of the dollar. The process was a bit complicated, but here is how it worked. The exchange value of the dollar depended upon its gold value. Following the increase in gold price, Americans now had to pay $35 for the same amount of foreign goods and services that they previously bought with an ounce of gold when it was priced at $20—in effect a 75 percent increase in the price of imports. At the same time, foreign purchasers got a good deal designed to promote exports because the foreign currency equivalent to an ounce of gold now bought $35 worth of American goods and services instead of just $20 worth. Of course, more than one country could play this game, and many did. As a result round after round of **competitive devaluations** characterized the 1930s, as each country tried to establish a trade advantage over others—maximizing exports and minimizing imports. It was a zero-sum political game that countries played, seeking gains at the expense of others.

The net effect of such policies was a drastic reduction in international trade and foreign investment as the worldwide economy continued to stagnate. These economic events were followed in a few years by the onset of another world war in 1939, which many observers at the time and since have understood at least partly as a consequence of the self-serving, nationalistic or neomercantilist political-economic policies pursued throughout the 1930s.

Lessons drawn from this experience led during World War II to political plans for establishing a new international monetary regime that would make possible a reopening of international trade and investment across national borders. Instead of zero-sum thinking, achieving positive gains through expanded trade and commerce took center stage. In game-theoretic terms, there was a visible shift from the zero-sum political game of the Depression years to a positive-sum political game to guide country players in the postwar period. All could gain in principle from international monetary collaboration.

One outcome of this thinking was establishment of an International Monetary Fund (IMF) by international agreement at a conference held in 1944 at Bretton Woods, New Hampshire. British economist John Maynard Keynes and his American counterpart, Harry Dexter White, were the key proponents of alternative plans. In proposing to allow

> **T**he real losers from Russia's disastrous initial flirtation with global capitalism [in the 1990s] were its middle classes. Not quite rich enough nor quite dishonest enough to squirrel their money away in, say, Cyprus, their hard work was destroyed by devaluation. By one estimate, within a month of the crash, sixty thousand professionals in Moscow were either laid off, sent home on "temporary unpaid leave," or forced to take salary cuts of one third.
>
> **John Micklethwait and Adrian Wooldridge**
> A Future Perfect: The Challenge and Promise of Globalization (New York: Random House, 2003), 249.

It's Been Said...

---

[3]For an excellent discussion of this period, see Charles P. Kindleberger, *The World in Depression, 1929–1939* (Berkeley: University of California Press, 1973).

the new IMF political authority to create reserves (to which Keynes and his followers gave the nickname *bancor*), the Keynes plan was far more liberal than the White plan, which preferred to rely on gold and key currencies for reserves and opposed conferring any such reserve-creation authority on the new IMF. Given the political-economic prominence of the United States in these negotiations, the American view was more influential in determining the final outcome. Nevertheless, a version of Keynesian thinking was evident in the 1960s when member countries authorized the IMF to create SDRs, or Special Drawing Rights (see the discussion of SDRs later in this chapter).

The task the IMF was given at Bretton Woods, which prevailed during the institution's first quarter-century, was to oversee and manage an international monetary regime of relatively fixed exchange rates. It did this by relying on key currencies like the U.S. dollar, which were readily exchangeable into gold or other currencies. As such, a new gold-exchange standard came into existence with the U.S. dollar at its center—in effect a dollar-gold-exchange standard with the dollar still priced at its 1934 level of $35 an ounce. As in the sterling-gold-exchange standard of the late nineteenth and early twentieth centuries, relatively few actual gold exchanges occurred among national monetary authorities. Most countries held their reserves in the form of U.S. dollar deposits, understood to be at least as good as gold, or even better because these deposits also earned interest.

This would last until 1971 when the United States, confronted by long-standing balance-of-payments deficits and now a substantial deficit in its trade balance as well, decided to go off the gold-exchange standard and made the unilateral political choice to abandon fixed exchange rates. It allowed the value of its currency to **float,** or be set based on market supply and demand. American officials complained that over the years the dollar had become overvalued, which as a practical matter meant that U.S. exports were too expensive to foreigners and imports too cheap to Americans. As a result, the volume of U.S. exports could not keep up with the ever-increasing volume of American imports. By contrast, many other countries were seen as having undervalued currencies, giving them a decisive trade advantage—promoting their exports to (while discouraging imports from) the United States.

With its trade balance slipping into deficit, American officials chose to devalue the dollar by letting its value float, depreciating it in currency markets. Because the exchange values of many other currencies were tied to what had become a floating dollar, their values also fluctuated. A new international monetary regime of flexible exchange rates had come into existence. Fierce debates, however, occurred among monetary authorities as to just how flexible these rates should be.

Fixed exchange rates were credited with having contributed to the enormous growth in international commerce since the end of World War II. On the other hand, they were also blamed for leading to financial crises when currencies were viewed in currency markets as either overvalued or undervalued in relation to other currencies. A compromise position, managed flexibility, allows for some intervention in currency markets by monetary authorities to stabilize or otherwise influence exchange rates.

Faced with what they understood as destabilizing fluctuations in exchange rates, in the 1970s and 1980s members of the European Communities (EC) developed a monetary arrangement to stabilize rates among themselves even as their currencies floated collectively in relation to the dollar. As the EC became incorporated in the 1990s in a new European Union (EU), an outgrowth of earlier monetary collaboration was the establishment of an economic and monetary union. This included a common central bank located in Frankfurt managing a new currency, the euro, viewed as the leading competitor or potential competitor to the dollar as a global key currency.

International Liquidity and Currencies

Liquidity is a financial term referring to having cash available or an ability to raise such funds readily by selling assets. Maintaining international liquidity, a central IMF task, means providing member countries in need with access to financial assets that can be exchanged for currencies necessary to meet their payments obligations. Financial assets held as reserves by national monetary authorities include gold, SDRs (see box on p. 384), and hard currencies.

Hard currencies are those major currencies (e.g, the U.S. dollar, British sterling or pound, Japanese yen, and the European Union's euro) readily accepted and used by countries for making their payments transactions. What made them hard in earlier times was their convertibility to gold (or dollars, which in turn were readily convertible to gold) by national treasuries or at their central banks. By contrast, **soft currencies** lacked this convertibility and thus were less accepted.

Now we refer to hard currencies simply as those readily accepted and exchangeable for one another and thus easily used to buy any country's currency whenever needed. In an effort to improve their acceptability, monetary authorities of countries with soft currencies sometimes peg or link these currencies to the dollar or one or another of the hard currencies, allowing their soft currencies to rise and fall in value in the same way as the leading hard currencies do. As a result, their otherwise soft currencies are more readily accepted in commercial transactions.

International Organizations and International Monetary Regime Maintenance

The IMF has its headquarters in Washington, D.C.—separate from but physically next to the headquarters of the World Bank. Although the World Bank specializes in making loans for investment in economic reconstruction and development (see Chapter 12), the focus of the IMF is on the finance of trade—assisting member countries to manage their payments obligations to each other. Another institution, the Bank for International Settlements (BIS) in Basel, Switzerland, is a bank for central bankers who engage in buying, selling, lending, and borrowing each other's currencies as needed to sustain international commerce.

Established in 1930, BIS members include many of the same countries that belong to the IMF. Governments and their treasury officials are typically the principals in the IMF, whereas central bankers are the main players in the BIS. Over the years central bankers participating in the BIS have played an active, often pivotal role in actually making some of the financial arrangements agreed to by treasury and other government officials of IMF member countries.

If there is a shortfall in the supply of foreign currencies available, banks (and governments) can turn to their central banks—national institutions that service the banking needs of both member banks and government treasuries. Countries normally keep reserves of foreign currencies (and gold that can be used to buy these currencies), but sometimes these reserves become depleted, as when charges for imported goods and services and other payments far exceed earnings from exports and other sources. When that happens, member countries can draw on their accounts or borrow from the International Monetary Fund (IMF), which is in a position to keep its members in cash (i.e., maintain international liquidity).

The IMF makes advances of hard currencies that can readily be exchanged for whatever currency may be needed to finance transactions. As the IMF itself likes to say,

The International Monetary Fund building in Washington, D.C.

Special Drawing Rights (SDRs)

Policy makers in the 1960s and 1970s addressed the availability of reserves to finance payments in international trade, concluding that reliance on growth in gold, dollars, and other hard currencies was not sufficient. Building on ideas set forth earlier by John Maynard Keynes and other economists, the IMF was authorized by its member countries to create **Special Drawing Rights (SDRs),** dubbed by journalists at the time as "paper gold." In fact, SDR allocations to each IMF member country amounted to a new line of credit that could be drawn on without challenge in a time of need. Because countries having SDRs in their IMF accounts can readily exchange them at any time for hard currencies like the U.S. dollar, Japanese yen, and other **convertible currencies,** they are "as good as gold" and thus also can be included as part of a country's official reserves in the same way that gold and hard currencies are counted. So far, the IMF has been authorized to create and allocate SDRs worth a total of about $30 billion.

---

it operates in much the same way as a credit union by offering its member countries a variety of different kinds of loans and other mechanisms to meet their financial needs. If countries did not have such a source of short-term finance for balancing their payments, they probably would be forced to impose exchange controls, severely limiting the amount of domestic currency used to acquire foreign currencies, thus restricting purchases from abroad and disrupting international commerce.

Advances by the IMF are just that—advances that must be repaid, usually with interest. The IMF has about $300 billion in deposits by its members, which it can use to provide hard currencies to members in need. The amount of each country's required deposit or "quota" is different, depending on the size of its economy and trade requirements. The quota size also determines the voting power a member has on the board of governors that provides policy guidance and direction to the executive board, the IMF managing director, and the IMF staff. In effect, this gives political primacy in the IMF to countries with the largest economies, notably the United States and other Group of Seven members. With 18 percent of the vote, the United States has the largest number of votes. Given the requirement for an 85 percent voting majority on important matters, the European Union members voting as a block and the United States voting alone all enjoy the political advantage of an effective veto on major policy questions and other organizational decisions.

Each member of the IMF meets its contribution quota by putting on deposit 25 percent of the amount in convertible currencies, gold, or SDRs—Special Drawing Rights (see accompanying box)—and the remaining 75 percent of the quota by deposit of the country's own currency. When in need, the first 25 percent can be drawn without question (which amounts to a line of credit), but drawings beyond that amount are usually subject to certain conditions.

These conditions are the politically difficult part. In time, these IMF-prescribed remedies are expected to lay a firm basis for producing a viable economy able to sustain growth and finance trade. In the short run, however, these measures often call for substantial government belt tightening—tighter fiscal policies (e.g., cutting expenditures and increasing taxes) and tighter monetary policies (e.g., raising interest rates and constraining growth in the domestic money supply). Unfortunately, such policies, designed to dampen economies, cut inflation, curb imports, and foster greater efficiency in use of factors of production—so-called **structural adjustments** in the fundamental elements of an economy—also impose enormous costs. Critics refer to such policies as "neoliberal"—driven by market-oriented understandings that force national economies to "adjust" to external or global pressures in the world economy coming from the economically powerful states that use their leverage in the IMF, World Bank, WTO, and other institutions to force compliance with these standards. Businesses, for example, may not readily find capital to finance plans for expansion or may even close, and workers may lose jobs and have difficulty finding new employment. These economically difficult times brought on by such IMF-prescribed "neoliberal" austerity measures may well have politically explosive consequences for governments complying with IMF loan conditions. The IMF has also been the target of much criticism for insisting on these stringent requirements as conditions for advances to borrowing countries. Critics see these structural adjustment measures as retarding economic growth and development in Third World countries with unfair, often dire consequences to the peoples affected by these "neoliberal" policies.

The Effects of National Macroeconomic Policies

Fiscal policies deal with government budgetary matters (how much and how to tax and spend), whereas monetary policies address government measures that affect size and growth of the money supply and level of interest rates. Together fiscal and monetary policies are sometimes referred to as macroeconomic policies because they affect the national economy taken as a whole.

No matter how necessary imposing fiscal and monetary restraints may seem to finance experts, compliance with loan conditions can be extraordinarily difficult. Certainly this was the case for Indonesia, Thailand, South Korea, and other countries caught in the Asian financial crisis during the late 1990s. For its part, however, Malaysia found its own way out of IMF-imposed austerity by breaking IMF rules and imposing exchange controls—limiting the amount of ringit, the Malaysian currency, that could leave the country and be spent abroad. By adopting this monetary policy, Malaysia managed its payment obligations through government actions to limit the amount that could be spent abroad for imports or other purposes.

Imposing exchange controls is a monetary policy for managing a country's payments obligations to other countries. These controls usually take the form of domestic banking regulations in Country X that limit purchase of foreign currencies that can be used to finance imports, other purchases, or investments abroad. People leaving a country also are limited in the amounts of the country's currency they physically can take with them lest these funds be spent abroad. With less money spent abroad, there are fewer payment obligations to meet when the central banks or treasuries of other countries seek hard currencies or other reserves in exchange for amounts of currency from Country X they have acquired.

As discussed earlier, trade of goods and services in classical theory is based on differences in cost of production and market value of products themselves, not on the value of money used to purchase them. Thus it was convenient for classical economic theorists to assume the neutrality of money—that money has no independent impact on the costs of production or market value of goods and services. In fact, money is anything but neutral in the real world. Changes in exchange value, for example, have a direct influence on the prices of exports and imports and thus on the demand for and supply of them. Accordingly governments and their national monetary policies do influence both domestic and international trade (see box on the next page).

From the IMF perspective, **exchange controls** come at a great cost. If countries in economic difficulties impose exchange controls (as many did before the IMF became effective as a lending agency), the net effect will be reduction in imports and thus on the global volume of trade, adversely affecting economic growth as well. Moreover, other countries can no longer sell their products freely to countries limiting imports through exchange controls. When export sales go down, profits and jobs are lost. These are real costs borne by other countries, which economists refer to, as noted earlier, as negative *externalities.*

Resorting to exchange controls thus runs the political and economic risk that countries adversely affected by this policy may choose to retaliate economically by discriminating against the exports of countries adopting such measures. In short, those opposing resort to exchange controls as a way of managing a country's payments not only see such a policy as reducing the volume of trade but also argue that it is an unfair way of shifting some of the costs of structural adjustments in one's own economy to the shoulders of others. Be that as it may, defenders of managing a country's payments through exchange controls see it as a more desirable, somewhat less intrusive remedy than either bearing the social and political consequences of fiscal and monetary austerity, or worse yet, directly blocking trade by imposing high tariffs or quotas against imports from other countries—an approach sure to invite retaliation in kind.

externalities
Positive or negative effect on others of decisions made or actions taken, as when a state makes a monetary or trade decision which, however much it may benefit the state and its economy, has a negative effect on the economy of other states.

Domestic Effects and Externalities of National Monetary Policy

Following is a list of domestic and external effects of political choices to change a country's monetary policy—specified here in terms of both interest rates (the cost of borrowing money) and the money supply (the amount of money in circulation).

Interest Rates Up
(tightening monetary policy; growth in money supply decreased)

Domestic Effects (ceteris paribus)

- Dampens domestic economy; slows growth by raising the cost of capital (e.g., borrowing capital for investment in productive enterprises is more expensive at higher interest rates)
- A curb on inflation (slower growth/less demand tends to keep prices stable or at least slow price increases; less money in circulation means there is less to spend)
- Increases fiscal cost of servicing national debt (government pays more interest given higher rates)
- Encourages short-term net capital inflow (as when capital flows in to take advantage of relatively higher interest rates domestically)
- Tends to increase exchange value of domestic currency (increasing capital inflows to take advantage of relatively higher interest rates tends to increase demand for country's currency)
- Stimulates imports; discourages exports (i.e., higher exchange value means imports tend to be cheaper domestically, exports more expensive to foreigners)
- Discourages long-term investment in domestic economy by foreigners (i.e., cost of domestic assets more expensive when purchased with foreign currencies)

External Effects (ceteris paribus)

- Stimulates foreign production by promoting imports (see previous examples)
- May "export" inflation by dampening domestic economy while stimulating foreign production for export
- More difficult for Third World and other debtors to pay their obligations

Interest Rates Down
(loosening monetary policy; growth in money supply increased)

Domestic Effects (ceteris paribus)

- Stimulates domestic economy; encourages growth by lowering the cost of capital (e.g., borrowing capital for investment in productive enterprises is cheaper at lower interest rates)
- Could spur inflation (faster growth/greater demand tends to put upward pressure on prices; more money in circulation means there is more to spend)
- Decreases fiscal cost of servicing national debt (government pays less interest given lower rates)
- Encourages short-term net capital outflow (as when capital flows out to take advantage of relatively higher interest rates abroad)
- Tends to decrease exchange value of domestic currency (increasing capital outflows to take advantage of relatively higher interest rates abroad tends to decrease demand for country's currency)
- Stimulates exports; discourages imports (i.e., lower exchange value means exports tend to be cheaper to foreigners, imports more expensive domestically)
- Encourages long-term investment in domestic economy by foreigners (i.e., cost of domestic assets cheaper when purchased with foreign currencies)

External Effects (ceteris paribus)

- Dampens foreign production by promoting exports (see previous examples)
- Tends to dampen inflation pressures abroad by stimulating domestic production and curbing imports
- Easier for Third World and other debtors to pay their obligations.

Political Choices: How Much Capital Should the IMF Have and for What Purposes?

Decisions on how much capital the IMF should have and for what purposes are essentially political choices made by member countries represented in the IMF's board of governors and its executive board. Indeed, the IMF's central function is to have the necessary funds available to lend to countries in balance-of-payments difficulties, thus precluding their resort either to erecting tariffs, quotas, and other barriers to trade or to imposing exchange controls. The IMF also facilitates dismantling exchange controls already in existence when countries are making the adjustments necessary to open their domestic economies and participate more fully in global trade and other forms of commerce.

To do all this—as a practical matter to be able to perform its core task of maintaining international liquidity as well as make funds available for other purposes specified by international agreement of its member countries—the IMF requires enormous capital resources. Because 75 percent of the quota contributions made by member countries is in their own currencies, the amount of "hard currency" available for lending is considerably less than half of some $300 billion the IMF has on deposit from quota subscriptions.

IMF lending resources were initially expanded in the 1960s when a new mechanism, the General Arrangements to Borrow (GAB), was constructed to supplement drawings on quotas. Eleven capital-rich countries originally put up GAB funds, which now total about $23 billion that can be lent to IMF members needing balance-of-payments assistance. Following the same model, twenty-five member countries decided to contribute hard currencies to another facility, the New Arrangements to Borrow (NAB), which was established in 1997, doubling total resources available under these arrangements to a combined total of some $46 billion.

The IMF also has a gold stock of more than 100 million fine ounces (its market value fluctuates from day to day, but at, say, $300 an ounce, this is worth more than $30 billion), which the IMF board of governors can authorize be sold to acquire hard currencies. The political decision to create Special Drawing Rights or SDRs—so-called "paper gold"—and allocate them to member countries (see box on SDRs earlier in the chapter) also expanded capital resources that now amount to close to an additional $30 billion.

As a lending institution, the IMF charges interest on drawings or borrowing of its funds. Member countries actually earn interest on their quota contributions when their currencies are borrowed by other countries. The interest rates charged to borrowing countries, however, are truly **concessionary**—well below rates countries would be charged if they borrowed in financial markets. Over the years, the specific purposes for which the IMF may lend funds have expanded substantially, particularly for low-income, less-developed countries.

For example, since the 1980s some eighty low-income, less-developed countries have been eligible to receive special treatment by borrowing funds for ten-year terms from the IMF's Enhanced Structural Adjustment Facility at below-market or concessionary interest rates (just one-half of one percent). The condition for such loans is that borrowing countries use the money for structural adjustment tasks—implementing a three-year program designed to provide a foundation for sustained economic growth, thus enabling them to meet their payments obligations. A total of close to $10 billion in loans has been disbursed to more than fifty needy countries by this facility, with new lending projected at more than a billion dollars a year. The source of these funds is capital-rich and other more economically developed countries that are willing to contribute.

The IMF may extend contingency lines of credit to countries not presently in balance-of-payments difficulties but that are concerned that the effects of financial turmoil in other countries might spread to them. The IMF also has special lending authority for countries recovering from war and other civil conflicts, as well as emergency assistance or compensatory financing when earthquakes, hurricanes, floods, droughts, frosts, insect and other pest infestations, or other natural disasters adversely affect exports or disrupt normal trade and payments transactions. The IMF not only lends money in such circumstances but also renders technical assistance toward establishing or reestablishing the financial infrastructure that may have been destroyed or weakened by political or economic turmoil brought on by natural disasters or armed conflict.

Understanding itself as an agent for global trade and commerce, the IMF sees this role as encompassing technical tasks as well as fostering market-oriented values in member or would-be member countries willing to avail themselves of such assistance. Accordingly, the IMF contributes to developing effective central banking and treasury institutions, collecting and refining statistical data on economic activities, and training officials who can perform technical monetary tasks. Perhaps even more significantly, as an agent of socialization the IMF joins other international organizations and governments in efforts to integrate these officials within an expanding, worldwide culture of values shared by professionals or technical experts dealing with monetary matters so essential to sustaining and increasing global trade and other forms of commerce. These technical experts can be understood as constituting an **epistemic community** conversant with each other across state boundaries whether in direct meetings or by telecommunications.

Political Choices: What Next for the WTO?

Just as an international monetary regime sets forth rules for the exchange of currencies and the finance of international commerce, an international trade regime also has rules relating to how exports and imports are bought and sold, transported, paid for, and delivered. Many of these rules have standing as customary international law and are enforceable in suits brought in national courts.

As discussed in Chapter 9, the topic of rules for international commerce is not a new one. Grotius (1583–1645) addressed the topic, and both customary international law and the Law of the Sea Treaty identify territorial waters, define rights of passage for commercial vessels, and underscore the primacy of freedom of navigation on the high seas. Similar rules with the force of international law apply to trade across land and by air.

As discussed in Chapter 10, political opposition, particularly in the United States, blocked efforts after World War II to establish an International Trade Organization (ITO) as a companion institution to the International Monetary Fund and World Bank. Instead, negotiating arrangements known as the General Agreement on Tariffs and Trade (GATT) produced periodic international conferences (or rounds, as they were called) that worked toward reduction of tariffs, quotas, and other barriers to trade, especially those erected in the 1930s when protectionist sentiments had reigned supreme.

Even in the absence of an international organization or specialized agency for trade, participating countries (including the United States) made great progress in liberalizing global trade—opening markets between and across national borders. Most of the existing trade agreements are the result of the 1986–1994 Uruguay Round negotiations, signed at the Marrakesh ministerial meeting in April 1994. There are about sixty agreements and decisions, totaling 550 pages. Marrakesh is where the World Trade Organization (WTO) was established as a single institutional framework designed to encompass the GATT, as modified by the Uruguay Round, and all agreements and arrangements concluded under its auspices. The WTO's essential mission is to ensure that trade flows as smoothly, predictably, and freely as possible. In addition to agreements reached on trading rules, WTO official tasks include "administering trade agreements, acting as a forum for trade negotiations, settling trade disputes, reviewing national trade policies, assisting developing countries in trade policy issues through technical assistance and training programs, and cooperating with other international organizations."

The WTO structure is headed by a Ministerial Conference meeting held at least once every two years. A General Council headquartered in Geneva oversees the operation of the agreement and ministerial decisions. Its key function is to act as a Dispute Settlement Body and a Trade Policy Review Mechanism dealing with the full range of trade issues covered by the WTO. Hence, member countries may bring complaints against other members to the WTO's dispute-settlement process. The framework requires a "single undertaking approach" to the results of the Uruguay Round. Therefore, membership in the WTO entails accepting all the results of the Round without exception by some 150 member countries.

Nevertheless, open-trade (if not entirely free-trade) advocates still saw much work to be done. In addition to further reductions in trade barriers, curbing bribery or other illicit practices and assuring global respect for intellectual property rights (patents and copyrights) are issues high on the agenda of both private interests and those wishing to promote growth in international commerce. Moreover, advocates want to head off fears of trade wars or any thought of return to the mutually exclusive, regional trading blocs that had prevailed in the 1930s. Bringing many newly market-oriented countries into the global trading regime was another important motivation in the 1990s for moving beyond GATT to forming a new World Trade Organization (WTO).

Major disputes do surround the WTO, as evidenced by demonstrators at a WTO ministerial meeting held in Seattle in 1999. WTO opponents were highly critical of trading policies that in their view do not afford sufficient weight to protecting the environment. Labor interests challenged WTO policies that open trade at the expense of workers who lose their jobs in what they argue is unfair global competition brought on by corporate exploitation of foreign workers who are paid very low wages and often suffer poor working conditions in labor-intensive industries abroad. Environmental activists and labor rights advocates thus found common cause in these anti-WTO demonstrations. These challenges from outside the WTO are matched by conflicts within. Not only are unfair trade practice complaints frequently made by member countries against each other, but members also differ philosophically on practical goals. Some members, like the United States, argue for open markets as free as possible of government intervention or protectionism. Other members argue not so much for free trade but rather for managed trade that avoids some of the environmental, labor, and other pitfalls encountered in a free-trade environment. From this perspective, the WTO can serve as a forum for discussing and negotiating managed-trade arrangements in which governments intervene in markets to reduce costs to interested parties. Despite the GATT's and WTO's tremendous success in reducing trade barriers over the years and the resulting increase in overall global prosperity, the collapse of the Cancun, Mexico, conference in September 2003 was an ominous sign. The chief goal of the conference was to lower trade barriers in areas where freer trade would help poor countries the most, particularly in agriculture. Suffice it to say there was enough blame to be shared by rich countries, poor countries, and nongovernmental organizations for this serious failure to maintain momentum in the expansion of the international trade regime.

Regional Economic Integration and Global Commerce

Economic efforts to increase the level of global prosperity have been taken at the regional as well as international level. The post–World War II European experience has been a test-bed for ideas, concepts, and theories as to how to increase regional integration. What has occurred in Europe since the end of World War II in 1945 is one of the more amazing international developments. Here we have a continent twice devastated by world wars, fueled by the nationalist fires and ambitions of century-long rivalries, and divided by the cold war, but now an economic giant. For realists, the success of the Western European economic enterprise was essentially due to the security protection provided by the United States. There is much truth to that, but pluralists are quick to point out that realists expected economic **integration** and cooperation to slow down or collapse once the unifying threat of the Soviet Union and its allies had passed. Such a crisis of authority for the European Union has not happened. Why not?

The underlying assumption of much of the work on European integration has been quite simple: enhanced economic ties and exchanges not only will have positive benefits in terms of economic prosperity but will have political benefits as well. A critical objective of regional integration therefore is the prospect of enhancing peace among states. In the first decade or so after World War II, Jean Monnet and Robert Schuman from France and German Chancellor Konrad Adenauer were among the important advocates of a new Europe. These elites had made no secret of their objectives and plans for constructing a new Europe. Reacting to the devastation wrought by two world wars, they were trying to put in place an alternative set of positive, constructive relations among former enemies. By fostering economic integration efforts they were trying at a very practical level to establish new, cooperative links between France and the Federal Republic of Germany, core players in the continental European economy. Theirs was an incremental, step-by-step strategy for attaining economic integration goals over time. A principal motivation was their expectation of a positive impact on political relations among European states to be drawn from progress toward greater economic integration.

As discussed in Chapter 6, **functionalists** note that international organizations are formed from the recognition that certain tasks need to be performed, such as monetary exchange, trade, multilateral investment, mail service, or parceling out telecommunications frequencies. **Neofunctionalists** focus on the political processes orchestrated by politically connected specialists or elites. To the neofunctionalist, integration doesn't just happen, it arises by design. More recently and along the same lines, Andrew Moravcsik

Case & Point

CHINA

If there is one country that figures prominently in the speculation of what international relations and world politics will look like in the next few years, it is China. Despite unprecedented access to China in the past twenty-five years by scholars, businesspeople, journalists, diplomats, and tourists, the country conjures up many different and conflicting images. For some, China is epitomized by its economic miracle and the skyscrapers of Shanghai, the spread of cell phones, and dusty construction sites. Others point to the repression of pro-democracy demonstrators in Tianamen Square in 1989 and the continual repression of dissidents as evidence of the "real China." The diversity and complexity of this giant country provide evidence to support almost any point of view.

What most observers would probably agree on, however, is that the single biggest challenge for the current Chinese leadership is the need to deliver continual economic growth or risk political turmoil. The economic reforms that began in the late 1970s generated catch-up growth—gains from disbanding agricultural communes and the resultant influx of cheap labor to low-end manufacturing firms made for double-digit economic growth. Those days are gone, as growth rates in the manufacturing sector have slowed and agricultural productivity has reached its limits due to a severe shortage of water. The gap in the standard of living between the city and the countryside is a serious problem, as is the growth in corruption and widespread environmental degradation.

Many businesspeople, however, see China simply as a vast market, its 1.3 billion citizens potential customers for a wide variety of consumer goods. International businesses, the United States, the European Union, and other advanced industrial countries lobbied for China's admittance to the World Trade Organization (WTO). Bipartisan U.S.

Case & Point

(continued)

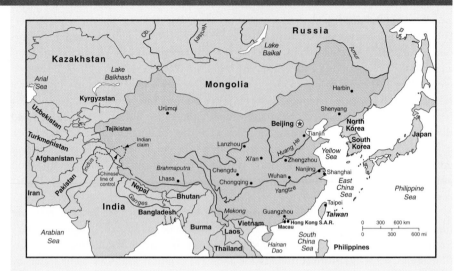

FIGURE 11.D

political support resulted in Congress granting permanent normal trading relations (PNTR) status to China in May 2000. Both China and its trading partners, it was claimed, would benefit in economic terms from the tariff-reduction and market-widening proposals. But there was a political argument as well—by being brought into the global trading system, China will no longer be the self-isolated Middle Kingdom but rather a vested partner in a stable global economic system. This follows the logic of economic liberalism and arguments for the pacifying effects of global interdependence. Furthermore, although not usually voiced, is the view that economic development will help to undermine the authoritarian regime in Beijing. Trade with foreigners will supposedly add pressure to the further development of the rule of law. Hence supporters of PNTR status for China managed to combine economic self-interest with claims of being supportive of human and political rights in China.

Some realist critics dismiss the economic liberalism argument as historically unfounded and empirically incorrect. The simple proposition that the benefits of economic exchange make war too costly to pursue seems intuitively plausible, yet in an anarchic world fear will be ever-present, and hence so will be the possibility of war.

Other critics, however, take a different tack, arguing that in the pursuit of trade benefits the world is too willing to overlook China's human rights abuses. By granting PNTR and admitting China to the World Trade Organization, advanced industrial states were, in effect, placing their seal of approval on the regime. Why, it was asked, should the advanced industrial democracies give up a carrot (admittance to the WTO and PNTR) that could be used to improve human rights in China?

Point: Too often we read interpretations of China only from outsiders. For Chinese perspectives that deal with the topics mentioned here, see Yong Deng and Fei-Ling Wand, *In the Eyes of the Dragon: China Views the World* (Savage, MD: Rowman and Littlefield, 2000).

claims liberal intergovernmentalism is the best perspective through which to view the major turning points in European integration. He argues that state preferences are chiefly determined by interdependence, opportunities for international economic exchange, and the dominant interests in a national society, with actual substantive integration outcomes resulting from hard bargaining among state elites.[4]

An internal logic to the economic integration process identified by neofunctionalists is apparent in the European integration experience. For example, free trade and commerce in the 1950s expanded in one economic sector (a customs union known as the European Coal and Steel Community, or ECSC). Commercial transactions and ties, however, also spilled over into other economic sectors that in turn were used by commercial and politically connected elites in 1958 to create an enlarged European Economic Community (EEC) as well as a European Atomic Energy Community (EURATOM) to advance peaceful, economic uses of nuclear energy. The ECSC, EEC, and EURATOM—referred to collectively as the European Communities (EC)—carried out their integration tasks for more than thirty years before being incorporated into what is now referred to as the European Union (EU). Another example of spillover occurred when a common agricultural policy (CAP)—painstakingly developed in the late 1960s and early 1970s to set farm prices and price supports within the EEC—came apart. The key precipitating event was when the dollar, to which European currencies were then tied, was allowed to fluctuate in value. To reconstruct a new CAP, integration spilled over into the monetary sector with the creation of a European Monetary System to stabilize currency exchange rates, a necessary step to stabilize prices for agricultural commodities traded within the EEC (see Table 11.2).

Integration also can occur in response to external challenges. Movement from a Customs Union to a Common Market in 1992 and achievement of a European Economic and Monetary Union were not driven by the internal logic indicated by neofunctionalist theory. These changes were due more to calculations by politically relevant elites that Europe would have to deepen the level of economic integration in order to remain competitive with the United States, Japan, and other countries in twenty-first-century high-technology and other global markets.

EC and EU Enlargement: Widening the Geographical Scope versus Deepening the Level of Integration

An ongoing debate within Europe involves the issue of whether the widening of the membership of the EU should be pursued if it comes at the expense of deepening the level of integration among member states. Britain's first attempt to join the EC, for example, was rebuffed in 1967 by France under President Charles de Gaulle (1958–1969) that saw the United Kingdom as more closely tied to the United States and the British Commonwealth than to continental Europe. After reconsideration of the matter by successor governments in France as well as by the five other EC members, accession to the EC by the United Kingdom, Ireland, and Denmark finally took place in 1973, thus marking the first round of enlargement. Greece joined in 1981, Portugal and Spain in 1986, and in 1995 came the immediate post–Cold War accessions by Austria, Finland, and Sweden—Norway choosing to maintain a more independent posture and thus remain outside what had now become the European Union (EU).

[4]Wayne Sandholtz and Alec Stone Sweet, eds., *European Integration and Supranational Government* (New York: Oxford University Press, 1998); and Andrew Moravcsik, *The Choice for Europe* (London: UCL Press, 1998).

TABLE 11.2

A Regional Integration Ladder

Descent on the ladder denotes movement from relatively shallow to ever-deeper levels of integration. Participants may choose to minimize the degree of integration, staying on upper rungs, or they may decide to deepen the level of integration by moving to lower rungs.

		CHARACTERISTICS (CHARACTERISTICS ARE CUMULATIVE AS RUNGS DESCEND)
First Rung	*Free-Trade Area*	*Goal:* no tariffs or other trade barriers (e.g., North American and European Free Trade Areas [NAFTA and EFTA])
		+
Second Rung	*Customs Union*	*Goal:* common external tariff against imports (e.g., European Economic Community, EEC, established in 1958)
		+
Third Rung	*Common Market*	*Goal:* free movement of factors of production (land, labor, and capital) within integration area (e.g., Europe 1992, Single European Act)
		+
Fourth Rung	*Economic and Monetary Union*	*Goal:* common currency and integrated economic policies (e.g., European Union Treaty agreed to at Maastricht in 1991, also calling for common foreign and security policy; implemented by Amsterdam Treaty signed in 1997 and effective in 1999)
		+
Fifth Rung	*Full Political Union*	*Goal:* complete economic and political integration (e.g., federations like the United States, a model for some advocates of European integration, but others oppose stepping into this deepest form of integration)

The most extensive enlargement round occurred in 2004 with decisions on widening to include much of Central and Eastern Europe, previously in the Soviet sphere of influence (the Czech Republic, Hungary, Poland, and Slovakia); the Baltic states, previously part of the Soviet Union itself (Estonia, Latvia, and Lithuania); a part of the former Yugoslav Federation (Slovenia); and two Mediterranean states (Cyprus and Malta). In the waiting line are two other central European states (Bulgaria and Romania) as well as Macedonia and Turkey, the latter continuing its long-term, uphill struggle for membership.

For many years, critics of EC or EU enlargement noted that increasing the membership and thus widening its European scope risked undermining efforts to deepen integration—moving beyond a customs union to a common market, economic and monetary union, and common social as well as foreign and security policies. Not only was collaboration among larger numbers of states understood to be more difficult than

Practicing World Politics

International organizations play important roles in trade and monetary aspects of global and regional economies. Visit some of their websites:

Global

World Trade Organization (www.wto.org)

International Monetary Fund (www.imf.org)

Bank for International Settlements (www.bis.org)

World Bank (www.worldbank.org)

U.N. Conference on Trade and Development (www.unctad.org)

World Intellectual Property Organization (www.wipo.int)

Organization of Petroleum Exporting Countries (www.opec.org)

Regional

Andean Group (www.comunidadandina.org)

Asia-Pacific Economic Cooperation (www.apec.org)

Association of Southeast Asian Nations (www.aseansec.org)

Caribbean Community and Common Market (www.caricom.org)

Economic Community of West African States (www.ecowas.int)

European Union (europa.eu.int and, in the United States, www.eurunion.org)

Mercosur (Common Market Southern Cone, South America) (www.mercosur.org.uy)

North American Free Trade Association (www.nafta-sec-alena.org)

U.N. Regional Economic Commissions

Africa (Addis Ababa) (www.uneca.org)

Europe (Geneva) (www.unece.org)

Latin America (Santiago) (www.eclac.org)

CHECKING OUT WEB SITES OF INTER-NATIONAL ORGANIZA-TIONS

forging agreements among a few had proven to be, but also the asymmetries in levels of economic development and socioeconomic diversities among a larger membership were seen as posing substantial challenges to keeping ever-deeper integration on track.

Although the EC members were often referred to as the "Common Market" countries, a true common market—a step deeper on the integration ladder than a customs union that entails free flow within the community of the land, labor, and capital "factors of production"—technically did not come into existence until full implementation in 1992 of the EC's 1987 agreement on a set of commercial and related regulations known more formally as the Single European Act (SEA). Work also was underway to create a European Union (EU) with common currency by the end of the 1990s, coordinating social policy and developing a common foreign and security policy (CFSP)—goals set in December 1991 and formally agreed in the February 1992 Treaty of Maastricht. The subsequent treaties of Amsterdam (1997) and Nice (2001) addressed organizational matters—an effort to streamline bureaucratic procedures and make other institutional adjustments to the expanded EU role.

To say the least, the EU has made great progress in its quest not only to widen but also to deepen the level of integration. Agricultural policy has always been a problematic issue, particularly given strong political pressures from farmers to continue or expand agricultural protection or subsidy. Admission of new members adds to the challenge in the decades-long effort to develop and implement a Common Agricultural Policy (CAP)—coordinating price structure and taking other cooperative measures to facilitate trade while accommodating farm-sector interests.

On monetary matters, great progress was marked in 2002 with the euro becoming the EU currency managed by a common central bank; however, asymmetries in fiscal and monetary policies and a political preference for retaining a greater degree of independent political control over such matters led the United Kingdom and Denmark also to opt out of the monetary union. That said, the euro has already become the major currency EU leaders sought not only to facilitate trade, investment, and other forms of commerce across the European continent but also to enhance the EU's economic standing regionally and globally in relation to the United States.

Finally, the quest for a common foreign and security policy remains a substantial challenge as does the effort to establish an agreed EU constitution, which continues notwithstanding rejection by French and Dutch voters in particular. Some progress, however, has been made on security since the decision in 1999 to assume the tasks previously performed by the West European Union (WEU), although critics argue that the effort has not received the funding the program needs to establish a viable all-European, independent defense capability. Of even greater concern to many was the decision in 2003 by the United Kingdom to join the United States in the invasion and subsequent occupation of Iraq (and the decision by France and Germany not to do so), thus effectively splitting the EU with adverse impact on plans for deepening the level of foreign and security policy integration.

Some realists have noted that perhaps the United States succeeded too well in encouraging European integration—not only does the European Union have the potential to be a formidable economic bloc, but Europeans have developed an ingrained aversion to large military budgets and the use of military force. To put it another way, the Europeans have managed to create for themselves a Kantian peace based upon negotiation and cooperation, and they don't want to jeopardize it. The United States, however, being a superpower, supposedly lives in a Hobbesian world with conflict the essential characteristic. Where the two might clash, however, is in the economic realm. The EU now stretches from the Arctic to the Mediterranean and from the Irish Sea to the Black Sea. It comprises 450 million persons and accounts for more than one-fifth of global economic activity. For this reason alone, realists foresee difficult times in U.S.–European relations.

Is Europe Unique?

Our focus in this section has been on European economic integration because it is the region that has made the most progress toward these goals. Most importantly, the idea of a war among Western European countries is almost to the point of being far-fetched. The interesting question is, "Why haven't we seen similar progress toward economic and political integration in other areas of the world?" Much more modest efforts include the North American Free Trade Agreement (NAFTA), the Central American

European Union

= Member states   58 = Joining dates

MAP 11.1   *European Union*

Free Trade Agreement (CAFTA), the West African Economic Community (ECOWAS), the Common Market in the Southern Cone of South America (MERCOSUR), the Andean Group, the Central American Common Market (CACM), the Association of Southeast Asian Nations (ASEAN), and other regional integration organizations. Compared to the EU, these are much more modest efforts that do not even have as an objective the levels that already have been achieved in Europe, much less those that are anticipated by European integration advocates.

For example, the much-celebrated Canada–Mexico–United States NAFTA accord has only the relatively modest ambition of gradually establishing a regional free-trade area. In this context it also provides for greater mobility of capital and some harmonization of business practices and standards. As yet there has been no serious discussion, however, of moving to a customs union with a common external tariff, much less a common market that would allow for the free flow of labor across borders. This makes the European efforts to establish and sustain an economic and monetary union with a common currency—a much deeper level of integration than ever attempted in other regional integration projects—even more impressive. The next challenge is to integrate the more recent entrants to the EU and the harmonization of a wide range of economic and monetary policies.

Perhaps the post–World War II circumstances in Western Europe were unique. As noted, the United States provided a security guarantee against the communist East and encouraged the Europeans to focus on economic recovery. The Marshall Plan certainly helped to jump-start economic recovery. The fact that the states were contiguous geographically was also a factor, a situation quite different than in Asia. The common aspirations of European elites were also important, and perhaps the common historical European values, despite the Fascist experiences in Germany, Italy, and elsewhere, also made a difference. In more recent years, the strong grounding in democratic values and traditions has encouraged the rise of a civil society, with many transnational European organizations encouraging social interactions below the level of the state.

Will the continual integration of Europe encourage the development of regional economic blocs and lead to mercantilist competition? This possibility is constantly raised and debated. Developing and maintaining trade within a region can (but need not) divert trade or displace other commercial relations outside of the regional context. Advances at the regional level should be viewed in the broader context of the continual fast pace of globalization. To the extent that they create trade and promote economic development, regional efforts—however ambitious or however modest—do contribute to the continued functioning of capitalist political economy on a global scale.

Conclusion

Economics has been called the dismal science, not just because of an inherent pessimism accompanying many economic theories or theorists but also because of a certain opaqueness of presentation seemingly impervious to penetration by general readers. To many people economics may well be a dismal science, but it is nonetheless an enormously important undertaking if we are to understand what is taking place in an increasingly globalized world. The importance of economics underscores its link to politics—in particular the processes leading to authoritative decisions and implementation of economic policies by governments and international organizations. That is why the focus in the chapters in Part IV is on political economy, a term that explicitly recognizes the political dimension of economic matters in domestic as well as international and global contexts.

Afterword

Political Economy and Foreign Trade
David Ricardo
(1772–1823)

In this short selection from his Principles of Political Economy and Taxation *(1817), David Ricardo provides commentary on political economy and foreign trade. As with Adam Smith before him (and Karl Marx to follow), Ricardo writes in the genre of the classical economists who represent the value of what is produced as a function of the labor put into its production. (Later in the 19th and early 20th centuries, neoclassical economists will turn instead to supply and demand, market-based understandings of value.) What is important here, however, is Ricardo's focus on the idea of comparative advantage—that a country will tend to produce both for domestic production and export those commodities it has the capacity to produce more cheaply than other countries. When countries specialize by producing according to their comparative advantage or relative efficiency, aggregate or overall production quantities of all commodities are enhanced.*

Other things equal, the consumers have more to consume. This is Ricardo's core argument for laissez faire*—free trade unencumbered by government intervention in either domestic or international markets. But even Ricardo acknowledges that other factors may affect the "natural" trade equilibrium. Beyond production improvements that may shift comparative advantage in production of a particular product from one country to another, there are "bounties" or taxes on imports—tariffs that countries may impose to protect domestic producers of a particular product, thus distorting production and supply in favor of less-efficient producers. Excise and other taxes that discourage exports of certain commodities also distort trade flows that otherwise would occur. Moreover, Ricardo admits that variations in the exchange value of money is another variable that can impact adversely on what would be the "natural" flow of trade and commerce.*

Present-day critics of this Ricardian free-trade theory go beyond these factors, objecting among other things to uneven (and thus unfair or unjust) distribution of gains from trade, adverse terms of trade (relative price advantages for capital-rich country producers of manufactures, especially high-technology items, compared to the prices capital-poor country producers of agricultural and mineral commodities can expect to receive), and "neoliberal" policies that in order to maintain the financial viability necessary for international trade force capital-poor countries to endure severe austerity (e.g., such "adjustment" measures as reduced government spending, higher taxes, and higher interest rates) that impose enormous costs on all segments of society, particularly the poor. All that said, the following passages from Ricardo's major work establish an important benchmark referred to by both advocates and critics of free trade. English spellings are left intact and italics have been added to emphasize certain points in Ricardo's argument.

The produce of the earth—all that is derived from its surface *by the united application of labour, machinery, and capital, is divided among three classes* of the community; namely, *the proprietor of the land, the owner of the stock or capital necessary for its cultivation, and the labourers* by whose industry it is cultivated.

But *in different stages of society, the proportions of the whole produce of the earth which will be allotted to each of these classes, under the names of rent, profit, and wages,* will be essentially different; depending mainly on the actual fertility of the soil, on the accumulation of capital and population, and on the skill, ingenuity, and instruments employed in agriculture.

To determine the laws which regulate this distribution, is the principal problem in Political Economy. . . .

On Foreign Trade

No extension of foreign trade will immediately increase the amount of value in a country, although it will very powerfully contribute to increase the mass of commodities, and therefore the sum of enjoyments. As the value of all foreign goods is measured by the quantity of the produce of our land and labour, which is given in exchange for them, we should have no greater value, if by the discovery of new markets, we obtained double the quantity of foreign goods in exchange for a given quantity of ours. . . . *Under a system of perfectly free commerce, each country naturally devotes its capital and labour to such employments as are most beneficial to each. This pursuit of individual advantage is admirably connected with the universal good of the whole. By stimulating industry, by regarding ingenuity, and by using most efficaciously the peculiar powers bestowed by nature, it distributes labour most effectively and most economically: while, by increasing the general mass of productions, it diffuses general benefit, and binds together by one common tie of interest and intercourse, the universal society of nations throughout the civilized world.* It is this principle which determines that wine shall be made in France and Portugal, that corn shall be grown in America and Poland, and that hardware and other goods shall be manufactured in England. . . .

England may be so circumstanced, that to produce the cloth may require the labour of 100 men for one year; and if she attempted to make the wine, it might require the labour of 120 men for the same time. *England would therefore find it her interest to import wine, and to purchase it by the exportation of cloth.* To produce the wine in Portugal, might require only the labour of 80 men for one year, and to produce the cloth in the same country, might require the labour of 90 men for the same time. It would therefore be advantageous for her to export wine in exchange for cloth. This exchange might even take place, notwithstanding that the commodity imported by Portugal could be produced there with less labour than in England. Though she could make the cloth with the labour of 90 men, she would import it from a country where it required the labour of 100 men to produce it, because *it would be advantageous to her rather to employ her capital in the production of wine, for which she would obtain more cloth from England, than she could produce by diverting a portion of her capital from the cultivation of vines to the manufacture of cloth.* Thus England would give the produce of the labour of 100 men, for the produce of the labour of 80. . . .

I have been supposing the trade between two countries to be confined to two commodities—to wine and cloth; but it is well known that many and various articles enter into the list of exports and imports. By the abstraction of money from one country, and the accumulation of it in another, *all commodities are affected in price, and consequently encouragement is given to the exportation of many more commodities.* . . .

Besides the improvements in arts and machinery, there are various other causes which are constantly operating on the natural course of trade, and which interfere with the equilibrium, and the relative value of money. *Bounties on exportation or importation, new taxes on commodities*, sometimes by their direct, and at other times, by their indirect operation, disturb the natural trade of barter, and produce a consequent necessity of importing or exporting money, in order that prices may be accommodated to the natural course of commerce; and this effect is produced not only in the country where the disturbing cause takes place, but, in a greater or less degree, in every country of the commercial world. . . .

We have assumed, for the purpose of argument, that money always continued of the same value; we are now endeavouring to shew that besides the ordinary variations in the value of money, and those which are common to the whole commercial world, there are also partial variations to which money is subject in particular countries; and in fact, that *the value of money is never the same in any two countries*, depending as it does on relative taxation, on manufacturing skill, on the advantages of climate, natural productions, and many other causes. . . .

Key Terms

Other Concepts

Additional Readings

Not surprisingly, trade and finance are closely linked as one can see in Barry Eichengreen, *Globalizing Capital* (Princeton, NJ: Princeton University Press, 1996); Mark R. Brawley, *Turning Points: Shaping the Evolution of the International Political Economy* (Ontario, Canada: Broadview Press,1998); and Eric Helleiner, *States and the Reemergence of Global Finance* (Ithaca, NY: Cornell University Press, 1994).Trade is also a domain of conflict as discussed in Michael T. Klare, *Resource Wars: The New Landscape of Global Conflict* (NY: Henry Holt & Co./Owl Books, 2001) and Tim Lang and Michael Heasman, *Food Wars: The Global Battle for Mouths, Minds and Markets* (London and Sterling,VA: Earthscam, 2004).

For further background reading, see Robert Gilpin's chapters on international political economy, money and international finance, trade, and multinational corporations in *The Political Economy of International Relations* (Princeton, N.J.: Princeton University Press, 1987) and his two more recent volumes—*Global Political Economy: Understanding the International Economic Order* (Princeton, NJ: Princeton University Press, 2001) and *The Challenge of Global Capitalism: The World Economy in the 21st Century* (Princeton, NJ: Princeton University Press, 2002). Robert O. Keohane and Joseph S. Nye deal with trade, money, and the oceans in *Power and Interdependence*, 3rd ed. (Boston: Little Brown, 1977, 2001), and Keohane also focuses on institutions and theories of cooperation in the world political economy in his *After Hegemony* (Princeton, N.J.: Princeton University Press, 1984). Keohane's institutionalist thesis is further developed in his *Power and Governance in a Partially Globalized World* (London: Routledge, 2002).

A widely used text presenting even the most difficult and complex international or global economic ideas in plain English is Paul R. Krugman and Maurice Obstfeld, *International Economics: Theory and Policy*, 6th ed. (Reading, Mass.: Addison-Wesley, 2002). Also easily read are H. Robert Heller's relatively short *International Trade: Theory and Empirical Evidence* (Englewood Cliffs, N.J.: Prentice-Hall, 1968, 1973) and Charles P. Kindleberger's now classic, nonmathematical presentations on international political economy that include *Foreign Trade and the National Economy* (New Haven, Conn.:Yale University Press, 1962), *Power and Money* (New York: Basic Books, 1970), *The World in Depression, 1929–1939* (Berkeley: University of California Press, 1973, 1986), *World Economic Primacy: 1500 to 1990* (Oxford, UK: Oxford University Press, 1995), and *A Financial History of Western Europe* (London: Allen & Unwin, 1984, and Oxford: Oxford University Press, 1993).

For a highly readable account of the development of both classical and neoclassical thought in economics, read Robert B. Ekelund Jr. and Robert F. Hebert, *A History of Economic Theory and Method*, 4th ed. (New York: McGraw-Hill, 1975, 2004). See also the chapters on trade and finance in David N. Balaam and Michael Veseth, *Introduction to International Political Economy*, 2nd ed. (Upper Saddle River, NJ: Prentice-Hall, 2001).

Chapter 12

The Political Economy of Investment and Sustainable Development

Optimists and Pessimists

Technology, in the form of computers and information, drives growth in advanced-industrial and postindustrial service economies in increasingly globalized markets. Given these circumstances, the gap between capital-poor and capital-rich countries grows wider and wider. Prospects of narrowing, much less closing, the gap seem dimmer and dimmer. "The rich get richer and the poor stay poor (or worse, get poorer)"—or so says the conventional wisdom.

But, according to some optimists, these are different times. They see harnessing information technology for productive purposes as by no means the exclusive preserve of capital-rich countries. They see possibilities in at least some less-developed, lower-income economies that acquire the know-how in advanced-production processes that capitalize on information technologies—putting labor and natural resources to work and leapfrogging to ever-higher levels of production and productivity. In Panama, for example, women weave intricate animal or geometric designs on shirts and dresses. "Weaving *molas* is an important part of my life," one young Panamanian notes, "This is more than just a *mola*. It is part of women's development, of our economic well-being, and most important of Panamanian culture." She and her colleagues were speaking at a U.N.–sponsored program designed to teach computer technology in order to sell their products on the Internet. In doing so, they bypass the retailers and retain 60 to 70 percent of their profit as opposed to the 10 percent they would get through retailers.[1]

Naysayers are quick to point out that any such gains, if achieved at all, will no doubt be reserved for only a small segment of populations in the Third World economies of the South. Advanced information-based technologies are labor saving, but labor is precisely what Third World countries have in

---

[1]World Bank, available at www.un.org/Pubs/ourlives/bank.htm.

abundance. These pessimists (or are they only being realistic?) see dual economies as the best that can reasonably be achieved—a minority of 30 percent or more relatively well off, with the majority of the population still suffering from varying degrees of poverty. Vast numbers of people measured in billions or hundreds of millions (as in China and India) with high population growth rates pose formidable challenges not so easily met. Notwithstanding substantial gains, some 80 percent of China is still a peasant society. According to the pessimists, the advantages still go to the already capital-rich countries of the North with their smaller, relatively well-educated and trained labor forces.

Social justice demands better levels of living than most of the world's more than six billion people now enjoy. Human rights to a full life and socioeconomic well-being require not only ***sustainable economic development*** and growth on a truly global scale but also a more equitable distribution of wealth—lofty objectives sought by economic development advocates. To the contrary, wishful thinking aside, pessimists see economic growth as both consuming resources that cannot be replaced and polluting the environment, making it extraordinarily difficult (if not impossible) to sustain growth, much less extend economic development to all the world's peoples.

Beyond assuring some basic, minimum level of living, is the world (or at least large parts of it) to abandon the effort, get off the ever-increasing growth-and-development train, and seek some new way of defining the quality of life? It is an interesting thought, taken more seriously by those who see the exhausting pace prescribed by market capitalism as having eroded core values and the overall quality of life. For understandable reasons, more low-income countries still seem eager to get better seats on—not get off—the growth-and-development train. Progression from local to express and then to "bullet-train" class seems to be the more common worldwide aspiration. But how realistic is this goal?

sustainable economic development
Economic growth that continues over time and also improves social conditions but does not deplete natural resources or cause environmental damage that would undermine or preclude continuing economic growth.

In this chapter, we review the data and disturbing facts of Third World poverty, noting the enormous obstacles to be overcome to achieve development. We begin with essentially conventional or mainstream accounts of the global political economy but end with emphasizing economic structuralist perspectives.

Third World Poverty and Capital Formation

Most of the Third World is, quite frankly, invisible to the West. When it makes the news it is invariably bad news—poverty, wars, famines, AIDS. The facts are stark and difficult to comprehend. Approximately 1.2 billion people—a fifth of humanity—subsist on less than one dollar a day. Women and children account for the majority. Seven hundred million people live in the forty-two most indebted, poverty-stricken countries. Even though barter, exchanges of one agricultural good for another, is the common way of subsistence as opposed to the use of currency, living standards are appallingly low compared to that of the industrialized North. Malnutrition accounts for the fact that 30 percent or more of children under 5 years old suffer from severe or moderate stunting and contributes to more than half of the deaths of children under 5 years old in developing countries. Twenty-one million children do not attend school.[2] Examples of extreme poverty are found throughout the Third World but particularly in more than thirty African countries identified in data collected by the U.N. Development Programs.

As mentioned in Chapter 10, Adam Smith (1723–1790) saw the wealth of nations lying not in their stock of gold or other treasure but rather in their productive capacity—effectively combining capital with land (natural resources) and labor (human resources) for production of goods and services. Figure 12.1 shows the distribution of GNP (gross national product per capita) in the world. All countries have labor, yet in many countries of the Third World it is uneducated and poorly trained. Land may be essentially deserts, mountains, and jungles, with natural resources few and far between. Capital formation on a national basis depends heavily on domestic savings, but millions of people are more worried about their next meal than saving for the future. Of these three *factors of production,* it is the stock of capital that not surprisingly figures most prominently in capitalism and in discussions of how to jump-start Third World economic development. Sources of capital include:

- Aid provided as grants
- Loans (as well as debt forgiveness)
- Direct foreign investment
- Trade preferences

Aid

Official development assistance (ODA) or aid from governments and international organizations continues to be an important source of investment capital for many

factors of production
Land, labor, and capital are essential elements that are combined to produce the goods and services that constitute economic output.

---

[2]See the UNICEF annual *The State of the World's Children*, available at www.unicef.org/sowc.

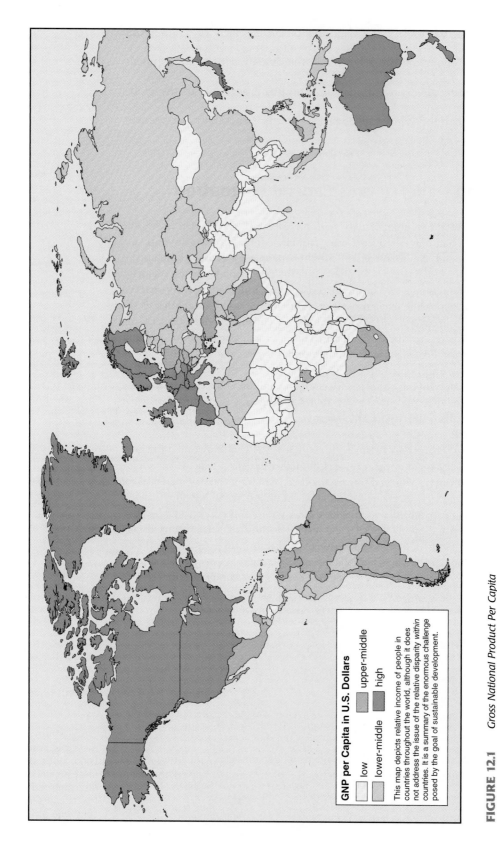

FIGURE 12.1 *Gross National Product Per Capita*

Net official development assistance (ODA) and borrowed funds are important sources of capital for investment as when a country improves its infrastructure of roads, rail, seaports, airports, power, telecommunications, and other utilities—all of which expand the country's capacity for economic growth. Properly invested, foreign aid and borrowed funds can contribute substantially to economic development; however, whether invested wisely or not, servicing debt (making payments of interest and principal on time) can be a heavy burden, particularly for capital-poor states that find themselves overextended and in need of debt relief. One indicator of debt burden is to calculate total debt as a percentage of gross domestic product (GDP) for a country's economy as a whole. Another indicator is the debt service ratio— the percentage of annual export earnings used to make payments of principal and interest on all external borrowings. All such debt payments, of course, constitute a drain on capital that otherwise would be available for further domestic investment. The table presents a sample of countries representative of debt burdens in national economies of varying size and level of development in different regions.

TABLE 12.1
Foreign Aid, Debt, and Economic Development

	TOTAL AID RECEIVED (NET ODA IN US $ MILLIONS)	TOTAL AID RECEIVED (NET ODA AS % OF GDP)	EXTERNAL DEBT (AS % OF GDP)	DEBT SERVICE RATIO (DEBT PAYMENTS AS % OF EXPORTS)
Latin America				
Brazil	376	0.1	11.4	68.9
Colombia	441	0.5	8.6	40.2
Mexico	136	<0.1	6.8	23.2
Panama	35	0.3	13.6	19.7
Peru	491	0.9	5.9	32.8
Venezuela	57	0.1	7.9	25.6
Asia				
Bangladesh	913	1.9	1.5	7.3
China	1,476	0.1	2.4	8.2
India	1,463	0.3	2.6	14.9
Indonesia	1,308	0.8	9.8	24.8
Pakistan	2,144	3.6	4.8	17.8
Philippines	560	0.7	11.8	20.2
Thailand	296	0.2	15.6	23.1
Vietnam	1,277	3.6	3.4	6.0
Africa				
Côte d'Ivoire	1,069	9.1	7.1	14.1
Egypt	1,286	1.4	2.3	10.3
Nigeria	314	0.7	3.4	8.6
South Africa	657	0.6	4.5	12.5

Source: Adapted from U.N. Development Programme, *Human Development Report, 2004* (New York: Oxford University Press, 2004), 198–201.

developing countries. (See Table 12.1, columns 1 and 2.) Table 12.2 lists providers of foreign aid. Note the low level of official development assistance as percentage of gross domestic product in terms of the United States.

For years, states and international organizations have provided a total of approximately $1 trillion in aid to the Third World. The logic was straightforward. It was assumed that such aid would boost recipient countries' growth rates and hence help millions escape poverty. Unfortunately, many studies have failed to find a strong link

TABLE 12.2
Principal Foreign Aid Donor Countries

Official Development Assistance (ODA) from capital-rich countries in the North is an important source of capital for investment in capital-poor countries in the South and in other countries receiving such aid. In addition to examining the total or aggregate amount of foreign aid disbursed for development purposes, indicators of the degree of commitment by capital-rich countries to development assistance are annual development assistance as a percent of gross national income (GNI) of the donor country (the 0.7% international goal met or surpassed only by Denmark, Luxembourg, the Netherlands, Norway, and Sweden) and development assistance on a per capita or per person basis in the donor country (for which no international goal has been set). The data below are for high per capita income, capital-rich donor countries with the largest economies—the Group of Seven countries that have the highest GNPs—as well as other relatively high per capita income, capital-rich countries albeit with economies smaller in aggregate size (i.e., lower GNPs than those of the "Group of Seven" countries).

	TOTAL ODA (US $ MILLIONS)	ODA AS % OF GNI	ODA (US $/PERSON IN DONOR COUNTRY)
Group of Seven			
United States	13,140	0.13	46
Japan	9,731	0.23	76
Germany	4,980	0.27	60
France	5,125	0.38	86
Italy	2,157	0.20	37
United Kingdom	4,581	0.31	78
Canada	2,011	0.28	64
Other Donor Countries			
Australia	916	0.26	47
Austria	488	0.26	61
Belgium	996	0.43	97
Denmark	1,540	0.96	286
Finland	434	0.35	83
Ireland `	360	0.40	93
Luxembourg	139	0.77	316
Netherlands	3,068	0.81	190
New Zealand	110	0.22	28
Norway	1,517	0.89	333
Portugal	293	0.27	28
Spain	1,559	0.26	38
Sweden	1,848	0.83	207
Switzerland	863	0.32	118

Source: Adapted from U.N. Development Programme, *Human Development Report, 2004* (New York: Oxford University Press, 2004), 196.

between the amount of aid and faster economic growth. Why not? First, a good deal of the aid was not really concerned with stimulating economic growth. During the Cold War the Soviet Union, United States, and their allies were primarily concerned with propping up friendly governments. To this day, Israel and Egypt are the two major recipients of U.S. foreign aid. Nor were the economic and financial competencies of governments a primary consideration. Second, donors often send inappropriate types of aid. Some, for example, prefer to direct aid to conspicuous prestige projects such as dams. Even small donations are regularly ill advised—Somalis have received heartburn pills and Mozambican peasants high-heeled shoes. Nomads of northwestern

Kenya, long pestered by poorly planned charitable projects, refer to their own government as well as foreign aid workers as *ngimoi:* "the enemy." Third, wars in the Third World often destroy the best-laid development plans. Finally, there is no doubt that corruption, incompetence, and poor economic policies have squandered large amounts of donor cash.

Yet all is not hopeless. Botswana, for example, gained independence in 1966. At the time, one British official rather undiplomatically termed it "a useless piece of territory." Foreign aid initially kept the new government going. Then diamonds were found in the desert, but the government did not squander its newfound wealth. Profits were plowed into infrastructure, education, and health care. Foreign investment was welcomed, and private business allowed to flourish. Aid projects proceeded only if it were likely they would provide sustainable development. From 1966 to 1991, Botswana's economy grew at one of the fastest rates in the world. A key reason was the fact that government ministers were for the most part honest and competent. As the economy slowly diversified, aid donors began to look for other, needier recipients.[3]

> If it were true that the poor were just like the rich but with less money, the global situation would be vastly easier than it is. As it happens, the poor live in different health conditions and must overcome agronomic limitations that are very different from those of rich countries. Those differences, indeed, are often a fundamental cause of persisting poverty.
>
> **Jeffery Sachs**
> *Harvard University economist, as cited in "Helping the World's Poorest," Economist, August 14, 1999, 17.*

It's Been Said...

Loans

In addition to loans by government, banks, and nongovernmental organizations, a conventional source of capital has been the World Bank. Formally the International Bank for Reconstruction and Development (IBRD), the institution was established along with the International Monetary Fund (IMF) at an international conference at Bretton Woods, New Hampshire, in 1944. The World Bank's immediate post–World War II goal was economic recovery and reconstruction of major European and Asian economies devastated by the war. Located in Washington, D.C., next to the IMF, the World Bank's focus since the 1950s and 1960s has been on loans for economic development to capital-poor countries. The World Bank's capital comes from contributions—a multilateral form of foreign assistance by capital-rich member countries that want to use this institution as a vehicle for lending to less-developed countries. Since it began operations after World War II, the World Bank has loaned more than $400 billion. In addition to loans at near-market rates, the World Bank engages in extensive lending at **concessionary,** below-market rates to capital-poor countries through its affiliate, the International Development Association (IDA). World Bank loans for private-sector projects in developing countries are made through its International Finance Corporation (IFC) affiliate.

To facilitate lending and direct investment to countries where investors fear takeover of their assets by **nationalization** or **expropriation** or face political instability or other political risks, the Multilateral Investment Guarantee Agency (MIGA) is an investment-insurance affiliate that provides political-risk insurance programs. Disputes between governments and private investors can also be submitted for mediation or conciliation to the World Bank's International Center for Settlement of Investment Disputes (ICSID).

---

[3]"Helping the Third World," *Economist*, June 26, 1999, 24.

Regional lending for development also occurs through such separate international organizations as the Inter-American Development Bank (IADB), Asian Development Bank, African Development Bank, and now the North American Development Bank. Privately held investment banks are also participants, often benefiting from research on investment projects undertaken by multilateral institutions.

Payments of interest and principal on loans to foreign governments or banks can constitute a substantial drain on capital, particularly if developing countries have borrowed too heavily. When global interest rates take a significant turn upward, additional strain is placed on Third World countries trying to service (make payments on) existing debt or refinancing and securing new loans. Countries facing financial difficulties, perhaps in danger of being forced to default on their loan payments, often seek debt forgiveness (for examples of debt, see Table 12.1, columns 3 and four).

Failing that, they ask for cooperation from governments or international or private lending institutions as they try to reschedule or refinance these obligations with new long-term loans at concessionary, below-market interest rates. As noted in Chapter 11, such concessionary loans are really a form of grant aid because interest earned from a proportion of the loan invested at higher market rates can actually be used to service the loan. Debtor countries do have some leverage over their lenders, however. Because lenders stand to lose all if borrowers default, the former are usually willing to accommodate reasonable requests from the latter, particularly if these concessions give some assurance that the loan eventually will be repaid. Table 12.3 (p. 411) shows investment capital received by selected countries.

Direct Foreign Investment

Multinational corporations (MNCs), investment firms, and international banks seeking profits or returns on investment are a third source of capital. In terms of multinational corporations, direct foreign investment involves building a foreign subsidiary whose assets are controlled by the parent company. Annual revenues of many MNCs are larger than the GDPs of many states. MNCs are also a potential source for the transfer of technologies they use in their production processes if carried out in Third World countries. Of course, proprietary interests of the MNCs often lead them to maximize their profits while minimizing technology transfers. Nevertheless, they are an important source of capital as well as training for domestic labor forces. Continuing and seemingly endless debate goes on between MNC advocates, who see these corporations as well as domestic firms providing jobs and contributing substantially to development, and those who contest this view, seeing MNCs as essentially predatory, engaging in whatever levels of exploitation governments and local elites will tolerate. Critics claim that one reason MNCs organize their operations multinationally is to avoid or circumvent obstacles or barriers imposed by particular states (see the box on p. 412 on transfer pricing). Nevertheless, private direct investment, portfolio investment, and bank lending accounted for approximately $145 billion dollars in capital investment in Third World countries during 2000.

New International Economic Order (NIEO)
A policy resolution of developing countries calling for a new international economic order—an international economic system more favorable to their interests.

Trade

Aside from aid, loans, investment (and occasionally debt forgiveness), **trade preferences** have been a key element of the agenda for a *New International Economic Order (NIEO)* advanced by Third World countries in the South and articulated over

TABLE 12.3
Investment Capital for Economic Development in Selected Countries

Economic development depends on the investment of capital, whether this capital is created from domestic savings or comes from other countries. In this table "net" flows refers to inflows of capital from abroad minus outflows of capital to other countries. As the term implies, *direct investments* refer to funds put directly into businesses, infrastructure, or other enterprises by investors. A favorable or positive trade balance (exports > imports) is another source of capital inflow; an unfavorable or negative trade balance (imports > exports) drains capital from the country.

	GROSS NATIONAL INCOME (GNI IN US $ MILLIONS)	FOREIGN DIRECT INVESTMENT (US $ MILLIONS)	NET PRIVATE CAPITAL FLOWS (US $ MILLIONS)	TRADE BALANCE (US $ MILLIONS)
Latin America				
Brazil	479	16,566	9,861	−7,696
Mexico	637	14,622	10,261	−9,150
Panama	13	57	180	−408
Peru	58	2,391	3,131	−1,116
Asia				
Bangladesh	55	47	132	739
China	1,590	58,990	47,107	52,836
India	568	3,030	4,944	4,656
Indonesia	173	−1,513	−6,966	6,085
Kazakhstan	27	2,583	4,431	−69
Malaysia	94	3,203	4,807	7,190
Pakistan	69	823	379	3,597
Thailand	136	900	−1,992	7,965
Vietnam	39	1,400	759	−604
Africa				
Côte d'Ivoire	11	230	117	767
Egypt	94	647	437	622
South Africa	126	739	783	−1,456

Source: Adapted from World Bank, *World Development Report, 2005* (New York: Oxford University Press, 2005), 256–57, 262–63.

several decades in the U.N. Conferences on Trade and Development (UNCTAD) and in other forums. Efforts that began in the 1960s and 1970s to build an NIEO looked for ways to bridge the great North–South divide. It is not surprising that the General Assembly was at the core of NIEO efforts because Third World countries have had a controlling majority there after decolonization, and the creation of new states in Africa and Asia in the 1960s tipped the balance of votes in that chamber toward the South.

In a challenge to Ricardian free-trade theory as a basis for policy, Third World discontent was expressed concerning the uneven or asymmetric distribution of wealth created through free trade—an arrangement that critics claimed clearly favored the North. For one thing, as discussed in Chapter 11, the **terms of trade** between exporters favor the North's manufactured and higher-technology goods and services over the single-commodity agricultural or mineral exports or relatively low-technology

terms of trade
The ratio of export prices from one country to those of another. Developing countries claim that, over time, the prices of their commodities and other exports tend to fall while the price of manufactured goods exported to them by advanced industrial countries tends to rise.

MNCs, Politics, and the State: The Complex Case of Transfer Pricing

It is fair to say that since the end of World War II, the most controversial aspect of international political economy has been the rise of the multinational corporation (MNC). Some see MNCs as eventually superseding the nation-state, muting nationalism by providing economic benefits to all. Others view MNCs as rapacious imperialists, exploiting the weak and poor in their quest for greater profits. The truth is somewhere in between these two views. In direct, open conflict between MNCs and the state, the state will in principle generally prevail, as it always has the option of closing down the corporation's operations. MNCs realize this and prefer to avoid such confrontations. Conflict between states and MNCs therefore tends to be more subtle and is usually reported on the business page, not the front page, of daily newspapers.

To illustrate potential conflict between a state and a multinational corporation, consider the following scenario. XYZ Corporation's automobile assembly plant **subsidiary** in the country of Ruralia needs to import engines, computer parts, and other higher-technology components manufactured in XYZ subsidiaries located in more industrially developed countries.

As it turns out, there is a difference in tax rates on profits in these countries. Because XYZ Corporation is a rational actor that tries to maximize its gains (or minimize its losses), the corporation can be expected to reduce its tax exposure—maximizing legally the amount of profit it makes in countries with lower tax rates. It may choose to do this through **transfer pricing**—increasing or decreasing the prices its subsidiaries charge each other for components.

Its assembly plant is in low-tax, less-developed Ruralia, a country chosen both because of its relatively low taxes and an abundant supply of relatively unskilled, lower-cost labor. The local government has intentionally set the tax rate low to attract investment by multinational corporations as part of its own economic development plan.

Although the Ruralian government would like XYZ Corporation to put in more than just an assembly plant, it recognizes that at least the assembly plant will employ a substantial number of Ruralians who would not otherwise have these jobs. Opponents who see XYZ and other MNCs as exploiting local labor, damaging the environment, or imposing foreign cultural preferences on Ruralians are not as strong politically as local investors and businesses that favor the plant. Some of these interests will participate in the venture directly, whereas others expect to gain indirectly due to the plant's positive contribution to local economic growth. The argument in favor of XYZ is that foreign investment contributes to a rising tide that raises all ships.

Thus, notwithstanding some domestic opposition, XYZ's investment in an assembly plant is compatible with both corporate and state objectives. In short, XYZ Corporation and the Ruralia government are rational (or purposive) actors seeking to make a good business deal. One side may get the better deal, but both see the investment as a potential or expected gain.

Manufacturing computers, carburetors, or other engine components that involve higher technologies, by contrast, requires greater capital investment in machinery, employing relatively fewer but higher-skilled and higher-paid workers than those needed for assembly plants. Countries like Industritania with higher-skilled and higher-paid labor forces are often higher-tax countries as well.

In this circumstance, the corporation's internal sales prices of computers, carburetors, or other engine components needed by the assembly plant subsidiary in Ruralia are set legally at or near cost, thus minimizing profit from producing these components in the high-tax country. Setting lower prices also reduces the tariff or tax that must be paid on the value of components imported by the assembly plant subsidiary in Ruralia, which has relatively high tariffs to protect its new, emergent industries as they compete in global markets.

When the automobiles have been assembled in Ruralia, they are sold or exported at market prices. Because components were imported so cheaply, and labor and other production costs were also held down, profit as the difference between revenue from sales and the overall costs of production is maximized in Ruralia and minimized in Industritania. Because of liberal capital outflow rules, XYZ Corporation spends some of its gain on new investment in Ruralia but moves most of it out of the country, using some to finance investments in other subsidiaries and **repatriating** the rest to its corporate headquarters to pay corporate shareholders and other stakeholders.

In this example, Industritania lost tax revenue on profits: Had components manufactured there been exported at market prices well above cost, revenues would have been higher. XYZ Corporation can expect the Industritanian government to object, particularly if XYZ exports components to its Ruralia subsidiary below production cost, thus avoiding payment of any tax at all to Industritania. On the other hand, Ruralia gains by having more profits to tax, even though its tax rate remains low.

When their interests diverge, governments may try through policy, law, and regulation to control multinational corporate operations. The complexity of financial transactions such as transfer pricing among subsidiaries of the same corporation in several countries makes regulation extraordinarily difficult. Moreover, if the corporation finds the local government too hostile, it may choose to close its plants and take operations elsewhere.

---

manufactured goods offered by most Third World countries. Prices for these Third World exports barely hold their own or tend to decline over time. By contrast, First World manufactured and higher-technology goods and services tend to hold their own or increase in price over time.

Hence, the South has sought trade preferences from the North as part of the NIEO. The argument is that beginning or infant industries in the South may need the protection of tariffs or other barriers to trade until they have grown sufficiently to be competitive in global markets. At the same time, these countries want advanced industrial or postindustrial societies not to discriminate against Third World exports by imposing trade barriers against them. Third World countries in effect have argued for unfettered access to First World markets for their exports, without fear of reprisal if in the early stages of industrialization they are allowed to discriminate against First World exports. In point of fact, the value of annual agricultural subsidies in rich nations is more than three times the yearly aid flow to poor countries, causing losses to producers in the Third World. Worse yet, the most protected industries in high-income economies include agriculture and textiles, precisely those sectors in which many poor countries are most competitive.[4]

Foreign-exchange earnings that come from exports can be used to purchase capital goods from the advanced industrial and postindustrial economies that produce them. Indeed, trade balances favorable to a Third World country are an important source of capital that can be invested for economic development purposes. By contrast, when Third World countries continue to run negative trade balances, capital that could have been invested in their domestic economies is drained off. That is why favorable terms of trade and trade preferences are so important, particularly to Third World countries trying to acquire capital for industrial or other economic development.

---

[4] "Ranking the Rich," *Foreign Policy*, May/June 2003, 63.

A New International Economic Order (NIEO)?

The arrows in this figure depict the direction of net capital flows less-developed countries in the South prefer. Critics note that net capital flows in fact often move in the opposite direction when MNCs send their profits or returns on investments back to the North, and when countries in the South run negative trade balances and must repay their loans (often at market rates), and owners of capital in the South choose to invest in the North, where they expect to realize greater returns.

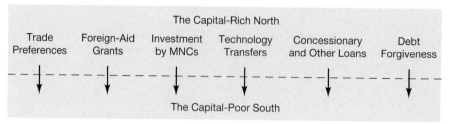

FIGURE 12.2   *Foreign Sources of Capital*

Special trade arrangements have in fact been made and preferences granted, most notably under agreements known as the Lomé Conventions (named for negotiations conducted in the African country of Togo) by European Union members with Third World "ACP" countries in Africa, the Caribbean, and the Pacific, many of which are former colonies of European powers. As mentioned in Chapter 11, critics have been quick to claim that these trade concessions, although of some benefit to the South, also effectively tie these states to the former colonial powers in what amount to **neocolonial** relations that work to the net advantage of Europe.

One approach to securing more favorable terms of trade is to form a **cartel** or joint arrangement that allows member states to influence the price of a commodity by regulating its supply to the world market. Efforts to form cartels among coffee producers and tin or other agricultural and mineral exporters have been relatively unsuccessful due to difficulty in enforcing compliance with cartel production targets and quotas. The ready availability of substitute suppliers outside of cartel arrangements has compounded these difficulties. Moreover, a rising price for one mineral or agricultural product may lead consumers to substitute and import another less-expensive product. If coffee becomes too high in price, for example, some consumers may switch to tea.

One exception to this generally negative record for cartels, at least for a few years, was the Organization of Petroleum Exporting Countries (OPEC), a cartel that was successful in substantially raising the world price of oil in the 1970s. These "oil shocks," as they were called, immediately and dramatically improved the terms of trade of cartel members; however, the industrial world's heavy dependence on imported oil at ever-higher prices significantly raised overall costs of production in oil-buying countries and thus contributed to fueling inflation on a global scale. Efforts were undertaken to find new oil supplies and to develop alternative energy sources. Powerful First World countries also brought great pressures to bear on those OPEC members they could influence.

The dollar price of oil was relatively static in the 1980s and 1990s, actually declining in real terms when we take inflation into account. The OPEC cartel thus has not been as successful as in its early years due to a number of factors. First, rivalry among OPEC members and a desire to produce more oil for export than allowed by cartel agreements kept OPEC production targets higher than they might have been and effectively added enough oil to world supplies to keep prices from rising. Due in part to its security and economic relations with the United States and other Western countries, Saudi Arabia (which has the world's largest oil reserves) has remained committed to maintaining an ample supply to world markets. Second, development of oil fields under the North Sea between Britain and Norway, at Prudhoe Bay in northern Alaska, and more recently in the central Asia–Caspian Sea area have added to world oil supplies. Finally, although aggregate demand for oil has continued to increase over the decades, it is less than what it would have been thanks to some development of alternative energy sources and energy-efficiency measures.

A great frustration for many in Third World countries, therefore, is the degree to which they are caught in a seemingly inescapable structure of **dependency** on capital-rich First World countries. There seems to be no escape. Adverse terms of trade are difficult to reverse, and producing qualitative manufactures that will compete favorably with those produced by firms in technology-endowed and capital-rich countries is a formidable task. Some **newly industrializing countries (NICs)**—for example, South Korea, Taiwan, Singapore, Hong Kong (now part of China), and Brazil—have been able to break into world markets for manufactured goods or such technology-intensive services as banking and insurance by combining substantial domestic capital formation, imported technologies, and access to a lower-wage but skilled and conscientious labor force.

Case & Point

THE INTERNET AND THE THIRD WORLD

An important reflection of globalization is the spread of global communication. The Internet epitomizes this global connectivity. But what about the Third World? Developing countries lack easy access to computers, infrastructure to support their use, and skilled users. Does the Internet therefore represent yet again a technological advancement that leaves the poorest of the world even further behind? As a result of the Rio Conference in 1992, the U.N. Development Programme (UNDP) launched the Sustainable Development Networking Programme (SDNP) designed to help bridge the information gap between the haves and have-nots. The program was met with much initial skepticism both within and outside the United Nations. How, it was asked, does information technology aid sustainable development? How does one get an illiterate farmer from his field to a computer? The answer is, "You don't."

The key intermediaries are NGOs that pass on useful information to the farmer. In Mexico, for example, the SDNP has established an information center for corn producers where farmers can learn online what the market price of corn is in the capital. The goal is to help them avoid underselling their crops. Similar information centers have been established in Jamaica, Guatemala, Honduras, and Costa Rica. The long-term goal is for communities eventually to manage the information centers on their own. As one advisor to the SDNP has commented, "You cannot drop information technology like a bomb and run away. That does not work. You have to train people, show them how to use it in a way that can help them, and that takes time, a lot of time."*

Point: It remains to be seen how important the Internet will be in terms of aiding sustainable development, but modest international efforts are under way.

*Esther Braun, "Internet: A Tool for Sustainable Development," *U.N. Chronicle*, No. 2 (1999), 77.

A study in contrast: Masai tribes-men in Kenya try out a laptop computer.

Most Third World countries have not been so successful, as their domestic firms find it difficult to compete in global trading markets or are shut out of rich countries that protect their agricultural and textile industries. Some have formed regional free-trading areas such as the Economic Community of West African States (ECOWAS) among lower-income countries in West Africa, the Southern Cone Common Market (MERCOSUR) in South America, the Andean Group, the Caribbean Community and Common Market (CARICOM), the Central American Common Market (CACM), and the Association of Southeast Asian Nations (ASEAN). For its part, Mexico has joined the United States and Canada, two First World countries with about ten times its per capita income, in a North American Free Trade Agreement (NAFTA). Given these economic asymmetries in levels of development, Mexico has faced substantial difficulties, as reflected in its having to defend the peso, its currency, with heavy foreign borrowings from time to time. Mexico's hope, of course, is that NAFTA will be a means of access to capital and to the huge, relatively wealthy Canadian and American markets for selling its goods and services over the long term.

Other Constraints

As we have seen, there are a number of sources for capital available to many developing countries. But if the solution to global poverty and underdevelopment was simply the provision or generation of more capital for investment, the challenge, though daunting, would seem to be achievable. Why, despite all of the aid, loans, foreign investment, and trade preferences, have so many Third World states still been unable to make much headway against underdevelopment? A number of possible interrelated factors that impinge directly on economic prosperity deal with the domestic and regional issues faced by these states. We will examine the following: population size, environmental degradation, health care, and war (other factors, such as the status of women, will be addressed in Chapter 14).

Population Growth   Economies that grow depend on a continuing investment of capital. Populations that grow too fast consume whatever surplus would have been produced for capital investment. Planners who want to lift the capacities of Third World political economies to provide a better level of living for their peoples seek to reduce birth rates even as improved medical and health conditions also reduce death rates.

Populations have continued to grow at a very rapid rate in Third World countries, although substantial progress has been made, as annual growth rates as high as 3 percent or more in the 1960s have been trimmed substantially in most countries. With a 3 percent growth rate, population doubles in just about a quarter-century, but a 2 percent growth rate slows this doubling time to only about three and a half decades. By contrast, population is actually declining in some First World countries. The 0.6 percent average growth rate in the First World taken as a whole means that it will take a much longer time—some 120 years—to double their numbers at this relatively slow rate (see Figure 12.3).

A 1994 U.N. conference held in Cairo on population issues and economic development was part of an international consensus-building process that included governmental representatives of U.N. member states, U.N. and other international organization delegates and staff members, and representatives of numerous nongovernmental

Demographic Nightmare?

In 1973 a Frenchman, Jean Raspail, published a futuristic and highly controversial novel, *Camp of the Saints*. In the novel, the Belgian government responds compassionately to accounts of a widespread famine in India, brought into homes around the world through the marvels of modern global communications, by adopting a number of poor young children. When thousands of desperate mothers descend on the Belgian consul general's residence, begging him to take their children to a better life, a startled Belgian government reverses its decision. As a result, a charismatic "untouchable" calls on the poor to make their way to the Western paradise: "The nations are rising from the four corners of the earth," he says, "and their number is like the sand of the sea. They will march up over the broad earth and surround the camp of the saints and the beloved city."

Commandeering every seaworthy ship available, the hordes of the poor make a horrific voyage around Africa and into the Mediterranean. French sailors are unable to bring themselves to sink this decrepit armada, and the destitute pour ashore as the French flee the south of France and soldiers desert their army units. The novel points to two global realities—an imbalance in resources between the haves and the have-nots and similarly unbalanced demographic trends. If these trends continue, the author makes clear that mass migration such as he describes will eventually overwhelm the West or force it into responding in a brutal and morally questionable fashion.

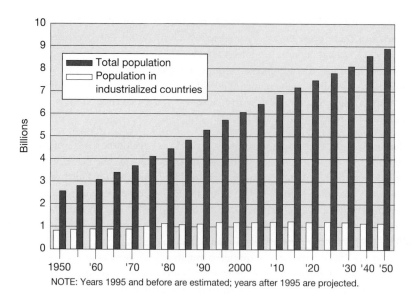

NOTE: Years 1995 and before are estimated; years after 1995 are projected.

FIGURE 12.3   *Population Growth in Industrial and Developing Countries*

organizations (NGOs). Significant differences of view on what was to be done were readily apparent. The Chinese policy of one child per family was scrutinized closely by those concerned that enforcement (which for all intents and purposes has lapsed) could easily violate human rights, particularly should violators face punitive sanctions or even forced sterilization. Many delegates preferred an approach focusing on empowering women by educating them in the use of contraceptives, medications, and other birth-control devices. Another objective for many was to make birth-control technologies readily available free of charge or at relatively low cost. A separate NGO forum was also attended by almost 4,000 individuals representing 200 nongovernmental organizations.

Slower-growing (but also better-educated and trained) populations coupled with substantial capital investment are key ingredients in the recipe for economic development and continued growth for any economy. Success in curbing population growth removes a significant obstacle or impediment to economic development. Excessive military spending, engaged in by many Third World countries, also drains important resources that could be used for more productive economic development purposes.

Environment   Relatively unconstrained efforts to achieve rapid economic growth can undermine the continued sustainability of economic development. The sheer size of populations in countries now industrializing magnifies the environmental impact of economic development. The adverse environmental impact of industrialization seen in First World societies with populations in the millions when the industrialization process was well under way in the nineteenth and early twentieth centuries can be expected on an even greater scale of damage if China (with more than 1.2 billion people) and India (with some 900 million people) continue to follow the same approach to industrialization in the first decades of the twenty-first century as they did in the last half of the twentieth century.

In addition to bearing the burden of soaring population, agricultural productivity can be destroyed through erosion and misuse of fertilizers, water supplies can be contaminated, and other forms of pollution can wreak havoc on agricultural and other forms of production. Resource depletion; reduction of wildlife, fishery, and seafood stocks; and other forms of environmental degradation can make continued production unsustainable even at present levels. In northern Africa, desertification continues. Arable land goes out of production as populations increase. These issues were at the core of U.N.–sponsored meetings in Rio de Janeiro in 1992 and at follow-on meetings attended by representatives of governments and international organizations. About 17,000 individuals, including 2,400 representatives of NGOs, held separate but simultaneous meetings in Rio on these same environmental and sustainable development issues. Subsequent conventions and programs have been instituted under U.N. auspices.

Health   It is truly ironic that, as some Third World countries worry about the danger of overpopulation to economic viability and quality of life, other countries fear the opposite—a precipitous decline in population due to the alarming increase in infectious diseases, which account for almost half of mortality in developing countries. In some cases the disease is relatively new (AIDS), while in other cases the diseases are reemerging (tuberculosis and malaria). What is frightening to many scientists and doctors is the rapid growth in the number of infectious diseases apparently resistant to antimicrobial

Practicing World Politics

Regional organizations play important roles in formulating and implementing strategies on development and the environment. Visit some of their Web sites:

REGIONAL ORGANIZATIONS ON SUSTAINABLE DEVELOPMENT

    Andean Group (www.itcilo.it)

    Asia-Pacific Economic Cooperation (www.apec.org)

    Association of Southeast Asian Nations (www.asean.org)

    Caribbean Community and Common Market (www.caricom.org)

    Economic Community of West African States (www.cedeao.org)

    European Union (europa.eu.int; in the United States, www.eurunion.org)

    Mercosur (Common Market Southern Cone, South America) (www.mercosur.com)

    North American Free Trade Association (www.nafta-sec-alena.org)

U.N. Regional Economic Commissions

    Africa (Addis Ababa) (www.un.org/Depts/eca)

    Asia and the Pacific (Bangkok) (www.unescap.org)

    Europe (Geneva) (www.unece.org)

    Latin America (Santiago) (www.ecla.org)

Regional Development Banks

    Inter-American Development Bank (www.IADB.org)

    Asian Development Bank (www.adb.org)

    African Development Bank (www.afdb.org)

    North American Development Bank (www.nadb.org)

drugs. This is not simply a problem for developing countries. Given the speed, ease, and volume of international trade and travel, diseases such as SARS have become a true hallmark of globalization.

The extent of the global HIV/AIDS epidemic is hard to fathom. It killed more than three million persons in 2003. Five million more persons acquired HIV that same year, bringing to forty-two million the number of people living with the virus around the world. Sub-Saharan Africa is in the worst straits:

- The region accounts for nearly three-quarters of the global population living with HIV/AIDS.
- By 2010, about half of all the orphans in sub-Saharan Africa will have become orphans because of HIV/AIDS.
- More than half of those orphaned by HIV/AIDS are between the ages of 10 and 15.
- More than 29 million Africans are infected with HIV, and the disease kills more people each year than all the continent's wars combined.[5]

As adults are struck down and children are orphaned, villages become ghost towns, and economic productivity plummets at the same time overburdened and underfunded clinics and rudimentary health care programs attempt to deal with the disaster.

The death toll caused by malaria in Africa is not as high as that caused by AIDS. But, in the memorable words of a Tanzanian researcher, it is equivalent to seven Boeing 747s, filled mostly with children, crashing into Mount Kilimanjaro each day. In the 1950s and 1960s, malarial mosquitoes were in retreat in most of Africa and Asia. It is estimated that hundreds of millions of lives were saved, but the use of the pesticide DDT involved a trade-off, as it also killed millions of birds and animals and poisoned the environment. Malaria seems to be, however, flying underneath the radar in terms of global awareness. It is private money, not public, that pays for most treatment and prevention measures and the search for a vaccine.[6]

In the case of AIDS, global awareness is high. At a special session of the U.N. General Assembly in June 2001, members adopted a Declaration of Commitment and time-bound targets to which governments and the United Nations are supposed to be accountable. Approximately two-thirds of the Global Fund to Fight AIDS, Tuberculosis and Malaria goes to fight AIDS. This battle was given a boost when President George W. Bush, in the 2001 State of the Union speech, pledged $15 billion, of which $1 billion will go directly to the Fund. The rest will be distributed over five years to private organizations and directly to governments in target countries. The organization UNAIDS, however, notes that much more money needs to be raised, even as AIDS spending in poor countries has risen tenfold between 1997–2003 with these countries providing over a third of the total. What is clearly lacking, however, is a sustained financial commitment to finding an effective AIDS vaccine. In 2001, less than two percent of the twenty billion dollars spent on AIDS prevention, treatment, and research across the world was devoted to the search for a vaccine. For pharmaceutical companies, the search for a vaccine is costly and potentially a liability nightmare. Furthermore, the demand for the vaccine would be greatest in those countries least able to pay for it.[7]

---

[5] "AIDS Orphans," *U.N. Chronicle,* No. 2 (2004), 9.

[6] "Africa's Other Plague," *Economist,* May 3, 2003, 13.

[7] "AIDS," *Economist,* June 28, 2003, 77; Michael Specter, "The Vaccine," *The New Yorker,* February 3, 2003, 59.

Grandmother in Malawi cares for her grandchildren whose parents died of AIDS. © UNICEF

Conflicts   Excessive military spending, engaged in by many Third World countries, also drains important resources that could be used for more productive economic development purposes. Worse yet, many of the weapons purchased are used in brutal civil wars, military interventions, and conflicts with neighboring states. Most wars now fought are civil wars, and most are in the poorest countries, Between 1960 and 1999, there were fifty-two major civil wars. In almost every case, they left a legacy of persistent poverty and disease in their wake.[8]

Economic Structuralist Critiques and Perspectives

Pluralists or liberals and realists of all persuasions may hold differing perspectives as to the utility of aid, loans, investment, trade concessions, technology transfers, and debt forgiveness. But both tend to take for granted the framework within which these economic activities take place—the global capitalist system. There are, however, radical critiques of this system that are theoretically grounded in quite different assumptions and world views.

Dependency Theory

Some of the more provocative work in the economic structuralist tradition was produced by Latin Americanists in the 1960s and 1970s. They have come to be referred to collectively as dependency theorists. Several of these writers were associated with the Economic Commission on Latin America (ECLA) and the U.N. Conference on Trade and Development (UNCTAD). They were concerned with the important problem of explaining why Latin America and other Third World countries were not developing

---

[8]Paul Collier, *Breaking the Conflict Trap: Civil War and Development Policy* (Washington, D.C: World Bank and Oxford University Press, 2003).

MARXIST PERSPECTIVES ON THE PLIGHT OF THE THIRD WORLD

Applying Theory

Marxists are not at all surprised by the depressed state of affairs in many Third World countries. In the Marxist view, the **bourgeoisie,** or capitalist class, uses its base in the capital-rich North to reach out to its class allies in the South for new markets in which to sell and new workers and peasants to exploit. In short, the *bourgeoisie* in the North joins with *bourgeois* elements at the top of societies in Third World countries in exploitative joint ventures. In advanced, global capitalism, older colonial forms of imperialism have been replaced by multinational corporations and banks, the present-day agents of the owners of capital who are able to use neocolonial ties and channels to facilitate their efforts.

In this Marxist perspective it is the class structure of dominance that explains the misery of peasants and workers in Third World countries. The prevalence of malnutrition and disease, high infant mortality rates, and low life expectancies constitute a relatively silent but particularly brutal form of **structural violence** against the common peoples. To Marxist revolutionaries, this analysis is sufficient motivation for action against an oppressive, worldwide class structure.

Karl Marx (1818–1883), born and reared in Trier in present-day Germany, wrote extensively on political-economic history and the practice of capitalism. Much of his research and writing took place during his stay in London where he was able to observe firsthand the kind of labor exploitation in early industrial capitalism that also inspired the literary contributions of Charles Dickens. Marx was both a political-economic theorist and a revolutionary who challenged the capitalist or *bourgeois* interests of his time. Present-day theorists who focus on the South's dependency on the North and the resulting exploitation of peoples in the Third World owe an intellectual debt to Marx, even if they do not share all of Marx's premises.

as had been predicted by mainstream economists. Why wasn't the North American–Western European experience being repeated?

The focus of the ECLA and UNCTAD economists was initially quite narrow. They examined the unequal terms of trade between LDCs that exported raw materials and northern industrialized countries that exported finished manufactured goods. They questioned the supposed benefits of free trade. The ECLA at one point favored the diversification of exports, advising LDCs to produce goods instead of importing them. This policy did not result in the anticipated amount of success and, in fact, increased the influence of foreign multinational corporations brought in to facilitate domestic production.

Some writers cast their recommendations in terms of nationalism and state-guided capitalism. Others, however, more boldly emphasized political and social factors within the context of a capitalist economic system that binds Latin America to North America. Development, it was argued, is not autonomous. If it occurs at all, it is reflexive—subject to the vagaries and ups and downs of the world's advanced economies. Choices of Latin American countries are restricted or constrained as a result of the dictates of capitalism but also due to supporting political, social, and cultural relations. The result is an *economic structure* of domination. This multifaceted web of dependency reinforces unequal exchange between the northern and southern parts of the hemisphere. Opportunities for the LDCs are few and far between because LDCs are allocated a subordinate role in world capitalism. Dependency has succinctly been defined as a "situation in which a certain number of countries have their economy conditioned by the development and expansion of another . . . , placing the dependent countries in a backward position exploited by the dominant countries."[9]

Some economic structuralists use Marxist terminology and Leninist insights to explain this situation of dependency. More important than relations between states are transnational class coalitions linking elites in industrially developed countries (the center) with their counterparts in the South (or periphery). This version of class analysis emphasizes how transnational ties within the global bourgeois or capitalist class work to the disadvantage of workers and peasants in the periphery. Multinational corporations and international banks, therefore, are viewed from a much different perspective than that of a realist or pluralist. To the pluralist, especially "liberal institutionalists," MNCs and international banks appear merely as other, potentially benign, actors. To the realist, they tend to be of secondary importance because of the emphasis on the state-as-actor. To economic structuralists who were part of the dependency perspective, however, they are central players in establishing and maintaining dependency relations.

One doesn't hear as much about dependency theory these days, at least not in the United States. There are a number of reasons. First, empirical studies have shown that terms of trade (the prices of exports relative to those of imports) have not always deteriorated for producers of commodities. Second, critics have raised the question of whether dependency creates social and economic backwardness or whether it is economic and social backwardness that leads to a situation of dependency. In short, there is the issue of causality—whether dependency is the cause of backwardness or whether it is an effect of this condition. Third, some of the protectionist policies engendered by dependency theory were failures, leading to inefficiency and stifled technological progress. Finally, in the 1980s Latin America began a period of trade liberalization policies. Some sectors thrived, others lagged; some countries experienced dramatic growth, others disasters. But under the pressure of globalization, protectionist policies could not be sustained, and Latin American presidents were active participants in World Trade Organization (WTO) meetings that called for further trade liberalization and the reduction of trade barriers and, more recently, in the new Central American Free Trade Agreement (CAFTA). Nevertheless, critics of these regimes continue to see them as serving U.S. and other First World interests at the expense of countries in the Third World. The decline in attention to dependency theory is understandable, they say, since this academic discourse is unpopular in capital-rich countries that object to any critique of neoliberal policies that serve their interests at the expense of capital-poor countries.

Capitalist World-System Theory

The dependency theorists pointed the way for scholars who write in what is known as the **capitalist world-system** perspective. This perspective is another form of economic structuralism that differs from dependency in at least two ways. First, world-system theorists are not only concerned with the lack of Third World development but also wish to understand the economic, political, and social development of regions throughout the entire world. Developed and underdeveloped states, winners and losers, all are examined in attempts to explain the global existence of uneven development.

---

[9]Theotonio dos Santos, as cited in J. Samuel Valenzuela and Arturo Valenzuela, "Modernization and Dependency: Alternative Perspectives in the Study of Latin American Underdevelopment," *Comparative Politics 10*, no. 4 (July 1978): 544.

Second, the goal is to understand the fate of various parts of the world at various times in history within the larger context of a developing world political economy. Latin America, for example, is not unique. Its experience is an integral part of the capitalist world-system. The priority is to understand the global system from a historical perspective. Only then can the fates of particular societies or regions of the globe be understood. World-system theorists, therefore, were interested in the nature and effects of globalization long before the end of the Cold War and the subsequent popularization of the term "globalization."

Advocates of this view are not necessarily Marxists, and in fact some adherents differ from classical Marxism in key respects. But world-system theory is essentially grounded in the Marxist conception of social reality because of its emphasis on the primacy of the economic sphere and the role of class struggle. Rather than focusing on domestic class structure, however, the emphasis is on an international hierarchy and the struggle among states and transnational classes.

The writings of Immanuel Wallerstein represent the most ambitious world-system work and have been the catalyst for an extensive amount of subsequent research. In attempting to understand the origins and dynamics of the modern world economy and the existence of worldwide uneven development, he aspires to no less than a historically based theory of global development, which he terms world-system theory.[10]

Wallerstein begins by analyzing the emergence of capitalism in Europe, tracing its development into a capitalist world-system that contains a core, a periphery, and a semiperiphery. The core areas historically have engaged in the most advanced economic activities, such as banking, manufacturing, technologically advanced agriculture, and ship building. The periphery has provided raw materials—minerals, timber, and the like—to fuel the core's economic expansion. Unskilled labor is repressed, and the peripheral countries are denied advanced technology in those areas that might make them more competitive with core states. The semiperiphery is involved in a mix of production activities, some associated with core areas and others with peripheral areas. The semiperiphery also serves a number of other functions, such as being an outlet for investment when wages in core economies become too high. Over time, particular countries or regions of the world may gravitate between core, peripheral, and semiperipheral status.

Class structure varies in each zone depending on how the dominant class relates to the world economy. Contrary to the liberal economic notion of specialization based on comparative advantage, this division of labor requires as well as increases inequality between regions. States in the periphery are weak, in that they are unable to control their fates, whereas states in the core are economically, politically, and militarily dominant. The basic function of the state is to ensure the continuation of the capitalist mode of production.

Given the inexorable nature of capitalism, Wallerstein and his followers were probably less surprised than most theoreticians at the virtual collapse of most of the communist Second World. In a post–Cold War volume, Wallerstein attempts to place the events of 1989–1991 in historical perspective. Liberalism—an ideology he identifies as associated with the capitalist world-system—has served as a "legitimating geoculture." On North-South relations, he depicts the North's wealth as largely "the result of a transfer of surplus value from the South." Vulnerability in a capitalist world economy comes from "a ceaseless accumulation of capital" that approaches its limit "to the point

---

[10]Immanuel Wallerstein, *The Capitalist World-Economy* (Cambridge, Cambridge University Press, 1979).

where none of the mechanisms for restoring the normal functioning of the system can work effectively any longer." Grossly unequal distribution of material gains contributes to multiple strains in the world-system and undermines state structures, notably "their ability to maintain order in a world of widespread civil warfare, both global and state level."[11] Hence Wallerstein sees a direct connection between the continual deepening of global capitalism, crises of political authority, and increased conflict.

Conclusion

Fostering economic growth and sustaining economic development on a global scale will remain formidable challenges throughout the coming decades. Some have suggested that we must redefine development needs to be more consistent with quality-of-life criteria rather than a seemingly never-ending quest for economic growth. Whether economic well-being, the environment, social justice, human rights, the natural environment, and the overall improvement of the human condition can be served at lower economic growth rates is not altogether clear. It is indeed a tall order.

Realists recognize the reality of Third World poverty and the developmental gap between North and South. They doubt, however, whether this gap will be major cause of international conflict, the primary realist concern. (The issue of resource wars will be discussed in the next chapter.) Furthermore, if developmental problems are to be mitigated, then it will be states that will take the lead and be the final arbiters of whatever global policies are devised. International organizations and nongovernmental organizations can play a role, but only states have the requisite economic clout to improve the situation.

Pluralists or liberals (to include liberal institutionalists) usually have a greater interest in international political economy than do most realists, at least in terms of the Third World. For them, states tend to think in terms of short- and medium-term objectives, lacking a longer time horizon. This is where international organizations such as the United Nations and nongovernmental organizations can play a role by institutionalizing the longer-term interests of states. Economic structuralists are most at home with issues of global development. Their major contribution has been to highlight an alternative theoretical perspective on the development of the global political economy. When development is placed in historical context, provocative arguments are put forward that draw our attention to alternative ways of interpreting the poverty of the vast majority of humanity. It is this global poverty, of course, that remains one of the most significant twenty-first century challenges as both capital-rich and capital-poor countries proceed down the paths of what they hope will be sustainable development.

---

[11]Immanuel Wallerstein, *After Liberalism* (New York: New Press, 1995).

Afterword

The General Theory
John Maynard Keynes

(1883–1946)

In the following excerpt from The General Theory of Employment, Interest and Money *(1935), Keynes addresses the "social philosophy towards which the General Theory might lead." Writing in the midst of an economic depression, Keynes rejects socialism in his search for a way to preserve economic liberalism and individual rights. This was to be done through what he saw as necessary government intervention in the marketplace to get economies moving again. A neoclassical economist, Keynes writes with the understanding that market value is a function of supply and demand—individuals and firms assumed to be fully informed rational actors seeking to maximize their gains (utility or profits) in such economic transactions as buying, producing, and selling. In* The General Theory, *Keynes goes beyond the supply-demand concerns of microeconomics on prices paid for quantities of product brought to different markets. Instead, he deals theoretically with production and employment in a country's economy as a whole, the subject of macroeconomics—a focus on aggregates like national income that are affected by such government actions as spending, taxing or borrowing (fiscal policy), or measures that affect the money supply and interest rates (monetary policy). In the passages below, Keynes provides justification for moving away from* laissez-faire *policies—leaving economic matters to the market—and carves out instead a role for government in an effort to advance economic growth with positive increases in consumption, investment, production, and employment. Moreover, Keynes also sees economic prosperity at home resulting from such domestic measures taken by governments as facilitating maintenance of liberal trade and commerce internationally. Italics have been added to emphasize key points in this excerpt from* The General Theory.

The outstanding faults of the economic society in which we live are its failure to provide for full employment and its arbitrary and inequitable distribution of wealth and incomes. . . .

It is not the ownership of the instruments of production which is important for the State to assume. If the State is able to determine the aggregate amount of resources devoted to augmenting the instruments and the basic rate of reward to those who own them, it will have accomplished all that is necessary. . . .

Our criticism of the accepted classical theory of economics has consisted not so much in finding logical flaws in its analysis as in pointing out that its tacit assumptions are seldom or never satisfied, with the result that it cannot solve the economic problems of the actual world. But if our central controls succeed in establishing an aggregate volume of output corresponding to full employment as nearly as is practicable, the classical theory comes into its own again from this point onwards. . . .

The central controls necessary to ensure full employment will, of course, involve a large extension of the traditional functions of government. Furthermore, the modern classical theory has itself called attention to various conditions in which the free play of economic forces may need to be curbed or guided. But there will still remain a wide field for the exercise of private initiative and responsibility. Within this field the traditional advantages of individualism will still hold good.

Let us stop for a moment to remind ourselves what these advantages are. They are partly advantages of efficiency—the advantages of decentralisation and of the play of self-interest. *The advantage to efficiency of the decentralisation of decisions and of individual responsibility is even greater,* perhaps, than the nineteenth century supposed; and the reaction against the appeal to self-interest may have gone too far. But, above all, *individualism,* if it can be purged of its defects and its abuses, *is the best safeguard of personal liberty in the sense that, compared with any other system, it greatly widens the field for the exercise of personal choice.* . . .

Whilst, therefore, *the enlargement of the functions of government,* involved in the task of adjusting to one another the propensity to consume and the inducement to invest, would seem to a nineteenth-century publicist or to a contemporary American financier to be a terrific encroachment on individualism. *I defend it,* on the contrary, both *as the only practicable means of avoiding the destruction of existing economic forms in their entirety and as the condition of the successful functioning of individual initiative.* . . .

I have pointed out . . . that, under the system of domestic *laissez-faire* and an international gold standard such as was orthodox in the latter half of the nineteenth century, there was no means open to a government whereby to mitigate economic distress at home except through the competitive struggle for markets. For all measures helpful to a state of chronic or intermittent under-employment were ruled out, except measures to improve the balance of trade on income account. . . .

If nations can learn to provide themselves with full employment by their domestic policy . . . , *there need be no important economic forces calculated to set the interest of one country against that of its neighbours.* There would still be room for the international division of labour and for international lending in appropriate conditions. But *there would no longer be a pressing motive why one country need force its wares on another or repulse the offerings of its neighbour,* not because this was necessary to enable it to pay for what it wished to purchase, but with the express object of upsetting the equilibrium of payments so as to develop a balance of trade in its own favour. *International trade* would cease to be what it is, namely, a desperate expedient to maintain employment at home by forcing sales on foreign markets and restricting purchases, which, if successful, will merely shift the problem of unemployment to the neighbour which is worsted in the struggle, but *a willing and unimpeded exchange of goods and services in conditions of mutual advantage.*

Is the fulfilment of these ideas a visionary hope? Have they insufficient roots in the motives which govern the evolution of political society? Are the interests which they will thwart stronger and more obvious than those which they will serve?

I do not attempt an answer in this place. It would need a volume of a different character from this one to indicate even in outline the practical measures in which they might be gradually clothed. But if the ideas are correct—an hypothesis on which the author himself must necessarily base what he writes—it would be a mistake, I predict, to dispute their potency over a period of time. At the present moment people are unusually expectant of a more fundamental diagnosis; more particularly ready to receive it; eager to try it out, if it should be even plausible. But apart from this contemporary mood, *the ideas of economists and political philosophers, both when they are right and when they are wrong, are more powerful than is commonly understood. Indeed the world is ruled by little else. Practical men, who believe themselves to be quite exempt from any intellectual influences, are usually the slaves of some defunct economist. Madmen in authority, who hear voices in the air, are distilling their frenzy from some academic scribbler of a few years back.* I am sure that the power of vested interests is vastly exaggerated compared with the gradual encroachment of ideas. Not, indeed, immediately, but after a certain interval; for in the field of economic and political philosophy there are not many who are influenced by new theories after they are twenty-five or thirty years of age, so that the ideas which civil servants and politicians and even agitators apply to current events are not likely to be the newest. But, soon or late, *it is ideas, not vested interests, which are dangerous for good or evil.*

Key Terms

sustainable economic development   *p. 404*
factors of production   *p. 405*

New International Economic Order
   (NIEO)   *p. 410*
   terms of trade   *p. 411*

Other Concepts

concessionary rates *p. 409*
nationalization *p. 409*
expropriation *p. 409*
trade preferences *p. 410*
subsidiary *p. 412*

transfer pricing *p. 412*
repatriation *p. 413*
neocolonialism *p. 414*
cartel *p. 414*
dependency *p. 415*

newly industrializing
    countries (NICs) *p. 415*
bourgeoisie *p. 422*
structural violence *p. 422*
capitalist world-system *p. 423*

Additional Readings

For statistical data, see the U.N. Development Program's annual *Human Development Report* and the World Bank's *World Development Report*. Both are published annually by Oxford University Press and available on the U.N. Web site. We also highly recommend the annual *State of the World* publication by the Worldwatch Institute.

For further background reading, see Robert Gilpin's chapters on multinational corporations and the issue of dependency and economic development in *The Political Economy of International Relations* (Princeton, NJ: Princeton University Press, 1987) and his two more recent volumes—*Global Political Economy: Understanding the International Economic Order* (Princeton, NJ: Princeton University Press, 2001) and *The Challenge of Global Capitalism: The World Economy in the 21st Century* (Princeton, NJ: Princeton University Press, 2002). On multinational corporations, development, North-South relations, OPEC, and other commodity cartels, see Joan E. Spero and Jeffrey A. Hart, *The Politics of International Economic Relations* (New York: St. Martin's Press, 1996). An anthology of articles on global power and wealth is Jeffry A. Frieden and David A. Lake (eds.), *International Political Economy* (New York: St. Martin's Press, 1995). See also Howard J. Wiarda and Harvey F. Kline, *An Introduction to Latin American Politics and Development* (Boulder, CO: Westview Press, 2001) and Carol Lancaster, *Transforming Foreign Aid* (Washington, D.C.: Institute for International Economics, 2000).

An anthology that includes diverse readings reflecting liberal, Marxist, rational-choice, and regime-oriented understanding of global political economy is George T. Crane and Abla Amawi (eds.), *The Theoretical Evolution of International Political Economy* (New York: Oxford University Press, 1997). On development and related global problems, see David N. Balaam and Michael Veseth, *Introduction to International Political Economy,* 2nd ed. (Upper Saddle River, NJ: Prentice-Hall, 2001), especially parts IV and V. Also of interest is Stefan Elbe, *Strategy in the Age of AIDS,* Adelphi Paper 359 (London: IISS, 2003). See also Hazel Henderson, *Beyond Globalization: Shaping a Sustainable Global Economy* (Bloomfield, CT: Kumarian Press, 1999).

Global economic institutionalization is the subject of Douglass C. North, *Institutions, Institutional Change and Economic Performance* (Cambridge: Cambridge University Press, 1994) and his earlier works *The Rise of the Western World Performance* (Cambridge, UK: Cambridge University Press, 1973) and *Structure and Change in Economic History* (New York: W.W. Norton, 1981). For a superb anthology on this, see also Miles Kahler and David A. Lake (eds.), *Governance in a Global Economy* (Princeton, NJ: Princeton University Press, 2003). See also Akira Iriye, *Global Community: The Role of International Organizations in the Making of the Contemporary World* (Berkeley: University of California Press, 2002).

Finally, on conflict related to production matters, see Michael T. Klare, *Resource Wars: The New Landscape of Global Conflict* (New York: Henry Holt & Co./Owl Books, 2001) and Tim Lang and Michael Heasman, *Food Wars: The Global Battle for Mouths, Minds and Markets* (London and Sterling, VA: Earthscam, 2004).

Chapter 13

The Global Environment

Imagine a village in England. On the edge of the village is a pasture commonly owned by the local herdsmen. It is a peaceful scene, as cows contently munch the grass and produce milk and calves. Gradually the size of the herd expands. As long as there is enough grass for the number of grazing cows, the carrying capacity of the commons is fine. But what happens as the grass becomes depleted and the herd continues to grow in number? Everyone sees that, at the current rate, the entire commons will be destroyed, and all will suffer. What to do? Focus on selfish short-term benefits? If everyone does that, the commons will rapidly disappear. Reduce the size of one's herd so the commons can replenish itself? That's all very fine, assuming everyone does the same. But can one trust others to do the same? Just as demonstrated in the discussion on Rousseau's fable about the deer hunters in Chapter 3, immediate self-interest may clash with the long-term common interest. The commons represents a ***collective or public good***, meaning one that cannot be withheld from any member of the group. The *tragedy of the commons* is that the situation encourages short-term consumption of a good, even though it will undermine the value of the good in the long-term. Or consider a more contemporary situation. SUVs are very popular vehicles. They evade the fuel efficiency standards for regular automobiles by being built on truck chassis. As gas guzzlers, they increase dependence on foreign oil. People know this, yet reason that, "What real difference can it make if I turn in my SUV for a fuel-efficient, gas-electrical hybrid car if no one else does? After all, the SUV is ideal for taking the kids to school and sporting events, and it is also safer on the road due to its size and weight."

A Global Perspective

Both examples make the point about the challenge of international action to improve the condition of the global environment. Everyone agrees that the environment should be protected, and it is recognized that this is a collective action problem. Discussions of the environment, however, raise a number of interesting and difficult questions:

- Is the environment a national security issue? An international security issue? Or should it be even more broadly construed as a **human security** issue, one that focuses more on individuals no matter where they live as opposed to viewing them as citizens of particular states?

- Who pays the cost? Should industrial states make the major adjustments as they consume most of the natural resources and produce the most pollution?

- What to do? How do we evaluate the trade-offs between, for example, the environment and the economy? It is all very well to worry about the spreading of deserts in Africa, but do we tell the local herdsmen and farmers not to cut down scrub brush for cooking fires and not to expand the size of their herds as precious grassland is trampled and destroyed?

- Who makes these decisions? Can or should the United Nations or transnational nongovernmental environmental organizations tell a sovereign state what to do?

- What are the potential unintended consequences of environmental policies? There are numerous examples where scientific expertise promised a solution to an environmental or economic problem, only to create a new one. For example, Nile perch was introduced into Lake Victoria, Uganda. This large predator drastically reduced native fish populations and caused extinction of as many as 200 indigenous species of cichlid fish.

- Because environmental threats in many cases are slow to develop, how does one mobilize political support to address an issue that for many people is off in the distant future?

In this chapter, we provide brief overviews of the major global environmental concerns as enumerated by the U.N. Environmental Program (UNEP).[1] We will then turn to the contentious matter of the relation between environmental issues and security and the status of global collective action to mitigate the worst aspects of global environmental pollution.

Atmosphere

The discovery of the ozone "hole" in the atmosphere in 1985 led to many years of debate over its importance and what to do about it. The ozone layer absorbs most of the harmful ultraviolet-B radiation from the sun. Depletion of the ozone layer allows more harmful rays to reach Earth, resulting in more skin cancer, eye cataracts, weakened immune systems, reduced plant yields, and damage to ocean ecosystems. In the early 1970s, researchers suggested that nitrogen oxides from fertilizers, supersonic aircraft, and chlorofluorocarbons (CFCs) break apart in the atmosphere and release chlorine atoms that cause ozone depletion. International agreements aim to reduce and eventually eliminate CFC production. Even so, CFCs already produced (e.g., freon in old air conditioners, refrigerators, and spray cans—many of which are rusting in garbage dumps) will continue to pollute the upper atmosphere. Measurements taken of the ozone layer over the Antarctic show a weakening of the ozone layer. No hole has appeared elsewhere. The first general ozone agreement, the Vienna Convention for the Protection of the Ozone

collective or public goods
The allocation of, and payment for, goods that, once provided, cannot easily be denied to others.

human security
The emphasis is on security of all human beings, not the more common, and limited, focus on national or state security.

---

[1]UNEP, *Global Environmental Outlook 3* (UNEP, 2002), available at www.unep.org/geo.

Layer, was simply a pledge to protect the ozone layer. Specific commitments are listed in the 1987 Montreal Protocol. Even with full compliance of the Montreal Protocol, scientists believe the ozone will remain particularly vulnerable for at least the next decade.

Industrial societies consume enormous quantities of oil, gas, coal, or wood (so-called fossil fuels) in factories, households, and transportation vehicles of all kinds. Burning these hydrocarbon fuels contributes to acid rain—production of carbonic, hydrochloric,

Applying Theory

UNDER-STANDING ENVIRON-MENTAL CHALLENGES

In his study of organizations, J. D. Thompson noted how uncertainties can make decision making difficult. If we apply his insights to environmental problems like global warming, we find uncertainty among atmospheric scientists about possible outcomes as well as the relative importance of different causes for global climate change. Given this uncertainty, it is extraordinarily difficult to form a global political consensus on what is to be done, particularly because proposed remedies are usually very costly.

By contrast, the scientific understanding of ozone-layer depletion caused by chlorofluorocarbon (CFC) emissions has been far clearer, making a political consensus on

remedies to be implemented much easier to achieve in what became the Montreal Protocol and later the Vienna Convention, which eliminate or reduce CFC emissions. Somewhere in between global warming and ozone-layer depletion in terms of degree of uncertainty is the case of increased acidification of precipitation—acid rain.

Thompson's matrix (Figure 13.A) may help us understand these problems analytically as we explore building political consensus nationally and globally on appropriate remedies. In which of the four cells would you place global warming, ozone-layer depletion, and acid rain? Or are you even uncertain about how to categorize them?

Preferences Regarding Possible Outcomes

	Certainty	Uncertainty
Certainty	A	B
Uncertainty	C	D

Beliefs About Cause-Effect Relations

FIGURE 13.A   *Decision-making Matrix*
Source: J. D. Thompson, *Organizations in Action* (New York: McGraw-Hill, 1967), pp. 134-135.

and sulfuric acids that fall to earth mixed with rainwater, thus increasing the acidity of soils, lakes, and streams and killing fish, trees, and other forest plant life. States have taken some steps to reduce the atmospheric pollution that contributes to acid rain (as in reducing sulfur content in industrial smokestack emissions or curbing auto emissions) and have tried to deacidify affected areas by adding calcium carbonate or other bases to lakes and streams. The problem, however, remains an enormous one as scientists try to identify more precisely the causes of undesired effects and suggest possible remedies or approaches to policy makers.

Even more devastating in terms of climatic consequences is the degree to which burning hydrocarbon fuels contributes to global warming. If atmospheric scientists are correct (and there are only a few who disagree), burning such fuels over many decades increases the overall volume of carbon dioxide in the atmosphere, creating a greenhouse effect or thermal blanket that keeps more heat from escaping into space. Clearing rain forests and other forested areas exacerbates the problems by removing an important, natural recycling mechanism—trees and other plant life take carbon dioxide in and release oxygen as part of the photosynthesis process. Even a degree or two in overall global temperature increase can produce seasonal variation, rainfall, and other effects that can reduce or even eliminate agricultural production in some regions, flood some landscapes, create deserts in other areas, and increase sea levels (due to melting polar ice caps) with consequent flooding of coastal and other low-lying areas. The prospect of "runaway climate change" also increases dramatically if global temperature rises more than 2°C, according to the International Climate Change Taskforce (2005), co-chaired by U.S. Senator Olympia Snowe and British Member of Parliament Stephen Byers. Such catastrophic climate change would cause rising sea levels, large declines in food production, water shortages, irreversible damage to ecosystems including the Amazon rain forest, and shutdown of the Gulf Stream that gives Europe its temperate climate.

Land

The main driving force leading to pressure on land resources has been increasing food production. Today food is needed for more than 2 billion more people than lived on the Earth three decades ago. Inefficient irrigation schemes can cause salinization and alkalization of soil, resulting in an estimated 10 million hectares of irrigated land abandoned annually. Humans also contribute to land degradation through poor soil management practices, deforestation, removal of natural vegetation, use of heavy machinery, overgrazing of livestock, and improper crop rotation.

Forests

Deforestation is caused by the expansion of agricultural land; overharvesting of industrial wood, fuelwood, and other forest products; and overgrazing. Underlying these practices are such factors as poverty, population growth, markets, and trade in forest products. Forests also can suffer from natural factors such as insect pests, diseases, and fire. The net loss of the global forest area (deforestation plus reforestation) in the last decade of the twentieth century was about 94 million hectares, the equivalent of 2.4 percent of total world forests. Deforestation of tropical forests is almost 1 percent annually. The 1972 U.N.–sponsored conference in Stockholm, Sweden, recognized forests as the largest and most complex and self-perpetuating of all ecosystems. The need for sound land- and forest-use policies was emphasized as well as the introduction of forest management planning. Most of these recommendations remain unfulfilled, particularly due to the competing demands for environmental conservation and economic development and subsistence. Some 75 million people live in the three largest tropical wilderness areas: the Upper Amazon, the Congo River Basin, and the New Guinea–Melanesia complex of islands. Population in these areas is growing at 3.1 percent per year, more than double the world average.

Biodiversity

The extent of the loss of biodiversity is calculated against what is termed the natural rate of extinction. Unfortunately, the loss of biodiversity is many times higher due to land conversion, climate change, pollution, and the harvesting of natural resources. Land conversion is most intensive in tropical forests, but other contributing factors to the loss of biodiversity include waste and pollution, urban development, and wars. As much as 40 percent of our modern pharmaceutical medicines are derived from plants or animals. The rosy periwinkle from Madagascar, for example, produces substances effective in fighting two types of cancers—Hodgkin's disease and leukemia. But it is rapidly disappearing as its environment is being destroyed to supply firewood and farmland to impoverished people.

Scientists have noted an apparent increase in the decline and extinction of species over the past thirty years. Lack of data does not allow for a precise determination of how many species have become extinct in the past several decades, but it is estimated that 24 percent of mammals and 12 percent of bird species are currently globally threatened. With continued global warming that upsets ecosystems throughout the world, some estimate the extinction of as many as half of the Earth's species of plants and animals in a matter of decades!

Freshwater

Approximately one-third of the world's population lives in countries that suffer from what scientists term moderate-to-high water stress. This is defined as a situation where water consumption is more than 10 percent of renewable freshwater resources.

Hauling their buckets, jugs, and jerricans filled at a communal well, these women begin their long trek home.

Practicing World Politics

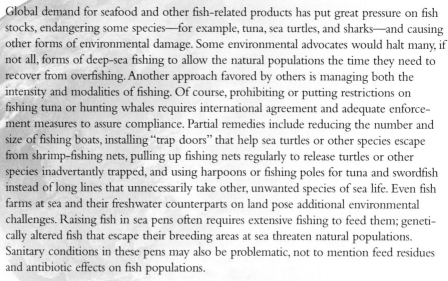

THE OCEANS AND GLOBAL FISHERIES

Global demand for seafood and other fish-related products has put great pressure on fish stocks, endangering some species—for example, tuna, sea turtles, and sharks—and causing other forms of environmental damage. Some environmental advocates would halt many, if not all, forms of deep-sea fishing to allow the natural populations the time they need to recover from overfishing. Another approach favored by others is managing both the intensity and modalities of fishing. Of course, prohibiting or putting restrictions on fishing tuna or hunting whales requires international agreement and adequate enforcement measures to assure compliance. Partial remedies include reducing the number and size of fishing boats, installing "trap doors" that help sea turtles or other species escape from shrimp-fishing nets, pulling up fishing nets regularly to release turtles or other species inadvertantly trapped, and using harpoons or fishing poles for tuna and swordfish instead of long lines that unnecessarily take other, unwanted species of sea life. Even fish farms at sea and their freshwater counterparts on land pose additional environmental challenges. Raising fish in sea pens often requires extensive fishing to feed them; genetically altered fish that escape their breeding areas at sea threaten natural populations. Sanitary conditions in these pens may also be problematic, not to mention feed residues and antibiotic effects on fish populations.

On the demand side, environmental advocates urge people to avoid consumption of endangered fish species and publish updated lists on such Web sites as www.montereybayaquarium.org. Related websites that offer information on oceans and global fisheries include the Ocean Conservancy (www.cmc-ocean.org), the National Audubon Society/Living Oceans Program (www.audubon.org/campaign/lo), the World Wildlife Fund (www.worldwildlife.org), the Natural Resources Defense Council (www.nrdc.org), and Environmental Defense (www.environmentaldefense.org).

By the mid-1990s, eighty countries, constituting 40 percent of the world's population, suffered from serious water shortages. With population growth comes industrial development and the expansion of irrigated agriculture, resulting in increased water demands. The flip side of the coin is untreated water. About 1.1 billion persons lack access to safe water, and 2.4 billion lack access to adequate sanitation. The result is hundreds of millions of cases each year of water-related diseases and more than 5 million deaths. Water management programs vary from place to place, and there has been a move to emphasize demand as opposed to supply management by introducing pricing policies.

Coastal and Marine Areas

Marine and coastal degradation is the result of increasing pressure on both land and marine natural resources as well as the use of the oceans to deposit wastes. The root causes are increased population growth, urbanization, industrialization, and tourism in coastal areas. It is estimated that some 37 percent of the world's population lives within 60 kilometers of the coast. This is more than the entire world population in 1950. Sewage remains the largest source of global ocean contamination, and coastal sewage discharges have increased dramatically in the past three decades. Blooms of toxic phytoplankton are increasing in frequency, intensity, and geographic location. In several enclosed or semienclosed seas, including the Black Sea, plant and animal life is dying. Finally, there is particular concern about the possible effects of global warming on coral reefs. During the intense weather of *El Niño* in 1997–1998, extensive coral bleaching occurred worldwide. Some reefs recovered quickly, but others in the Indian Ocean, Southeast Asia, the far western Pacific, and the Caribbean suffered high mortality rates, in come cases more than 90 percent.

The Environment and Security

A key question is whether environmental issues undermine international security. This requires us to bring politics back into the discussion. The Project on Environmental Change and Acute Conflict, which involved the efforts of thirty researchers from ten countries, asked three specific questions: (1) Do decreasing supplies of resources such as clean water and arable land provoke interstate "resource wars"? (2) Does large-scale migration caused by environmental stress lead to "group-identity" conflicts, particularly ethnic clashes? (3) Does severe environmental scarcity increase economic deprivation, disrupt key institutions, and hence contribute directly to civil strife and crises of authority?[2] All three questions directly deal with war, identity, and crises of authority, major themes of this book.

Conventional wisdom suggests that resource wars are rather prevalent. But scarcity of renewable resources such as forests and cropland rarely cause resource wars between states. It is rather conflict over nonrenewable resources that occurs. Examples include Japan's attempts to secure oil, minerals, and other resources in China and Southeast Asia during World War II and, in part, Iraq's invasion of Kuwait in 1990 to secure disputed oil fields. Oil and minerals are understandably of greater concern to states, as they can more easily be converted into state power than can land, fish, and forests.

The most likely renewable resource to generate conflict among states is freshwater in lakes, rivers, and aquifers shared by two or more states. No society can survive without adequate water supplies. In the Middle East and Southwest Asia, the Jordan, Tigris-Euphrates, and Indus rivers provide the only significant sources of water to the approximately 500 million persons who live in the area, and the number is expected to double by 2050.[3] Shared water resources that have caused disputes include the Nile, Jordan, and Euphrates rivers in the Middle East; the Indus, Ganges, and Brahmaputra rivers in south Asia; and the Rio Grande, Colorado, and Parana rivers in the Americas.[4] Because rivers often pass through more than one state, they are a constant source of potential tension. States upstream may not only pollute the water; as a means of coercive diplomacy, they may also threaten to dam the river, thus reducing downstream flow. Particularly in those cases in which the state downstream believes it has the military capabilities to rectify the situation, the chances for conflict increase.

In 1986, for example, North Korea announced it would build a hydroelectric dam on a tributary of the Han River, which flows down to South Korea's capital of Seoul.

---

[2] The framework, evidence, and conclusions of this impressive effort are presented in Thomas F. Homer-Dixon, "Environmental Scarcity and Violent Conflict: Evidence from Cases," *International Security*, v. 19, no. 1 (Summer 1994): 5–40.

[3] Michael T. Klare, *Resource Wars: The New Landscape of Global Conflict* (New York: Holt and Company, 2001), 161.

[4] Peter H. Gleick, "Water and Conflict: Fresh Water Resources and International Security," *International Security*, v. 18, no. 1 (Summer 1993), 80.

TABLE 13.1
Freshwater Dependency

PERCENTAGE OF FRESHWATER ORIGINATING OUTSIDE OF BORDER	
Egypt	96%
Hungary	95
Botswana	94
Cambodia	82
Syria	76
Paraguay	70
Lithuania	45
Ukraine	40
Pakistan	36
Argentina	30
Jordan	28
Israel	21

Source: Percentages calculated from statistics (drawn from multiple sources) by the World Resources Institute.

South Korea feared the dam could be used to limit its water supplies or perhaps as a military weapon if the dam were destroyed and most of Seoul flooded. In the Middle East, the Euphrates flows from Turkey through Syria and Iraq and into the Persian Gulf. Syria and Iraq both rely on the Euphrates for drinking water, irrigation, industrial use, and hydroelectric power. In 1974, Iraq threatened to bomb the al-Thawra dam in Syria, claiming the dam had reduced Iraq's share of the water. Then, in 1990, Turkey completed the Ataturk dam, the largest of twenty-one proposed dams in a major water supply plan to improve hydroelectric power and irrigation. Both Syria and Iraq protested, viewing the project as a potential source of Turkish coercive diplomacy. The fears were perhaps not unwarranted—in mid-1990 the president of Turkey threatened to restrict water flow to Syria in the hope of forcing Syria to end support for Kurdish rebels operating in southern Turkey. While Turkey later disavowed the threat, the fact remains that completion of the Turkish projects reduces water to Syria by up to 40 percent and to Iraq by up to 80 percent.[5] Numerous other states also depend on surface water from outside their borders. (see Table 13.1).

The second question—whether there is a link between "group-identity" conflicts and large-scale migration caused by environmental stress—is supported by substantial empirical evidence. The link in any particular case has to be carefully traced as the environmental factors that may lead people to migrate occur slowly over time, just as the social and political problems that arise in a host country also may take time to develop; there is no sudden explosion of ethnic conflict. In fact, ethnic conflict may not even occur, as in many cases immigrants simply suffer quietly in isolated misery.

---

[5]*Ibid.*, 88–89.

But the situation is quite different in such cases as Bangladesh and northeast India. Over the years, large numbers of Bangladeshi have moved to India, causing group-identity conflicts. Degradation of the soil is less problematic than the increasing size of the Bangladeshi population. The United Nations estimates that Bangladesh's current population of more than 120 million will nearly double to some 235 million by the year 2025. Almost all of the arable land is already under cultivation, and land scarcity and poverty are exacerbated by flooding. It is estimated that migrants from Bangladesh have increased the population of neighboring regions of India by 12 to 17 million, with at most 2 million accounted for by migration resulting from the 1971 war between India and Pakistan that created Bangladesh.

This massive influx of peoples has affected land distribution patterns, economic relations, and the balance of political power among ethnic and religious groups. The result has been intergroup conflict and violence. In the state of Assam, for example, members of the Lalung tribe have accused Bengali immigrants of taking the best farmland. In 1983, during an election campaign, nearly 1,700 Bengali were massacred in the village of Nellie. Similar tensions exist in Tripura, where the Bengali influx has reduced the original Buddhist and Christian inhabitants to less than 30 percent of the population. This change in the local balance of power led to an insurgency between 1980 and 1988 that ended only after the central government agreed both to return land to the native Tripuris and work to stop the influx of Bangladeshi.[6]

The third question—whether severe environmental scarcity increases economic deprivation, disrupts key institutions, and hence contributes directly to civil strife and crises of authority—is partially supported by empirical evidence. The first part of the equation—environmental scarcity leading to economic deprivation—is well established. Soil erosion in upland Indonesia costs the agricultural economy about half a billion dollars in loss of income per year. The destruction of the dry land in Burkina Faso in Africa reduces the country's gross domestic product by an estimated 9 percent a year due to fuelwood loss, lower yields of crops, and reduction in numbers of livestock.

China provides an interesting example as it is best known for its booming economy—at least in the coastal regions—over the past twenty-five years. It is estimated that the combined costs of environmental degradation are about 15 percent of China's gross national product. The cost derives from such factors as lower crop yields because of water, soil, and air pollution; higher death rates from air pollution; lost farmland caused by soil erosion and construction; flooding and loss of soil nutrients from erosion and deforestation; and loss of timber because of poor harvesting practices.[7]

The last part of the equation concerning the political effects of environmental scarcity and economic deprivation applies to the state. Particularly in the Third World, the effect has been to undermine the legitimacy and hence the authority of certain states. Given the precarious finances of many governments, the loss of water, soil, and forests results in demands for new dams, irrigation systems, and reforestation programs. If those living in the countryside do not receive adequate government support, rural poverty increases. This may lead to an exodus to the city in the often vain hope of finding a better livelihood. The demands then take the form of calls for housing, transportation, food, and employment. With the increase in urban population come subsidies that strain financial coffers and misallocate capital. Such state intervention often breeds corruption and tends to concentrate financial and political power in the hands of a small elite.[8]

[6]Homer-Dixon, "Environmental Scarcity," 21–23.

[7]*Ibid.*, 24.

[8]*Ibid.*, 25.

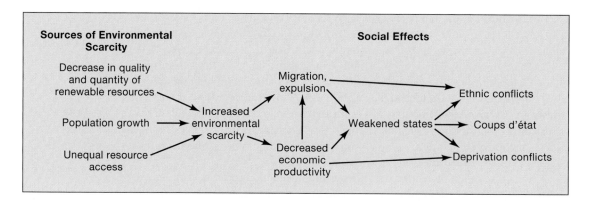

FIGURE 13.1   *Some Sources and Consequences of Environmental Scarcity*

Source: Thomas F. Homer-Dixon, "Environmental Scarcities and Violent Conflict: Evidence from Cases," *International Security,* vol. 19 no. 1 (Summer 1994): 5–40. © 1994 by the President and Fellows of Harvard College and the Massachusetts Institute of Technology.

When the elites are drawn from one ethnic group, urban unrest is possible, if not likely. This is not to suggest that conflict in the Third World is simply a function of environmental scarcity and economic deprivation. The idea that poverty in and of itself leads to political violence has proven simply to be untrue. Other factors, such as conceptions of what is economically just, perceptions of economic and political opportunities, the coercive power of the state, and the ability of political elites to exploit and politicize the poverty issue, all play a role. But such scarcity certainly exacerbates the myriad of problems faced by people of the Third World and works to undermine the legitimacy of many developing states.

We would also note the link between resources and civil wars. In such domestic power struggles, financing is obviously a key factor. In 2000, a U.N. report was issued on illicit diamond trafficking and arms procurement by the UNITA rebel group in Angola. The report noted "Diamond revenues constitute the essential component of UNITA's ability to wage war." That same year, a World Bank study was issued on the relation between "natural resource predation" and the incidence of civil war. Based on a statistical analysis of all major internal conflicts between 1960 and 1995, the greatest risk factor for civil war was not ethnic antagonism, but the availability of easily procured "lootable" resources.[9]

In sum, environmental scarcity will only worsen over the next few decades as population growth leads to a decrease in the quantity and quality of renewable resources with some groups enjoying disproportionate access to them. The population explosion will occur in the developing regions of the world, those least able to deal with such a development. The political and social effects are outlined in Figure 13.1. Finally, nonrenewable resources such as precious minerals will continue to be fought over to finance wars and civil wars.

---

[9]U.N. Security Council, *Report of the Panel of Experts on Violations of Security Council Sanctions against UNITA,* U.N. doc. S/200/203, March 10, 2000; Paul Collier, "Economic Causes of Civil Conflict and Their Implications for Policy," unpublished paper, World Bank, Washington, D.C., June 15, 2000. Both cited in Klare, *Resource Wars,* 210–211.

International Organizations and the Environment

In our discussion of states and national security, we noted that realists claim the anarchic structure of the international system makes it difficult for states to work together. National interests and anarchy emphasize what divides states and people from one another. In the case of the physical environment, however, it is apparent to even the most obtuse leader that environmental concerns transcend state borders. Industrial pollution in one country can drift downstream or blow across borders; environmental degradation can lead to economic refugees looking for a better life; the implications of global warming and ozone-layer depletion affect people around the world. Not surprisingly, pluralists and liberal institutionalists have been particularly interested in tracking the drafting and implementation of environmental international agreements and analyzing the evolution of international norms and their role in the construction of environmental regimes. (See Table 13.2.)

As noted at the outset of this chapter, even when the environmental implications of industrial and economic practices are accepted, agreement on what needs to be done can be difficult to achieve. Many Third World countries, for example, suffer from massive unemployment and underemployment and resent being told by developed countries that industrialization is bad for the environment, particularly when during their own early phases of industrialization these latter countries paid little or no heed to the impact of their activities on the environment.

In an attempt to reconcile Third World emphasis on economic development and First World expressed concern for the global environment, we have noted that the concept of *sustainable development* has gained increasing acceptance. Sustainable development is based on the premise that there needs to be a balance between consumption and population size within overall limits imposed by nature. Environmental degradation can also impede production of food and other goods and services needed to sustain increasing populations. Without an improvement in resource and environmental stewardship, development ultimately will be undermined, as eventually there will be little or nothing left of nature to be exploited. But without accelerated economic growth in the poorest countries in the near term, environmental policies will fail, as the poor peasants are likely to exploit the land to the maximum merely in order to survive. Trying to implement such a balancing act is not a function of the "ignorant" poor failing to understand the implications of their actions; for example, ranchers and farmers in developed countries often also focus on the near term, tending to discount considerations that lie in the future. Indeed, given the massive scale of their agricultural and industrial production and extraordinarily high consumption patterns, it is the advanced economies in wealthier countries that have the greatest adverse impact, resulting in resource depletion, pollution, and other forms of environmental degradation. In any event, to avoid turning the concept of sustainable development into a buzzword or slogan lacking any meaningful content, hard thinking has to take place on the trade-offs between protecting the environment and economic development. Such a dialogue is not simply a matter of scientific evidence, but political debate as well, because it is through politics that policies will be decided.

Since Rio, a growing body of actors—governments, nongovernmental organizations, the private sector, civil society, and the scientific and research community—have responded to environmental challenges in a variety of ways . . . Nevertheless, despite progress on several fronts, from a global perspective the environment has continued to degrade during the past decade, and significant environmental problems remain deeply embedded in the socio-economic fabric of nations in all regions. Progress towards a global sustainable future is just too slow. A sense of urgency is lacking. Internationally and nationally, the funds and political will are insufficient to halt further global environmental degradation.

U.N. Environment Programme,
Global Environment Outlook-1,
available at www.unep.org/unep/eia/geo1.

It's Been Said...

TABLE 13.2
*Selected International
Environmental Regime
Agreements*

ENVIRONMENTAL AGREEMENTS RELATING TO ATMOSPHERIC REGIMES

Air Pollution	Convention on Long-Range Transboundary Air Pollution (1979)
Air Pollution: Nitrogen Oxides	Protocol to the 1979 Convention on Long-Range Transboundary Air Pollution Concerning the Control of Emissions of Nitogen Oxides or Their Transboundary Fluxes
Air Pollution: Sulphur	Protocols to the 1979 Convention on Long-Range Transboundary Air Pollution on the Reduction of Sulphur Emissions or Their Transboundary Fluxes by at least 30 percent (1985); further reductions (1994)
Air Pollution: Volatile Organic Compounds	Protocol to the 1979 Convention on Long-Range Transboundary Air Pollution Concerning the Control of Emissions of Volatile Organic Compounds or Their Transboundary Fluxes
Ozone Layer	Montreal Protocol on Substances That Deplete the Ozone Layer and Vienna Convention for the Protection of the Ozone Layer
Climate Change	U.N. Framework Convention on Climate Change
Environmental Modification	Convention on the Prohibition of Military or Any Other Hostile Use of Environmental Modification Techniques

ENVIRONMENTAL AGREEMENTS RELATING TO REGIMES FOR THE HIGH SEAS

Law of the Sea	U.N. Convention on the Law of the Sea (LOS)
Marine Dumping (London Convention)	Convention on the Prevention of Marine Pollution by Dumping Wastes and Other Matter
Marine Life Conservation	Convention on Fishing and Conservation of Living Resources of the High Seas
Ship Pollution	Protocol of 1978 Relating to the International Convention for the Prevention of Pollution from Ships (MARPOL) (1973)
Whaling	International Convention for the Regulation of Whaling

ENVIRONMENTAL AGREEMENTS RELATING TO REGIMES FOR LAND AREAS

Antarctic: Environmental Protocol	Protocol on Environmental Protection to the Antarctic Treaty
Desertification	U.N. Convention to Combat Desertification in Those Countries Experiencing Serious Drought or Desertification, particularly in Africa
Hazardous Wastes	Basel Convention on the Control of Transboundary Movements of Hazardous Wastes and Their Disposal
Tropical Timber	International Tropical Timber Agreements (1983 and 1994)
Wetlands	Convention on Wetlands of International Importance, Especially as Waterfowl Habitat (also known as Ramsar)
Organic Pollutants	Stockholm Treaty on Persistent Organic Pollutants (2000)

AGREEMENTS FOR OTHER ENVIRONMENTAL REGIMES		TABLE 13.2 *(continued)*
Biodiversity	Convention on Biological Diversity	
Endangered Species	Convention on the International Trade in Endangered Species of Wild Flora and Fauna (CITES)	
Comprehensive Nuclear Test Ban	Bans all nuclear tests in the atmosphere, underground or under water, or in outer space	

Sources: U.N. Environmental Programme and *The World Fact Book* (Washington, D.C.).

As noted previously, U.N.–sponsored conferences have addressed many of these issues. The U.N. Conference on Environment and Development held in Rio de Janeiro, Brazil, in 1992 is a good example of a forum that brought diverse governmental and nongovernmental actors together. As the formal U.N. members, states controlled most of the action, but parallel meetings by nongovernmental actors also contributed substantially to the professed consensus reached on a sustainable development approach, assuring a sensitivity to the environmental impacts of economic activities and demographics. The distillation of this consensus was the Rio Declaration later endorsed by the U.N. General Assembly and the creation of the Commission on Sustainable Development, an intergovernmental body of some fifty-two members that serves as a focal point within the U.N. system for coordination of various U.N. programs.

From the perspective of some environmental activists, however, much of the Rio Conference consisted of world leaders posturing and mouthing platitudes about their concern for the environment. Hundreds of pages of proposals for international and national action were produced, but not much has happened. For the poorest countries, the problem is not simply lack of will but lack of resources to implement a program of sustainable development that balances economic and environmental needs at a time when population continues to grow. Environmental activists note, however, that the sustainable development concept also places developed countries on the hook. These countries, after all, far and away consume more both per capita and in the aggregate than do those in the developing world. Indeed, it is not always certain whether Third World population growth rates or the expanding appetites for the consumption of raw materials on the part of the industrial nations is the greater danger. (Figure 13.2 illustrates this point.)

A related international effort was undertaken in 1994 at a meeting under U.N. auspices in Cairo, Egypt, to address global population growth in relation to economic development, the environment, and social concerns. Although a Cairo declaration addressing measures to slow population growth rates eventually passed, conflicting views were not easily reconciled—some Islamic countries even refused to send representatives to the conference. As such, some international conferences may well reflect the absence of consensus among the parties. Table 13.3 lists examples of U.N. conferences that have examined global political economy and society.

Even when an international consensus is worked out, such as in the Law of the Sea negotiations in the late 1970s, which dealt with navigation rights and economic uses of offshore waters and the seabed, domestic political processes may preclude ratification of treaties and other agreements reached. Treaties may go for decades without ratification

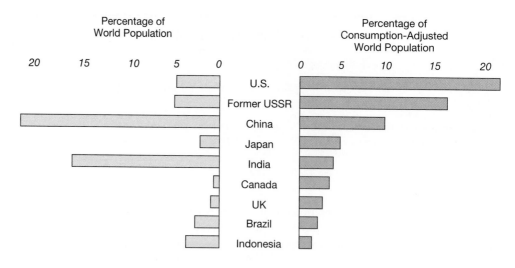

FIGURE 13.2   *Population and Consumption*
Source: The Commission on Global Governance.

when effective domestic opposition is in place. Reservations or interpretations appended to international agreements can even alter concessions made by negotiators or change substantial portions of agreements made in the give-and-take of international negotiations. Of course other parties may not accept such changes made unilaterally by individual countries.

TABLE 13.3	Conference diplomacy under U.N. auspices has brought states, nongovernmental organizations (NGOs), and individuals together to address issues of common concern in the global economy and society.
U.N. Conference Diplomacy on Global Political Economy and Society	

MAJOR CONFERENCES

World Summit for Children, New York, 1990

Survival, protection and development of children, setting goals for children's health, nutrition, education, and access to safe water and sanitation

U.N. Conference on Environment and Development, Rio de Janeiro, 1992

Continuing work that began in 1972 at the U.N. Conference on the Human Environment in Stockholm, this Earth Summit developed Agenda 21—a global blueprint for sustainable development (dealing with poverty, excess consumption, toxic and other hazardous wastes from production processes, alternative energy sources, greater reliance on public transportation systems, environmental impact of national economic decisions, etc.); drafted a Declaration on Environment and Development; prepared a Statement of Forest Principles; and took up both the U.N. Framework Convention on Climate Change and the Convention on Biological Diversity

World Conference on Human Rights, Vienna, 1993

Reaffirmed international commitment to human rights, strengthening mechanisms for monitoring and promoting human rights globally; led to the appointment of the first U.N. High Commissioner for Human

TABLE 13.3
(continued)

Rights; made human rights integral to U.N. peacekeeping missions; linked democracy, development, and human rights

International Conference on Population and Development, Cairo, 1994

Worked toward consensus on family planning as part of development programs, seeking education and empowerment of women as the most effective way to reduce population growth rates and promote sustainable development, reaffirming that voluntary family planning decisions are a basic human right, and encouraging donor countries to increase funding for population-related activities. Follow-up special session of the U.N. General Assembly held in June 1999

World Summit for Social Development, Copenhagen, 1995

Committed governments to eradicating poverty "as an ethical, social, political and economic imperative"; raised the negative side of economic globalization—growing gaps between rich and poor, shrinking social safety nets, and increasing insecurity about jobs and social services in both developed and developing countries; formulated a plan for meeting basic human needs, reducing economic and social inequalities, and providing sustainable livelihoods

Fourth World Conference on Women, Beijing, 1995

Addressed advancement and empowerment of women in relation to women's human rights, women and poverty, women and decision making, the girl-child, violence against women and other areas of concern; supported effort to fight violence against women and afford them greater legal protection. Follow-up special session of the U.N. General Assembly in June 2000

Second U.N. Conference on Human Settlements (Habitat II), Istanbul, 1996

Adopted a global plan and policy guidelines to improve living conditions in urban and rural settlements and to implement the "full and progressive realization of the right to adequate housing," identifying mayors and other local officials as key players in implementation of the Habitat action plan

The Millennium Assembly of the United Nations, New York, 2000

Set forth "animating" vision "to strengthen the role of the United Nations in meeting the challenges of the twenty-first century" for the United Nations in the new era of "global society"—underscoring the relation between development on the one hand and peace and security on the other, promoting peace and sustainable development; agenda included disarmament and other aspects of peace and security, development and poverty eradication, human rights. Separate "Millennium Forum" for NGOs and other individuals

SELECTED LIST OF OTHER U.N. CONFERENCES ON GLOBAL ECONOMY AND SOCIETY

U.N. Global Conference on the Sustainable Development of Small Island Developing States, 1994

International Conference on Natural Disaster Reduction, 1994

World Summit on Trade Efficiency, 1994

Ninth U.N. Congress on the Prevention of Crime and the Treatment of Offenders, 1995

Conference on Highly Migratory Fish Stocks, 1995

World Food Summit, 1996

Ninth U.N. Conference on Trade and Development (UNCTAD IX), 1996

Earth Summit+5, 1997

(table continues)

TABLE 13.3
(continued)

U.N. Conference on the Establishment of an International Criminal Court, Rome, 1998

General Assembly Twentieth Special Session—World Drug Problem, 1998

General Assembly Special Session on Small Island Developing States, 1999

Third U.N. Conference on the Exploration and Peaceful Uses of Outer Space, Vienna, 1999

General Assembly Special Session on the International Conference on Population and Development, New York, 1999

General Assembly Special Session on Social Development and Beyond, Geneva, 2000

U.N. Workshop on Energy Efficiency, Global Competitiveness, and Deregulation, 2000

Development Finance for the World's Least Developed Countries, 2001

World Conference against Racism, Racial Discrimination, Xenophobia, and Related Intolerance, South Africa, 2001

U.N. General Assembly Declaration of Commitment to Fight AIDS, 2001

Transnational Organizations and the Environment

The impact of transnational nongovernmental organizations (NGOs) on environmental issues is perhaps more evident than in any other area of global politics. At the international conferences in Rio and Cairo, private transnational organizations influenced the agenda, actively participated, and pressured states to hold these conferences in the first place. They have also played an important watchdog role in a wide variety of functional areas, ranging from environmental protection of the oceans and forests, Antarctica, and the ozone layer, always reminding political leaders of their public commitments. Such environmental organizations as the World Wildlife Fund, Greenpeace, Conservation International, Friends of the Earth, World Business Council for Sustainable Development, Earth Council, and the International Council for Local Environment Initiatives exemplify the diversity of actors that compose global civil society.

Transnational organizations demonstrate that instruments of power are not solely available to the state. One instrument has been modern communications. Greenpeace, for example, has created wonderful photo opportunities for journalists by climbing aboard whaling ships, parachuting from smokestacks, and floating hot air balloons into nuclear test sites. Greenpeace has its own media facilities, allowing it to produce video spots and photographs for news organizations. Through dramatic actions and publications, Greenpeace and other environmental organizations can change public perceptions of the activities of states as well as nonstate actors. A good example involves Greenpeace's antiwhaling efforts. They have changed whaling's original image of man versus vicious, Moby Dick–like monsters of the deep, substituting the image of rapacious hunters slaughtering peaceful, nurturing mammals.

Using the power of modern communications to alter how people view topics of potential international concern requires money, an obvious source of power in the world. Since the 1970s the budgets of the largest transnational environmental groups are greater than the amount spent by most states on environmental issues. Some of these

NETWORK	DATE LAUNCHED	DESCRIPTION
Sponsored by NGOs: Association for Progressive Communications (APC) (www.apc.org)	1990	Links NGOs promoting human rights and environmental justice
OneWorld Online (www.oneworld.net)	1995	A "supersite" that links to hundreds of websites to provide information on development
Global Forest Watch (www.wri.org/gfw)	1999	Linking to NGOs in five countries to monitor the world's large, intact "frontier forests"
Sponsored by U.N. Agencies: UNEPNet (UNEP) (www.unep.net)	1997	Links eight UNEP offices and at least nine other partner institutions by satellite to improve the flow of global environmental information
Global Urban Observatory (Habitat) (www.urbanobservatory.org)	1998	Links researchers worldwide to compile statistics and examples of best practices in urban management
HORIZON Solutions Web site (UNDP, UNEP, UNFPA, UNICEF, IDRC, Harvard, Yale) (www.solutions-site.org)	1999	Provides case studies on solutions to problems of water, waste, energy, transportation, toxic chemicals, public health, industry, desertification, biodiversity, air pollution, and agriculture

TABLE 13.4
Selected Global Environmental Networks

Source: Molly O'Meara, "Harnessing Information Technology for the Environment," in Lester Brown et al., *State of the World 2000* (New York: W. W. Norton, 2000), p. 139.

organizations have budgets equal to—or sometimes close to double—that of the U.N. Environmental Programme. In the 1990s, for example, Greenpeace International and the World Wildlife Fund had annual budgets of some $100 million and $200 million respectively, while UNEP's yearly budget was only about $75 million.

Table 13.4 describes various environmental networks.

Finally, initial successes of such organizations are often followed by further successes. Greenpeace and the World Wildlife Fund have enrolled over six million members around the globe, supported by a well-developed staff and cadre of scientific experts able to contest the arguments and evidence put forward by state bureaucracies and corporations. These experts often provide input into the development of programs such as the Global Environment Outlook, sponsored by the U.N. Environment Programme. Such NGOs illustrate that the state is not the only focus for collective efforts to affect world politics.[10]

Governance therefore is not necessarily synonymous with government.[11] Transnational environmental organizations contribute to global governance through their influence on how publics, states, and corporations perceive international issues. Such organizations rely not on force but rather on persuasion to help change and define the boundaries and conceptions of what are considered "good" ecological policies. In other words, they work to restructure the "environment" within which environmental policies

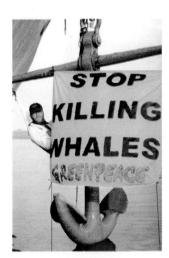

Greenpeace activist on a Japanese whaling ship.

[10]Paul Wapner, "Politics Beyond the State: Environmental Activism and World Civic Politics," *World Politics,* 47, no. 3 (April 1995): 315 (footnotes 12 and 13), 320–321.

[11]James N. Rosenau, "Governance, Order and Change in World Politics," in James N. Rosenau and Ernst-Otto Czempiel, eds., *Governance without Government: Order and Change in World Politics* (Cambridge: Cambridge University Press, 1992).

Practicing World Politics

DEVELOPMENT AND THE ENVIRONMENT

In addition to the U.N.'s main Web page (www.un.org), see the U.N. Environmental Programme (www.unep.org) and the U.N. Development Programme (www.undp.org) sites. See also the World Bank (www.worldbank.org) and the U.N. Conference on Trade and Development (www.unctad.org). On workers' rights concerning health, safety, working conditions, and child labor, see the International Labor Organization in Geneva (www.ilo.org). For the U.S. government site on environmental matters, see the Environmental Protection Agency (www.epa.gov). Nongovernmental organizations on these subjects include Greenpeace (www.greenpeace.org), the World Wildlife Fund (www.worldwildlife.org), World Watch (www.worldwatch.org), Conservation International (www.conservation.org), and Friends of the Earth (www.foe.org in the U.S.; in Canada, www.foecanada.org), and other national chapters linked to these sites. A U.S.–focused NGO concerned with the environment is the Sierra Club (www.sierraclub.org).

are framed, by politicizing such actions as whaling or pollution, issues that historically have been viewed as simply economic in nature. Most importantly, transnational environmental organizations have used this noncoercive power in efforts designed to change the behavior of states and corporations.

Global Population

Although we have noted that a number of factors place stress on the global environment, the key underlying factor is the growing world population. Some demographers project that within three decades or so world population will have passed nine billion persons. The concern, however, over the carrying capacity of the earth is certainly not new. Thomas Malthus (1766–1834), a minister and social analyst, published "An Essay on the Principle of Population" on the eve of the nineteenth century in 1798. He published a shorter summary in 1830 for "those who have not had the leisure to read the whole work."[12] Noting the "prodigious power of increase in plants and animals," Malthus observed that human "population, when unchecked, increases in a geometrical progression of such a nature as to double itself every twenty-five years."[13]

He worried that food supplies would not keep pace with population growth. How would humanity cope with its tendency "to increase, if unchecked, beyond the possibility of an adequate supply of food?" He foresaw "diseases and epidemics, wars, infanticide, plague, and famine."[14] Malthus acknowledged that technology would contribute to increased food production; but, at some point, he believed that human ingenuity would run up against the Earth's limits to produce, resulting in awful consequences for the human condition.

In the almost two centuries since Malthus made these predictions, global population has grown dramatically from the hundreds of millions of his time to more than six billion people today. Through industrialization and modern medicine, population has continued

---

[12]See Thomas Malthus, *An Essay on the Principle of Population* and *A Summary View of the Principle of Population* (London: Penguin Books, 1982, 1985), p. 221.

[13]*Ibid.*, 223, 238.

[14]*Ibid.*, 250, 268.

Estimating Population Growth

Annual population growth rate (usually expressed as a proportion or percentage) for a given population is calculated by subtracting the number of deaths from the number of births at the end of a given year and dividing that figure by the total population at the beginning of that year.

A convenient way to estimate the impact of population growth rate on total population over time is the "Rule of 72," which is also used by financial analysts as a quick rule of thumb in estimating the effect of compound interest rates on the growth of principal over time. The length of time in years that a population can be expected to double is 72 divided by the growth rate. Thus a 2 percent growth rate means that population can be expected to double in 36 years (72 divided by 2), assuming of course that the 2 percent rate remains constant over the period.

It is easy to overestimate future population size by projecting present growth rates. Reduction in population growth rates will slow the doubling time. Because population growth rates tend to decline as societies industrialize, there is a danger in projecting present population growth rates for Third World countries too far into the future. Unexpected catastrophes due to natural disasters, widespread famine, disease, or warfare will also have a negative impact on population growth rate. On the other hand, if assumptions on reduced population growth rates are too optimistic, future population size can just as easily be underestimated.

to grow even more significantly. From the 1820s to the 1920s the global population doubled and reached two billion. From 1925 to 1976 it doubled again to four billion. By 1990 the figure was 5.3 billion, increasing by more than 700 million people in the last decade of the twentieth century. Doubling populations when numbers are in the millions is challenging enough; doubling when the base is in billions is potentially catastrophic. Indeed, current estimates for the end of the twenty-first century put the numbers in a wide range from about 11 billion to more than 15 billion people. Can Earth sustain so many? Are there limits to growth? Figure 13.3 graphically presents data on world population growth.

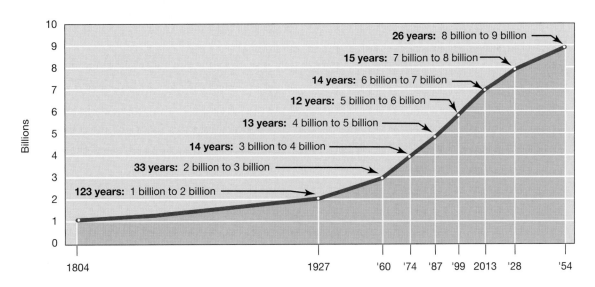

FIGURE 13.3   *World Population Increase*

Source: U.N. Population Division.

In the early 1970s, a nongovernmental organization known as the Club of Rome sponsored studies and conferences on limits to growth. The push for industrial development that got underway in Europe and North America in the nineteenth-century world of Thomas Malthus had enormous impact on the environment as forests were cleared, resources mined, and factories put into operation. Consumption of nonrenewable energy resources and other minerals increased dramatically, reducing stocks and adding to ground, sea, and air pollution levels.

Production of goods and services for increasing numbers of peoples has had adverse environmental impact, but continued development thus far has still been sustainable. The negative environmental impact of the industrial revolution, however, was less than it would have been had population levels been as high as they are today. If the more than 1.3 billion people currently in China and some 900 million now in India (not to mention projected increases in these numbers and additional billions in other less-developed countries) continue to industrialize following the European, American, or Japanese models, the result could be truly devastating, not only for these countries but also for the world as a whole. Resource depletion and environmental degradation on a global scale could undermine any capacity to continue producing at ever-increasing levels. Renewable resources would also suffer from growing scarcity as demand dramatically increases, with obvious implications in terms of arable land, fisheries, and the degradation of aquifers, rivers, and lakes. Development in these circumstances would not be sustainable. The limits predicted by Malthus might finally be reached.

Conclusion

Interest in the global environment as a topic in international relations and world politics is relatively new. Access to natural resources has always been of concern to realists analyzing competition among states, but such topics as ozone depletion, biodiversity, and water pollution seem to many realists to border on the trendy or faddish. This is quite different from the perspective of many pluralists or liberals, who see the environment as another important chessboard of international politics. Not only are environmental issues directly tied to economic and development concerns, but they may also stimulate conflict among states and groups.

The environment is also a topic that raises the issue of "What is meant by security?" To pursue a policy based on a narrow definition of "national security" may be counterproductive if the issue at hand transcends borders and requires international cooperation. Avoiding the "tragedy of the commons" is in everyone's interest. If so, "international security" or "human security" may therefore be the most appropriate concept when discussing the global environment.

Afterword

On Population
Thomas Robert Malthus

(1766–1834)

Parson Malthus, a religious man of the cloth, spent much of his professional life studying systematically and writing extensively about human population growth in relation to the societal problem of feeding these geometrically increasing numbers of people. According to Malthus, "Population, when unchecked, increases in a geometrical ratio. Subsistence [i.e., food] increases only in an arithmetical ratio." Put another way, in the absence of measures that might be taken to slow its rate of growth, population tends to outpace the food production necessary to sustain the whole of humanity. Indeed, his commentary below foreshadows present-day efforts to achieve sustainable development. The passages are drawn from his "Essay on the Principle of Population" (1798) and his restatement or "Summary" provided in 1830. The challenge is to draw from the earth resources necessary for increasing levels of production and improved human wellbeing while, at the same time, avoiding resource depletion and environmental degradation which, in turn, will undermine capacity for further production. The application of technology to agriculture, particularly in capital-rich countries, has extended the food-production limits of which Malthus wrote so pessimistically; however, the twenty-first century world as a whole does still suffer from widespread malnutrition (and even starvation) to be found today primarily in capital-poor countries. In the passages below, italics have been added for emphasis of key points in the argument.

Population, when unchecked, increases in a geometrical ratio. Subsistence increases only in an arithmetical ratio. A slight acquaintance with numbers will shew [i.e., show] the immensity of the first power in comparison of the second. By that law of our nature which makes food necessary to the life of man, the effects of these two unequal powers must be kept equal. This implies *a strong and constantly operating check on population from the difficulty of subsistence. This difficulty must fall somewhere and must necessarily be severely felt by a large portion of mankind.* . . .

The passion between the sexes has appeared in every age to be so nearly the same that it may always be considered, in algebraic language, as a given quantity. *The great law of necessity which prevents population from increasing in any country beyond the food which it can either produce or acquire,* is a law so open to our view, so obvious and evident to our understandings, and so completely confirmed by the experience of every age, that we cannot for a moment doubt it. The different modes which nature takes to prevent or repress a redundant population do not appear, indeed, to us so certain and regular, but though we cannot always predict the mode we may with certainty predict the fact. *If the proportion of births to deaths for a few years indicate an increase of numbers much beyond the proportional increased or acquired produce of the country, we may be perfectly certain that unless an emigration takes place, the deaths will shortly exceed the births;* and that the increase that had taken place for a few years cannot be the real average increase of the population of the country. *Were there no other depopulating causes, every country would, without doubt, be subject to periodical pestilences or famine.*

The only true criterion of a real and permanent increase in the population of any country is the increase of the means of subsistence. . . .

Elevated as man is above all other animals by his intellectual faculties, . . . he may increase slower than most other animals; but food is equally necessary to his support; and if his natural capacity of increase be greater than can be permanently supplied with food from a limited territory, his increase must be constantly retarded by the difficulty of procuring the means of subsistence.

The main peculiarity which distinguishes man from other animals, in the means of support, is the power which he possesses of very greatly increasing these means. But this power is obviously limited by the scarcity of land—by the great natural barrenness of a very large part of the surface of the earth—and by *the decreasing proportion of produce which must necessarily be obtained from the continual additions of capital applied to land already in cultivation.*

It is, however, specifically with *this diminishing and limited power of increasing the produce of the soil,* that we must compare the natural power of mankind to increase, in order to ascertain whether, in the progress to the full cultivation and peopling of the globe, the natural power of mankind to increase must not, of absolute necessity, be constantly retarded by the difficulty of procuring the means of subsistence; and if so, what are likely to be the effects of such a state of things. . . .

It may be safely asserted, therefore, that *population, when unchecked, increases in a geometrical progression of such nature as to double itself every twenty-five years* [i.e., Malthus calculates an unconstrained annual population growth rate on the order of three percent—Eds.]. This statement, of course, refers to the general result, and not to each intermediate step of the progress. Practically, it would sometimes be slower, and sometimes faster. . . .

But, if the natural increase of population, when unchecked by the difficulty of procuring the means of subsistence, or other peculiar causes, be such as to continue doubling its numbers in twenty-five years; and the greatest increase of food, which . . . could possibly take place on a limited territory like our earth in its present state, be at the most only such as would add every twenty-five years an amount equal to its present produce; it is quite clear that a powerful check on the increase of population must be almost constantly in action. . . .

The rate of increase [in population] *would be checked, partly by the diminution of births, and partly by the increase of mortality. The first of these checks may, with propriety, be called the* preventive check *to population; the second, the* positive check; *and the absolute necessity of their operation in the case supposed is as certain and obvious as that man cannot live without food.* . . .

The distress which would obviously arise in the most simple state of society from the natural tendency of population to increase faster than the means of subsistence in a limited territory, is brought home to the higher classes of an improved and populous country in the difficulty which they find in supporting their families in the same rank of life with themselves; and to the labouring classes, which form the great mass of society, in the insufficiency of the real wages of common labour to bring up a large family. . . .

If the preventive check to population—that check which can alone supersede great misery and mortality—operates chiefly by a prudential restraint on marriage; it will be obvious . . . that direct legislation cannot do much. Prudence cannot be enforced by laws, without a great violation of natural liberty, and a great risk of producing more evil than good. But still, the very great influence of a just and enlightened government, and the perfect security of property in creating habits of prudence, cannot for a moment be questioned. . . .

Key Terms

collective or public good   human security   *p. 432*
  p. 431

Additional Readings

To understand the roots of global agenda setting on what we now call sustainable development, good early sources are the *Brundtland Commission Report,* published as World Commission on Environmental and Development, *Our Common Future* (Oxford, UK: Oxford University Press, 1987), as well as the *Brandt Commission Report* (more formally the *Report of the Independent Commission on International Development Issues*), a document available in libraries and also published as *North-South: A Program for Survival* (Cambridge, MA: The MIT Press, 1980). The idea of sustainable development is a response to the more pessimistic view of there being very real limits to growth, a thesis presented in the

1970s by a transnational NGO, the Club of Rome. See Dennis L. Meadows et al., *The Limits to Growth* (New York: Signet Books, 1972). Cf. Donald H. Meadows, Dennis L. Meadows, and Jørgen Randers, *Beyond the Limits: Confronting Global Collapse, Envisioning a Sustainable Future* (Post Mills, VT: Chelsea Green Publishing, 1992). More recent environmental crisis predictions also include Stephen Sloan, *Ocean Bankruptcy: World Fisheries on the Brink of Disaster* (Guilford, CT: The Lyons Press, 2003) and Stephen Byers (British Member of Parliament) and Olympia J. Snowe (U.S. Senator), co-chairs, *Meeting the Climate Challenge*—work of the International Climate Change Taskforce (2005), which is available on the Web.

Publications of the United Nations organization, the World Bank, the U.N. Development Program, the U.N. Environmental Program, and other international organizations are rich sources available in libraries and usually advertised on these organizations' web sites. For the relation between economic production and the environment—questions of environmental degradation and resource depletion—one may consult Charles S. Pearson, *Economics and the Global Environment* (Cambridge: Cambridge University Press, 2000), Bryan G. Norton, *Searching for Sustainability* (Cambridge: Cambridge University Press, 2003), Paul Robbins, *Political Ecology: A Critical Introduction* (Oxford, UK: Blackwell, 2004), Lester R. Brown, *Eco-Economy: Building an Economy for the Earth* (New York: W.W. Norton, 2001), and Eric A. Davidson, *You Can't Eat GNP: Economics as if Ecology Mattered* (Cambridge, MA: Perseus, 2000).

For a historical overview relating to the biological impact of European imperialism throughout the world, see Alfred Crosby, *Ecological Imperialism: The Biological Expansion of Europe, 900–1900* (Cambridge, UK: Cambridge University Press, 1993). On disease as a global environmental issue, consider John M. Barry, *The Great Influenza* [1918], (New York: Penguin, 2004), Jeanne Guillemin, *Biological Weapons: From the Intervention of State-Sponsored Programs to Contemporary Bioterrorism* (New York: Columbia, 2005), and Jennifer Brower and Peter Chalk, *The Global Threat of New and Reemerging Infectious Diseases* (Santa Monica, CA: RAND Corporation, 2003).

To deal with environmental matters on a worldwide scale, some propose strengthening the capacity of global governance or other forms of international and transnational collaboration. See, for example, Jon M. Van Dyke, Durwood Zaelke, and Grant Harrison, *Freedom for the Seas in the 21st Century: Ocean Governance and Environmental Harmony* (Washington, D.C.: Island Press, 1993) and Hilary French, *Vanishing Borders: Protecting the Planet in the Age of Globalization* (New York: W.W. Norton, 2000).

Chapter 14

"The concept of nation requires that all its members should form as if it were only one individual."

FRIEDRICH SCHLEGAL,
GERMAN CRITIC AND WRITER,
1772–1829

Religion, Nationalism, and Conflicting Identities

M igjen Kelmendi is a well-known Kosovo Albanian writer and journalist. In March 1999, Serbian police began to clear out Pristina, the Kosovar capital. Kelmendi, assuming he was marked for execution, borrowed a baby and pretended to be part of a family. On March 31, he began a journey he could never have imagined. The police went from house to house and ordered everyone out. Some three thousand people were herded down the street to the railroad station. "They were driving us like cattle. The children were screaming and the elderly were very slow," he said. They passed down Pristina's main street. "The saddest bit was that along the way I saw bunches of people, Serbs. They looked at us with complete indifference. It was unimaginable." When they got to the train station, there were already 25,000 to 30,000 people there, all waiting for trains to take them to the border with neighboring Macedonia. Just before midnight, the crowd heard NATO planes wheeling across the night sky. "People began to clap. They were shouting 'NATO! NATO!' and saying 'They will help us.' Then we heard shooting very close to us. Everyone fell silent immediately."[1]

---

[1]Tim Judah, "Inside the KLA," *New York Review of Books*, June 10, 1999, 19.

What am I? What are you? What are our identities? Are you an Englishman? A Brit? A European? If you are American, are you a Native American or are you also of some European, Asian, African, or other origin? Are you a Christian, Jew, Muslim, or Buddhist? Does it matter? Should it matter? Do these distinctions that define our identities set us into mutually exclusive, often conflicting, groups, or do we let our common human identity transcend these differences?

As will become clear in this chapter, questions relating to religious, national, ethnic, tribal, clan, or other human identities are universal. Human beings are social creatures, as Aristotle observed, a fact that has both up and down sides. For the most part, we live and work together cooperatively, divided only by relatively small differences or conflicts. The great achievements of humankind have depended on our ability to pool talents and resources in social groups of one kind or another. At the same time, however, human beings who are organized into separate, conflicting groups can be the source of mutually destructive activities, as has been evident in recent years in parts of Africa and Asia.

An ongoing debate revolves around the question of whether identities are essentially primordial in origin, passed down through generations and a given almost as much as our genetics. Conversely, social constructivists argue that identities are formed, created, malleable, and subject to change and self-definition. Where one comes down on this issue has a dramatic impact on whether one is pessimistic or optimistic about the ability of groupings of individuals to live in relative harmony. From the perspective of international relations and world politics, the world is conventionally divided into single **nation-states, multinational states,** and *nations* dispersed in two or more states. Individuals may derive a sense of security or other value from having a particular national or ethnic identity, but this ethnic identification may make others (particularly minority groups) feel insecure. Mutually exclusive communities within, between, or across state boundaries appear to be the source of conflict based on these national, ethnic, religious, historical and cultural, racial and physical, or other differences. Conflicts may smolder for decades (and even centuries), breaking out as interstate or civil wars, insurgencies, terrorism, or other forms of revolutionary violence.

This chapter begins a discussion concerning one of the most vexing and important issues in world politics at the beginning of the twenty-first century: conflicts relating to state sovereignty, national identity, and human rights. A whole host of questions arise:

- In the name of upholding the concept of state sovereignty, should the aspirations of a minority ethnic group for an independent country be ignored?
- On the other hand, if national self-determination is embraced across the board, then will the world witness increasing fragmentation of the international state system? If so, is this such a bad thing in the age of globalization?
- If, in the name of sovereignty, a state claims the outside world has no right to interfere in its policies against an indigenous minority, what does this mean in terms of protecting human rights around the globe? Does a state's reliance on claims of "national security" trump arguments made in the name of "human security"?

Such questions are not part of an abstract academic enterprise. For example, Kosovo has long been part of the Republic of Yugoslavia or Serbia (the principal part of what remains of Yugoslavia) and Chechnya an integral part of the former Soviet Union (and now the Russian Federation). Why then did NATO claim that humanitarianism was a reason for going to war against Serbia but stood by when the Russians attempted to quell national separatism in Chechnya?

nations
People with a common identity who have formed a nation-state or usually aspire to do so.

We begin by considering the role of religion in global politics. This is followed by a discussion of nationality and ethnicity as concepts used to describe identities peoples may have within and across the formal boundaries of states. We illustrate the obvious fact that the world is replete with conflicts and controversies related to religion, nationality, ethnicity, and race. We then turn to a discussion of approaches designed to foster peace among differing nationalities. Given the confines of a single chapter, we make no attempt to be exhaustive on this subject but do provide representative examples of these national, ethnic, and racial cleavages that often divide societies and peoples across state and communal boundaries. Matters of human rights will be discussed in the next chapter.

Religion

One impact of the Cold War was to overshadow the role of religion in global politics. Although from the perspective of some in the West, the Cold War was a battle between Christianity and other religions against "godless communism," most people saw it in nonreligious terms as a battle between two visions of the appropriate political and economic forms of governance—Western-style democracy and market capitalism versus centrally directed state-socialist or communist economies.

Historically, however, religion has at times played a major role in international politics. The attempt of Christian crusaders to "liberate" the Holy Land in the Middle Ages— and the efforts to repel the "infidels" on the part of the Muslims—is one example. The seventeenth-century Thirty Years' War on the continent and the English civil war also concerned significant religious issues involving Protestants versus Catholics. Not confined to Europe, religious conflict spread to the western hemisphere and later to Africa, Asia, and the Pacific, as Protestant and Catholic missionaries competed with each other in a quest to save the souls of the indigenous "heathens."

In more recent times, the Iranian revolution of 1978–1979 and the coming to power of Shiite Muslim religious leaders were seen as possible harbingers of things to come. But observers of international relations almost universally failed to foresee the significant challenge to modern, secular regimes posed by a global resurgence of religious ideas and movements at the end of the twentieth century. What is fascinating about this global phenomenon is that it is occurring within diverse cultures, different types of political systems, and in countries with varying levels of economic development.[2] Figure 14.1 graphs the relative numbers of people who identify with the religions of the world.

The global rediscovery of religion has some obvious and some contradictory implications. First, transnational organizations such as the Roman Catholic Church, the World Council of Churches, and the Society for the Propagation of Islam would presumably assume more important roles. The pronouncements of various religious organizations over the years, of course, have supposedly had universal application, no matter where the flock may reside. But thanks to modern telecommunications technologies, religious organizations have found it even easier to communicate their messages. Their global religious networks reach out across and beyond the more confining borders of states. It seems, however, that it is not the mainstream religions that have benefited most from the communication revolution but rather some of the more extreme elements who preach religious intolerance if not hate toward adherents of other religious faiths.

Second, transnational religious movements and beliefs also strengthen the development of transnational identities not constrained either by state borders or secular nationalism. For

---

[2]Scott Thomas, "The Global Resurgence of Religion and the Study of World Politics," *Millennium*, v. 24, no. 2 (1995): 289.

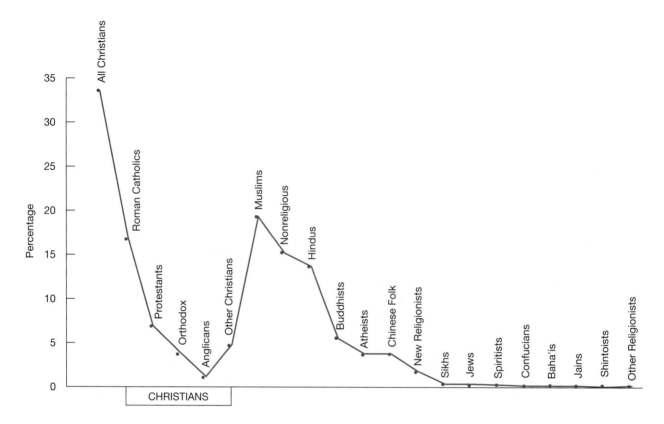

FIGURE 14.1   *Religions of the World*
Based on data in the 1997 *Britannica Book of the Year* (Chicago: 1997), 311.

some, religious identity is more important than any particular national identity. To these people, loyalty to God comes first with the state a more distant second or third.

Third, if such a trend continues, its implications for global conflict are uncertain. On the one hand, some religious movements have spearheaded peace movements and crusades for human rights and justice. On the other hand, one author suggests that religious identity could be a key component of a broader clash of civilizations[3] with the fault lines of conflict, for example, between civilizations or cultures influenced by Judeo-Christian religious traditions and those influenced by Islam.

Finally, we wish to observe that from a realist perspective, religion remains less important than other factors in relations among states. While religious groups will undoubtedly continue to influence government policies around the globe, realists would argue that the governments themselves will continue to operate in the international system on the basis of national interests and security—factors discussed in Chapter 3. Even the Iranian and the now defunct Afghani Taliban governments, for all their Islamic pronouncements, have used religion not as the exclusive road map for foreign policy but rather as a means to guide and facilitate pursuit of power and basic domestic and foreign policy objectives. Realists argue that very often secular

---

[3]Samuel P. Huntington, "The Clash of Civilizations," *Foreign Affairs*, v. 72, no. 3 (1993): 22–49.

objectives are cast in religious garb in order to make them more appealing to peoples of various nationalities.

From the pluralist or liberal perspective, religious diversity is not inevitably associated with conflict. As we will see in the case of national identities, many pluralists hold out the prospect that international organizations, transnational nongovernmental organizations, and increasing globalization may reduce or ameliorate conflict among religious groups professing diverse faiths. Religious diversity, in their view, is one of the defining elements of an emerging global civil society.

For economic structuralists influenced by Karl Marx, economic class identities should dominate. But Marxists have always recognized (and bemoaned) the pervasive power of religion to act as a veritable opiate to induce "false consciousness" on the part of the working class. Social constructivists, as noted above, see religious identification as something that is socially constructed and not a given. There is nothing inherently violent or pacifist about any particular religion. For feminists, most mainstream religions are understandably viewed with skepticism or challenge due to the generally submissive and supportive role customarily assigned to women.

Islam

There is no doubt that at least in the Western world, Islam is viewed by many less familiar with its teachings with a certain amount of trepidation. Unfortunately, Islamist extremism is often associated with terrorism. Islam is the religious identity of more than 1.2 billion Muslims—one out of every five human beings or some 20 percent of humanity in some fifty countries. Islam extends across the globe from Morocco on Africa's western Atlantic coast to Malaysia, Indonesia, and the Philippines in southeast Asia. A western religion that spread eastward in the first century after the *hegira* (or *hejira*) when Muhammad made his way in A.D. 622 from Mecca to Medina, Islam shares the same monotheistic Middle East roots as Christianity and Judaism, which preceded it on the world stage. Indeed, the Bible (both Old and New Testaments) are considered sacred texts. However, it is the Koran (in some transliterations from Arabic, the *Qur'an*) that is at the core of Islam, understood to be the word of God passed by the angel Gabriel to the prophet Muhammad. Muslims annually celebrate this enlightenment of Muhammad in the late October and November holy days of Ramadan. Written in Arabic, the language in which it was first transcribed, the Koran is the most sacred of texts to Muslims. Even non-Muslims able to read Arabic see the poetry and prose of the Koran as a work of great literary art.

To Muslims, Muhammad is the last of the prophets, the others including Adam, Noah, Abraham (the first Muslim), Moses, and Jesus. That there is only one God, named Allah (the name in Arabic for God), was an Islamic reaction not only to polytheistic religions (worship of multiple gods) then prominent in the Middle East but also to the Christian belief of God as a trinity of three divine persons. In this regard, to Muslims Jesus was a holy man—a prophet of God like Muhammad, but not God in himself. Accordingly, among their obligations the first is that all Muslims are to recite the *Shahadah* as an article of their monotheistic faith: "I bear witness that there is no God but Allah and Muhammad is His Prophet" (in Arabic *Ash hadu an La ilaha illa 'llah, Muhammad ar rasul Allah*). Indeed, this statement of faith is the most important obligation in Islam. Even in ordinary conversation, when Muslims say they are hoping or planning for something to happen, they frequently add the word *Insha'llah*—"if it is God's will," or more simply "God willing." Another common expression in everyday Arabic is *Alhumdulillah,* or "Praise God."

The joy of youth: Malaysian boys studying the Koran.

Friday congregational worship.

Muslims also have four other duties. One is *to pray* five times a day (at dawn, noon, midafternoon, dusk, and before midnight but after darkness has set in—normally with head covered, shoes off, and kneeling on a carpet in the direction of the holy city of Mecca where Muhammad was born in A.D. 570). Another is *to give alms* or charitable contributions, thus putting more abstract notions of generosity and humanitarianism routinely into practice (for those financially able, contributions should be at least 1/40th or 2.5 percent of one's total wealth; using total wealth rather than annual income as a base often means a much greater sacrifice by the truly wealthy than a tithe based on 10 percent of annual income typically required in some Christian or other religious communities). Moreover, one is *to fast* in daytime (from dawn to dusk) as an act of self-denial during the holy month of Ramadan. Finally, at least once in one's life, one should make the *Hajj*—a pilgrimage to Mecca in Saudia Arabia—if one can. The *Kaabah* is located there—a sanctuary or small cube-like structure in the Great Mosque of Mecca that contains the sacred black stone believed to have been given by God to the patriarch Abraham, father to both the Arabs and the Israelites.

God's guidance and the rules by which one is to live one's life are to be found not only in the Koran but also the life of Muhammad in the *Hadith* (sayings) and *Sunnah* (deeds) of the prophet. Upon these sources rests the *Shariah,* or Islamic law, that extends beyond the mosque in many Muslim countries to society as a whole. To be a Muslim is to be "one who submits" (the meaning of *Muslim*) to the will of God. Islam not only allows but also encourages trade and commerce so long as transactions between buyer and seller are just or equitable. Indeed, along with conquest, trade was a most important vehicle for the rapid spread of Islam to the far reaches of the world in the seventh, eighth, and subsequent centuries. In this understanding, so long as one is honest or just, to become wealthy through commerce is a good thing, pleasing to God. That said, much as in pre-Reformation Christian communities, making money through lending and charging interest is contrary to Islamic teaching. Mobilizing capital for investment through equity shares, joint ventures, or other creative approaches thus avoids direct loans for which interest would have to be paid.

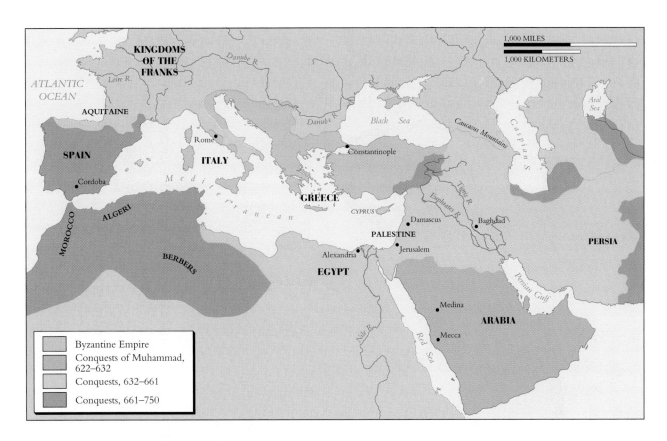

MAP 14.1   *Muslim Expansion around the Mediterranean. The teachings of the Prophet Muhammad (570–632) and the military conquests led by him and his followers reversed the spread of Christianity around the Mediterranean with startling speed.*

Islam shares with Judaism many ideas and practices in common, including male circumcision (traceable in the Hebrew tradition to Abraham's command, though not mentioned in the Koran) as well as prohibitions against eating pork—a practice that has its functional origins in concern for hygiene and disease prevention. As with other religions, culture often matters in defining how Muslims actually practice their religion in daily life. Muslims are also prohibited from drinking wine (most, but not all, seeing this as including other alcoholic spirits as well). How the *Shariah* is interpreted is in fact also subject to cultural variations with some interpretations differing across the vast Islamic world.

The mosque is both a place of prayer close to Earth as one kneels and bows deeply in a prostrate position as well as a place for learning how to deal practically with day-to-day moral issues. A very down-to-earth religion, Islam is thus concerned with the affairs of day-to-day living, which also includes both work and commercial activities. This interest in practicality also underscores Islam's earliest interest in science and knowledge (the Koran's opening command that one should read and thus educate the mind).

A deep, religiously based commitment to knowledge also explains why Euclidian geometry and the writings of Plato, Aristotle, and other Greeks were retained throughout

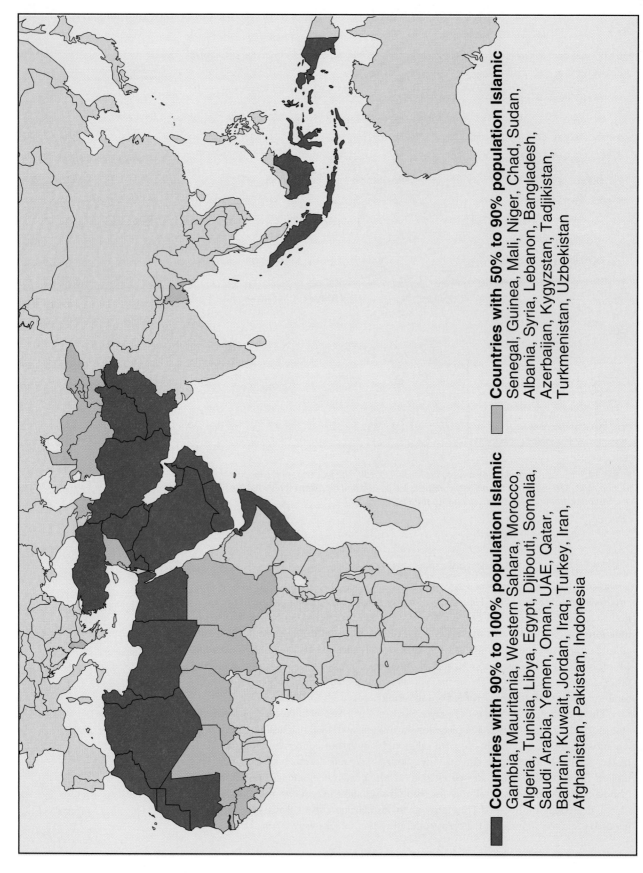

Countries with 90% to 100% population Islamic
Gambia, Mauritania, Western Sahara, Morocco, Algeria, Tunisia, Libya, Egypt, Djibouti, Somalia, Saudi Arabia, Yemen, Oman, UAE, Qatar, Bahrain, Kuwait, Jordan, Iraq, Turkey, Iran, Afghanistan, Pakistan, Indonesia

Countries with 50% to 90% population Islamic
Senegal, Guinea, Mali, Niger, Chad, Sudan, Albania, Syria, Lebanon, Bangladesh, Azerbaijan, Kyrgyzstan, Tadjikistan, Turkmenistan, Uzbekistan

MAP 14.2   *The Islamic World*

the Muslim period in Egypt and elsewhere in the Arab world long after the fall of the Roman Empire and the European "dark ages" that followed. This created a favorable academic environment that no doubt contributed to discovering algebra and the concept of zero in mathematics; perfecting an ability to perform cataract removal and other delicate surgeries unheard of in Europe during the late Middle Ages; developing a medical art and science that understood details of human anatomy—skeletal, nervous, and circulatory systems. By the early eleventh century Islamic scholars already had found fault with the ancient Greek Ptolomeic view of Earth as the universe's center, an understanding held long before formulations of a solar system offered by the Polish astronomer Nicholas Copernicus (1473–1543) and his later Italian counterpart Galileo Galilei (1564–1642). Consistent with this commitment to knowledge, great universities were established in Damascus, Baghdad, Bukhara, Seville and Cordoba in Spain, and Cairo (which became the intellectual center for Islam).

As with Christianity and Judaism, which came before it, Islam also has its sectarian divisions. Most Muslims are Sunni; however, most in Iran are Shiah, a division that dates from a dispute on succession to the prophet in the century after the prophet's death. Shiah Islam holds that Ali was selected by Muhammad as successor (a claim disputed by Sunnis). Ali was succeeded in the line of the prophet by other *imams*, the twelfth of whom was Muhammad al Mahdi, whom Shiites believe disappeared but never died; his immanent presence is understood as a source of guidance to the present-day religious leadership.

Indeed, the Islamic clergy plays an important role, particularly in the Shiite understanding of Islam. The Mahdi eventually shall reappear one day to establish a new Islamic golden age. Although different in details, this belief is similar in some respects to the Judaic belief in the coming of a messiah or in Christianity the second coming of Jesus (also accepted by Muslims). Most Sunnis reject such ideas as heretical and, with a few exceptions, place much less emphasis on the clerical role.

One such exception is the Wahhabi sect in Saudi Arabia, which takes a very strict view of Islam's commands. Particularly in rural areas of the desert kingdom, clergy educate the populace religiously and enforce compliance with the *Shariah,* informed as it is by this particular interpretation of the Koran, *Hadith*, and *Sunnah.* Religious leaders authorized to do so from time to time when circumstances dictate may issue a decree (or *fatwah*) for religious guidance on various topics to include calling for *jihad* or holy struggle as against infidels, whether non-Muslims or Muslims, who have strayed from their religious obligations.

The establishment of *madrassas,* or religious schools, is seen by many faithful as a blessing. A large number are funded by Saudi Wahhabists in countries such as Pakistan where public schools are often poor or nonexistent, and the *madrassas* provide meals for the young boys who attend. The curriculum, however, essentially emphasizes the rote memorization of the Koran. It was out of such *madrassas* that the leader of the Taliban, Mullah Omar, and a number of his associates emerged. While much is made of the potential of conflict between Islam and other faiths, of equal concern should be the internal struggle within Islam. Muslim fanatics, or *jihadists,* have carried out fearful acts of violence in the name of Islam, and voices have been raised that such persons are threatening to hijack Islam and use it to justify their extreme world view. Religious intolerance, of course, is not restricted to Muslim *jihadists*. In 2002, Hindus in Gujarat, India, killed several hundred Muslims with the collaboration of local officials. Anti-Semitism is on the rise in Europe, and all too often there is an unfortunate tendency to equate all of Islam with terrorism in the United States and European countries.

Nations, Ethnic Groups, and States

While the role of religion in international politics has only recently been rediscovered, the concepts of *nation* and *state* have been at the forefront of studies of global politics for years. A certain amount of confusion, however, continues to exist over their meanings and the meanings of related terms.

The terms *nation* and *state* are frequently used interchangeably as if they were synonyms. To use the terms this way, however, is to miss important differences. As noted earlier, the term *state* is a legal concept that refers to a population administered by a government (or other administrative authority) on a given territory with a claim to sovereignty recognized by other sovereign states. When a particular state is composed of a single *nation* or people with a common identity, we call it a *nation-state* because the people who compose the "nation" live on the territory of that "state." Nation and state are coterminous or overlapping, as in the United States where most of the people consider themselves to be American, notwithstanding the diversity of racial, ethnic, and cultural differences among them.

Race refers to identifiable physical differences used to categorize people, whether or not individuals share a common identity. Although race can be a basis for identity, it is also a very problematic basis for establishing unity. Racial distinctions that are used to justify divisiveness, discrimination, or unequal treatment are common enough. In the extreme, **racism** can also lead to **genocide**—the mass murder of people because of their race or other identity. Because of this, many prefer not to draw racial distinctions among peoples at all; it is better from this perspective to identify only with the human race. Focusing on a common humanity avoids the scourge of racism that may come from accentuating separate identities based on physical or other differences.

The distinction between a nation and an ethnic group is often difficult to make. One reason is that the terms are subjective; people themselves are the ones who make the choice when they define their identities in either national or ethnic terms. Adding to the confusion, the two terms are frequently used interchangeably. In the United States, people tend to identify nationally as Americans while at the same time holding other ethnic identities that define them as individuals or groups within society.

Nationality involves a significant degree of self-definition and refers to a people with a sense of common identity, if not destiny. In other words, a nation is whatever a group of people says it is. This common identity may be the result of such diverse factors as race, ethnicity, religion, culture, shared historical experiences, or some combination of these. When this common identity has political consequences and serves as a basis for national mobilization, the result is *nationalism.*

Nations and Nationalism

The birth of modern nationalism is generally traced back to the eighteenth century. More than a mere change of political regime and authorities, the French Revolution that began in 1789 was a watershed of political ideas and ideologies—some democratic and others authoritarian—that would take root throughout Europe and later spread primarily through colonialism throughout the rest of the world. The mobilization of the masses in politics, which had previously been the exclusive domain of upper classes or elites, was one important legacy; nationalism was another.

Local (and even national) identities were not new to Europe. In the fifteenth century, Machiavelli had written in *The Prince* that the ruler of the city of Florence, Lorenzo de Medici, needed to use his resources to unify Italy and thus avoid continual warfare

nationalism
Devotion to the interests of one's nation, usually to the exclusion of other competing identities.

among Italian city-states and invasion or other intrusions by France and Spain. Because they were without unity, Machiavelli observed rather emotionally that Italians had been "more enslaved than the Hebrews, more oppressed than the Persians, and more scattered than the Athenians." They were "without a head, without order, beaten, despoiled, lacerated, and overrun," having "suffered ruin of every kind."[4] Machiavelli is honored in present-day Florence for having been among the first advocates of Italian unity.

In fact, however, unification of Italy would have to wait until the 1880s. It was the French in their revolution and its aftermath who first put to practical use the notion of nationalism to inspire an entire nation of people to act as a unit. This idea dominated much of the nineteenth and twentieth centuries.

In past centuries, French and English kings had raised armies to fight one another, but they had relied heavily on professionals or mercenaries in their employ. Departing from this tradition, Oliver Cromwell's "new model army" was raised from the general population during the 1640s to fight the king's forces in the English civil war. This very successful approach was used to fill the ranks of Napoleon's mass armies as they set forth on military campaigns across the European continent. The French employed a draft—conscription for national service (the *levée en masse*)—as an effective means to raise popular armies galvanized in their fervor by nationalism and nationalist appeals. It was a model followed in Europe and elsewhere (often with disastrous consequences) throughout the nineteenth and twentieth centuries.

Nationalism can be a benign force or even make a contribution to peace, as when fostering a common national identity within a state, and is used to overcome conflicts in an ethnically or racially diverse population. It has also been used to unify a people and lead to the formation of a single nation-state, as was true in Germany and Italy in the 1870s and 1880s and Israel in 1948.

The Italian patriot and revolutionary Giuseppe Mazzini (1805–1872) and the Hungarian Jewish newspaper correspondent Theodor Herzl (1860–1904) are representative of writers in the nineteenth-century nationalist genre.[5] Mazzini argued that God had "divided humanity into distinct groups upon the face of our globe, and thus planted the seeds of nations." He wrote that Italians were a people "speaking the same language, endowed with the same tendencies, and educated by the same historic tradition" and Italy "the home that God has given us, placing therein a numerous family we love and are loved by, and with which we have a more intimate and quicker communion of feeling and thought than with others."

In a similar line of argumentation, Herzl asserted that Jews throughout the world "are a people—*one* people." He and fellow Jewish nationalists, or Zionists, referring to ancient biblical lands that were home to the Israelites, called for "restoration of the Jewish State." Observing that "no nation on earth has endured such struggles and sufferings," he saw "the distinctive nationality of the Jews" as best preserved within a Jewish state.

Early nineteenth-century nationalism in Latin America took the form of independence movements that ended Spanish and Portuguese empires there. Nationalist political movements in the 1940s, 1950s, and 1960s also succeeded in ending European colonial rule in most of Africa and Asia.

Nationalism, however, can also serve darker purposes when it is used at the expense of others and contributes to civil strife and warfare. In these circumstances, there is a mutual exclusivity or intolerance of differing national and ethnic groups. Extreme

---

[4]Niccolo Machiavelli, *The Prince*, Ch. xxvi.

[5]Quotes are taken from Mazzini's *The Duties of Man* and Herzl's *The Jewish State,* as reprinted in Michael Curtis, ed., *The Great Political Theories,* vol. 2 (New York: Avon Books, 1962, 1981), 237–248.

Genocide in the Twentieth Century

The twentieth century witnessed many appalling instances of genocide—killing of people based on racial or ethnic differences. Chief among these was the Holocaust, Nazi Germany's persecution, enslavement, and methodical elimination of European Jews. Approximately six million Jews, along with Gypsies, communists, and others deemed by the Nazis to be "undesirables" died under Nazi rule from 1933 to 1945, often in such notorious slave labor and death camps as Treblinka, Auschwitz, and Dachau. Other ethnic groups have suffered from genocide as well. Beginning in 1894, nearly 200,000 Armenians were slain in two years by Turkish soldiers and police. In 1909 the renewed massacre of Armenians began again and ended only because of the intervention of outside powers, including the United States. Armenian support for the Allied cause in World War I led to the estimated elimination of one million Armenians. More recently, ethnic conflict in the African state of Rwanda resulted in the massacre of at least 500,000 Tutsi at the hands of the Hutus. Genocide in the former Yugoslavia has also claimed large numbers of Muslims, Croats, Serbs, and Kosovars as victims.

The gates of the Nazi concentration camp at Auschwitz. The sign above them reads "Arbeit Macht Frei"—"Work Makes You Free."

nationalism, often expressed by those feeling that their people have been oppressed, usually fosters an intolerance of others, particularly if they are seen as the oppressors.

In some cases, as in Germany during the 1930s, the extreme-nationalist appeal may take the illusory form that the oppressed are actually a superior people who have been downtrodden unjustly by so-called inferiors. Adolf Hitler's twentieth-century ultranationalist and racist supremacy arguments went well beyond those of Johann Fichte (1762–1814) and other eighteenth- and nineteenth-century German nationalist writers. Hitler (1889–1945) and his National Socialist movement portrayed Jews, Slavs, Gypsies, and other non-Germanic peoples as racially and culturally inferior. Germans were said to be Aryans—a "master race"—who deserved to be treated as such and given the territory needed to expand and grow. Nationalism pushed to this racist extreme was the rationale used in an attempt to "justify" Germany's aggression against non-German nation-states in World War II and the Holocaust, in which more than six million Jews as well as Slavs, Gypsies, and others were murdered or worked to death.

Countries that enjoy a relatively strong sense of unity (as is true for most Americans in the United States) tend to characterize additional identities among peoples as *ethnic* distinctions rather than seeing them as differences in nationality. Thus Native Americans, Hispanics, Jews, and other Americans of European, African, or Asian origin are referred to customarily as ethnic groups, although some Native Americans see themselves as

ethnic, ethnicity
A common, often cultural, identity of a group of people who usually also identify themselves with a larger society.

"nations" within the United States. Whatever their differences, they still identify themselves as Americans.

In this usage, ethnic groups retain a separate identity within the larger, more ethnically diverse nation. Members of ethnic groups may speak the same language, share
cultural values, or even have physical similarities; however, all of these groups still maintain an overarching or common national identity.

Although most French are of European origin, many of African or Asian deriva-
tion (often from local elites in nineteenth- and twentieth-century French colonial
populations) consider themselves as French nationals despite racial differences with
those of European origins. More homogeneous as a nation-state than either the United
States or France is Japan. Indeed, with the exception of a small proportion of Korean
or other origin, most of Japan's population share a common language, history, culture,
physical characteristics, and national identity.

Things get more confusing when we talk of a state made up of several "countries,"
as in the United Kingdom (U.K.), which is composed of England, Scotland, Wales, and
Northern Ireland (see Map 14.3). States are countries, but not all countries are states.
After all, Scotland and England, which already had established dominance in earlier centuries over Wales and Ireland, did not unite as a single state until they finally became a
united kingdom in 1707. English and Scottish monarchs were almost always at odds and
had often been at war with each other. Although the United Kingdom is a single state,
frictions and conflicts among the different national or ethnic groups continue to the present day. Scottish nationalists, a minority within Scotland, certainly see "Scottishness" as
much more than a mere ethnic distinction. If they had their way, their country would
again become a separate state. It remains to be seen whether the creation of Scottish and
Welsh parliaments at the end of the 1990s to handle many regional affairs will satisfy
nationalist sentiment or simply spur demands for eventual complete independence.

Binational States

Very often two or more nations exist within the borders of a single state. After World
War I, the victorious allied powers created a single Czechoslovak state from some of the
territory that had been part of the just-defeated Austro-Hungarian empire. Physically
the same people, Czechs and Slovaks shared the same language and, although there were
some Protestants and Jews in the population, most were Catholics.

Of course this focus on physical, linguistic, and religious similarities overlooked
significant cultural differences related to their separate development over some 500 years.
Among other factors, for example, Czechs were subject more to Austrian and Slovaks
more to Hungarian influences. Complicating reconciliation of these Czech-Slovak
cultural differences were ethnic (at times "national") differences between Bohemian
Czechs in the western part and Moravian Czechs in the eastern part of the present-day
Czech Republic.

Separate identities between Czechs and Slovaks proved to be more than just ethnic differences, leading in 1993 to the formal breakup of Czechoslovakia into separate
Czech and Slovak states. Czechoslovakia is thus an example of a **binational state** that
has become separate Czech and Slovak nation-states.

There are other binational states, by contrast, that thus far have stayed together. One
example is Belgium, with its separate Flemish- and French-speaking national groups.
Some see the Belgian state as being composed of two separate countries or nations—
Flanders to the north with its Flemish-speaking Flemings and Wallonia to the south
with its French-speaking Walloons. Different language groups in a particular country

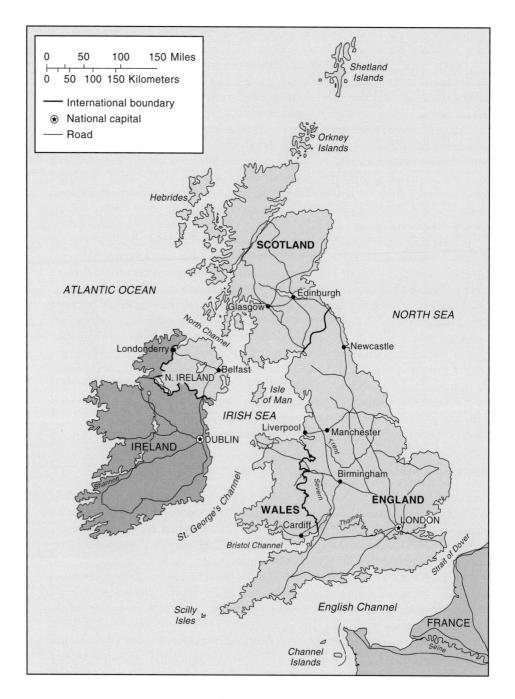

MAP 14.3   *The United Kingdom and Ireland*

usually are an indicator of diverse cultures with different histories and, as a result, separate national identities.

Keeping Belgium together as a single state has been a formidable challenge for more than a century and a half. A common religious affiliation (most Belgians are Catholics) has not been enough. Indeed, the Church in Belgium has come to reflect

Flemish-Wallonian cultural differences. In such circumstances, choosing a common form of governance proved to be as difficult in the twentieth century as in the nineteenth. In the winter of 1830–1831, the great powers meeting in London brought in a king from one of the German states (Leopold of Saxe-Coburg) in an effort to keep the country together. The monarchy of Belgium continues its efforts (as it has for over 170 years) to perform the same national-unity function.

The king of the Belgians—now seen as very much a Belgian himself—is neither a Fleming nor a Walloon. As chief of state, the Belgian king symbolizes Belgian national unity; his role is to take concrete steps to help maintain some degree of unity among Flemings and Walloons. At the same time, however, the Belgian government has increasingly become fractured into separate sets of institutions servicing the separate Flemish and Wallonian national groups. Even universities have been divided along national lines.

Canada is yet another example of a binational state with its separate English- and French-speaking national groups. Some Canadians say "binational" is inaccurate because it excludes Canada's Inuit, the Arctic peoples, or other native Americans referred to by many Canadian ethnologists as "first nations." In any event, the extent to which these peoples identify themselves as "Canadians" or choose instead to have separate national identities is a crucial distinction if we are to understand the complexity of the Canadian society. Of course, a feeling of national unity as Canadians, notwithstanding considerable national diversity, contributes to keeping the country together. In other words, as the Canadian example demonstrates, it is possible to have different levels of national identity. Thus one can be Canadian first and English- or French-speaking Canadian second. More troublesome for national unity, however, is when French- or English-speakers see themselves as separate (and separable) nations. In 1995, for example, a referendum in Quebec to create an independent state was barely defeated.

Multinational, Multitribal, and Other Multiethnic States

Switzerland is an example of a relatively successful multinational state composed of German-, French-, Italian-, and Romansch-speaking Swiss. (Romansch, a language closely related to Latin, the language of the Roman empire, survives among a minority of Swiss, mainly in the very mountainous area in the southeast part of the country.) The Swiss confederation allows a considerable degree of local autonomy, while still allowing broad Swiss identification.

In fact, Swiss citizenship is not established by the central government in Bern; it is determined instead by the canton (the state or provincial level) and more specifically by the local *Gemeinde* (to use the German word) or community of one's family at birth. Key to keeping the country together over centuries has been decentralization of as many matters as possible. Over time, however, there has been agreement to collaborate in such matters as establishing a common currency and to cooperate centrally in other ways to promote commerce, maintain common defenses (although with considerable local authority), and conduct a common foreign policy.

Unsuccessful examples of multinational states include the former Soviet Union and the former Yugoslavia, both of which have broken apart into separate states since 1991. Given a changed international climate and much domestic turmoil after the end of the Cold War, national groups in both countries found that most of the obstacles to separatism had been either removed or weakened substantially. Use of coercive means to maintain unity—actions by the police and armed forces—failed in both countries. Both cases are worthy of further comment.

MAP 14.4

The ethnic composition in the former Yugoslavia. The rapid changes in Eastern Europe during the close of the 1980s intensified long-standing ethnic tensions in the former Yugoslavia. This map shows where Yugoslavia's ethnic population lived in 1991, before internal conflicts escalated.

The Disintegration of Yugoslavia   From what was Yugoslavia, separate Slovene and Croat states emerged quickly in the north. Macedonia, north of Greece, followed suit, while Serbia and Montenegro, with their predominantly Serbian populations, stayed together as the residual of what had been Yugoslavia. Fierce fighting broke out in Bosnia-Herzegovina among Muslims, Croats, and Serbs, with Muslims losing most of their territory to the other parties (see Map 14.4).

Like Czechoslovakia, Yugoslavia was created after World War I in an attempt to create a common national identity among "south Slavs" (the word *Yugoslavia* itself referring to a land of south Slavs). Beyond linguistic similarities, these Slavic-speaking peoples had little else in common. Serbs and Croats, for example, though in physical appearance the same people speaking a common language (Serbo-Croatian), wrote with different alphabets. Croats were predominantly Roman Catholics (as were Slovenes and the other populations that had been part of the Austro-Hungarian empire). By contrast, Serbia and Montenegro had been part of the Ottoman (or Turkish) empire composed of Orthodox Christians and Muslims. It was not easy to set aside cultural cleavages that had developed over centuries when these peoples were subject to such different imperial influences.

Notwithstanding atrocities conducted against each other during World War II by elements of Croat and Serb populations, Josip Broz Tito was able to forge a greater degree of national unity in postwar Yugoslavia than previously had been thought possible. Tito, a nationalist war hero and a Croat, had fostered collaboration with Serbs as fellow "Yugoslavs" in World War II against a common enemy, the Germans, then occupying much of the country. Tito and his Yugoslav Communist Party followers worked after the war until his death in 1980 to build Yugoslav national unity, trying as much as possible to reduce national and cultural differences to mere ethnic distinctions among fellow Yugoslav "workers."

As events in the 1990s demonstrated, however, the idea of Yugoslav nationalism had never really displaced separate Serb, Croat, Slovene, Muslim, or Macedonian national identities. Even in Tito's lifetime, no matter what one was expected or had to say in public, most people in the country considered themselves Serb, Muslim, Macedonian, Croat, or Slovene first, Yugoslav second. Thus when the opportunity for secession emerged, Slovenes, Croats, and later the Macedonians all withdrew from the Yugoslav federation. Slovenes and Croats received diplomatic or other support for secession from Austria, Hungary, and Germany—a sympathy based no doubt on pre–World War I associations, when Croatia and Slovenia had been part of the Austro-Hungarian empire. It is significant that these historically based ties survived the East-West divisions of the Cold War and had been maintained, often informally, over many decades.

That fighting became concentrated in Bosnia-Herzegovina is not surprising. Historically, by the nineteenth century this area between Serbia and Croatia had become the frontier that divided the Austro-Hungarian and Ottoman empires. In their expansionary phase, the Ottoman Turks had reached as far north as Vienna, where they were finally turned back in 1683, beginning a gradual retreat southward over several centuries. Although the remains of the Austro-Hungarian and Ottoman empires were dismantled after World War I, the legacy of their separate imperial influences was felt by present-day Balkan peoples, leaving them with separate national identities not easily displaced even now after some eighty or more years.

There are those who argue that nationality, ethnicity, and historically based cultural differences are merely excuses used to justify **irredentism** and aggression. No doubt some leaders do know how to manipulate their populations by national and ethnic appeals that mesh nicely with other objectives. On the other hand, even in these cases, that leaders are able to mobilize people on these grounds suggests that national and ethnic difference are, in fact, real to the peoples involved and not just artificial constructions.

The Breakup of the Soviet Union   Comparing the breakup in the early 1990s of Czechoslovakia, Yugoslavia, and the Soviet Union, the most peaceful transition was the establishment of separate Czech and Slovak republics and the most violent was both civil war and war among newly recognized states in the former Yugoslavia. The Soviet case fits between the two.

Violence and the use of force were present in early Soviet efforts to forestall secession by the Baltic and other republics. In the turmoil after an abortive military coup in Moscow in 1991, many of the republics elected to go their separate ways rather than remain in the Soviet Union. Efforts were made to provide only for a loose association for those republics joining in a Commonwealth of Independent States (CIS).[6] Given their separate, strong national identities and earlier histories of greater independence,

---

[6]Republics joining the Russian Federation in the commonwealth were Belarus, Ukraine, Kazakhstan, Turkmenistan, Uzbekistan, Kyrgystan, Tajikistan, Moldova, Armenia, and Azerbaijan.

Case & Point

CYBER YUGOSLAVIA

The country of Cyber Yugoslavia has been created on the Internet. At this site you can apply for a passport, read the constitution, and vote on issues. The main page provides the following overview of this virtual country (www.juga.com):

This is Cyber Yugoslavia. We lost our country in 1991 and became citizens of Atlantis. Since September 9, 1999, this is our home. We don't have a physical land, but we do have nationality, and we are giving citizenship and passports. Because this is Atlantis, we are allowing double and triple citizenship. If you feel Yugoslav, you are welcome to apply for CY citizenship regardless of your current nationality and citizenship, and you will be accepted. Please read our Constitution for the details. If you are just curious, you are welcome to visit as tourists.

This land will grow as our citizens wish. Neither faster nor slower. Neither more, nor less. So, this site will always be under construction. For a solid country to grow, even a virtual one, it takes some time.

When we have five million citizens, we plan to apply for U.N. member status. When this happens, we will ask for 20 square meters of land anywhere on earth to be our country. On this land, we'll keep our server.

Point: While whimsical, Cyber Yugoslavia actually raises the important question of what is meant by the term "nationality." Is it a physical characteristic or a state of mind?

---

the Baltic republics (Estonia, Latvia, and Lithuania) opted out of even this relatively weak association with Russia. The most violence occurred within Russia itself in Chechnya, which continues to be an ongoing human tragedy.

An aim of communist ideology had been to eliminate not only class but also ethnic and national distinctions that divided workers within and among fellow "socialist" states and eventually throughout the world as a whole. Open talk of separate national identities had been forbidden or discouraged in the Soviet Union and in the socialist states of East-Central Europe and elsewhere. Instead international (and transnational) solidarity of factory workers, peasants, and other "toilers" was the goal.

Reality was quite different, as indicated by the fast pace by which Hungary, Poland, Czechoslovakia, Romania, Bulgaria, and East Germany curtailed their Cold War economic and military ties with the Soviet Union to pursue their separate national agendas. The pace at which these ties were dissolved was to be surpassed only by the speed with which the Soviet Union itself broke apart into separate national republics. National identities suppressed even by the Tsars (as in Ukraine, for example) could now find their clear expression in the form of newly independent countries recognized as sovereign states and members of the United Nations.

Dominance by Russians, whether under the Tsars or under Marxists-Leninists after the 1917 Bolshevik Revolution, had been the experience of many nationalities. In its most extreme form the pan-Slavic movement that began in Tsarist days attempted to replace separate identities with a common identity among all European Slavs.[7] In fact, Slavic

---

[7]Slavic countries in East-Central Europe—those identified by Slavic-language group—include Russia, Belarus, Ukraine, Poland, the Czech and Slovak Republics, Bulgaria, and the republics of the former Yugoslavia. Decidedly non-Slavic are Hungary, Romania, and Albania.

peoples had had separate histories for more than a thousand years, their basis for common identity being similarity in language that suggested common historic or tribal origins.

Perceptions by many that pan-Slavism was really a cover for Russian domination of East-Central Europe were reinforced by efforts under Stalin to "Russify" non-Russians within the Soviet Union. Russification—a clear departure from the ideological notion that nationality was to be displaced by worker solidarity—ranged from active promotion to coercive imposition of Russian language and culture upon non-Russians. Later abandoned as a policy, its net effect had been to reinforce national antagonisms within the Soviet Union. A return to policies fostering unity, while acknowledging ethnic, linguistic, and cultural diversity, did not alter the reality that it was the Russians who continued to possess the bulk of political power and authority throughout the Soviet Union.

The important point is that separate national identities had survived all efforts to replace them either with notions of a worker solidarity intended to transcend national and ethnic distinctions or by such national-suppression policies as Russification. It is not surprising, therefore, that East-Central European states broke from Moscow when able to do so and separate nation-states also came to displace what had been a multinational Soviet state. The Russian Republic remains multinational in certain areas such as Chechnya, where a military campaign against separatists has led to years of internal strife, terrorism, human rights abuses, and corruption.

Multinational and Multiethnic States in the Third World   The boundaries of states in much of Africa, Asia, and Latin America were determined by divisions agreed upon by the former colonial or imperial powers for reasons often having very little to do with respecting national, tribal, ethnic, or other local identities. In fact, containing peoples with diverse identities within the same borders allowed colonial powers to maintain control by capitalizing on these differences, thus making national unity against their rule more difficult to achieve. This was particularly true in Africa where in Nigeria, for example, boundaries of this former British colony include three separate tribal groups (Ibo, Yoruba, and Hausa-Fulani) that outnumber the populations of many countries. After independence and the departure of British administrators and security forces from Nigeria, civil war broke out there with fighting among tribal groups continuing into the 1970s. "Nigerian" as a national identity has proven to be elusive at best. People continue to identify by tribal group and resent advantages taken by some groups over others. Map 14.5 shows the social complexity of Africa divided by tribal boundaries.

While one could call Nigeria a multinational state, it is referred to more commonly as a multiethnic or multitribal state. It is interesting to note that in the case of Africa, it is common to use the terms **tribes** and **tribalism** rather than *nations* and *nationalism*. For some observers *tribalism* carries negative (if not pejorative) connotations, while *nationalism* has more positive overtones. Hence the massacres that occurred in Rwanda in 1994 were ascribed to tribalism, whereas much of the slaughter occurring in the former Yugoslavia in the 1990s was generally attributed to Serbian or Croatian nationalism. Whether the different use of terms is an accurate reflection of regional or local preferences or instead is indicative of bias or ignorance on the part of the observer is often unclear.

> *The brutality of the conflicts in Kosovo, East Timor, and Rwanda—and the messiness of the international responses to them—obscures the larger shift from confrontation toward accommodation. But the trends are there: a sharp decline in new ethnic wars, the settlement of many old ones, and proactive efforts by states and international organizations to recognize group rights and channel ethnic disputes into conventional politics. In Kosovo and East Timor, intervention was chosen only after other means failed. The fact that the United States, NATO, the United Nations, and Australia intervened was itself a testament to the underlying premise that managing ethnic conflict has become an international responsibility.*
>
> **Professor Ted Robert Gurr**
> *"Ethnic Warfare on the Wane,"* Foreign Affairs, 79, no. 3 (May/June 2000): 52–53.

It's Been Said...

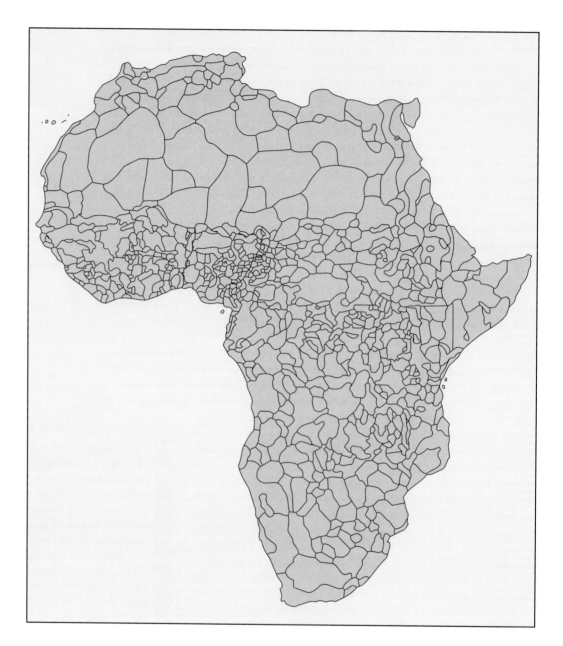

MAP 14.5   *Africa: Tribal Boundaries*

Source: George Demko, Agel Jerome, Eugene Boe, *Why in the World: Adventures in Geography* (New York: Anchor Books, 1992).

By no means are Nigeria and Rwanda isolated cases in Africa or elsewhere, especially in the Third World. Divisions by tribe or clan in Africa are often much stronger than any pretense to national unity. To avoid civil war and other forms of ethnic strife as have occurred in places as diverse as Nigeria, Rwanda, Burundi, Ethiopia, Somalia, Chad, Liberia, and the Sudan, postcolonial governments have tried with varying degrees of success to build working arrangements to manage this diversity.

While tribalism is associated with Africa, group identities in many countries throughout the rest of the Third World are often characterized in terms of ethnicity. Hence civil strife occurs involving Sikh, Tamil, and other ethnic minorities in India and in Sri Lanka (the island state known as Ceylon when it was part of British India). The potential for (or reality of) ethnic strife persists in Indonesia, Malaysia, and other multiethnic societies in South and Southeast Asia, as elsewhere in the Third World. Again, what is characterized as nationalism in Europe is often termed tribalism or ethnicity in other regions.

Neocolonialism refers to foreign influence by the former colonial power that persists despite an end to its physical, controlling presence. Although neocolonialism is sometimes criticized, some unity among elites has been found through their linguistic, cultural, and commercial ties with the former colonial powers, particularly in Africa and Asia. Quite apart from local identities along tribal, familial, or other ethnic affiliation, elites who initially came to power in these countries had developed strong European associations. To varying degrees they acquired either British, French, Belgian, Dutch, or Portuguese linkages that have been retained in the postcolonial period to the present day. As a practical matter, the European colonial language provided a means of communication across tribal and linguistic groups. In addition, aspects of European social and political values were either blended with or grafted onto local cultures and customs.

English, for example, is the common language of the political, social, and commercial elites in both Indian and Pakistani societies. After World War II, when the British and local nationalists negotiated independence in India in 1947–1948, a decision was made to divide India and Pakistan along Hindu-Muslim lines as separate countries. **Partition** into different states did not prevent war, continuing tensions, and more recently, a nuclear weapons development competition between the two. Moreover, partition still left India itself as a very heterogeneous society with many ethnic divisions.

Nation-States and Nations without States

As noted at the outset of this chapter, it is possible for a nation to exist without being associated with a particular state. The Irish were a nation without a state until 1922, when nationalists finally were successful in establishing a separate state after several centuries of British rule. Omitted from the new Irish Republic, however, were six of the nine counties in the northern region known as Ulster. Protestant majorities in Ulster with their historical ties to Scotland and the English crown remained under British protection as part of the United Kingdom.

Although the strife in Northern Ireland is commonly understood as being strife between Catholics and Protestants, the conflict is really not about religion per se. Religious difference between the two communities is only a surface-level indicator of much deeper historical, cultural, and political cleavages underlying recurrent **intercommunal** strife.

The aim of some Irish nationalists to drive the British out of Ireland has continued since the 1920s. Known collectively as the Irish Republican Army or IRA, these nationalists are really a collection of diverse nongovernmental factions, some of which have been as hostile to the Irish government in Dublin as to the British government in London. Indeed, the police and military forces of both countries collaborate routinely to curb those IRA factions prone to engage in violent activities. The best known—the Provisional Irish Republican Army, or PIRA—has engaged in a terrorist campaign over more than three decades beginning in 1970. Negotiations brought a tenuous peace to Northern Ireland by the end of the 1990s. Efforts have continued to establish home rule in Northern Ireland and the eventual reconciliation of two communities historically divided by fear, suspicion, and hatred.

Until the creation of Israel in 1948, Jews were dispersed in any number of countries (as they still are). The late nineteenth- and twentieth-century Zionist movement sought a state (or at least a homeland) for Jews in the ancient biblical lands. The horror of the

Holocaust of the 1930s and 1940s in which some six million Jews died in concentration camps primarily in Germany and occupied Poland contributed to the international decision to create a Jewish state in Israel. Although many ethnic Jews have chosen to retain American or other national identities, those who wish to make their homes in Israel have been able to emigrate there and formally become Israeli nationals.

Palestinians and Kurds are two national groups (many of the latter having distinct tribal identities as well) without single states to call their own. The Kurds were promised a state in the peace settlements after World War I, but have remained dispersed in and near mountainous areas of Iran, Iraq, Syria, Turkey, Azerbaijan and elsewhere in the trans-Caucasus region of the former Soviet Union.

Palestinians, a population with many highly educated people, live in a number of countries including Israel, Jordan, southern Lebanon, Syria, and the Gulf states. Palestinians also remain in the Israeli-occupied territories taken in the June 1967 war, primarily in and around Jerusalem and on territory on the West Bank of the Jordan River, which is referred to by those Israelis laying ancient claim to the area as the biblical lands of Judea and Samaria. One also finds Palestinians in many cities throughout the Middle East, where they often hold highly skilled positions as well as providing clerical, information technology, and other commercial services.

Palestinians and Kurds, as minorities in the countries in which they live, have suffered from severe forms of discrimination. Turkish government policy at one time was to deny the very existence of Kurds as a separate national group, referring to them instead as "mountain Turks." Many Palestinians felt dispossessed of their homes and homeland in Palestine when Israel was established as a Jewish state in 1948. Aside from routine forms of discrimination, governments have conducted military campaigns and other attacks against Kurdish and Palestinian groups.

For their part, involvement in insurgent or terrorist activities by Kurds and Palestinians have added to hostilities, promoting further discord and no doubt encouraging

Unrepresented Nations

Nations without states may form various expatriate associations to lobby governments in other countries for the creation of an independent homeland. This certainly was the case with many European colonies following World War II. There is, however, an Unrepresented Nations and Peoples Organization (UNPO) associated with the United Nations. Also known as the U.N. Council for Oppressed Nations (UNCON), it was founded in 1991 to represent and promote the interests of minority groups and occupied territories not officially recognized by the United Nations. Membership is extended to groups with distinct linguistic and cultural heritages who are not U.N. members and otherwise would not have access to institutions that address the international community. There are currently more than fifty members whose population totals 100 million persons.

The founding charter was signed by representatives of Armenia, Crimea, Estonia, Georgia, Turkestan, and the Volga region in the former Soviet Union; Australian Aborigines; Native Americans; West Irians and West Papuans in Indonesia; Kurds; Cordillera minorities in the Philippines; the Greek minority in Albania; and non-Chinese in Taiwan and Tibet. Several of the original members—Estonians and Latvians—have become member states in the United Nations. The General Assembly of the UNPO meets annually and appoints a Steering Committee. The secretariat is located in The Hague, Netherlands. For further information, see www.unpo.org.

Applying Theory

NATIONALISM, WAR, AND ETHNIC CONFLICT

A tremendous amount of literature has been produced on nationalism. Typologies abound, and numerous hypotheses, frameworks, and theories have been advanced to explain the origin of nationalism and the conditions under which it contributes to international conflict. David A. Lake and Donald Rothchild have developed an interesting framework and argument concerning the circumstances under which ethnic conflict arises.

They argue that many popular explanations are incomplete or simply wrong. Ethnic conflict is not caused directly by intergroup differences, ancient hatreds, or the stresses of modern life caused by a global economy. For them, intense ethnic conflict is most often caused by collective fears of the future. This occurs when states lose their ability to arbitrate between groups or provide credible guarantees of protection for groups. In other words, a crisis of confidence in the state or the actual specter of state failure is the key underlying factor they identify for the rise in ethnic conflict. The effects of international anarchy—fear and a feeling that self-help is the only option—take effect at the societal level of analysis. Groups may arm out of a sense of fear, but the result is to stimulate competition among groups, raising the collective fear factor even higher. Groups become suspicious of the intentions of other ethnic groups—the security dilemma is at work. State weakness, therefore, is a precondition for violent ethnic conflict within states, just as the absence of a superordinate authority in the international system of world politics is a permissive cause of war (see Chapter 5).

Once groups begin to fear for their safety, other factors come to the fore. Of particular importance is the rise of ethnic activists and political entrepreneurs who build on group fears. Political memories and historical symbols are stirred and utilized to whip up nationalist feeling and gain broader support. Such entrepreneurs cannot achieve their goals on their own. In one sense, they are as much a product as a producer of ethnic fears. Yet individuals such as Milosevic in Serbia certainly exacerbate ethnic tensions and contribute to polarization within societies. Once political minorities realize they cannot rely on the state for their protection, they usually look outward to the international community for protection. The international response has been, in the minds of Lake and Rothchild, feeble and unconvincing. With the possible exception of Kosovo, states are reluctant to intervene to end systematic, state-sanctioned ethnic killing. When they do, as in Rwanda, it is often after hundreds of thousands of people have already died.

Stephen Van Evera is particularly interested in the impact of nationalism on the stability of the international system and its contribution to international war. He has suggested that four primary attributes of a nationalist movement determine the potential to produce violence. First is the movement's political status: Is statehood attained or not? If the nationalist movement does not have a state, he argues this raises the risks of war in the international system. A struggle for national freedom can produce wars of secession, risking the conflict spilling over into the international arena. For example, 15 of the 104 nationalities of the former Soviet Union have achieved statehood, but the other 89 have not. Chechnya is one example. Such stateless nationalities total approximately 25.6 million people, or 10 percent of the former USSR's total population. Furthermore, even if a nationalist movement successfully creates a new state, the seeds of future conflict may be planted if other groups are displaced. For example, Zionism's displacement of the Palestinian Arabs in 1948 set the stage for later Arab-Israeli wars as well as terrorist activities. Finally, successful nationalist leaders may reject the old "rules of the game" of interstate politics, creating regional instability.

The second factor that determines the potential of a national movement producing violence is the movement's stance toward its national diaspora (the dispersion or scattering of persons across different lands): if the movement has a national state, will it try to incorporate its nationals via territorial expansion or by encouraging immigration? The latter policy has been pursued after World War II by both German and Israeli governments. The territorial expansion route was pursued by pre-1914 pan-Germanism and by pan-Serbianism in the 1990s.

The third factor is the movement's attitude toward other independent nationalities: Is it one of tolerance or hegemony? In other words, does the nationalist ideology respect the freedom of other nationalities or does it assume a right or duty to rule them? Hegemonic nationalism is the rarest and most dangerous variety. The obvious examples are interwar Nazi nationalism in Germany, fascist nationalism in Mussolini's Italy, and militarist nationalism in imperial Japan.

Fourth is the nationalist movement's treatment of its own minorities: are the rights of minorities respected or abused? The nationalism of many immigrant nations (such as the United States and Canada) tend to be relatively more minority respecting. By contrast, nonimmigrant nationalisms tend to discriminate against or even suppress or oppress their minorities. For example, Iraqi and Turkish policy against the Kurds, China's actions in Tibet, and Serbian oppression of Slavic Muslim and Albanian (Kosovar) minorities.

According to Van Evera, these four attributes constitute a "danger scale," highlighting the level of danger posed by any given nationalism. If all four attributes are positive or benign, such nationalisms may actually dampen the risk of war. Conversely, if all four attributes are negative or malign, the nationalism at issue is bound to clash with others, increasing the risk of war.

Sources: David A. Lake and Donald Rothchild, "Containing Fear: The Origins and Management of Ethnic Conflict," International Security, vol. 21, no. 2 (Fall 1996): 41–75; Stephen Van Evera, "Hypotheses on Nationalism and War," International Security, vol. 18, no. 4 (Spring 1994): 5–39.

further recriminations against them. At least in the Palestinian case, the 1990s witnessed a move toward a degree of political autonomy in the West Bank and Gaza strip. Terrorism, however, was continued by Palestinian factions such as Hamas. Most Palestinians hope that the current trend toward self-rule in areas of the West Bank will eventually lead to an independent Palestinian state with worldwide recognition of its sovereignty.

Approaches to Dealing with Nationalism and Ethnicity

National Self-Determination

national self-determination
The view that a people with a common identity have the right to be independent from outside control, as in establishing a state.

The principle of **national self-determination**, advocated by American President Woodrow Wilson and other leaders after World War I, was used as a criterion for determining the boundaries of states in their efforts to redraw the map of Europe. The aim was to create nation-states to take the place of the defeated German, Austro-

Hungarian, and Turkish empires that had dominated East-Central Europe. Each nation was to have its own state.

However well intentioned, the national-self-determination principle has been abused. Hitler, for example, claimed in 1938 that the Sudetenland—that part of Bohemia in Czechoslovakia in which German-speaking people lived—should be a part of Germany. Hitler got his way at a 1938 summit conference held in Munich. After all, and quite apart from German aggressive designs on the territory of Czechoslovakia, supporters of the Munich concession could point to the arrangement merely as a line-drawing adjustment to post–World War I maps, an exercise consistent with the principle of national self-determination.

In recent years, with the seeming explosion of ethnic conflict within some states, the international community is forced to come to terms with two conflicting principles: respect for territorial sovereignty of the state and the right of national self-determination. During the cold war this was less of a problem. When political independence movements in the Third World struggled to end colonialism, they were not calling for the partition of a state but rather its complete independence from foreign rule. Leaders in emerging Third World states agreed to respect colonial borders. There were exceptions: Tibetans in China, the Ibos in Nigeria, and Kashmir in India. Still, the one major successful breakup of an existing state during the cold war occurred in 1971 when Bangladesh, with India's help, shattered the unity of Pakistan at the cost of tens of thousands of deaths and the flight of ten million refugees to India.

Limiting self-determination was actually endorsed unanimously by the U.N. General Assembly in the 1970 Declaration of Principles of International Law Concerning Friendly Relations among States. This resolution sought to sustain the international stability resulting from reaffirmation of the primacy of the sovereign state over people on its own territory. The end of the Cold War, however, has seen substantial erosion of this idea. The outbreak of nationalist sentiment, particularly the unraveling of the Soviet Union with the recognition of the independence of the Baltic states and other republics in central Asia, set a different precedent: self-determination could be achieved even at the expense of the unity of an existing state. What was largely a voluntary and peaceful development in the former Soviet Union, however, played out quite differently as the former Yugoslavia broke apart in the early 1990s, spawning a series of Balkan wars accompanied by widespread civil strife. In the case of sub-Saharan Africa, during the Cold War both Moscow and Washington as well as former European colonial powers worked to keep their favorite strongmen in control as the two superpowers engaged in fierce global competition. In the 1960s and 1970s, China also competed for favor in Africa and elsewhere in the Third World. With the end of this strategic competition on the African continent, countries such as Zaire or Congo were no longer strategic battlegrounds, and outside powers seemed to lose interest in the fate of many of these ethnically diverse states.

Alternative Approaches to Maintaining Unity in Binational, Multinational, and Multiethnic States

With varying degrees of success or failure, several different strategies or approaches have been adopted to manage two or more nations within a given state. Keeping binational and multinational states together in intercommunal peace and mutual acceptance has proven to be a formidable task wherever it has been tried. What can be done to stem a potential tide of ethno-nationalist conflicts that threaten to undermine regional if not international stability?

The Green Line divided Beirut's Christian and Muslim sectors for fifteen years. The sign, showing the now deceased Pope John Paul II beside a map of Lebanon, reads in both Arabic and French, "Lebanon, more than a country, it's a message," and is one of the many that greeted the Holy Father on his visit to Beirut in May 1997.

Partition   Partition or formal separation can be used to stop or reduce national and ethnic strife, at least for a limited time. Separating national and ethnic groups into distinct, mutually exclusive communities—drawing solid-line boundaries around them—is at best a short-term approach or coping mechanism as long as they remain within a single state. It is not by any means a long-term solution to the problem of national and ethnic or racial strife.

Intercommunal fighting in Lebanon in the 1970s and 1980s, for example, could be stopped only by creating what amounted to strict territorial zones for different religious and cultural groups, policed by Syrian and other troops as well as multinational peacekeepers. At best, such informal or de facto partition could produce only a very fragile peace, which easily could (and did) break down again into intercommunal warfare. Similarly, *de jure* or formal, legal division into separate Pakistani and Indian states in 1948 did not resolve differences between Muslim and Hindu communities either. As already noted, hostilities (actual warfare or continual threat of warfare) have remained a fairly constant condition in Pakistani-Indian relations. These conflictual relations, moreover, have contributed substantially to efforts by both countries to acquire nuclear-weapons capabilities, which now poses a threat to security in South Asia that goes well beyond differences between India and Pakistan.

Similarly, dividing peoples by national and ethnic identity into separate states in the former Yugoslavia did not promote peace. Civil strife became international war as each new state sought to expand or defend its territorial base. Not surprisingly, some of the worst fighting occurred in Bosnia, the state that was most ethnically diverse. Again, when faced with such conflicts, a cease-fire with strict divisions among the parties may be necessary to halt bloodshed in the short run, but partition alone (whether within or between states) has not provided a foundation for long-term peace anywhere.

One of the most severe examples of separation policies was racial division of blacks and whites in South Africa. Universally criticized for its injustice, South African **apartheid,** a policy of strict racial segregation, allowed a white minority to maintain a dominant position over the black majority. Moreover, as a white-dominated state, South Africa became isolated from neighboring black African states, giving the latter ample incentive to support antigovernment, black nationalist groups in South Africa. Ending formal apartheid by the early 1990s, of course, did not resolve black-white problems, much less tribal and other differences within the black majority. Efforts were in fact taken in the 1990s to expose abuses by all parties during the apartheid period in an attempt to achieve reconciliation. As elsewhere, prospects for a long-term peace in

South Africa rest instead on improved economic well-being and greater social tolerance or acceptance across ethnic communities, aspirations always much more easily stated than achieved.

Assimilation   Another strategy or approach, sometimes a very oppressive one, is **assimilation** of diverse populations into a single national grouping. This may entail denying that national differences exist at all or, if they do, denying their legitimacy as separate identities. As noted, assimilationist policies were adopted in the Soviet Union during Stalin's time in an effort to "Russify" non-Russian peoples. The Iraqi government under Saddam Hussein conducted military campaigns to suppress or maintain control over the non-Arab Kurdish population in the northern part of the country. Turkish policies mentioned previously that denied Kurds a separate identity, referring to them merely as "mountain Turks," are another example of assimilationist policy.

The United States has also tried to assimilate diverse populations, establishing "American" as a common national identity. Earlier in its history, particularly in the nineteenth century, military campaigns were conducted to gain control over Native American populations, later placing them on reservations. This policy of formal exclusion gradually changed, as many Native Americans were encouraged to leave the reservations and become part of the larger American society.

Slavery in the United States lasted until the 1860s and effectively denied African Americans in slave states any degree of autonomy. Racial segregation policies that formally separated blacks from whites, particularly in the American South, survived into the 1960s. Segregationists did not intend that blacks ever see themselves as a separate nation (as many American Indians did); the goal of segregationist policies was to impose on blacks a separate (and lower) status within American society. Similarly, mainstream civil rights reformers opposed the few who advocated separation into different, racially distinct states or societies. The aim instead was racial integration, a view perfectly consistent with assimilationist strategy.

Consistent with the assimilationist idea, Indians are referred to in present-day parlance as Native Americans and blacks as African Americans, in much the same way as European and Asian populations came to be identified as Polish-Americans, Irish-Americans, Italian-Americans, Norwegian-Americans, Japanese-Americans, Chinese-Americans, and so forth. There are those, of course, who object to any such hyphenation of the American nationality, preferring the complete assimilation or unity implied by the single term *American*. But those who want to retain ethnic identities as part of the American fabric, particularly those living in and identifying as part of ethnic communities, do not object to hyphenation or ethnic labels in which they take pride. Thus from this perspective to acknowledge explicitly that one is of Japanese, Finnish, Hispanic (or Latino) origin, for example, is still to be very much an American.

Wherever assimilationist policies have been relatively successful, adopting a common national identity has not necessarily meant dropping all other identities. There can still be unity in diversity. Separate ethnic and racial identities have survived, if not flourished, in the United States. The important point, however, is that almost all members of these groups still commonly identify themselves as "Americans." The common bond is a commitment to the idea of being an American or to

> *Clearly, blind love for one's own country—a love that defers to nothing beyond itself, that excuses anything one's own state does only because it is one's own country, yet rejects everything else only because it is different—has necessarily become a dangerous anachronism, a source of conflict and, in extreme cases, of immense human suffering.*
>
> **Vaclav Havel**
> *playwright and former President of Czech Republic,* New York Review of Books, *June 10, 1999, 4.*

It's Been Said...

the democratic ideals expressed in the national Constitution, not to any single or separate ethnic identity.

A commitment to multiculturalism allows for the richness of cultural diversity while still retaining an overarching national identity. It is when cultural diversity is interpreted as separatism that controversy ensues. One sees this in the United States in the debate over national language. Most assimilationists in the United States, for example, acknowledge that different ethnic and cultural groups have a right to speak Spanish, Mandarin or one of the other Chinese dialects, Italian, Vietnamese, or whatever. On the other hand, they voice opposition to giving other languages equal status with English. To be bilingual or multilingual is a matter of choice, not a requirement for other Americans who choose to communicate only in English. They refer to English as the traditional, spoken language in the United States that cuts across—and thus contributes to uniting—different ethnic, cultural, or other identities. The controversy is particularly acute in major cities such as New York and Miami or in the American Southwest where large numbers (in some cases approaching a majority) of people speak languages other than English.

Consociationalism in Multinational Unitary States   In a unitary state, all political power and authority come to rest in the institutions of a central government. Although almost all countries have at least one or more ethnic minorities in their societies, those coming closest to being single nation-states—states with one common or overarching national identity and lacking deep national and ethnic divisions—may choose to vest central government institutions with significant political power and authority. This is the case in France, Japan, the Scandinavian countries, the Republic of Korea, and most nation-states throughout the world.

On the other hand, when unitary states are composed of two or more nations or strong ethnic communities, a **consociational** model may be the means for maintaining peace and keeping the state together. Through agreements and formal rules that share or divide the powers and positions of government among different national and ethnic groups, consociationalism typically allows a maximum of local autonomy for the different communities within binational and multinational states.

Prior to its breakdown into civil war in the 1970s, Lebanon was viewed by many as a model of consociational arrangements among different cultural communities. Strict rules were followed for several decades that allocated positions of political authority and representation among the different Christian and Muslim communities. It proved extraordinarily difficult to renegotiate these arrangements, partly because any such alteration was seen by many Christian Lebanese as undermining their position in favor of increasing the representation of one or another of the Muslim communities. Differences among familial and other factions vying for power in the different communities contributed to the complexity of recasting political relationships. The interests of outside states as diverse as Syria, Iran, and Israel made an already difficult problem next to impossible to resolve. Intercommunal bloodshed, direct and indirect interventions by outside powers, and de facto partition of the different communities ensued. Although consociationalism can contribute to unity and civility among diverse peoples within a state, the Lebanese example underscores how fragile these arrangements can be.

Belgian accommodation of different Flemish and Wallonian interests has required continual attention. Establishing duplicate governmental ministries, political parties, and even universities for the separate Flemish- and French-speaking communities is an approach consistent with the consociational model. A central government has remained in Brussels even as there has been considerable decentralization of political authority to the separate communities.

If diverse communities are to stay together within a single state, considerable efforts are required continually over time to refine, modify, correct, and legitimize these power-sharing and power-dividing arrangements. Political elites must be dedicated to maintaining the system as opposed to exacerbating ethnic tensions.

Federal and Confederal Approaches   As noted, unitary states establish single, centralized governments. By contrast, a federal state is one composed of separate state or provincial governments that have important functions to perform independently but must coexist with a strong central government that may well take the upper hand on many matters. The United States is an example of a federation, although the reasons for Americans choosing federalism were not related to problems of nationality and ethnicity. The American rationale for establishing a federated state had more to do with distrust of unchallenged centralized power, geographic distances that were significant in the eighteenth century when the U.S. Constitution was written, and a desire to provide for security as well as some degree of local autonomy to states that had developed historically as separate colonies.

In Canada, on the other hand, the rationale for federalism goes beyond such geographic and other concerns to provide a vehicle for managing differences between separate French-speaking and English-speaking communities. Thus francophone Quebec has a separate distinction and some local authority even as it remains part of the Canadian federation. Separatists, thus far still a minority, find present arrangements unsatisfactory. Efforts have been made, however, to accommodate the national and ethnic concerns they represent. Agreements have been made protecting separate language and cultural identities and allocating additional funds and more local authority over issues of importance to the different provinces. These agreements have served a similar function to the consociational arrangements discussed above, which is to keep different peoples together within a single (in this case, federal) state.

The terms perhaps can be best understood as different points on a continuum. The distinction between federation and **confederation** is not always clear cut. Federations and confederations are both composed of states, republics, provinces, cantons, or other political units with their own separate governments. Confederations, however, have much weaker central governance than federations and put relatively more political authority at local levels. In short, confederalism takes a major step further in the direction of greater local autonomy through decentralization.

Decentralized governance, for example, has been a key ingredient in Switzerland's success in keeping its Italian-, French-, German-, and Romansch-speaking peoples together in a single state—a confederation. Cantons the size of American counties retain considerable authority over education, health care, law enforcement, and even the conveying of citizenship. Important functions are entrusted to central authorities—making a common foreign policy, planning for defense against invasion by outside powers, and maintaining the country's economic and monetary systems. Even these are subject to scrutiny by authorities representing local interests.

Rather than having a single president of the Swiss Confederation, for example, there is a seven-person presidency that (similar to consociational arrangements in some unitary states) assures representation in national councils of diverse interests among the different cantons. This is in addition to a national legislature constituted to bring representatives together to deal with issues that cannot be dealt with at the local (or cantonal) level. Important questions are frequently given to the people to vote on directly in a referendum. Such direct democracy is consistent with a "town meeting" tradition still practiced, particularly in smaller Swiss cantons.

The USSR, or Union of Soviet Socialist Republics, formally had been a federation, even though in practice political authority always had been concentrated within the central leadership of the communist party. Given this experience, breakaway national republics found even confederation too strong a set of ties for their political taste. With the collapse of the Soviet Union, the most that could be worked out was agreement on establishing a **commonwealth**—a very loose association of sovereign states.

Social and Economic Approaches to Intercommunal Peace

How can intercommunal conflicts be halted? Over a half century of experience in United Nations and other multilateral efforts to establish and maintain peace in places as diverse as Cyprus, the Sinai, and the Balkans, three functions have been identified. A first step is to establish peace. Diplomatic efforts to end fighting among the groups is the peacemaking function. An alternative or supplement to diplomatic efforts is the function of peace enforcement—the threat or actual use of force by local or multilateral authorities (as when actions are taken under U.N. auspices) designed to stop the fighting and halt or at least reduce bloodshed among national or ethnic groups. This may be followed by peacekeeping, a maintenance function that typically involves monitoring or enforcing in a neutral fashion a cease-fire or peace already agreed to by the contending parties. The problem with all three, however, is that they are stopgap or short-term measures and do little to address the underlying causes of intercommunal strife.

When the social orientation of human beings takes a turn toward the mutual exclusivity of different national, ethnic, or other group identities, we are usually observing a problem with deep psychological or social-psychological roots. From peace theory we learn that *prospects for peace are greatest if there at least can be an acceptance or tolerance of people with diverse identities*. Some degree of intercommunal tolerance or acceptance is a minimal condition for maintaining peace over time.

Of course, no easy remedy can be found to solve problems of national, ethnic, or racial strife. In the short term, we may need to draw lines on maps to partition or separate people just to keep them from fighting. Peace theorists do look, however, to a longer-run transformation of these solid lines that divide peoples (dividing them from one another in mutually exclusive categories) into dotted or permeable lines that allow for passage across intercommunal boundaries of people, their ideas, and economic resources. This prescription for peace is based on liberal principles. The idea is hardly new.

That there can be tolerance or acceptance of diverse peoples has roots in the seventeenth- and eighteenth-century Enlightenment, in the **cosmopolitan** sense of unity among peoples that prevailed in the Middle Ages, and in the ancient Greco-Roman Stoic idea that whatever our differences, it is common humanity that unites us. Such tolerance or acceptance of cultural diversity and different identities within, between, and across societies is a minimum condition for a durable domestic peace. Difficult as it may be to achieve, this intercommunal peace can be strengthened still further when social relationships go beyond mere tolerance to a higher level of mutual respect for diverse cultures.

A durable peace, of course, cannot rest on mere assertion, however pleasing or enlightened cosmopolitanism may sound. When it has been achieved it is the outcome of policies pursued patiently over time. Although peacemaking, peace enforcement, and peacekeeping provide security in the short term by stopping the violence and bloodshed of intercommunal strife, it is not enough merely to establish law and order through the use of force or otherwise. Two kinds of development—social and economic—are necessary to provide a firm, long-term basis for lasting peace among diverse peoples.

Social development means establishing over time a greater degree of mutual acceptance or tolerance among different peoples. It involves education, cultural exchanges, communications, and other constructive efforts that over decades tend to bring diverse peoples together. Commercial and professional ties, friendships, and marriages that cross intercommunal lines are indicative of a relatively high level of social development. Social development involves values that are usually slow to change. Education of younger generations, reeducation of older generations, and building new human associations across communal lines are core tasks in social-developmental efforts. This is the core of the social constructivist perspective on identity, which is equally applicable to societal relations as it is to international relations. Social constructivism emphasizes the ability of people to redefine how they look at the world and hence their conception of how they relate to others. One's identity is not something one is simply born with, but is the result of inter-actions with society. As the term suggests, identity is a matter of social—that is, shared—construction.

Even so, measures intended to promote greater tolerance or acceptance proceed at a glacial pace, with progress measured only over decades. Older generations are least likely to change their outlook, particularly if they have experienced the human costs of civil strife or intercommunal warfare. Memories are long. Such memories often block the best-designed reconciliation efforts. In such circumstances, peace practitioners adopt a patient stance, waiting for the eventual passing of older generations, while at the same time hoping to foster cosmopolitan values among younger generations. To a considerable degree, this has been the approach followed in Western Europe after World War II. Even though old antagonisms have not been eliminated entirely, there is today a much higher degree of tolerance or mutual acceptance than many would have thought possible among the Germans, French, British, Belgians, Dutch, Danes and other Scandinavians, Spaniards, Italians, Greeks, and others.

This Western European achievement did not just happen; it was the result of a decided effort to change the mutual exclusivity of national and ethnic mind sets. European international organizations were established and expanded into what is now the European Union (EU). In addition to the specific purposes of particular organizations or channels of communication across national borders, the attempt was to go beyond the national and ethnic divisions that had contributed to the bloodshed of two major world wars in the first half of the twentieth century.

Economic development that reduces disparities in levels of living among different communities is also an essential ingredient. It is difficult to have open frontiers when disparate economic levels on different sides of borders result in migration of large numbers of people from poorer countries or areas to richer ones.

Even the better-off economies of advanced industrial countries have limits on how many immigrants they can absorb before suffering real economic costs. This is as true in North America as in Europe. Thus attempts have been made to restrict the flow of labor from Mexico into the United States. In Europe there are limits in place on flows of people from Eastern countries moving to Germany and other highly developed Western countries. Only when levels of economic development have become somewhat less disparate (if not equalized) may it be possible to open borders to unrestricted movements of peoples. In the case of Europe, there is no doubt that immigration from the Third World has exacerbated tensions at a time when many economies are in difficulty. No one expects many African states, for example, to achieve a level of economic development sufficient to encourage those without economic prospects to stay home.

The problem is that we are talking, in some cases, of no less than a long-term international endeavor and commitment to save failed states and their peoples. In this regard, some advocates favor an international "conservatorship" to administer critical government functions of "failed states" until the country can govern itself. But how long might that take if ethnic war has destroyed the social and economic infrastructure? How patient would outside powers be? Even if basic state functions are reestablished, how can the memories of ethnic violence be muted in the case of those who have witnessed atrocities perpetrated on their communities?

Some may think, therefore, that to rely on social and economic development over time to be simply a utopian approach to countries ravaged by ethnic conflict. It may be. On the other hand, to proceed as if national and ethnic strife are insoluble problems would be a self-fulfilling prophecy. Although there is no certainty that social and economic development conducted in a physically secure environment will put national and ethnic strife to rest, the degree of civility among nations that has been achieved in Western Europe supports the view that such social and economic development policies can be fruitful.

Conclusion

From the perspective of many realists, nationalism, or serving the national interest, is perhaps the single biggest reason the state will continue into the indefinite future. Crises of authority may cause a state to be torn in two, but the result will be the seceding territory joining a neighboring state or the creation of a newly independent state. Similarly, if a state motivated by extreme nationalism and an expansionist ideology successfully conquers a neighbor, the result is simply a larger state. The point is that whether nationalism helps to keep a current state together or tears it apart, the end result is the same—a state. Nationalists are not interested in transferring power and sovereignty upward to an international organization, let alone a world government. They also are suspicious of regional associations among states, which helps to account for the fact that even in the European Union people still tend to call themselves Germans, French, or English first, not "European."

Pluralists or liberals also recognize that nationalism is a primary cause of conflict in the world. But they tend to be more optimistic about the possibility of taming nationalism despite the Yugoslavia disaster. This will not happen by either avoiding or somehow transcending politics; it will happen *through* politics. Following the logic of the social constructivists, people can learn from the past and from past mistakes. International organizations and regimes can facilitate the more orderly conduct of interstate relations. Nongovernmental organizations and the growing global civil society provide other voices for moderation in the relations among peoples. The state will not wither away, as predicted by orthodox Marxists and idealistic world federalists. The state and the people it encompasses within its borders will continue to be a major focus of identity. But that does not necessarily mean that the state's function is to be the vehicle for expressing national prejudices against other states and peoples.

Nationalism, therefore, is one of the most significant phenomena in world politics. With the end of the Cold War, the suppressed nationalisms of Central and Eastern Europe (to include the former Soviet Union) burst forth. On the one hand, national- ism can be a force for unity and solidarity and be supportive of democracy, as has continued to be the case in the Czech Republic after its peaceful break with Slovakia. On the other hand, it can also tear a society apart, as we have seen in the former Yugoslavia. Nationalism can buttress existing political authority or be the rallying cry of those who wish to overthrow it. It can be a progressive as well as a repressive force, fostering at the same time unity at home and wars of aggression abroad. As we have seen, the constitutive elements of nationalism vary from case to case. Despite its im- portance and the amount of research and thought conducted on the subject, it remains complex, elusive and often difficult to grasp.

Appendix

Convention on the Prevention and Punishment of the Crime of Genocide (1948)

As knowledge of the extent of mass murder—the Holocaust of the Nazi period—became more widely known in the aftermath of World War II, consensus grew to support specifying genocide as a crime under international law. Tragically, genocide continues to occur as an extreme form of intercommunal or national and ethnic strife. We include the following legally binding articles on states to prevent and punish genocide—defined below as acts intended "to destroy, in whole or in part, a national, ethnical, racial or religious group." Italics have been added to emphasize key passages or phrases.

Article I   The Contracting Parties confirm that *genocide, whether committed in time of peace or in time of war, is a crime under international law* which they undertake to prevent and to punish.

Article II   In the present Convention, genocide means any of the following *acts committed with intent to destroy, in whole or in part, a national, ethnical, racial or religious group*, as such: (a) *Killing* members of the group; (b) *Causing serious bodily or mental harm* to members of the group; (c) Deliberately inflicting on the group *conditions of life calculated to bring about* its *physical destruction in whole or in part*; (d) Imposing *measures intended to prevent births* within the group; (e) *Forcibly transferring children* of the group to another group.

Article III   The following acts shall be punishable: (a) Genocide; (b) Conspiracy to commit genocide; (c) Direct and public incitement to commit genocide; (d) Attempt to commit genocide; (e) Complicity in genocide.

Article IV   Persons committing genocide or any of the other acts enumerated in article III shall be punished, whether they are constitutionally responsible rulers, public officials or private individuals.

Article V   The Contracting Parties undertake to enact, in accordance with their respective Constitutions, the necessary legislation to give effect to the provisions of the present Convention, and, in particular, to provide effective penalties for persons guilty of genocide or any of the other acts enumerated in article III.

Article VI   *Persons charged with genocide* or any of the other acts enumerated in article III *shall be tried by a competent tribunal* of the State in the territory of which the act was committed, or by such international penal tribunal as may have jurisdiction with respect to those Contracting Parties which shall have accepted its jurisdiction.

Article VII   Genocide and the other acts enumerated in article III shall not be considered as political crimes for the purpose of extradition. The Contracting Parties pledge themselves in such cases to grant extradition in accordance with their laws and treaties in force.

Article VIII   Any Contracting Party may call upon the competent organs of the United Nations to take such action under the Charter of the United Nations as they consider appropriate for the prevention and suppression of acts of genocide or any of the other acts enumerated in article III.

Article IX   Disputes between the Contracting Parties relating to the interpretation, application or fulfilment of the present Convention, including those relating to the responsibility of a State for genocide or for any of the other acts enumerated in article III, shall be submitted to the International Court of Justice at the request of any of the parties to the dispute....

Key Terms

nations   *p. 456*
nationalism   *p. 464*

ethnic, ethnicity   *p. 466*

national self-determination
  p. 478

Other Concepts

nation-states   *p. 456*
multinational states   *p. 456*
race   *p. 464*
racism   *p. 464*
genocide   *p. 464*
binational state   *p. 467*
irredentism   *p. 471*

tribe,   *p. 473*
tribalism   *p. 473*
neocolonialism   *p. 475*
partition   *p. 475*
intercommunal   *p. 475*
apartheid   *p. 480*
assimilation   *p. 481*

consociational   *p. 482*
confederation   *p. 483*
commonwealth   *p. 484*
cosmopolitan   *p. 484*
social development   *p. 485*
economic development
  p. 485

Additional Readings

The amount of work published on nationalism is daunting. We recommend an anthology edited by Walker Connor, *Ethnonationalism: The Quest for Understanding* (Princeton, NJ: Princeton University Press, 1994). See also Elie Kedourie, *Nationalism,* 4th ed. (Oxford, UK: Blackwell, 1993); E. J. Hobsbawn, *Nations and Nationalism Since 1780: Programme, Myth, and Reality* (Cambridge: Cambridge University Press, 1990); and Ernst B. Haas, "Nationalism: An Instrumental Social Construction," *Millennium* (January 1994): 505–45 and *Nationalism, Liberalism, and Progress,* 2 vols. (Ithaca, NY: Cornell University Press, 1997 and 2000). While taking account of the downside, work by Haas on this subject also underscores the positive impact and potential of nationalism and national identity as social constructs that serve the welfare of a nation's people.

A controversial, provocative discussion of global conflict among "civilizations" is Samuel P. Huntington, *The Clash of Civilizations & The Remaking of World Order* (New York: Simon & Schuster, 1996, 1998). Instead of casting conflicts so broadly as clashes among civilizations, we prefer to see intercommunal or sectarian conflicts more closely tied to particular societies—grounded in different cultures or identities. More than just a religion, for example, Islam is a most important cultural influence on some 20 percent of human beings living in different societies across the globe. See Bernard Lewis, *What Went Wrong? The Clash Between Islam and Modernity in the Middle East* (New York: Perennial/Harper Collins, 2003) and his *The Crisis of Islam* (New York: Random House, 2003, 2004), Sohail H. Hashmi, *Islamic Political Ethics: Civil Society, Pluralism, and Conflict* (Princeton, NJ: Princeton University Press, 2002), Vartan Gregorian, *Islam: A Mosaic, Not a Monolith* (Washington, D.C.: Brookings Institution, 2003), and Mir Zohair Husain, *Global Islamic Politics,* 2nd ed. (New York: Longman, 2003).

In the extreme, intercommunal strife takes the form of genocide. See Samantha Power, *A Problem from Hell: America and the Age of Genocide* (New York: Basic Books, 2002), Tony Kushner and Katharine Knox, *Refugees in an Age of Genocide* (London: Frank Cass, 1990), and on Cambodia, Afghan refugees in Pakistan, and Zaire, see Stephan John Stedman and Fred Tanner (eds.), *Refugee Manipulation: War, Politics, and the Abuse of Human Suffering* (Washington, D.C.: Brookings Institution, 2003). On conflict resolution, see Stephen John Stedman, Donald Rothchild, and Elizabeth M. Cousens (eds.), *Ending Civil Wars: The Implementation of Peace Agreements* (Boulder, CO: Lynne Rienner, 2002).

Chapter 5

"To establish conditions under which justice and respect for the obligations arising from treaties and other sources of international law can be maintained."

FROM THE PREAMBLE TO THE CHARTER
OF THE UNITED NATIONS

Humanitarianism:
Human Rights
and Refugees

Aung San Suu Kyi is one of the most famous political activists in the world today. Due to her defense of human rights and nonviolent opposition to the military regime in Myanmar (formerly known as Burma), she was awarded the Nobel Peace Prize in 1991. Viewed as a threat to state security, she was held under house arrest from July 1989 to July 1995. The daughter of the revered father of Burmese independence, Suu Kyi returned to Burma in 1988 to take care of her dying mother. She became actively involved in the democracy movement, helping to form the National League for Democracy (NLD). The NLD is the largest legally recognized political party. The military, however, which came to power in a bloody military coup in September 1988, reigned supreme.

Nonviolent resistance to martial law led to a series of arrests in 1989. In July of that year Suu Kyi and her colleagues had planned a Martyrs' Day March but called it off when extensive military preparations were evident. Returning home she found eleven truckloads of troops waiting for her. During most of her six years of house arrest, she was denied access to the outside world. In April 1995 she was finally allowed two visits from her husband and sons, the first in over two years. Her husband, terminally ill with cancer and living in London, applied for a visa in 1999 to pay a farewell visit to his wife in Myanmar, his first in three years. The junta refused, hoping Suu Kyi would go to Britain instead. Suu Kyi's husband died in March 1999, but she has continued to work for democracy and human rights in Myanmar. In May 2002 she was released from nineteen months of house arrest in her barricaded villa in Yangon.

We live in a world of some six billion people, a large proportion of whom suffer from political oppression, social discrimination, poverty, starvation or malnutrition, disease, and early death. Freedom from want is an elusive goal in much of the world, where poverty is the norm, life expectancy is much lower than in high-income countries, and infant mortality is still very high. Insecurity reigns supreme, and there is relatively little prospect of eliminating either the fact or fear of political and other abuses. Many human rights advocates lament how President Franklin Roosevelt's "four freedoms" enumerated in his 1941 State of the Union address—freedom of speech and expression, freedom of religion, freedom from want, and freedom from fear—seem so unattainable for most of the world's population.

We approach the subject of human rights in this chapter by examining how rights or values can be considered universal and not just representations of particular cultural or national preferences. In this regard, it is important for Americans (or the nationals of any country, for that matter) to understand the lack of universal agreement on *which* rights or *whose* rights ought to be protected. We also examine the problem of refugees not simply in terms of human rights but also as a potentially destabilizing element in international relations and world politics.

We deal explicitly with human rights as part of the human condition and in relation to concepts of justice and state sovereignty. After an overview of historical and contemporary human rights abuses, we examine how human rights can be understood not only from the U.S. perspective but also from the perspectives of different cultures. Lists of human rights have been made in universal declarations, covenants, and other documents of the United Nations and regional organizations such as the Council of Europe, the European Union (EU), the Organization of American States (OAS), and the Organization of African Unity (OAU). We close by returning to the issue of how the evolving doctrine of internationally protected human rights poses a challenge to traditional conceptions of sovereignty, and we examine the role of transnational organizations in globalizing the issue of human rights.

Human Rights and the Human Condition

A belief in certain inalienable human rights is at the core of our understanding of the human condition. Yet the human condition is beset by widespread abuses related to intercommunal strife, politically oppressive regimes, and deeply set prejudices within and across different societies and cultures. We focus in this section on some of these circumstances that produce widespread human rights violations.

Racial and ethnic discrimination is a global problem. South African apartheid or racial-separation policies were implemented by white-minority governments against the black majority population until the 1990s. Suppression of a majority by a small, powerful minority made the South African case particularly egregious.

Much more common in various countries, however, are racial, national, and ethnic prejudices that result in oppression of minority populations. These are not just Third World issues. Europe, Japan, and North America also offer considerable evidence of discriminatory practices on racial or ethnic lines.

For its part legalized, racially based slavery in the United States lasted until President Lincoln's Emancipation Proclamation of 1863 and Amendment 13 to the U.S. Constitution, passed in 1865, prohibited the practice. Outlawing slavery, of course, did not eliminate racial discrimination. Legalized racial segregation continued until

Supreme Court rulings beginning in 1954 and passage of the Civil Rights Act of 1965. Notwithstanding considerable progress toward equal rights, there is still substantial evidence of continuing racial discrimination in various forms.

Some societies value free expression and religious choice, but others do not. Brutality directed against other human beings, by no means a new phenomenon, seemed nevertheless to intensify during the 1980s and 1990s, as evidenced by the 1989 massacre of demonstrators at Tiananmen Square in the Chinese capital of Beijing; the slaying of peasant villagers in the southern Mexican state of Chiapas and in El Salvador, Honduras, Nicaragua, Haiti, and other parts of Central America and the Caribbean; the breakup of Yugoslavia and the intercommunal violence among Croat, Serb, and Muslim populations that followed; and intertribal atrocities committed in the Sudan, Ethiopia, Rwanda, and elsewhere in Africa. These incidents gained worldwide attention not just as localized atrocities but also because they are indicative of a pattern of intercommunal violence throughout the world.

Massive numbers of migrant populations—especially economic refugees seeking work and a place to live for themselves and their families—have swelled the ranks of other refugees, most of whom are seeking asylum or protection from various forms of political oppression throughout the world. These growing numbers challenge even those countries historically sympathetic to their plight. Widespread national and ethnic strife in Africa, the Balkans, the Gulf, the Transcaucasus, South and Southeast Asia, and the Caribbean have produced literally millions of displaced persons who have been forced, or who have fled, from their home areas, often across national borders. In sub-Saharan Africa alone, the U.N. High Commission for Refugees (UNHCR) has counted more than six million displaced persons—more than 10 percent of the region's population.[1]

Not all countries share a deep commitment to admitting immigrants seeking asylum or refugee status, but even those that do face practical limits to their population-absorption capacities; large-scale immigration pressures typically are balanced by governments that also are concerned about the impact of immigration on the welfare of their own citizens. The United States certainly has grappled with this issue, given pressures from populations fleeing regimes in Cuba, Haiti, and other locations in Central America and the Caribbean. In addition, there are large numbers of employment-driven migrations from Mexico, many of them illegal.

Widespread gender discrimination also denies equal rights to women. The term *gender discrimination* hardly captures the nature of existence for the vast majority of women in the Third World, where a combination of culture, laws, and religion not only deprive women of basic human rights but also relegate them in some places to almost subhuman status. In parts of Latin America, Asia, or Africa, women suffer from endless discrimination that begins even before birth with forced abortions of female fetuses in some countries. Infanticide, the practice of killing newborn girls, is a common rural phenomenon in India and China. For cultural as well as economic reasons, boys are preferred. Government policies that limit overall family size have had the unintended consequence of encouraging resort to female abortion and infanticide in these circumstances. They have also led to the development of the notorious "Dying Rooms," which are orphanages filled almost entirely with abandoned female infants and girls.[2]

Even if a baby girl survives the first few years, life continues to be precarious. As children, girls are fed less than their brothers, often only table scraps. Genital mutilation,

[1] For the most recent data on refugees, see the UNHCR Web site (www.unhcr.ch).
[2] See www.gendercide.org/case_infanticide.

Case & Point

WOMEN IN THE THIRD WORLD

- An estimated 500,000 women die of pregnancy-related causes each year, more than 90 percent of them in the Third World.
- 100,000 women die each year from unsafe abortions, almost all in the Third World.
- The World Health Organization estimates that seventy million women, most of them Africans, have undergone some form of female circumcision.
- In 1991 bridal dowry disputes led husbands and in-laws to kill more than 5,000 wives in India.
- Approximately 855 million people in the world are illiterate (almost one-sixth of humanity); two-thirds of them are women.
- Of the 1.3 billion persons living in absolute poverty, 70 percent are women.

IN SOUTH ASIA

- One of every eighteen women dies of a pregnancy-related cause.
- More than one of every ten babies dies during delivery.

IN NEPAL AND BANGLADESH

- One in every five girls dies before age five.

IN INDIA

- Approximately 25 percent of the twelve million girls born each year die by age fifteen.

Point: As difficult as life may be for the vast majority of humanity, it is even more trying for females.

Source: UNICEF

a severely damaging ritual often referred to euphemistically as "female circumcision," is widely practiced in parts of Africa. Women also are provided with less medical care and are much less likely to be taken to a hospital for treatment compared to their brothers. The largest obstacle to advancement of women is lack of educational opportunities. Throughout the Third World, even if girls are allowed to attend school, they are withdrawn sooner than boys so they can carry water, work in the fields, raise younger siblings, and do other domestic chores. In Pakistan, where schools are segregated by sex, only one-third are for women, and one-third of those have no building. Three out of four women cannot read or write. There has also been a recent rise of Islamic fundamentalism in Pakistan—what some refer to as the "Koran and Kalashnikov" culture—in part due to the spillover effect of the Taliban regime that ruled Afghanistan for so many years. Many mullahs have increased in power and preach against any developments meant to improve the status and condition of females.[3]

Deeply rooted cultural values or prejudices are, of course, not easily changed, even when laws are passed to condemn such practices. In some cases, however, laws have been passed that actively discriminate against women. In some African countries, there are laws

---

[3]www.rferl.org/nca/features/2001/12/06.

*Women of the town of Koena,
Burkina Faso.*

that prohibit women from owning houses. In old age, these trials and indignities often become worse. In India a woman's identity is so intertwined with that of her husband that
if she should outlive him, she is often treated as a nonentity. In some parts of the country
women are forced to marry the dead husband's brother so that property stays in the family. Small wonder that one study states that in India half the women age 60 and older are
widows, and their mortality rate is three times that of married women the same age.[4]

Such conditions and extreme practices are not commonplace in advanced industrial societies. Yet women still have not achieved equality of opportunity or position in
the workplace or in other aspects of social life in these countries. Progress has been
made on these issues but only at a very slow pace. One international effort to publicize
the problems facing women around the globe has been through U.N.–sponsored conferences. One held in Beijing, China, in September 1995 aimed to develop a worldwide
strategy to advance the situation of women. Parallel to this official conference was a
Non-Governmental Organizations Forum on Women that attracted some 35,000 participants, 2,000 organizations, and 4,000 journalists. This gave the forum perhaps even
more press coverage than the official conference received.

---

[4]"Born Oppressed," *Washington Post,* February 14, 1993, p. A48.

Justice: The Universality of Human Rights versus State Sovereignty

Quite apart from how we may feel about human rights abuses, do we have any obligation to act or any right to do so, particularly if actions conflict with the prerogatives of sovereign states? Indeed, international or transnational actions in support of human rights often directly challenge or violate state sovereignty. For example, NATO's war against Serbia over Serbian actions in Kosovo clearly violated state sovereignty because Kosovo was recognized by most all states as being a province of the Yugoslav Republic. Still, injustices offend the human conscience and cry out for corrective action. If justice is understood universally as fairness,[5] is there agreed or common cause for external action on behalf of human rights? Or does their sovereignty (affirmed by Article 2, Section 7 of the U.N. Charter) legally preclude intervention in the domestic affairs of states, however just a cause might be?

To what extent, then, need we be concerned with the **welfare** of other human beings in different cultural, socioeconomic, and geographic settings? Are there grounds for such concerns that go beyond the bounds of a given state or society? Is it enough to be concerned about justice and human rights within one's own country? Should we seek application of universal norms of justice and human rights? Is the human condition properly a global or **supranational** concern?

It is an understatement to say that there is no consensus on the answers to these questions. A traditional response is that sovereign states have an exclusive right to address such questions within their own jurisdictions. Others would argue that universal norms (some of which now are part of international law) apply across national borders. The existence of human rights from this perspective concerns international or global society as a whole, not just an internal matter for particular states to manage or handle.

We may be more likely to address human rights or questions of justice in global terms if we see the world as composed of individuals (or tribes, classes, or other groups of people) rather than of states. By contrast, if we adopt a more abstract, state-centric view, we may see demands for justice and respect for human rights in other countries as unwarranted intrusions into their domestic affairs.

A further significant complication is the absence of agreement on what human rights are (much less on what constitutes justice, either within a particular society or across national boundaries). Efforts have been made to define human rights in formal terms, as in the U.N. Declaration of Human Rights and in the documents of such regional organizations as the Council of Europe, the Organization for Security and Cooperation in Europe, the European Union, the Organization of American States, and the Organization of African Unity.

Human Rights and the Liberal Tradition

The degree of emphasis on human rights in U.S. foreign policy has varied from one governmental administration to another and even within administrations. Regardless of the degree of emphasis, the U.S. approach has been criticized because of its distinctly American point of view. The American focus on individual rights, a concern deeply embedded in its liberal tradition, tends to overlook **communitarian,** group, or class rights that occupy a more prominent place in other political cultures.

[5]See John Rawls, *A Theory of Justice* (Cambridge, MA: Harvard University Press, 1971).

Americans also tend to place more weight on liberty and its relation to order than on the egalitarian and socioeconomic issues emphasized in other countries. Notwithstanding what may be the best of intentions, American foreign policy pronouncements on human rights that project an individually oriented, ***libertarian*** focus are sometimes taken as yet another imposition of American values on others. The severest critics call it quite simply cultural imperialism. As such, U.S. and other national efforts in the human rights field have often been interpreted as intrusions on the sovereign prerogatives of states not sharing the same perspectives on these issues.

The American understanding of human rights stems in large part from the ideas of seventeenth- and eighteenth-century Enlightenment thinkers and the American historical experience itself. One of the best summations of this thesis is Louis Hartz's now-classic book, *The Liberal Tradition in America*.[6] Hartz notes that the United States, unlike Europe, lacked any direct experience with feudalism and its hierarchic authority structure. European medieval society was dominated by an aristocracy with antidemocratic values. By contrast, the new American political culture had embedded within it what Hartz calls "the liberal idea."[7] What then is the nature of "liberal society" from the American point of view?

The term ***liberal*** as used by Hartz in its classic meaning should not be confused with contemporary American political usage that places "liberals" and "conservatives" into opposing categories. Although modern-day American social liberals and conservatives differ on many political issues, they are all "liberals" in the classical meaning of the term used by Hartz; that is, they share a belief in **individualism,** a commitment to individuals as human beings worthy of regard in themselves and not just as part of larger groups or classes.

Individualism built further on notions of equality among individuals; however, this egalitarianism would not readily support a redistribution of property or other socialist design. Alexis de Tocqueville, an early-nineteenth-century French observer of the American scene, commented how the egalitarian spirit in the United States existed among individuals who were part of a very individualistic society.

Because the United States had not experienced feudalism in its national history, the country lacked even the vestiges of aristocratic titles and deference to authorities that, by contrast, were integral parts of European societies. Feudalism, of course, had long since given way to preindustrial market capitalism in Europe, but many of the class inequalities of feudalism had survived into the modern era.[8] Notwithstanding actual differences among individuals in wealth and opportunity in the United States, its society and culture exhibited a stronger spirit of equality than in most early nineteenth-century European societies.

---

[6]See Louis Hartz, *The Liberal Tradition in America: An Interpretation of American Political Thought since the Revolution* (New York: Harcourt, Brace & World, 1955).

[7]That "the absence of feudalism and the presence of the liberal idea" are key factors in "an analysis of American history and politics" is a core thesis in the entire book, first discussed by Hartz on pp. 20–23. It is incorrect to identify the plantation system (with its reliance on slavery as the principal source of labor) merely as a form of feudalism; democratic structures and values, though obviously denied to slaves, were nevertheless characteristic of the rest of society. It was, of course, a contradiction that was understood by many of the men who drafted the U.S. Constitution and Bill of Rights. Slaveholders included such notables as George Washington and Thomas Jefferson.

[8]See Alexis de Tocqueville, *Democracy in America,* Henry Reeve, trans. (New York: Schocken Books, 1961). The first English translations were published in 1835 and 1840, accompanied by introductions written by the English liberal and political philosopher John Stuart Mill. In developing his thesis, Louis Hartz draws directly from Tocqueville's observations of early American society.

libertarian
A philosophical position emphasizing individual rights, often preferring specific limits or restraints on government.

liberalism
A political philosophy with origins in the seventeenth and eighteenth centuries that emphasizes individual liberty, which originally was to be achieved through a minimal state.

To many Americans of Tocqueville's time, government was a necessary evil at best. As he noted, "Whenever the political laws of the United States are to be discussed, it is with the doctrine of sovereignty of the people that we must begin."[9] The best way for people as equal individuals to remain sovereign was to constrain the authority and power of government. In the America that Tocqueville observed, it was the "people"—understood not in some abstract way as society as a whole but rather as individual "citizens" (or groups of them)—who were "the real directing power."[10]

The framers of the U.S. Constitution, educated in the Greek and Roman classics, also drew heavily from the writings of such Enlightenment thinkers as Montesquieu and Locke. Following the late Greek historian Polybius (ca. 203–120 B.C.), Montesquieu developed the idea of separation of powers in his *Spirit of the Laws*. This idea would be adopted in the U.S. Constitution as a means of keeping central government from growing too strong at the expense of the governed. Human rights were to be conserved by restricting government's size and involvement in the private affairs of individual citizens.

Locke advocated an important but relatively minimal role for government at the service of individuals, primarily the protection of their lives, liberties, and property. Consistent with Locke, the U.S. Constitution explicitly prohibits government infringing on individual rights; citizens grant their consent to be governed and do not delegate all their rights to government. Isaiah Berlin and other political writers have called this a "negative" construction of libertarian rights. Liberties are negatively maintained by constraining government rather than by empowering it in some positive way to serve individual rights. The government role was thus to be as small as possible. The framers of the U.S. Constitution understood that this liberal philosophy of governmental *laissez-faire* offered the most consistent and effective means of protecting individual liberty.

In the course of its history, American government in practice would depart from this strict *laissez-faire* philosophy, particularly in the twentieth century. Even the meaning of the term *liberal* in its American context took on a more positive orientation toward governmental action for social and economic purposes. By contrast, American **conservatives** have articulated greater skepticism toward governmental activism, preferring to underscore their preference for governmental *laissez-faire*.

The key point is that what survived alongside new and expanded governmental attention to social and economic issues was a tendency for Americans to see and deal with human rights in individualist terms. American liberals and conservatives have differed on the means by which individuals are to be served and the role government is to play in this regard, but both groups have retained their classical liberal focus on individuals. Thus, laws passed since the 1930s have government do such things for individuals as guarantee a minimum wage, provide for a safer workplace, give unemployment and disability compensation, establish retirement pensions, offer job training, make higher-education loans and grants, and provide medical care.

Even advocacy of civil rights in the United States has been based primarily on the Constitutional view that individuals as citizens are entitled to **equal protection** under the law. With few exceptions (e.g., group rights for Native Americans or the right of organized labor to bargain collectively), Americans have been much less comfortable with recognizing rights on a group or class basis. Even collective bargaining by labor unions was understood as a tactical means for representing individual worker interests;

---

[9]*Ibid.*, p. 48.
[10]*Ibid.*, pp. 193–194.

Student activists construct a "Goddess of Democracy and Freedom," taking the Statue of Liberty as their model. The goddess was in place in Tiananmen Square shortly before tanks drove students from the square in June 1989.
Reuters/Ed Nachtrieb.

groups of individuals were understood in this context as being more effective than individuals standing alone in disputes with managers or owners of firms.

Arguments in favor of socioeconomic rights for large groups, classes, or society as a whole have enjoyed far less support in American thinking and practice than claims in favor of individual political rights and liberties. Even though the doctrine of **eminent domain** allows public need to supersede individual property rights (e.g., when government takes private property in order to build a highway or school), the law upholds individual rights at the same time by specific provisions to assure just compensation. Such property is also to be taken in a nondiscriminatory way; no individuals are supposed to receive either more favorable or unfair treatment compared to anyone else.

Human Rights across Cultures

It should not be surprising, therefore, that Americans (whether social liberals or conservatives) tend to view human rights through these same individualist and liberal lenses, focusing more on individual rather than collective rights and liberties. Not everyone agrees with this decidedly American perspective. In fact, when we examine the issue as it is addressed in different cultures, we find a lack of consensus on *whose* rights and *what* rights are bases for legitimate claims.[11]

---

[11]See Ernst B. Haas, *Global Evangelism Rides Again: How to Protect Human Rights without Really Trying* (Berkeley: University of California Institute of International Studies, 1978).

Some cultures perceive rights less in relation to individuals than to tribes, classes, or other groups. The state and society as a whole also may claim to have rights. States thus claim to be sovereign with rights to exercise complete jurisdiction over their domestic affairs and to be independent or autonomous in the conduct of their foreign affairs. The existence of rights belonging to the world's population taken as a whole—human civilization or humankind (to include generations not yet born)—is a claim quite different from the liberal idea that rights are primarily an individual matter.

Does a tribe, for example, have rights as a tribe that supersede rights claimed by individuals, whether or not they are members of the tribe? Can the same be said of society as a whole in relation to the individuals, tribes, classes, or other groups of which it is composed? For human civilization as a whole? Unfortunately there is no consensus across societies and cultures on this question of *whose* rights are to take priority when they conflict.

Cross-cultural disagreement also exists even on what rights are to be considered human rights. Consistent with their focus on individual, civil or political, and legal rights, Americans often fault foreign governments for failure to provide adequate **due process** or equal protection of the laws. This is particularly troublesome for Americans who are arrested while traveling abroad who may not have the same rights to a fair and speedy trial as at home and may suffer mistreatment or what they consider to be cruel and unusual punishments.

A celebrated case in which Singapore administered severe corporal punishment by caning an American youth who was found guilty of vandalism is by no means unique. In any given year, more than 2,500 Americans are incarcerated abroad for crimes or alleged crimes, often involving drug use or trade. Complaints concerning abuses of rights claimed by these American citizens in custody abroad are commonplace. The U.S. State Department's Bureau of Consular Affairs monitors the issue, but U.S. consular officials stationed abroad must rely for the most part on persuasion to extricate Americans unjustly implicated or mistreated. The host government and local authorities claim complete jurisdiction or sovereign authority over the acts of individuals committed on their own territory, regardless of the citizenship of these alleged offenders or convicted felons.

This American focus on legal and political rights (especially relating to life, liberty, and property), which puts much less emphasis on claims to social, cultural, and economic rights, is by no means universally shared. For citizens merely to be equal before the law is considered in many other cultures to be too narrow and a rather abstract construction of human rights. If they have human rights sensitivity at all, human welfare or social security in its fullest sense may be more highly valued.

Do people have sufficient food, clothing, shelter, medical care, and other necessities? From this perspective, ignoring or doing little about conditions that promote disease, hunger, and high mortality rates are understood as human rights violations of greater consequence than the more abstract legal and political rights concerning liberty or property. This priority stands quite apart from whether rights are understood in individual terms or as applying to tribes, classes, or other groups in a given society.

Culturally Specific Rights and Values

It is sometimes tempting to adopt a moral or **cultural relativism** and assert that rights or any other values can be understood only within their separate cultural contexts. Cultural relativists reject claims to human rights as universal, arguing that such universal

Case & Point

CHILDREN AND HUMAN RIGHTS

The worldwide population of children under the age of 14 who work full time is estimated to exceed 200 million. Pakistan illustrates the gap between a government's declared commitment to protecting the welfare of its children and its actual policies. According to the Human Rights Commission of Pakistan, some eleven to twelve million children work full time, about half under the age of 10. They are found in virtually every factory, workshop, and field in situations best characterized as indentured servitude. The carpet-making industry is a good example. According to UNICEF, between 500,000 and one million Pakistani children between the ages of 4 and 14 work long hours as full-time carpet weavers, accounting for up to 90 percent of the workforce.

A carpet master in the Punjab village of Wasan Pura states that he aggressively pursues boys from poverty-stricken families who are between the ages of 7 and 10: "They make ideal employees. Boys at this stage of development are at the peak of their dexterity and endurance, and they're wonderfully obedient—they'd work around the clock if I asked them. I hire them first and foremost because they're economical. For what I'd pay one second-class adult weaver I can get three boys, sometimes four, who can produce first-class rugs in no time." The low cost of child labor allows Pakistan to undersell its foreign competitors that prohibit child labor.

A Pakistani human rights nongovernmental organization known as the Bonded Labor Liberation Front (BLLF) has worked hard since its founding in 1988 against bonded and child labor, liberating some 30,000 adults and children from brick kilns, carpet factories, and farms. It has won some 25,000 court cases against unscrupulous employers.

Point: The plight of children in the Third World at times fails to receive the amount of publicity that other human rights cases receive.

Source: www.theatlantic.com/atlantic/issues/96/feb/pakistan

---

claims are artificial constructions. To a relativist, values cannot be separated from the cultural context. Who is to say which culture's values should supersede another's?

It is not hard to show that different cultures (and subcultures within a given society) have different ways of thinking about and doing things. For example, the time of day and the size and content of different meals considered appropriate varies across cultures and subcultures. How one eats—with one's hands, with chopsticks, or with fork, knife, and spoon—is also quite variable. We refer to such practices as customs or manners. Even though there may be a correct way to act in a particular cultural context, we usually do not understand the values associated with manners or customs as having *moral* content.

Other values in a particular cultural context may be part of its moral code. Thus respecting the elderly as a group or as individuals may be seen as a moral obligation in some cultures but not in others, at least not to the same degree. The same is true for children (see Map 15.1). Providing for some minimum level of living may be understood in moral terms as social responsibility in some cultures, whereas others prefer to hold individuals primarily responsible to provide for themselves.

Thus many societies hold governments, whether democratic or authoritarian in character, responsible for assuring at least a basic level of living and welfare for their people, but this is not a universally held view. In American society, for example, there

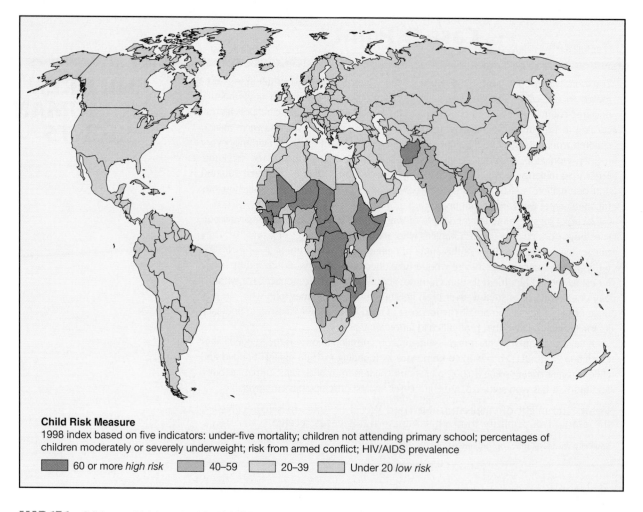

Child Risk Measure
1998 index based on five indicators: under-five mortality; children not attending primary school; percentages of
children moderately or severely underweight; risk from armed conflict; HIV/AIDS prevalence

 60 or more *high risk* | 40–59 | 20–39 | Under 20 *low risk*

MAP 15.1   *Children and Adolescents at Special Risk*
Source: UNICEF

may be a higher value placed on equality of opportunity rather than on fairness of
socioeconomic outcomes. Although Americans disagree among themselves on such
matters, many who are well off may not feel there is any individual or societal obligation to assist those who are not. This perspective views charity as properly a voluntary effort undertaken primarily by individuals, not by governments. Value is often
placed on the marketplace as the best mechanism for allocating goods and services, a
view challenged, of course, by Americans with greater **social-liberal** (or social-
democratic) commitments.

　　The American approach to such matters not only differs from most other
advanced industrial countries, which expect a larger government role in assuring a
greater degree of socioeconomic welfare, but also from many less-developed countries,
which have social security systems based on tribal or clan loyalties. The more *laissez-
faire* perspective still prevalent in the United States is not in any way typical of the rest
of the world.

Toward Global Society and Values That Transcend Diverse Cultures

Although some values do vary across cultures from one society to another, does this mean that all values are dependent on certain societal or cultural contexts? Do any values apply to human beings or humanity as a whole independent of cultural context?

Students of philosophy observe that if we really believe in a strict cultural relativism—that values and rights are only to be defined by separate cultures and can have no independent standing of their own—then we are saying in effect that there is no such thing as morality or ethics. Can morality, ethical principles, and human rights really be said to exist if they can be changed so readily within and across cultures and subcultures? Is there no basis independent of a given society or culture for moral or ethical standards of behavior?

One significant problem with moral or cultural relativism is that it gives us no universal basis for condemning atrocities and such human tragedies as the Holocaust. Just because eliminating the Jews as a people may have been considered legitimate within a Nazi political subculture, this belief did not make it right. Even if we have difficulty agreeing on many other values, *genocide* is so offensive to the human spirit that it is condemned as mass murder on universal, not just on cultural, grounds. Any rational human being, regardless of cultural origin, would understand the immorality of such atrocities.

What about a religious basis for universal human rights? Islam, Christianity, Judaism, Hinduism, Buddhism, and other religions do not just limit themselves to their followers but frequently also make universally applicable moral claims. As a practical matter, rejection of religion by some and the absence of theological consensus even among the followers of various religious groups prevent us from using particular religions as the solitary bases for common, worldwide acceptance of human rights and other moral claims.

Instead, many writers have tried to identify secular or non-religious bases for their universalist positions. Aristotle identified certain virtues exhibited by virtuous persons we might emulate. Also attributed to Aristotle is the ethical maxim "do no harm." For his part, the eighteenth-century German philosopher Immanuel Kant identified what he called **categorical imperatives,** or absolute obligations, that he argued had applicability to all reasoning human beings, regardless of religious or other cultural differences. Thus, according to Kant, we should follow only those maxims that we would be willing to make into universal laws. This "categorical imperative" binds all human beings. Regardless of cultural or religious identity, rational human beings would not want to legitimize murder, lying, stealing, or other forms of dishonesty by making them into universal "laws" or maxims to guide human conduct. Even though human beings engage in such activities, they cannot be considered right by rational human beings in any cultural context.

In short, a difference is recognized between how human beings *should* act and how they *do* act. Kant also understood as universal the obligation to treat human beings as ends worthy in themselves, not just as means to other ends. From the Kantian perspective, this categorical imperative is also universally binding as a moral or ethical guide to behavior, even though it too is often violated. Again, even though the actual conduct of human beings deviates from these norms or maxims, they are not any less morally binding. According to Kant, human beings have a duty to follow those ethical principles that are discoverable through their rational faculties.

genocide
Mass murder of a people typically because of their racial, ethnic, religious, or other particular identity.

Children behind a barbed wire fence at the Nazi concentration camp in Auschwitz.

Kant was not the only writer to provide a secular basis for universal norms of right conduct. The nineteenth-century English **utilitarians** Jeremy Bentham and John Stuart Mill argued that we should act in accordance with the maxim of assuring the greatest good (or greatest happiness) for the greatest number. Utilitarians take this abstract principle and apply it to a wide range of human circumstances, including a defense of liberty and other human rights as representing the greatest good for the greatest number.

The seventeenth-century English writer John Locke reasoned that human beings have certain **natural rights** to life, liberty, and property, which they surrender only as part of a **social contract.** The notion among social-contract theorists that, quite apart from cultural context, human beings have rights as part of their nature obviously provides another secular ground for making universalist moral claims. To Locke (and to Thomas Jefferson, who followed Locke's lead), human rights are thus part of human nature. The citizenry or people who empower governments in the first place must therefore strictly limit the authority of governments to abridge them. In fact, governments are created in part to guarantee certain **civil rights,** which are those rights that individuals have as members of the societies to which they belong.

Locke and Jefferson clearly put particular emphasis on individual liberties, although another social-contract theorist, the eighteenth-century French-Swiss writer Jean-Jacques Rousseau, placed relatively greater emphasis on equality and on the obligations to one's community. In his "Discourse on the Origin of Inequality," Rousseau found fault with the division of property among individuals, believing it to be the source of much that is wrong in society. That "the fruits of the earth belong to all and the earth to no one" is at once egalitarian and communitarian, a universalist moral.

At the same time, in his *Social Contract* Rousseau argued in favor of liberty, lamenting that "man is born free" but that "everywhere he is in chains." Rousseau's thoughts on such matters are more complex, of course, than merely providing an endorsement of liberty and equality. He saw human beings as part of a larger community or society in which decisions are to serve the "general will" or interest of society as a whole, rather than the particular wills or interests of certain individuals.

The important point for this discussion, however, is that some human rights advocates in Europe and elsewhere have been influenced by this mode of thought. They have tended to offer a vision of a just world society based more on egalitarian and communitarian values than is present in the more individualist, Lockean mode of thought. John Rawls, a late twentieth-century theorist in the social-contract tradition, comes closer to Rousseau in his focus on the equity or fairness we would expect in a just society. If human beings did not know in advance how they would fare (behind what Rawls referred to as a "veil of ignorance" as to what their personal circumstances might be), what rules would they establish to assure fair or just outcomes?[12]

The lack of intellectual agreement among social-contract theorists, utilitarians, Kantians, and others who think about values in universal terms is part of the global confusion on such matters. This lack of consensus on human rights—how we are to understand rights and values and what we are to do about them—underlies the global debate on what commitments and obligations we have to fellow human beings throughout the world. Disagreement on what and whose human rights ought to be recognized hinders the construction of a just world society.

From Theory to Fact

English, French, and American theories of rights, developed in the seventeenth and eighteenth centuries as part of liberal revolutions then under way in these societies, remain important as philosophical underpinnings of present-day, global concerns about justice and human rights. The idea of agreeing on principles of human rights and then declaring them as binding obligations is also consistent with a ***positivist*** view. From this perspective, whether or not rights exist as part of human nature, their existence as civil rights can be declared as a positive act. Indeed, when states ratify treaties to this effect, human rights become binding as part of international law.

The idea of constraining government authority by the positive assertion of rights is contained in the English Magna Carta (1215), by which the English nobility set limits on their own monarch. The English civil war of the 1640s was followed by a period of turmoil that finally resulted in Parliament's restoration of a constitutional (or limited) monarchy in 1688, proclaiming an English Bill of Rights in 1689. The American understanding of rights was profoundly influenced by the British experience in general and English and Scottish writers in particular. The Declaration of Independence (1776) and the addition of a Bill of Rights to those rights specified in the original draft of the U.S. Constitution underscored an American commitment to the civil rights and liberties of individuals.

Following in this liberal tradition, a Universal Declaration of the Rights of Man was proclaimed in 1789 by the French revolutionary National Assembly. The eighteenth-century English writer Thomas Paine, who was widely read by Americans at the time, provided an eloquent defense of the French position on human rights.[13] In doing so, he directly contradicted the conservative Edmund Burke, then a member of Parliament, who saw the French Revolution as dangerous in the extreme. Paine justified French claims by expounding a theory of natural human rights. Going beyond individual rights and liberties, Paine also provided justification for egalitarian and communitarian claims.

---

[12]See Rawls, *A Theory of Justice.*
[13]Thomas Paine published *Rights of Man* in two parts in 1791 and 1792.

positivism
The concept that law is what lawmakers, following constitutional procedures, define it to be.

The Universal Declaration of Human Rights (1948) included in this chapter and subsequent efforts to codify human rights as treaty obligations owe much to an historical legacy of constitutional liberalism in which governments were constrained and citizen rights were declared. On this and following pages a few of these are presented. Because of their global influence in the nineteenth and twentieth centuries, this bedrock of predominantly Anglo-American and French ideas has provided the foundation for the universal declaration and international conventions on human rights promulgated since 1945.

Whether or not we are satisfied with one or another of the intellectual justifications that have been offered for the universality of human rights in Kantian, natural, utilitarian, religious or other terms, we should take note of several positivist constructions since the end of World War II. These are part of a growing body of human rights principles, some of which have the binding character of international law. Consistent with its preamble, Articles 1 and 55 of the U.N. Charter (1945) established the principle of "universal respect for, and observance of human rights and fundamental freedoms for all without distinction as to race, sex, language, or religion." Many of these rights were also specified in the Universal Declaration on Human Rights, passed by the U.N. General Assembly in 1948.

The declaration did not establish these specified rights in international law with the binding force of a treaty. Some have argued, however, that the declaration did give formal recognition to rights as they have come to be accepted in practice and thus have become in effect part of **customary international law.** Whatever the outcome of this argument among international lawyers, what is most important for our purposes in this chapter is that by vote of the United Nations General Assembly, sovereign states formally acknowledged the legitimacy of human rights as *universal* rights.

Former American Ambassador to the U.N. Eleanor Roosevelt, a principal architect and advocate of the universal declaration, joined with others in seeking to legitimize the idea that rights exist independently of particular sovereign states and their respective societies. Not surprisingly, given the dominant position of the United States in world politics at the time, the declaration conformed more to American and other Western preferences for individual, political rights in the liberal tradition and gave relatively less emphasis to communitarian and socioeconomic interpretations of human rights.

Nevertheless, six of the thirty articles in the universal declaration did address such socioeconomic and cultural rights, but even these were cast largely in individual rather than collective terms.[14] Further specification of these rights was contained in two 1966 covenants that entered into force in 1976—one for civil and political rights and the other for economic, social, and cultural rights. Reference in these later documents to "peoples" indicated some acceptance that rights could be understood in terms of collectivities, not just individuals.

In any event, these two covenants, built as they are on the foundation of the U.N. Charter and the Universal Declaration of Human Rights, are the main pillars of the United Nations's human rights "structure." Other documents include the International Convention on the Elimination of All Forms of Racial Discrimination (1966), the Convention on the Elimination of All Forms of Discrimination against Women (1979), Convention against Torture and Other Cruel, Inhuman or Degrading Treatment or Punishment

---

[14]Articles 22–27 specifically address social security, rights to work and leisure, adequate standard of living, education, and participation in cultural life.

(1984), and a Convention on the Rights of a Child (1989). Documents produced by the U.N. Educational, Scientific, and Cultural Organization (UNESCO), the International Labor Organization (ILO), the World Health Organization (WHO), and other specialized agencies have contributed directly and indirectly to the corpus of this emergent U.N. human rights regime. See Table 15.1 for a list of documentary sources that specify human rights.

Machinery for Human Rights Issues and Cases

Sovereign states have jealously guarded their legal jurisdiction and have been very reluctant to surrender such authority to international institutions on all types of cases,

1948	Universal Declaration of Human Rights
1948	Convention on the Prevention and Punishment of the Crime of Genocide
1949	Geneva Conventions for Amelioration of the Condition of the Wounded and Sick Members of Armed Forces in the Field Amelioration of the Condition of Wounded, Sick and Shipwrecked Members of Armed Forces at Sea Treatment of Prisoners of War Protection of Civilian Persons in Time of War
1951	Convention Relating to the Status of Refugees
1966	International Covenant of Civil and Political Rights
1966	International Covenant on Social and Cultural Rights
1966	International Convention on the Elimination of All Forms of Racial Discrimination
1977	Protocols to the Geneva Conventions (see 1949 above) Protection of Victims of International Armed Conflicts Non-International Armed Conflicts
1979	Convention on the Elimination of All Forms of Discrimination against Women
1984	Convention against Torture and Other Cruel, Inhuman or Degrading Treatment or Punishment
1989	Convention on the Rights of the Child
1989	Second Optional Protocol to the International Covenant on Civil and Political Rights (aiming at abolition of the death penalty)
1999	Optional Protocol to the Convention on the Elimination of Discrimination Against Women
2000	Optional Protocols to the Convention on the Rights of Children (children in armed conflict, the sale of children, child prostitution, and pornography)
2002	Optional Protocol to the Convention Against Torture and Other Cruel, Inhuman or Degrading Treatment or Punishment

TABLE 15.1
Selected Documents Defining a Global Human Rights Regime

including human rights. A Permanent Court of International Justice (PCIJ) was established under the League of Nations in 1922 at The Hague in the Netherlands. Its jurisdiction was limited to cases involving states. Legal accountability of individuals was left to the courts of individual states. Germany's invasion of Poland in 1939 marked the de facto end of the PCIJ, which was officially disbanded in 1946.

Following World War II, a new International Court of Justice (ICJ) or World Court was established at The Hague in the Netherlands as a principal organ of the U.N. organization and successor to the earlier PCIJ. The ICJ also meets to hear only those cases brought voluntarily by states agreeing to submit to its jurisdiction. Moreover, the ICJ does not have jurisdiction in cases involving individuals; the ICJ's jurisdiction thus fully respects the sovereignty of states.

Even the Universal Declaration of Human Rights has been viewed with a certain degree of skepticism. It was easy to agree on high principles when the matter of enforcement was left unresolved. Nowhere in the Declaration was it mandated that a member state had the right to intervene in another country's affairs to stop human rights abuses; state sovereignty still ruled.

Individual accountability for such crimes against the law of nations as piracy on the high seas was established in international legal practice centuries ago. It was left, however, to the domestic courts of states to try pirates and other alleged offenders of the law of nations. War crimes trials of individuals following World War II under the International Military Tribunal at Nuremberg, Germany, set an enormously important precedent for the assertion of international jurisdiction over such cases. The Nuremberg Tribunal was given its authority in 1945 by the victorious "Big Four" Allied powers or "united nations" of World War II—the United States, Soviet Union, the United Kingdom, and France—which had just defeated the German Reich and its allies. War crimes trials were also conducted in Tokyo under U.S. occupation authority over Japan.

Practicing World Politics

THE INTERNET: CHECKING OUT SOME WEB SITES ON INTERNATIONAL JURISPRUDENCE

A principal organ of the United Nations Organization, the International Court of Justice at The Hague in the Netherlands (www.icj-cij.org) contains basic documents, the current docket, and decisions of the Court. The U.N. home page (www.u.n..org) provides access to human rights and international criminal tribunal reports. In particular, see the U.N. High Commissioner on Human Rights (www.unhchr.org).

Founded in 1952, the International Commission of Jurists in Geneva (www.ICJ.org) is a nongovernmental organization site that advocates the rule of law, promotes protection of human rights, and has consultative status with the U.N. Economic and Social Council; the U.N. Educational, Scientific, and Cultural Organization (UNESCO); the Organization of African Unity; and the Council of Europe. For reports of progress on human rights in regional contexts, see also the Council of Europe (www.coe.fr) and, more specifically, its human rights pages (www.dhdirhr.coe.fr); the European Union (europa.eu.int); the Organization for Security and Cooperation in Europe (www.osce.org); the Organization of American States in Washington, D.C. (www.oas.org); and the Organization of African Unity in Addis Ababa, Ethiopia (www.oau.oua.org).

Shown on November 15, 1945, in the dock at the courtroom at Nuremberg during the early months of the year-long trial of the Nazi war criminals, are, from left to right: Herman Goering, Rudolf Hess, Joachim von Ribbentrop, Wilhelm Keitel, and Alfred Rosenberg.

The Nuremberg Tribunal dealt not only with war crimes ("violations of the laws or customs of war") but also with two new crimes under international law—crimes against peace ("planning, preparation, initiation or waging of a war of aggression"), and crimes against humanity ("murder, extermination, enslavement, deportation, and other inhumane acts committed against any civilian population"). The concept of crimes against humanity was affirmed further when the General Assembly adopted the Convention on the Prevention and Punishment of the Crime of Genocide in December 1948. The convention declared genocide to be a crime under international law and stated that persons charged with genocide shall be tried "by a competent tribunal." After adjournment of the Nuremberg Tribunal, states reassumed first jurisdiction in such matters, but a precedent for international hearing of criminal cases involving individuals had been set.

Calls for new international war crimes trials have occurred from time to time. A number of issues that need to be resolved include the following: How broad should the scope of the court's jurisdiction be? Should the court be established on a regional or global basis? How should the judges be selected? What should be the rules of evidence?[15]

Global horror over atrocities in Bosnia and elsewhere in the former Yugoslavia finally produced enough pressure for war crimes trials to be organized, the first since Nuremberg after World War II. The statute establishing the International Criminal Tribunal for the Former Yugoslavia (ICTY) was adopted by the U.N. Security Council in May 1993. The tribunal was mandated to prosecute persons responsible for serious violations of basic international humanitarian laws (war crimes, crimes against humanity, and genocide). The Tribunal is an independent body consisting of sixteen judges, an Office of the Prosecutor, and staff of more than 1,300 persons from eighty-three countries.

---

[15]John F. Murphy, "International Crimes," in Christopher Joyner, ed., *The United Nations and International Law* (Cambridge: Cambridge University Press, 1997), 380.

A U.N. investigative commission reported to the Security Council in 1994 its findings of "crimes against humanity" that "constitute genocide" in Bosnia.[16] Human rights violations were committed by all sides, but the principal victims were Bosnian Muslims. The report indicated that among the tactics used was rape of women "for the purpose of terrorizing and humiliating them often as part of the policy of 'ethnic cleansing.'" Beyond regrouping and forcing movements of peoples based on their ethnic identities, humiliation of women apparently was part of "a systematic rape" campaign designed to break up Muslim families and communities because of the shame rape victims would carry, particularly in these more traditional Muslim communal settings. Further victimization of innocent rape victims by shunning, ostracizing, or holding them somehow responsible or guilty is common enough in many societies. To use this vulnerability as a calculated tactic in the destruction of a people, however, is what makes mass rape part of an overall program of genocide. In March 1998, the Tribunal's Office of the Prosecutor announced the extension of its jurisdiction over events also occurring during the armed conflict in Kosovo. Trials began two years later.

A major weakness of the Tribunal has been the fact that it has no constabulary to enforce its indictments. It must rely on the voluntary cooperation of states, including the very governments whose officials it seeks to prosecute. In effect, the Tribunal has had to rely on NATO forces to enforce its rulings. In the case of Bosnia, NATO forces were given the authorization, but not the responsibility, for apprehending indicted war criminals. Significantly, the June 1999 peace plan to end the war in Kosovo did not give NATO forces a mandate to arrest Slobodan Milosevic, the president of Serbia and an indicted war criminal. Milosevic was eventually arrested, and his long, drawn-out trial began in February 2002. Other key Serbian officials indicted for war crimes remain at large. Nevertheless, the Tribunal has gained the grudging respect even of its critics. Those found guilty of crimes against humanity received sentences ranging between five and forty years of imprisonment.[17]

Similarly an International Criminal Tribunal for Rwanda (ICTR) was established in Tanzania to prosecute those suspected of committing genocide and other serious human rights violations during Hutu-Tutsi tribal warfare in 1994. Specifically listed offenses include widespread murder of civilians, torture, and mass rape. More than sixty persons have been arrested. The first-ever sentencing for the crime of genocide by an international court occurred in 1998. Two individuals, including the former prime minister of Rwanda, were given life sentences.[18] An interesting development in recent years has been so-called "hybrid courts." In Kosovo, East Timor, and Sierra Leone, courts composed of local and international judges apply a mix of local and international law.

An international conference in Rome did take a major step forward in 1998 when it formulated as a treaty for signature and ratification a new statute for an International Criminal Court (ICC) with global jurisdiction, complementary to national courts, for genocide, war crimes, and crimes against humanity. Unlike previous war crimes courts with jurisdiction limited to specific conflicts, the ICC is a permanent institution. Unlike the International Court of Justice (ICJ), it is not an organ of the United Nations. Three countries openly stated they would not vote for the establishment of the ICC—the United States, Israel, and China. U.S. negotiators claimed they feared American soldiers and peacekeepers abroad could be brought before the court on politically motivated charges. In May 2002, a month after the ICC formally came

---

[16]See Paul Lewis, "Word for Word: The Balkan War-Crimes Report," *New York Times,* June 12, 1994.

[17]From http://www.un.org/icty/glance/index.htm (dated 9 January 2004).

[18]From http://www.ictr.org/default.htm (dated 9 January 2004).

into existence, President George W. Bush informed the United Nations that the United States would not ratify the agreement, raising questions about the court's legitimacy. Gains in criminal accountability before international courts have not been matched, however, by expansion of international jurisdiction for civil cases (as when individuals or corporations sue each other for violations of contracts, torts, and other offenses, or when allowed by domestic law, try to sue or petition governments for redress of grievances). For the most part, civil law remains the domain of states exercising jurisdiction within their territorial boundaries.

Regional Human Rights Efforts in Europe

Efforts to build upon the base established by the Universal Declaration have continued within the United Nations, expanding the scope of rights to include social, economic, and cultural concerns that retain—but go well beyond—the liberal, individual commitments embodied in the original declaration. Further specification of rights by treaty (and thus with a firmer basis in international law) has been achieved by states participating on regional bases in the Council of Europe, the Organization for Security and Cooperation in Europe (OSCE), the European Union, and the Organization of American States.

Some of these regional efforts have made substantial progress in the human rights field. Members of the Council of Europe (an international organization formed in 1949 and located in Strasbourg, France) are democratically oriented European states seeking to expand civil society and the rule of law. In 1950, the Council adopted the European Convention for the Protection of Human Rights and Fundamental Freedoms. As an international organization composed of European democracies, the Council oversees the work of an executive agency (the European Commission on Human Rights) and a judicial arm (the European Court of Human Rights), both of which are located in Strasbourg. Only member states or the Commission may actually bring cases before this court. Europeans as individuals, however, may petition the European Commission on Human Rights after exhausting domestic legal remedies. In turn, the Commission (or states) may refer such matters to the European Court of Human Rights. Although individuals thus do not have direct access to this court, individual cases deemed worthy by the Commission or states belonging to the Council of Europe may be heard. Moreover, the European Court of Human Rights not only may award compensation to individuals for damages but also may exercise limited judicial review by requiring states to change domestic laws found in violation of the Convention.

Not to be confused with the Council of Europe and its European Court of Human Rights is the European Union's European Court of Justice (ECJ), located in Luxembourg. In the European Union's legal system, ECJ rulings supersede domestic laws of EU members when these laws are in conflict with EU law. Significantly the ECJ hears not only cases brought by states and EU institutions but also cases brought by or against individuals or corporations (so-called natural or legal persons, respectively). Thus, in addition to states and EU institutions, individuals and corporations may take cases directly to the European Court of Justice without having secured the consent of their national authorities. Indeed, its caseload has grown substantially in recent years, ruling on thousands of cases involving contract and other economic issues, some of which have had human rights aspects. International courts in Europe have thus acquired some jurisdiction for certain civil and criminal cases involving persons. It should also be noted that the European Union has a Charter of Fundamental Rights, and acceptance of these rights is a precondition for countries who seek to join the EU.

It's Been Said...

Relying on regional courts and asserting legal arguments and decisions that overrule national courts is mainly a European development. In addition to the Council of Europe and the European Union, the human rights obligations assumed by OSCE member states have been invoked many times since the Act of Helsinki (1975) that specified these rights in the first Conference on Security and Cooperation in Europe (CSCE). With more than fifty members, the OSCE also includes the United States and Canada and almost all countries in Europe from the Atlantic to the Urals. Review conferences allow an opportunity for the airing of human rights violations and the application of public and private pressures for their correction. During the 1980s, for example, the United States and other Western states used various CSCE review conferences to criticize the USSR and other Eastern European states for human rights violations.

More recently, however, human rights questions have been dealt with as part of the OSCE's commitment to the "human dimension." This refers to commitments made by OSCE participating states to ensure full respect for human rights and fundamental freedoms. Since 1990, the OSCE has developed institutions and mechanisms to promote respect for these commitments, such as the Office for Democratic Institutions and Human Rights. The current approach of the OSCE is to assist states in living up to their obligations rather than isolating them.

Whether within the OSCE, other international organizational settings, or in bilateral diplomacy, public airing of human rights violations usually contributes very little to correcting these violations. In fact, such publicity often contributes to a hardening of the offending state's position lest it lose face in submitting to such public rebuke. China, for example, has been reluctant to change its policies despite foreign criticism. It is true that accusing states may use human rights to score propaganda points against alleged offenders, but this is use of the human rights issue for other purposes.

States and governments genuinely committed to rectifying perceived human rights abuses usually find confidential, behind-the-scenes diplomacy—however forceful—more effective in achieving these ends. Positive incentives for compliance may be offered in these quiet, diplomatic efforts on behalf of human rights. Of course, accusing states may also choose to use the threat of public exposure as a negative tactic. It may become necessary to act on the threat, however, when quiet efforts have failed.

In the final analysis, the OSCE and its human rights charter can claim at least some degree of credit for changes since the fall of the Berlin Wall in 1989 and the subsequent demise of the Soviet bloc and the Soviet Union itself. Indeed, democratic reforms and human rights assurances offered by the new governments in many of these countries have enabled them to join the Council of Europe with its more developed legal structure for human rights cases. These are modest but still very positive developments that seemed unthinkable just a few years earlier.

Other Regional Human Rights Efforts

Efforts in Latin America and Africa, in contrast to Europe, have been far more modest. Human rights obligations were specified in 1948 as part of inter-American law in the OAS Charter and the American Declaration of the Rights and Duties of Man. The Inter-American Commission on Human Rights was created in 1960, and in 1969 the American Convention on Human Rights established an Inter-American Court of Human Rights.

Practicing World Politics

In addition to the U.N. home page (www.un.org), see the U.N. High Commissioners for Human Rights (www.unhchr.ch) and Refugees (www.unhcr.ch), the U.N. Development Program (www.undp.org), and the U.N. International Children's Emergency Fund (www.unicef.org). On workers' rights concerning health, safety, working conditions, and child labor, see the International Labor Organization in Geneva (www.ilo.org). Nongovernmental organizations involved with these subjects include Amnesty International (www.amnesty.org), Human Rights Watch (www.hrw.org), and the American Civil Liberties Union (www.aclu.org). You might also want to take a look at the journal *Human Rights Review*.

THE INTERNET: CHECKING OUT SOME WEB SITES ON HUMAN RIGHTS

OAS Charter revision in 1970 gave the Inter-American Commission a greater role in human rights matters, which was underscored by OAS approval in 1979 of a revised statute for the Commission. The Commission engages in human rights education and awareness efforts and receives petitions and complaints, even from private persons; it may publicize human rights violations, but it has no real enforcement authority. For its part, the Inter-American Court of Human Rights, located in Costa Rica, has heard a small number of cases but has not played the decisive role of its European counterparts in carving out authority over member states on human rights matters. Its opinions have tended to be advisory in nature.

The human rights structure of the African Union is even less developed on a continent plagued by violence and atrocities committed within and among states. Nevertheless, the 1981 African Charter on Human and People's Rights (the "Banjul Declaration") did enter into force in 1986. In addition to individual and collective rights, a list of duties to humanity and to state and society also was prescribed. The mandate to the African Commission on Human and Peoples' Rights was explicitly limited to interpretation, promotion, and protection of human rights. No judicial arrangements or enforcement authorities were provided. Nevertheless, it has played a role in publicizing human rights violation such as by sending a fact-finding mission to the Darfur region of the Sudan in 2004 and establishing a venue for peace talks.

NGOs and Human Rights

Particularly in the post–World War II era, states, international organizations, and nongovernmental organizations have all contributed to raising the international profile of human rights. For some states, pointing out human rights violations in another state may be a matter of principle, or it may simply be a way to embarrass a government. At times, a state may issue a condemnatory statement due to the efforts of NGOs such as Amnesty International, which relies heavily on global letter-writing campaigns, press releases, and publications to shame governments into releasing political prisoners or shame other states into making good their publicly stated support for human rights.

The origins of Amnesty International date to 1961 when a London lawyer, Peter Benenson, read about a group of students in Portugal who had been arrested for toasting freedom in a restaurant. This event prompted him to launch an "Appeal for Amnesty," calling for the release of all people imprisoned because of their peaceful

Case & Point

LANDMINES

In Ottawa, Canada, in December 1997, 122 governments signed a treaty banning antipersonnel landmines. Much of the credit for this achievement was due to an alliance of NGOs and sympathetic governments. A major media campaign highlighted the role of landmines in contributing to humanitarian crises. It is estimated that there are 250 million antipersonnel landmines in the arsenals of 108 countries. The major arsenals are in China (110 million), Russia (60 to 70 million), Belarus (estimated tens of millions), the United States (11 million), the Ukraine (10 million), Italy (7 million), and India (4 to 5 million). Some 115 million landmines are currently laid in sixty-eight countries. The cost of buying one landmine is between $3 and $10; the cost of removing one landmine is between $300 and $1,000. It is estimated that 8,000 to 10,000 children are killed or maimed by landmines each year.

Subsequent to the signing of the agreement, the International Campaign to Ban Land Mines (ICBL) was awarded the Nobel Peace Prize. The ICBL is a global network of more than 1,000 NGOs active in more than seventy-five countries. The goal is to prevent the further manufacturing, deployment, and selling of landmines, and eventually to remove them from state arsenals. The United States has not signed the treaty, but it also has not produced any landmines since 1997 and has banned exports of these weapons.

Point: The ICBL is a prime example of the persuasiveness if not the power of NGOs.

For more information on landmines, go to www.icbl.org.

---

expression of beliefs, politics, race, religion, or national origin. The campaign caught on and spread to other countries. By the end of 1961 Amnesty International had been formed. Amnesty's initial activities involved letter-writing campaigns on behalf of prisoners of conscience. Groups of volunteers were assigned to a particular prisoner whose fate was closely monitored. Unfortunately, few of these letters were ever answered, so in the late 1960s adoption groups were formed at the local level. These groups adopted a particular prisoner, country, or issue and helped with publicity, education, and fund-raising at the grassroots level. Outreach activity included churches, schools, businesses, professional organizations, and labor unions. New members and more financial contributions aided Amnesty's growth. In the early 1980s, the number of college campus groups expanded. Today Amnesty International has more than one million members, subscribers, and regular donors in more than 160 countries and territories.

The largest human rights organization in the United States is Human Rights Watch. The organization was founded in 1978 as Helsinki Watch. Local human rights groups in Moscow, Warsaw, and Prague had been established in the mid-1970s to monitor their governments' compliance with the Helsinki accords. Not surprisingly, they came under pressure from the communist governments, and Helsinki Watch was created to provide support for these embattled groups. A few years later, Americas Watch was created to monitor human rights abuses in North and South America. The strategy of Human Rights Watch is straightforward—painstaking documentation of abuses and vigorous advocacy in the media and halls of governments and international organizations.

As the organization notes: "Our goal is to make governments pay a heavy price in reputation and legitimacy if they violate the rights of their people."[19]

Amnesty International is only the best-known NGO working for human rights. Indeed, recent years have seen a veritable explosion in such organizations: 38 in 1950, 72 in 1960, 103 in 1970, 138 in 1980, and 275 in 1990. Not only is the number of groups significant but also the fact that these NGOs form coalitions and communication networks to link them together continuing from the twentieth into the twenty-first century. The growth of the Internet has certainly facilitated this networking by providing data and information on Web sites. Now anyone can easily gain access to information about the latest advocacy campaigns or learn how to become directly involved in supporting human rights around the globe. These human rights organizations are in turn linked to domestic movements and organizations in countries suffering from human rights abuses.

Refugees

Migration and *refugee* issues are no longer the sole concern of midlevel bureaucrats and advocates of human rights; they have become a topic of conversation and negotiation among heads of state. This is because these issues have generated conflict both within and between states, no matter what the underlying cause for an outflow of migrants might happen to be. International migration has implications for sovereignty, stability, and security for a growing number of states. In fact, the issue promises to become even more salient due to three political, economic, and environmental trends that cause international migration.

First, with the end of the Cold War, barriers to movement were lifted for many people living in former communist states. As the Soviet empire collapsed and independent states came into existence, new minorities were created within these borders who now feel less secure. One option is for minorities to create secessionist movements and demand their own states; another option is to migrate. This scenario is all too familiar to many people living in Africa and South Asia, areas that have been plagued by civil wars.

Second, the huge gap in income and employment opportunities among countries motivates thousands of persons to become economic migrants. Western Europe has been particularly concerned in recent years over the immigration issue. In the 1970s and early 1980s, about 100,000 people left the Warsaw Pact countries for the West for essentially political reasons, and they were welcomed there. But, as communism began to collapse, the number of migrants rose dramatically as their motivation became economic as well as political. In 1989 alone, 1.2 million people left the former Warsaw Pact states. The economic restructuring and privatization process in the former Soviet Union and Eastern Europe may also increase the number of those who want to migrate. While many people may seek to move to Western Europe, other countries such as Poland may see their own economic reform efforts hampered by a dramatic influx of immigrants.[20] In the developing world there are similar concerns among the so-called economic "Little Tigers" or NICs—newly industrializing countries—in Asia and among the oil-producing countries of the Middle East.

migration
The movement of peoples from one country or area to others; immigration involves arrivals, emigration, departures.

refugees
Persons displaced because of war (usually) or other political or economic causes. Refugees may flee or be forced to leave a country, or they may be internally displaced persons within their own state.

---

[19]From www.hrw.org/about/info/gna.html.

[20]F. Stephen Larrabee, "Down and Out in Warsaw and Budapest: Eastern Europe and East–West Migration," *International Security,* v. 16, no. 4 (Spring 1992): 5–6.

Vulnerable refugees waiting for emergency aid at the makeshift site in Djoran, eastern Chad.
UNHCR/H. Caux/01.2004

Finally, drought, floods, and famines may also stimulate migration. According to one estimate, two million Africans were displaced in the mid–1980s due to drought alone. This does not even take into account refugees created by conflict in such places as Somalia, Rwanda, and Burundi. One can begin to sense the magnitude of the problem.[21]

In this section we focus on refugees, who can be viewed as one type of immigrant. While a true immigrant is influenced by both push and pull factors such as better options in another country, refugees are unwillingly forced from their homes. The most generally accepted definition of a refugee comes from the United Nations: A refugee is a person who "owing to a well-founded fear of being persecuted for reasons of race, religion, nationality, membership of a particular social group or political opinion, is outside the country of his nationality and is unable, or unwilling to avail himself of the protection of that country."[22]

Thanks to the wonders of modern global communications, refugees trek across our television screens on a regular basis. The report may come from Africa, Asia, Latin America, or Europe, but the image is always the same—men, women, and children trudging down dusty roads, their few possessions on their backs or in horse-drawn carts or dilapidated automobiles and trucks. No matter who the unfortunate inhabitants may be, refugee camps share similar characteristics—smoky cooking fires, endless rows of tents, skinny children with saucer-sized eyes, and long lines of the ill and infirm waiting

---

[21]Myron Weiner, "Security, Stability, and International Migration," *International Security,* v. 17, no. 3 (Winter 1992/93): footnote 5.

[22]The definition comes from the 1951 U.N. Convention Relating to the Status of Refugees.

patiently to see a specialist from organizations like Doctors Without Borders. Most reports include the obligatory thirty-second interview with the representative from the U.N. High Commissioner for Refugees (UNHCR), who once again emphasizes the need for a sustained global response to the latest humanitarian crisis. Other refugees are not so lucky. Some refugees are separated from their families and subjected to armed attacks and exploitation.

The humanitarian response to refugee crises is in part a moral argument. How can the comparatively wealthy of the world sit idly by and watch fellow human beings exist in unspeakable conditions and subject to extreme deprivations? But watching the endless replay of refugee crises and scenes of famine sometimes induces **compassion fatigue.** Eventually, television viewers may feel that investing emotion and money in what seems to be an inalterable fact of life on this planet is pointless.

Some refugees are victims of natural disasters such as drought, floods, or typhoons. The fact of the matter is, however, that most refugee crises are not a function of acts of God or weather but of politics. Political turmoil is most often the root cause of the crisis, dictating the type and level of international response. In 1971, for example, ten million East Pakistani refugees fled to India, most not returning until the creation of an independent Bangladesh. The disintegration of the former Yugoslavia displaced some four million people within the former communist state and scattered another half million across Europe. Throughout many other areas of the world men, women, and children flee their homelands because of armed conflict, intimidation, and repression.

Particularly when the political conflict has racial, religious, and ethnic overtones, those who have been expelled from their homeland will find it increasingly difficult to integrate into neighboring host nations or be resettled in distant countries. But thanks to modern means of travel, those refugees with the financial wherewithal have the ability to travel by sea or air to more distant lands. Those who manage to reach their destination are often viewed with fear and resentment. Others are kept in a legal limbo.

The exodus of refugees is as old as repression. It was not until 1951, however, that the Office of the U.N. High Commissioner for Refugees was established, principally in response to the large number of refugees fleeing the oppression of Eastern European communist regimes. These refugees were resettled and generally integrated into Western states, aided by sympathy for their plight as well as cultural and ethnic affinities. As a result of this experience, international standards concerning the treatment of refugees were adopted and are reflected in the 1951 U.N. Convention Relating to the Status of Refugees.

This convention states that the international community will treat refugees as a distinct category of human rights victims who should be accorded special protection.

World Actors

In Chapter 1, we raised the issue of "What about individuals in world politics? Can they make a real difference, especially if they are not in a high profile policy position?" An extraordinary individual who has made a significant impact on the world is Dr. Paul Farmer, Harvard professor, infectious-disease specialist, and anthropologist. His life's calling has been to diagnose and cure infectious diseases and bring modern medicine to those who need it most; whether working with the poorest of the poor in Haiti, Peru, Cuba, Russia, or elsewhere, he has widely influenced and motivated many others to follow his philosophy that "the only real nation is humanity." For an excellent biography of Paul Farmer, see Tracy Kidder, Mountains beyond Mountains: The Quest of Dr. Paul Farmer. A Man Who Would Cure the World *(New York: Random House, 2003).*

PAUL FARMER

Afghan refugees return from Pakistan following the fall of the Taliban in 2002. UNHCR/P. Benetar/03.2002

As noted, refugees are defined as people who have been forced for political, racial, or ideological reasons to flee their home countries. According to the Convention, the host nation should not compel refugees to return to their homes if doing so would place them in danger of persecution. Furthermore, refugees have the right to apply for asylum and be given a chance to plead the political nature of their plight. While their appeal is in process, refugees are to be granted adequate assistance. The convention was essentially written with the European case in mind, but since the United Nations was involved, nods were made toward universalizing these norms.

In the 1960s, however, the focus of international efforts began to shift to the Third World, which had been undergoing the pains of decolonization and wars of national liberation. Compared to later years, the early reaction of African states and the international community to the displacement of hundreds of thousands of people went relatively smoothly, in part because many African states shared a common colonial experience. Regional norms for the treatment of refugees were embodied in a 1969 Organization of African Unity agreement, and the 1951 Convention added a protocol in 1967.

In the 1970s, however, the size and complexity of the problem dramatically increased in a manner the signatories of the 1951 Convention could not have foreseen. In terms of sheer numbers, little can match the ten million refugees from East Pakistan in 1971. But with the era of decolonization almost over, political conflicts now involved independent Third World states. Developed countries increasingly looked askance at asylum seekers from countries that had achieved independence years before as well as from countries with no historical ties to a European state. What did the developed world owe to these people? Were these refugees seeking **political asylum,** or were they actually economic refugees or, less charitably, fortune seekers?[23] Could they contribute economically, socially, and culturally to the host nation, or would they simply be a drain on resources?

Such questions and attitudes are found in Europe, which has had to absorb the brunt of refugees resulting from the end-of-Cold-War fall of communism, but they also resonate in immigration debates in the United States and Canada. Downturns in the

---

[23]Jean-Pierre Hocke, "Beyond Humanitarianism," in Gil Loescher and Laila Monahan, eds., Refugees and International Relations (Oxford, England: Clarendon Press, 1990), 39–40.

business cycle marked by sluggish economic growth rates particularly tend to heighten public awareness of the numbers of refugees and legal or illegal immigrants competing with citizens for employment and other opportunities.

An International Regime for Refugees

As noted, the 1951 Convention was the first international and transnational response to the refugee problem. Since that time, basic norms concerning the treatment of refugees have been institutionalized in refugee-receiving nations and also in the complex structure of international and private transnational organizations that attempt to deal with the problem. In other words we can speak of an international regime, or agreed set of rules, for dealing with refugees. As with all such regimes, it requires the support of the major powers that dominate world politics. As such, the norms and programs of the regime effectively cannot run counter to the interests of these key states. The United States, for example, was initially quite suspicious of yielding authority to UNHCR. Over time, however, it has become apparent to most states that the network of international agencies and voluntary organizations is critical if the refugee problem is not going to spin out of control. Unilateral *ad hoc* responses to crisis conditions are deemed unsatisfactory.[24]

Nevertheless, the treatment of refugee groups under this international regime varies widely. A number of factors come into play, all of them involving politics:

- Domestic support for certain refugees in the receiving country
- The publicity the refugees receive
- The financial cost incurred by accepting them
- Foreign policy concerns of the receiving country in terms of the country of origin or other interested countries

During the Cold War, for example, local conflicts drew in outside powers. These conflicts generated large numbers of refugees in the Horn of Africa, southern Africa, and Central America. The United States and other donor countries responded out of humanitarian concern but also for reasons of national interest and broader foreign policy objectives. As the former U.S. Coordinator for Refugee Affairs stated in 1982, refugee policy helped to counter Soviet expansionism because it could be used to "wean away client states from Soviet domination."[25] Similarly, Western Europe welcomed refugees from the Eastern bloc who, by voting with their feet, symbolically demonstrated the bankruptcy of communist regimes in the East. In some cases, such as in Central America, support for refugees went beyond humanitarian assistance and a desire to score propaganda points; refugees were armed and sent back to fight their oppressors. In general, therefore, states will be more positively disposed toward involvement in refugee crises if they believe their interests and foreign policy objectives are at stake—no surprise to a realist.

The interests of the major donors to U.N. programs—the United States, Western Europe, Japan, Australia, and Canada—in particular ultimately decide the nature and extent of the international refugee regime. The UNHCR and voluntary transnational

---

[24]Gil Loescher, "Introduction: Refugee Issues in International Relations," in Loescher and Monahan, eds., *Refugees and International Relations,* 9.

[25]*Ibid.,* 12.

organizations therefore are constrained in what they can do given limited resources.[26] Voluntary organizations in an age of instantaneous global communication, however, can help sway domestic public opinion. This was evident in the case of the conflict and resultant creation in 1995 of refugee camps in Rwanda, Africa. Based upon a cold, hard calculation of U.S. national security interests, there was little reason to expect U.S. relief and logistical support to such a country. The American public and leadership, however, were willing to help, in part due to humanitarian concerns and worldwide appeals on the part of international and transnational refugee-relief organizations. By this time, however, 800,000 Rwandans had been murdered.

It is not only foreign policy considerations that influence the attitude of potential host and donor countries. Refugees can also be created by regimes that want to rid themselves of political dissidents or other undesirables. This was the case in Vietnam's expulsion of hundreds of thousands of Vietnamese of Chinese origin in the early 1980s as well as Fidel Castro's expulsion of criminals and mentally ill people in 1980 during the Mariel boatlift. Once such an action occurs, states may attempt to score political points such as anticommunist states did by accepting the Vietnamese boat people in the 1980s.[27]

The international refugee regime essentially deals with the appropriate responses expected of states, IOs, and NGOs *after* a crisis has occurred. Indeed, the UNHCR's mandate prohibits it from protesting against the cause of refugee outflows, allowing it to respond once refugee flight has happened. Little headway has been made in dealing with the roots of refugee crises, although doing so might help the international community extricate itself from a reactive mode. The problem is evident: to prevent refugee crises may require outside powers to intervene before people flee or are expelled from their country; however, any such interference violates the sovereignty of such states.

Quite apart from legal considerations, in the post–Cold War era the advanced industrial states have relatively little appetite for intervention. This is the case in particular with the Third World, where the West sees few if any vital interests. Yet it is in the Third World that refugee crises will most likely continue to occur. Not just plagued with drought and famine, the Third World is the primary setting for armed conflict. From 1945 to 1990, for example, there were over 100 internal and interstate wars in the Third World. Since 1945, nearly twenty million people have died in wars or as a result of civil strife and the use of force. Out of this total, some 200,000 or about 10 percent occurred in Europe in conflicts such as the Greek civil war in the late 1940s and Soviet military intervention in Hungary in 1956. The rest died from wars in the Third World.[28] Even taking into account the deaths caused by conflicts in the former Yugoslavia and Chechnya in the Russian Federation, interstate wars are primarily a Third World phenomenon, and this is where refugee crises will most likely continue to occur.

It has also been in the Third World where outside interventions have challenged the concept of sovereignty held by political leaders and many analysts of the international state system. In 1991, the U.N. Security Council passed Resolution 688, demanding that the Government of Iraq "allow immediate access by international humanitarian organizations to all those in need of assistance." Subsequent U.N. resolutions and state actions regarding Haiti, Rwanda, and Somalia overrode the principle of

---

[26]*Ibid.*, 9–10.

[27]*Ibid.*, 13.

[28]Steven R. David, "Why the Third World Still Matters," *International Security*, v. 17, no. 3 (Winter 1992/93): 131. See also Guy Arnold, *Wars in the Third World since 1945* (London: Cassell Publishers, 1991).

noninterference in the domestic affairs of states on the legal ground that these conflicts also endangered international peace and security, a condition allowing U.N.–authorized actions consistent with Article 42 of the U.N. Charter. Compared to the Cold War and given their humanitarian concerns, the major powers are now much more willing to acknowledge that events that take place within a country can constitute a threat to regional and international peace and security, although it may be difficult to identify a threat to a particular state's "national security." Notwithstanding difficulties encountered during the U.N. peacekeeping effort in Somalia and the international consensus that the U.N. peacekeeping effort failed to halt the war in the former Yugoslavia, the West still was willing to introduce NATO troops into Bosnia in December 1995 and go to war with Serbia over Kosovo in 1999.

For international and transnational organizations dealing with refugee problems, such concerns over sovereignty issues pale in comparison to the sorts of challenges they face in the post–Cold War international environment. First, refugee crises have increased in number and severity, leading to the understandable perception that the situation is out of control.

Second, traditional solutions and procedures appear to be inadequate in the current environment. For example, voluntary repatriation of refugees to their homes is virtually impossible when the country is plagued by continual war and economic devastation. At the same time, few host countries are willing to allow refugees to take up permanent residence in their countries. In fact, even U.N. officials are now beginning to recognize that the very success of resettling Vietnamese boat people in the 1980s as well as the expensive long-term assistance programs for refugees in Africa have actually made the global situation worse, as states that create refugees believe they have no responsibility for finding viable solutions. For example, what will happen to displaced Muslims and Croats whose land was seized by Serbs, or the Azeris of Nagorno-Karabakh whose territory in the trans-Caucasus region north of Iran and Iraq was seized by neighboring Armenia?

Third, donor states are grumbling over the increasing costs of these humanitarian missions. In one year for example, UNHCR received $1.3 billion in contributions, and this does not include the large sums of money provided to other international organizations such as World Food Programme and the International Committee of the Red Cross nor the money spent by nongovernmental organizations or bilateral state programs.

Finally, the conventional categories used since the early 1950s have proved inadequate to deal with the refugee crises of the current era. Traditionally, humanitarian organizations made fairly rigid distinctions between refugees, returnees, internally displaced persons, and the resident population. But in the border areas of a number of African countries such as Sierra Leone, Ethiopia, and Somalia, people from all four categories live side by side in similarly appalling circumstances. The same situation exists in parts of Bosnia-Herzegovina. In this case the UNHCR, which has always seen itself as an organization concerned with refugees, has provided food and shelter to persons besieged in their own communities. Little has been done to resolve the legal status of displaced persons, some of whom may be able to return to their homes, but thousands of others who cannot or will not return.

Conclusion

Perhaps international human rights efforts and attempts to deal with refugee crises in recent years need to be assessed not so much for what they have accomplished in concrete terms but rather in terms of the contribution to developing a universal consensus on human rights and proper responses in what is still an anarchic world society. The U.N.–sponsored World Conference on Human Rights held in Vienna in 1993, however, illustrated the different interpretations of human rights concepts. In particular, there was an obvious gap between Western norms and those of many developing countries.

The difficulty in pursuing international human rights is particularly evident when it is discussed in the context of some of the other themes addressed in this book. By definition, a concern for human rights raises the basic issue of what the term *sovereignty* means today. If, as we have noted, the internal aspect of sovereignty traditionally has meant that how a state treats its own citizens is a matter of domestic jurisdiction, then criticizing a state on the grounds of human rights violations undermines the concept of sovereignty. Although some states such as China or Myanmar may continue to claim that no state, international organization, or transnational organization has the right to criticize how it treats its dissidents, the reality of the world today is that they do.

The violation of a person's rights due to his or her political beliefs and activities is relatively easy to condemn. In other cases it is not quite as easy. Consider, for example, how the AIDS epidemic in Africa has begun to change the international debate about human rights. AIDS can not only devastate a country's workforce and worsen its economic prospects, it can also weaken its military forces. How far should a state go to prevent the spread of AIDS? In the case of Cuba, for example, mandatory testing, immigration controls, and quarantine were implemented, testing Western human rights precepts about an individual's dignity and privacy. How should a state balance the rights of AIDS or other victims with its concurrent responsibilities for economic and national security? Do foreigners have the right to criticize a state's decision and demand an end to discriminatory policies and proclaim that access to health care and treatment should be a basic human right?

Reconciling diverse interpretations of human rights is not an easy task. Nevertheless we can expect to see continuing efforts to cast human rights and human rights enforcement in global terms. This quest is pursued not just by diplomats but also by such NGOs as Asia Watch, Americas Watch, Human Rights Watch, Amnesty International, and other similarly motivated transnational and domestic interest groups. Even if states are reluctant to act, such NGOs and movements continue to give human rights issues a high profile, contributing to an emerging global civil society. Assuming such trends continue, the idea that basic human rights of individuals are not the exclusive domain of a state but also are a legitimate concern of the larger international community will continue to be strengthened.

Afterword

Morality and Politics
Immanuel Kant
(1724–1804)

Kant stands as one of the strongest philosophical advocates of morality in politics in general and human rights in particular. In this brief excerpt appended to a much larger argument on the ways and means of Perpetual Peace, *Kant rejects the idea that expediency—what is practical or pragmatic—in politics must displace moral principle in either domestic or international politics. In this passage he underscores the importance of human rights, asserting that "the rights of men must be held sacred, however much sacrifice it may cost the ruling power." Kant's critics call his approach utopian. For his part, the late British writer Edward Hallett Carr wrote in his now classic* The Twenty Years' Crisis, 1919-1939 *of the seemingly ceaseless tension policy-makers necessarily face between the power and interest of realist politics, on the one hand, and the moral or ideal on the other. Italics have been added to the excerpt below to underscore key points in Kant's statement on moral principle and human rights. The complete essay from which these shortened paragraphs are drawn may be found readily on the web or in Immanuel Kant,* Perpetual Peace, *Ed. Lewis White Beck (Indianapolis and New York: Bobbs-Merrill Company, 1957).*

Taken objectively, *morality is in itself practical*, being the totality of unconditionally mandatory laws according to which we ought to act. . . . There can be no conflict of politics, as a practical doctrine of right, with ethics, as a theoretical doctrine of right. . . .

  Politics says, "Be ye wise as serpents"; morality adds, as a limiting condition, "and guileless as doves." If these two injunctions are incompatible in a single command, then politics and morality are really in conflict; but if these two qualities ought always to be united, the thought of contrariety is absurd, and the question as to how the conflict between morals and politics is to be resolved cannot even be posed as a problem. Although the proposition, "Honesty is the best policy," implies a theory which practice unfortunately often refutes, the equally theoretical "Honesty is better than any policy" is beyond refutation and is indeed the indispensable condition of policy. . . .

  True politics can never take a step without rendering homage to morality. Though politics by itself is a difficult art, its union with morality is no art at all, for this union cuts the knot which politics could not untie when they were in conflict. *The rights of men must be held sacred*, however much sacrifice it may cost the ruling power. *One cannot compromise here and seek the middle course of a pragmatic conditional law between the morally right and the expedient. All politics must bend its knee before the right.* But by this it can hope slowly to reach the stage where it will shine with an immortal glory.

Appendices

Human Rights, Humanitarian Law, and the Treatment of Prisoners and Detainees

We include below two documents relating to treatment of human beings who may find themselves caught in the midst of war or various forms of civil strife. The first of these documents is the preamble and opening articles binding on states party to the international convention prohibiting torture and other forms of inhumane treatment. As in warfare, in a period of similarly high insecurity due to terrorist acts, governments may be drawn to using torture as a tactic in interrogations of prisoners and other detainees. Notwithstanding the high premium placed on securing information intended to prevent recurrence of such attacks, the anti-torture convention makes clear that any such use of "ends justify the means" argumentation is contrary to international law. Excerpts from the second document—the Fourth Geneva Convention (1949)—specify how civilians caught in conflicts are to be treated humanely. (The other three of the 1949 Geneva conventions focus on humane treatment of members of the armed forces—prisoners of war, the wounded, sick, and shipwrecked.)

Convention Against Torture and Other Cruel, Inhuman or Degrading Treatment or Punishment

The States Parties to this Convention,

Considering that, in accordance with the principles proclaimed in the Charter of the United Nations, recognition of the equal and inalienable rights of all members of the human family is the foundation of freedom, justice and peace in the world,

Recognizing that those rights derive from the inherent dignity of the human person, Considering the obligation of States under the Charter, in particular Article 55, to promote universal respect for, and observance of, human rights and fundamental freedoms,

Having regard to article 5 of the Universal Declaration of Human Rights and article 7 of the International Covenant on Civil and Political Rights, both of which provide that no one may be subjected to torture or to cruel, inhuman or degrading treatment or punishment,

Having regard also to the Declaration on the Protection of All Persons from Being Subjected to Torture and Other Cruel, Inhuman or Degrading Treatment or Punishment, adopted by the General Assembly on 9 December 1975 (resolution 3452),

Desiring to make more effective the struggle against torture and other cruel, inhuman or degrading treatment or punishment throughout the world,

Have agreed as follows:

Article 1

1.   For the purposes of this Convention, *torture means any act by which severe pain or suffering, whether physical or mental, is intentionally inflicted on a person for such purposes as obtaining from him or a third person information or a confession, punishing him for an act he or a third person has committed or is suspected of having committed, or intimidating or coercing him or a third person, or for any reason based on discrimination of any kind, when such pain or suffering is inflicted by or at the instigation of or with the consent or acquiescence of a public official or other person acting in an official capacity.* It does not include pain or suffering arising only from, inherent in or incidental to lawful sanctions.

2.   This article is without prejudice to any international instrument or national legislation which does or may contain provisions of wider application.

Article 2

1.   Each State Party shall take effective legislative, administrative, judicial or other measures to prevent acts of torture in any territory under its jurisdiction.

2.   *No exceptional circumstances whatsoever, whether a state of war or a threat or war, internal political instability or any other public emergency, may be invoked as a justification of torture.*

3.   An order from a superior officer or a public authority may not be invoked as a justification of torture.

Article 3

1.   *No State Party shall expel, return . . . or extradite a person to another State where there are substantial grounds for believing that he would be in danger of being subjected to torture.*

2.   For the purpose of determining whether there are such grounds, the competent authorities shall take into account all relevant considerations including, where applicable, the existence in the State concerned of a consistent pattern of gross, flagrant or mass violations of human rights.

Article 4

1.   Each State Party shall ensure that all acts of torture are offences under its criminal law. The same shall apply to an attempt to commit torture and to an act by any person which constitutes complicity or participation in torture.

2.   Each State Party shall make these offences punishable by appropriate penalties which take into account their grave nature.

Article 5

Each State Party shall take such measures as may be necessary to establish its jurisdiction over the offences referred to in article 4. . . .

Geneva Convention IV

Relative to the Protection of Civilian Persons in Time of War (1949)

The undersigned Plenipotentiaries . . . for the purpose of establishing a Convention for the Protection of Civilians in Time of War, have agreed as follows:. . .

Article 2   In addition to the provisions which shall be implemented in peace-time, *the present Convention shall apply to all cases of declared war or of any other armed conflict which may arise between two or more of the High Contracting Parties, even if the state of war is not recognized by one of them. The Convention shall also apply to all cases of partial or total occupation of the territory of a High Contracting Party, even if the said occupation meets with no armed resistance. . . .*

Article 3   In the case of armed conflict not of an international character occurring in the territory of one of the High Contracting Parties, each Party to the conflict shall be bound to apply, as a minimum, the following provisions: (1) *Persons taking no active part in the hostilities*, including members of armed forces who have laid down their arms and those placed hors de combat by sickness, wounds, detention, or any other cause, *shall in all circumstances be treated humanely, without any adverse distinction founded on race, colour, religion or faith, sex, birth or wealth, or any other similar criteria.* To this end *the following acts are and shall remain prohibited* at any time and in any place whatsoever with respect to the above-mentioned persons: (a) *violence to life and person*, in particular murder of all kinds, mutilation, cruel treatment and torture; (b) *taking of hostages*; (c) *outrages upon personal dignity, in particular humiliating and degrading treatment*; (d) the passing of sentences and the carrying out of executions without previous judgment pronounced by a regularly constituted court, affording all the judicial guarantees which are recognized as indispensable by civilized peoples. (2) The wounded and sick shall be collected and cared for. An impartial humanitarian body, such as the International Committee of the Red Cross, may offer its services to the Parties to the conflict. . . .

Article 4   *Persons protected by the Convention are those who, at a given moment and in any manner whatsoever, find themselves, in case of a conflict or occupation, in the hands of a Party to the conflict or Occupying Power of which they are not nationals. . . .*

Article 5   Where in the territory of a Party to the conflict, the latter is satisfied that an individual protected person is definitely suspected of or engaged in activities hostile to the security of the State, such individual person shall not be entitled to claim such rights and privileges under the present Convention as would, if exercised in the favour of such individual person, be prejudicial to the security of such State. Where in occupied territory an individual protected person is detained as a spy or saboteur, or as a person under definite suspicion of activity hostile to the security of the Occupying Power, such person shall, in those cases where absolute military security so requires, be regarded as having forfeited rights of communication under the present

Convention. In each case, *such persons shall nevertheless be treated with humanity and*, in case of trial, *shall not be deprived of the rights of fair and regular trial* prescribed by the present Convention. They shall also be granted the full rights and privileges of a protected person under the present Convention at the earliest date consistent with security of State or Occupying Power. . . .

Article 10   The provisions of the present Convention constitute no obstacle to the humanitarian activities which the International Committee of the Red Cross or any other impartial humanitarian organization may, subject to the consent of the Parties to the conflict concerned, undertake for the protection of civilian persons and for their relief.

Article 30   *Protected persons shall have every facility for making application to the Protecting Powers, the International Committee of the Red Cross, the National Red Cross (Red Crescent, Red Lion and Sun) Society of the country where they may be, as well as to any organization that might assist them.* These several organizations shall be granted all facilities for that purpose by the authorities, within the bounds set by military or security considerations. Apart from the visits of the delegates of the Protecting Powers and of the International Committee of the Red Cross . . . the Detaining or Occupying Powers shall facilitate, as much as possible, visits to protected persons by the representatives of other organizations whose object is to give spiritual aid or material relief to such persons.

Article 31   *No physical or moral coercion shall be exercised* against protected persons, in particular *to obtain information* from them or from third parties.

Article 32   *The High Contracting Parties specifically agree that each of them is prohibited from taking any measure of such a character as to cause the physical suffering or extermination of protected persons* in their hands. *This prohibition applies not only to murder, torture, corporal punishments, mutilation and medical or scientific experiments not necessitated by the medical treatment of a protected person, but also to any other measures of brutality whether applied by civilian or military agents.*

Article 33   No protected person may be punished for an offence he or she has not personally committed. Collective penalties and likewise all measures of intimidation or of terrorism are prohibited. Pillage is prohibited. Reprisals against protected persons and their property are prohibited.

Article 34   The taking of hostages is prohibited.

Article 37   Protected persons who are confined pending proceedings or subject to a sentence involving loss of liberty, shall during their confinement be humanely treated. . . .

Article 38   With the exception of special measures authorized by the present Convention . . . the situation of protected persons shall continue to be regulated, in principle, by the provisions concerning aliens in time of peace. In any case, the following rights shall be granted to them (1) they shall be enabled to receive the individual or collective relief that may be sent to them. (2) they shall, if their state of health so requires, receive medical attention and hospital treatment to the same extent as the nationals of the State concerned. (3) they shall be allowed to practise their religion and to receive spiritual assistance from ministers of their faith. (4) if they reside in an area particularly exposed to the dangers of war, they shall be authorized to move from that area to the same extent as the nationals of the State concerned. (5) children under fifteen years, pregnant women and mothers of children under seven years shall benefit by any preferential treatment to the same extent as the nationals of the State concerned.

Article 42   The internment or placing in assigned residence of protected persons may be ordered only if the security of the Detaining Power makes it absolutely necessary. If any person, acting through the representatives of the Protecting Power, voluntarily demands internment, and if his situation renders this step necessary, he shall be interned by the Power in whose hands he may be.

Article 43   Any protected person who has been interned or placed in assigned residence shall be entitled to have such action reconsidered as soon as possible by an appropriate court or administrative board designated by the Detaining Power for that purpose. . . .

Article 71   No sentence shall be pronounced by the competent courts of the Occupying Power except after a regular trial. Accused persons who are prosecuted by the Occupying Power shall be promptly informed, in writing, in a language which they understand, of the particulars of the charges preferred against them, and shall be brought to trial as rapidly as possible. . . .

Article 72   Accused persons shall have the right to present evidence necessary to their defence and may, in particular, call witnesses. They shall have the right to be assisted by a qualified advocate or counsel of their own choice, who shall be able to visit them freely and shall enjoy the necessary facilities for preparing the defence. Failing a choice by the accused, the Protecting Power may provide him with an advocate or counsel. . . .

Article 73   A convicted person shall have the right of appeal provided for by the laws applied by the court. He shall be fully informed of his right to appeal or petition and of the time limit within which he may do so. . . .

Article 80   Internees shall retain their full civil capacity and shall exercise such attendant rights as may be compatible with their status.

Article 84   Internees shall be accommodated and administered separately from prisoners of war and from persons deprived of liberty for any other reason.

Magna Carta (1215)

His barons and members of clergy in revolt over costly, unsuccessful military ventures and other grievances, England's King John finally agreed to grant them certain rights in a formal document written in Latin and known as the Magna Carta, which he signed in the year 1215. Most of its sixty-three articles deal with issues important at the time—for example, provision for "standard measures of wine, ale, and corn" or prohibition against taking "wood for our castle, or for any other purpose, without the consent of the owner."

Included among the clauses in this selection, however, are a few that have had lasting significance as part of the foundation of rights and liberties that have been reaffirmed in succeeding centuries and in other countries around the world. Rights to trial, due process of law, and equitable punishment for offenses are among those addressed. Importantly, these rights were not just reserved to a few, but were extended to subjects throughout the kingdom.

John, by the grace of God King of England, Lord of Ireland, Duke of Normandy and Aquitaine, and Count of Anjou, to his archbishops, abbots, earls, barons, justices, foresters, sheriffs, stewards, servants, and to all his officials and loyal subjects, Greeting.

Know that before God . . .

(1) We have granted . . . that the English Church shall be free, and shall have its rights undiminished, and its liberties unimpaired. . . .

(2) The city of London shall enjoy all its ancient liberties and free customs, both by land and water. We also will and grant that all other cities, boroughs, towns, and ports shall enjoy all their liberties and free customs. . . .

(3) Ordinary lawsuits shall not follow the royal court around, but shall be held in a fixed place. . . .

(4) For a trivial offense, a free man shall be fined only in proportion to the degree of his offense, and for a serious offense correspondingly. . . .

(5) Earls and barons shall be fined only by their equals, and in proportion to the gravity of their offense. . . .

(6) If a free man dies intestate [that is, without a will], his movable goods are to be distributed by his next-of-kin and friends, under the supervision of the Church. The rights of his debtors are to be preserved. . . .

(7) In future no official shall place a man on trial upon his own unsupported statement, without producing credible witnesses to the truth of it. . . .

(8) No free man shall be seized or imprisoned, or stripped of his rights or possessions, or outlawed or exiled, or deprived of his standing in any other way, nor will we proceed with force against him, or send others to do so, except by the lawful judgment of his equals or by the law of the land.

(9) To no one will we sell, to no one deny or delay right or justice. . . .

(10) We will appoint as justices, constables, sheriffs, or other officials, only men that know the law of the realm and are minded to keep it well. . . .

(11) To any man whom we have deprived or dispossessed of lands, castles, liberties, or rights, without the lawful judgments of his equals, we will at once restore these. . . .

(12) All fines that have been given to us unjustly and against the law of the land, and all fines that we have exacted unjustly, shall be entirely remitted. . . .

(13) All these customs and liberties that we have granted shall be observed in our kingdom in so far as concerns our own relations with our subjects. Let all men of our kingdom, whether clergy or laymen, observe them similarly in their relations with their own men. . . .

(14) It is accordingly our wish and command that the English Church shall be free, and that men in our kingdom shall have and keep all these liberties, rights, and concessions, well and peaceably in their fullness and entirety for them and their heirs, of us and our heirs, in all things and all places forever. . . .

Given by our hand in the meadow that is called Runnymede, between Windsor and Staines, on the fifteenth day of June in the seventeenth year of our reign [that is, A.D. 1215].

Declaration of the Rights of Man and of Citizens (1789)

The liberal character of the French Revolution at its outset is captured in this document. Reflecting a continental European tradition, the list of rights goes beyond individual liberties to focus on equality, adding a communal dimension. Thomas Paine's Rights of Man (1791), written in opposition to Edmund Burke's criticisms of the French Revolution, actively promoted these ideas in the United States as well as in England.

. . . The National Assembly doth recognise and declare . . . the following sacred rights of men and of citizens:

(1) Men are born, and always continue, free and equal in respect of their rights. Civil distinctions, therefore, can be founded only on public utility.

(2) The end of all political associations is the preservation of the natural and imprescriptable rights of man; and these rights are liberty, property, security, and resistance of oppression.

(3) The nation is essentially the source of all sovereignty; nor can any individual, or any body of men, be entitled to any authority which is not expressly derived from it.

(4) Political liberty consists in the power of doing whatever does not injure another. The exercise of the natural rights of every man has no other limits than those which are necessary to secure to every other man the free exercise of the same rights; and these rights are determinable only by the law.

(5) The law ought to prohibit only actions hurtful to society. What is not prohibited by the law should not be hindered; nor should anyone be compelled to that which the law does not require.

(6) The law is an expression of the will of the community. All citizens have a right to concur, either personally or by their representatives, in its formation. It should be the same to all, whether it protects or punishes; and all being equal in its sight, are equally eligible to all honours, places, and employments, according to their different abilities, without any other distinction than that created by their virtue and talents.

(7) No man should be accused, arrested, or held in confinement, except in cases determined by the law, and according to the forms which it has prescribed. All who promote, solicit, execute, or cause to be executed, arbitrary orders, ought to be punished, and every citizen called upon, or apprehended by virtue of the law, ought immediately to obey, and renders himself culpable by resistance.

(8) The law ought to impose no other penalties but such as are absolutely and evidently necessary; and no one ought to be punished, but in virtue of a law promulgated before the offence, and legally applied.

(9) Every man being presumed innocent till he has been convicted, whenever his detention becomes indispensable, all rigour to him, more than is necessary to secure his person, ought to be provided against by the law.

(10) No man ought to be molested on account of his opinions, not even on account of his religious opinions, provided his avowal of them does not disturb the public order established by the law.

(11) The unrestrained communication of thoughts and opinions being one of the most precious rights of man, every citizen may speak, write, and publish freely, provided he is responsible for the abuse of this liberty, in cases determined by the law.

(12) A public force being necessary to give security to the rights of men and of citizens, that force is instituted for the benefit of the community and not for the particular benefit of the persons to whom it is intrusted.

(13) A common contribution being necessary for the support of the public force, and for defraying the other expenses of government, it ought to be divided equally among the members of the community, according to their abilities.

(14) Every citizen has a right, either by himself or his representative, to a free voice in determining the necessity of public contributions, the appropriation of them, and their amount, mode of assessment, and duration.

(15) Every community has a right to demand of all its agents an account of their conduct.

(16) Every community in which a separation of powers and a security of rights is not provided for, wants a constitution.

(17) The right to property being inviolable and sacred, no one ought to be deprived of it, except in cases of evident public necessity, legally ascertained, and on condition of a previous just indemnity.

The U.S. Bill of Rights (1791)

The English Bill of Rights was composed in 1689, a year after William and Mary assumed the crown upon Parliament's invitation in what is commonly referred to as the Glorious (and bloodless) Revolution. The monarchy, however, was subject to certain limitations set down by Parliament, which had at last established its supremacy. Moreover, the civil and political rights of Englishmen that had evolved since the Magna Carta were reaffirmed in this document. As British subjects prior to the revolution of

1776–1783, the American constitutional framers brought this liberal English civil and political rights tradition to their deliberations, incorporating constitutional limitations on governing authority.

Thomas Jefferson and others lobbied for the addition of a Bill of Rights to the U.S. Constitution, which was ratified and went into effect in 1789. In addition to these first ten amendments are excerpts of three others ratified after the U.S. Civil War and three more ratified in the twentieth century as a more inclusive statement of civil rights and liberties to which American citizens as individuals are constitutionally entitled.

(1) Congress shall make no law respecting an establishment of religion, or prohibiting the free exercise thereof; or abridging the freedom of speech, or of the press; or the right of the people peaceably to assemble, and to petition the Government for a redress of grievances.

(2) A well regulated Militia, being necessary to the security of a free State, the right of the people to keep and bear Arms, shall not be infringed.

(3) No Soldier shall, in time of peace be quartered in any house, without the consent of the Owner, nor in time of war, but in a manner to be prescribed by law.

(4) The right of the people to be secure in their persons, houses, papers, and effects, against unreasonable searches and seizures, shall not be violated, and no Warrants shall issue, but upon probable cause, supported by Oath or affirmation, and particularly describing the place to be searched, and the persons or things to be seized.

(5) No person shall be held to answer for a capital, or otherwise infamous crime, unless on a presentment or indictment of a Grand Jury, except in cases arising in the land or naval forces, or in the Militia, when in actual service in time of War or public danger; nor shall any person be subject for the same offence to be twice put in jeopardy of life or limb; nor shall be compelled in a criminal case to be a witness against himself, nor be deprived of life, liberty, or property, without due process of law; nor shall private property be taken for public use, without just compensation.

(6) In all criminal prosecutions, the accused shall enjoy the right to a speedy and public trial, by an impartial jury of the State and district wherein the crime shall have been committed, which district shall have been previously ascertained by law, and to be informed of the nature and cause of the accusation; to be confronted with the witnesses against him; to have compulsory process for obtaining witnesses in his favor, and to have the Assistance of Counsel for his defence.

(7) In Suits at common law, where the value in controversy shall exceed twenty dollars, the right of trial by jury shall be preserved, and no fact tried by jury, shall be otherwise re-examined in any Court of the United States, than according to the rules of the common law.

(8) Excessive bail shall not be required, nor excessive fines imposed, nor cruel and unusual punishments inflicted.

(9) The enumeration in the Constitution, of certain rights, shall not be construed to deny or disparage others retained by the people.

(10) The powers not delegated to the United States by the Constitution, nor prohibited by it to the States, are reserved to the States respectively, or to the people.

* * *

(13) [1865] . . . Neither slavery nor involuntary servitude, except as a punishment for crime whereof the party shall have been duly convicted, shall exist within the United States, or any place subject to their jurisdiction. . . .

(14) [1868] . . . All persons born or naturalized in the United States, and subject to the jurisdiction thereof, are citizens of the United States and of the State wherein they reside. No State shall make or enforce any law which shall abridge the privileges or immunities of citizens of the United States; nor shall any State deprive any person of life, liberty, or

property, without due process of law; nor deny to any person within its jurisdiction the equal protection of the laws. . . .

(15) [1870] . . . The right of citizens of the United States to vote shall not be denied or abridged by the United States or by any State on account of race, color, or previous condition of servitude. . . .

(19) [1920] . . . The right of citizens of the United States to vote shall not be denied or abridged by the United States or by any State on account of sex. . . .

(24) [1964] . . . The right of citizens of the United States to vote . . . shall not be denied or abridged by the United States or any State by reason of failure to pay any poll tax or other tax. . . .

(26) [1971] . . . The right of citizens of the United States, who are eighteen years of age or older, to vote shall not be denied or abridged by the United States or by any State on account of age. . . .

Universal Declaration of Human Rights

Adopted by the U.N. General Assembly Resolution 217A (III) of 10 December 1948

Preamble

Whereas recognition of the inherent dignity and of the equal and inalienable rights of all members of the human family is the foundation of freedom, justice and peace in the world,

Whereas disregard and contempt for human rights have resulted in barbarous acts which have outraged the conscience of mankind, and the advent of a world in which human beings shall enjoy freedom of speech and belief and freedom from fear and want has been proclaimed as the highest aspiration of the common people,

Whereas it is essential, if man is not to be compelled to have recourse, as a last resort, to rebellion against tyranny and oppression, that human rights should be protected by the rule of law,

Whereas it is essential to promote the development of friendly relations between nations,

Whereas the peoples of the United Nations have in the Charter reaffirmed their faith in fundamental human rights, in the dignity and worth of the human person and in the equal rights of men and women and have determined to promote social progress and better standards of life in larger freedom,

Whereas Member States have pledged themselves to achieve, in cooperation with the United Nations, the promotion of universal respect for and observance of human rights and fundamental freedoms,

Whereas a common understanding of these rights and freedoms is of the greatest importance for the full realization of this pledge,

Now, therefore,

The General Assembly,

Proclaims this Universal Declaration of Human Rights as a common standard of achievement for all peoples and all nations, to the end that every individual and every organ of society, keeping this Declaration constantly in mind, shall strive by teaching and education to promote respect for these rights and freedoms and by progressive measures, national and international, to secure their universal and effective recognition and observance, both among the peoples of Member States themselves and among the peoples of territories under their jurisdiction.

Article 1

All human beings are born free and equal in dignity and rights. They are endowed with reason and conscience and should act towards one another in a spirit of brotherhood.

Article 2

Everyone is entitled to all the rights and freedoms set forth in this Declaration, without distinction of any kind, such as race, colour, sex, language, religion, political or other opinion, national or social origin, property, birth or other status.

Furthermore, no distinction shall be made on the basis of the political, jurisdictional or international status of the country or territory to which a person belongs, whether it be independent, trust, non-self-governing or under any other limitation of sovereignty.

Article 3

Everyone has the right to life, liberty and security of person.

Article 4

No one shall be held in slavery or servitude; slavery and the slave trade shall be prohibited in all their forms.

Article 5

No one shall be subjected to torture or to cruel, inhuman or degrading treatment or punishment.

Article 6

Everyone has the right to recognition everywhere as a person before the law.

Article 7

All are equal before the law and are entitled without any discrimination to equal protection of the law. All are entitled to equal protection against any discrimination in violation of this Declaration and against any incitement to such discrimination.

Article 8

Everyone has the right to an effective remedy by the competent national tribunals for acts violating the fundamental rights granted him by the constitution or by law.

Article 9

No one shall be subjected to arbitrary arrest, detention or exile.

Article 10

Everyone is entitled in full equality to a fair and public hearing by an independent and impartial tribunal, in the determination of his rights and obligations and of any criminal charge against him.

Article 11

1. Everyone charged with a penal offence has the right to be presumed innocent until proved guilty according to law in a public trial at which he has had all the guarantees necessary for his defence.
2. No one shall be held guilty of any penal offence on account of any act or omission which did not constitute a penal offence, under national or international law, at the time when it was committed. Nor shall a heavier penalty be imposed than the one that was applicable at the time the penal offence was committed.

Article 12

No one shall be subjected to arbitrary interference with his privacy, family, home or correspondence, nor to attacks upon his honour and reputation. Everyone has the right to the protection of the law against such interference or attacks.

Article 13

1. Everyone has the right to freedom of movement and residence within the borders of each State.
2. Everyone has the right to leave any country, including his own, and to return to his country.

Article 14

1. Everyone has the right to seek and to enjoy in other countries asylum from persecution.
2. This right may not be invoked in the case of prosecutions genuinely arising from non-political crimes or from acts contrary to the purposes and principles of the United Nations.

Article 15

1. Everyone has the right to a nationality.
2. No one shall be arbitrarily deprived of his nationality nor denied the right to change his nationality.

Article 16

1. Men and women of full age, without any limitations due to race, nationality or religion, have the right to marry and to found a family. They are entitled to equal rights as to marriage, during marriage and at its dissolution.
2. Marriage shall be entered into only with the free and full consent of the intending spouses.
3. The family is the natural and fundamental group of society and is entitled to protection by society and the State.

Article 17

1. Everyone has the right to own property alone as well as in association with others.
2. No one shall be arbitrarily deprived of his property.

Article 18

Everyone has the right to freedom of thought, conscience and religion; this right includes freedom to change his religion or belief, and freedom, either alone or in community with others and in public or private, to manifest his religion or belief in teaching, practice, worship and observance.

Article 19

Everyone has the right to freedom of opinion and expression; this right includes freedom to hold opinions without interference and to seek, receive and impart information and ideas through any media and regardless of frontiers.

Article 20

1. Everyone has the right to freedom of peaceful assembly and association.
2. No one may be compelled to belong to an association.

Article 21

1. Everyone has the right to take part in the government of his country, directly or through freely chosen representatives.

2. Everyone has the right to equal access to public service in his country.
3. The will of the people shall be the basis of the authority of government; this will shall be expressed in periodic and genuine elections which shall be by universal suffrage and shall be held by secret vote or by equivalent free voting procedures.

Article 22

Everyone, as a member of society, has the right to social security and is entitled to realization, through national effort and international co-operation and in accordance with the organization and resources of each State, of the economic, social and cultural rights indispensable for his dignity and the free development of his personality.

Article 23

1. Everyone has the right to work, to free choice of employment, to just and favourable conditions of work and to protection against unemployment.
2. Everyone, without any discrimination, has the right to equal pay for equal work.
3. Everyone who works has the right to just and favourable remuneration ensuring for himself and his family an existence worthy of human dignity, and supplemented, if necessary, by other means of social protection.
4. Everyone has the right to form and to join trade unions for the protection of his interests.

Article 24

Everyone has the right to rest and leisure, including reasonable limitation of working hours and periodic holidays with pay.

Article 25

1. Everyone has the right to a standard of living adequate for the health and well-being of himself and of his family, including food, clothing, housing and medical care and necessary social services, and the right to security in the event of unemployment, sickness, disability, widowhood, old age or other lack of livelihood in circumstances beyond his control.
2. Motherhood and childhood are entitled to special care and assistance. All children, whether born in or out of wedlock, shall enjoy the same social protection.

Article 26

1. Everyone has the right to education. Education shall be free, at least in the elementary and fundamental stages. Elementary education shall be compulsory. Technical and professional education shall be made generally available and higher education shall be equally accessible to all on the basis of merit.
2. Education shall be directed to the full development of the human personality and to the strengthening of respect for human rights and fundamental freedoms. It shall promote understanding, tolerance and friendship among all nations, racial or religious groups, and shall further the activities of the United Nations for the maintenance of peace.
3. Parents have a prior right to choose the kind of education that shall be given to their children.

Article 27

1. Everyone has the right freely to participate in the cultural life of his community, to enjoy the arts and to share in scientific advancement and its benefits.
2. Everyone has the right to the protection of the moral and material interests resulting from any scientific, literary or artistic production of which he is the author.

Article 28

Everyone is entitled to a social and international order in which the rights and freedoms set forth in this Declaration can be fully realized.

Article 29

1. Everyone has duties to the community in which alone the free and full development of his personality is possible.
2. In the exercise of his rights and freedoms, everyone shall be subject only to such limitations as are determined by law solely for the purpose of securing due recognition and respect for the rights and freedoms of others and of meeting the just requirements of morality, public order and the general welfare in a democratic society.
3. These rights and freedoms may in no case be exercised contrary to the purposes and principles of the United Nations.

Article 30

Nothing in this Declaration may be interpreted as implying for any State, group or person any right to engage in any activity or to perform any act aimed at the destruction of any of the rights and freedoms set forth herein.

Key Terms

libertarian   p. 497
liberal   p. 497

genocide   p. 503
positivism   p. 505

migration   p. 515
refugees   p. 515

Other Concepts

welfare   p. 496
supranational   p. 496
communitarian   p. 496
individualism   p. 497
conservative   p. 498
equal protection   p. 498
eminent domain   p. 499

due process   p. 500
cultural relativism   p. 500
social-liberal   p. 502
categorical imperatives   p. 503
utilitarian   p. 504
natural rights   p. 504
social contract   p. 504

civil rights   p. 504
customary international
   law   p. 506
compassion fatigue   p. 517
political asylum   p. 518

Additional Readings

Political essays, speeches, and documents on human rights may be found in Micheline R. Ishay (ed.), *The Human Rights Reader* (London and New York: Routledge, 1997). See also her more recent *History of Human Rights: From Ancient Times to the Globalization Era* (Berkeley: University of California Press, 2005). For a discussion of the evolution of human rights regimes, see Jack Donnelly, *Universal Human Rights in Theory and Practice,* 2nd ed. (Ithaca, NY: Cornell University Press, 1989, 2003) as well as his *International Human Rights,* 2nd ed. (Boulder, Co: Westview Press, 1993, 1997).

Other general works on human rights include Tim Dunne and Nicholas J. Wheeler, *Human Rights in Global Politics* (Cambridge: Cambridge University Press, 1999), Claude E. Welch, Jr., *Protecting Human Rights in Africa: Strategies and Roles of Nongovernmental Organizations* (Philadelphia: University of Pennsylvania Press, 1995), and Thomas Pogge, *World Poverty and Human Rights* (Cambridge, UK: Polity Press, 2002).

On the role of the United Nations, see Philip Alston, ed., *The United Nations and Human Rights* (New York: Oxford University Press, 1992) and Johannes Morsink, *The Universal Declaration of Human Rights: Origins, Drafting and Intent* (Philadelphia: University of Pennsylvania Press, 1999). See also Paul Gordon Lauren, *The Evolution of International Human Rights: Visions Seen* (Philadelphia: University of Pennsylvania Press, 1998). For a world view that sees human rights as a core element of global politics, see Richard Falk, *On Humane Governance* (University Park: Pennsylvania State University Press, 1995). A quick overview of international law on human rights is Thomas Buergenthal, *International Human Rights in a Nutshell,* 3rd ed. (St. Paul, MN: West Publishing Co., 1995, 2002). On NGOs see William Korey, *NGOs and the Universal Declaration of Human Rights: A Curious Grapevine* (New York: St. Martin's, 1998).

Lectures delivered at Oxford University on human rights related to religion, cross-cultural and comparative perspectives, gender, and other topics are in Olwen Hufton (ed.), *Historical Change and Human Rights* (New York: Basic Books, 1995). A classic treatment of the subject rooted in political philosophy that deals with the public and private realms, work, dignity, and various human activities is Hannah Arendt, *The Human Condition* (Chicago: University of Chicago Press, 1958). On refugees the UNHCR Web site [www.unhcr.ch] provides up-to-date information, statistics, and the magazine *Refugees*. On human rights, see also the UNHCHR Web site (www.unhchr.ch).

On human rights and humanitarian law in wartime, see Jackson Nyamuya Maogoto, *War Crimes and Realpolitik* (Boulder, CO: Lynne Rienner, 2004), Iris Chang, *The Rape of Nanking: The Forgotten Holocaust of World War II* (New York: Penguin, 1997), on the international criminal tribunal in the former Yugoslavia, Pierre Hazan, *Justice in a Time of War*, trans. James Thomas Snyder (College Station: Texas A&M Press, 2004), and Danilo Zolo, *Invoking Humanity: War, Law and Global Order* (London and New York: Continuum, 2000, 2002). The moral hazards of military privatization—moving many military functions to the private sector—are treated in P. W. Singer, *Corporate Warriors: The Rise of the Privatized Military Industry* (Ithaca, NY: Cornell University Press, 2003).

Human trafficking is discussed in David Kyle and Rey Koslowski, *Global Human Smuggling* (Baltimore, MD: Johns Hopkins University Press, 2001). On torture, see Karen J. Greenberg and Joshua L. Dratel, *The Torture Papers: The Road to Abu Ghraib* (Cambridge: Cambridge University Press, 2005), Sanford Levinson, *Torture: A Collection* (Oxford, UK: Oxford University Press, 2004), Mark Danner, *Torture and Truth: America, Abu Ghraib, and the War on Terror* (New York: New York Review of Books, 2004), and Geoffrey Robertson, *Crimes Against Humanity: The Struggle for Global Justice,* rev. ed. (New York: The New Press, 1999).

Chapter 16

Questions in Lieu of Conclusions

Final Words

We end where we began. When the communist hammer-and-sickle flag was lowered from the Kremlin on December 25, 1991, there was a dramatic increase in speculation on the future of international relations and world politics. Such efforts included newspaper pundits and political leaders as well as scholars. Given the failure of seasoned observers to foresee the end of the Cold War, one would have thought that humility might have kept these same crystal-ball gazers from prognosticating about world politics in the twenty-first century. History has a way of confounding our best efforts to divine what lies ahead.

After World War I, for example, optimists thought that interstate war could be banished through such mechanisms as collective security. They were tragically wrong. Pessimists thought that the Cold War would end in a hot war—a catastrophic nuclear exchange between the United States and the Soviet Union. Fortunately they too were wrong. In fact in most cases straight-line extrapolations of current trends are generally incorrect.

More generally, nineteenth-century techno-optimists, looking toward the twentieth century, anticipated the marvels that applied science and technology would achieve. These marvels turned out to be a mixed blessing. Mobilizing the machinery of industrial capitalism certainly has brought great rewards, empowering individuals and groups and providing higher standards of living for many. On the other hand, economic development has had heavy environmental and social costs as well. Industrialization and new technologies also have produced armed forces ever more destructive, raising the human costs of warfare to an unprecedented, terribly high level, making the twentieth century (especially during the two world wars in the first half) the bloodiest and most destructive period in human history.

In this concluding chapter, we resist the temptation to make specific predictions about the twenty-first century. Instead, we pose a series of questions for the reader's consideration, in some cases providing speculative answers as seen through the perspectives or lenses of realists, pluralists or liberals, economic structuralists, and, where applicable, scholars in the English School, social constructivists, and feminists.

Is the world becoming a more peaceful or a more violent place?

The answer depends on the part of the world toward which one is looking. In terms of interstate relations, large parts of Europe certainly have become a zone of peace. It is hard to imagine an interstate war breaking out. The historical antagonisms of France, Germany, and Great Britain are simply that—historical. As pluralists or liberals have argued, the logic of regional integration has been played out in the ever-expanding European Union. Violent conflict in Europe has been most evident outside the European Union in the Russian Federation (Chechnya) and during the 1990s in the former Yugoslavia. The true test of the stability of Europe may be if an economic recession were to turn into a true economic depression. Would the EU member states work together to get beyond the crisis or would there be a regional and global return to the "beggar-thy-neighbor" policies of the 1930s? As a practical matter, and despite political setbacks that occur from time to time, most of the economies of the European Union are so deeply integrated today that it is hard to imagine any such disintegration of the union even in difficult economic circumstances. Some realists do predict, however, that over time the sheer size of the EU and its economic power likely will make it a political and economic (or even military) rival to the United States. So goes the logic of balance-of-power theory: when powerful states exercise their power (as the United

States does), this gives incentives to others to balance (in an effort to constrain) further exercise of this power.

It would take a Hollywood scriptwriter to come up with a scenario that leads to conflict in North America among Canada, Mexico, and the United States—another zone of peace. Armed conflict is highly unlikely, notwithstanding tensions due to cross-border immigration, resentment of U.S. economic and political might, and concerns in both Canada and Mexico about strong U.S. cultural influences. Within Latin America, the Marxist-Leninist revolutionary ideologies of the 1960s and 1970s had lost their appeal by the 1980s. Prior to that time, a number of observers deemed the insurgencies in Bolivia, Peru, El Salvador, Nicaragua, and elsewhere as part of a larger trend toward "inevitable revolutions" supported by peasants and workers—*los de abajo* (those at the lower socioeconomic rungs of society). Part of the reason for such predictions was the widespread prevalence of authoritarian dictatorships and military juntas, often backed by the United States and seen as representing the interests of the elites or upper classes at the expense of the masses. Economic stagnation was one reason for the eventual demise of many of these regimes, and free market policies seemed to "neoliberal" advocates to go hand -in- hand with the eventual expansion of civil society and in many cases the development and spread of democratic institutions. Today, however, although economic problems continue to dominate the agendas of Latin American states, it is difficult to see these as contributory to the outbreak of war. Instead, domestic conflicts in these countries seem more likely to take the form (as in Venezuela) of challenges from the left against right-of-center regimes committed to neoliberal policies depicted as disadvantaging large sectors of the population to the benefit of the few on top.

Elsewhere in the world there continues to be the threat of interstate conflict. In Africa there is the phenomenon of failed states, meaning governments that have little if any control over their own territories, that cannot establish civil order on a firm footing, and that suffer from warlordism, private armies, and tribal or ethnic conflicts that spill over national borders, sometimes (as in central Africa and the Sudan) becoming genocidal. Failed states unable to maintain law and order or provide other governmental services not only are not capable of preventing civil war or dealing effectively with other forms of intercommunal strife, but also cannot preclude neighboring states from intervening in their domestic affairs.

Asia remains a likely venue for a major interstate war. India and Pakistan, both nuclear armed states, are the main concern in south Asia; however, both countries also have a stake in moderating their conflicts, given the threat of mutual mass destruction that could result from interstate warfare. The region is also rife with ethnic conflicts as, for example, between Tamils (Hindus) and Sinhalese (Buddhists) in Sri Lanka or between Muslims and Hindus in India and in the Kashmir region along the border between India and Pakistan.

For some realists, the continual increase in China's economic power is a matter of serious concern, particularly since such progress also facilitates expansion of military capabilities. At some point in future decades, some fear Chinese power may even rival the United States. The long-term future of Taiwan—viewed by Beijing as a "renegade province"—remains unresolved. For its part, the United States holds to its position that although Taiwan is legally a part of China, it can continue to enjoy its autonomy well into the future. The United States has a large stake in managing relations with both Beijing and Taipei to maintain the status quo, lest the conflict lead to a war not in the interest of any of the parties.

North Korea and its nuclear weapons capabilities in northeast Asia are a constant cause of concern to countries in the region, as are nuclear weapons programs pursued by Iran in southwest Asia at the easternmost edge of what we more commonly refer to as the Middle East. Extending from Morocco in the west across North Africa, the Mediterranean coast, and Arabia to the Gulf states, the Middle East continues to be a region in which still unresolved interstate and intercommunal conflicts stand as a major challenge to world peace. Beyond Palestinian and other Arab-Israeli issues are divisions along Sunni-Shia and other sectarian lines in Islamic states and conflicts between Iran (an Islamic Shia, but non-Arab state) and Israel as well as against some Arab states, particularly those in the Gulf. Indeed, the 1980s witnessed a bloody interstate war along the border between Iran and Iraq—a conflict that has since been overshadowed by U.S.-led, multistate coalitions against Iraq to liberate Kuwait from Iraqi occupation in 1991 and to change the Iraqi regime in 2003. Of course, the presence of the world's largest known oil reserves in the Middle East, concentrated primarily in Saudi Arabia and other Gulf states, makes the region enormously important to the global economy. This oil dependence on the Middle East by states outside the region can easily lead to armed intervention should diplomacy fail and the flow of oil either be cut off or put in jeopardy.

Whether in the Middle East or elsewhere, the prevalence of military force and other forms of violence as "remedies" for conflicts reflect to many feminists a masculinist take on dealing with these problems. Rather than reaching for the gun, more effective approaches to conflict resolution would seem to be a more promising modality for dealing with these complex matters. From this perspective, peaceful means of conflict resolution are far preferable to military options, which tend to create (or deepen) more problems than they resolve.

Finally, it might come as a surprise (and anger) to many Americans, but around the globe the United States and its interventionist policies are perceived by many to be the greatest threat to regional and global stability and thus to world peace! No matter which party controls the White House or Congress, public opinion polls in foreign countries show a consistent fear or animosity concerning the use not only of American military power, but also of American economic might. For many outside the United States, globalization is really Americanization—seen by them as an arrogant attempt to impose American political, economic, and social values as if they were (or should be) universally held, effectively reconstituting the world in the image of the United States. Although most Americans reject such characterizations as distortions, dealing with these adverse perceptions of the exercise of U.S. power remains a major challenge.

Whether one is an optimist or a pessimist about whether the world is becoming more peaceful or violent is in part a function of the perspective one adopts. For many realists, competition, conflict, and war seem almost inevitable in an anarchic international system with no overarching power to enforce harmony. On the other hand, many members of the English School are self-professed realists who accept such concepts as power and balance of power but, despite recognizing the challenges posed by international anarchy, do not see international politics necessarily as a continuing "war of all against all." Instead of this purely Hobbesian view, they see states quite capable of acting in a Grotian way with enlightened self-interest guiding a global *society* of states and other actors—agreed-upon international rules, institutions, procedures, and norms for engaging in cooperation or managing conflicts.

Pluralists or liberals tend also to be more optimistic than realists. While for realists the glass is seemingly half empty, for pluralists typically it is at least half full. International institutions can help to smooth the workings of the interstate system and relations among non-state actors as well. Particularly in the economic realm, such "liberal institutionalists" can point to how the monetary, capital investment, and trade regimes constructed after World War II worked well to aid European and Asian recovery and expand economic prosperity in other parts of the world as well. The same can be said for managing world health, civil air and maritime transportation, telecommunications, development, agriculture, law enforcement, human rights, arms control, and a wide variety of other "functional" matters of great importance to the security and well-being of humankind. To liberal institutionalists, international organizations are core players that provide a venue for multilateral negotiations, often providing information that facilitates the completion of agreements. Furthermore, transnational nongovernmental organizations concerned with such issues as human rights and the global environment have varying degrees of influence on governmental policies. Often ignored by states, they have increasingly linked themselves to international organizations, seeking to influence their agendas and support their work on matters of concern to these NGOs.

Given the fact that social constructivists believe states can redefine their interests even under conditions of international anarchy, they are understandably also on the optimistic end of the spectrum, yet fully realize the challenge of moving the world toward a more peaceful status. Their focus is not so much on the cost-benefit, enlightened self-interest calculations of liberal institutionalists as it is on the ideas, norms, or values that become institutionalized in international or world politics over time, sometimes becoming embedded in international or other organizational forms. For example, commitment to multilateralism as an approach to dealing with diverse issues is one such norm that one can find institutionalized in such regional organizations as the European Union or in the United Nations, the World Bank, International Monetary Fund, World Trade Organization, World Health Organization, and many other worldwide or global organizations.

For economic structuralists, the inexorable logic of the "capitalist world system" continues to be in play. Capitalism, the critical element of globalization, continues its creatively destructive path, penetrating every place on Earth. For classical and neoclassical economists an expanding world economy may be all well and good, but economic structuralists—influenced by the Marxist tradition of economic thought—return again and again to the vast social and economic disparities we can observe both within and among societies. Neoliberal economic policies are seen as advantaging the capital-rich at the expense of the capital-poor, further impoverishing the latter. The apparent lack of viable economic alternatives for the poor is a matter for condemnation—indicative to many economic structuralists of the ultimate failure of capitalism to provide for the welfare of the vast majority of humanity.

Will the state wither away? Will international organizations and nongovernmental organizations play a more prominent role in IR and world politics?

From the realist perspective, the state most likely will remain pretty much as it is without either surrendering to world government or passing much more of its authority to other regimes or institutions. The state has proven to be a very durable and attractive set of institutions for people of all political persuasions, for several reasons.

First, with the exception of anarchists, most revolutionaries of the left and reactionaries on the right historically aim not for the abolition of the state but rather for the overthrow of its current rulers, perhaps seeking fundamental changes in society as well. They share a strong belief that there is nothing wrong in principle with the state that *they* could not fix if they were in charge.

Second, the nation-state has been able to provide something no other entity has been able to match—a sense of political and social identity. One might admire an international organization or an NGO, but they cannot compete with the emotional power of nationalism, and they are certainly hard to love. One might argue that religion can provide a source of transnational identity, just as Christianity and Islam did in the Middle Ages and Islam in particular may still be doing today. But then the question becomes, "Is this identification with religion a substitute for identification with the nation-state, or a supplement?"

Finally, most states seem to be able to provide people with one other valuable commodity—a sense of security (or at least a greater degree of security than if states and their governments were not present). While globalization and increasing global interdependence have reduced the ability of states to limit or negate external economic, social, and political influences, states still overwhelmingly control the use of force. From the realist perspective, therefore, if the state is becoming increasingly obsolete, one would certainly not know it by the sheer number of new states that have been created in the more than half-century since the end of World War II (from about 60 then to close to 200 at present)—evidence that counters claims that the state is somehow fading away. When states break up, as happened to the Soviet Union, Yugoslavia, and Czechoslovakia in the 1990s, new states are formed to replace them. Moreover, even when states achieve greater degrees of integration, as in the European Union, members not surprisingly still retain their identities as sovereign states, with grants of authority to EU institutions limited to what is necessary to perform the functions member states want them to perform.

From the pluralist or liberal perspective, the state continues to exist well into the future, but it does so in functionally truncated or reduced form. In the economic realm, global interdependence makes for a seemingly borderless world, and crises of authority continue to affect states to varying degrees. In this more complex future architecture, states and their governments operate alongside other international, transnational, and local actors—both governmental and nongovernmental. States still retain substantial authority, albeit for fewer tasks, relegating others to more central, either global or regional institutions. States also serve as important go-betweens as they coordinate global, regional, and local efforts. State-as-coordinator is a very important future role, although it is quite different from the position of states as they first emerged in the late Middle Ages and have remained for several centuries—functionally diffuse actors, claiming exclusive sovereign authority, and performing a wide array of tasks for their societies. Taken as a whole, therefore, the apparent architecture or structure of world politics would be one of multiple overlapping international regimes with global and regional responsibilities for a wide range of social, economic, and political tasks. At least that is how liberal institutionalists might understand it. The responsibilities, norms, and values inherent in these regimes would be influenced by not only states but also transnational or nongovernmental organizations and movements that are part of a growing global civil society.

For economic structuralists, the logic of capitalism continues to play out on the world stage. Despite the emphasis on this transnational economic dynamic and recognition that the ability of states to control their economic destiny is limited, the state remains for the foreseeable future the preeminent actor in world politics. Scholars in the English School would agree, although they share with pluralists and liberals a belief in the importance of international norms as a means to regulate conflict among states. Even social constructivists understand the importance of states as a social construction that has developed to its present form over the course of centuries. They are, perhaps, more optimistic than those with other perspectives in world politics, tending to see that in a world of states it is still possible (though by no means inevitable) for interests to be redefined by states in such a way as to enhance the possibility of world peace and economic and social well being.

Are interdependence and globalization inevitable?

Interdependence is an attribute or characteristic of globalization involving the relations among states and other actors that, at least in principle, is measurable. The degree of interdependence among states and other actors has always varied, depending on the states involved and the issue at hand. States can indeed take unilateral action to sever, for example, economic relations. The worldwide depression of the 1930s was a time when the level of interdependence among states was low compared to earlier decades. As noted earlier, asymmetrical interdependence—a situation where one or more parties are more affected than others—can be a source of vulnerability, particularly if the weaker parties have no viable alternatives. For example, the United States and Saudi Arabia are economically interdependent—the United States needs oil and the Saudi regime needs dollars as well as external support for its security in a troubled region. If the Saudi regime were overthrown and a hostile government came to power vowing to cut off oil to the West, the United States would certainly remain vulnerable and likely suffer substantial economic damage, but would still be in a position to cultivate alternative sources of oil. Others might be less able to find alternative sources of supply, at least not quickly enough to avoid suffering economic consequences of even greater severity.

Globalization can be understood as a continuing, multifaceted historical *process* that, as the term suggests, has global implications. Its defining characteristic is in the economic realm, particularly the spread of capitalism and such associated liberal values as an emphasis on the individual and the important roles individuals (and individual firms) play in economic growth and development. To the extent that globalization is a purveyor of economic processes that improve the lot of humanity, it is obviously of benefit. Transportation and telecommunications advances have facilitated global reach not just economically, but also over a wide range of social, cultural, and political issues. On the other hand, to the extent that globalization exacerbates economic distress and undermines the economic livelihood of persons, it is viewed by many as the bane of the present-day world. But how does one measure such effects? The same holds true with the rapid dissemination of information and, with it, cultural and social values. Are they contaminating local cultures and societies? Or are they offering, for example, women the opportunity to break out from repressive social and economic conditions? For some, globalization is a major reason many regimes are faced with crises of authority. For others, such crises of authority are an opportunity to sweep away the old and replace it with something better. For example, the Internet has been an important means to spread Western political and social values to young people around the world, including those in Iran who may chafe under the repressive rule of religious mullahs. The Internet has also been a critical tool for human rights activists to disseminate information to the outside world of the conditions in China and elsewhere. But the Internet has also allowed terrorists and criminals in their separate networks to communicate, plot, and plan various nefarious acts.

Is the proliferation of weapons of mass destruction inevitable?

There would seem to be some grounds for optimism on this front. The former apartheid regime in South Africa and, more recently, Libya have renounced nuclear research programs that were moving toward weapons designed for military use. Unfortunately that has been more than counterbalanced by the proliferation of nuclear weapons technology, most evident in the case of Pakistan and its dealings with North Korea and Iran.

As noted in Chapter 7, an effective nuclear nonproliferation regime needs to work not only on the supply side, but also on the demand side by reducing the motivation of states to acquire nuclear weapons. Ideally, this would mean reducing the insecurity and fear that often permeates interstate relations. Of similar concern are chemical and biological weapons, the former of which are found in the arsenals of many states. The major concern, however, is if terrorists either acquire or produce weapons of mass destruction. Science knows no boundaries, and the availability of requisite information to create lethal toxins and chemicals is unfortunately enhanced by the Internet. It is difficult enough to monitor the activities of states, doubly so if the activity is being done by a few individuals in a basement or garage or by insurgents or terrorists operating in a remote, clandestine location.

Will terrorism become the preeminent international security issue and create crises of authority for governments?

Some would argue that terrorism is already the number-one threat to international security. While this might be a parochial American view due to the catastrophic events of 9/11, there is no doubt that the specter of Islamist or *jihadist* terrorism in particular is haunting more than the United States, as evidenced by terror attacks in Europe as well. Coupled with weapons of mass destruction, deterrence of terrorism carried out by transnational, nonstate groups is extraordinarily difficult, if not impossible. We must remember, however, that terrorism is a violent tactic that is as old as humanity. It will not go away. What has changed over time are the underlying factors that come together in various combinations to give terrorism distinct characteristics at any given point in history. Disaffection born of globalization might not lend itself to any solution if globalization is an ongoing, complex process that is beyond the control of states, international organizations, or transnational nongovernmental organizations.

On the other hand, the political circumstances and grievances that provide much of the fuel for terrorism may be at least somewhat susceptible to actions taken to dampen these fires of hatred and envy. As noted above, the Arab-Israeli situation is one example, and the India-Pakistan dispute over Kashmir another. The desire for political independence among ethnic movements in various parts of Asia and Africa and resultant repressive government policies leading to cycles of violence is yet another. In many of these cases, it is not terrorism that is leading to crises of authority but rather crises of state legitimacy that breed terrorism. Saudi Arabia, home of fifteen of the nineteen 9/11 hijackers, is one example of a movement within a country hostile not just to its own regime, but also to the United States and other countries. There will always be men and women with apocalyptic visions of destruction and revenge with no interest in dialogue or compromise. But the best way to marginalize such persons is for a concerted global effort to ameliorate the underlying political, social, and economic conditions that breed the foot soldiers of terrorist movements, whatever the banner, religion, or cause they claim to support. This is an agenda whose end state is much easier to postulate, of course, than the means required to achieve it. Still, attention to the grievances (real or imagined, just or unjust) that spawn and sustain terrorist movements is probably the only way effectively to reduce the likelihood of these terrorist attacks.

Will the global environment continue to deteriorate?

It is hard to be optimistic. Concern for the environment is justified and laudatory. But the environment is under increasing strain due to two major factors: the inexorable growth of the world population coupled with the associated need to provide and improve the economic livelihood of these greater numbers of people. The state and non-state actors discussed in this book all have their limitations when it comes to tackling such global challenges as the environment. International organizations remain weak as global governing structures and are often viewed with skepticism—if not suspicion—by states concerned with maintaining their sovereignty and sovereign prerogatives. For their part, states and their governments claim the right to address global problems, but they are less qualified for this task than collective, concerted action taken on a global scale would be. Resources deplete and the environment degrades. Pollution drifts or flows across borders, the Earth becomes warmer, stocks of fish deplete or vanish. Some environmental experts see rapid and catastrophic climate change with rising sea levels, greatly reduced levels of agricultural production, and massive extinction of diverse species of plants and animals as a very real possibility.

Transnational nongovernmental organizations are playing an increasingly important role in an expanding global civil society, but it is arguable how representative they are. Do they really represent "humanity" or simply the interests of their memberships? Developing consensus on what is to be done is no easy task. There might be agreement on what the problem is, but not necessarily on remedies or ways to deal with it effectively. "Who will bear the cost?" is not simply an economic question but a political one. So, while scientific evidence may be the starting point for discussion and debate, it is the political process that will determine what policies (if any) are ultimately decided on.

Is human security a useful analytical concept? Does it provide policymakers with guidance?

While national security has traditionally referred to the security of a state (and international security to common security concerns among states), human security involves shifting the unit of analysis down to ordinary people. The problem with the concept, some say, is that its analytical utility is virtually nil if it consists of little more than a laundry list of concerns—human rights, the environment, disease, poverty, freedom from fear, psychological well-being, and so on. Are some issues more important than others? Is there an appropriate rank order? Or is the concept little more than a rallying cry for various nongovernmental and international organizations? On the other hand, advocates of human security see concerns for human rights, welfare, and the overall human condition as frequently displaced by the defense and security concerns of states. Human security helps us refocus on what matters most for human beings.

Will human rights improve around the world?

While nonstate actors or movements such as insurgencies and various criminals, pillagers, and mobs may violate human rights, more often than not it is states that are the primary violators of the rights of their own citizens or that fail to enforce even their own standards. On the other hand, while NGOs may play an important role in reminding states of their professed commitment (or lack thereof) to human rights, they ultimately cannot enforce their application in the absence of actions by states or through the work of international organizations. The extension of human rights will have to be achieved through various mechanisms involving states, not by bypassing them. On the other hand, this is, to put it mildly, a difficult challenge.

An even more problematic challenge involves the human rights of women in most areas of the world. Women are not only faced with discriminatory laws regarding marriage, property, and family; they also are faced with cultural attitudes that restrict their life chances in work or professional development. Exploitation of children, whether by corporations or by more traditional labor-intensive enterprises, is another major challenge faced by human rights advocates and the people they represent. Even if a government professes adherence to a human rights convention, the actual ability to enforce those standards upon its populace can be highly problematic in many countries.

Do we have any responsibility to a broader humanity? Or only to ourselves, family, community, or state?

These are, of course, not empirical questions. They are normative, ethical, even philosophical questions. But let us assume one wishes to take some step, however modest, to improve the human condition. What can be done that isn't simply a "feel good" gesture? There is actually much truth to the cliché "Think globally, act locally." In other words, one does not have to live overseas or in another country to be engaged in issues of global importance. Although one need not quit school or one's job and devote years of life to the greater good, however defined, we certainly commend and applaud those who do continue to make so many personal sacrifices to advance one aspect or another of the human condition. Throughout this book we have provided Web site URLs that can link us to many international and transnational or nongovernmental organizations that are working to improve the human condition. It is, after all, through collective action that the weak "I" becomes the strong "we."

Final Words

We must note that whatever the nature of twenty-first century world politics, the problems that confront humankind do not lend themselves to easy solutions. Unquestioned faith that growing economic and technological interdependence will somehow lead us to a better world politically and socially is naive. Similarly, to believe that world politics will remain essentially unchanged is reminiscent of the confidence of feudal lords who were blind to the rise of the then-new sovereign state and the capitalist form of political economy.

Human beings have the cognitive capacity to analyze situations, plan ahead, and take action. The surest way to reduce the chances of something terrible happening on the world stage is to predict it will occur and make sure your prediction receives wide publicity. If you are lucky, those with the power and understanding to do so will take action and (one hopes) make your prediction wrong. In other words, it is likely that a *laissez-faire* approach to world problems will not gain ground, and collective efforts in fact will be made to tackle these difficult problems, particularly since most of them cannot be adequately addressed by states acting alone. This may result in genuine concerns generated by telecasts of people starving to death, dying of disease, or being killed in war. Or it may be a more calculated decision based on concerns for personal, national, or international security in an increasingly globalized world where security, however defined, seems problematical. But the fact of the matter is that global problems require collective responses. However tentative, partial, and frustrating this process might be, there is no real alternative.

We hope this book has helped the reader to begin thinking about the nature of international relations and world politics as the twenty-first century unfolds. While much of the past may be prologue, one needs to keep a critical eye out for emerging trends as well, whatever the perspective or image one may adopt for understanding these challenges. That the end of this twenty-first-century story will be a happy one is by no means a foregone conclusion. We remain convinced, however, that constructive, concerted efforts taken on a global basis have the potential for building a sustainable, worthwhile future for humankind.

Additional Readings

The only consensus in the literature on what the future holds is that there will continue to be significant challenges to the human condition as security, economy, identity and other human issues remain high on the global agenda. Although not everyone agrees with him, Samuel P. Huntington sees "civilizations" in deep conflict, a thesis he argues in *The Clash of Civilizations & The Remaking of World Order* (New York: Simon & Schuster, 1996, 1998). Terrorism is not going away anytime soon as Walter Laqueur sees the future in his *No End to War: Terrorism in the 21st Century* (New York: Continuum, 2004). For his part, Bernard Lewis looks toward the Middle East and asks *What Went Wrong? The Clash Between Islam and Modernity in the Middle East* (New York: Perennial/ Harper Collins, 2003). The implications for proliferation of weapons of mass destruction are debated in Scott Sagan and Kenneth Waltz, *The Spread of Nuclear Weapons*, 2nd ed. (New York: W.W. Norton, 1995, 2002). Somewhat more positive takes on the future are in Scott A. Hunt, *On the Future of Peace: On the Front Lines with the World's Great Peacemakers* (San Francisco: Harper Collins, 2004) and Mary Kaldor, *Global Civil Society: An Answer to War* (Cambridge: Polity, 2003).

The literature alleging an American imperium under continuing unipolarity that puts the United States in the lead position is large and growing. For example, see Chalmers Johnson, *The Sorrows of Empire: Militarism, Secrecy, and the End of the American Republic* (New York: Metropolitan Books, 2004) and his earlier *Blowback: The Costs and Consequences of American Empire* (New York: Metropolitan Books, 2003), G. John Ikenberry (ed.), *America Unrivaled: The Future of the Balance of Power* (Ithaca, NY: Cornell University Press, 2002), Richard A. Falk, *The Declining World Order: America's Imperial Geopolitics* (London: Routledge, 2004), Andrew J. Bacevich, *American Empire: The Realities and Consequences of U.S. Diplomacy* (Cambridge, MA: Harvard University Press, 2002), and Michael Hardt and Antonio Negri, *Empire* (Cambridge, MA: Harvard University Press, 2000). For different perspectives on this question of American power and interest, see Robert Kagan, *Of Paradise and Power: America and Europe in the New World Order* (New York: Knopf, 2003) and Charles Kupchan, *The End of the American Era: U.S. Foreign Policy and the Geopolitics of the 21st Century* (New York: Knopf, 2002).

GLOSSARY

actor   A participant or player. In international relations or world politics actors include states, international organizations, multinational corporations and banks, and other non-governmental (or non-state, transnational) organizations.

alliance   A formal agreement between two (bilateral) or more states (multilateral) to cooperate in security matters; a formal security coalition of states with specified commitments.

ambassador   (*See* mission)

anarchists   People who believe there should be no centralized political authority as such authority abuses the rights of individuals. Historically, anarchists have been against the governments of states. Many anarchists are non-violent; however, the nineteenth-century People's Will in Russia is an example of an anarchist terrorist group.

anarchy   The absence of political authority. International politics or the international system is said to be anarchic as there is no world government—no central or superordinate authority over states, which retain their sovereign rights. (*See also* sovereignty)

ancien regime   The ruling order in pre-Revolutionary (1789) France. More generally the term refers to the old order or former constitutional regime in an earlier time by which a state was previously governed.

Andean Group   International organization established in 1969 to promote economic integration. Members now include Bolivia, Colombia, Ecuador, Peru, and Venezuela.

apartheid   A policy of discrimination and strict racial segregation or separateness in society. The term is associated primarily with the former white-dominated state of South Africa.

APEC (Asia-Pacific Economic Cooperation)   Established in 1989, inclusive Asia and Pacific rim association of states with periodic summit meetings on economic and other policy issues. Members include Japan, China, Russia, Taiwan, and South Korea in Northeast Asia; Australia, Brunei, Indonesia, Malaysia, New Zealand, Papua New Guinea, the Philippines, Singapore, Thailand, and Vietnam in Southeast Asia and western Pacific; and the United States, Canada, Mexico, Peru, and Chile in the Americas along the eastern-Pacific rim.

appreciate, appreciation   When a currency or other asset increases in value over time we say it appreciates. (*See also* depreciate, depreciation)

Arab League   Founded in 1945, this pan-Arab international organization facilitates cooperation among its Arab-state members and advances Arab causes in relation to Palestine and other issues. Original members were Egypt, Iraq, Lebanon, Saudi Arabia, Syria, Yemen, Palestine (representatives of Palestine Arabs), and Jordan. Members now also include Morocco, Mauritania, Algeria, Tunisia, Libya, Sudan, Somalia, Djibouti, Oman, United Arab Emirates (UAE), Qatar, Bahrain, Comoros and Kuwait.

armed conflict   A struggle involving the use of weapons and force.

armed intervention   (*See* intervention)

arms control   Negotiations designed to reduce the quantity or quality of certain types or classes of weapons or the geographical area or circumstances under which they may be possessed or used; more broadly, arms control may also include confidence- and security-building measures intended to reduce the likely use of weaponry by lowering the risk of war. Reasons for pursuing arms control include: (1) curbing arms race competition; (2) saving money; (3) reducing the risk of war; (4) reducing the damage done by war; and (5) securing either some mutual advantage or other advantage over an opponent. (*See also* functional approaches)

arms transfers   The sale or giving away of weapons from one political entity (usually a state) to another.

Article 51 (of the UN Charter)   If attacked, states have the inherent right of individual or collective self-defense.

artificial intelligence   Generally associated with advanced computers that are able to conduct computations in a manner similar to the human brain.

ASEAN (Association of Southeast Asian Nations)   Formed in 1967, this international organization tries to advance regional peace and security, especially through economic cooperation. Regional security has also been added to the ASEAN agenda. Original members were Indonesia, Malaysia, the Philippines, Singapore, and Thailand. Membership now also includes Brunei, Vietnam, Laos, Myanmar (Burma), and Cambodia.

assimilation   A strategy to create a single national identity out of diverse populations. It may be repressive (as with the efforts under Stalin's communist Soviet Union) or non-coercive.

asylum   Allowing a refugee to stay in a country to which he or she has fled out of fear of political repression or fear for one's life in one's home country. (*See also* extraterritoriality)

asymmetry, asymmetric   Lacking precise correspondence or relation—that is, symmetry—between or among components. An interdependence relation is said to be asymmetric if Party A is more dependent on Party B than Party B is on Party A.

autarky   An independent posture of self-sufficiency without dependence on other actors. Autarky occurs when a state attempts as a matter of policy to exist in economic isolation from other states.

authority   A legitimate right to direct or command and to make, decide, and enforce rules. The term *authority* has a moral or legal quality and, as such, can be distinguished from control by brute force or by coercion. (*See also* power)

balance of payments   Accounting concept by which the international economic transactions (inflows and outflows) of states and their corporate and private elements are tracked. Balance of payments includes export and import of merchandise goods and services (balance of trade), capital investment and other "invisible" or financial flows, and official reserve transactions (gold, certain national currencies acceptable as reserves, and Special Drawing Rights in the International Monetary Fund). "Balance" is achieved when reserves flow in or out to cover differences in other accounts, as when a country exporting more than it imports receives foreign currency that it can hold as a financial reserve.

balance of power A key concept among realists that refers to a condition of, or tendency toward, equilibrium among states. Realists differ on whether the equilibrium or balance is created by diplomats or statesmen (that is, by influencing balance of power as a policy); is useful as a rational basis for justifying policies; and occurs as a natural outcome of international politics, whether or not diplomats or statesmen intend such an outcome. A dynamic equilibrium refers to an inherent systemic tendency to return to equilibrium each and every time the balance is upset. Due to its multiple definitions, some critics question the utility of the concept—if balance of power means so many different things, then does it mean anything at all? (*See also* equilibrium)

balance of trade One account in the balance of payments, it is the difference between a country's *exports* (what is sold abroad) and its *imports* (what is purchased from abroad). A negative balance of trade exists when imports of goods and services exceed exports; a positive balance of trade exists when exports exceed imports.

ballistic missiles Missiles that when launched follow a trajectory to the ground subject to gravitational forces; depending upon its range, a ballistic missile may hit targets nearby or in a neighboring or distant country.

banks Organizations that perform various financial services, including lending money at interest for purchases or capital investment. International (or multinational) banks are key players in the global political economy.

barter (*See* money)

bellicism A term constructed from the Latin word *bellum* (war), sometimes used to refer to the belief in the value or utility of force or war as a preferred instrument of policy.

bilateral diplomacy (*See* diplomacy)

binational state (*See* state)

bipolar, bipolarity (*See* structure)

blockade (*See* economic leverage)

bourgeoisie The capitalist (and, at the time of its emergence, the "middle") class. The bourgeoisie is the class defined in Marxian terms by its relation to the means of production—its ownership of capital, including factories and other machinery of production in a capitalist mode of production. (*See also* class struggle)

boycott (*See* economic leverage)

capabilities Resources or power any international actor can bring to bear to achieve its goals and defend its interests.

capital Savings that can be used for investment in the means for producing goods and services, typically expenditures for plant and equipment.

capital controls Restrictions placed by a state on the export of money or wealth. (*See* capital goods)

capital formation New and continuing investment in *capital gods* for production and consumption.

capital goods Refers to goods used in the production of other goods or services, e.g., the machinery and tools in a factory.

capitalism An economic system, form of political economy, or mode of production that emphasizes money, market-oriented trade, and capital investment for further production. Capitalism is also associated with a set of values or culture that sustains it. Commonly the term refers to private ownership of the means of production and a free market; however, as presented here, capitalism may be understood in global terms, taking different forms in different societies at different times. Capitalism is often further subdivided into the different forms it has taken over some 500 years—*early, industrial,* and *post-industrial. State* capitalism refers to collective ownership of capital or other property by "the people" or by the state or government as opposed to being privately owned. *Free-market* capitalism refers either to the absence or, more accurately, the minimization of government intervention or regulation of merchandise, service, capital or other financial exchange transactions. In Marxist usage, a *mode of production.* (*See* mode of production)

capitalist world-system An approach to international relations that emphasizes the impact of the worldwide spread of capitalism; a focus on class and economic relations and the division of the world into a core, periphery, and semi-periphery. *See also* core, periphery, semi-periphery, class.

Caribbean Community and Common Market (CARICOM) Formed as a free-trade association in 1965, it assumed its present title in 1973. Participants include British dependency Montserrat and a number of British Commonwealth members—the Bahamas, Antigua and Barbuda, Barbados, St. Kitts and Nevis, Dominica, St. Lucia, St. Vincent, Grenada, Trinidad and Tobago, Jamaica, Guyana, and Belize—plus the Dominican Republic, Haiti, and Surinam as observers.

cartel An association among financial, commodity-producing, or industrial interests, including states, for establishing a national or international market control, setting production levels and increasing or stabilizing the prices of such diverse products as oil, tin, and coffee.

categorical imperative Concept associated with the work of the East Prussian philosopher and ethicist Immanuel Kant, that one ought to act "according to the maxim that you can at the same time will [such conduct] to be a universal law" and that one should treat others "as an end as well as a means, never merely as a means."

causes, causality, causal Factors that occur prior to and appear to produce certain outcomes or effects. Some causes may be *necessary,* but not *sufficient* to produce a given effect; some are *efficient*—the proximate, immediate, or direct cause(s), while others are *permissive* underlying cause(s) that allow certain outcomes or effects to occur, as when international *anarchy* or the absence of central authority over states is said to pose no obstacle to the onset of war between or among them. What is to be explained causally (for example, war) is referred to as the *dependent* variable and the factors that account for or causally explain a phenomenon such as war are referred to as the *independent* variables.

Central American Common Market (CACM) Formed in 1960 to liberalize trade, its members are Costa Rica, El Salvador, Guatemala, Honduras, and Nicaragua.

Chargé d'Affaires (*See* mission)

Chief of Mission (*See* mission)

city-state (*See* state)

civil liberties Freedoms guaranteed to citizens typically by the constitution and laws of a state and society. (*See also* civil rights)

civil rights Claims typically made by or on behalf of individuals concerning their equal status and role as citizens. (*See also* civil liberties)

civil war   (*See* war*)*

class   A unit in society with identifiable interests or characteristics that differentiate it from other such units. In Marxist usage, the term is defined by relations to the means of production—in capitalism the *bourgeoisie* by its ownership of capital and workers or *proletariat* by their labor; in feudalism the *aristocracy* by its ownership of land and the *peasantry* by its labor.

class conflict, class struggle   A concept associated with Marxism that emphasizes the inevitable clash of interests between classes, which are defined in terms of their relations to the means (how goods, services, and value are produced) in a particular mode of production or form of political economy such as feudalism or capitalism. Marx, for example, analyzed the class struggle between the *bourgeoisie* (owners of capital, especially factories) and the *proletariat* or working class (defined by its labor).

classical economics, political economy, economists   Although they understood the importance of finance capital and capital goods in early capitalism, Adam Smith, David Ricardo and other 18th and 19th century classical writers saw value in goods and services produced as the result of labor put into the production process, a labor theory of value. Specialization and division of labor that enhances efficiency in domestic production, free trade, and specialization in production for export based on comparative advantage are among the concepts developed by the classical economists. (*See also* neoclassical economics)

coalition   A formal or informal grouping of actors that share some common purpose or purposes. Alliances and some international organizations (particularly those that are exclusive or less inclusive) are examples of *formal* coalitions; however, *ad hoc* coalitions among states or other actors that also form from time to time both *outside of* and *within* alliances and international organizations are often more transient or less durable than formal coalitions. (*See also* alliance)

coercion   (*See* power)

coercive diplomacy   (*See* diplomacy)

cognition, cognitive   The process by which human beings acquire knowledge through perception, reasoning, and (some would say) intuition.

collateral damage, death and destruction   Damage to human beings and property coincident to or following the intentional destruction of military targets; the damage is not confined to the intended targets, but spills over to harm other victims and property.

collective defense   A function performed by alliances that pool power or capabilities of state members to balance or countervail against the power of other states, alliances, or other coalitions. The right to individual and collective defense is legally recognized by Article 51 of the UN Charter. (*See also* Article 51; collective security)

collective goods   Refers to goods (or services) to which others (including other states) cannot be excluded even though they have not contributed to paying for them. For example, the security produced by an alliance can be understood as a collective good. This security benefits non-alliance members, referred to as *free riders,* because they have not made direct payments or other contributions to the collective alliance effort. Sometimes referred to as *public goods,* provision of collective goods is often by state or governmental authorities.

collective security   The term is used commonly as if it were synonymous with *collective defense;* however, such usage overlooks the important distinction that, in principle, collective security is based on international law-enforcement obligations whereas collective defense is merely a form of balance-of-power politics. Under collective security, states agree to enforce international law by confronting any aggressor with the preponderant power that comes from pooling their collective efforts. A variety of diplomatic, economic and other measures including the use of force may be employed. Unlike *collective defense* or *balance of power* policies, collective security is understood as a law-enforcement or police activity. Unlike an *alliance* that is directed against adversaries, the goal in collective security is to encourage international law-abiding behavior by states, dissuading them from committing aggression or other illegal actions taken against other states. As an all-inclusive or "universal" organization open to membership by all states, the League of Nations in the period between World War I and World War II was organized around this concept of collective security through collective law enforcement. Its successor, the United Nations, learned from League failures to stop aggression, and provides not only a collective-security framework under Security Council jurisdiction, but also allows states to enter balance of power-based alliances or other collective-defense arrangements, particularly if collective security fails to prevent aggression or other breaches of international law. (*See also* collective defense)

collectivization   Refers typically to expropriation of private property as has occurred particularly in present-day and former Marxist-Leninist regimes. In the agricultural sector, not only was land taken from its owners, but the labor of farm workers or peasants was aggregated or put together on so-called collective farms.

colonialism   (*See* imperialism*)*

command economy   (*See* markets)

commodity   Broadly, any article bought or sold; agricultural products, metals, and other minerals are often referred to as commodities and are traded in bulk on commodities exchanges.

common market   Level of economic integration that in addition to the free trade of goods and services among members (as in a free-trade area) and common external tariffs on imports from non-member countries (as in a customs union), there is also free movement across the borders of member states by all three factors of production—land, labor, and capital. (*See* integration)

commonwealth   A loose association of sovereign states that, notwithstanding their differences and desire for independence or autonomy, have some over-arching identity that makes the association meaningful. Examples include the British Commonwealth of Nations, made up of former colonies and dominions, as well as the Commonwealth of Independent States, made up of former Soviet republics.

communism   A mode of production in Marxist theory or the ultimate form of political economy in a classless society in which the state withers away as each person works maximally according to ability, receiving the fruits of collective labors in accordance with need. (*See also* mode of production)

communitarian   While compatible in principle with an orientation toward individual or libertarian concerns, the communitarian focus is more on collective or group service obligations to one another in society.

comparative advantage   Economic free-trade principle associated with David Ricardo's work in classical economics. Ricardian economics holds that countries tend to specialize in producing those goods and services for export in which they are most efficient or have a comparative advantage, importing from other countries those goods and services in which their production is relatively less efficient. In a free-trade environment there would be, according to theory, a global specialization or division of labor with aggregate productivity maximized.

compassion fatigue   As a result of recurrent crises over time, scenes of famine and refugee camps tend to lose their impact on audiences.

compellence   Term coined by Thomas Schelling to refer to diplomatic efforts often using force (or threats of force) to compel other states to do what they would not otherwise do. By contrast, *deterrence is* directed more passively to keep other states from doing something or from undertaking an undesirable action through threat of punishment if such action were undertaken. (*See also* coercive diplomacy; deterrence)

competitive devaluation   (*See* devalue)

compliance   (*See* verification)

comprador class   A term referring originally to the stratum of native businessmen in various Asian countries (including China) who served as local agents for foreign, colonial business interests. In contemporary usage, it refers to the aggregate of business elites in a Third World country or countries who maintain close links with their counterparts in the industrial countries of the First World. Particularly in Marxist usage, the term is used to explain relations of exploitation by the bourgeoisie of Third World workers and peasants.

concentration of forces   (*See* principles of war)

concept   A construct or idea of a general or abstract nature that may, for example, refer to a particular phenomenon such as *war, power;* or *authority.*

Concert of Europe   Nineteenth-century association of states that devised the rules of great-power competition following the Napoleonic Wars and settlement at the Congress of Vienna (1815). (*See also* collective security)

concessionary, concessionary rate   Often a form of *foreign aid,* an interest rate below market rates that allows the recipient of loan proceeds to take a portion of the loan for reinvestment at market rates, compounding the gains from higher interest and applying the proceeds toward amortization of principal.

confederation, confederalism   A loose federation or association of component states or provinces; the confederal concept can be used to integrate societies often divided by regional, national-ethnic or other cleavages.

Conference on Security and Cooperation in Europe (CSCE)   (*See* Organization for Security and Cooperation in Europe)

confidence- and security-building measures (CSBMs)   Agreed-upon mechanisms among states aimed at improving security over time by building trust. Notice of military exercises, allowing adversaries and others to observe them, providing for scheduled and surprise inspections of military installations on a reciprocal basis, and an open information environment are among the CSBMs that have been established, particularly in Europe. (*See also* transparency)

conflict   Disagreement; the opposition or clash of units. Conflicts may be nonviolent or at varying degrees or levels of violence. Some theorists see the management of conflicts that cannot be resolved as being central to establishing and maintaining peace. Conflicts in international relations or world politics exist between or among states, national or ethnic communities, tribes, etc.

conservative   In Edmund Burke's definition, conservatives distrust change, particularly any radical transformation of existing arrangements in society. Reliance is on traditional, established, ways of doing things. Incremental or reformist rather than revolutionary activities are preferred if any changes are needed. Many present-day social conservatives doubt the efficacy of social engineering or other governmental programs that would effect substantial changes in the status quo, preferring instead to rely more on private, nongovernmental efforts.

consociational   Refers to formal arrangements for sharing power in society among diverse national, ethnic, or other groups.

constructivist   (*See* social constructivism)

consul, consul general   (*See* mission)

consulate   (*See* mission)

consumption   In economics, the use of goods or services that have been produced. Some of what is produced is not consumed, but rather is set aside or saved for investment in future production efforts. There is thus an inverse relation between consumption and savings or investment; the more that is consumed, the less will be left for saving and investment.

containment   The grand strategy of the United States designed to deal with the Soviet Union during the cold war. Through support to democratic states and forces, the building-up of robust military forces, the creation of military alliances, and supporting capitalist economic development, it was hoped the Soviet Union specifically and communism in general could be "contained" or confined within existing borders.

convertible currency   Readily accepted in exchange for other currencies; originally meant a "hard" currency readily exchangeable for gold and thus other currencies.

core   A term sometimes used synonymously with *center,* a reference to the industrialized countries in the global political economy. The term is also sometimes used to refer to the elites or dominant classes. The *periphery* consists of the less-developed countries or areas of Asia, Latin America, and Africa. The periphery plays a subordinate but important role in a worldwide capitalist division of labor by providing raw materials and cheap labor. As capitalism develops, countries can move from periphery to core or slip from core to peripheral or *semiperipheral* status, which refers to an intermediate position between core and periphery.

cosmopolitan, cosmopolitanism   Outward or worldly in orientation, avoiding local and ethnocentric prejudices; the "citizen of the world" with human associations across the frontiers of states and other jurisdictions.

cost   A loss as opposed to a benefit; something paid as opposed to something received.

Council of Europe   International organization that promotes democracy in the European area.

counterforce targets   (*See* targeting)

counter-offensive   (*See* offensive)

counterproliferation   Active measures to reduce or eliminate existing weapons systems and nuclear, chemical, and biological agents as opposed to simply preventing the spread of such weapons, technology, and knowledge which is associated with nonproliferation.

countervalue targets   (*See* targeting)

country team   (*See* mission)

credibility   (*See* deterrence)

crisis   A situation characterized by surprise, high threat to values or interests, and short decision time.

crisis of authority   A loss of legitimacy on the part of a government or other actor. A result may be the breakdown of order as people refuse to follow the orders of those who claim to be in positions of authority. (*See also* authority)

crisis diplomacy   (*See* diplomacy)

critical theorists, theory   Associated with Jürgen Habermas and the "Frankfurt School" in Germany that offered a theory of social reality based on the dialectic of knowledge and power, arguing that theory must be connected to practice. This also entailed a critique of positivist–empiricist approaches to knowledge, with critical theorists claiming all knowledge is historical and political in nature. Current "dissidents" in the field of international relations have also drawn, among others, from Antonio Gramsci's own version of critical theory, Ludwig Wittgenstein's work on linguistics and hermeneutics, and the post-structuralist perspective of such writers as Michel Foucault. Critical theory challenges the stated and unstated assumptions and alleged objectivity of mainstream social science. Ideologies that represent particular interests, while masquerading as "theories," are especially suspect. Such theories are depicted deceptively as if they were objective portrayals of sociopolitical time and space. Critical theorists reject the pretense to objective knowledge—the logical positivism of the "Vienna Circle" advanced in the interwar period and followed by many social scientists in subsequent decades. The rigid division between normative and empirical theory is illusory. Moreover, what we think we know really is a function of language and sociopolitical context. Critical theory calls for interpretive understanding of time and space, an insight drawn originally from Max Weber's work in social science methodology.

crusades   Efforts in the eleventh, twelfth, and thirteenth centuries by European Christians including the use of force in the Middle East to regain the Holy Land and religious shrines that had fallen under Islamic influence and control.

cujus regio ejus religio   Latin phrase referring to the peace settlement at Westphalia (1648) that ended the Thirty Years' War among German and other states by establishing the principle by which the religion of the inhabitants of a state would be determined by the prince to whom they were subject. Beyond this issue, such authority was indicative of the growing strength of states and the evolving concept of sovereignty. (*See also* sovereignty)

cultural imperialism   (*See* imperialism)

cultural relativism   (*See* relativism)

cultures of violence   Refers to values in societies or subgroups that accept or even legitimize the use of violent means to attain social ends.

customary international law   Established practice over time by states gives a customary base for international law. Thus centuries of practice had established diplomatic immunity and other diplomatic rights.

customs union   Level of economic integration in which states not only have agreed to eliminate tariffs on imports and other barriers to trade among themselves, but have also established a common external tariff imposed on imports from non-members of the customs union. (*See* integration)

cyberterrorism   Computer-based attacks on information systems designed to destroy or manipulate data banks or cause the system to crash with the goal of furthering a political agenda.

decision   Choosing among often competing alternatives or options; making a judgment or drawing a conclusion. A *rational* decision making process is one in which alternative means to achieve certain objectives are evaluated and the best (or at least satisfactory) option or options for attaining these objectives are selected. (*See also* policy)

defense   Security against attack or threat of attack. In *strategic defense* against attack by nuclear or other weapons of mass destruction, defenses include both active and passive measures. *Active defense* includes actual *warfighting* capabilities such as fighter-interceptor aircraft, surface-to-air missiles (SAM), and anti-aircraft artillery (AAA) against invading bombers; anti-ballistic missiles (ABM) against incoming missiles as in national missile defense; and surface ships and attack submarines in anti-submarine warfare (ASW). An even more offensive form of active defense is construed to include intercontinental (ICBM), submarinelaunched (SLBM), or other ballistic missiles directed preemptively against an enemy's own offensive ballistic missiles or launch-control system before launching has occurred. Although related to a country's overall warfighting posture, *passive defense* does not include warfighting activities *per se.* Such passive measures include deploying radar and other means to detect and thus provide warning of attack. *Civil defense,* such as notifying populations to take cover or moving them to blast or other fall-out shelters, is an additional passive defense measure. Strategic defense can be designed to protect specific targets an enemy might attack (sometimes called *point defenses)* or large expanses of territory (sometimes called *area defenses).*

delegation   (*See* mission)

demand   In economics, the desire for a good or service and the ability to pay for some quantity of it at a certain price or range of prices. (*See also* elasticity)

démarche   A diplomatic representation, request, or protest from one government to another.

democratic centralism   An organizing principle in Leninist or communist parties that allows participation by party members on issues under discussion, but requires party members to adhere to decisions once they are made by higher party authorities. The *politburo* is usually the highest level of party decision-making and thus retains central authority over subordinate levels of party organization and membership.

demographics, demography   Measures relating to population, including overall numbers; life, death, and social statistics; categorization (such as national, ethnic, tribal, racial, cultural affiliations); and, more broadly, implications of such variables for human beings as form of political economy or political regime, war or domestic strife, and climate change or other environmental factors.

dependency   The concept that low-income countries (sometimes referred to as Third World or South) are economically subordinated to serve primarily the interests or advantage of high-income countries (sometimes referred to as First World or North). In class-analytical terms, workers and peasants on a worldwide scale are subordinated and exploited to varying degrees by capital-owning classes or *bourgeoisie* in their own and in First World countries.

dependent variable   (*See* causes, causality, causal)

Depreciate, depreciation   When a currency or other asset decreases in value over time we say it depreciates. (*See also* appreciate, appreciation)

Deputy Chief of Mission   (DCM) (*See* mission)

détente   An easing or relaxing of tensions between states, as in the late 1960s and 1970s between the U.S. and Soviet Union and their respective allies.

deterrence   Threat of the use of force aimed at persuading another actor not to do what it intends or may like to do; a psychological effect on an opponent that results in a rational decision to desist because of the expected consequences of attacking or starting a war. Deterrence usually involves threat of *punishment;* however, in some usages it refers *to denial*—that other states are deterred because they expect an effective military response to their actions, know they cannot achieve their objectives through the use of force, and thus rationally do not try to do so. To be effective, deterrence threats must be *credible* or believed by policy makers in the threatened country as being real (and not just bluffs)—that is, that they would be carried out. *Extended deterrence* refers to deterrence threats designed to protect other countries in addition to the country making the deterrence threats, as when a great power makes deterrence commitments to its allies, thus effectively putting them under its security "umbrella." In *strategic* or *nuclear deterrence, minimum* or *finite* deterrence refers to a country maintaining a relatively small number of nuclear or other weapons of mass destruction for use in making deterrence threats. Critics of minimum deterrence usually argue that the small numbers of such weapons may make them vulnerable to preemptive destruction or that threats from such countries may not be credible.

devalue   To reduce the exchange value of a country's currency, as when one unit of a country's currency that could buy ten units of another currency yesterday can buy only eight units today, representing a 20 percent devaluation. Because devaluation effectively reduces the export price of goods and services produced domestically and sold to other countries, some countries may choose to devalue merely to gain a competitive advantage (for example, a good selling for one currency unit cost foreign importers ten units of their currency yesterday, but today only eight units—a 20 percent discount that may undercut the price foreign producers can offer). *Competitive devaluations* occur when foreign countries match a devaluation in one country with devaluations of their own to even the score or gain an advantage of their own. Experience with competitive devaluations in the 1930s, for example, had the net effect of substantially reducing the overall volume of world trade. (*See also* exchange rate)

development   The process associated with economic growth or the industrialization of societies. As used in this text, a distinction is drawn between economic and social development. (*See also* economic development; social development; sustainable development)

diplomacy, diplomat   The management of international relations by negotiations; the method by which these relations are adjusted and managed by ambassadors and envoys; the business or art of the *diplomat,* who is the official representative of states and international organizations who defends state or organizational interests through negotiation. To do their job, diplomats require *diplomatic immunity,* a reciprocal privilege among states by which diplomats are not subject to arrest, prosecution, or penalty in the foreign state to which they are assigned. Such *reciprocity* among states is essential if countries are to maintain and conduct business with one another. To expel a diplomat, the state must declare him or her *persona non grata* (person not welcome); in such cases the person is forced to leave the country and is removed from the *diplomatic list* maintained by the host country. *Bilateral diplomacy* involves two states whereas *multilateral diplomacy* involves three or more states. *Preventive diplomacy* refers to efforts taken to address international problems with constructive approaches, avoiding if possible the deterioration of relations that could lead to armed conflict. *Good offices* can be offered by a third-party state whose diplomats assist in getting two disputant states to communicate, cease hostilities, work toward conflict resolution, or keep the peace. *Crisis diplomacy* involves negotiation between actors often characterized by surprise, high threat to values or interests, and short decision time, as occurred, for example, in the October 1962 Cuban missile crisis, when the U.S. and Soviet Union came to the brink of nuclear war. *Coercive diplomacy* refers to veiled or explicit threats of economic sanctions or military actions designed to influence diplomats or policy makers in other states to do something they would not otherwise do. (*See* compellence *and, by contrast, see also* deterrence; *see also* extraterritoriality *and* asylum)

diplomatic immunity   (*See* diplomacy)

disarmament   The reduction of armaments or weapons of war, ultimately to zero in *general and complete disarmament.*

dissuade, dissuasion   To persuade other states from a position of strength not to do something they might otherwise do; dissuasion is usually seen as using both positive and negative measures, but falling short of *deterrence* (that is, making threats to punish another state or states if they commit aggression or pursue some other undesirable policy). (*See also* deterrence; compellence; coercive diplomacy)

division of labor   In international trade, the specialization in production of goods and services in which some countries as more efficient producers have a *comparative advantage* that may result in what amounts to a division of labor among countries in world markets, with some countries producing some things for export while importing other goods and services from foreign producers. The concept is drawn from production efficiencies in domestic economies achieved through specialization and the resulting division of labor and is associated with Ricardian free-trade theory. (*See also* comparative advantage)

division of powers As between a central government and the governments of constituent parts such as provinces or states. (*See also* state, federal)

dual or double-effect principle (*See* just-war theory)

due process The citizen's expectation of or right to fairness, especially in relation to government, often operationalized in the form of procedures that, if followed, have a higher likelihood of assuring a fair or just outcome.

East During the Cold War years, *East* referred to the Soviet Union and other Marxist-Leninist countries, mainly those in Eastern Europe, that were part of an *East-West* struggle or conflict. A more traditional meaning is the Orient or countries of Asia. (*See also* West)

East African Community (EAC) Formed in 1967 in an effort to strengthen economic ties in the region; members are Kenya, Uganda, and Tanzania. An East African Development Bank also serves these three countries.

East-West (*See* East; West)

economic and monetary union Economic integration to a high degree that includes not only a customs union and common market, but also centralized monetary policy making, as in a single central bank and coordination of fiscal (tax and government expenditure) policy decision-making.

Economic Community of West African States (ECOWAS) Formed in 1975 in an effort to liberalize regional trade. Members include Benin, Burkina Faso, Cape Verde, Cote d'Ivoire, the Gambia, Ghana, Guinea, Guinea-Bissau, Ivory Coast, Liberia, Mali, Mauritania, Niger, Nigeria, Senegal, Sierra Leone, and Togo.

economic development The sustained expansion of production in an economy that raises the standard of living for the citizenry. (*See also* development)

economic infrastructure Production-support factors such as roads, seaports, airports, public transportation, and telecommunications that enhance a country's ability to sustain production and develop economically.

economic leverage Carrots and sticks used to influence, persuade, or coerce another state to do something or to stop doing something. *Foreign aid* includes grants, loans, trade preferences, or military assistance provided by one country to another, often with the hope of the provider gaining something in return such as political support for its foreign policy agenda. *Economic sanctions* include such coercive means to influence a state's behavior as a *boycott* (not purchasing the other country's exports) or going one step further with an *embargo* (prohibiting not only a government's agencies, but non-government or private firms as well, from dealing with the country being embargoed). Although they may have value symbolically, boycotts and embargoes are often ineffective unless all states that have major economic dealings with the country collaborate. A *blockade* is the physical imposition of ships, troops, or air power to prevent goods from entering or leaving the country.

economic liberalism (*See* liberalism)

economic and monetary union The deepest form of economic integration short of full political union; in addition to free trade, a common external tariff, and free movement of factors of production, an economic and monetary union integrates (or at least coordinates) fiscal and monetary policy, usually establishing a common currency and central bank to manage it. (*See* integration)

economic sanctions (*See* economic leverage)

economic structuralism, globalism, globalists, A perspective that one must comprehend the global context within which states and other entities interact. Understanding the overall economic or class structure of the international system means one must examine more than the distribution of power among states (realists) or chart the movements of transnational actors and the internal political processes of states (pluralists). While important, such actors, processes, and relations are part of a world shaped by global social and economic forces whose impact is not always readily apparent in the day-to-day world of domestic and international political competition. (*See* also Marxism-Leninism, structural violence)

economies of scale Efficiencies that come from larger quantities or mass production resulting in lower costs.

economy The production, distribution, and consumption of goods and services. Discussions of the economy generally focus on a particular state and society, but the growth of an international or global economy has expanded the focus to regional and global economies and the interdependency and interconnectedness of economies and economic actors such as multinational corporations and banks that cross national boundaries. Economic concerns can also be viewed from the perspective of individuals or groups.

economy of forces (*See* principles of war)

egalitarian A democratic focus on rights to *equality* either in terms of opportunity or outcome for individuals, groups, tribes, classes, etc. (*See also* equal protection)

effect Outcome of some cause or causes. (*See also* causes)

elasticity Ratio of the change in quantity of demand (or supply) caused by a change in price or income, the former referred to as price elasticity and latter income elasticity of demand (or supply).

elite The upper stratum or strata of a society.

embargo (*See* economic leverage)

embassy (*See* mission)

eminent domain A government's right to take private property for public use, usually with compensation for the owner.

emissary One who officially represents a state; he or she may be an ambassador, or someone specially designated to convey a government's wishes, concerns, or demands.

empires (*See* imperial system)

empirical, empirical theory Factual or known through observation; theories are interrelated propositions that aim to explain or predict what is observed. *Explanation* involves accounting for, or understanding causes of, such phenomena as war, arms races, and regional integration. In a loose sense, *prediction* amounts merely to forecasting, but in a strict sense it implies explanation sufficient to anticipate outcomes, given the presence of certain variables or conditions. Empirical theories are differentiated from value-oriented, prescriptive or normative theories. (*See also* normative theory, cause)

English School   Scholars influenced by the earlier work of Martin Wight, Hedley Bull, F. H. Hinsley and others. The school focuses on the societal aspects of international relations rather than seeing politics in purely abstract, systemic terms. Power, law or rules based on enlightened self-interest, and emergent global norms are all part of an anarchical international society.

epistemic community   Associations typically across national borders among knowledgeable persons or experts in particular (often very technical) fields; these are networks of personal contacts established and maintained over time in various settings—international meetings and conferences, joint research projects, contacts in international and nongovernmental organizations, and direct communications facilitated by the internet.

epistemology   Refers to a theory of knowledge: how we come to know what we think we know about the world and what we observe in it, a pursuit that leads us to adopt various methods and methodologies for testing and expanding our knowledge. (*See also* ontology)

equal protection   Refers to a civil right claimed by citizens (as in the United States) to equal protection of the laws—the equality of treatment citizens have a right to demand or expect before the law. (*See also* egalitarian)

equilibrium   When various elements of a system are in balance, as in a *balance of power among states*. (*See also* balance of power)

espionage   The act of spying on others, as in efforts to obtain secret intelligence. *Sabotage is* destruction of property, sometimes including loss of lives, or disruption of normal operations, typically by an agent or others working for a foreign government or cause. (*See also* intelligence collection)

ethnic, ethnicity   A common, often cultural, identity of a group of people who usually also identify themselves with a larger society that includes other groups within the nation as a whole; ethnic ties can cross the formal boundaries of states. In common usage, ethnicity is usually differentiated from nationality; that is, an over-arching identity that includes diverse ethnic and other groups in society and is often associated with a particular state, as in a *nation-state*.

European Community, European Communities (EC)   (*See* European Union, EU)

European Free Trade Area (EFTA)   Composed of non-European Union members, the organization originally formed as an alternative to what is now the European Union.

European Union (EU)   A collaborative association of European states previously known as the European Communities (EC)—the European Coal and Steel Community (ECSC), European Economic Community (EEC), and European Atomic Energy Community (EURATOM). Since agreeing at a summit meeting in December 1991 in the city of Maastricht in the Netherlands to move beyond a customs union and common market toward a full economic and monetary union, the association of states is now referred to as the European Union. Members include the original six—France, Germany, Italy, Belgium, Netherlands, and Luxembourg—and nine later additions—Austria, Denmark, Finland, Greece, Ireland, Portugal, Spain, Sweden, and the United Kingdom. Countries in Central and Eastern Europe have (or will be) admitted as members.

exchange controls   Limits placed on the amounts of domestic currency that can be exchanged for other currencies as in placing constraints on purchases of imports or the amount of domestic currency that can be taken out of the country.

exchange rate   The value of one currency in terms of another currency, as when one unit of a given currency can be exchanged for ten units of another.

executive agreement   Agreements made between the leaders of two or more countries that do not have the more formal characteristics of treaties. Leaders of democratic states often find such agreements preferable to treaties which, in the case of the United States, require the consent of two-thirds of the Senate before the treaty comes into force.

explanation   (*See* empirical theory)

exports   (*See* balance of trade)

expropriation   When a state nationalizes or takes private property; the state is obligated under international law to give just compensation for any property seized; however, states do not always choose to comply with this requirement. (*See also* nationalization)

extended deterrence   (*See* deterrence)

externality   When a state or other actor takes an action that has an intended or unintended impact (positive or negative) on another actor. For example, a negative externality occurs when Country A devalues its currency (making it less in value compared to other currencies), hence making the price of foreign imports more expensive and less likely to be purchased from abroad by importers in Country A.

extradition   Governments often have agreements or otherwise request another government to transfer and release persons to its own custody as when, for example, persons accused of crimes have sought refuge in another country.

extraterritoriality   The legal fiction that an embassy or consulate and the ground it stands on are part of the sovereign territory and property of the foreign country. As a result, the host government is not supposed to enter the grounds, for example, in pursuit of dissidents. Embassies and consulates, therefore, may serve as places of *asylum* for refuge for host-country citizens seeking protection. (*See* diplomacy; asylum)

factor endowments   (*See* factors of production)

factors of production   Land (including natural resources), labor, and capital are the *factors* essential to the production of goods and services. Countries vary significantly in the amounts of these different factors they possess. These different *factor endowments* may make some more efficient in the production of certain goods or services than others, which may result in specialization in accordance with the principle of *comparative advantage*. (*See also* comparative advantage)

federal, federalism, federation   (*See* state)

feminism, feminist   An approach to theory that takes into account the constructive and collaborative potential of human beings, often rejecting such cold, abstract analysis as found in neorealist and other structural explanations; the focus is more on multilateral relations rather than unilateral or hegemonic dominance. In the policy realm, feminism also seeks the empowerment of women, putting women on an equal plain with men.

feudalism, feudal system   Diverse group of governmental units from ninth to fourteenth century Europe, including trading associations, merchant banks, local feudal barons, emperor of the Holy Roman Empire, and the Christian Church. A prime example of a *pluralist* era. In Marxist usage, a mode of production. (*See also* mode of production)

finite, minimum deterrence (*See* deterrence)

first-, second-strike capability In nuclear strategy, first-strike capability does not mean simply an ability to strike first. Only if a country's strategic arsenal has robust defenses in addition to substantial offenses will it be in a position to launch an attack against another nuclear-weapons state, nullifying or reducing to a tolerable level the damage that would be sustained by a retaliatory counter-attack. As such, it is said to have a *first-strike capability*. Put another way, it is the military ability to blunt or withstand counterattack and to win or prevail in any such nuclear confrontation that is the acid test of whether a country has a first-strike capability which, in turn, could be used as leverage against other states. A *second-strike capability* refers merely to being able to absorb a nuclear first strike with sufficient retaliatory forces surviving to launch a counter-attack. A country without second-strike capability faces the problem that its retaliatory forces could be destroyed before they were launched, thus giving an incentive to launch a retaliatory strike on earliest warning of an attack, even before the attack is confirmed. By contrast, nuclear deterrence relations are generally more stable if the parties have a second-strike capability, because no country would have to launch its retaliatory forces until confirming that it had, in fact, been attacked. (*See also* deterrence)

First World (*See* Third World)

fiscal policy National budget decisions and actions on taxing and spending. (*See also* monetary policy, macroeconomics)

float When governments do not intervene in currency markets, allowing currency exchange rates to move flexibly in response to market forces (supply and demand).

fog of war The sum of all uncertainties and unpredictable occurrences that can happen so rapidly in war.

force Military measures intended to coerce other state(s) against their will.

force posture Numbers, types, locations, and other qualitative factors concerning a state's military forces.

foreign aid (*See* economic leverage)

foreign policy (*See* policy)

free markets (*See* capitalism)

free rider (*See* collective goods)

free trade, free-trade area In the purest sense, free trade is commerce unobstructed by tariffs, quotas, or other barriers to trade, particularly the absence of government interference in market transactions. A free-trade area includes states that have eliminated (or are in the process of eliminating) tariffs, quotas, or other barriers to trade. (*See* integration)

friction Clausewitz observed that, when implemented, war plans in practice may not work as expected due to a number of real-world, often unexpected factors he referred to collectively as friction.

functional approaches (to controlling or managing conflicts) include (1) maintaining effective communications between adversaries; (2) establishing confidence- and security-building measures (see entry), and (3) conducting peacekeeping operations.

functionalism, functionalist Functionalist theories posit that international organizations form when functions need to be performed; for example, postal exchange led in the nineteenth century to creation of the Universal Postal Union; maintenance of international liquidity led to creation of an International Monetary Fund (IMF); management of telecommunications on a global scale led to construction of the International Telecommunications Union, and so forth. Neofunctionalism, by contrast, looks beyond functions that need to be performed and puts more emphasis on politics, especially within and across elites, as essential to understanding how international regimes and organizations are constructed and maintained.

game theory A decision-making approach based on the assumption of actor rationality in a competitive situation, in which each party tries to maximize gains or minimize losses. Some games are zero-sum while others are variable- or positive-sum. (*See also* zero-sum)

gender The classification of beings as masculine, feminine, or neuter. From the feminist perspective, gender distinctions are often viewed as being socially constructed as opposed to being determined by nature.

genocide Mass murder of a people typically because of their racial, ethnic, or particular identity. No other example compares in magnitude or brutality to the *Holocaust* of the 1930s and 1940s in Germany and other countries in central Europe, which was responsible for the deaths of some six million Jews as well as Slavs, Gypsies, homosexuals, and others considered undesirable by National Socialist (Nazi) authorities in Germany. More recent examples in the 1990s have occurred in the Balkan republics of the former Yugoslavia, among Tutu and Hutsi tribes in Rwanda and Burundi in sub-Saharan Africa in the Sudan.

global civil society The gradual emergence worldwide of the rule of law and networks of relationships among people around a world composed of both state and non-state actors to include non-governmental organizations (NGOs) that aggregate individual interests within states, operating across the border of any single state. The explosion in the number of NGOs in recent years exemplifies this trend, as does the ability of individuals to communicate with one another through such technological means as satellite links and the Internet. The concept of global civil society captures the idea that global politics is much more than just the interactions of states; people are not just the subjects of state authorities, but as parts of worldwide organizations and as individuals able to move and communicate globally, they also influence both governmental and nongovernmental decisions and actions.

globalization The continual increase in transnational and worldwide economic, social, and cultural interactions that transcend the boundaries of states, aided by advances in technology.

global politics (*See* world politics)

global warming An increase in the volume of carbon dioxide in the atmosphere, contributing to a "green-house" or insulating effect that traps heat from the sun's rays and raises the average temperature around the world. Changes of only a degree or two can have substantial or even catastrophic climatic effects with changes in rainfall patterns affecting agriculture and polar ice cap melt raising sea level, threatening lower-lying coastal areas. Burning of hydrocarbon fuels and destruction of rain forests are among the causes usually cited for global warming.

good offices   (*See* diplomacy)

government   Administrative unit or units that exercise authority in a political unit, making decisions and taking actions. A *puppet government* is one installed by an outside or occupying power, usually involving indigenous collaborators; the Vichy regime in France during World War II, for example, was subject to daily influence and ultimate control by the National Socialist (Nazi) regime in Germany. When a state has been invaded and occupied a *government in exile* may be set up in a foreign country; during the Nazi occupation of World War II, General Charles deGaulle located the French government in exile in London.

government in exile   (*See* government)

gross domestic product (GDP)   The total value or sum of goods and services produced *domestically* usually within a given year. It amounts to GNP minus return on foreign investment, since the latter is a measure of foreign, rather than domestic, production. (*See also* gross national product)

gross national product (GNP)   The total value or sum of a country's output of goods and services. Usually calculated on an annual basis, it is the sum of consumption, investment, government spending, and exports minus imports.

Group of Eight (G-8)   (*See* Group of Seven)

Group of Seven (G-7)   States having the world's largest market economies—the United States, Japan, Germany, France, the United Kingdom, Italy, and Canada. The Russian Federation is now included in the group, now often referred to as the G-8. Leaders of these countries hold periodic summit meetings where macroeconomic and other policy issues are discussed.

groupthink   A mode of thinking that people engage in when they are deeply involved in a cohesive in-group, when the members' strivings for unanimity override their motivation to appraise realistically alternative courses of actions. (The social psychologist Irving Janis is credited with important work on this subject as well as coining the term.) Indicators of groupthink include social pressure to enforce conformity, limiting discussion to a few alternatives, failing to examine initial decisions, and making little effort to seek information from outside experts. It is assumed that groupthink enhances the possibility of poor foreign policy decisions. By contrast, measures taken to avoid groupthink—bringing alternative views and perspectives legitimately into consideration—can have an opposite, positive effect on foreign policy making.

guerrilla warfare   War conducted by irregulars or *guerrillas,* usually against regular, uniformed forces, employing hit-and-run, ambush, and other tactics that allow smaller numbers of guerrillas to win battles against numerically superior, often heavily-armed regular forces. Guerrilla warfare can be particularly successful if the guerrillas can rely on popular support from the people. (*See also* war)

Gulf Cooperation Council (GCC)   Formed in 1981, this international organization addresses economic and security issues of concern to Arab Gulf member states—Bahrain, Kuwait, Oman, Qatar, Saudi Arabia, and the United Arab Emirates. Iraq and non-Arab Iran are not members.

hard currencies   Money preferred for use in settling obligations among countries because it is readily convertible from one currency to another and can be kept by national treasuries as monetary reserves. The U.S. dollar is a key hard currency as is the European euro and the Japanese yen. (*See also* soft currencies)

hegemonic state system   (*See* state)

hegemony, hegemonic   Relations of dominance as when a major power exercises hegemony over countries within its sphere of influence. A state exercising hegemony is sometimes called a *hegemon.*

Heckscher-Ohlin theorem   Holds that because different countries have diverse factor endowments (different amounts of land, labor, and capital), they likely will export those goods or services in which their combination of these production factors gives them a comparative advantage.

humanitarian intervention   (*See* intervention)

human security   focus is on individuals no matter where they live as opposed to viewing them as citizens of particular states or nations.

hypothesis   A proposition subject to empirical test for its veracity. (*See* causes, causality, causal)

idealism   A tradition of political thought that emphasizes what unites (as opposed to divides) peoples. Traced back to the philosophical school of thought known as Stoicism, it is also associated with the writers Hugo Grotius and Immanuel Kant, who searched for such universal, uniting concepts as international law or moral principles. A high value orientation in idealism has led many writers to present it as different from, even the opposite of, realism in foreign policy, which focuses primarily on national interest and power considerations. This rigid idealist-realist dichotomy can be misleading, however, since many realists also incorporate value considerations in their analyses and prescriptions.

ideal (or pure) type   A concept developed by the German sociologist Max Weber to describe an extreme, or pure, case that is not found in this form anywhere but that serves as an analytical benchmark useful in comparing real-world cases.

identity   Consists of the answer to the question "Who am I and with whom do I identify?" In international relations the answer is usually in terms of identification with a nation that may or may not be associated with an existing state. Identity, however, can be transnational such as religious or gender identification.

imperial (suzerain) system   Separate societal units associated by regular interaction, but with one among them asserting political supremacy and the others formally or tacitly accepting this claim as, for example, in the Roman empire under the Caesars. In feudal Europe and after, when a state or ruler had some authority or control over other countries or lesser political entities, these political units were said to be under the suzerainty of that state or ruler.

imperialism   In its classic meaning, a position or policy of preeminence or dominance with respect to foreign elements as in the Roman or British empires. Imperialism in earlier centuries involved the establishment of colonies staffed by personnel (administrators, military troops, missionaries) from the imperial country or *metropole,* which reflected what is known as *colonialism.* Although most of these former colonies have formally become independent states, the relations of economic, social, cultural, and even political dominance by the former colonial power remain, a phenomenon often called *neocolonialism.* Influence or dominance by a former colonial or other great power by virtue of the capabilities it has over less powerful states is sometimes referred to by critics as economic, social, or cultural imperialism.

imports   (*See* balance of trade)

independent state system   (*See* state)

independent variable   (*See* causes, causality, causal)

individualism   Associated with *liberalism,* the belief that individuals have particular value in themselves and for what they can do: People as individuals have more importance than the groups, tribes, communities, or societies to which they may belong. (*See also* liberalism)

infant industry   As a country develops economically, new industries may form that in the early stages are not competitive in global markets with well-established industries of the same type from other countries. As such, governments may choose to protect these infant industries from foreign competition by imposing tariffs or quotas against imports or seeking trade preferences by other countries that allow infant-industry firms to export on favorable terms to these foreign countries.

influence   (*See* power)

insurgency   (*See* war)

insurgent warfare   (*See* war)

intelligence, intelligence collection   The overt or covert gathering of information by intelligence operatives from human sources or photography, electronic emissions, intercepted communications and other transmissions gathered by *national technical means (NTM)* in ground stations and on ships at sea, aircraft or earth satellites *Strategic intelligence* supports the formulation of strategy, policy, plans and operations at the national level, providing intelligence of use to policy makers and senior military commanders and their staffs. *Operational intelligence* supports planning and conducting military campaigns to accomplish objectives in a particular contingency or within a particular region. (*See also* espionage)

integration   The process by which such political units as states come together in varying degrees of unity, often to serve specific functions or purposes. Thus economic integration may range from defining a free trade area or customs union to agreeing on terms for a common market or economic and monetary union. (*See also* free trade area, customs union, common market, economic and monetary union)

intercommunal   Relations between communities with separate identities often within the same society. These can be friendly relations or, conversely, can involve strife including violent acts by members of one community against the other, as between Protestants and Catholics in Northern Ireland, Hutu and Tutsi tribes in Rwanda, or Croats, Muslims, and Serbs in Bosnia.

interdependence   A situation whereby actions and events in one state, society, or part of the world affect peoples elsewhere. For interdependence to exist, there must be some degree of mutual dependence, or reciprocal ties and effects among the parties involved. In most cases interdependence is *asymmetric,* meaning one party is more affected than the other. Interdependence relations can exist among states or involve other actors such as transnational organizations or individuals, with channels of interaction or links that transcend the boundaries of states and their respective societies.

interest section   (*See* mission)

interests   Security and welfare considerations constitute the interests often expressed as goals or objectives that any actor in world politics (whether a state, an international organization, multinational corporation, or some other nongovernmental organization) may seek to pursue. The term *national interests* is associated with states, and all states at a minimum typically seek not only to survive, but also to achieve economic vitality (or at least viability) and the protection of what they deem to be their core values. Given the general nature of interests, *objectives* are more specific goals that any international actor may choose to pursue. For example, a concern for the security and welfare of a state with a long coastline that depends on foreign trade would likely lead its policymakers to view protection of sea lanes as an important national objective.

International Atomic Energy Agency (IAEA)   International organization located in Vienna and established in 1956 with responsibilities for peaceful uses of nuclear energy while, at the same time, precluding use of these technologies or otherwise acquiring nuclear weapons by countries not now possessing them. (*See also* Nuclear Non-Proliferation Treaty)

international commerce   Trade of goods and services between and among states and their societies.

international governmental or inter-governmental organizations (IGOs)   (*See* international organizations)

internationalization   Increasing trade, communication, investment, and other interactions between or among *states* and their societies. When we refer to internationalization we think in terms of national identities, a view that can be contrasted with *globalization* that transcends or goes beyond states and their respective corporations or other organizations, taking a broad or global view of such matters. (*See also* globalization)

international law   Laws that transcend borders and apply to states as well as to individuals (natural persons) and organizations or corporations (legal persons). Sources of international law are *treaties or conventions* that bind states to these formal agreements even when their existing governments change, *customary practice* that has been established by states over time, the *writings of jurists* (justices or judges) such as those on the International Court of Justice, and *general principles* such as those to be discovered through reason or found in the *jus naturale*—laws of nature that some writers see as superseding those laws of individual states that contradict these general principles. The idea of a *jus gentium*—laws applicable to all of humanity, nations, and individuals—dates at least from the time of the Roman Empire and is to be found in Stoic thought.

international law of war, international law of armed conflicts   International law governing warfare and the use of force in international relations requires legitimate reasons for using force and places specific limitations on the actual use of force. (*See also* just-war theory, doctrine)

international liquidity   *See* liquidity (international)

international monetary regime   The rules on how money is exchanged and international liquidity is maintained as well as associated multilateral institutions (such as the International Monetary Fund and Bank for International Settlements)

international organizations   The multilateral institutions created by states in order to pursue common objectives that usually cannot be achieved as easily (or as well, if at all) by states acting unilaterally; for example, the European Union and its component institutions and the United Nations and its associated agencies, including the World Health Organization, World Bank, International Monetary Fund, International Civil Aviation and Maritime Organizations, and so forth. Sometimes called international governmental or intergovernmental organizations (IGOs), members of international organizations are states, which differentiates them from transnational or non-governmental organizations (NGOs). (*See also* non-governmental organization, NGO)

international politics   The *political* focus is on choices made by actors with authority to do so on issues external to states or that cross the frontiers or boundaries of state jurisdiction. (*See also* international relations; world politics)

international regime   The set of rules and associated institutions or international organizations, if any, that have been constructed by states to coordinate, manage, or regulate their relations in a particular issue area. Some regime rules have the binding character of international law, but others are followed by states because they simplify international relations by routinizing many recurring transactions or are seen as generally being in the state's enlightened self-interest. States may enforce regime rules on non-state actors. An *international monetary regime,* for example, specifies the rules for exchanging currency among states, making provision for maintaining international liquidity through credit arrangements by which some states or institutions like the International Monetary Fund in Washington lend currencies to states in balance-of-trade or balance-of-payments deficit. Other institutions associated with this regime include the Bank for International Settlements in Basel, Switzerland, as well as central banks and treasuries of states participating in the international regime. (*See also* international security regime)

international relations   Generally refers to relations among states—the total of political, social, economic, cultural, and other interactions. Realists tend to feel most comfortable with this state-centric definition of the term because they customarily view states as far more important or significant than non-state actors. (*See also* international politics, world politics)

international security   In its narrowest construction, the term refers to defense matters among states and their respective societies. In its broadest sense, it encompasses a very wide range of issues that affect the welfare of human beings—not just defense, but also economics, health, environment, human rights, and other social questions that cross national boundaries. Critics of broad definitions argue that if *security* as a concept can be construed to mean so many things, then as a practical matter it means nothing. They prefer to retain the more traditional distinction between *security* (and related defense issues) and *welfare* issues.

international security regime   A particular type of international regime with rules and associated institutions, if any, concerning some defense-related or other security concern of member states. For example, a nuclear nonproliferation international security regime exists in an effort to curb the spread of nuclear weapons and weapons-related technologies to non-nuclear states while, at the same time, it is committed in principle to working toward nuclear disarmament by those states already possessing such arms. The International Atomic Energy Agency (IAEA) in Vienna is a key institution associated with this regime. (*See also* international regime; Nuclear Non-Proliferation Treaty)

international systems   An aggregation of similar or diverse entities united by regular interaction that sets them apart from other systems; for example, the *interstate* or *international system* of states or *world politics* understood as a system composed of both state and non-state actors.

international terrorism   (*See* terrorism)

interstate war   (*See* war)

intervention   Interference in the domestic affairs of another state by diplomatic, economic, military, or other means. *Armed* or *military intervention* is a particular kind of intervention. Even though it has often occurred under one pretext or another, intervention in civil wars—understood as unresolved domestic affairs—is prohibited by international law. By contrast, intervention in a war between states in defense of the side suffering from aggression is allowable under the UN Charter, Article 51, that acknowledges the right of states to individual or collective self-defense. Some interventions are for *humanitarian* purposes, concerning welfare, rights, justice, or other factors relating to the condition of human beings.

investment   In business terms, the input of money or saved resources to maintain or expand productive capacity and, in turn, to generate a profit or return on investment for the investor.

invisible hand   The idea drawn from Book IV of Adam Smith's *Wealth of Nations* that competitive markets are self-regulating; that the allocation of factors of production for bringing goods and services to market can be efficiently achieved without government intervention or other actions that would affect these market transactions.

irredentism, irredentist   Seeking to acquire neighboring or other territories in another state, particularly if it is populated by peoples with a common national or ethnic heritage. (*See also* revanchism)

irregulars   (*See* war)

jus ad bellum   (*See* just-war theory)

jus gentium **(law or laws of nations)**   (*See* international law)

jus in bello   (*See* just-war theory)

jus naturale **(natural law, law or laws of nature)**   (*See* international law)

just-war theory, doctrine   Relying on Platonic thought, Cicero developed one of the earliest formulations of just-war theory: just wars ought to be fought justly. This idea would be developed over the centuries into a Christian doctrine by Augustine, Aquinas, Suarez, Gentilis, Vitoria, and others. Grotius adapted this thinking to an international law of war, which would become more formalized in succeeding centuries. The Hague and Geneva Conventions, for example, are based on or rely very heavily on earlier just-war theory. *Jus ad bellum* refers to the right to use force or go to war in the first place, which must satisfy all of the following conditions:

(1) *just or legitimate cause* for using force, (2) that waging war is a *proportionate* response to the provocation or cause for war, (3) that the decisions for war are made by *legitimate authority,* (4) that *peaceful remedies have been exhausted,* and (5) because warfare results in destruction of lives and property that it will not be undertaken unless there is at least some *chance of success*—that using force or waging war is at best a legitimate *means* to redress a grievance; it is not a legitimate *end* in itself. *Jus in bello* refers to limitations on actual conduct in warfare, including obligations: (1) to *spare noncombatants* (sometimes referred to as innocents), (2) to exercise restraint so that the means used in war are *proportionate* to the ends sought and do not produce needless death and destruction, (3) to use only those *weapons that are not immoral in themselves* (that is, indiscriminate weapons or those that cause needless suffering), and (4) to see *military necessity as a limiting rather than expansive principle.* Sometimes the same actions in warfare can have both positive, morally legitimate effects (as in destroying a military target without any unnecessary loss of life or property) and morally negative or evil effects, as when there is also *collateral damage*—loss of life or destruction of property. According to the *principle of dual or double-effect* such actions are legitimate only if the positive or legitimate purpose is intended, efforts have been taken to minimize collateral damage, the collateral damage caused is not disproportionate, and it occurs at the same time or after the positive effect (a provision to assure that positive or morally legitimate ends do not rely on evil means, but that evil consequences are merely another effect). To be effective, both the *jus ad bellum* and *jus in bello* rely heavily on the *right intention* of policy makers who try to follow these guidelines. In practice these principles, contrary to the requirement for *right intention,* have frequently been violated or manipulated in such a way as to justify or rationalize all forms of misconduct. Defenders of just-war theory acknowledge this criticism, but argue that if war cannot be avoided altogether, these principles at least offer a means for reducing the barbarity of war, as long as policy-makers choose to follow them.

kiloton   (*See* targeting)

laissez-faire   The classical liberal idea that governments should not intervene in markets because competitive markets are understood to be self-regulating. (*See also* invisible hand)

law of war   (*See* international law; international law of war; just-war theory)

legitimacy   In terms of *domestic politics,* the right to rule or be obeyed based on legal grounds or, more commonly, in the eyes of the citizenry based on custom or consent. Legitimacy may apply to a form of government or regime (as when a particular constitution has legitimacy) or to the authorities presently in power. Lacking legitimacy, rulers often have to rely on coercion to enforce obedience, finding it difficult to carry out domestic policies, and perhaps foreign policies as well. In international politics *legitimacy* often refers to whether a government, particularly a new government of a state, is recognized by other governments of foreign states as the proper representative or agent of the state in question. After a revolution or *coup d'état,* the governments of other states may choose to withhold recognition in an effort to deny legitimacy to the new government or regime.

levels of analysis   A way to organize thinking about and analysis of world politics. Individuals, groups, states and their societies, or the overall international system are separate points of focus, each illuminating some aspect of international relations. Such levels of analysis help scholars to be systematic in their approach to understanding world politics. In examining a phenomenon such as war, for example, the observer may identify possible causes as a characteristic of the international system, states and their societies, groups or individuals.

liberal   (*See* liberalism)

liberalism   Political philosophy with origins in the seventeenth and eighteenth centuries that emphasizes individual liberty to be achieved through a minimal state. A *laissez-faire* government—one that provides for law and order but is otherwise relatively more constrained or restricted, particularly from intervention in markets—is said to be politically and economically liberal. In both domestic and international economy, liberalism implies commitment to free-market principles generally without government intervention, including advocacy of international free-trade policies. In more recent times, liberalism has taken on a more social meaning, particularly in the United States, with reference to enhancing individual rights and well-being, typically through government action or programs.

liberalization   In the economic realm, a reduction of barriers making it easier for the import and export of goods and services, investment, and commerce in general.

libertarian   A philosophical position emphasizing individual rights, often preferring specific limits or restraints on government.

liquidity (international)   In monetary affairs, the ease with which foreign currencies are available for countries so they can settle their accounts with other countries.

long-cycle theory   An explanation of international system change in which it is argued that the global political system goes through distinct and identifiable historical cycles or recurrent patterns of behavior. The dominance of any particular state corresponds to a "long cycle," with war tending to mark the end of one cycle and the beginning of another.

macroeconomics   Focus is on how the economy as a whole works in relation to such aggregates as gross national product (GNP), gross domestic product (GDP), etc. How government fiscal and monetary policy affects these aggregates, levels of employment, and inflation are also macroeconomic concerns. (*See also* microeconomics, fiscal policy, monetary policy)

managed trade   Rather than leave trade to free markets, states choose to intervene, establishing understandings or making trade arrangements with other states, often to serve economic development, employment or other domestic considerations.

market prices   The monetary value at which exchange takes place freely in accordance with supply of goods and services offered to market and demand for them.

market rates   Usually refers to interest or discount rates, rates of return on investment, currency exchange rates, or other financial rates set freely in markets in accordance with supply and demand for securities (e.g., stocks and bonds), deposits in financial institutions, foreign currencies, and other financial instruments.

markets   Refers to the exchange of goods, services, money and other financial instruments between buyers and sellers. Governments play a role in markets through the policies they pursue concerning fiscal (taxing and spending) and monetary (managing the money supply and affecting interest rates) matters. "Free" markets refer to those left to the private or nongovernmental actors, eliminating (or at least minimizing) government interference. In practice, the degree and kind of government actions in markets varies widely. (By contrast, in "command" economies as in Marxist-Leninist regimes government plays a strong directive or controlling role by allocating human and natural resources and capital, setting production targets, overseeing production and distribution, and regulating prices.) Facilitated by liberalization as well as technological improvements in telecommunications and transportation, markets have become increasingly globalized. (*See also* liberalization, global civil society)

Marxism-Leninism   A body of thought inspired by the German Karl Marx and the Russian revolutionary Vladimir Lenin. Marx stressed the importance of economic and material forces and class analysis. He emphasized the dialectical, clashing, unfolding of history. He predicted that contradictions in each historical epoch eventually led to the rise of a new dominant class. Lenin, building on Marx's work, argued that contradictions in capitalist societies made *imperialism* inevitable, leading to war among capitalist states as they fought over colonial resources and territory throughout the world.

mass   (*See* principles of war)

means of production   The combinations of land, labor, and capital used to produce goods and services. In Marxist understanding, classes are defined by their relations to the means of production; for example, in feudalism the aristocracy is identifiable by its ownership of land and the peasantry by its labor; in capitalism, the bourgeoisie owns capital (factories, machinery, and financial assets related to production), the workers contributing labor. (*See also* factors of production; mode of production)

megaton   (*See* targeting)

mercantilism, mercantile   A theory of early capitalism that saw the wealth of a nation as a function of the amount of gold and other treasure that it could accumulate. Accordingly, running trade surpluses (more exports than imports), while finding new gold in mines or accepting it in payment for goods or services became national economic policy. In his *Wealth of Nations* (1776) Adam Smith challenged this view, arguing that the true wealth of a nation was to be found in its productive capacity, not its treasure. Present-day *neomercantilist* policies pursued by some states try to maximize trade surpluses, accumulating large monetary-reserve balances.

MERCOSUR (Mercado Comun del Sur)   Formed in 1991, this international organization promotes economic integration among Argentina, Brazil, Chile, Paraguay and Uruguay.

methodology   The approach one takes to an academic study; modes of research and analysis, as in the use of historical and comparative case studies, or the use of statistics as in formal hypothesis testing or causal modeling of variables.

microeconomics   Focus is on how markets work, how supply and demand relate and how prices are set. Sometimes referred to as price theory. On the supply side, for example, the number of firms matters in explanations of behavior in particular markets with notable variation as to whether the market in question is an oligopoly (several dominant firms), duopoly (two dominant firms), monopoly (one dominant firm), pure competition (no dominant firms), etc. Structural realism (or neorealism) draws explicitly from these microeconomic insights in developing what is referred to as microtheory on behavior in international systems in which the number of dominant states (multipolar, bipolar, unipolar) is similar in concept to the number of dominant firms in particular markets. (*See also* structural realism, macroeconomics)

migration   The movement of peoples from one country or area to others. Some *immigration* (arrivals) and *emigration* (departures) occur routinely; however, in the absence of obstacles, political refugees and economically deprived peoples are likely to move in large numbers.

military (force-employment) doctrines   The approaches developed over time by military or other security experts to the effective use of armed forces for specified purposes; for example, doctrine may hold that full-scale use of tactical air forces against military targets in another country be preceded by attacks against that country's air-defense capabilities in order to establish air superiority or command of the air which, when established, will allow the full-scale attack to proceed without effective opposition.

military necessity   Principle in warfare that battlefield success depends on destroying or weakening an adversary's warfighting capabilities. A narrow construction of military necessity restricts actions in war to only those required for destruction or weakening of an enemy's warmaking capability; however, some have used (or abused) the principle to justify or rationalize any number of actions in war, including atrocities committed against civilian populations.

minimum deterrence   (*See* deterrence)

Missile Technology Control Regime (MTCR)   An international security regime with rules that restrain transfer of missiles and missile-related technologies. (*See also* international regime; international security regime)

mission   A country's official foreign representation to another country or an international organization. A *delegation* is an official government representation to an international organization or conference. The *ambassador* is a state's highest ranking representative, assigned to the country's *embassy* in another state or its *mission* to an international organization. The ambassador is also the personal representative of a state's president or prime minister. The *Chief of Mission* is the highest ranking diplomat at a mission, usually the ambassador. The *Deputy Chief of Mission* (DCM) is the number-two ranking diplomat at a mission. *Chargé d'Affaires is* a French term that usually refers to the DCM or number-two ranking diplomat at a mission when the Chief of Mission is not present or has left the capital or country. *Country team* is an American management concept that aids in coordinating the work of the many agencies represented at a U.S. mission. In principle country-team meetings allow for discussion of issues, enhancing the overall effectiveness of the mission. *Consul general* is the title of the official in charge of a *consulate,* which is a mission (usually subordinate to the country's embassy in the capital of the host country, but in a different city) that deals with citizen services whether for their own country, the host country, or those of other foreign countries (for example, issuance of visas to foreign nationals desiring rights to enter the home country for tourist, student, or business purposes or to emigrate and acquire citizenship; visitation to citizens in foreign jails and prisons, promotion of commerce such as trade and investment; and so forth). *Consular sections* also perform similar functions within the embassy in the capital city. When diplomatic relations are first established or are being *normalized* after a period in which they have been broken, a consulate may be the first mission established, later upgrading the level of representation to an embassy with exchange of ambassadors, when *normalization* of relations is complete. When two countries have severed diplomatic relations and closed their respective missions, an *interest section* is often established in a mutually friendly or disinterested country's embassy to maintain an avenue for some minimal contact (for example, the U.S. relies on its interest section in the Swiss embassy in Havana as a point of contact for dealing with the Cuban government, should it be necessary).

mode of production   The form of political economy associated with the production of goods and services at different historical periods—a term used in Marxist understanding of ancient slavery, feudalism, and capitalism as different modes of production. (*See also* means of production)

monetarists   Those putting emphasis on understanding how money supply (volume of money in circulation, the "velocity" of money exchange or transaction flows, interest rates, currency exchange rates, etc.) affect the economy as a whole and markets in particular. As between monetary and fiscal policy, greater emphasis is placed on the former. (*See also* monetary policy, microeconomics, macroeconomics, exchange rate)

monetary policy   National decisions and actions that affect the money supply, interest rates, and exchange rates. (*See also* fiscal policy, macroeconomics, monetarist, exchange rate)

money   An instrument that provides a store of value and serves as a medium to facilitate exchange in market transactions. In the absence of money, exchange of goods and services is by trading one for another, referred to as barter.

multi-ethnic state   (*See* state)

multilateral diplomacy   (*See* diplomacy)

multilateralism   Working international issues jointly rather than unilaterally by a single state; a means to achieve mutual gains as in developing mutually acceptable norms and institutions. Associated with international relations as well as the idea of an emerging *global civil society.*

multinational banks   (*See* banks)

multinational corporation (MNC)   A corporate firm based or headquartered in one country but producing goods or services and conducting other operations in two or more countries.

multinational state   (*See* state)

multipolar, multipolarity   (*See* structure)

multi-tribal state   (*See* state)

mutually assured destruction   (MAD) (also referred to as mutual assured destruction) The nuclear deterrence doctrine that avoids resort to war by reciprocal threat of punishment through an unacceptable level of (or mass) destruction, should either party commit aggression or take other hostile action against the other that would provoke such a response.

nation, nationality   People with a common identity who have formed a nation-state or aspire to do so. (*See* nation-state; ethnic, ethnicity)

nationalization   The taking by governments of private property for public ownership or use. Owners suffering such loss of assets may or may not be compensated; however, consistent with international law such takings are supposed to be accompanied by fair compensation as well as being nondiscriminatory (for example, not singling out or targeting a particular firm or a particular foreign country's nationals). (*See also* expropriation)

nation-state   (*See* state)

national interest   (*See* interest)

national self-determination   The view that a people with a common identity have the right to be independent from outside control, as in establishing a state for such a national group.

national technical means   (See verification)

nationalism   Promoting national identity, usually to the exclusion of other, competing identities and legitimizing actions of state taken for national purposes. Nations without states often solidify movements to establish a nation-state around nationalist themes.

natural law   A philosophical view that claims there are laws inherent in nature that transcend any laws made by mere mortals. Such thinking is closely tied to the writings of Augustine, Aquinas, and other Christian writers of the late Roman empire and Middle Ages.

natural rights   Reference to the theory that human rights in nature can be discovered through reason. Social-contract theorists such as Locke and Rousseau saw rights in this naturalist understanding; however, utilitarians such as Bentham and Mill argued that human rights rested on other grounds also discoverable through reason, that human rights constitute the greatest good or happiness for the greatest number. (See utilitarian)

neoclassical economics, political economy, economists   Late 19th and early 20th century developments in economic thought departed from the labor theory of value held by classical economists, seeing value in a market context with price as the outcome of demand for and supply of particular products (goods or services). Utility and marginal utility (the value to be found in each additional unit of a good or service), marginal cost in relation to marginal revenue, and elasticity of supply and demand are examples of concepts in market analysis developed by neoclassical economists. The English writer Alfred Marshall and the French writer Leon Walras were among the most prominent early neoclassical contributors. (*See also* classical economics)

neocolonial, neocolonialism   (*See* imperialism)

neofunctionalism, neofunctionalist   (*See* functionalism)

neoliberal institutionalism   Like realism, neoliberal institutionalism is utilitarian and rational in orientation—states are treated as rational egoists and interstate cooperation occurs when states have significant interests in common. The goal is to discover how, and under what conditions, institutions matter. As such, neoliberal institutionalism addresses both security and nonsecurity or welfare issues. In this regard, institutions provide information, reduce transaction costs, make commitments more credible, establish focal points for coordination, and aid in the operation of reciprocity and multilateralism among states. The term *institution* may also refer not just to organizations, but also to such accepted patterns of recurrent or institutionalized relations as *multilateralism*.

mercantilism, neomercantilist   (*See* mercantilism, mercantile)

netwar   Conflicts in which the combatant is organized along networked lines or employs networks for operational control and other communications. Such networks provide lucrative targets to an adversary.

neutrality, neutral   Neutral states do not take sides in an international dispute or war or join an alliance. Some, like Switzerland, claim *permanent* neutrality. Others choose to be neutral, or perhaps more accurately, *nonaligned* as a tactical choice that serves its interest at a particular time.

New International Economic Order (NIEO)   Project developed under UN auspices, particularly in the 1960s, 1970s and 1980s, that called for trade preferences, concessionary loans, capital investment and other measures by economically advanced countries, thus contributing to Third World development.

newly industrializing country (NIC)   Countries such as Brazil, Taiwan, Singapore, South Korea, or Malaysia whose rapid economic growth over the past 30 years made the label *Third World* inappropriate. These countries exhibit strong *market* orientations, develop industrially, and heavily emphasize *exports*.

Nonaligned Movement (NAM)   Composed of those Third-World states wishing to avoid cold-war alliances with the United States, the Soviet Union or other major powers, the NAM originated formally in the 1955 Bandung (Indonesia) Conference. Early leaders included India's Nehru, Yugoslavia's Tito, and Indonesia's Sukarno.

nongovernmental organization   (NGO) Transnational organizations have a standing independent of governments, often with diversified membership, and work to fulfill specific political, social, or economic objectives that may benefit or have some positive or negative impact on a wide range of persons. Examples include Amnesty International (human rights) and Doctors Without Borders (medical support for health care crises in the Third World). Because of their nongovernmental character, NGOs also include multinational corporations and banks; labor unions; privately owned telecommunications, newspaper, and other print media firms; churches and other religious organizations; and so forth. (*See also* international organizations)

normative theory   Value-oriented or philosophical theory that focuses on what ought to be. As such it is usually different from *empirical* theories which try to explain the way things are or predict what they will be. (*See also* empirical, empirical theory)

norms   Values that states or peoples over time take seriously and by which they are influenced; for instance, a belief in universal human rights. Norms may also erode over time; for example, the prohibition against intervention in the internal affairs of a state.

North, South   North refers to advanced-industrial and post-industrial, high-income, First-World countries and societies generally in northern parts of the northern hemisphere (with such notable exceptions as Australia and New Zealand), the South being composed of the less industrially developed, lower-income, Third-World countries that tend to be located further south, including most countries in the southern hemisphere.

North American Free Trade Agreement   (NAFTA) Free-trade area or association among the United States, Canada, and Mexico. (*See also* free-trade area)

North Atlantic Treaty Organization   (NATO) Formed in 1949 during the cold war, NATO is an alliance or collective-defense organization now headquartered in Brussels, Belgium. Its members include Belgium, Canada, Czech Republic, Denmark, France, Germany, Greece, Hungary, Iceland, Italy, Luxembourg, Norway, the Netherlands, Poland, Portugal, Turkey, Spain, the United Kingdom, and the United States. Since the end of the Cold War, other Central and Eastern European states have become members or established links with NATO in a Partnership for Peace. In addition to its UN Charter Article 51 collective-defense status, NATO also performs collective-security, peacekeeping, and other tasks under UN auspices. (*See also* Article 51; collective defense; collective security)

Nuclear Non-Proliferation Treaty (NPT)   Convention that prohibits transfer of nuclear weapons and nuclear-weapons technologies to non-nuclear countries, pledging nuclear countries to work constructively toward nuclear disarmament.

objectives   (*See* interests)

offense, offensive, counter-offensive   To initiate actions that threaten or attack another state or to posture military forces to take such actions. A credible offensive posture requires robust defenses as well. If attacked, a state may choose to take defensive measures first as it prepares to launch a *counter-offensive*.

ontology   Refers to one's world view: the essence of things and the properties of existence in the world as we understand them. As human beings, we often bring to the study different assumptions and presuppositions about the way things are and how they relate. (*See also* epistemology)

opportunity cost   When a decision is made to do one thing, the cost of not pursuing some alternative course of action; for example, in national budgets, money spent for one program is no longer available for spending on some other program, the latter being an opportunity cost.

Organization for Security and Cooperation in Europe (OSCE)   Growing out of a series of conferences (CSCE) that began in the 1970s, the OSCE is a widely inclusive international organization that includes most European countries in the Atlantic-to-Urals area as well as the United States and Canada. Confidence- and security-building as well as cultural, commercial, and human rights issues have been core concerns on its agenda.

Organization for the Prohibition of Chemical Weapons   Designed to verify that state signatories of various chemical weapons conventions are abiding by the agreements.

Organization of African Unity (OAU)   Pan-African international organization that includes both Saharan and sub-Saharan states.

Organization of American States (OAS)   Pan-American international organization that includes North, Central (and Caribbean), and South American states.

Organization of Arab Petroleum Exporting Countries (OAPEC)   Formed in 1968, this international organization includes Arab OPEC members Algeria, Bahrain, Egypt, Iraq, Kuwait, Libya, Qatar, Saudi Arabia, Syria, Tunisia and the United Arab Emirates.

Organization of Petroleum Exporting Countries (OPEC) Formed in 1960, this international organization performs like a *cartel,* setting production limits in an attempt to regulate supply and prices on the global market. Member states now include Algeria, Libya, Nigeria, Indonesia, Iran, Iraq, Kuwait, Qatar, Saudi Arabia, United Arab Emirates, and Venezuela. (*See also* cartel)

overvalued currency   Overvalued currencies are those in which a country's currency exchange rate is too high because it stimulates imports by making the price of imports below market (relatively inexpensive to domestic consumers) and, by contrast, discourages or dampens exports by making the price of exports relatively expensive to would-be buyers from abroad. (*See also* undervalued currency)

pacta sunt servanda   (*See* treaty)

pacifism   The rejection of the use of force, war, and other forms of violence against other human beings.

parliamentary government   A form of government in which the head of the government (the prime minister) and cabinet are also members of the legislature. In the United Kingdom, for example, there is a fusion of powers between the executive and legislative branches. (*See also* presidential government)

partition   Division and separation of peoples, particularly those with a propensity or demonstrated record of engaging in intercommunal violence; there is, for example, partition between Greek- and Turkish-speaking inhabitants of Cyprus. *De facto* partition (partition as a matter of fact) occurs when peoples divide and separate themselves into separate areas; *de jure* partition (partition as a matter of law) is a more formal set of legally binding division and separation arrangements.

peace   Definitions include the absence of war; a situation of security, order, or stability; and harmonious relations among states and other actors.

peacekeeping   Task performed by UN or other multilateral forces in an effort to keep conflicting parties from resorting (or returning) to armed hostilities. Related functions are *peace monitoring* and *peace enforcement* of terms between the conflicting parties. Finally, *peace making* refers to measures, including the use of armed force, to establish a ceasefire and basis for a more durable peace.

per capita income (PCI)   The mean or average income for each person. Calculated on an annualized national basis it is gross national product or gross domestic product divided by the total population.

periphery   (*See* core)

persona non grata   (*See* diplomat)

pluralism, pluralists, liberalism   An image of world politics that emphasizes the multiplicity of international actors—states, international organizations, and transnational organizations—challenging the realist preoccupation with the state. Pluralists or liberalism do not view the state as a unitary, rational actor, but rather as a battle ground for conflicting bureaucratic and other interests, subject to the pressures of both domestic and transnational interest groups. (*See* also neoliberal institutionalism, liberalism)

polarity   (*See* structure)

policy   Decisions and actions taken by governments or other authoritative actors. Some policies of states deal with domestic, societal matters; externally oriented decisions and actions are the domain of foreign policy. (*See also* decision)

political asylum   Protection granted to individuals who face persecution, violation of human rights, or other denial of civil rights and liberties in their home and other countries.

political culture   The norms, values, and orientations of a society's culture that are politically relevant; for instance, many societies traditionally defer to political authorities in making domestic and foreign policies. Other, more participatory political cultures reflect a public interest in political matters with individuals, groups, and organizations attempting to influence political decisions.

political economy   The intersection of politics (or authoritative choice) with economics, which is concerned with seemingly unlimited wants in a world of relative scarcity of resources.

political exception rule   Used by states to justify their refusal to extradite a suspected terrorist to another country when they believe the act was done for political (not criminal) reasons.

political liberalism   (*See* liberalism)

positive sum   (*See* zero-sum; game theory)

positivism   (1) The concept that law is what law makers, following constitutional procedures, define it to be. In international law, treaties and conventions are a key source of this human-constructed law. A positive-law tradition, as in Anglo-American law, differs from the natural-law tradition in some continental European countries and their former colonies, which see legal principles as discoverable through reason in relation to natural law. (2) Positivism may also refer to a modern or scientific methodology by which truth claims are formalized and hypotheses are subject to rigorous empirical test.

power   The actual or potential influence or coercion a state (or other actor) can assert relative to other states and non-state actors because of the political, geographic, economic and financial, technological, military, social, cultural, or other capabilities it possesses. *Influence* is the ability to get a state or other unit to do something it would otherwise not do through its deference to the relative capabilities or status of the requesting party, by explicit promises or provision of rewards, or by threats or actual punishment. *Coercion* is the ability to force another state or other unit to do something it would not otherwise do through the threat or use of force or other sanctions. Particularly from a realist perspective, power is the currency of world politics. (*See also* authority)

power transition theory   An explanation of change in the international system that can be traced back to Thucydides. It is argued that there is a tendency for the powers of member states to change at different rates because of political, economic, and technological developments. In time, the differential growth of power of the various states causes a fundamental redistribution of power in the system, usually due to a war when an ascending power challenges the hegemony of the dominant power.

prediction   (*See* empirical theory)

presidential government   Strong powers reside in the office of the president as chief executive separate from legislative authority; presidential governments include the United States and France. (*See also* separation of powers; parliamentary government)

preventive diplomacy   (*See* diplomacy)

principles of war   Associated with the Prussian Clausewitz, the Frenchman Jomini, and others, such warfighting criteria or principles have been specified as guides for planners and commanders. These include principles of the *objective* (what is the goal, clearly stated and understood), *offensive* (aimed at destroying or substantially weakening an enemy's warmaking capability), *mass or concentration of forces* (avoiding weak fronts through excessive dispersion of forces), *economy of forces* (not wasting finite military resources), *maneuver* (to include mobility), *surprise* (gaining an offensive advantage), *security* (including defense of one's forces from surprise or other decisive attack), *simplicity* (avoiding excessive, unnecessary complexity), and *unity of command* (with the locus or loci of authority clearly specified and understood).

price elasticity   (*See* elasticity)

privateering, privateer   As when privately owned, armed ships have governmental authority to attack enemy shipping, typically in wartime

privatization vs. socialization   The former is an effort or program to shift ownership to nongovernmental or private hands, and the latter, by contrast, to publicly or state-owned means of production. (*See also* means of production, factors of production, and markets)

profit   Net revenues, derived from subtracting outlays or costs from gross revenues or income. (*See* also surplus value)

proletariat   (*See* class struggle)

protectionism   Policies intended to favor the market position of a country's industries and other producers by imposing tariffs or quotas on imports, subsidizing production, and other measures. (*See also* free trade, markets)

public goods   (See collective goods)

public opinion   The views of the citizenry on issues of public interest and concern. When public opinion supports a government's domestic and foreign policies, the political capabilities of the state are enhanced. Loss of public support may undermine the legitimacy of policies and the political authorities responsible for them.

puppet government   (*See* government)

race, racial, racism   Distinctions based primarily on physical similarities and differences such as skin color, although cultural and other factors may also be significant. Racism usually refers to assertions of alleged superiority by one racial group over another.

raison d'Etat, Staaträson   French and German terms, respectively, that indicate the realist justification for policies pursued by state authorities. First and foremost of these justifications or criteria is security, followed by other interests and associated objectives.

rational choice   To act rationally requires a rank ordering of preferred goals, consideration of all feasible alternatives to attain these goals in the light of existing capabilities, and consideration of the costs and benefits associated with using particular methods to attain particular goals. The assumption is often made in international relations research that actors do indeed act rationally. This assumption is made in order to develop hypotheses and to produce insights, theoretical explanation and prediction.

real terms   Since the value or purchasing power of a currency changes over time, particularly due to inflation, statistics expressed in *real terms* are those that factor inflation out of calculations. For example, for comparative purposes GNP or GDP statistics over a ten-year period may be expressed in constant or uninflated dollars, converting each year's actual totals to the same value expressed in the value of dollars in a particular, specified year. Thus one can refer to 2001 dollars or 1991 dollars, using one or the other as the benchmark for comparison.

realism, realists   An image of international relations or world politics that can be traced back more than two thousand years. Realists tend to hold a rather pessimistic view, emphasizing the struggle for power and influence among political units acting in a rational, unitary manner in pursuit of objectives grounded in their separate, often divergent interests.

Realpolitik   A German term referring to foreign policy ordered or motivated by power politics. As Thucydides commented on the conflict between ancient Athens and Melos, the strong (Athens) do what they will and the weak (Melos) do what they must.

reciprocity   (*See* diplomat)

refugee   Persons displaced because of war or other political or economic causes. (*See also* political asylum)

regime   Domestically, another term for government or a particular form of government, as in a *democratic regime* or *authoritarian regime*. (*See also* international regime)

relativism (moral or cultural)   The belief that moral or ethical principles are not universal, but rather are tied to particular situational or cultural contexts.

repatriation   In economics, a multinational corporation taking its profits out of a country in which it has invested and sending them back to the home country.

reserves (monetary)   Cash or assets easily converted into cash held out of use by a bank, company, or state to meet expected or unexpected demands.

revanchism   A militaristic movement or philosophy aimed at reclaiming lost lands. (*See also* irredentism)

sabotage   (*See* espionage)

savings   Production minus consumption is surplus that can be saved or invested. (*See also* surplus value)

second-strike capability   (*See* first-, second-strike capability)

Second World   (*See* Third World)

security   For realists, the basic survival and protection of the state. Pluralists or liberals have a more expansive definition, also applying the concept to individuals and groups of people. In fact, the state may be not a provider of security, but rather a threat to the security of many people.

security dilemma   As states spend more on defense, even if only for defensive purposes, their opponents may feel threatened and increase their own defense spending. An increasing spiral of defense spending does not in fact increase security, as each party feels more and more threatened.

semiperiphery   (*See* core)

separation of powers   A form of government in which power is divided among two or more branches of government; for example, the United States, with executive, legislative, and judicial branches. (*See also* state, federal, presidential government)

slavery   A social system or form of political economy based on involuntary servitude. In Marxist usage, reference is to ancient *slavery* as a *mode of production*. (*See also* mode of production)

stake holder   Denotes an ownership stake in a given firm. Because it is a broader, more inclusive term, *stake holder is often preferred to stock holder.*

social constructivism   A theoretical perspective on international relations and world politics that claims values and ideas or concepts (such as balance of power or multilateralism) are constituted or constructed over time such that they acquire legitimacy or acceptance as the way international relations are (or ought to be) conducted. Ideas and concepts about international relations do not exist somehow in nature; they are not "givens" or essential attributes but are rather of human origin and humanly constructed. The world is what states (and others) choose to make of it.

social contract   The idea that human beings, acting in their own enlightened self-interest, would agree to bind themselves to one political or governing arrangement or another.

social democratic   A political perspective that, while favoring liberty, puts greater emphasis than libertarians do on equality and community as values to be realized in social policy. Social democrats also tend to rely on government programmatic approaches to social questions. (*See also* libertarian)

social development   Concept used in this text for dealing with intercommunal conflict that refers first to building an acceptance of people in other communities, states, or societies as fellow human beings, expanding from this base to developing relations based on mutual respect, trust, and other higher values. (*See also* development)

social liberalism, social liberal   A political perspective that, while sharing the commitment to individualism, puts emphasis on government programs or other social actions as means to improve the position or conditions of individuals. By contrast, classical liberalism is *laissez-faire,* minimizing the role of government.

socialism   Public (as in state or governmental) ownership of the means of production, particularly major industries or utilities. In Marxist usage, a *mode of production*. (*See also* mode of production)

society of states   The view of some realists that at certain times in history states have agreed upon basic rules, norms, and international laws to govern their relations. The nineteenth-century Concert of Europe is one example.

soft currencies   Money not readily convertible from one currency to another and, as a result, may or may not be accepted as payment for international obligations. Although small amounts may be kept on hand, soft currencies normally are not counted as monetary reserves. (*See also* hard currencies)

South   (*See* North, South)

Southern Cone   (*See* MERCOSUR)

sovereign, sovereignty   A claim to political authority based on territory and autonomy, historically associated with the modern state. Internally it is the right claimed by states to exercise exclusive political authority over a defined geographic space or territory; it also includes the claim to a right to autonomy. No external actor such as another state enjoys authority within the borders of the state. A sovereign state claims a right to exercise *internal* sovereignty over its territory and *external sov*ereignty in terms of relations with other states—no one has the right to tell a state how to conduct its domestic or foreign relations. States differ in power, but as sovereign entities they are, in principle, legal equals.

Special Drawing Rights (SDRs)   Once dubbed by journalists as "paper gold," SDRs are an IMF line of credit member countries can draw on for getting foreign currencies needed for making international payments; as such, SDRs can be counted as part of the country's monetary reserves.

Staaträson   (*See raison d'Etat*)

stability, destabilizing   Some theorists compare unipolar, bipolar, and multipolar international systems in terms of which is more or less stable. Stable deterrence relations are said to depend on maintaining second-strike capabilities that would allow either party to absorb a first strike prior to choosing whether and how to retaliate. By contrast, when one party fears it has lost (or will lose) its second-strike capability this may be *destabilizing,* because it may be prone in a crisis to launch first or to launch on warning of an attack, even before it has confirmed that an attack has actually taken place.

state   Consists of a territory with defined boundaries, a population (with or without a common identity), a government or administration, and recognition as a sovereign state by other sovereign states. The state is viewed as the key actor in international or world politics. A *nation-state* is a single people with a common identity (nation) who live in a given state (such as Japan or Germany). *Non-state nations* such as the Kurds have aspired to the creation of a Kurdish nation-state; Kurdish peoples are to be found in Turkey, Syria, Iraq, Iran, and in former Soviet republics in the trans-caucasus region. A *binational state* includes a society with two nations or national identities (such as the Flemish-speaking and French-speaking "nations" in Belgian society); an example of a *multinational* or *multi-ethnic state* is the Russian Federation with its Russian majority and non-Russian minorities; and a *multi-tribal state* like Nigeria that includes Yoruba, Ibo, and Hausa-Fulani tribal identities. A *city-state,* as suggested by the term itself, refers to a city that has many of the attributes of a modern state, including a government, armed forces and foreign and domestic policies. Historic city-states include Sparta and Athens in ancient Greece and Venice and Florence in Renaissance Italy. A unitary state has only one government with all significant executive, legislative, and judicial power concentrated at the national level (for example, Japan, France, and the United Kingdom). By contrast, a *federal state* or *federation is* one in which there is a *division of power* between the central government and constituent governments in states or provinces (for example, the United States, Canada, and the Federal Republic of Germany). A *welfare state* is one in which extensive government programs exist to provide for the well-being or welfare of the population. The term *hegemonic state system* refers to a condition in which one or more states enjoy a position of dominance over other states in the international or interstate system (such as Athens and Sparta in the fifth century B.C. or, quite apart from their own rivalries, the collective hegemony of five European powers for several decades following the Congress of Vienna in 1815). By contrast, the term *independent state system* refers to political entities that claim and can retain the ultimate authority and ability to make both foreign and domestic policies without external interference.

state capitalism *(See* **capitalism)**   (*See* capitalism)

state of nature   A philosophical construct referring to a time prior to the creation of civil society—a world without governmental authority, also an analogy to the *anarchic* structure of the international system. An important concept, particularly for realists who follow the thinking of Hobbes, as it raises the issue of how order and stability can be achieved in an international system of states competing for power and prestige.

strategic defense   (*See* defense)

strategy, tactics   Strategy usually refers to an overall plan for the use of various capabilities to accomplish objectives, whereas tactics are usually specific or particular measures for accomplishing tasks consistent with these strategic purposes.

structural adjustment   As when fiscal and monetary policies (cutting spending, increasing taxes, raising interest rates, etc.) are used to curb or dampen an economy deemed to be "overheated"; such policies often have adverse effects in the short run on businesses, employment, and return on investment, although the objective of such austerity policies is to provide a foundation for sustained economic growth over the longer term. (*See also* fiscal policy, monetary policy, macroeconomics)

structural violence   Refers, particularly in contemporary Marxist thought, to the oppression and poor living conditions of victims of class domination that result in lower life expectancy, sustained poverty, malnutrition, and disease.

structure (systemic), structural realism (neorealism)   In realist thought about international systems, particularly structural or "neorealist" theorizing, structure refers to the distribution of power among states. Thus a world subject to the influence of one great power is *unipolar;* to two principal great powers is *bipolar* and to three or more is *multipolar.* (*See also* the discussion in microeconomics)

suboptimal   Less than the best choice or outcome, although it may be deemed good enough.

subsidiary   A subordinate firm or unit of larger corporation.

supply   What is available for purchase (brought to market) at a given price or range of possible prices, whether currency (such as U.S. dollars), commodity (such as oil), manufactured goods (such as automobiles and computers), or a service (such as airline transportation, education, or banking). (*See also* elasticity)

supranational   Beyond or above the level of a state. If one were created, a world government would be a supranational authority, governing the relations among states and other actors in world politics.

surplus value   In Marxist usage, the value of goods and services produced comes from the labor put into their production. After paying wages (which tend toward subsistence or minimum levels) and other costs, the remainder is *surplus* that can be pocketed or invested by the owners of land or capital. *See* profit)

surprise   (*See* principles of war)

survivability   In nuclear deterrence theory, a second-strike capability depends upon the ability of some proportion of retaliatory forces to avoid destruction and thus survive a first strike, particularly a surprise attack. Survivability can be enhanced by increased numbers of dispersed forces, hardening or shielding weaponry against attack, putting weapons underground or underwater, and making at least some weapons mobile.

sustainable development   Increased economic production puts increasing pressure on resources and adds pollution, which can undermine continued development. Rapid population growth adds further strain. For economic development to continue or be sustained over the long term, attention must be paid to these resource, environmental, and demographic constraints.

system   (*See* international systems)

tactics   (*See* strategy)

targeting   Process of selecting certain objects or *targets* against which military force is directed. Selecting military targets (such as tank and troop concentrations, railroad junctions, air fields, command posts, and so forth) is referred to as *counterforce* targeting, while selecting industrial targets and population centers is referred to as *countervalue* targeting. When particular targets are struck, some damage may spill over to kill people and destroy property—so-called *collateral damage.* Different targets require different weaponry and modes of attack. Nuclear weapons are measured in terms of yield or explosive force as *kilotons* (equivalent to thousands of tons of TNT) or *megatons* (millions of tons of TNT).

tariffs   Taxes placed by a government on imported goods from other countries.

telemetry   (*See* verification)

terms of trade   The value or prices of a country's exports compared to the value or prices of imports. Third-World or low-income countries, for example, often have adverse terms of trade. The agricultural or mineral commodities they produce for export tend to have relatively static or declining prices whereas the manufactures and other products they import tend to be rising in price.

terrorism   Politically motivated violence, designed to influence an audience beyond the immediate victim and perpetrated by clandestine state agents or by subnational or transnational groups. *Domestic* terrorism involves a domestic terrorist group attacking against a domestic target. By contrast, *international* terrorism goes beyond the borders of any one state with respect to the terrorist group, target attacked, or territory on which the incident is planned or takes place. Thus, if Jihad terrorists attack an Egyptian government building in Cairo, it is domestic terrorism. But if the same group attacks foreign tourists in Cairo, it is an act of international terrorism.

theory   (*See* empirical theory, normative theory)

Third World   A term devised during the Cold War era referring to less-developed countries, many of which being part of the so-called "nonaligned movement," meaning they did not wish to choose sides between the capitalist West or *First World* and the socialist or communist *Second World.* The term *Third*

World also had the positive meaning among French socialists in the 1960s that, like the *"third estate"* of common people at the time of the French Revolution, the bulk of the world's population in the Third World need not remain at the bottom of the heap. The First World—sometimes referred to as "the West" or "the North"—includes North America, much of Europe, and Japan. With the collapse of communism in many countries at the end of the Cold War, the terms "First" and "Second" World are used less frequently.

trade   (*See* balance of trade, trade barriers, trade preferences, comparative advantage, Hekscher-Ohlin theorem)

trade barriers   Restrictions placed on the import of foreign goods or services. The barrier may be a tariff (tax) or quota (quantitative limitation) on imports, or a non-tariff barrier such as health standards on imported meats that effectively exclude them from the domestic market.

trade preference   A special arrangement that allows easy access on a cost-competitive basis by a foreign producer to a country's domestic market; for example, European Union members have granted trade preferences to Third World countries, particularly to their former colonies.

tragedy of the commons   Circumstances in which people have an incentive to increase personal consumption of a collective good even though such consumption will reduce the supply of that good. An analogy applied to the global environment. (*See* collective goods)

transfer pricing   Scheme by which a corporation with subsidiaries or divisions in different countries can price components manufactured or exchanged between one division or subsidiary and another *within* the same corporation to minimize tax exposure, maximize profits, or repatriate earnings to the corporate home-country. Transfer-pricing schemes are sometimes contrary to the interests of the governments and states in which an MNC operates.

transgovernmental   Relations involving links, ties, or even coalitions among bureaucratic or other official actors of different states.

transnational   (*See* transnational organizations and movements)

transnational criminal organizations (TCOs)   (*See* transnational organizations and movements)

transnational organizations and movements   Non-state actors that cross state borders. They include: (1) institutions pursuing their own economic goals such as international banks and multinational corporations (MNCs); (2) non-governmental organizations (NGOs) with a strictly humanitarian agenda (e.g., Doctors Without Borders) or organizations with broader political, social, or environmental agendas and constituencies (such as Amnesty International or Greenpeace); and (3) terrorist groups that operate across borders as well as transnational criminal organizations (TCOs).

transparency   Refers to an open-information environment even among adversaries so that each state can know what the others are doing through exchange of information, intelligence, and other means. (*See* confidence- and security-building measures)

treaty   A written agreement or contract between two or more states pledging adherence to any number of commitments, including arms reduction, trade arrangements, the pursuit of collective security via an alliance, health standards, protection of the environment, and so forth. In international law, treaties are binding (*pacta sunt servanda*) even though there is no global or international enforcing authority *per se.*

trend   A recurrent pattern observable over time that may differ from what was typical or expected in an earlier period.

tribe, tribalism   Tribes are social or societal units with an authority structure and shared or common identity in a society (for example, Tutsis and Hutus are competing tribes in Rwanda and Burundi; Ibo, Yoruba, and Hausa-Fulani are tribal groupings in Nigeria). Tribalism refers to the culture of tribal life, particularly a commitment to it.

ultimatum   A statement issued from one state to another demanding compliance, specifying that certain actions be taken or halted, usually within a specified time period.

undervalued currency   Undervalued currencies are those in which a country's currency exchange rate is too low because it discourages or dampens imports by making the price of imports above market (relatively expensive to domestic consumers) and, by contrast, stimulates exports by making them relatively inexpensive to would-buyers from abroad. (*See also* overvalued currency, exchange rates)

uneven development   The gains from economic growth tend to be asymmetric with some countries or parts of countries gaining more than others.

UNHCR   (*See* United Nations)

unipolar, unipolarity   (*See* structure)

unit of analysis   What is being studied; for example, a state or a decision-making unit.

unitary state   (*See* state)

United Nations (UN)   Formed in 1945, an international organization that includes almost all (some 193) of the world's states as members. Principal organs include the General Assembly, Security Council, Secretariat, Economic and Social Council, Trusteeship Council, and International Court of Justice. *Specialized agencies affiliated with the UN through the Economic and Social Council* include the following international organizations: World Bank (or IBRD, International Bank for Reconstruction and Development), International Monetary Fund (IMF), International Labor Organization (ILO), Food and Agricultural Organization (FAO), Educational, Scientific, and Cultural Organization (UNESCO), International Civil Aviation Organization (ICAO), Universal Postal Union (UPU), International Telecommunications Union (ITU), World Meteorological Organization (WMO), International Maritime Organization (IMO), World Trade Organization (WTO), and the Industrial Development Organization (UNIDO), and others. *Organizational units tied to the UN General Assembly* include the United Nations High Commissioner for Refugees (UNHCR), the High Commissioner for Human Rights (UNHCHR), the Conference on Trade and Development (UNCTAD), International Children's Emergency Fund (UNICEF), Development Programme (UNDP), Environment Program (UNEP), World Food Program (WFP), Population Fund (UNFPA), and others.

utilitarian   A philosophical school associated with Jeremy Bentham and John Stuart Mill based on the principle of the greatest good or happiness for the greatest number.

variable-sum   (*See* zero-sum; game theory)

verification   Finding out whether another party to a treaty or other agreement is living up to its obligations. Arms control treaties and agreements have relied when possible on onsite inspections, but also on *national technical means* (NTM) of verification (such as high technology ground stations, ships, aircraft and satellites). For example, intercepting *telemetry*—communications sent to ground stations by missiles in flight—can yield important information or intelligence about operational characteristics of the missile. Verification is typically the first step; negotiating to assure compliance when violations have been discovered is the next step. (*See also* national technical means)

voluntarist, voluntarism   A philosophical position that reality is created by human will; that humans can affect, if not control, their destinies. In international relations, it generally means that decisionmakers have effective choice and are able to influence outcomes. *Social constructivism*, for example, can be understood as a voluntarist formulation to the extent that knowingly or otherwise it is human beings and their ideas that shape the institutions and processes that constitute international or world politics. (*See also* social constructivism)

war, warfare, warfighting   War is organized armed conflict between or among states *(interstate war)* or within a given state or society *(civil war)*. *Guerrilla warfare* is a type of war involving *irregular,* usually non-uniformed fighters; *guerrillas* may be associated with either civil or interstate wars. *Insurgency* is armed resistance to a government's authority.

weapons proliferation   The sale, transfer, or indigenous production of various types and classes of weapons. An example would be nuclear weapons. When states acquire larger and larger stockpiles of weapons we refer to vertical proliferation; when weapons or weapons technologies (whether nuclear, biological, chemical, or "conventional") are transferred laterally to other countries we refer to horizontal proliferation.

welfare issues   Socioeconomic, human rights, and other issues associated with improving the human condition.

welfare state   (*See* state)

West   Generally the countries of North America, Western Europe and, paradoxically, Japan, because of its level of industrial development and its links to other advanced capitalist states. (*See also* East)

Western European Union (WEU)   Security organization formed by European states in the 1948 Brussels pact. For security matters the WEU acts as agent for the European Union, the latter having decided to absorb WEU defense functions in its own right.

world federalism   The goal of individuals favoring a world government that would have authority over constituent states. Some world federalists posit more modest goals such as achieving greater criminal and civil accountability before international courts, matters historically reserved to states.

world government   (*See* world federalism)

world (or global) politics   The term favored by those who emphasize the multidimensional or pluralist nature of international relations today, which includes not simply states, but also a wide diversity of international and nongovernmental, transnational organizations, other groups, and individuals; not simply the physical security of the state, but also environmental, human rights, and demographic issues. (*See also* international politics; international relations)

world system   Term associated with the work of Immanuel Wallerstein and his colleagues, focusing on capitalism as a world system, a perspective influenced by Marxist understandings of a capitalism as a global system.

zero-sum   Concept in game theory that one side's gain amounts to the other's loss. *Variable sum* games allow both parties to gain or both to lose asymmetrically (by differing amounts); in *positive-sum* games, both parties win. One approach to conflicts is to transform them such that both (or all) parties see them as *positive-sum* games in which all may win. (*See also* game theory)

INDEX

O

P

X

Y

Z